KT-416-877

# a-z
## of careers
## & jobs

C0000 002 468 318

Monday: 10.36am : 55°51.9'N 4°15.4'W

# A breakthrough in engineering

There's no standing still at Rolls-Royce. As the world's leading provider of power systems for use on land, at sea and in the air, we are perpetually in motion – always looking for new and better ways to keep moving forward. That's how we know that university isn't for everyone. That sometimes, it's better just to get on with your career – to get stuck into something real, to develop valuable skills, to earn sought-afte qualifications, to get paid. A Rolls-Royce Engineering Apprenticeship will give you all these things and more. So get moving. Find out more and apply at www.rolls-royce.com/apprenticeships

**Trusted to deliver excellence**

www.rolls-royce.com/careers

Apprenticeships
National Awards 2009
Highly commended

ROLLS
ROYCE
Rolls-Royce

# Apprenticeships at Rolls-Royce

A Rolls-Royce Engineering Apprenticeship is a genuine alternative to university – giving you the chance to develop valuable skills, gain qualifications, earn a good salary and work with some of the world's leading engineers.

To find out more, come to our open day or visit
**www.rolls-royce.com/apprentices**

---

## 'My apprenticeship gave me a broad vision of the whole company.'

Louise Craig has just completed her apprenticeship at Rolls-Royce's East Kilbride factory. For the first six months she worked in a training centre where she learnt to operate various engineering machines. During this time she gained her SVQ levels 1 and 2. She then moved to the factory where she shadowed fitters on the shop floor, worked on aeroplane parts, learnt the principles of business awareness and studied for her SVQ level 3.

'We spent three months at a time in different sections of the factory,' she says. 'Amongst other things, I worked on engine build, module build and component refurbishment, and this gave me a broad vision of the whole company, not just one small area. So at the end of my apprenticeship I'd gained an overall awareness of the engineering process, from when a part comes into the factory to when it goes back to the customer.

'But the apprenticeship wasn't all factory based. I spent time working with schools, colleges and at career fairs, encouraging women from the UK and overseas to consider the challenge of an engineering apprenticeship with Rolls-Royce.

'I've just been accepted on an Assembly and Manufacturing Leadership scheme. This is a fast track programme based in Derby, and may lead to a substantive role in the company. It involves secondments to other sites around the country, and I'll also get the opportunity to study for a Master's degree in Engineering Business Management at Warwick University. So the future's bright, and I can't wait to get to grips with the next set of challenges.'

advertisement feature

St Mary's
University College
Twickenham
London

Whether its Management to Media, Sociology to Sport, or Teaching to Tourism, St Mary's offers degrees for your future career. See our website for the full offer.

St Mary's University College
Waldegrave Road, Strawberry Hill, Twickenham TW1 4SX

Tel 020 8240 2314  www.smuc.ac.uk

St Mary's is a small well resourced University College in a leafy suburb of London. Established in 1850 we have a long history and tradition behind our quality courses and a beautiful campus. Renowned for our teacher training and health and sport related courses, we also offer a wide range of other degrees that could set your career off on the right path.

You could benefit from study placements abroad, work experience options and teaching from respected and experienced staff. Many of our courses can be combined and are flexible so that you can shape the course as your interests develop.

You can see our virtual tour of St Mary's and course information on our website **www.smuc.ac.uk**. Why not come to visit us at one of our Open Days.

advertisement feature

# THE TIMES

# a-z
## of careers
## & jobs

**17th edition**

Edited by:
**Susan Hodgson**

KoganPage

LONDON  PHILADELPHIA  NEW DELHI

| HOUNSLOW LIBRARIES | |
|---|---|
| **BED** | |
| C0000 002 468 318 | |
| Askews | 05-Mar-2010 |
| 331.702094 | £14.99 |
| | |

**Publisher's note**

Every possible effort has been made to ensure that the information contained in this book is accurate at the time of going to press. Neither Kogan Page nor the editor can accept responsibility for any errors or omissions, however caused. No responsibility for loss or damage occasioned to any person acting, or refraining from action, as a result of the material in this publication can be accepted by the editor, the publisher or any of the authors.

First published in Great Britain in 1984 by Kogan Page Limited
Seventeenth edition 2010

Apart from any fair dealing for the purposes of research or private study, or criticism or review, as permitted under the Copyright, Designs and Patents Act 1988, this publication may only be reproduced, stored or transmitted, in any form or by any means, with the prior permission in writing of the publishers, or in the case of reprographic reproduction in accordance with the terms and licences issued by the CLA. Enquiries concerning reproduction outside these terms should be sent to the publishers at the undermentioned address:

Kogan Page Limited
120 Pentonville Road
London N1 9JN
www.koganpage.com

© Kogan Page, 1984, 1986, 1988, 1991, 1992, 1994, 1995, 1997, 2000, 2002, 2004, 2005, 2006, 2007, 2008, 2009, 2010

The views expressed in this book are those of the author, and are not necessarily the same as those of Times Newspapers Ltd.

**British Library Cataloguing in Publication Data**

A CIP record for this book is available from the British Library.

ISBN 978 0 7494 5980 2
E-ISBN 978 0 7494 5981 9

Typeset by Saxon Graphics Ltd, Derby
Printed and bound in Great Britain by MPG Books Ltd, Bodmin, Cornwall

**ALLEN & OVERY**

**Start at the top**
A Career in Law

When it comes to eggs, it's more than just a question of etiquette. Edward VI certainly thought so. That's why he decreed that any person found breaking a boiled egg at the sharp end would be sentenced to 24 hours in the village stocks.

☐ Law or ☐ Non-law?

Law and business are full of surprises. Whether you are exploring the modern implications of existing laws, or working to find legal solutions to new situations, you'll need to be open-minded, creative and commercial. At Allen & Overy, we are working at the forefront of today's evolving legal landscape, helping to shape and frame the environment in which business, and life itself, is conducted.

# Breaking with tradition

You don't need to have studied law to become a lawyer, but business sense, curiosity and a commitment to excellence are essential.

Answer: Non-law

www.allenovery.com/careeruk
Allen & Overy means Allen & Overy LLP and/or its affiliated undertakings.

WINNER
TARGETjobs
National Graduate Recruitment
Awards 2009
Sector award law - solicitors

THE TIMES
TOP 100
GRADUATE EMPLOYERS

# ALLEN & OVERY

With 5,000 people working across 31 major cities worldwide, and more than half of these outside the UK, Allen & Overy truly is a global firm. Our international reach gives us the ability to provide world class expertise combined with local knowledge enabling us to work on some of the most exciting and complex transactions. We are renowned for the high quality of our Corporate, Banking and International Capital Markets advice, but also have major strengths in areas such as Litigation, Tax, Employment and Benefits, and Real Estate.

Life at Allen & Overy is about more than just the work we do – our team environment encourages both professional and social relationships. Being involved in cutting-edge, high profile deals with clients who are household names means there's no doubt you'll work hard, but at Allen & Overy we help you to balance that with social, cultural and sporting activities.

## Our Training Contract

Within this broad range of expertise we offer a training contract characterised by flexibility and choice – our training programme is widely regarded as the best in the City and continues throughout your career at Allen & Overy following qualification. Our aim is to recruit, train and develop successful lawyers who want a long-term career with Allen & Overy.

All our future trainees take the Allen & Overy-specific LPC at The College of Law in London. The course has been specially designed to equip you with the skills and knowledge needed to be a successful solicitor, and is set in the context of the type of transactions Allen & Overy lawyers are involved in. The modules you take will focus on our core practice areas, to ensure your time at law school is the best possible preparation for your training contract with Allen & Overy. It will provide you with a sound technical and theoretical background for your career with us. The

advertisement feature

Allen & Overy LPC also means that you will develop strong bonds with your new colleagues and build friendships from day one.

You will have a tailored training contract, designed to give you the best start to your career. Given the strength of our international finance practice, we require our trainees to spend a minimum of 12 months in at least two of the following departments: Banking, Corporate and International Capital Markets. There is also the opportunity for trainees to spend six months of their training contract in one of our international offices or the in-house legal department of a major client.

## Vacation Programmes

Choosing the right career is a big decision. There are lots of questions you need to ask yourself. What type of law do I want to practise? What type of firm would suit me best? What will the work really be like? The best way to answer these questions is to get first-hand experience of life in a law firm and this is exactly what our vacation programmes offer.

During your placement you will assist a partner or senior associate on real deals. You will sit in two departments (one during the shorter Winter scheme) and we will ask you in advance what area most interests you. You will also work with fellow vacation students on a case study project designed to sharpen your research skills and expose you to our broad range of practice areas.

Alongside your legal work you will take part in workshops and attend presentations and talks aimed at informing you about our work and helping you to develop the skills you need to be a successful commercial lawyer such as negotiation, presentation and interview skills. There will also be plenty of time to socialise with other Allen & Overy people during your placement.

Placements are held in our London office during the summer and winter vacations.

For details of all our vacancies visit
www.allenovery.com/careeruk.

advertisement feature

# SkillsActiveCareers

SkillsActiveCareers is the number one contact for information and advice on working in the active leisure, learning and well-being sector, offering clear and comprehensive advice to all those wanting to enter and progress through a career in Sport & Recreation, Health & Fitness, Playwork, The Outdoors and Caravan industries.

Around
## 634,000
people work together
in the sector.
If all employees were standing
together, they would fill
Wembley Stadium
over 7 times.

Around
## 30%
of the workforce have
achieved a level 4/5
NVQ or equivalent
qualification.
But, around 29% are not
qualified at level 2.

Around
## 7.5million
coached in 2007/08 to
improve their sports
performance.
There are 1.2million coaches
in the UK.

With so many young people wanting to get into the sector, coupled with an array of entry options, what advice is the correct advice?

# Visit: www.skillsactive.com/careers

**1** You can view our interactive careers map:

**2**

Ask Dougie!

Dougie is our virtual careers advisor who is available to give you a rough guide as to what jobs you may wish to consider in the sector.

**3** Read real life case studies from people who are already working, and progressing their career in the active leisure and learning sector.

## Active Advice for an Active Career

The sport and active leisure sector is one of the most rewarding sectors to work. You need a multitude of skills from customer service and communication, to IT, management and leadership. Thousands of students graduate each year with a qualification in the sector but not necessarily the right skills. The challenge is to obtain industry-related certificates and work experience whilst studying.

The development of vocationally-based courses offers the best of both worlds – academic learning and hands on training. Apprenticeships are a great way to start a career in the sector; at 16 you learn the practical skills needed plus gain the managerial skills and knowledge required to move up the career ladder.

Young people will be able to specialise in the area of sport and active leisure whilst still at school thanks to the introduction of the Diploma in Sport and Active Leisure in 2010, offering the skills needed to work in the sector, along with academic qualifications in English, maths and IT.

Visit **www.skillsactive.com/careers**

advertisement feature

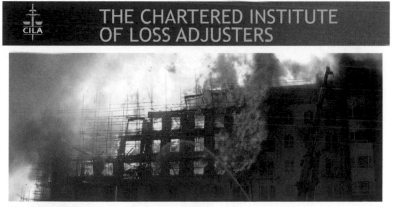

# THE CHARTERED INSTITUTE OF LOSS ADJUSTERS

## Have you considered becoming a Chartered Loss Adjuster?

A little known profession with a great reputation and excellent career prospects.

**THE CHARTERED INSTITUTE OF LOSS ADJUSTERS**
Warwick House, 65-66 Queen Street, London EC4R 1EB • Email: info@cila.co.uk

For more information visit www.cila.co.uk or call 020 7337 9960

Have you ever considered becoming a Chartered Loss Adjuster, a little known profession with a great reputation and excellent career prospects?

There are so many aspects to the everyday working life of a Loss Adjuster. No day is ever the same. One day at the scene of a fire, explosion, flood or other catastrophe and the

next investigating the theft of a significant work of art or perhaps flying to the Caribbean to assess hurricane damage to a major bank or hotel.

Being a Chartered Loss Adjuster demonstrates that you are a member of an exclusive professional body with the opportunity to work anywhere in the world.

Loss adjusting is one of the most varied and interesting careers. You need to have the ability of remaining calm when others may be in crisis, needing your help and support in the immediate aftermath of a major life changing situation.

There are several routes to qualification aimed at candidates from a variety of backgrounds with differing capabilities.

Full details are set out on the Institute's website at www.cila.co.uk

advertisement feature

# Preface

It is often said, possibly with good reason, that there is too much choice in the modern world. What people perhaps mean when they say 'too much choice' is too much confusion and not enough clear information upon which to base a decision. This is especially true when it comes to making career choices, since the results of choices can be long lasting and significant. Whether you are picking which GCSEs or A levels to study, considering university or college courses, seeking your first job, or contemplating a change of direction, good, clear information about jobs and careers is essential.

The current job market is competitive and challenging. Many people are facing tough choices and difficult situations beyond their control. Being well informed is one way to take some control of your own situation. Find out what job and career opportunities there are. A well informed candidate for any position is likely to produce a more effective CV and give a more convincing performance at an interview. Having a good careers research tool if you have to make a change of job or career through no fault of your own could also be a vital first step in getting back on the career ladder.

This guide draws together a wide range of information on all kinds of jobs. It may give you ideas you have never considered before. It helps you to compare what qualifications you need, what you may already have in terms of personal qualities and skills, and what you want, eg salaries. It also gives you all the right starting points to carry out more detailed research and gather further information. It will prove a useful starting point to realising your career ambitions at any stage of your working life.

*Susan Hodgson*
*Careers consultant*

# Abbreviations

| | |
|---|---|
| A level | Advanced level |
| AS level | Advanced Special level |
| AVCE | Vocational A level |
| CAM | Communication, Advertising and Marketing Foundation |
| Edexcel | Edexcel Foundation |
| Edexcel (BTEC) | Comprises ULEAC (University of London Examination and Assessment Council) and BTEC (Business and Technology Education Council) |
| GCE | General Certificate of Education |
| GCSE | General Certificate of Secondary Education |
| GSVQ | General Scottish Vocational Qualification |
| H grade | Higher grade (SCE) |
| HNC/HND | Higher National Certificate/Higher National Diploma |
| HTC | Higher Technical Certificate |
| LSC | Learning and Skills Council |
| NC/ND | National Certificate/National Diploma |
| NVQ | National Vocational Qualification |
| QCA | Qualifications and Curriculum Authority |
| SCE | Scottish Certificate of Education (equivalent to GCSE) |
| SNC/SND | Scottish National Certificate/Scottish National Diploma |
| SQA | Scottish Qualifications Authority |
| SVQ | Scottish Vocational Qualification |
| TEC | Training and Enterprise Council |
| UCAS | Universities and Colleges Admissions System |

# Qualifications

Scottish readers should be aware that in order to simplify the text the editor has referred to qualifications required in terms of GCSEs, A levels and NVQs or equivalent. NVQs are directly equivalent to SVQs but Scottish National and Higher Qualifications are not equivalent to GCSEs and A levels. A new qualification, the Advanced Higher, does equate to A level but most universities still express their entry requirements in terms of the Higher. Full details of all Scottish qualifications can be found on the SQA website. The easiest way to compare the points awarded for A levels and Highers is using the Universities and Colleges Admissions Service (UCAS) tariff calculator. Relevant Scottish sources of further information have been included where appropriate.

## Overseas international qualifications

The National Recognition Centre (comparability of international qualifications) (NARIC) can provide a letter outlining how your overseas qualifications equate to UK qualifications. There is a charge for this service: £86.50 for paper applications, £80.25 if you apply online. Large organisations that deal with many overseas applicants may be able to give you some guidance too.

National Recognition Centre (comparability of international qualifications) (NARIC) Oriel House, Oriel Road, Cheltenham, Gloucestershire GL50 1XP; 0870 990 4088; www.naric.org.uk

# Useful points of contact

www.ucas.ac.uk
This is the central organisation which provides information about and processes applications for higher education courses. UCAS also offers advice on funding your studies.

www.ukpass.ac.uk
A new online service which enables you to research thousands of taught postgraduate courses.

wwwcityandguilds.com
City & Guilds awards a wide range of qualifications across nearly 30 industries in the UK. You can find information on courses for 14–19-year-olds, adult learners and people looking for professional development opportunities.

www.crb.gov.uk
The Criminal Records Bureau (CRB) is the organisation which carries out the checks on anyone who has applied to work with children, young people or vulnerable adults. The website gives details about the procedure and includes an online application facility.

## The National Minimum Wage
The current rates are £4.88 for workers aged 18 to 21, £5.80 for workers aged 22 and over.

**norland**college

CARING FOR CHILDREN

Train at the world famous
Norland College, Bath, for a
rewarding career in childcare

**Norland College Open Days**
Saturday 13 March 2010
Saturday 16 October 2010
Saturday 20 November 2010
Drop in anytime between 10.30am and 2.30pm

www.norland.co.uk

Norland College was founded in 1892 by Emily Lord, a woman who believed that the care of children should centre on the child and be loving and nurturing. Although there have been enormous changes in society since that time, the values and philosophy behind these ideals are still relevant today. Norland College is internationally recognised as the leading provider of childcare training and education.

Norland College offers the following two full-time courses both of which qualify students to work with children:

- **BA (Hons) Early Childhood Studies (Norland)** (a post A Level course run in association with the University of Gloucestershire). This course provides an opportunity to undertake degree level study in a supportive environment within an institution whose sole focus is childcare. Modules include Children's Language and Literacy and the Creative Child. Students can go on to study to

advertisement feature

become primary school teachers, nurses, or Early Years Professionals.

- **Diploma in Early Childhood Studies (DCE) (CACHE)** (a post GCSE course). This course involves the study of child development and how to observe and plan effectively for young children up to the age of 8. Units include Play and Learning in Children's Education and Keeping Children Safe. This qualification can lead to jobs as nannies or Early Years Practitioners in nurseries. Because the DCE awards 360 UCAS points at distinction level, students also have the option to progress on to university.

Norland offers a unique training experience to its students. On both courses the amount of 'hands-on' experience is greater than that found on typical childcare courses. Every other week, and when not in lectures, students spend five consecutive days in an Early Years placement. Students may also spend time in the college's own nursery, 'Norland Nursery' which cares for and educates children from four months to 5 years old. Here they can experience best practice taught at the college in a real working environment.

Students on both courses also work towards the 'Norland Diploma'. The Norland Diploma is made up of lectures in Practical Skills (for example making up bottle feeds and learning how to bath a baby), Creative Skills (for example making a baby mobile and planning a children's birthday party) and Home Economics (learning how to cook nutritious and tasty food for children).

Employment prospects are excellent for Norland graduates. With its own in-house employment agency, 'Norland Agency', the college can provide students with a unique route from training to life-long employment.

Norland provides unparalleled training and opportunities to maximise the full potential of students and that of the children in their care.

To find out more, please visit our website **www.norland.co.uk**, email **enquiries@norland.co.uk** or phone **01225 466202**.

Norland College, York Place, London Road, Bath BA1 6AE

advertisement feature

# With over 42 years of publishing, more than 80 million people have succeeded in business with thanks to **Kogan Page**

# www.koganpage.com

You are reading one of the thousands of books published by **Kogan Page**. As Europe's leading independent business book publishers **Kogan Page** has always sought to provide up-to-the-minute books that offer practical guidance at affordable prices.

**KoganPage**

## MMU School of Law

Manchester
Metropolitan
University

A £15million state-of-the-art building, at the heart of the second largest legal centre in the country, and an excellent reputation for producing quality graduates.

- With a renowned academic team, the School of Law at MMU is well respected, and offers a comprehensive portfolio of legal studies, including undergraduate law degrees, with full and part-time study available.

- We can offer various study options to suit your lifestyle; a wide range of optional subjects; regular feedback, personal tutors and careers advice; and friendly supportive teaching staff with close links to the legal profession.

- The School of Law also works to help provide skills and expertise for those who cannot easily access legal advice through their pro bono work.

For more information contact:
Telephone: 0161 247 2978
E-mail: law@mmu.ac.uk

www.mmu.ac.uk/law

## Manchester Metropolitan University

The School of Law at Manchester Metropolitan University is one of the largest and most well regarded in the UK, enjoying a reputation for the quality and range of its courses.

"We are proud of the diversity of our student population, and of the successes achieved by our students during their time at MMU and afterwards. Whether you are studying in order to enhance your career opportunities or purely for interest, the aim on our comprehensive range of programmes is to make the challenging experience of studying law both enjoyable and rewarding." Miceál Barden, Head of School of Law

The School is housed in the Sandra Burslem building, a £15 million state-of-the-art purpose-built building designed specifically to meet the needs of law students.

We offer a full range of legal education courses from undergraduate law programmes through to postgraduate professional programmes leading to qualifications to enter the legal profession as a trainee solicitor or pupil barrister.

There are opportunities for postgraduate study in a wide range of legal specialisms, particularly in the area of socio-legal studies. We also offer short courses and consultancy for the legal profession and for private and public sector organisations.

Manchester is the second largest legal centre in the country, so our students are well placed to interact with the legal profession and with practitioners of legal skills in other sectors of employment. The School maintains strong links with the local and regional legal profession.

Our students benefit from the expertise and commitment of highly qualified teaching and administrative staff, including well regarded authors, award-winning researchers and those with wide professional experience. Staff prioritise the needs of students, seeking to ensure that they succeed in their studies. We are especially proud of our learning and pastoral support for students, and of the opportunities our part-time programmes offer for students to learn flexibly around their other commitments.

advertisement feature

The School is committed to playing its part in offering access to free legal services for those who would otherwise be denied it. This pro bono work is an important element of the School's commitment to the local community and all students will be offered the opportunity to participate in our pro bono activity.

The School of Law is based on the central university All Saints campus, just off Oxford Road, and is close to Manchester City Centre, the legal district and the Law Courts.

All our programmes have pastoral care arrangements, with dedicated pastoral care tutors.

## Case study

### Ayo James LLB (Hons)

"The support that you get from the staff here in the School of Law is amazing, and I have always found that if I had a query or problem, it was always answered. I have made a number of exceptional links through the School and schemes that they have put on, and I am so grateful to them for what they have done for me."

### Why study at MMU?

- State-of-the-art study facilities
- Many members of staff are qualified solicitors and barristers with strong links to the local legal profession
- Close to the heart of Manchester's legal community
- Located next to the University Sports facilities
- Excellent careers support
- Emphasis on small group interactive teaching
- Excellent pastoral as well as academic support
- Most courses available in full and part-time modes
- 24 hour access to electronic learning materials
- Active and successful research culture

MMU School of Law
t: +44 (0)161 247 3046
e: law@mmu.ac.uk
www.law.mmu.ac.uk

advertisement feature

Share your ideas.

There's a time and place for sharing ideas – and RM is one of them. But that's hardly surprising. As the leader in IT-for-education, it's our job to create technology that both educates and entertains. Which helps kids to focus in class. And that's something that takes plenty of imagination.

So don't be surprised if we put your ideas into action at an early stage. We're a company that likes to give our graduates real responsibility from day one. If you've got a great idea, we want to hear it – no matter what part of the business you happen to be in.

We're looking for graduates to join us in a wide range of roles. Product Development, Software Engineering, Project Management, Finance, Product Management…the list goes on. If you have a 2.1 or above, at least 260 UCAS points, and would like to find out more, visit **www.rmgraduates.com**

**RM.** *REINVENTING* THE CLASSROOM

TOP IT EMPLOYERS

*Microsoft* GOLD CERTIFIED

THE SUNDAY TIMES BEST GREEN COMPANIES

# RM is the UK's leading provider of hardware, software and support services to the education sector.

## About RM

Here, we are guided by a simple vision. To help teachers to teach and learners to learn. To make this happen, we insist on two things; Using the best technology and encouraging and developing our people to become the very best at what they do. The scope of our work is huge. Whether developing award-winning hardware, life-enhancing software, or entire ICT strategies for local authorities, we're at the forefront of every aspect of educational technology.

## Opportunities

We recruit for a wide range of roles - from Software and Systems Engineers to Sales Consultants and Project Managers. You'll need a minimum of a 2:1 and 260 UCAS points, but it's your personal qualities, experience and aptitude we look at most closely. Things like problem-solving skills, your ability to work in a team and gain a real feel for what the customer wants are all important. It's about the person as well as the degree.

People here at RM are the very backbone of what we do – so an open and supportive working culture, along with an awareness of our social and environmental responsibilities make for a pretty great place to work.

## Development

Expect to enjoy real support from day one. Our 2010 intake will get the chance to enjoy our brand new Graduate Development Program. Focused on your induction into the business and starting with an off-site induction, the program will continue to support you through on-the-job training and mentoring as well as through specific technical training courses. You'll have the chance to receive a respected professional accreditation early on in your career. You'll also benefit from more general courses to develop your professional skills (such as presentation, time management and leadership).

**www.rmgraduates.com**

advertisement feature

# Think...
## ...about
# Podiatry

**Podiatry is a healthcare profession, which has developed from its origins in Chiropody. It involves assessment, diagnosis and treatment of patients with foot and lower limb disorders.**

### Who do Podiatrists treat?

It is not only the elderly who have problems with their feet! Podiatrists treat patients of all ages, and from all walks of life.

### Training

- To become Registered you must complete a degree in Podiatry. This can be done at one of 13 institutions across the UK.

- Places for UK Residents are funded by the NHS and SHEFC. They will pay your tuition fees and offer you a means tested bursary.

- Entry requirements for the degree courses vary but generally applicants need to have 2 A Levels or equivalent, one of which must be science based.

- Following the degree most students find employment very quickly in a variety of environments, including the health service, private practice and the retail sector.

If you would like further detailed information please visit our website at:

## www.feetforlife.org

or contact:

**The Society of Chiropodists & Podiatrists**
1 Fellmongers Path, Tower Bridge Road, London SE1 3LY
Telephone: 020 7234 8620  E-mail: enq@scpod.org

The Society of Chiropodists & Podiatrists (SCP)

Podiatry is a medical discipline that focuses on the assessment; diagnosis and management of lower limb health problems.

Podiatrists diagnose and manage problems ranging from gait disorders in children to foot pathologies in the elderly; from overuse injuries in sport to ulceration in patients with diabetes.

An application of biomechanical assessment and techniques for the manufacture of orthotic insoles enable podiatrists to treat athletes with a range of injuries. They also use exercises and heat therapies to treat soft tissue injuries, and knowledge of local anaesthetics combined with surgical skills to resolve a variety of nail pathologies. A detailed understanding of vascular and neurological assessment techniques, along with woundcare skills, allow them to make a considerable contribution in the prevention of amputation in high-risk patients.

Podiatry is a regulated profession and in order to be eligible for Health Professions Council registration and, therefore, employment within the NHS you need to undertake a recognised course of study.

There are 13 schools across the country that offer full-time and some offering part-time bachelor of science honours degrees in Podiatry. The full-time course takes three or four years to complete depending on where you choose to study. The part-time course is usually completed over four and a half years.

The minimum entry requirements vary from school to school so you must check with the institutions you are interested in. However, the following general principles apply:

- The tariff point score ranges up to 300 across the schools
- You are generally required to have a minimum of 2 preferably 3 A-levels one of which should be science, preferably biology based.
- PE may be considered by some institutions as an alternative
- For those taking Scottish Highers the general entry is 4 Highers. One of these must be biology and generally biology or chemistry are preferred.

For further information on podiatry log on to www.feetforlife.org

# www.prospect4u.co.uk

## Careers for you at Prospect 4U

Your number one place for careers information in the process and manufacturing sector

Choose... Building Products

Choose... Coatings

Choose... Quarrying & Mining

Choose... Glass

Choose... Ceramics

Choose... Print

Choose... Paper

Choose... Furniture

Choose... Wood

## Get started...

The process and manufacturing sector is full of exciting and rewarding career opportunities.

You can find all the information you need about getting started in any of these innovative industries by visiting:

## www.prospect4u.co.uk

Visit www.prospect4u.co.uk and find out:

✓ Detailed information on working within each industry

✓ Information on qualifications and training

✓ Different careers you could choose and salary expectations

✓ Case studies from people already working in this sector

✓ Links to help you get started

**proskills**
MAKING SKILLS WORK

**Proskills UK Group**
Centurion Court, 85b Milton Park, Abingdon, Oxon, OX14 4RY
Tel: 01235 833 844 • Fax: 01235 833 733 • info@proskills.co.uk

Choose
proskills
**CAREERS**

# Process and Manufacturing

## Building Products

The industry comprises of two main sub-sectors:

Clay Building Products – which include bricks, roofing tiles, clay pipes and paving blocks

Precast Concrete Products – these make up the British infrastructure such as bridges, culverts, street furniture, cladding of buildings and flooring

- The Building Products sector comprises around 3,000 UK workplaces
- It is a £6.9 billion industry
- The industry employs around 51,000 employees

Jobs include plant operations, engineers, production, apprentice, technicians, sales and management.

Salary: £12,000 - £85,000+

## Coatings

The Coatings industry includes manufacturers of decorative and industrial paints, powder coatings, printing inks, and wall coverings. Coatings are produced for many things we use, including the automotive sector, marine, wood finishing, DIY paints, packaging, and coatings for plastics and printing inks for newspapers.

- The Coatings industry comprises of some 1,000 workplaces
- The industry employs around 21,000 people across the UK
- 65% of companies employ less than 10 people
- It is a £3.9 billion industry

Jobs include Production, Operations, Quality control, Maintenance & Management

Salary: £11,000 - £75,000+

## Extractive and Mineral Processing

The sector provides the essential raw materials for use by the construction industry, agricultural, manufacturing and the energy production industry.

- The UK is the European leader in the recycling of aggregates;
- It is a £9.7 billion industry
- Aggregates account for 70% of the 300 million tonnes of minerals produced each year
- The industry employs around 86,000 individuals in 10,000 UK workplaces

Jobs include mining, civil, engineering, geology, logistics, IT, sales, HR, planning, management, admin & finance.

Salary: £10,000 - £100,000+

## Furniture

The industry is traditionally segmented into three primary sectors:

Domestic - serving the public through retail outlets;

Office - desks, seating, tables and other office items;

Contract - furniture for public areas such as hospitals, schools, hotels and airports.

These can be broken down into the following sub-sectors: Cabinet, Upholstery, Kitchen, Bathroom, Bedroom, Restoration, Reproduction, Soft Furnishings and Other (i.e. components such as chair legs).

- The furniture industry comprises around 12,000 UK workplaces
- The furniture industry employs in excess of 145,000 individuals
- It is a £10.9 billion industry

Careers range from cabinet maker, hand crafts, finisher, polisher, restorer & upholsterer to design & Purchasing, sales and shop owner.

Salary: £12,000 - £75,000+

## Glass

The industry covers the manufacture of flat glass, container glass, domestic glass, decorative glass, automotive and specialist glass.

Companies range from high-tech scientific glass makers, through a whole range of Glass Processors to more traditional Stained Glass Conservation specialists. Glass is used in applications as diverse as packaging, decoration, automotive manufacture and architecture.

- There are in excess of 21,000 UK workplaces in the glass & glazing sector
- The industry employs around 168,000 people
- It is a £3.1billion industry

Careers include glassmaker, automotive glazer, production, management, distribution & sales and there are also opportunities for finance, HR and admin roles.
Salary: £14,000 - £80,000+

## Glazed Ceramics

The industry includes the following sub-sectors:

Tableware, giftware, sanitary ware, wall and floor tiles, craft potters, technical and industrial ceramics.

In addition, ceramics are used in many mechanical and electrical components; the nuclear industry even uses Glazed Ceramics in the production of moderators and controls in nuclear reactors!

- The Glazed ceramics sector comprises approximately 1,200 UK workplaces
- The industry employs almost 30,000 employees
- It is a £1.2 billion industry

Careers include design, operative, lab tech, production & distribution.
Salary: £12,000 - £75,000+

## Paper

The industry can be broadly divided into four areas:

Paper Making; Recovered Paper; Corrugated and Tissue Grade.

Forestry, paper and packaging are among the most sustainable industries in existence. Forests are planted and re-planted and are one of the main contributors to absorbing $CO_2$.

- The UK Paper industry comprises 3,600 workplaces
- The industry employs around 99,000 people
- It is an £11 billion p.a. industry

Careers include manufacturing, fibre preparations, operatives, engineers, quality technician, production and operations as well as sales, finance and HR.
Salary: £12,000 - £75,000+

## Print

The industry produces a wide and varied spectrum of products ranging from newspapers, books and magazines to money, passports, signage and printed packaging.

- The Print industry comprises around 27,000 UK workplaces
- It is a £12.6 billion industry
- The industry employs in excess of 205,000 people across the UK

Jobs include administration, sales, graphic design, production, finishing, operations & studio management.
Salary: £10,000 - £75,000+

## Timber / Wood

This sector dominates the supply of softwood and hardwood in the UK. Products also include plywood, fibreboard, MDF and particleboard.

- The vast majority of wood purchased in the UK comes from sustainably managed forests.
- The wood products industry is worth over £11 billion
- Approximately 60% of wood or wood products are used in construction
- The timber industry employs approximately 115,000 employees

Careers in the industry can include design, architecture, science, logging, environmental, journalism, PR, accounting, IT and sales.

**For more information on jobs, careers and skills visit Proskills UK at www.prospect4u.co.uk**

advertisement feature

## ACCOUNTANCY

(*see also* Taxation)

Members of the accountancy profession are involved in the financial transactions of businesses, including the preparation and verification of accounts, auditing and analysis.

## Accountant

Accountants work with and have expert understanding of a wide range of financial questions, issues and procedures. They work in many different settings, including small high street accounting firms, local and central government departments, management consultants and for the finance departments of commercial and industrial organisations from small businesses to huge multinationals. They deal with such questions as taxation, business forecasting, monitoring financial performance, advising on investments, acquisitions and mergers and good daily financial management. They also audit the paperwork and computer records of organisations to make sure that all financial transactions are accounted for and comply with the law.

Because accountants cover such a wide area of expertise, there are several different specialist branches within the profession. They work in one of the following three areas.

### Management accountant

Chartered management accountants, usually referred to as management accountants, work in commerce and industry. They work with a company or organisation monitoring and planning budgets, preparing information for external auditors, overseeing credit control, monitoring financial performance and making suggestions about future business development. They work closely with other members of the management team. They may be qualified Chartered Accountants, Chartered Certified Accountants or Management Accountants.

# YOUR ROUTE TO A SUCCESSFUL CAREER IN BUSINESS.

## Certificate in Finance, Accounting and Business

Develop your understanding of finance, accounting and business fundamentals and enhance your CV to stand out from the crowd in a competitive job market. The certificate can also be used as a stepping stone towards the ACA, one of the leading business and finance qualifications from the ICAEW.

It can be completed in less than one year; whilst you study or whilst you're reviewing your career opportunities. There are no entry requirements, credits for prior learning are available and there are several choices on how you study.

**To find out more:**
**T +44 (0)1908 248 040**
**www.icaew.com/cfab**

THE INSTITUTE
OF CHARTERED
ACCOUNTANTS
IN ENGLAND AND WALES

# Your route to success

Have you considered where your future career lies? Do you want to work in a varied and dynamic business arena? Are you looking to enhance your CV? Then maybe a professional qualification from the ICAEW could be your route to success.

The Institute of Chartered Accountants in England and Wales (ICAEW) is a world leader in the accountancy and finance profession. We have a range of qualifications that you can complete independently, or whilst supported by an employer, which are recognised and respected around the world.

## The Certificate in Finance, Accounting and Business

The Certificate in Finance, Accounting and Business (CFAB) is open to all, regardless of academic background or experience. The business skills you will learn are highly relevant in all business sectors, providing you with your many vital career options.

CFAB provides an essential understanding of the fundamentals of finance, accounting and business it can also be used as an entry route into the ICAEW's ACA, one of the leading professional business and finance qualifications.

There are also exemptions available, which means you could complete CFAB in less than 12 months. The modules include: business and finance; management information; accounting (compulsory); law; assurance and principles of taxation. These modules also make up the knowledge exams of the ACA qualification.

## The ACA qualification

The ACA qualification can lead to a varied career in finance and business. Look closely enough and you'll find that many of the world's top business advisers are chartered accountants.

The ACA equips you with the skills and knowledge needed to work in a variety of roles, in a diverse business environment. You'll gain a solid foundation in finance, business, marketing, economics, management and information systems, opening the door to a wide range of career paths once qualified.

## Earn while you learn with the ACA

ACA training is a mixture of classroom learning and work experience. When studying for the ACA you will work for an ICAEW authorised training employer. These employers are in all business sectors, including; practice (chartered accountancy firms) commerce and the public sector. Your employer will generally fund all of your training, allow you study leave and pay you a competitive salary which can increase as you pass your ACA exams.

## Routes to ACA training

There are several options open to you, depending on where you are in your study. You may find you can study for the ACA straight from school or university, via CFAB, or after taking the AAT (Association of Accounting Technicians) qualification.

**Find out more about your routes to success**

Visit **www.icaew.com/cfab** • E careers@icaew.com • www.icaew.com/careers

advertisement feature

### Accountant in private practice

Accountants working in private practice assess, monitor and advise on the financial status of private businesses. They work for freelancers, for small firms or for large practices offering their services to fee-paying clients.

Practitioners are either qualified as Associate Members of the Institute of Chartered Accountants in England and Wales (ICAEW), the Institute of Chartered Accountants in Scotland (ICAS), the Institute of Chartered Accountants in Ireland (ICAI), or the Association of Chartered Certified Accountants (ACCA). Members of the Association of International Accountants (AIA) also do private practice work.

One specific role within accountancy is that of the auditor. Auditors are responsible for checking the financial records of every kind of business and organisation and they are not employees of that organisation. External auditors must be qualified Chartered Accountants or international accountants.

### Accountant in the public sector

Chartered public finance accountants (public sector accountants) control and assess the efficiency of public spending. Working for example in health trusts, local authorities, universities and central government departments, they examine the cost-effectiveness of policies, manage budgets, conduct internal audits and advise on policy.

Knowing in what kind of environment you would work and what specialist knowledge you wish to apply will help you choose which of the branches of accountancy is most appropriate for you.

## Qualifications and Training

Each of the professional bodies offering training asks for slightly different entry qualifications. It is, however, possible to offer some general useful guidelines. Trainee accountants are taken on by employers of many kinds, but they also have to fulfil the entry criteria for the appropriate professional body.

With the exception of a few people with three grade As at A level, the vast majority of trainee accounts are graduates. A good honours degree in any subject is fine, although business, mathematics and technical subjects are strongly represented in the profession. If your degree includes a lot of maths, you may be exempt from some of the professional exams. Many employers set numeracy tests as part of their selection process.

You should have five GCSEs grades A or B and two A levels. Many accountancy firms require you to have 280 to 300 UCAS points if you wish to become a Chartered Accountant. All the accounting professional bodies do offer alternative entry routes for mature students and for applicants who are already qualified accounting technicians.

Management accountants do not have to be graduates, but a good honours degree in a mathematical or business subject may offer exemptions from some of the professional examinations.

Accountants qualified with any of the professional accountancy bodies can work in the public sector, but the most relevant organisation is the Chartered Institute of Public Finance and Accountancy (CIPFA). If you don't have another accountancy qualification you must have three GCSEs grades A to C and two A levels and you must have maths and English at either GCSE or A level.

All the accountancy professions offer similar training routes where you have to complete three years' supervised work and take professional exams at two levels.

## Personal qualities and skills

Accountants have to be good at working with numbers but they must also be very good communicators. They have to be able to understand complex information and also to explain complicated information to people who don't have detailed financial knowledge. They must be persistent, and assertiveness is as important as tact and discretion.

## Salaries

Starting salaries vary considerably, depending on location, size of firm and type of accountancy, but start at around £23,000 to £28,000 for trainees in London and the South East; £17,000 to £24,000 is more typical elsewhere. On qualifying, salaries increase significantly – £40,000 to £55,000 with a few years' experience. Salary packages often include benefits such as pay bonuses, share options and pension and private health plans. The professional bodies conduct regular salary surveys and you can obtain further information from them.

**info**

Association of Accounting Technicians, 140 Aldersgate Street, London EC1A 4HY; 0845 863 0800; www.aat.org.uk

Association of Chartered Certified Accountants, 29 Lincoln's Inn Fields, London WC2A 3EE; 020 7059 5000; www.accaglobal.com

Association of International Accountants, Staithes 3, The Watermark, Metro Riverside, Newcastle Upon Tyne NE11 9SN; 0191 482 0277; www.aia.org.uk

Chartered Institute of Management Accountants (CIMA), 26 Chapter Street, London SW1P 4NP; 020 8849 2287; www.cimaglobal.com

Chartered Institute of Public Finance and Accountancy (CIPFA), 3 Robert Street, London WC2N 6RL; 020 7543 5600; www.cipfa.org.uk

Financial Services Skills Council, 51 Gresham Street, London EC2V 7HQ; 0845 257 3772; www.fssc.org.uk

HM Revenue & Customs (HMRC); www.hmrc.gov.uk

The Insolvency Service, 21 Bloomsbury Street, London WC1B 3QW; www.insolvency.gov.uk

Institute of Chartered Accountants in England and Wales (ICAEW), Chartered Accountants' Hall, PO Box 433 EC2P 2BJ; 020 7920 8100; www.icaew.co.uk

Institute of Chartered Accountants In Ireland (ICAI); Burlington House, Burlington Road, Dublin 4; +3531 637 7200; www.icai.ie

Institute of Chartered Accountants of Scotland (ICAS), CA House, 21 Haymarket Yards, Edinburgh EH12 5BH; 0131 347 0100; www.icas.org.uk

Institute of Public Finance, No. 1 Croydon, 12–16 Addiscombe Road, Croydon CR0 0XT; 020 8667 1144; www.ipf.co.uk

National Audit Office, 151 Buckingham Palace Road, London SW1W 9SS; 020 7798 7000; www.nao.org.uk

# Accounting technician

Accounting technicians work in a variety of roles, often alongside profession-ally qualified Chartered Accountants. They are involved in the day-to-day practical work of accountancy and finance, including the preparation of infor-mation and accounts and the interpretation of computer information, such as audit tax and payroll. Accounting technicians are widely employed in public finance, industry and commerce, and private practice. Their roles range from accounts clerks to finance managers. A growing number of accounting tech-nicians provide a range of services direct to the public and manage their own practice. Many go on to qualify with the senior chartered accountancy bodies.

## Qualifications and Training

There are no set entry qualifications, but you must be confident with maths. Some employers may prefer you to have GCSEs (A–C) or equivalent in English and maths. Previous experience of office work and good IT skills, especially in creating spreadsheets, are also valuable.

You can start as an accounts clerk doing basic duties, and take work-based training or a part-time college course to qualify as a technician with the Association of Accounting Technicians (AAT) or Association of Chartered Certified Accountants (ACCA). You may not have to do the first stages of accounting technician training if you already have an A level or equivalent in accounting, previous relevant work experience or a basic book keeping quali-fication. AAT and ACCA qualifications comprise a foundation, an intermedi-ate and a technician stage. The AAT or the ACCA can advise you about where to find a training place. It is also sometimes possible to do an apprenticeship as an accounting technician.

## Personal Qualities and Skills

You must be thorough and methodical and enjoy working with figures. Good IT skills and the ability to work as part of a team are also very important. Some positions involve considerable responsibility and/or the pressure of deadlines.

## Salaries

There are often significant differences between salaries in London and the South-East compared to the regions. Starting salaries for trainees are between £15,500 and £20,000. Qualified technicians earn from £18,000 to £27,000. Accounting technicians with other management responsibilities can earn far more than this.

**info**

Association of Accounting Technicians, 140 Aldersgate Street, London EC1A 4HY; 0845 863 0800; www.aat.org.uk

Association of Chartered Certified Accountants, 29 Lincolns Inn Fields, London WC2A 3EE; 020 7059 5000; www.accaglobal.com

Financial Services Skills Council, 51 Gresham Street, London EC2V 7HQ; 020 7216 7366; www.fssc.org.uk

# ACTOR

*see* Performing Arts

# ACTUARY

Actuaries use their knowledge of mathematics, statistics, economics and business to assess financial risks and probabilities. Traditionally their work is mainly concerned with the topical issue of pensions, plus life assurance and other types of insurance, but they may also work in investment and other business areas where major financial risks are involved.

They create statistical and mathematical models to analyse past events and predict the financial outcome of different situations. For example, in insurance they may study accident rates or medical data to develop and price new insurance policies, making sure that there are sufficient funds to cover liabilities but allow the company to remain profitable.

Around 45 per cent of actuaries work for consultancies providing specialist actuarial services to businesses of every kind. They advise on business recovery, acquisitions and employee benefit schemes. Central government also has its own actuarial departments that provide actuarial support and information across central government, its agencies and the National Health Service.

## Qualifications and Training

To qualify as an actuary you must become a student member of one of the professional bodies; either the Faculty or Institute of Actuaries – referred to collectively as the Actuarial Profession. Minimum entry qualifications are three GCSEs grades A–C including English and two A levels one of which must be maths at grade B. If you have a second class honours degree in any subject, A level maths grade C is acceptable. If you have a degree in maths or actuarial science you do not need a maths A level. If your degree is in maths or a highly numerate discipline a third class honours degree is acceptable. In practice, entry to the profession is competitive, so the majority of entrants are graduates with good degrees.

Once you have completed your professional training, study and examinations you become a Fellow of either the Institute or Faculty. To qualify as a Fellow of the Faculty or Institute of Actuaries, you must pass 15 professional examinations. After one year's work experience and appropriate examinations you should reach associate membership and after three years' work experience and appropriate exams you should reach fellowship.

If you have a degree or postgraduate qualification in actuarial science, statistics or economics, you may be exempt from some or all of the exams at the Core Technical Stage and some at the next stage. Please contact the Institute of Actuaries for further details of exemptions.

## Personal Qualities and Skills

You need excellent maths and statistical skills and must be able to understand and explain complex information. You should have a thorough understanding

The Actuarial Profession
making financial sense of the future
Beyond the norm
Work for one organisation, influence countless others
The decisions and forecasts you make as an actuary will have a far-reaching impact. If you love solving problems and would relish the chance to make sure businesses are ready for anything, this is a profession like no other.
For more information, please go to www.actuaries.org.uk

# The Actuarial Profession
## *Work for one organisation, influence countless others*

Become an actuary and combine your problem solving and maths skills with communications and teamwork in an ever-changing financial environment. Actuaries identify solutions to business problems and manage assets and liabilities by analysing past events, assessing present risks and modelling the future.

Actuaries work in many areas that directly benefit the public through their work in life and non-life insurance, advising pension funds, savings, capital projects, investment, healthcare and risk management. Such work offers management opportunities, with actuaries having a commercial as well as technical role.

Although qualifying as an actuary is a demanding process, the rewards are considerable. An actuarial career offers a challenging, well respected and well paid future. Graduate entry salaries are offered between £23,000 to £30,000, and chief actuaries can earn £150,000+.

To qualify as an actuary, trainees need to be intelligent; most actuaries possess either a first or upper second class numerate degree. The most successful actuaries also have good communication skills. The minimum entrance requirement is grade B at A level or equivalent in maths. Qualification involves passing the professional examinations of The Faculty and Institute of Actuaries. Trainees take the examinations at their own pace, usually whilst working for an actuarial employer. Exemptions from some of the examinations may be awarded to students who have achieved an appropriate standard in a relevant degree, or have studied actuarial science at postgraduate level.

There are many opportunities for actuaries to use their skills, in the UK and overseas and the demand for actuarial skills continues to grow. The qualification is an excellent base for a business career that is widely recognised throughout the financial world.

*To find out more about an actuarial career:*

Tel: **01865 268 228**
Email: **careers@actuaries.org.uk**
Or visit **www.actuaries.org.uk**

advertisement feature

of business and economics, be a great communicator and be aware of the bigger picture while paying attention to fine detail.

## Salaries

Trainee actuaries start on around £30,000. This rises to between £35,000 and £50,000 for part-qualified associate actuaries. Qualified actuaries with at least five years' experience can earn between £55,000 and £75,000 and some salaries in the profession reach more than £100,000.

**info**

The Actuarial Education Company, 31 Bath Street, Abingdon, Oxfordshire OX14 3FF; 01235 550005; www.acted.co.uk

The Actuarial Profession, Napier House, 4 Worcester Street, Oxford OX1 2AW; 01865 268200; www.actuaries.org.uk

The Association of Consulting Actuaries, Warnford Court, 29 Throgmorton Street, London EC2N 2AT; 020 7382 4954; www.aca.org.uk

Faculty of Actuaries, Maclaurin House, 18 Dublin Street, Edinburgh

EH1 3PP; 0131 240 1300; www.actuaries.org.uk

Financial Services Skills Council, 51 Gresham Street, London EC2V 7HQ; 020 7216 7366; www.fssc.org.uk

Insurance Careers: www.insurancecareers.org

Computer Economics Limited and Remuneration Economics, Survey House, 51 Portland Road, Kingston upon Thames, Surrey KT1 2SH; 020 8549 8726; www.celre.co.uk

# ADVERTISING

(*see also* Market Researcher and Public Relations Officer)

Communication is the heart of this complex industry, providing a wide range of openings, many with agencies that plan, organise and run advertising campaigns. Working on behalf of clients, advertising agencies study the product or service to be advertised and its market. They then plan how it should be sold and distributed, and how the media might be used to the best advantage in this process.

# Account executive

Account executives are responsible within the agency for a particular client or group of clients. They interpret the client's wishes; coordinate and supervise the work of others within the agency, such as creatives, account planners, copywriters and scriptwriters; seek advice from other experts such as media executives; and then present the ideas most likely to meet with the client's approval.

## Account planner

Account planners consider the client's brief and work to identify the ideal audience and optimum method of getting the client's message across. They analyse market research and other data and provide the creative team with the information that will help them develop the most effective campaign. They may also work on forward planning for the agency, identifying likely future clients based on market data they have researched.

## Art editor/executive director

This position involves coordinating the work of the creative department, which converts the client's original intentions into a visual form for approval. Others, including copywriters, may elaborate upon this.

## Artist

(*see also* Art and Design)

Agency artists prepare initial visual layouts of adverts, posters and displays, and produce final artwork for printing. They need to be competent in using design software.

## Copywriter and scriptwriter

The writers in the agency produce headings, text, jingles and copy for articles in journals, and scripts for films and commercials. Copywriters often work closely with the Art Editor and visualisers.

## Media executive

Media executives work as media buyers and media planners to ensure that advertising campaigns reach their target audiences. Media planners work out where advertising will be most effective – television, radio, posters, newspapers, magazines and of course, the internet. They must keep abreast of the changing market; the growth in internet advertising is a prime example of this. Media buyers try to get the best possible deals for their clients when placing advertising with this wide variety of media.

### Qualifications and Training

Advertising is a fiercely competitive sector, especially in the current economic climate. Most entrants to jobs in advertising have either a degree or an HND. Any subject is acceptable, but some employers prefer related subjects including advertising, business studies, marketing, English or consumer science. Smaller agencies may take you without a degree, particularly if you have some relevant work experience. Work experience is extremely valuable, it shows you how agencies work and makes you a stronger applicant, but this experience is hard to come by. You may want to consider doing voluntary work for an agency. Some agencies offer formal work experience schemes and details of these appear on the Institute of Practitioners in Advertising website. There are many courses in marketing, communications and media studies at many levels. These may provide useful background, but they won't necessarily make you more employable. There are a few highly respected postgraduate courses in advertising including a diploma in copywriting at West Herts College and a postgraduate diploma in advertising at Falmouth College of Art and Design.

The majority of training is on the job, learning from colleagues, and you are usually considered to be a trainee for about two years. The IPA offers induction courses and continuing professional development courses and the Chartered Institute of Marketing offers a range of part-time and distance learning courses for those who are already working in the sector.

Since September 2008 a limited number of schools and colleges have introduced new Vocational Diplomas in creative and media studies. These can be taken at foundation, higher or advanced level. These courses combine academic study and training with an employer.

## Personal Qualities and Skills

Excellent communication skills at every level are extremely important. Being able to deal with people, write clearly and work creatively are all essential skills. Many roles require you to be persuasive and tactful, and to be a media planner you need to be highly numerate. Advertising is a highly pressured business so you have to be thick-skinned and keep calm when chasing deadlines.

**info**

Account Planning Group, 16 Creighton Avenue, London N10 1NU; 020 8444 3692; www.apg.org.uk

The Advertising Association (AA), 7th Floor North, Artillery House, 11–19 Artillery Row, London SW1P 1RT; 020 7340 1100; www.adassoc.org.uk

British Interactive Media Association (BIMA), Briarlea House, Southend Road, South Green, Billericay, Essex CM11 2PR; www.bima.co.uk

Chartered Institute of Marketing (CIM), Moor Hall, Cookham,

Maidenhead, Berks SL6 9QH; 01628 427500; www.cim.co.uk

The Communication Advertising and Marketing Education Foundation (CAM), Moor Hall, Cookham, Maidenhead, Berkshire SL6 9QH; 01628 427 120; www.camfoundation.com

The Creative Circle, 22 Poland Street, London W1F 8QQ; 020 7734 9334; www.creativecircle.co.uk

Creative and Cultural Skills, 4th Floor, Lafone House, The Leathermarket Weston St, London SE1 3HN; 0207 015 1800; www.ccskills.org.uk

## Salaries

Starting salaries range from £18,000 to £25,000 depending on your role. Trainee account executives tend to earn more than trainee media planners and buyers. Salary also depends on size of the agency. Many agencies are based in London and the South-East. In the regions, starting salaries range from £15,000 to £20,000. Senior account executives can earn £100,000, but averages are closer to £43,000 to £50,000. Advertising has suffered in the current recession and salaries have not risen as fast in the past 18 months.

# AERIAL INSTALLER

Aerial installers fix aerials to roof structures along with the necessary cabling to feed televisions, VCRs and radio receivers. Many installers also offer cable and satellite dish installation, and a number of businesses specialise in these areas as well as offering standard communication aerial installation.

## Qualifications and Training

No formal qualifications are necessary, but many employers would expect a good general standard of education; some companies like you to have three or four GCSEs grades A–C. Training is on the job, but the main trade organisation in the sector, the CAI, has developed a good range of basic and more advanced training courses. It offers short courses in basic radio and TV installation, basic satellite dish installation and motorised dish installation. It also offers courses on customer relations and training in working safely at heights. Through the CAI you can work for NVQ levels 2 and 3. Level 2 is aimed at installing aerials and communications equipment on individual private properties. The level 3 qualification is for technicians who are installing systems to blocks of flats, commercial premises and large organisations such as hospitals or schools. For aerial installers, there is a City & Guilds Certificate in Digital Television Aerial Installation at level 2. Many installers go on to do other courses in electronics engineering, maintenance engineering or communications engineering. There is a wide range of courses, full and part time, in all these areas.

## Personal Qualities and Skills

You have to be very practical, have good numeracy skills and be quite happy working up high. You should be able to get on well with people. You need to be a good problem solver and a thorough and meticulous worker.

E-skills UK, 1 Castle Lane, London SW1E 6DR; www.e-skills.com

Confederation of Aerial Industries, Fulton House Business Centre, Fulton Road, Wembley Park,

Middlesex HA9 0TF; 020 8902 8998; www.cai.org.uk

Local Jobcentre Plus and Connexions careers office.

info

## Salaries

Salaries during training or apprenticeship range from £16,000 to £18,000. After two or three years' experience salaries are between £20,000 and £23,000. They can be higher if you are working on large commercial premises rather than domestic properties.

# AGRICULTURE

(*see also* Farming)

The work in agriculture involves cultivating crops and raising livestock for food, energy and raw materials.

# Agricultural contractor

Agricultural contractors work in many farming operations including harvesting, crop spraying, weeding, lambing and sheep shearing – in short, all those tasks where extra labour is needed for a particular task or a particular season.

## Qualifications and Training

You don't normally need specific entry qualifications, but you do need experience of those aspects of agricultural operations in which you wish to take on contract work. There are several relevant courses available for anyone who wishes to gain qualifications. These include BTEC First Diplomas in Agriculture and BTEC National Diplomas in Agriculture, City & Guilds National Certificate in Agriculture, C&G Advanced National Certificate in Agriculture, NVQ levels 2 and 3 in Agricultural Crop Production, NVQ levels 2 and 3 in Mixed Farming, and NVQ levels 2 and 3 in Livestock Production.

For some tasks, such as operating chainsaws or using pesticides, you are legally required to be trained and competent. The National Proficiency Test Council (NPTC) awards certificates of competence for chainsaw use. The NPTC offers many short courses in ploughing, crop spraying and other agricultural skills.

## Personal Qualities and Skills

You must be practical, able to solve problems and able to handle and maintain machinery. You should be able to work with different teams of people and adapt to new situations readily.

**info**

Lantra, Lantra House, Stoneleigh Park, Nr Coventry, Warwickshire CV8 2LG; 0845 707 8007; www.lantra.co.uk

National Proficiency Tests Council (NPTC), Stoneleigh Park, Stoneleigh, Warwickshire CV8 2LG; 024 7685 7300; www.nptc.org.uk

## Salaries

Salaries vary according to the level of skill required for the work you are carrying out. Some agricultural contractors are paid very close to the minimum wage, but average earnings are between £14,000 and £22,000 a year. Overtime can often be earned, because there are very busy times of year – harvesting, crop spraying, etc – contrasted with some very quiet times.

## Agricultural engineering

*see* Engineering

## Agricultural surveying

*see* Surveying

# AMBULANCE SERVICE

Most of the work in the ambulance service is directly with patients, providing pre-hospital care and transportation in response to emergency and urgent calls, or providing transport for those unable, for medical reasons, to make their own way to hospital. There are two distinct areas of front-line work: accident and emergency, and patient transport services.

## Ambulance care assistant

Ambulance care assistants usually work in the patient transport service of an ambulance trust, where they drive disabled, elderly and vulnerable people to and from outpatient clinics, daycare centres and to routine hospital admissions. They are sometimes called PTS drivers. They may have to lift or assist patients in and out of vehicles and they have to ensure that their patients are comfortable and safe.

## Ambulance technician

Ambulance technicians normally work alongside a paramedic, attending scenes of accidents and other emergencies. Supervised by a paramedic, an ambulance technician carries out a wide range of emergency treatments, treating burns, wounds, fractures and heart attacks. As well as treating patients, ambulance technicians have to liaise with patients' relatives, with members of the public and with staff from other emergency services.

# Emergency medical dispatcher

Emergency medical dispatchers handle emergency 999 calls from the public and from GPs. Some ambulance services split this role into call takers and dispatchers. Where this is the case, call handlers take down details accurately, quickly and calmly. Dispatchers then decide how best to deal with this situation – how many vehicles to send, for example. In some ambulance services, the same person is responsible for taking down details, logging them onto a computer and sending out the ambulances.

# Paramedic

Paramedics are the senior ambulance service healthcare professionals at an accident or a medical emergency. They assess a patient's condition and give essential and often lifesaving treatment. They use a range of sophisticated equipment and can administer drugs, drips and oxygen. They are trained to resuscitate and stabilise patients and they may also drive ambulances, since they usually work in teams of two to a vehicle.

# PTS call handler

PTS (Patient Transport Service) call handlers work in the non-emergency part of ambulance services, organising routine transport to take patients to and from hospital appointments and home after discharge. They deal with requests for appointments and ensure the most efficient use of the available vehicles.

## Qualifications and Training

Entry qualifications for ambulance care assistants and for emergency medical dispatchers vary between ambulance trusts – many do require GCSEs, NVQs and/or relevant work experience. PTS call handlers don't need academic qualifications, though each ambulance service does set its own entry requirements. Training is on the job and covers how to use communications equipment and customer care skills. Drivers of non-emergency and emergency vehicles must hold a full, clean, manual driving licence.

Ambulance technicians have often worked as ambulance care assistants first. An alternative route is to obtain a post as a trainee ambulance technician. Academic requirements for this vary between different ambulance services, but GCSEs grades A–C are often required. Paramedics qualify either by training first as an ambulance technician, or by doing a diploma, foundation degree or degree course in paramedic science. Appropriate courses are approved by the Health Professionals Council.

Training relevant to particular roles is given on the job and through special training courses on lifting and handling patients, advanced driving, etc. Ambulance technicians and paramedics need regular training to keep them up to date with new equipment, drugs and knowledge of dealing with emergency situations.

## Personal Qualities and Skills

Most NHS salaries are linked to a graded pay structure. The NHS Careers website gives detailed information for each job title, showing which pay bands a particular job falls into. The pay structure is based on skills and responsibilities attached to each job. An ambulance care assistant working in the NHS earns from £13,300 to just under £17,500. A paramedic earns between £19,600 and £26,000 a year. A fully qualified ambulance technician earns around £20,000 a year. Many ambulance jobs also attract antisocial working hours payments. There are additional allowances for working in Inner and Outer London.

Ambulance Service Association, Capital Tower, 91 Waterloo Road, London SE1 8RT; 020 7928 9620; www.asa.uk.net

British Paramedic Association, 28 Wilfred Street, Derby DE23 8GF; 01332 746356; www. britishparamedic.org

Health Professions Council, Park House, 184 Kennington Park Road London SE11 4BU; 020 7582 0866; www.hpc-uk.org

NHS Careers, PO Box 376, Bristol BS99 3EY; 0845 606 0655; www.nhscareers.nhs.uk

NHS Learning and Development; 08000 150 850; e-mail: learning@nhscareers.nhs.uk

Skills for Health, 1st Floor, Goldsmiths House, Broad Plain, Bristol BS2 0JP; 0117 922 1155; www.skillsforhealth.org.uk

**info**

# ANIMALS

(*see also* Veterinary Science *and* Zoology)

There is a wide range of occupations that involve working with animals. An obvious prerequisite for anyone wanting to work in this field is to have a love of animals and concern for their welfare.

# Animal care worker

Animal care workers feed, groom, clean, exercise and generally care for small animals of many kinds. They may also have to keep records and to deal with members of the public. They work in many different settings including kennels, catteries, animal rescue centres, open farms and animal sanctuaries. They also work as kennel assistants at quarantine centres and as auxiliaries at animal hospitals.

## Qualifications and Training

The right attitude and some relevant experience – either paid or voluntary – are more important than qualifications. Some organisations may require you to have passed GCSEs, especially if you may want to go on to part-time study. Work with animals is popular; a good way to improve your chances of success is to do some relevant voluntary work. See Info panel to find out where to volunteer. There are EDEXCEL/BTEC certificate and diploma courses available in animal care; for these you will need three GCSEs grade A–C including a science.

## Personal Qualities and Skills

You must be kind and gentle when handling animals, but you must also be calm and confident. You need to be patient and you can't be squeamish. While being caring is essential, you must be resilient enough not to get too easily upset when dealing with badly treated or neglected animals. You need to be practical, you might need record-keeping skills and you should be good at dealing with humans as well as animals.

## Salaries

Pay is often low in this sector, especially with charitable organisations, which want to minimise staff costs. Your pay is often around minimum wage level, but it can rise to £13,000 to £16,000 with experience and responsibility.

**info**

Lantra, Lantra House, Stoneleigh Park, Nr Coventry, Warwickshire CV8 2LG; 0845 707 8007; www.lantra.co.uk

RSPCA, Wilberforce Way, Southwater, Horsham, West Sussex RH13 9RS; www.rspca.org.uk

PDSA, Whitechapel Way, Priorslee, Telford, Shropshire TF2 9PQ; 0800 917 2509; www.pdsa.org.uk

Blue Cross, Shilton Road, Burford, Oxfordshire OX18 4PF; 01993 822651; www.bluecross.org.uk

College of Animal Welfare, London Road, Godmanchester, Cambridgeshire PE29 2LJ; 0870 062 1122; www.caw.ac.uk

Animal Care College, Ascot House, High Street, Ascot, Berkshire SL5 7JG; 0870 730 8433; www.animalcarecollege.co.uk

Volunteering England; www.volunteering.org.uk

Volunteer Scotland; www.volunteerscotland.info

# Animal groomer

Animal grooming is a growing industry, with more dog and cat owners using the services provided by grooming salons, of which there are 2,000 in the UK. Most are small private businesses, and some are part of other establishments, including pet shops, garden centres, and boarding and breeding kennels. Some mobile groomers visit animals in their own home.

Each breed has different requirements and there are many types of coat, which all require specialist skills and techniques. The work involves bathing, shampooing, drying, clipping, trimming and brushing a variety of long- and short-coated animals. Specialist procedures include nail clipping, teeth cleaning, ear care and treatments for parasites.

## Qualifications and Training

There are two main routes into training: a fee-paying course at a private grooming training centre or learning on the job. Candidates with practical animal-grooming experience may enrol for the City & Guilds Dog Grooming Certificate 775. This two-part exam, with a written paper and a practical element, tests candidates' skills on three different types of animal. This qualification shows employers that the groomer has had correct training and gives customers confidence that he or she is competent.

The Advanced Grooming Diploma tests the expertise and skill required of the experienced groomer working in a commercial environment. A good working knowledge of the Kennel Club Breed Standards, styles and trimming techniques is required in order to pass all components. The exam consists of a written paper and seven practical modules, which can be taken over a period of time until all seven are complete, working at a timescale to suit the individual.

## Salaries

These vary from area to area, and hours and rates of pay are negotiable. A general range is £10,000 to £15,000, but more if you run your own business.

British Dog Groomers Association, Bedford Business Centre, 170 Mile Road, Bedford MK42 9TW; 01234 273933; fax: 01234 273550; www.petcare.org.uk; e-mail: info@petcare.org.uk

Lantra Connect, Lantra House, Stoneleigh, Warwickshire CV8 2LG; 0045 707 8007; www.lantra.co.uk; Local Job Centre Plus and Careers/ Connexions Centres

**info**

# Animal technician

Animal technicians are a specialised and distinct group of professionals who are responsible for the care and welfare of animals used in biomedical research. Governments around the world require that new medicines have been extensively tested on animals before allowing human clinical trials. Testing is also undertaken on veterinary medicines and other products which may have an effect on human health. Animal technicians are responsible for caring for the animals, undertaking observations, sampling for the scientific studies, and ensuring that the strict laws controlling their use are followed at all times. Applicants should have a genuine desire to work with animals and must demonstrate concern and respect for their well-being.

## Qualifications and Training

The minimum entry qualifications are five GCSEs at grade C or above, but some entrants have A levels or a degree. The Institute of Animal Technology offers five levels of qualification, from a basic one-year certificate to a post-graduate MSc. You can get exemption from certain modules of these courses if you can offer sciences at A or degree level. These qualifications can be taken as distance learning modules or at local colleges through day release courses.

## Personal Qualities and Skills

You have to be comfortable handling animals and you must be kind, caring and calm when doing so. You also have to accept that you will have to do things that are stressful for animals, so you need to be prepared for this. You must be practical, thorough and meticulous, since you have to record scientific information accurately.

## Salaries

Salaries for trainees range from £12,000 to £15,000 and from £15,000 to £20,000 for qualified technicians, but there is no national agreed rate for this work. A senior laboratory manager can earn up to £35,000.

info

Institute of Animal Technology,
5 South Parade, Summertown,
Oxford OX2 7JL; www.iat.org.uk

Lantra, Lantra House, Stonelelgh
Park, Nr Coventry, Warwickshire
CV8 2LG; 0845 707 8007;
www.lantra.co.uk

# Assistance dog trainer

Assistance dog trainers and instructors train dogs to help people with physical disabilities, hearing or sight impairments, or who are prone to seizures, to live independently. There are four types of assistance dogs. Guide Dogs for the Blind help people to avoid obstacles, find entrances, stairs, etc. Disability assistance dogs do such things as pick up a telephone, press an emergency button or load a washing machine. Hearing dogs alert people to sounds such as a doorbell or a telephone. Seizure alert dogs watch for tell-tale signs of an impending seizure, warn their owners and care for them if a seizure does occur. Most trainers are employed by the four relevant charities; they are listed in the Info panel. Trainers work closely with dogs to teach them the skills they need and then they work with the dog and the human with whom it is going to live to teach that person how to use the dog and also how to care for it properly.

## Qualifications and Training

You must be at least 18 years old and have a full, clean driving licence. Academic and other requirements vary between the different employer organisations, so you should contact them for details. In general, you will need qualifications which are relevant to your client group, eg know British Sign Language if you are working with hearing impaired people and their assistance dogs. GCSEs grades A–C may be required and some employers prefer one of your subjects to be a science.

## Personal Qualities and Skills

You must have great patience and a real understanding of and interest in animal behaviour. You should also get on really well with people, who often need a lot of encouragement and support when they first acquire an assistance dog. You should be practical, well organised and good at thinking up solutions to problems.

## Salaries

Starting salaries are around £11,000 a year, rising to £15,000 with experience. Salaries for trainers working with hearing dogs are a little bit higher.

Guide Dogs for the Blind, Head Office, Hillfields, Burghfield Common, Reading, Berks RG7 3YG; 0118 983 5555; www.guidedogs.org.uk

Hearing Dogs for Deaf People, The Grange, Wycombe Road, Saunderton, Bucks HP27 9NS; 01844 348100; www.hearing-dogs.co.uk

Support Dogs, 21 Jessops Riverside, Brightside Lane, Sheffield S9 2RX;

0870 609 3476; www.support-dogs.org.uk

Canine Partners, Mill Lane, Heyshott, Midhurst, West Sussex GU29 0ED; 0845 658 0480; www.c-p-i.org.uk

Dogs for the Disabled, The Frances Hay Centre, Blacklocks Hill, Banbury, Oxfordshire OX17 2BS; 08700 776600; www. dogsforthedisabled.org

info

# Dog handler

Dog handlers work for the police, the armed services, HM Revenue & Customs, fire and rescue services and private security firms. There are many examples of the kinds of work in which dogs and dog handlers are involved. Police dogs track missing people, help control crowds or guard prisoners. In the Army dogs are used to find injured people, guard premises and equipment and even search for landmines. Doing customs work, handlers get their dogs to sniff out drugs, tobacco and food. In the prison service dogs are mainly used for guarding activities. The fire service sometimes uses dogs to search for survivors after fires and other disasters. Private security firms mainly use dogs to patrol and guard premises and equipment.

## Qualifications and Training

In most organisations you are not taken on as a dog handler. You start like any other recruit and dog handling is a specialist area for which you may then get the opportunity to train. You need to check the entry requirements of the other different career paths, but many will require you to have at least four GCSEs grades A–C, including maths and English. Check the info panel and other career entries in this guide.

## Personal Qualities and Skills

It is essential that you love working with dogs, that you are confident and sure of yourself when handling them. The bond that builds up between handler and dog is often very strong and you may have to spend a lot of time working on your own, just with your dog. Depending on the organisation you are working for, you may have to work in stressful or dangerous situations, or in uncomfortable and unpleasant conditions. You also need to be good at communicating with people.

## Salaries

With a wide range of different employers, the salary range is equally wide. A rough guide would be around £15,000 for new dog handlers and up to £25,000 or more for handlers with experience and other management responsibilities.

**info**

Police service portal; www.police.uk

Security Industry Authority (SIA), PO Box 9, Newcastle upon Tyne NE82 6YX; 0870 243 0100; www.the-sia.org.uk

RAF Careers; 0845 605 5555; www.rafcareers.com

National Search and Rescue; www.nsarda.org.uk

British Army; 08457 300111; www.army.mod.uk

HM Revenue & Customs; www.hmrc.gov

# Farrier

If a horse needs new shoes a farrier is the person who makes and fits these shoes. Working mainly with metal, though some shoes are made from plastic and other modern materials, farriers measure, shape and fit shoes to every kind of horse and pony. While there are not large numbers of opportunities in this work, riding and keeping horses has become increasingly popular over the last decade, so there are some opportunities in this highly specialised work.

## Qualifications and Training

To practise as a farrier you have to register with the Farriery Council and the only training route is a four-year apprenticeship which you must serve with a qualified farrier who is also registered to provide training. There are usually around 100 apprenticeships offered each year and the Farriery Training Agency may be able to help you find one of these. During your apprenticeship you also spend 23 weeks on block release at one of four approved colleges. Your apprenticeship leads to an NVQ level 3 in Farriery. You need four GCSEs grades A–C in order to start an apprenticeship and you also have to pass a medical. You have to pay for this medical yourself.

## Personal Qualities and Skills

Your have to be confident handling and enjoy working closely with horses of all sizes and temperaments. You have to have good practical skills and be able to work quickly and accurately. You have to have good people skills too. You may have to point out a health problem with a horse's leg or foot that the owner has not noticed. Since almost all farriers are self-employed you also have to be able to run your own business.

## Salaries

Apprenticeship pay rates are set annually by the Farriery Training Council and are linked to the National Minimum Wage. First-year apprentices aged 16 earn £2.70 por hour, fourth-year apprentices earn £5 an hour. There are also differences according to how old you are when you start your apprenticeship. Qualified farriers are self-employed and earn between £19,000 and £31,000.

info

Lantra, Lantra House, Stoneleigh Park, Nr Coventry, Warwickshire CV8 2LG; 0845 707 8007; www.lantra.co.uk

National Association of Farriers, Blacksmiths and Agricultural Engineers, The Forge, 10th Street, Stoneleigh Park, Nr Coventry, Warwickshire CV8 2LG; 02476 696595; www.nafbae.org

Farriery Training Agency, Sefton House, Adam Court, Newark Road, Peterborough PE1 5PP; 01733 319770; www.farrierytraining.co.uk

Farriers Registration Council, Sefton House, Adam Court, Newark Road, Peterborough PE1 5PP; 01733 319911; www.farrier-reg.gov

# Groom

Grooms look after all aspects of the horse's welfare. Their duties include grooming and strapping, mucking out, feeding, cleaning tack, saddling up, exercising and leading both mounted and dismounted, elementary veterinary care and sick nursing, preparation for and travelling with horses by road, sea and air, and care of the horse when at grass. Grooms work in racing stables, hunting establishments, private stables, studs and breeding concerns, riding schools, occasionally (seasonally) with polo ponies and at trekking centres.

## Qualifications and Training

No formal qualifications are necessary but it is recommended that grooms take the British Horse Society examinations stages 1, 2 and 3 in Horse Knowledge and Care, which comprise the Grooms Certificate. Alternative options are NVQs in Horse Care, levels 1, 2 and 3.

Training is usually on the job and should be sufficient to prepare students for exams. There are also courses of varying lengths to prepare students for particular exams; however, the fees are often high. Funding may be available for the achievement of British Horse Society qualifications providing that the person is not eligible for any other type of funding.

## Personal Qualities and Skills

A love of horses is essential, plus patience and the willingness to work long hours and perform many routine tasks. A heavy goods vehicle driving licence may be an advantage.

## Salaries

Stable staff generally earn the national minimum wage. In some cases food and accommodation may be free, in others they may be deducted from the wage. The hours may be long. The BHS issues guidelines on salaries for those with BHS qualifications; details are on their website.

# Jockey

Jockeys ride race horses in competitions on flat ground or over jumps (national hunt). They may ride for one race horse trainer or for several, and owners and trainers are interested in getting the best jockeys for their horses. Jockeys are also involved in preparing the horses for races, exercising them to bring them to best possible racing condition. Jockeys have to build up knowledge of individual horses, understand racing conditions, how the ground will affect performance and work out the most effective racing strategy.

## Qualifications and Training

Most jockeys start as stable hands working for trainers in racing yards. There are no specific academic requirements to become a stable hand; if you want to become a jockey there are strict weight limits, about 9 stone 7lb for a jump jockey and 8 stone for flat racing. You then have to persuade a trainer to take you on as either an apprentice jockey for flat racing, or a conditional jockey if you plan to become a jump jockey.

You can prepare for work in a racing yard by doing the NVQ level 1 and 2 Racehorse Care Residential Course. This course is free if you are aged between 16 and 25. There are NVQs levels 1 and 2 available in racehorse care. You can do these at a residential course at the British Racing School or the Northern Racing College. Places on these courses are highly sought after and are free if you are aged between 16 and 25. Day release courses in racehorse care are also available at some local colleges. Details of these are given on the British Horseracing Board website.

The key to being taken on to train as a jockey is that you must have exceptional riding skills in order to get yourself noticed by a trainer.

As an apprentice or conditional jockey, you train on the job. The trainer takes responsibility for where and what horses you ride and decides when you are competent and ready to race-ride (usually after about two years). You can then apply to the Horseracing Regulatory Authority for a licence to ride.

## Personal Qualities and Skills

You must have a love of horses as well as of riding, since in your early days you will be involved in a lot of horse care, and for good riding you need to be able to build up a real bond with your animals. You must be confident, physically brave, determined, able to cope with disappointment and good at dealing with people as well as with horses.

## Salaries

As a stable hand you earn around £8,000 and if you decide to become a groom rather than a jockey your earnings rise to around £10,000 and £15,000. Jockeys' earnings include a percentage of prize money and a fee for each ride. Experienced and successful jockeys can also earn money through sponsorship. Many jobs in racing yards provide free or subsidised accommodation.

Association of British Riding Schools (ABRS), Queens Chambers, 38–40 Queen Street, Penzance, Cornwall TR18 4BH; 01736 369440; www.abrs-info.org

British Horseracing Board (BHB), 151 Shaftesbury Avenue, London WC2H 8AL; 020 7152 0000; e-mail: info@careersinracing.com; www.careersinracing.com

British Horse Society (BHS), Stoneleigh, Deer Park, Kenilworth, Warwickshire CV8 2XZ; 0870 120 2244; www.bhs.org.uk

British Racing School (BRS), Snailwell Road, Newmarket, Suffolk CB8 7NU; 01638 665103; www.brs.org.uk

Horseracing Regulatory Authority (HRA), 151 Shaftesbury Avenue, London WC2H 8AL; 020 7189 3800 (NB: calls to this number may be recorded); www.thehra.org

Jockeys Employment and Training Scheme (JETS), 39b Kingfisher Court, Hambridge Road, Newbury, Berkshire RG14 5SJ; 01635 230410; www.jets-uk.org

Lantra, Lantra House, Stoneleigh Park, Nr Coventry, Warwickshire CV8 2LG; 0845 707 8007; www.lantra.co.uk

Northern Racing College (NRC), The Stables, Rossington Hall, Great North Road, Doncaster, South Yorkshire DN11 0HN; 01302 861000; www.northernracingcollege.co.uk

Thoroughbred Breeders' Association, British Stud Staff Training Scheme, Stanstead House, The Avenue, Newmarket, Suffolk CB8 9AA; 01638 661321; www.thoroughbredbreedersassociation.co.uk

info

# Kennel work

Kennel staff ensure that the animals in their care have clean accommodation, are fed a regular and nutritious diet, are kept clean and well groomed and are given sufficient exercise. Where animals are sick or recovering from an operation, the kennel staff must also be able to provide adequate nursing care.

There are a number of different types of kennel – greyhound kennels train dogs for racing, hunt kennels for hunting – and they involve a lot of outdoor work, exercising the dogs and perhaps travelling to meetings. There are quarantine kennels licensed by the Department for the Environment, Food and Rural Affairs (DEFRA) and breeding kennels where duties also include weaning and training puppies, preparing dogs for shows and possibly handling them. Boarding kennels look after animals while their owners are away. Some of the racing and quarantine kennels are large operations situated near racing stadia, airports and ports, but others may be smaller, family-run concerns.

## Qualifications and Training

No formal qualifications are needed to work in kennels and most employers prefer school leavers to train on the job. The NVQ level 2 in Animal Care and the National Small Animal Care Certificate are nationally recognised by the industry and provide a good base for further study. Many training organisations and agricultural colleges throughout the country offer these qualifications. Entry requirements vary depending on the institution.

## Personal Qualities and Skills

Good health, general fitness and stamina are required for this manual, physically demanding, outdoor work. Kennel staff must be unsentimental about animals but at the same time have a genuine concern for their well-being; they require patience and a placid but firm nature. A willingness to work long days, weekends and public holidays is also required.

## Salaries

Kennel workers earn around £10,000 to start with. Experienced kennel workers earn between £12,000 and £15,000.

info

College of Animal Welfare, London Road, Godmanchester, Cambridgeshire PE29 2LJ; 0870 062 1122; www.caw.ac.uk

Lantra, Lantra House, Stoneleigh Park, Warwickshire CV8 2LG; 0845 707 8007; www.lantra.co.uk

Dogs Trust, 17 Wakely Street, London EC1V 7RQ; 020 7837 0006; www.dogstrust.org.uk

Animal Care College, Ascot House, High Street, Ascot, Berkshire SL5 7JG; 0870 730 8433; www. animalcarecollege.co.uk

# Riding instructor

Riding instructors teach people, individuals or groups, how to ride horses. They may also accompany riders who hire horses by the hour, and be required to help train horses and look after them, cleaning tack and stables. The work includes teaching in riding schools and clubs and in summer camps, training competition riders and occasionally sitting as a judge or examiner.

## Qualifications and Training

While you may not need formal qualifications to train you do need to work towards a series of certificated examinations offered by either the British Horse Society (BHS) or The Association of British Riding Schools (ABRS). Both offer several levels of qualification from preliminary to assistant instructor and instructor. There are three routes to working for these examinations: you may be able to get an apprenticeship; you could train as a private fee-paying student at riding stables; or you could attend a college course that includes BHS or ABRS qualifications. If you do opt for a college course, or manage to obtain an apprenticeship you may need three or four GCSEs. Whatever qualification you opt for, and whichever training method you choose, you will need to have a strong background in riding and in handling and caring for horses.

You can opt for further specialist training in work with riding for the disabled or riding holiday leadership.

## Personal Qualities and Skills

A love for and understanding of horses and good confident riding ability are essential. You also need to be good at communicating with people of all ages and different levels of ability. You should be observant, encouraging and sensitive. You must have a good awareness of safety issues.

**info**

Lantra, Lantra House, Stoneleigh Park, Nr Coventry, Warwickshire CV8 2LG; 0845 707 8007; www.lantra.co.uk

British Equestrian Federation (BEF); www.bef.co.uk

Riding for the Disabled Association, Norfolk House, 1a Tournament Court, Edgehill Drive, Warwick CV34 6LG; 0845 658 1082; www.riding-for-disabled.org.uk

Association of British Riding Schools (ABRS), Queens Chambers, 38–40 Queen Street, Penzance, Cornwall TR18 4BH; 01736 369440; www.abrs-info.org

British Horse Society (BHS), Stoneleigh Deer Park, Kenilworth, Warwickshire CV8 2XZ; Tel: 0844 848 1666; www.bhs.org.uk

## Salaries

Trainees and assistant instructors earn between £12,000 and £16,000 and qualified instructors earn £16,000 to £25,000. Earnings vary according to whether accommodation and meals are provided. Some experienced instructors are self-employed and with experience and a good reputation can earn more than £35,000.

# RSPCA inspector

Inspectors for the Royal Society for the Prevention of Cruelty to Animals (RSPCA) deal with complaints from the general public about the alleged ill-treatment of animals and also perform more routine tasks. Inspectors have no power to take an animal from its owner unless the owner legally signs it over. They may caution people and, in some circumstances, the organisation will ensure that cases go before the courts. Inspectors also visit boarding kennels, pet shops and riding schools. They can be involved in physical rescues, often working unsociable hours and driving considerable distances.

## Qualifications and Training

Applicants require GCSEs or equivalent in English and a science, a valid driving licence and the ability to swim 50 metres fully clothed. Experience of working with animals is desirable.

About 20 inspectors are recruited each year from over 2,000 applicants. Training lasts six months and covers animal welfare legislation, basic veterinary training, mountain and boat rescue techniques, investigation skills, interview techniques, court work, animal-handling techniques, media training and public speaking. After written examinations, students serve six months' probation before becoming fully qualified. Minimum age for entry is 22.

## Personal Qualities and Skills

Inspectors have to be very good at handling animals of all kinds. They must be calm, kind and authoritative. They need excellent interpersonal skills, must be able to be assertive, to deal with both sensitive and potentially confrontational situations. They must be able to speak in public, whether it is in court or in a classroom.

## Salaries

In the RSPCA the starting salary is just under £22,000 a year. Fully trained inspectors earn from £24,000 to £26,500. An accommodation allowance is included in the salary and there are additional allowances for officers working near London.

Volunteering England; www. volunteering.org.uk

Volunteering Scotland; www. volunteerscotland.info

RSPCA, Wilberforce Way, Southwater, Horsham, West Sussex RH13 9RS; www.rspca.org.uk

SSPCA, Braehead Mains, 603 Queensferry Road, Edinburgh EH4 6EA; 0131 339 0222; www. scottishspca.org.uk

info

# Stable hand

Stable hands (formerly known as 'stable lads') do a lot of labouring work, mucking out, fetching straw, filling haynets and sweeping. They must also learn to groom and exercise the horses, and usually become responsible for a certain number of their 'own'. On race days, a stable hand will accompany a horse, groom it, walk it round before the race and lead it into the winner's enclosure if it wins.

## Qualifications and Training

Most jockeys start as stable hands working for trainers in racing yards. There are no specific academic requirements to become a stable hand. If you want to become a jockey there are strict weight limits, about 9 stone 7lb for a jump jockey and 8 stone for flat racing. You then have to persuade a trainer to take you on as either an apprentice jockey for flat racing, or a conditional jockey if you plan to become a jump jockey.

You can prepare for work in a racing yard by doing the NVQ level 1 and 2 Racehorse Care Residential Course. You can do these at a residential course at the British Racing School or the Northern Racing College. Places on these courses are highly sought after and are free if you are aged between 16 and 25. Day release courses in racehorse care are also available at some local colleges. Details of these are given on the British Horseracing Board website.

The key to being taken on to train as a jockey is that you must have exceptional riding skills in order to get yourself noticed by a trainer.

As an apprentice or conditional jockey, you train on the job. The trainer takes responsibility for where and what horses you ride and decides when you are competent and ready to race-ride (usually about two years). You can then apply to the Horseracing Regulatory Authority for a licence to ride.

## Personal Qualities and Skills

You must have a love of horses as well as of riding, since in your early days you will be involved in a lot of horse care and for good riding you need to be able to build up a real bond with your animals. You must be confident, physically brave, determined and able to cope with disappointment, and good at dealing with people as well as with horses.

## Salaries

As a stable hand you earn around £8,000 and if you decide to become a groom rather than a jockey your earnings rise to between £10,000 and £15,000. Jockeys' earnings include a percentage of prize money and a fee for each ride. Experienced and successful jockeys can also earn money through sponsorship. Many jobs in racing yards provide free or subsidised accommodation.

**info**

Lantra, Lantra House, Stoneleigh Park, Warwickshire CV8 2LG; 0845 707 8007; www.lantra.co.uk

Horseracing Regulatory Authority (HRA), 151 Shaftesbury Avenue, London WC2H 8AL; 020 7189 3800 (NB: Calls to this number may be recorded); www.thehra.org

Jockeys Employment and Training Scheme (JETS), 39b Kingfisher Court, Hambridge Road, Newbury, Berkshire RG14 5SJ; 01635 230410; www.jets-uk.org

Northern Racing College (NRC), The Stables, Rossington Hall, Great North Road, Doncaster, South Yorkshire DN11 0HN; 01302 861000; www.northernracingcollege.co.uk

British Horseracing Board, 151 Shaftesbury Avenue, London WC2H 8AL; 020 7152 0000; www.careersinracing.com

British Racing School (BRS), Snailwell Road, Newmarket, Suffolk CB8 7NU; 01638 665103; www.brs.org.uk

# Zoo keeper

Keepers look after animals in zoos, mucking out their living quarters, preparing their food, feeding them and engaging in all other aspects of animal husbandry. There is increasing emphasis on education, public relations and research. Keepers work long hours – from 8 am to as late as 7 pm – much of the time outdoors and the work is often physically demanding.

## Qualifications and Training

You don't usually need academic qualifications, though some employers may ask for GCSEs grades A–C including English and one science subject. Most zoos expect you to have experience of working with animals and the main way to acquire this is through volunteering. Most zoos have volunteer schemes, though these are popular and competitive. The British and Irish Association of Zoos and Aquariums website gives contact details for all zoos and wildlife parks. If you want to work in a safari or wildlife park you will need a driving licence. Your application may be strengthened by acquiring one of the following: a BTEC First Diploma and National Certificate/Diploma in Animal Care or Animal Management, a City & Guilds National Certificate and Advanced National Certificate in Animal Care or NVQ levels 1 and 2 in Animal Care. Check individual colleges for entry requirements.

Some zoos may run apprenticeship schemes from time to time. Training is on the job and you may be able to work for some of the qualifications just listed on a day-release basis. Once you have worked as a zoo keeper for at least a year, you can do a two-year part-time block release foundation degree in Zoo Resource Management at Sparsholt College in Hampshire. You can do foundation degrees and degrees in Animal Management at some other colleges and universities.

## Personal Qualities and Skills

You must love animals and be good at assessing their condition and monitoring behaviour. You have to be practical, calm, confident, happy working in the open air and not squeamish about smells. You must be very alert and safety-conscious, especially when working with dangerous animals. You should be able to work as part of a team, be interested in science and the environment, and be able to communicate with members of the public in a friendly and informative way.

## Salaries

Salaries start from around £12,200 to £14,500. Experienced zoo keepers can earn from around £15,000 to over £21,000.

British and Irish Association of Zoos and Aquariums (BIAZA); www.biaza.org.uk

Sparsholt College, Sparsholt, Winchester SO21 2NF; 01962 776441; www.sparsholt.ac.uk

Lantra, Lantra House, Stoneleigh Park, Warwickshire CV8 2LG; 0845 707 8007; www.lantra.co.uk

info

# ANTHROPOLOGIST

Anthropologists study the development of human societies, making comparisons between different communities and cultures. This academic discipline is linked with the other social sciences and with evolutionary biology. Much of the work still concerns non-industrial, 'primitive' or rural cultures, but changes brought about by contact with more sophisticated outside influences and pressures from 'modern' societies are an important aspect of study and many anthropologists now undertake research in urban or industrial societies. The career involves a combination of research, teaching and finding out more about the people being studied by going to live with them over a period of time.

Increasingly, anthropologists are finding employment as consultants, for instance in the development, health and humanitarian fields and in such professions as journalism, human resource management, planning, tourism and heritage, museum curatorship and medicine.

## Qualifications and Training

A good degree in anthropology. Postgraduate study is usually required.

## Personal Qualities and Skills

Those wishing to embark on this career must normally be committed to an academic way of life, although there is growing demand outside universities. Field researchers must be prepared to spend long spells abroad, often in basic conditions. Physical and mental stamina is required, as well as independence and resourcefulness. Anthropologists must be prepared to work on their own. However, as anthropology has diversified, so the ways of working life adopted by anthropologists have become more varied too and they now work in every imaginable setting, from offices and daycare centres to out in the field. Linguistic ability is useful.

## Salaries

There is little clear salary data, but many anthropologists would earn similar rates to research workers in universities – around £18,000 to £20,000 for junior staff and up to £23,000 with experience. On field work overseas, earnings may include living and many other allowances.

**info**

Royal Anthropological Institute, 50 Fitzroy Street, London W1T 5BT; 020 7387 0455; fax: 020 7383 4235; www.therai.org.uk; e-mail: admin@therai.org.uk

# ANTIQUE DEALER

The buying and selling of antiques for profit entails expert knowledge of the field, combined with sound managerial and business sense. Comparatively few people make a living at this trade, and many businesses are family concerns. Dealers frequently specialise in particular types of antiques, and trade among themselves as well as with private buyers and sellers. Dealers may sell from shops, antiques markets, antiques fairs and from home. An increasing number trade on the internet using auction sites such as eBay as well as their own websites.

## Qualifications and Training

While there are no formal entry qualifications, experience in a sales room or an antique shop is extremely useful. Some antique dealers do have degrees in fine arts or applied arts and there are one or two specific postgraduate courses in understanding the arts and antiques market. Large dealers such as Christie's and Sotheby's do offer a few training places to graduates. Training is on the job if you are employed by a large auction house, but otherwise it is mainly through your own study, persistence and research.

## Personal Qualities and Skills

A real interest in antiques in general or a particular category – paintings, ceramics, furniture, etc – is absolutely essential. Many dealers are also collectors. You have to have a keen eye for detail, a professional, confident manner with people, and sound business sense. You may also need considerable capital to get yourself started.

## Salaries

There is wide variation in earnings because so many antique dealers are self-employed and have to make earnings through commissions on what they sell. Starting in an antique shop or an auction house sales room, salaries are from £12,000 to £19,000.

The British Antique Dealers' Association, 20 Rutland Gate, London SW7 1BD; 020 7589 4128; www.bada.org

Sotheby's Institute of Art; www. sothebysinstitute.com

Christie's; www.christies.co.uk/

info

# ARCHAEOLOGY

Archaeology is the examination of the human past through the study of buried remains and artefacts.

# Archaeologist

Archaeology – building up a picture of the past – is both an art and a science. Archaeologists use highly technical and scientific methods of discovery, analysis and identification to reconstruct and study men and women from the past using their material remains. The evidence is collected through fieldwork, including excavations, where clues are sought in objects, their surroundings, the ground itself and the remains of living things. The evidence is then analysed, subjected to experiment, assessed, identified, catalogued, conserved and possibly exhibited. Archaeologists usually specialise in a particular period, technique or geographical area. Opportunities for full-time, permanent positions are limited; consequently competition is fierce for the few jobs available. These are to be found in central and local government, museums and universities, independent units and trusts, as well as a variety of positions in commercial operations. Job availability is closely related to building and development work. Some work includes the opportunity to spend time abroad.

## Qualifications and Training

There are several degree courses in archaeology and most people who work as archaeologists will also have a postgraduate qualification and some work experience of volunteering on archaeological digs. There are also postgraduate courses in archaeological conservation.

## Personal Qualities and Skills

Archaeologists need to be practical, thorough and very careful and observant. They should be able to work well as part of a team, or as a team leader. They need to have a real passion for and commitment to their work.

## Salaries

Starting salaries for excavators and site assistants are between £13,500 and £15,500. Supervisors earn from £15,500 to £17,500. Senior archaeologists managing site projects earn £27,000 to £30,000. Archaeologists working in museums or in universities are paid according to local authority or lecturer pay scales.

**info**

Council for British Archaeology, St Mary's House, 66 Bootham, York YO30 7BZ; 01904 671417; www. britarch.ac.uk

Training Online Resource Centre for Archaeology (TORC); www.torc.org. uk

British Archaeological Jobs Resource; www.bajr.org

English Heritage www.english-heritage.org.uk

Environment and Heritage Service, 5/33 Hill Street, Belfast BT1 2LA; 028 9054 3034; http://www.ehsni. gov.uk

# Archaeological surveying

*see* Surveying

# ARCHITECTURE

Architecture is a profession requiring the practical combination of imaginative design with scientific and technological principles, to produce designs for new buildings and for the extension, or renovation, of those already existing.

# Architect

Architects are professional experts in the field of building design and construction. They advise individuals, developers, local authorities and commercial organisations on the design and construction of new buildings and the area around them. Architects are also involved in the restoration and conservation of historic and existing buildings. In its wider definition the professional association for architects, RIBA, says, 'Society looks to architects to define new ways of living and working, to develop innovative ways of using existing buildings and creating new ones.'

Architects create designs based on information supplied by the client on the function of the building, the proposed budget and the site. An architect needs to have an understanding of structure, finance, planning law and design, and in many building projects acts as the coordinator in a team of specialist consultants such as engineers, builders and interior designers. The architect works to the client's requirements and produces working drawings for the builder. These show dimensions, materials and how everything will be put together. An architect will also negotiate with local authorities and submit the designs to planning officers for approval. On large jobs there will be a team of architects working with engineers and other specialists, and it may take months to prepare all the drawings and schedules. Alternatively, very small jobs take only a few weeks. After the contract documents have been prepared and a builder selected, work begins on the site. The architect visits frequently as the building goes up. This can involve tramping around in boots and a hard hat, climbing up and down ladders as well as taking the chair at site meetings.

Opportunities exist for employment in private practice, with local authorities, in research, teaching, central government and some industrial organisations. Increasingly, interior design and companies working in associated fields employ architects as part of their team. Specialist areas can include domestic, public building and retail architecture. The use of computer-aided design packages plays a significant part in the work of architects.

## Qualifications and Training

Architecture is a graduate level profession, unless you have considerable experience as a building surveyor, architectural technician or architectural technologist. The usual route to qualifying as an architect is to do a three-year degree course in architecture ensuring that the course is registered with the Architects Registration Board (ARB). You then have to undertake at least two years' work In an architect's office. Having done this you have completed what is known as Stage 1. You then take a two-year diploma or Master's in architecture; this is referred to as Part 2. Having completed these stages you then sit an examination to achieve Part 3 and you can then apply to become a chartered architect. To gain a place on an architecture degree course you need five GCSEs grades A–C including maths, English and either physics or chemistry. You need three good A levels and many universities require one of these to be in a science subject.

## Personal Qualities and Skills

You need a very broad range of skills as an architect: you must have good scientific and mathematical ability, but you also need imagination, creativity and a flair for design. You need good IT skills, sound business awareness and an ability to communicate technical information and ideas to people without a technical background.

## Salaries

Salaries vary according to the size of practice you work for. The Royal Institute of British Architects provides a rough guide to what you can expect to earn during the various stages of training: the rates for first-year trainees are

£20,000 to £23,000; after completing your diploma you can earn £25,000 to £45,000; and registered architects with three to five years' experience can expect £40,000 to £45,000. Salaries in this sector often suffer when the financial and property markets are problematic.

**info**

Royal Institute of British Architects (RIBA), 66 Portland Place, London W1B 1AD; 020 7580 5533; fax 020 7255 1541; www.architecture.com; e-mail: info@inst.riba.org (There is a comprehensive careers section on the website.)

Architects' Registration Board (ARB), 8 Weymouth Street, London

W1N 3FB; 020 7580 5861; www.arb.org.uk; e-mail: information@arb.org.uk

Royal Incorporation of Architects in Scotland (RIAS), 15 Rutland Square, Edinburgh EH1 2BE; 0131 229 7545; www.rias.org.uk; e-mail:information@rias.org.uk

# Architectural technologist

Architectural technologists work alongside architects and other professionals as part of the building design and construction team. Technologists can negotiate the construction project from inception to completion. Specific, specialist skills could include surveying land and buildings, preparing and undertaking feasibility studies, presenting design solutions, analysing and detailing drawings, and managing and applying computer-aided design (CAD) techniques.

## Qualifications and Training

A degree in architectural technology, an HNC/HND in Building Studies (with specific additional units) or an NVQ level 4 in Architectural Technology lead to Associate Membership of the British Institute of Architectural Technologists (BIAT) and the designation ABIAT.

## Personal Qualities and Skills

Architectural technologists should be able to work both as part of a team and on their own initiative. Attention to detail is necessary, as is the ability to take account of other professionals' needs. Effective communication skills are necessary when working as part of the team, liaising with clients or tendering for contracts and they should feel comfortable with new technology and innovative concepts.

## Salaries

Salaries start at between £15,000 and £20,000, possibly more in London. With experience salaries rise to between £30,000 and £45,000. This sector has suffered in the current economic climate, so salaries have not risen much in the past two years.

Chartered Institute of Architectural Technologists (CIAT), 397 City Road, London EC1V 1NH; 020 7278 2206; Freephone (UK only) 0800 731 5471; www. biat.org.uk; e-mail: careers@biat.org.uk

**info**

# Model maker

*see* Film and Television Production

# ARCHIVIST

In the course of business many organisations and people create or collect archives. These include government agencies, local authorities, universities, hospitals, businesses, charities, professional organisations and families and individuals. Archives may be books or papers, maps or plans, photographs or prints, films or videos, or computer-generated records. Archives are intended to be kept permanently, to preserve the past and allow others to discover it.

It is the job of the archivist to preserve and exploit this archival heritage and the information contained within it. This includes assisting visitors or users, promotional work including exhibitions, presentations or media liaison, as well as the curatorial skills of selecting archives for preservation and interpreting them for archive users.

## Qualifications and Training

The main qualification is the postgraduate diploma in archive management, which is run at six UK universities. To be accepted on to one of these programmes you need a good honours degree, usually a 2.1. Any discipline is acceptable, but history, or a subject where you have had to research original source material, will be particularly useful. Many entrants start as records clerks or assistant archivists. In fact, such work experience is very important if you want to complete a postgraduate diploma. Many applicants also do quite a lot of voluntary work in order to strengthen their applications. Your paid or voluntary experience must be in an archive or records management department, not a library. The Society of Archivists keeps list of suitable paid and voluntary training places. Tracking down employers who can provide experience can be quite hard – universities and local government offices have some of the largest archive and records departments.

## Personal Qualities and Skills

A passionate interest in history and in original source material is essential. You should be logical, well organised and good at paying attention to detail. You meet all sorts of people in this work, so good communication skills and a real commitment to customer service are very important. At senior level you also need to be good at managing members of a team.

## Salaries

The Society of Archivists suggests a minimum of £20,000 for newly qualified archivists. Currently the range is £18,000 to £27,000. The higher salaries tend to be paid in academia. Senior archivists earn between £26,500 and £40,000.

**info**

The British Library, 96 Euston Road, London NW1 2DB; 020 7412 7332; www.bl.uk

Business Archives Council, c/o Ms F Maccoll, Rio Tinto plc, 6 St James Square, London SW1Y 4LD; 020 7753 2123; www.businessarchivescouncil.com

Museum, Libraries and Archives Council, 16 Queen Anne's Gate,

London SW19 9AA; 020 7272 1444; www.mla.gov.uk

The National Archives, Kew, Richmond, Surrey TW9 4DU; 020 8876 3444; www.nationalarchives.gov.uk

Society of Archivists, Prioryfield House, 20 Canon Street, Taunton TA1 1SW; 01823 327030; www.archives.org.uk

# ARMED FORCES

The United Kingdom armed forces are comprised of the Army, the Royal Air Force and the Royal Navy. The Royal Marines are also part of the Royal Navy. While their main roles are warfare and defence, the armed services take on many other roles. They can be involved in peace keeping, holding a line in areas of conflict. They may be involved in search and rescue after natural disasters such as earthquakes overseas. In the UK they may provide help after a natural disaster such as a flood.

While the three armed services employ many civilian staff most of their work is done by serving forces members, whether this work is catering, IT support, mechanical repairs to equipment, medical treatment or training and educating its own members.

# Army careers

While there are many army careers, opportunities can be split into these main areas: combat, engineering logistics, intelligence, music and ceremony, IT, medicine, human resources and finance.

There are two basic levels at which you can join the British Army either as a private, or as an officer. As a private you may be called a gunner or a signaller according to the regiment you belong to and the work you do. As an officer you start as an officer cadet. In either case there is a clear career structure through which you can climb, to regimental sergeant major as a private, and to lieutenant colonel as an officer.

Rank is the backbone of Army structure and defines your role and degree of responsibility. Soldiers and officers have different terms of rank and, broadly speaking, it is officers that have more leadership duties. But remember, many officers are drawn from the ranks – if you show potential in the Army, your efforts will not go unrewarded.

## Qualifications and Training

To join as a soldier you must be aged 16 to 33, pass a medical and meet nationality requirements. You don't normally need formal qualifications, though in some technical and engineering jobs you may. Your local Armed Forces Careers Office (AFCO) will be happy to talk to you in detail. They can also give you a multiple-choice test, sometimes referred to as the BARB test, which can indicate which particular roles you might be most suited to and find most satisfactory. If you are interested in joining, you have to attend a two-day series of selection tests and if you pass these you can then join up. Initial training, referred to as basic training, takes 12 to 14 weeks. After this you will receive further training connected with your specific role and duties and the kinds of activities in which your unit is engaged.

If you are applying to join as an officer, you must be aged 17 to 28 and must also pass a medical and meet nationality criteria. You need five GCSEs grades A–C including English, maths and either a science or a foreign language. This requirement is sometimes referred to as needing 35 ALIS points. You also need two A levels or equivalent equal to 120 UCAS points. The Army also runs graduate-entry training for officers. You then have to pass a three-day Army Officer Selection Board. If you are successful, you begin training as an Officer Cadet on the 44-week Commissioning Course (CC) at the Royal Military Academy, Sandhurst (RMAS). The course includes training in leadership and management, tactics, weapons and physical fitness. If you join as a professional officer already qualified as a nurse, doctor, vet, engineer, etc, you take a shortened course.

## Personal Qualities and Skills

For soldiers and officers self-discipline, confidence and initiative are important. You have to be physically fit, quick at reacting to situations and willing to work in highly dangerous or frightening situations. It is essential that you can work as part of a team. Officers and other ranks with leadership roles have to be able to motivate, lead and organise, encourage and discipline colleagues.

## Salaries

Pay is linked to rank, length of service and responsibilities. A soldier in training earns around £13,000. Once training is complete earnings are between £16,000 and £28,000. Some higher ranks earn up to £46,000. Non-graduate officer cadets start on £15,000, graduate officer cadets on £23,000. After training, salaries rise to £28,000 to £33,000. The highest ranks earn up to £100,000. There are also additional allowances for working overseas and subsidised accommodation may be provided.

# Royal Air Force careers

Like the Army, the Royal Air Force (RAF) is engaged in many different operations, but of course one of its main tasks is flying fixed-wing aircraft and helicopters over UK airspace and in actions all around the world, whether these
are under the auspices of NATO, the UN or other situations. Much of the work
involves flying and maintaining combat, reconnaissance and transport
aircraft. As well as roles associated directly with flying the RAF employs
catering staff, engineers, IT specialists, medical staff and administrators.
While there are many different opportunities the two basic levels of recruitment are RAF airman or woman (aircrew) and RAF officer. As an RAF airman
or airwoman, you would provide specialist support in one of the following
areas: aircrew – which includes non-commissioned aircrew and weapon
systems operators; engineering and technical – including roles like aircraft
technician; catering and hospitality – which includes roles such as catering
officer; security and defence – with jobs in fire-fighting and the RAF police;
medical and medical support – dental, nursing, medical and laboratory roles;
air operations support – for example air traffic controllers; and communications and intelligence – such as photographers and intelligence analysts. RAF
officers work in more than 20 roles, but some of the main ones are pilots, air
traffic controllers and engineers. The RAF also employs non-commissioned
officers in many flight and technical roles and as linguists.

## Qualifications and Training

To join as an airman or airwoman you do not need formal qualifications. You
must be over the age of 16. Upper age limits for joining vary according to the
role in which you will be working. You also have to be a UK citizen and you
have to pass a medical. Your local Armed Forces Careers Office will be able to
provide you with more detailed information. The requirements to join as an
officer vary and many applicants are graduates. You will have to pass a series
of rigorous selection tests including medical, psychological and intelligence
tests. For some roles, eg linguists, you will need relevant qualifications. Initial
training for airmen and airwomen is 14 weeks, 33 weeks for officers. There is
continuing training depending on your role and the operations and activities
in which you are involved. There are very often opportunities to gain professional and technical qualifications once you have joined up.

## Personal Qualities and Skills

A real interest in the RAF is a good starting point. All RAF personnel have to
be physically fit, well disciplined, and able to follow or give orders and be
good at working as part of a team. Many posts will demand technical or practical skills. Officers will need good leadership skills, be able to motivate and
keep other people working together. They will also have to be good at taking
responsibility and making quick decisions. All RAF personnel will have to be
prepared to work in difficult and dangerous situations.

## Salaries

Airmen and airwomen start training on a little over £13,000, with £16,500 when training is complete. Senior airmen and women at warrant officer level, the highest non-commissioned rank, can earn up to £44,000. New pilot officers earn £23,500, flying officers earn between £28,300 and £31,500, and squadron leaders earn up to £54,500.

# Royal Navy careers

The Royal Navy has operations on the sea (the surface fleet), in the air (the air corps) and in submarine under the water. There are two basic entry levels, either as a rating or as an officer. Like the other armed services the Royal Navy employs personnel in catering, medicine, dentistry, engineering, logistics, and finance and information technology.

## Qualifications and Training

You don't need formal qualifications to join as a rating, but good GCSEs may increase the variety of roles you can take on. For most ratings you have to be aged 16, but to train as a diver you must be 18. Some other posts have higher age limits. All new naval ratings undergo nine weeks of introductory training at HMS Raleigh in Cornwall. Officers need five GCSEs and 180 UCAS points or their equivalent. Some posts have a height requirement. Ratings have to be aged 16 to join and officers must be 17. For some officer posts you need to be older.

## Personal Qualities and Skills

All Royal Navy personnel must be good at working as part of a team. They must be physically fit and emotionally resilient – capable of living in fairly confined conditions close to other people. They must be good at taking orders and giving instructions, quick to react and have good practical skills. They must be capable of working in difficult and dangerous situations. Officers have to have all of these qualities combined with the ability to lead, encourage, motivate and organise others.

## Salaries

Starting salaries are from around £13,500 a year for ratings. Able ratings (the next rank) earn between close to £17,000 and £28,500 a year. Warrant officers earn up to £46,000.

# Royal Marines careers

Royal Marines are part of the Royal Navy. They take part in front-line combat (on land and at sea) and are sent at short notice to deal with emergency situations, which may include military operations or natural disasters. The basic entry level is as a commando. As a newly trained recruit, you would usually start as a rifleman. You might be based in a unit responding to emergencies around the world as part of the Joint Rapid Reaction Force, the Fleet Protection Group, guarding UK nuclear weapons or a Fleet Standby Rifle Troop, trained to board ships at sea. The Royal Marines recruits officers as well as commandos. Officers are responsible for leading units in all the activities mentioned above. They are also responsible for training and discipline. Many officers will be qualified professionals – engineers or doctors for example.

## Qualifications and Training

To join as a commando you must be aged 17, male and a British citizen. You do not need any formal qualifications, but you do have to pass a series of selection tests including a medical and a rigorous physical fitness test. Your initial training lasts 32 weeks and covers teamwork, survival, assault course and weapons training. To apply to become a Royal Marines Officer you must pass the rigorous three-day selection process, you must be aged at least 17, a British citizen and at least 1.51 metres tall. You also need three GCSEs grades A–C. There is also a graduate officer training programme operating in the Royal Marines. Training for officers consists of five stages, from basic training to amphibious craft training. At the end of your training period you will command a troop or unit.

## Personal Qualities and Skills

All Royal Marines personnel must be resilient, resourceful and determined. You need to be very good at working as part of a team, following or giving orders as appropriate. You must be physically very fit and able to cope with tough conditions. You need to be practical, quick to think and quick to react. Officers must be good leaders, able to keep a team working well together and able to motivate colleagues in challenging situations.

## Salaries

On entry, commandos earn around £13,300 a year. This can rise to between £16,259 and £27,600 a year after training. The most senior non-commissioned ranks can earn up to £45,000. Officers in training earn between £13,200 and £17,100 a year. Captains earn between £36,160 and £43,002. Colonels can earn up to £85,268.

**info**

British Army; 08457 300111; www. army.mod.uk

Royal Air Force Careers; 0845 605 5555; www.rafcareers.com

Royal Navy Careers; 0845 607 5555; www.royal-navy.mod.uk

Armed Forces Careers Office (NI), Royal Navy and Royal Marines,

Palace Barracks, Holywood, Co Down BT18 9RA; 028 9042 7040

Visit your local Armed Forces Careers Office (AFCO) for information on all the armed services and the career opportunities in each.

# ART AND DESIGN

There are many different careers in art and design and artists work with many different mediums. Popular areas include fashion and textiles, jewellery, furniture, interior design, graphic design, industrial design and photography. Less commercial applications include painting and sculpture.

# Artist

Artists communicate ideas, emotions and thoughts through visual mediums such as painting, print making, digital fine art or sculpture. They work with a wide range of materials, though most artists develop a preference for working with particular materials and in particular styles. They earn money by selling work which they either produce independently or by undertaking commissioned work. A few artists may be employed as artist in residence at a gallery or for some other organisation. Some work on community arts projects or as art teachers. As an artist, your work may also involve liaising with galleries, sourcing materials, coming up with new ideas, managing, marketing your work and building up a business.

## Qualifications and Training

While some artists have no formal qualifications, and may simply be self-taught and have a rare talent, the majority of artists will have a degree in an arts-related subject. There are many fine arts degrees in subjects including painting, digital fine art, print making, sculpture and photography. There are also degrees in art criticism and contextual art. To get onto an arts degree course you normally have to have completed a foundation year and prepare a portfolio of your work to demonstrate your artistic ability.

## Personal Qualities and Skills

You must have flair and imagination and a really strong desire to work with your chosen subjects and mediums. You have to be resilient, good at building up relationships with people, flexible and able to handle disappointment. You also need to be able to work on your own and sometimes to work long hours.

## Salaries

As a new artist it is very difficult to make a living entirely from your art. You can get advice on how to price your work, but many new artists assist more experienced artists and this work pays between £8 and £10 per hour. Salaries in teaching are between £23,000 and £35,000 depending on your level of experience and geographical location.

**info**

Arts Council, 14 Great Peter Street, London SW1P 3NQ, 020 7333 0100; www.artscouncil.org.uk

Design Council, 34 Bow Street, London WC2E 7DL; 020 7420 5200; www.designcouncil.org.uk and www.yourcreativefuture.org.uk; e-mail: info@designcouncil.org.uk

Creative and Cultural Skills, 4th Floor, Lafone House, The Leathermarket, Weston Street, London SE1 3HN; 020 7015 1800; www.ccskills.org.uk

# Graphic designer

A number of different disciplines come under the umbrella heading of graphic design. These can include design studies, film and animation work, typography and lettering, illustration, printing processes, display and exhibition work, technical graphics for engineering, calligraphy, packaging and design for advertising, corporate identity and multimedia. Graphic design incorporates drawing and presentation skills and requires an understanding of colour, lettering and patterns. Many graphic designers work in three dimensions using specialist computer software. A high level of technical skills is therefore expected along with design ability. A rapidly growing area in graphic design is the field of new media, with new opportunities in multimedia, digital imagery and computer-aided design/manufacture.

## Qualifications and Training

It is sometimes possible to get work as a graphic designer without formal qualifications, provided you have relevant experience and a really impressive portfolio of your design work – this is a highly competitive field. In practice, most graphic designers have either a degree in graphic design or in another art and design-related subject. To be accepted on many art and design degrees you also need a recognised foundation course. You will need to have or to get training in a number of relevant computer graphics packages, including Quark Xpress, Photoshop, Illustrator, Freehand and Dreamweaver. Local colleges offer courses in many of these, and the Chartered Society of Designers funds a programme of continuing professional development for designers who want to keep their skills and knowledge current.

## Personal Qualities and Skills

You must be creative and imaginative with drawing as well as computer graphics skills. You should have some knowledge of printing technology, be able to work to a budget and to deadlines, and be an excellent communicator.

## Salaries

Starting salaries for newly qualified designers are between £14,000 and £18,000. Experienced designers earn between £20,000 and £30,000. Someone with exceptional talent and a good reputation can earn more than this and many graphic designers are self-employed, working freelance.

**info**

The Chartered Society of Designers (CSD), 1 Cedar Court, Royal Oak Yard, Bermondsey Street, London SE1 3GA; 020 7357 8088; www.csd.org.uk

Creative and Cultural Skills, 4th Floor, Lafone House, The Leathermarket, Weston Street London SE1 3HN; 020 7015 1800; www.ccskills.org.uk

D&AD, 9 Graphite Square, Vauxhall Walk, London SE11 5EF; 020 7840 1111; www.dandad.org

Design Business Association (DBA), 35–39 Old Street, London EC1V 9HX; 020 7251 9229; www.dba.org.uk

The Design Council, 34 Bow Street, London WC2E 7DL; 020 7420 5200; www.designcouncil.org.uk

International Society of Typographic Designers (ISTD), PO Box 725, Taunton, Somerset TA2 8WE; 020 7436 0984; www.istd.org.uk

Society of Graphic Fine Art, 9 Newburgh Street, London W1V 1LH; www.sgfa.org.uk

# Illustrator

Illustrators use painting, drawing and multimedia technology to provide illustrations in a whole variety of media and for a wide range of clients. They might illustrate children's books, work for magazines in fashion forecasting, or create artwork for posters and story boards for advertising clients. They may design greetings cards or designs to appear on ceramics. They may work on corporate brochures and increasingly they work on multimedia materials. The aim of an illustration can be to entertain, inform or persuade. Many illustrators become specialists in a particular area such as scientific or technical illustrating.

## Qualifications and Training

To be successful as an illustrator, your portfolio of work is more important than formal qualifications. Many entrants have degrees in graphic design, fine art, fashion or similar, but this is not essential. Your portfolio and your ability to promote yourself and your work is very important. Illustrations don't just have to be creatively good, you have to be clear about the message or idea that they are conveying. This ability to translate an idea or a thought into a design is what clients look for.

## Personal Qualities and Skills

Design and artistic skills. Ability to develop good client relationships and to interpret client briefs. Ability to work in a variety of styles. Self-motivation and marketing skills.

## Salaries

Since illustrators work freelance, it is hard to give typical salary details, but the Society of Illustrators can give help and advice on how to charge and how to price your work.

**info**

Association of Illustrators, 2nd Floor, Back Building, 150 Curtain Road, London EC2A 3AR; 020 7613 4328; www.theAOI.com

Design Council, 34 Bow Street, London WC2E 7DL; 020 7420 5200; www.designcouncil.org.uk and www.yourcreativefuture.org.uk; e-mail: info@designcouncil.org.uk

# Industrial product designer

Trained designers work within industry with engineers who have created products. These range from household goods and furniture to specialised equipment for science, industry and commerce. Designers are concerned with creating products that both look attractive and are efficient and convenient in use. The competition for the sale of new goods, from suitcases or spectacles to CD players or cars, has resulted in an increased demand for the services of industrial designers.

## Qualifications and Training

Employers recruit from those with an HND or degree in a design-related subject; some courses offer specialist modules in industrial design. Entry to such courses is normally via a National Diploma course after GCSEs or a Foundation course at an art college after A levels. Applicants for art and design courses are expected to have a portfolio of their artwork when interviewed.

## Personal Qualities and Skills

As well as artistic ability, an understanding of mass-production processes is necessary; the industrial designer should also be able to work as part of a team, to schedule and recognise the needs of the consumer.

**info**

The Chartered Society of Designers (CSD), 1 Cedar Court, Royal Oak Yard, Bermondsey Street, London SE1 3GA; 020 7357 8088; www.csd. org.uk

Design Business Association (DBA), 35–39 Old Street, London EC1V 9HX; 020 7251 9229; www.dba.org.uk

The Design Council, 34 Bow Street, London WC2E 7DL; 020 7420 5200; www.designcouncil.org.uk

SEMTA, 14 Upton Road, Watford, Hertfordshire WD18 0JT; 0845 643 9001; www.SEMTA.org.uk

## Salaries

Salaries start at between £20,000 and £26,000, rising to £30,000 to £35,000 with a few years' experience.

# Interactive media design

(*see also* Information and Communication Technology)

Interactive media design is a new and highly popular area within art and design. There are now over 500 multimedia courses in the UK. Multimedia design draws on both technical and design skills, and is used in designs for interactive media products such as websites, CD ROMs, interactive TV and computer games. Career opportunities exist in a wide variety of organisations, from corporations with websites to specialist producers of computer games.

### Qualifications and Training

Technical and design skills are essential. Many general courses in Art and Design also have a multimedia option, though there are now specialist multimedia and interactive design courses available. The majority of employers expect an HND or degree.

### Personal Qualities and Skills

Strong design and IT abilities are essential, as are the ability to work within a team and to understand the requirements of the organisation if employed on a company website. The development of new multimedia products such as computer games and CD ROMs also requires an understanding of business and marketing principles.

### Salaries

Starting salary approximately £18,000, although experienced designers can achieve £40,000+.

British Computer Society, 1 Sanford Street, Swindon, Wiltshire SN1 1HJ; 01793 417417; www.bcs.org.uk

British Interactive Multimedia Association, 5–6 Clipstone Street, London W1P 7EB; 020 7436 8250; www.bima.co.uk

British Web Design and Marketing Association, PO Box 3227, London NW9 9LX; 020 8204 2474; www.bwdma.com

UK Web Design Association, Fareham Enterprise Centre, Hackett Way, Fareham, Hampshire PO14 1TH; www.ukwda.org

Skillset, Focus Point, 21 Caledonian Road, London N1 9GB; 020 7520 5757; www.skillset.org

*Careers and Jobs in IT* (Kogan Page)

info

# Interior designer

Interior designers work for commercial organisations as well as undertaking private commissions. They are responsible for the interiors of buildings (whereas an architect is responsible for its shell). Interior design can cover materials for floors and ceilings, fitments and fittings, and colour schemes, along with electrical and spatial planning. The commercial organisations may be offices, hotels, pubs, stores or banks. Interior designers may work with architects, have their own consultancies, or work in design units within large organisations.

## Qualifications and Training

Entry to art school and college via a Foundation course is the same as for an industrial product designer (see page 46). Once at art college, the student may specialise in interior design.

## Personal Qualities and Skills

A natural aptitude for art and the ability to work as part of a design team and to present work to customers are necessary.

## Salaries

Junior designers earn from £15,000 to £20,000. With experience this range rises to £25,000 to £45,000, though few achieve the top of the range. Interior designers working freelance set their own hourly rates.

**info**

Arts Council of Wales, 9 Museum Place, Cardiff CF10 3NX; 029 2037 6500; www.artswales.org.uk

The Chartered Society of Designers (CSD), 1 Cedar Court, Royal Oak Yard, Bermondsey Street, London SE1 3GA; 020 7357 8088; www.csd.org.uk

Design Nation, 41 Commercial Road, London E1 1LA; 020 7320 2895; www.designnation.co.uk

The British Interior Design Association (BIDA), 3/18 Chelsea Harbour Design Centre, Lots Road, London SW10 0XE; www.bida.org

Creative and Cultural Skills, 4th Floor, Lafone House, The Leathermarket, Weston Street, London SE1 3HN; 020 7015 1800; www.ccskills.org.uk

# Signwriter

Signwriters design and paint company names and logos on to shop fronts and the sides of vans and lorries; they may also paint estate agents' signboards and a wide variety of other temporary signs and notices. Signwriters increasingly use a range of materials and techniques, including computer technology, to create signs. The letters are often formed from plastics, metal or wood and stuck on to the background.

Some signwriters are in business on their own; others work for commercial signwriting companies.

## Qualifications and Training

There are no formal academic entry requirements for this type of work, but artistic talent combined with an interest in lettering is important. Some graphic design courses include typography and signwriting and provide wider training. Some commercial signwriting firms take on trainees and NVQs in Assembly, Fabrication and Manufacturing Processes and Signmaking are available at level 2.

## Salaries

Salaries start at around £12,000, rising to £17,000. The highest salaries are around £21,000 to £23,000.

British Signwriters and Graphics Association, 5 Orton Enterprise Centre, Bakewell Road, Orton Southgate, Peterborough, Cambs PE2 6XU; 01733 230033; www.bsga.co.uk

Creative and Cultural Skills, 4th Floor, Lafone House, The Leathermarket, Weston Street, London SE1 3HN; 020 7015 1800; www.ccskills.org.uk

info

# Art theraplst

*see* Therapy

# Arts administration

This is the administration and management of theatres, orchestras, opera houses, ballet companies and arts centres. The Arts Council, responsible for the promotion of art throughout the country, has its own administrative staff. The British Council, responsible for displaying British arts abroad, also employs a small number of staff.

## Qualifications and Training

Experience is often more important than formal qualifications, although a good general education is expected; many entrants are graduates. Commercial awareness plus a knowledge of and interest in the arts is essential. Postgraduate courses such as an MA in Arts Administration can be studied part- or full-time.

## Personal Qualities and Skills

You have to be good at dealing with the public and also with artists, so a full range of interpersonal skills is important. You must be well organised, a very good administrator and have good ideas about marketing, publicity and fund raising. Basic accounting skills are useful.

## Salaries

Salaries for trainees are between £12,000 and £19,000. More experienced staff earn £25,000 to £30,000. Pay is often linked to local authority pay scales.

**info**

Arts Council England, 14 Great Peter Street, London SW1P 3NQ; 0845 300 6200; www. artscouncil.org.uk

The Arts Marketing Association (AMA), 7a Clifton Court, Clifton Road, Cambridge CB1 7BN; 01223 578 078; www.a-m-a.co.uk/

Creative and Cultural Skills: the Sector Skills Council for the Creative and Cultural Industries, 4th Floor Lafone House, The Leathermarket, Weston Street, London SE1 3HN; 020 7015 1800; www.ccskills.org.uk

National Campaign for the Arts, 1 Kingly Street, London W1B 5PA; 020 7287 3777; www.artscampaign. org.uk

# ASTRONOMER

Astronomers study the sun, planets, stars, galaxies and other objects in the sky, analysing the radio, infrared, optical, ultraviolet, X and gamma radiations they emit, to find out how they work. Some of these radiations do not penetrate the earth's atmosphere, so observations by satellite are necessary as well as from the ground. Modern astronomical detectors are usually based on electronic methods and give results which can be analysed by computer.

## Qualifications and Training

To become a research astronomer, a good degree in physics or maths is necessary and it is possible to do degrees in astronomy or astrophysics. This is normally followed by postgraduate study and research. Various grants are available to support students undertaking such courses.

Astronomy-related careers at an engineering or technical level are also open to those with skills in applied physics, electronics, computer hardware and software, optics and mechanical engineering.

## Personal Qualities and Skills

Astronomers need curiosity and imagination; they must be able to make logical deductions from the available observations. Working long and unusual hours and travelling to remote observatories may also be involved.

## Salaries

A junior researcher in astronomy will earn between £20,000 and £25,000. Senior researchers earn more than £35,000. Senior lecturers and astronomers associated with prestigious research projects or working with technical organisations may earn far more than this.

The Library, Royal Astronomical Society, Burlington House, Piccadilly, London W1V 0NL; 020 7734 3307; www.ras.org.uk; e-mail: info@ras.org.uk

Public Information Officer, Royal Observatory Greenwich, National Maritime Museum, London SE10 9NF; 020 8858 4422; www.rog.nmm.ac.uk

# AUCTIONEER

(*see also* Land and Property)

The auctioneer's work involves the sale by auction of property of all kinds, including buildings (houses, farms and estates), livestock, and goods such as furniture, antiques, paintings, glass, toys, carpets and china. The work also entails valuations for various purposes, including investment and insurance.

## Qualifications and Training

An auctioneer's work involves the valuation of land and property, so surveying or valuation qualifications are necessary. There are two components to qualifying as a Chartered Surveyor or Valuer. First is successful completion of a Royal Institution of Chartered Surveyors (RICS) accredited degree or diploma, followed by enrolment onto the Assessment of Professional Competence (APC). The latter is two years' practical training while in employment, finishing with an RICS professional assessment interview. One-year full-time and two-year part-time postgraduate conversion courses are also available.

## Personal Qualities and Skills

Attention to detail is important for this job, together with a practical attitude and an aptitude for figures. In fine art auctioneering, a certain flair and the ability to distinguish a fake from the genuine article are essential.

## Salaries

Salaries for newly qualified valuers are around £20,000. Experienced valuers and auctioneers earn from £25,000 to £40,000. Any earnings linked to the property market and where commission is part of the package will be affected by the current economic climate.

Asset Skills, The Courtyard, 48 New North Road, Exeter, Devon EX4 4EP; 08000 567160; www.assetskills.org

Royal Institution of Chartered Surveyors (RICS), Surveyor Court, Westwood Way, Coventry CV4 8JE; 0870 333 1600; www.rics.org

# Train to become a Registered Hearing Aid Dispenser

**Provide the best quality service to help the hard of hearing live the life they want with the hearing they have**

- Fully funded Foundation Degree in Hearing Aid Audiology
- 2 year earn while you learn programme
- Fully salaried student position
- Guaranteed position available on professional registration
- Based in one of Hidden Hearing's Centres around the UK

**Further details and application form available at www.becomeahearingaiddispenser.co.uk**

HIDDEN HEARING
WE LISTEN, YOU HEAR

INVESTOR IN PEOPLE

**HIDDEN HEARING**

WE LISTEN, YOU HEAR

## REGISTERED HEARING AID DISPENSER

A Registered Hearing Aid Dispenser (RHAD) works within the private hearing healthcare sector often in a retail environment. Their primary role is to assess and treat hearing disorders recommending appropriate hearing solutions and rehabilitation plans for their clients. Many RHAD's work within hearing centres or shops while a number are mobile conducting domiciliary visits. In the main the client population are the elderly who suffer from age related hearing loss and other adults who have suffered hearing deterioration through loud noise or illness.

In the UK there are approximately 1200 Registered Hearing Aid Dispensers all regulated by the Health Professions Council. Due to the nature of modern life, the RNID reports that the numbers of hearing impaired adults in the UK is increasing while at the same time the average age at which a hearing solution is necessary is falling. This gives rise to an increasing market with insufficient professionals to meet the growing private sector demand.

In the private sector the professional body is The British Society of Hearing Aid Audiologists (BSHAA).

### Qualifications and Training

To join the professional register an individual will have to achieve a Foundation Degree in Hearing Aid Audiology. This qualification is offered by a number of UK Universities usually on a block release or distance learning basis and takes 2 years to complete. When not engaged in formal study, a student hearing aid dispenser would usually work alongside a qualified dispenser in a hearing centre practicing their competence under strict direct supervision. As a student's competence increases so their supervision changes to allow them to work alone with clients so that by the end of the Foundation Degree the student is fully competent in all aspects of the RHAD role.

Students will usually have passed a minimum of 5 GCSE examinations, at least 2 of which should be at Advanced Level, including a Science subject. Equivalent qualifications are also welcome. Accreditation of prior learning and relevant working experience can be taken into account for mature students who may not possess the necessary qualifications.

It is also possible for graduates with a BSc in Audiology or an existing NHS Audiology qualification to undergo a transition programme to work within the private sector. Once qualified it is an ongoing condition of registration that all

advertisement feature

RHAD's complete an ongoing programme of Continuing Professional Development that reflects the learning and development that a RHAD makes within their practice.

## Personal Skills and Qualities

Registered Hearing Aid Dispensers need to be able to communicate with people who have hearing difficulties together with client families and carers. They need to be able to demonstrate a caring and patient approach while at the same time being driven to achieve retail sales objectives. The nature of a client consultation requires a structured, logical and scientific approach following set procedures and standards while at the same time having the mental flexibility to adjust personal communication style and behaviour to suit the individual client's preferences and needs. Registered Hearing Aid Dispensers will need to be able to drive and to receive clearance from the Criminal Records Bureau or Independent Safeguard Authority to work with vulnerable members of the community.

## Salaries

Salaries for Student Hearing Aid Dispensers range from £12,000 to £13,000 per year rising with additional sales commission after full qualification and HPC Professional Registration. Employers have different educational assistance schemes some of which fully fund the Foundation Degree Programmes.

## Career Planning

The profession has a number of support roles that range from diary managers and tele-appointers through to assistant dispensing roles. The student RHAD role is a logical step in the career progression of these roles. Many RHAD's continue to develop their specialism throughout their career while others develop their people management and business skills to become team leaders, supervisors and managers fulfilling their aspirations for more senior roles.

## Additional Information

www.becomeahearingaiddispenser.co.uk

Hidden Hearing Limited, Meadow House, Medway Street, Maidstone, Kent. ME14 1HL Tele: 01622 690132

BSHAA, 9 Lukins Drive, Great Dunmow, Essex CM6 1XQ
See: www.bshaa.com

The Health professions Council (HPC), Park House,
184 Kennington Park Road London SE11 4BU
See: www.hpc-uk.org

advertisement feature

# AUDIOLOGIST

Audiologists work with patients as part of a multidisciplinary team of professionals. They identify, assess and treat hearing and/or balance disorders, recommending and providing appropriate rehabilitation and management. Most audiologists work in hospitals. Many choose to specialise in particular client groups such as babies, young children or older people. They may choose to specialise in particular conditions such as tinnitus or balance problems.

## Qualifications and Training

There are three main routes to qualifying as an audiologist: a BSc in Audiology, an MSc in Audiology or a Postgraduate Diploma in Audiology. To gain a place on either the MSc or postgraduate diploma courses you normally need a good degree, first or upper-second class, in a science subject. The BSc in Audiology takes four years, of which the third year is a clinical placement in an audiology department.

It is also possible for graduates with an appropriate science degree at first or upper-second class level to apply for training as a clinical scientist in audiology through the Clinical Scientist Training Scheme. Training takes four years and leads to the MSc or postgraduate diploma.

Clinical scientists in audiology who have successfully completed their training must register with the Health Professions Council (HPC) in order to practise.

## Personal Qualities and Skills

Audiologists need to be able to communicate with people of all ages. They need to be able to think logically and adopt a scientific approach combined with caring and patience.

## Salaries

Salaries for trainees are around £17,400, rising to £27,000. Salaries for audiological scientists are higher than for audiologists. All NHS salaries are paid on a graded scale, with increases for experience, skills and responsibilities.

The British Academy of Audiology, BAA Admin, Resources for Associations, Association House, South Park Road, Macclesfield, Cheshire SK11 6SH; 01625 504066; www.baaudiology.org

British Society of Audiology, 80 Brighton Road, Reading, Berkshire RG6 1PS; 0118 966 0622; www.thebsa.org.uk

Health Professions Council (HPC), Park House, 184 Kennington Park Road, London SE11 4BU; 020 7582 0866; www.hpc-uk.org

NHS Careers; 0845 60 60 655

info

# B

## BANKING AND FINANCE

There are several different types of bank. Retail or high street banks are the local banks with branches all over the country. Of course, all of these now have large call centre operations too. Retail banks serve individual customers, helping with all their personal banking needs. Investment or corporate banks provide financial services to large companies and other organisations.

## Bank cashier/customer service adviser

Bank cashiers, increasingly called customer service advisers, deal with all the daily enquiries made by customers in person, by telephone or via the internet. They work either in high street branches or at call centres. They are responsible for processing cash and cheques, entering account details onto computer systems and issuing foreign currency. They also book appointments for customers who need more specialised advice. Senior cashiers handle more complex enquiries and also supervise small teams of cashiers.

### Qualifications and Training

Each bank sets its own entry requirements. Some do not ask for specific qualifications, but they set entry tests which assess maths, English and computer skills. Many banks do require four or five GCSEs grades A–C including English and maths. Training is on the job and often includes options to study for NVQ levels 2 and 3 in Retail Financial Services, NVQ levels 1 and 2 in Contact Centre Operations or levels 3, 4 and 5 for contact centre professionals (if you work in a call centre) or NVQ levels 2 and 3 in Customer Service. Anyone interested in management may be able to study for one of the diploma courses listed in the 'Bank manager' entry below.

## Bank manager

Bank managers plan and deliver effective sales strategies and monitor the performance of new and existing financial products. Bank managers work

# Treasury - your career path to success

TREASURY, RISK AND FINANCE PROFESSIONALS

**ACT**

**Did you know that corporate treasurers manage the company's financial risk and are instrumental to the development of business strategy?**

If you want to work in a fast-paced environment and have the potential to be one of the top earners in finance, treasury is for you.

## Become ACT qualified and look forward to:

- managing millions and dealing with dynamic global markets
- continually developing your skills and being challenged daily
- directly shaping the organisation's business strategy

**www.treasurers.org/times10**

Association of Corporate Treasurers (ACT) – the professional body for treasury, risk and finance professionals.

## Kick-start your career with ACT professional qualifications

Treasurers manage the company's financial risk and are instrumental to the development of business strategy. The Association of Corporate Treasurers (ACT) is the international body for professionals working in treasury, risk and corporate finance. Our qualifications are a benchmark of technical competency which is why 89% of the FTSE 100 have ACT qualified staff at senior level.

## Treasury - your career path to success

For an ambitious candidate, treasury is a great career to embark on. Future steps on the treasury career ladder could include Group Treasurer, Finance Director and even Chief Executive. ACT qualified treasurers with experience can expect to earn a six-figure salary, with additional higher earning opportunities. You'll be one of the top earners in finance!

## Professional development as you work

Develop specialist knowledge in key areas including cash management, risk management, international treasury management and corporate finance. ACT qualifications combine self study with the option of face-to-face tuition and revision days. They are distance learning qualifications supported by a wide range of print and online learning materials and tools.

## Enrolment deadlines

See individual qualifications for further details.

Find out more at www.treasurers.org/timetoqualify

advertisement feature

either in high street branches, taking responsibility for day-to-day management, or in more specialised posts in corporate or commercial departments at regional or head office level. Their work involves talking to customers, offering advice and planning the workload of other staff in their branch or department. The financial services sector is now extremely competitive, so product sales are now a key part of the manager's role.

## Qualifications and Training

There are two routes to management – either joining a training scheme run by a bank, or by gaining promotion after joining the bank as a cashier/customer services adviser. Most banks expect management trainees to have a good honours degree in a business- or finance-related subject, but it is worth checking individual requirements. Some banks will accept A level entrants or applicants with HNDs. For anyone already working for a bank and wishing to get into management, being good at dealing with customers and having some supervisory experience are very important.

There are several professional qualifications you can work towards on a part-time basis. These include the Professional Diploma in Financial Services Management (Professional DFSM), the Applied Diploma in Corporate Banking and the Applied Diploma in Retailing Financial Services. Management training programmes in banks are normally quite structured and often include the requirement to study for one of the above qualifications.

## Personal Qualities and Skills

All bank staff need very good communication skills. You must be able to explain complex information and be assertive enough to disappoint people sometimes. You must have good IT skills and the ability to interpret figures and other financial information. In management you have to be able to take responsibility for motivating other staff and for implementing sales policies. As a cashier, you may well want to develop some supervisory and management skills by working towards becoming a senior cashier or a customer services adviser in a specialised area such as mortgages or personal investment.

**info**

British Bankers Association (BBA), Pinners Hall, 105–108 Old Broad Street, London EC2N 1EX; 020 7216 8800; www.bba.org.uk

Financial Services Skills Council, 51 Gresham Street, London EC2V 7HQ; 0845 257 3772; www.fssc.org.uk

ifs School of Finance, Institute of Financial Services, IFS House, 4–9 Burgate Lane, Canterbury, Kent CT1 2XJ; 01227 818609; www.ifslearning.ac.uk

## Salaries

Salaries for cashiers start at between £13,000 and £15,000, rising to £19,000 to £23,000 with experience. Earnings often include bonuses or commission for selling financial products to customers. Management trainees earn between £21,000 and £25,000. Some banks pay a joining bonus of between £3,000 and £5,000 to their graduate trainees. Experienced managers earn between £25,000 and £40,000. Bank staff in senior positions can earn up to £100,000. Many roles include the payment of bonuses.

# Building society customer service adviser

Building society customer service advisers (sometimes called cashiers) undertake very similar work to that of banking cashiers. They deal with all the daily enquiries made by customers in person or by telephone. They work either in high street branches or at regional offices. They are responsible for processing cash and cheques, entering account details onto computer systems and issuing foreign currency. They also book appointments for customers who need more specialised advice. Senior cashiers handle more complex enquiries and also supervise small teams of customer service advisers.

Despite the current similarity between banks and building societies, there are still more customers who apply for mortgages through building societies and who use building societies for longer term investments.

## Qualifications and training

Some building societies require applicants to have four GCSEs including English and maths. Others rely on their own selection tests. Experience of customer service work and handling cash are a big advantage, so having worked in any form of retail is very beneficial. Most training is on the job and well structured.

You often have the chance to combine your training with studying for a financial services qualification such as NVQ levels 2 and 3 in Retail Financial Services, NVQ/SVQ levels 2 and 3 in Customer Service or the Ifs School of Finance Customer Service Professional (CSP) award. As you gain qualifications, and with increased experience, there are often opportunities to train and specialise in financial or mortgage advice.

# Building society manager

Building society managers are responsible for running one or more branches of a high street building society. As well as the day-to-day management of their branch or branches they have to ensure that existing customers are happy, that new customers are acquired and that sales of new financial products are increased. They work with individual customers and develop business plans. They have to motivate staff and monitor sales performance.

## Qualifications and Training

Most building societies run management training schemes, but it is also possible to gain promotion to a management role if you are already working as a customer services adviser/cashier. Most management training schemes are only open to applicants with a good honours degree in a business- or finance-related subject. Check individual company requirements though, because some will accept management trainees with degrees in other subjects or with good A levels or HNDs.

Training is on the job and well structured, with opportunities to learn about different aspects of the role. Most trainee managers are either required or encouraged to study for one of the following qualifications: the Professional Diploma in Financial Services Management (Professional DFSM), the Applied Diploma in Corporate Banking or the Applied Diploma in Retailing Financial Services.

## Personal Qualities and Skills

For customer service staff and managers good interpersonal skills for dealing with enquiries are extremely important. You have to be able to convey complex financial information so that it is easily understood. Good computer skills are important and an ability to work accurately and carefully is necessary. Customer service staff aiming towards management roles and managers need to be able to take responsibility for leading and motivating staff teams.

## Salaries

Starting salaries are between £13,500 and £17,000 rising to £19,000 to £25,000 with experience. Salaries are higher in London. Management trainees earn between £21,000 and £25,000 while experienced managers earn up to £50,000. Senior managers in the organisation can earn up to £100,000. Benefits often include bonus sharing schemes, subsidised mortgages and share options. Earnings often include commission on financial products sold.

**info**

Financial Services Skills Council, 51 Gresham Street, London EC2V 7HQ; 0845 257 3772; www.fssc.org.uk

Building Societies Association, 6th Floor, York House, 23 Kingsway, London WC2B 6UJ; 020 7520 5900; www.bsa.org.uk

ifs School of Finance, Institute of Financial Services, IFS House, 4–9 Burgate Lane Canterbury, Kent CT1 2XJ; 01227 818609; www.ifslearning.ac.uk

# Commodity broker

Commodity brokers buy and sell commodities including tea, coffee, grain, oil, gas and metals. They work either for companies which specialise in dealing in commodities trading or for companies which produce and/or grow the commodities. As well as trading in the actual products, they trade in futures (commodities that will be produced or grown in the future). They have to monitor world markets, possibly visiting sites and countries where commodities are produced. They have to advise clients when to buy, when to sell and where to place themselves in the market. They also have to work closely with shipping, transport and insurance organisations.

## Qualifications and Training

While there are no specific entry qualifications, most successful applicants have a 2.1 degree in a relevant subject such as economics, maths, science, business or finance. The recruitment process can be very demanding, including several interviews and psychometric tests.

## Personal Qualities and Skills

You must be highly numerate and an excellent communicator. You have to be able to take decisions under pressure, accept responsibility and work as part of a team. Being able to live with job insecurity is also important; opportunities in this work fluctuate widely.

## Salaries

Salaries are between £35,000 and £50,000 and experienced brokers with a successful trading record can earn extremely high salaries. It is a volatile market, though, with a lot of associated risk.

eFinancialCareers Ltd,
Tabernacle Court, 3rd Floor,
16/28 Tabernacle Street, London
EC2A 4DD; 020 7997 7900; www.
efinancialcareers.co.uk

Financial Services Authority (FSA),
25 The North Colonnade,
Canary Wharf, London E14 5HS;
020 7066 1000; www.fsa.gov.uk

Financial Services Skills Council,
51 Gresham Street, London
EC2V 7HQ; 0845 257 3772; www.fssc.org.uk

IntercontinentalExchange (ICE),
International House,

1 St Katherines Way,
London E1W 1UY; 020 7481 0643;
www.theice.com/homepage.jhtml

London International Financial
Futures & Options Exchange (LIFFE),
Euronext.liffe, Cannon Bridge,
London EC4R 3XX; 020 7623 0444;
www.euronext.com/home_
derivatives/0,4810,1732_6391950,00.html

The London Metal Exchange,
56 Leadenhall Street,
London EC3A 2DX; 020 7264 5555;
www.lme.co.uk

info

# Economist

*see* Economist

# Financial adviser

Financial advisers provide advice on all aspects of financial planning to a wide range of clients. They work with individuals, corporate clients and other groups of people such as societies or charities. They can offer advice on such diverse matters as loans, mortgages, pensions, investments and other financial products and services.

Their work involves meeting clients and explaining financial products and services to them clearly and carefully. They have to assess people's different financial circumstances in order to advise on the most suitable products. They conduct in-depth research into different products and liaise closely with banks, building societies, insurance companies, etc – the financial product suppliers. They are often self-employed, so they also have to be good at marketing and promoting themselves and seeking out new clients.

There are approximately 75,000 financial advisers working in the UK, and almost half class themselves as independent rather than tied advisers. Being independent, however, does not necessarily mean being self-employed. Both tied and independent financial advisers may work for an organisation or may be self-employed. Many independent advisers work for firms which themselves are known as independent financial advisers.

Tied advisers work for financial services companies, insurance companies, investment firms, banks and building societies. Some are employed by estate agencies, law firms and by retailers that have developed financial services as a part of their business.

## Qualifications and Training

You don't have to be a graduate, though a degree in business studies, accountancy or financial services can give you an advantage. Many employers are happy to take people from a wide range of working backgrounds and do not require academic qualifications. You nearly always need a driving licence, and some employers set a lower age limit of 21 or older for trainees.

All entrants to the professions have to pass the Financial Planning Certificate examinations parts 1, 2 and 3 or the Certificate for Financial Advisers in order to be licensed by the Financial Services Authority. A lot of the training is provided on the job and when you start you often learn by shadowing a more experienced adviser.

## Personal Qualities and Skills

You need excellent communication skills, to be able to talk convincingly to corporate clients and sensitively to private individuals. You must be smart, well organised and highly motivated – this is a competitive sector. You need good numeracy and IT skills and the ability to deal with highly complex information.

## Salaries

The earnings of financial advisers employed by financial services companies are made up of a combination of a basic salary plus commission on products sold. Basic salaries are between £20,000 and £30,000. Achieving successful sales targets can raise salaries to between £30,000 and £60,000. In a difficult market place these commissions and target-related earning are much harder to achieve. Some independent financial advisers charge a fee to clients rather than earning commission on products sold.

Association of Independent Financial Advisers (AIFA), 2–6 Austin Friars House, Austin Friars, London EC2N 2HD; 020 7628 1287; www.aifa.net

Financial Services Authority, 25 The North Colonnade, Canary Wharf, London E14 5HS; 020 7066 1000; www.fsa.gov.uk

Financial Services Skills Council, 51 Gresham Street, London EC2V 7HQ; 0845 257 3772; www.fssc.org.uk

ifs School of Finance, Institute of Financial Services, IFS House, 4–9 Burgate Lane Canterbury, Kent CT1 2XJ; 01227 818609; www.ifslearning.ac.uk

Chartered Insurance Institute, 20 Aldermanbury, London EC2V 7HY; 020 8989 8464; www.cii.co.uk

info

# Investment work

## Investment analyst

Investment analysts analyse the financial markets to advise on the best investments for clients. Investment managers rely on their information. There are two main types of investment analyst. First are those who work for stockbrokers and undertake their own analysis to provide information for fund manager clients. The aim is to generate 'buy and sell' orders for the stockbrokers for whom they work. This is known as the 'sell side'. Second, there are those who work for investment management institutions. They provide ideas and information to enable their in-house fund managers to make the best decisions for their clients. This is known as the 'buy side'. The majority of investment analysts work on the 'sell side'.

## Fund manager

Investment fund managers invest the funds of other people – private clients and institutions, such as insurance companies, charities, independent schools and specialised research institutions. Managers must keep their clients' interests continually under review, offering advice on how to retain their clients' income and when to change investments. Investment fund managers may be employed by the larger institutions, or work in specialist firms that tend to serve smaller clients.

## Qualifications and Training

Investment banks and stock broking firms prefer to recruit graduates. A good honours degree in any subject is acceptable, but degrees in accountancy, business, economics or maths are especially relevant. Some investment analysts need in-depth knowledge of particular industry markets, so it may be useful to have experience in areas such as energy, engineering, mining or life sciences. Training is on the job and graduates are usually placed with a more experienced analyst and given other structured training. Initial training takes around three years.

# IG GROUP

# IG Group Holdings plc

**The Company** Established in 1974, IG Group Holdings plc is a world leader in financial derivatives trading and sports betting. The IG Group is a member of the FTSE 250. We have over 800 employees based in offices in the UK, Australia, Singapore, Europe, the USA and Japan. The UK operation is regulated by the Financial Services Authority and IG Index is the UK's leading financial spread betting firm offering prices in a huge range of indices, currencies, commodities and options, as well as thousands of individual shares and sports markets. IG Markets is the IG brand for its worldwide businesses and for trading Contracts for Difference (CFDs).

**Opportunities** IG Group recognises that its continued growth is highly dependant upon attracting and retaining high calibre employees and there are exciting, dynamic and fast-paced roles at IG in which employees can add value, whilst building upon their skills and developing their careers.

**Trainee Financial Dealers** are offered extensive training that covers all aspects of IG's financial dealing and financial sales operations. As part of this training, there is a requirement to take and successfully pass the Securities Institute Regulatory Paper. Upon successful completion of the training, permanent positions are offered within one of the Financial Dealing or Financial Sales teams.

**Client Services Co-ordinators** provide excellent customer service to IG's clients and they support the financial dealing desk. In addition to taking care of administrative duties relating to client accounts, responsibilities include responding to client queries and investigating and resolving client disputes.

**IT Graduate Trainees** are offered the opportunity to work with a number of different teams within IT Development. This will involve learning about finance, liaising with senior business representatives and learning some of the latest technologies. The role will require you to work on one or more of our performance critical systems; including our C++ calculation engines, our distributed highly available Java dealing platform, our REST based SOA, our high performance enterprise messaging or our cutting edge JavaScript and Ajax based award winning dealing front end. There is a wide range of technologies used within our department and we are seeking people who are excited about technology and are keen to put all that hard study into practice in an Agile, rewarding, challenging and dynamic environment.

**The Suitable Candidates** You will need at least 3 A levels at grade "B" or above and ideally have a 2.1 degree or above. You will need to be able to demonstrate that you are highly numerate, IT literate and have a real interest in betting and/or financial markets. Ideally, especially for the Trainee Financial Dealer role, you will have taken a gap year and/or have 1 to 2 years' postgraduate experience. As IG continues to expand across the globe, fluency in another language would be very useful. You will also need to work effectively under pressure and be prepared to work unconventional hours with an underlying enthusiasm to serve our clients. Candidates will be self-confident with a friendly outgoing manner and the ability to work as an effective team member.

**Pay and Benefits** Starting Salary circa £25,000 + Bonus + Good Benefits Package.

**To apply** please send your CV to hr@igindex.co.uk.
**Telephone:** 0207-896-0011 **Fax:** 0207-896-0010.
For more information about the company, please visit our website at **www.iggroup.com**.

## About the business

IG has travelled a long way from the niche business founded by entrepreneur Stuart Wheeler in 1974. IG remained small until 1998 and since then has enjoyed more than ten years of uninterrupted growth. An initial London Stock Exchange listing in 2000 was followed by a management buyout in 2003 when the founder sold his shares. IG Group re-listed in 2005. Revenue increased by 40% to £250m in 2009 while profit before tax rose by 33% to £131m.

Financial spread betting has grown exponentially over the past decade because it offers traders and investors a unique combination of flexibility, speed of execution and tax-free profits. It's all about leverage. Indices are derivative based – you don't need to own the underlying share – instead you buy and sell an index at a market price and profit or lose by any movements in these indices.

More than 38,000 IG clients log on every day to trade the financial markets. The 24-hour market is covered by 15 hours from London and nine hours from Melbourne. More than 90% of transactions are made online, using IG's browser-based trading platforms.

## Company culture

IG is seen as the market leader, an innovator, and the one to aspire to. IG people have grown up together over 10 years and that has generated a common purpose of learning, building and a passion for the business and for success.

The four board directors are very much hands-on and ideas are welcomed from anyone. IG considers its culture, and the way in which it has managed and brought in its people, to have driven its success.

Employees are given autonomy within their roles to show what they can do for IG, rather than the employee relying on IG to demonstrate what it can do for them. Everyone is expected to hit the ground running as soon as they join the company.

IG does not consider itself to be a traditional City trading culture. IT specialists and client services are just as important as dealers. There is meritocracy without a hierarchy.

## Innovation and creativity

IG has a culture of encouraging employees to suggest innovations and employees are rewarded for the best ones. IG was the first to introduce dealing from an iPhone and the first to create dealing directly from technical charts. IG Index also introduced the innovative and highly popular 'Bungee Bet', a unique limited risk bet. The employees that invented the product and the name won an Innovation Award.

## Innovation and creativity (continued)

IG is very proud of its trading platform 'PureDeal' which is considered by the industry and clients alike to be robust and intuitive to use. It is designed so that users can get started without needing to read a manual or call Client Services.

IG was the first to offer spreads on individual shares, out-of-hour indices, binary trades, and guaranteed stop-loss limits and continuously monitors what is working and what is not to ensure that it remains in front.

## Pay & Benefits

IG compares its packages with other financial institutions and it recognises that salary is important and therefore pays median to upper quartile.

Bonus is based on a communal pool driven by the overall profitability of the company. The pool is first apportioned by department, and then distributed to individuals, based upon their performance, by department heads.

There's a share incentive plan awarded each year to all UK staff. The company matches shares one-to-one up to £1,500.

IG contributes 10% into the pension if the employee contributes 5%. This is done as a salary sacrifice with Inland Revenue approved tax benefits and other benefits include private medical cover and permanent health insurance for everyone.

In addition, other benefits include free fruit every day and free 'coffee bar standard' coffee. All expenses paid parties at Christmas at fantastic venues are notable events and one of the highlights of the year and are very well attended

## Career development

IG offers good development routes in trading and finance. A new employee would need to spend 12-18 months immersed in it to contemplate a wider management role. A six-month probationary period is intended to find out if a new joiner enjoys it at IG. These months are intensive and dealers would be expected to work hard. They would be expected to sit 'bet tests' to ensure that they can cope with working on the Financial Dealing Desk and that they have the right judgement. After 12-18 months a graduate can expect to be appointed to a specific desk.

The majority of work related training is carried out on the job. However, IG runs training lectures on the market and on specific products and also offers the opportunities for employees to attend external courses to develop their skills and competence. There are also opportunities to take studying further with some studying for qualifications with chartered status and senior members working towards achieving their MBA's.

IG GROUP

## Career development (continued)

IG has seen those that joined as graduates go from London to Japan, Singapore and Australia and another helped set up the client services operation in Chicago. Peter Hetherington was the company's first ever graduate trainee employee and he is now IG's Chief Operating Officer. People who do well at IG have a good academic background with strong numeracy. They are proactive, team players, and not afraid to throw their hat into the ring. They 'own' problems, pick an issue up, and run with it. Progress is gauged through the line manager and the annual appraisal process.

## Corporate Social Responsibility

IG is committed to treating clients fairly. IG introduced 'price improvement,' where if a price moves in the fractions of a second between the client clicking a trade and it being executed, and they could have got a better price, then IG gives it to them. Other companies reject a client's trade if the price moves in favour of the client.

Spread betting is not for everyone and there are risks involved. IG does turn away clients, and assesses the appropriateness of a product for a client based on their previous trading experience. IG scores every new client. Low scores means a client has to join the Trade Sense education programme (a modular education programme which teaches new clients the fundamentals of spreadbetting and allows them to try it with lower-than-usual size bets) and need to have defined stop-loss limits so that they can never lose more money than they have on account.

IG is an equal opportunity employer. Graduate intakes are a very diverse group while the IT department, often made up of second, third or fourth jobbers from all over the globe, is the most diverse team in terms of age, background and ethnicity.

IG employees asked about recycling so this was taken on board and now there are bins for everything strewn around the offices. Bottled water was replaced with filtered tap water. All lights are switched off five minutes after leaving, and PC screens power down automatically. IG's offices were refurbished to be environmentally and ergonomically efficient. IG also calculates and monitors its carbon footprint.

There is an IG charity budget and employees get involved in a wide range of charity and sponsored events. The company gives people time off for volunteer work and is very happy to match what they raise.

Trainees are usually required or encouraged to study for relevant professional qualifications. Two of the most widely offered are the United Kingdom Society of Investment Professionals (UKSIP) Investment Management Certificate (IMC) and the Securities and Investments Institute (SII) Certificate in Securities and Financial Derivatives. Many analysts then carry on to study for more advanced diplomas.

## Personal Qualities and Skills

As an investment analyst you must have an enquiring mind and be persistent and thorough in your research. A broad range of interests including politics and economics as well as finance is important. You have to be confident dealing with people, one-to-one or at meetings with senior representatives of companies. You should be able to write clear, concise summaries of statistical data and other research findings.

## Salaries

Typical starting salaries are £35,000 in London, with bonuses of 20–100 per cent possible in the first three years, less in other parts of the UK. After five to eight years, salaries rise to £65,000–£100,000, with bonuses of 40–100 per cent possible. Salaries vary according to the nature and size of the company and geographical location. Salaries are higher with investment banks.

info

Association of Private Client Investment Managers and Stockbrokers (APCIMS), 114 Middlesex Street, London E1 7JH; 020 7247 7080; www.apcims.co.uk

Chartered Financial Analyst (CFA) Institute,10th Floor, One Canada Square, Canary Wharf, London E14 5AB; 020 7531 0751; www.cfainstitute.org

Financial Services Authority (FSA), 25 The North Colonnade, Canary Wharf, London E14 5HS; 020 7066 1000; www.fsa.gov.uk

Financial Services Skills Council, 51 Gresham Street, London EC2V 7HQ; 0845 257 3772; www.fssc.org.uk

London Investment Banking Association (LIBA), 6 Frederick's Place, London EC2R 8BT; 020 7796 3606; www.liba.org.uk

Securities and Investment Institute (SII), Centurion House, 24 Monument Street, London EC3R 8AQ; 020 7645 0600; www.securities-institute.org.uk

UK Society of Investment Professionals (UKSIP), 4th Floor, 90 Basinghall Street, London EC2V 5AY; 020 7796 3000; www.uksip.org

# Stockbroker

Stockbrokers buy and sell securities on the Stock Exchange on behalf of investors, who may be individuals but are increasingly institutions, such as banks, insurance companies, pension funds or unit trusts. They also advise clients on shares they hold and suggest good times to sell or buy. Stockbrokers work from their offices using the phone and internet to keep in touch with financial markets and news.

## Qualifications and Training

While there are no formal entry requirements most investment banks will only consider you if you have a 2.1 degree and some employers require an MSc or an MBA. Relevant subjects such as economics or business are preferred and the selection procedure is tough. If you do not have a relevant degree, it is really important that you are able to demonstrate your understanding of how financial markets work. Some people move from investment analysis or investment administration into stockbroking. To practise as a stockbroker you must register with the Financial Services Authority (FSA). The Financial Services Skills Council can provide you with a full list of all the qualifications which allow you to register. Investment banks and other firms which take on trainee brokers offer in-house training.

## Personal Qualities and Skills

A great aptitude with numbers and excellent communication skills are essential. You must be calm under pressure, able to take decisions and happy working on your own or as part of a team.

## Salaries

Salaries for trainees start from £26,000 to £35,000 rising to £50,000 to £80,000. Experienced and successful brokers can earn far more, but at the moment this type of work is going through a difficult period and job insecurity may balance out the high salaries.

Financial Services Skills Council, 51 Gresham Street, London EC2V 7HQ; 0845 257 3772; www.fssc.org.uk

Financial Services Authority, 25 The North Colonnade, Canary Wharf, London E14 5HS; 020 7066 1000; www.fsa.gov.uk

CFA Society of the UK, 90 Basinghall Street, London EC2V 5AY; 020 7796 3000; www.cfauk.org

Securities & Investment Institute (SII), 8 Eastcheap, London EC3M 1AE; 020 7645 0680; www.sii.org.uk

info

# Trader/dealer

Traders or dealers fall into three categories; each working in different ways and/or for different client groups. Flow traders buy and sell such products as shares, bonds, commodities and foreign exchange on the financial markets. They buy and sell on behalf of banks or other financial institutions' clients. They try to minimise risk and maximise profits for their clients. Proprietary traders trade on behalf of a bank or financial institution rather than its clients. They try to buy at low prices, and sell high. Flow and proprietary traders work mainly in dealing rooms, constantly tracking market performance and making decisions about when and what to buy and sell. Sales traders deal directly with clients, providing market information and promoting new financial ideas to clients. Their role includes preparing detailed reports based on market information – so is more research based than the work of flow traders.

## Qualifications and Training

This is now very much a graduate profession – you normally need a good degree, and while any subject is acceptable, business studies, economics, maths and politics are particularly useful. You may also get in if you have an HND or foundation degree in one of these subjects. This has been a highly competitive area and you are likely to face a rigorous selection process. If you have not gone on to higher education, it may be possible to work your way from an administrative job for a bank, or other financial organisation, especially if you are able to build up a good network of contacts. Most training is on the job, combined with in-house short courses or work towards financial sector qualifications.

## Personal Qualities and Skills

All traders have to be able to develop a really good knowledge of financial markets and to apply that knowledge. In other work than sales, a good trader should be able to take risks, but in a balanced way – weighing up benefits and dangers realistically. Traders working in dealing rooms have to be resilient and able to think quickly and take decisions under pressure. Traders working in sales have to build up excellent relationships with their clients.

**info**

Bank of England,
Threadneedle Street,
London EC2R 8AH; 020 7601 4444;
www.bankofengland.co.uk

eFinancialCareers Ltd,
Tabernacle Court, 3rd Floor,
16/28 Tabernacle Street,
London EC2A 4DD; 020 7997 7900;
www.efinancialcareers.co.uk

Financial Services Skills Council,
51 Gresham Street,
London EC2V 7HQ; 0845 257 3772;
www.fssc.org.uk

IntercontinentalExchange (ICE),
International House,
1 St Katherines Way,
London E1W 1UY; 020 7481 0643;
www.theice.com/homepage.jhtml

London International Financial
Futures & Options Exchange (LIFFE),
Euronext.liffe, Cannon Bridge,
London EC4R 3XX; 020 7623 0444;
www.euronext.com/home_
derivatives/0,4810,1732_6391950,00.
html

London Stock Exchange (LSE),
10 Paternoster Square,
London EC4M 7LS; 020 7797 1000;
www.londonstockexchange.com

Securities and Investment Institute
(SII), 8 Eastcheap,
London EC3M 1AE;
+44 (0) 20 7645 0600; www.sii.org.uk

## Salaries

Starting salaries are between £25,000 and £50,000 and with a few years' experience and a successful record salaries can become very high indeed, including large bonuses and other benefits.

# BEAUTY

Beauticians are predominantly, although not exclusively, female. There is a variety of occupations within the beauty sector, ranging from therapists who provide body and face treatment to make-up artists who work in film and television.

# Beauty sales consultant

### Qualifications and Training

You don't need formal qualifications to start training – your employer normally provides an introductory course. There are several NVQ level 2 courses available in beauty consultancy, for which you can study on a part-time basis. Previous experience in either retail or beauty therapy can also be very useful.

### Personal Qualities and Skills

You need to have excellent communication skills, to be able to talk to people, make them feel comfortable and encourage them to purchase products. You need to be practical and sensitive when applying make-up and other beauty products. You often have to organise your own product displays so you must be imaginative and have good visual awareness. You need to be highly presentable yourself – a good advert for what you are selling.

### Salaries

Trainees start on around £11,000 to £13,000, rising to £19,000 with experience. Consultants are often expected to achieve sales targets and earn part of their salaries through sales commission.

# Beauty therapist

(*see also* Hairdresser)

Beauty therapists work in salons, health clubs and private homes and, at the glamorous end of the market, for film, television and fashion magazines. Beauty therapists offer a range of treatments to their clients, such as facials, massage, make-up, manicures, waxing and body toning and tanning treatments. Beauty therapists who visit clients in their own homes have to be good business people, keeping accounts, ordering stock and keeping up to date with the latest developments. The top end of the market is highly competitive, but it is a profession that gives you a lot of flexibility. UK hairdressers and beauty therapists are generally highly thought of.

## Qualifications and Training

You normally need three or four GCSEs grades A–C and then there are several relevant qualifications including the City & Guilds diploma in beauty therapy, City & Guilds level 3 diploma in specialist beauty therapy, Edexcel national certificate and diploma in beauty therapy sciences, VTCT advanced diploma in beauty therapy, NVQ level 3 in beauty therapy. You can either go to a further education or private college full-time, or work as an assistant at a beauty salon and attend college part-time. Private college courses may be shorter and more intensive, but they are also expensive.

## Personal Qualities and Skills

As a beauty therapist you have to look neat, presentable and well groomed. You must be friendly, welcoming, and able to put clients at ease and you also need to be tactful and sensitive. You must be comfortable working in close physical proximity with your clients and you need reasonable stamina as you will be on your feet for most of the time. If you run your own business you need all the appropriate business skills too.

## Salaries

Beauty therapists earn between £12,000 and £18,000 while salon managers earn between £20,000 and £23,000. Beauty therapists often receive tips and they may also make commission from selling cosmetics and beauty products. Some beauty therapists are self-employed, in which case earnings vary according to how much work they undertake.

**info**

Hairdressing and Beauty Industry Authority (HABIA), Oxford House, Sixth Ave, Sky Business Park, Robin Hood Airport, Doncaster CN9 3GG; www.habia.org

International Therapist Examination Council (ITEC), 4 Heathfield Terrace, Chiswick, London W4 4JE; 020 8994 4141; www.itecworld.co.uk

# Body artist/tattooist

Body artists/tattooists working in studios or parlours draw designs of words, patterns and pictures on the bodies of customers. This form of body adornment has grown increasingly popular over recent years. The body artist either draws the design freehand or works from a transfer placed on the customer's skin. He or she then follows the outline with an electrically operated needle which delivers permanent ink dyes just under the skin.

## Qualifications and Training

No formal qualifications are required, but you will have to persuade a registered tattooist to take you on as an apprentice. It is illegal to tattoo if you are not registered with your local Environmental Health Department. This department should be able to provide you with names of local registered artists and the Tattoo Club of Great Britain can also help you with this. Training takes from one to three years, but it takes at least five years to become really competent.

## Personal Qualities and Skills

Body artists/tattooists must have a flair for design and also be very good at working with people. Customers may want a tattoo, but they are often a bit nervous about it. Body artists must be extremely careful about their art work, since the designs are permanent. They must also have scrupulous hygiene and health and safety awareness.

## Salaries

Trainees earn around £11,000 rising to £17,000 with considerable experience. It is possible to earn more than this if you develop a really good reputation and have obvious talent, or if you work in a highly fashionable studio.

Tattoo Club of Great Britain, 389 Cowley Road, Oxford OX4 2BS; 01865 716877; www.tattoo.co.uk

**info**

# Make-up artist

Make-up artists prepare and work on make-up and hair styling required for each individual such as artists, singers, dancers, actors and others appearing on television and in film production. Make-up artists also work in other environments such as on cruise liners, in beauty salons in large hotels, stage shows, fashion shows or in the medical profession, where they provide make-up to camouflage client injuries following an accident or surgery.

An experienced make-up artist will work on more versatile projects using elaborate make-up, wigs, and materials to change the shape of a face or create scars and wounds for television and film productions. This will require research and design of the make-up required for a production, through to completion ready for filming. It is necessary to be able to liaise closely with producers, directors, costume designers, hairdressers and the performers.

## Qualifications and Training

While there are no set entry qualifications, many applicants have degrees or HNDs in art and design-related subjects and/or beauty therapy and hairdressing qualifications. There is a wide range of training courses available and Skillset gives useful advice on these. Examples of some relevant qualifications include the BTEC/SQA National Certificate/Diploma in Performing Arts (Make-up), Vocational Training Charitable Trust (VTCT) level 3 Diploma in Theatre and Media Make-up, and International Therapy Examinations Council (ITEC) level 3 Diploma in Fashion, Theatre and Media Make-up. The London College of Fashion offers a foundation degree in make-up artistry. Most people start as a make-up assistant while doing one of the courses mentioned above.

## Personal Qualities and Skills

You need to have artistic flair and imagination. You must be practical, methodical and patient, but you must also be able to work quickly under pressure. You should be able to get on well with all sorts of people, and be confident and tactful, able to make suggestions and put people at ease. You should be good at working as part of a team.

**info**

Broadcasting Entertainment Cinematographic and Theatre Union (BECTU), 373–377 Clapham Road, London SW9 9BT; 020 7346 0900; www.bectu.org.uk

FT2 – Film & Television Freelance Training, Third Floor, 18–20 Southwark Street, London SE1 1TJ; 020 7407 0344; www.ft2.org.uk

Greasepaint, 143 Northfield Avenue, Ealing, London W13 9QT; 020 8840 6000; www.greasepaint.co.uk

International Therapy Examination Council, Heathfield Terrace, Chiswick, London W4 4JE; 020 8994 4141; www.itecworld.co.uk

London College of Fashion, 20 John Prince's Street, London W1G 0BJ; 020 7514 7344; www.fashion.arts.ac.uk

The Make-up Centre, Ealing Studios, Building D, Second Floor, Ealing Green, London W5 5EP; 020 8579 9511; www.themake-upcentre.co.uk

Producers Alliance for Cinema and Television (PACT), Proctor House, 1 Proctor Street, Holborn, London WC1V 6DW; 020 7067 4367; www.pact.co.uk

Revelations School of Make-up, Revelations House, Royal Oak Yard, off Little Underbank, Stockport, Manchester SK1 1JZ; 0161 476 5009; www.schoolofmakeup.co.uk

Scottish Screen, 249 West George Street, Glasgow G2 4QE; 0141 302 1700; www.scottishscreen.com

Skillset (Sector Skills Council for the Audio Visual Industries), Prospect House, 80–110 New Oxford Street, London WC1A 1HB; 020 7520 5757; www.skillset.org

Vocational Training Charitable Trust, 3rd Floor, Eastleigh House, Upper Market Street, Eastleigh, Hants SO50 9FD; 023 8068 4500; www.vtct.org.uk

## Salaries

There are recommended industry minimum pay rates for film and television work. Current rates are £184 per day for junior make-up/hair assistant and

£279 for make-up designer prosthetics. These rates are for peak-time drama television production and high-budget feature films. Rates are negotiable and individuals who are well regarded in the industry are in great demand and can command good money. It is such a competitive field that some make-up artists start out working for nothing or for low pay on budget productions.

# Nail technician

As greater numbers of people are going to salons to have either regular manicures or false nails or nail extensions applied, so there has been a growth in this specialist area of beauty therapy. There are now many salons which specialise purely in nail care, treatment and decoration. Nail technicians do manicures, apply, maintain and repair false nails and extensions, and decorate both natural and gel nails with polish or with painted artistic designs.

## Qualifications and Training

There are usually no formal qualifications required to get into this work, but some large salons may require you to have GCSEs in English, maths and a science. Many nail technicians are qualified beauty therapists who choose to specialise in nail technology. If this is not the case, then a good way to start is by working towards an NVQ level 1 in Beauty Therapy and then trying to gain work as an assistant in a salon. Once you have learnt the basics about nail care and nail treatments and decoration, there are further NVQs levels 2 and 3 in Nail Care and Nail Technology towards which you can work while employed.

## Personal Qualities and Skills

You have to be smart and presentable and have a friendly and pleasant manner. You should have good manual dexterity and an interest in colour and design. You should have a careful and patient approach to your work, and a good awareness of health and safety and hygiene issues.

## Salaries

Salaries range from £11,000 to £15,000 depending on geographical location. In some city centre salons with a really good reputation earnings can be more than £23,000. Many nail technicians are self-employed, as this is work that can be done from home or by visiting clients in their homes.

Association of Nail Technicians; 01322 555724; www.ant.uk.net

Hairdressing and Beauty Therapy Industry Authority (HABIA), Oxford House, Sixth Avenue, Sky Business Park, Robin Hood Airport, Doncaster DN9 3GG; 08452 306080; www.habia.org

info

# BIOLOGY

Those who work in the field of biology are concerned with the structure, processes and functions of living organisms.

# Biochemist

Biochemistry is the study of chemical substances and processes in living cells and tissues. Most biochemists work in laboratories though some make their careers in education or industry, in brewing, food technology, forestry, agriculture, dietetics, pharmaceuticals, management and planning.

Many biochemists are employed in hospitals, where they manage and develop the service and carry out research into disease. Pharmaceutical firms also employ biochemists to develop new drugs and study their effects on diseases and patients. Qualified biochemists are also employed in research institutions funded by the Medical Research Council, the National Institute for Medical Research and Biotechnology, and the Biological Sciences Research Council, as well as some funded by charities such as the Imperial Cancer Research Fund (ICRF).

## Qualifications and Training

Most biochemists are graduates with a degree in biochemistry or chemistry. Increasingly many applicants also have postgraduate qualifications in biochemistry or clinical chemistry. If you can get some work experience in a lab while studying for your degree this is also really useful. It is possible to work your way up by starting as a lab technician and doing a degree in biochemistry part-time.

If you choose to work for the NHS as a biochemist, you normally start training as a clinical biochemist and work for professional qualifications as a clinical scientist. In industry and research, once you are working as a trainee biochemist, your employer may encourage or require you to take further postgraduate qualifications.

## Personal Qualities and Skills

You need all the skills of a good scientist. You must be a good problem solver and be able to think creatively. You need to pay great attention to detail, follow procedures carefully and be highly observant. You should be practical with reasonable IT skills. You must be able to work as part of a team, or capable of working on your own. At senior level, your work may well involve management of other staff and various projects.

## Salaries

Starting salaries for trainees range from £25,000 to £28,000. Experienced biochemists can earn £35,000 to £55,000. In the NHS biochemists' salaries are linked to a clear graded structure. Research jobs in industry may offer higher salaries than those in the NHS and public sector.

Institute of Biology, 9 Red Lion Court, London EC4A 3EF; 020 7936 5900; www.iob.org

Institute of Biomedical Science, 12 Coldbath Square, London EC1R 5HL; 020 7713 0214; www.ibms.org

Biochemical Society, 3rd Floor, Eagle House, 16 Proctor Street, London WC1V 6NX; 01206 796 351; www.biochemistry. org

info

# Biomedical scientist

*see* Medical and Healthcare Science

# Biotechnologist

Biotechnologists work with agriculture, the food industry, medicine and the environment. They apply their knowledge of biological systems and structure in plants and animals to solve problems and develop products and processes in all these sectors. Applications of biotechnology are wide, but examples include developing vaccines and hormones to help treat inherited diseases, the study of human genetics, plants, animals and other organisms to understand the nature of inherited disease, and the development of genetic modification to alter certain properties of plants and seeds. Other examples include manufacturing enzymes that can preserve food, developing dyes and detergents for the textiles industry and developing microorganisms and plants that will clean land.

## Qualifications and Training

To work as a biotechnologist you need a degree in a subject such as biotechnology, bioscience, microbiology, biochemistry, chemical engineering or a related biological science. You should also consider which specific area of biotechnology interests you, eg food, agriculture or medicine, as some degree courses offer work placements in industry and having experience in the field that particularly interests you will be helpful when you come to apply for jobs. Since so much of the work is research based, you may also need an MSc or a PhD plus several years working as a laboratory assistant or a research assistant before you can progress to becoming a biotechnologist.

Training is on the job. Pharmaceutical companies often have in-house training schemes. Your training covers working with advanced technical equipment, computing skills and project management. If you don't join this sector with a postgraduate qualification, it is often possible to study for this on a part-time basis. Many postgraduate biotechnology courses allow you to focus on one area of the work and so develop specialised expertise.

## Personal Qualities and Skills

An enquiring mind and an interest in biology and chemistry are essential. You need to be a good, imaginative problem solver, but also highly meticulous and accurate in the way you work. Good IT and writing skills are also important. You have to be able to work well as part of a team, but also be good at working on your own without supervision.

## Salaries

Salaries for trainee biotechnologists are between £21,000 and £27,000. You may start on less as a junior research assistant or laboratory assistant. Senior biotechnologists earn £30,000 to £45,000.

**info**

Association of the British Pharmaceutical Industry (ABPI), 12 Whitehall, London SW1A 2DY; 020 7930 3477; www.abpi.org.uk

Biotechnology and Biological Sciences Research Council, Polaris House, North Star Avenue, Swindon SN2 1UH; 01793 413200; www.bbsrc.ac.uk

SEMTA (Science, Engineering and Manufacturing Technologies Alliance),14 Upton Road, Watford, Hertfordshire WD18 0JT; 0800 282167; www.semta.org.uk

Royal Academy of Engineering, 29 Great Peter Street, Westminster, London SW1P 3LW; 020 7227 0500; www.raeng.org.uk

# BOOKMAKER

As a bookmaker or in betting shop management, you work with people who are placing bets on everything from horse and greyhound racing results through to whether or not there will be a white Christmas. The majority of betting shops are part of large chains, but there are a few small, independent operators. This sector has done a lot to improve its image and make its outlets more appealing to customers, especially since the advent of online gambling.

## Qualifications and Training

While you may not need formal qualifications, especially if you start as a betting shop cashier, many off-course bookmakers take on management trainees who have HNDs, degrees or other qualifications. Business-related subjects are the most sought after. At any level, you are likely to have to take a maths test to check how well you deal with percentages and calculating odds. A background in retail or other customer service roles is useful and further training is available in marketing, business management and customer service.

## Personal Qualities and Skills

You need excellent customer service skills, a lot of common sense, good numerical skills and the ability to manage other people.

## Salaries

Trainee managers start on between £14,000 and £16,000, while branch managers earn between £17,000 and £40,000.

Association of British Bookmakers Ltd, Regency House, 1–4 Warwick Street, London W1B 5LT; 020 7434 2111; www.abb.uk.com

National Association of Bookmakers, PO Box 242, East Molesey, Surrey KT8 2WE; 01884 841859

People 1st, 2nd Floor, Armstrong House, 38 Market Square, Uxbridge, Middlesex UB8 1LH; 0870 060 2550; www.people1st.org

info

# BOOKSELLER

Booksellers work in a variety of stores: bookselling chains, book sections in large department stores, specialist bookshops selling books on a particular topic, academic bookshops on university or college campuses, or second-hand bookshops. The work involves dealing with customer enquiries, checking stock, dealing with publishers, ordering new material and marketing products. Bookshops have to compete with online booksellers which can often sell products more cheaply. This means that good booksellers have to be very effective in dealing with detailed customer enquiries, making helpful recommendations and sourcing products that are hard to track down. At a management level your work could also include managing staff, attending book fairs and organising publicity and promotional events.

## Qualifications and Training

No formal qualifications are necessary, but in practice many staff working in bookshops have either a degree or a diploma; business-related disciplines are very popular with employers. Bookshop chains offering management training based on their own entry requirements normally expect you to have five GCSEs grades A–C, A levels, or other academic qualifications. Training is normally on the job, with an induction course to get you started.

## Personal Qualities and Skills

You need a genuine interest in books and being widely read is a great help. You must enjoy dealing with people and be happy to answer questions and offer advice. You need good basic IT skills both for ordering stock and for researching product queries for customers. A flair for organising window and counter displays and a general interest in marketing are also very useful.

## Salaries

Starting salaries range from £13,500 to £17,500. Store managers and senior staff working for large chains earn between £24,000 and £45,000. Some companies also offer bonus schemes for achieving high sales.

info

Skillsmart Retail, Fourth Floor,
93 Newman Street, London W1T 3EZ;
0800 093 5001;
www.skillsmartretail.com

Book Careers; www.bookcareers.com

Book Marketing Limited (BML),
7 John Street, London WC1N 2ES;

020 7440 8930;
www.bookmarketing.co.uk

Booksellers Association of UK and
Ireland (BA), Minster House,
272 Vauxhall Bridge Road,
London SW1V 1BA; 020 7802 0802;
www.booksellers.org.uk

# BREWING

Brewing and brewery work describes the manufacture and production of beer and lager for the hospitality and retail sectors. Breweries can be large, supporting their own pub and hotel chains or they can be small, independent local breweries that sell to free houses and other customers. They can also be micro breweries where members of the public brew their own batches of beer under supervision and guidance from brewing professionals. While breweries employ a range of staff including marketing, finance and human resource professionals, the two groups of brewing specialists they employ are brewery workers and technical brewers.

## Brewery worker

Brewery workers or brewery operatives work under the supervision of technical brewers helping with the manufacture and production of beer or lager. In small breweries they are often involved in all the different processes of manufacture. Working for larger companies, they may specialise in one process. The work could include weighing and mixing ingredients, monitoring quality, packing and labelling products, cleaning equipment and loading and storing the beer ready for delivery to pubs, restaurants and shops.

### Qualifications and Training

You do not need formal qualifications, but GCSEs including science or another technical subject could be useful, especially if you would like to progress to more technical and supervisory work. Training is on the job.

### Personal Qualities and Skills

You have to be good at following instructions, observant and careful in your work. You need to be able to cope with routine work, while being prepared to be flexible as well. You are often working as part of a team and you may need to develop the skills of supervising others.

# Technical brewer

Technical brewers or brewing technologists are responsible for developing and overseeing the production of beers and lagers. They have to decide on the right mix of ingredients, the temperatures at which processes should take place and the length of time that each part of the brewing process should take. It is their responsibility to ensure the quality and consistency of the product and to analyse and correct problems when they do arise. They also have to source the right quality of raw materials and work within set budgets.

## Qualifications and Training

Most trainee technical brewers have degrees in relevant subjects. Useful subjects include biological science, chemistry, chemical engineering and food technology. There are a few degrees available in brewing and distilling technology. You may get into this work with a BTEC or HND.

## Personal Qualities and Skills

You need a combination of good technical skills, being methodical, careful and good at problem solving, along with excellent management skills.

## Salaries

Brewery workers start on £12,000 to £14,000 and technical brewers on £16,000 to £22,000. Senior technical brewers with management responsibility working for large breweries may earn £45,000 plus.

Institute of Brewing and Distilling, 33 Clarges Street, London W1J 7EE; 020 7499 8144; www.ibd.org.uk

Improve Ltd, Providence House, 2 Innovation Close, York YO10 5ZF; 0845 644 0448; www.improve-skills.

co.uk/improveltd.co.uk

British Beer and Pub Association, Market Towers, 1 Nine Elms Lane, London SW8 5NQ; 020 7627 9191; www.beerandpub.org

info

# BROADCASTING

(*see also* Film and Television Production *and* Performing Arts)

The following job descriptions and information cover the wide range of career options available in radio broadcasting. You should also look at the section on Film and Television Production as work like sound recording, research and editing is relevant to radio and television. You should also consult the TV, film and video entry if you are interested in work such as camera work, costume design and make-up artistry.

Radio in the UK covers a diverse range of broadcasting outlets. The BBC is the largest and broadcasts national and local stations. There are several commercial radio stations, national and local, and there is also community radio, hospital radio for example. There are also many independent production companies developing drama, documentaries and other programmes and they may produce work for public and commercial radio outlets. Broadcasts are many and varied, designed to inform, educate, update or entertain listeners, and the remit of each programme will be different. As well as the specific careers outlined below, you may also find openings in finance, administration, IT support and marketing – just as with any other organisation, large or small.

## Broadcast editor

Editors work to ensure that the finished programme is of the highest quality. For anything which is pre-recorded, editors go through the material, making sure the quality of sound is correct, that the programme fits exactly to time and that anything inappropriate is removed. If editing live programmes, they work with producers to ensure that everything runs smoothly and to time. Increasingly, even though radio is not a visual medium, editors work with other staff to put appropriate pictures, recordings and other material on a website associated with the radio broadcast.

## Broadcast journalist

(*see also* Journalism)

Broadcast journalists prepare and present news programmes and other factual programmes such as documentaries or consumer advice programmes. They may work for radio, television or the internet. Many develop in-depth knowledge of certain fields: education, science, economics or social issues, for example.

## Broadcast sound engineer

Sound engineers are responsible for recording any radio station's output. This may be in a studio or on location, eg the seashore for a nature documentary, a concert hall for a live recording of an orchestral work. Engineers work to ensure that maximum quality of sound is produced and that there are no breaks in transmission. The work involves ensuring that all the technical equipment is functioning properly, solving problems the second they arise and working very closely with producers, presenters and other studio staff.

## Broadcast sound technician

Sound technicians are part of the team that supports sound engineers. They help set up equipment and check and test that it is working properly. They may also work with the finished recording, cutting out unnecessary background noise, getting the levels right, or adding sound effects.

## Broadcast presenter

Presenters work at the front line of radio and television, entertaining or informing the audience. They work on many different types of programme, including current affairs, documentaries, special interest and game shows. They work in all areas of broadcasting – national and regional television and radio, satellite and cable channels. Another version of presenting is the role of continuity announcer. They are the people who make announcements between scheduled broadcasts. Presenters and announcers have to do a great deal of preparatory work and liaise closely with their production staff, so it is not simply a matter of presenting a programme.

## Broadcast researcher

Researchers work for producers, programme commissioners and presenters gathering all kind of background information required for a broadcast to be interesting, accurate or entertaining. This research may involve finding out more about potential interviewees, ascertaining who might be an ideal interviewee, and researching facts – historical, cultural or current affairs related.

## Producer and assistant producer

Radio producers are responsible for the content of audio broadcasts on radio, and increasingly through internet versions of radio broadcasts. The producer takes responsibility for the whole process. This starts with generating ideas and entails liaising with presenters, DJs, engineers and broadcasting assistants throughout the planning and the actual output of the programme. They are also responsible for ensuring that audience feedback and responses to a particular programme are gathered and used to inform the planning of future programmes. Assistant producers help producers with all aspects of the work, but often carry out more of the basic administration and organisation. It is usual to start as an assistant producer before gaining promotion to become a producer.

## Radio broadcast assistant

Broadcast assistants are referred to in the business as 'BAs'. Your work as a broadcast assistant would involve supporting all aspects of programme making and transmission. You would help presenters and producers with administration, technical support in the studio and generally help out wherever you can. You would often meet and greet guests and explain to them what to expect – especially if they are not familiar with studios and how they work.

### Qualifications and Training

For all jobs, any experience you can get in student broadcasting, volunteering to help on a hospital or other community station or any other relevant experience will be tremendously helpful and undoubtedly strengthen your application. You also have to be able to convince potential employers that it really is radio that interests you, above TV or any other platform.

### Broadcast journalist

You either need a relevant degree or postgraduate qualification, or a background in magazine or newspaper journalism. Some companies offer a very limited number of training schemes, and competition for these is fierce.

### Broadcast engineer

Broadcast engineers are normally graduates with degrees in electronics, electronic engineering or broadcast engineering. It may be possible to get a traineeship with an HND or foundation IT degree. It is sometimes possible for graduates of other disciplines to get into this work, but they need good A level maths and demonstrable technical/IT skills. Technician level training or entry is sometimes possible with five GCSEs, grades A–C including maths, English and a science.

### Broadcast researcher

Broadcast researchers usually have a degree, though the subject does not particularly matter. It is more important that you can demonstrate that you have good research and communication skills. Like all broadcasting jobs, competition for this work is fierce, so some researchers start work in other administrative roles and move into research.

### Radio broadcast assistant

While radio broadcast assistants don't necessarily need formal qualifications, this is such a competitive industry that many applicants do have A levels or degrees. Getting a job as a BA is a very useful first step on the ladder to work as an assistant producer and then producer.

### Producer and editor

Producers, assistant producers and editors come from a variety of backgrounds. Many are graduate entrants, with degrees or postgraduate qualifications in broadcast journalism or broadcast production, simply because there is such great competition for this work. Good technical qualifications, A levels or an HND can be an advantage if you don't have a degree.

## Personal Qualities and Skills

You have to be absolutely passionate about the medium. Listen to radio, learn about it and think about it. While there are some skills particular to specific roles, there are many skills and qualities essential to anyone working in radio. You have to have excellent communication skills and an ability to work well as part of a team. If you are in a front role such as announcer or presenter, you need self-confidence and an ability to think on your feet. If you are more behind the scenes, you need equally quick reactions – dealing with equipment failure or a guest who fails to arrive, for example. In all roles you have to be happy to cope with constant change and embrace changes in technology.

## Salaries

Salaries vary widely according to the job you do, your level of experience and the qualifications you have. Generally, early on in your career in broadcasting, salaries may be relatively low, but they tend to rise as your career progresses. Salaries for assistant-level jobs are around £14,000 to £20,000 in London, £12,000 to £18,000 in other areas. Senior producers can earn £30,000 to £40,000. Presenters work on individually negotiated contracts.

**info**

www.bbc.co.uk/newtalent/
www.bbc.co.uk/radio/
www.bbc.co.uk/training and development/

Broadcast Journalism Training Council, 18 Miller's Close, Rippingale near Bourne, Lincolnshire PE10 0TH; 01778 440025; www.bjtc.org.uk

Community Media Association, 15 Paternoster Row, Sheffield S1 2BX; 0114 279 5219; www.commedia.org.uk

Hospital Broadcasting Association; www.hbauk.com

The Media Association; www.mediaassociaitn.org.uk, gives listings of all hospital and community radio stations; useful source for voluntary work

Radio Academy, 5 Market Place, London W1W 8AE; 020 7927 9920; www.radioacademy.org

The Radio Centre, 77 Shaftsbury Avenue, London W1D 5DU; 020 7306 2603; www.radiocentre.org

Skillset, Focus Point, 21 Caledonian Road, London N1 9GB; 08080 300 900 (England and Northern Ireland); www.skillset.org

# BUSINESS ADMINISTRATION

The term 'business administration' covers all of the roles required to ensure the smooth running of the day-to-day functions of a business regardless of the business purpose. 'Business' refers to any type of organisation in the public, private or voluntary sector. The jobs range from the Company Secretary's duties (at director level) to the duties of the accounts staff and a variety in between.

# Administrative assistant

Administrative assistants undertake a wide variety of routine and clerical tasks in every kind of office and organisation. The same job shares many different job titles, including clerical assistant, clerical worker, office assistant, office junior and administrative support worker. It is very hard to describe a typical job, because you may be working in such different settings and dealing with such different office procedures. You may be the only administrative worker in a very small company, or you could be working in a hospital, a local authority department, a charity or a multinational company. There are some common threads to the work. These include processing paperwork, entering data into computer files, dealing with telephone queries, arranging filing systems, electronic and paper, dealing with incoming post and sending out correspondence, checking and updating records, photocopying and gathering and disseminating information. Some jobs involve considerable responsibility, with the opportunity to supervise, train and manage other members of staff.

## Qualifications and Training

Employers usually expect a good standard of general education and often require you to have four or five GCSEs grades A–C including English and maths. A lot of the training is on the job, because you will need to learn about an organisation's particular systems, procedures and structures. Administrative and clerical work can be a very good starting point for other careers in finance, human resources and many other fields. It is common to find people with A levels and degrees starting their careers in administration and clerical support, but this is by no means essential. College courses in administration leading to NVQ levels 1 and 2 awards may improve your chances.

## Personal Qualities and Skills

You need good written English skills, including good spelling and grammar. You may need to have good numeracy skills and you should have good basic IT skills. You need to be able to deal with people, cope with problems, but also concentrate on repetitive tasks.

## Salaries

Salaries vary considerably because this work is available with so many different types of employer. A fairly typical range of starting salaries is £12,000 to £16,000 depending on geographical location and size and type of employer. With experience salaries rise to between £16,000 and £23,000.

**info**

Council for Administration, Graphite Square, Vauxhall Walk, London SE11 5EE; 020 7091 9620; www.cfa.uk.com

# Company Secretary

The Company Secretary plays a major part in the organisation's governance. Duties include ensuring that the company complies with relevant legal and regulatory matters, administration of mergers and acquisitions, drafting contracts, advising the board of directors on company law and procedures and maintaining company records. Other duties can include pensions administration, personnel matters, shareholder issues, property management and finance.

## Qualifications and Training

Someone usually becomes a company secretary as a second career after working in law, accountancy or other aspects of business. Most of the professions from which company secretaries are drawn are graduate-level careers. The Institute of Chartered Secretaries and Administrators (ICSA) offers a series of certificate, diploma and professional development programmes. These can be studied part time or through distance learning. Which programme you choose is determined by how much relevant experience and what other professional qualifications you already possess.

## Personal Qualities and Skills

You need excellent written and spoken English and very good presentation skills. You should be able to deal with highly complex information and be very well organised. You need to be a good problem solver who can employ sound judgement.

## Salaries

Salaries start at around £35,000 – remember that this is normally a second career for most people. Salaries rise from £40,000 to £90,000 according to responsibilities and size and type of employer.

www.breakinto.biz

Council for Administration (CfA), 6 Graphite Square, Vauxhall Walk, London SE11 5EE; 020 7091 9620; www.cfa.uk.com

Institute of Chartered Secretaries and Administrators (ICSA), 16 Park Crescent, London W1B 1AH; 020 7580 4741; www.icsa.org.uk

# Personal assistant

(*see also* Secretary)

A senior secretary or personal assistant (PA) may work with one or more senior executives. Accurate skills in shorthand, audio typewriting, word processing and information management, and a knowledge of office-based software are desirable. The PA may also act as administrator, information centre, organiser of the manager's day, progress chaser, arranger of travel and meetings, receptionist and communicator (oral and written) internally and externally. A senior secretary or PA assumes responsibility without direct supervision and takes decisions within the scope of assigned authority.

## Qualifications and Training

A minimum of GCSEs in maths and English is usually required, but it is not uncommon for people with A levels or degrees to go into this work. Any relevant IT training courses on software packages for managing data or accounts are also useful. Some colleges run full-time and part-time secretarial and administrative courses to GNVQ levels 2 and 3. Courses can also be taken through part-time study while working, through the London Chamber of Commerce and Industry Examination Board (LCCIEB), Oxford, Cambridge and RSA Examination Board (OCR) and Pitmans Qualifications (City & Guilds), which offer relevant qualifications that take one to two years to complete. Personal assistant work spans everything from fairly junior jobs in small companies, to extremely responsible roles working with directors of large organisations. The training courses available reflect this, and courses are offered at several different levels.

## Personal Qualities and Skills

You must be friendly but discreet and diplomatic. You need to be extremely well organised and calm when you are under pressure or working to deadlines. Knowing when to use your own initiative is also important.

## Salaries

There is a lot of variation in salary determined by the size, type and location of the organisation for which you work and the position in that organisation of the person to whom you are personal assistant. £17,000 to £25,000 are fairly typical starting salaries, a little less outside London and the M25. A personal assistant to a senior manager can earn up to £40,000.

**info**

Institute of Qualified Professional Secretaries (IQPS), Suite 464, 24–28 St Leonards Road, Windsor, Berks SL4 3BB; 0844 800 0182; www.iqps.org

London Chamber of Commerce and Industry Examinations Board (LCCIEB), 112 Station Road, Sidcup, Kent DA15 7BJ; 0870 720 2909; www.lccieb.com

Oxford and Cambridge and RSA Examinations (OCR), 9 Hills Road, Cambridge CB2 1PB; 01223 553311; www.ocr.org.uk

Pitman Qualifications, City & Guilds, 1 Giltspur Street, London EC1A 9DD; 020 7294 2800; www.pitmanqualifications.com

# Receptionist

Receptionists work in hotels, large organisations and private firms, sometimes combining the job with the duties of telephonist. In hotels, they welcome the guests, make bookings and prepare the final accounts. They also deal with reservation correspondence and act as a general information office. In small hotels this can be handled by one person but in most, and especially the larger hotels, they work in a team headed by the Reception Manager. In large official organisations, such as a town hall or in firms with many staff, receptionists direct visitors to the correct department. In small firms the job is often combined with answering the phone, typing and franking the mail.

Medical receptionists work in a variety of environments. They need, in addition to the standard skills of a receptionist, a full understanding of the principles of medical ethics and confidentiality, knowledge of the NHS and social services, medical terminology and clinical procedures.

## Qualifications and Training

Formal educational qualifications are not necessary, but proficiency in English and maths is an advantage. For some posts knowledge of other languages is important. Many further education colleges offer one-year full-time courses and a range of part-time courses in reception skills. A range of qualifications is available, including NVQs at levels 1, 2 and 3 and Modern Apprenticeships.

The AMSPAR (see p. 91) diploma in health service reception is a nationally recognised professional qualification. It can be achieved by examination and is available from a wide network of approved centres throughout the UK.

## Personal Qualities and Skills

Receptionists should be friendly, pleasant with a good phone manner and neat appearance. They also need stamina, as they are often expected to work shifts that include evenings and weekends. They should have a real liking for people and a good memory for faces. Computer literacy is also important.

## Salaries

Receptionists earn between £12,000 and £17,000, more than this in London or if the work involves other duties and responsibilities. Hotel receptionists earn between £11,500 and £16,000. In large hotels with big reception teams, supervisory work can take earnings up to £22,000.

| | | |
|---|---|---|
| People 1st, 2nd Floor, Armstrong House, 38 Market Square, Uxbridge UB8 1LX; 0870 060 2550; www.people1st.co.uk | Local Job Centre Plus and Connexions/Careers Centres | **info** |

# Secretary

Secretaries work in all types of organisations. Sometimes they are assigned to one person, sometimes they provide support services for several people. Most secretaries need to have well-developed ICT skills but there is still a demand for those with shorthand and audio typing. As well as producing documents, secretaries undertake a range of organisational tasks such as arranging travel and meetings. They may also work as receptionists and deal with callers and queries by phone or e-mail. Those in senior positions may make decisions on behalf of managers.

## Bilingual secretary

A bilingual secretary is fluent in a second or third language and may work in commerce, overseas or as an employee of an international organisation. The work will include composing, reading and translating documents in the foreign language. They may use speaking/listening skills in their languages for telephone work, receiving visitors and interpreting at meetings.

## Farm secretary

In addition to normal secretarial work, farm secretaries will be responsible for completing complex forms, keeping records and accounts and calculating wages. A farm secretary may work for one employer, be freelance or be sent out by an agency to smaller farms.

## Legal secretary

Accurate skills have always been paramount for legal paperwork, but word processors have made the job easier. Legal secretaries are employed by barristers and solicitors in professional practice and in large commercial organisations.

## Medical secretary

Medical secretaries are good administrators, keep records, and handle correspondence and filing. They work in hospitals, for individual doctors/consultants and in health centres. Accuracy and confidentiality are essential, as is a thorough knowledge of medical terminology.

## Qualifications and Training

There is a range of full- and part-time courses available. Courses usually include word processing, audio, shorthand and office procedures. There are training opportunities for young people leading to NVQ levels 1, 2 and 3 in Administration.

GCSEs are usually required to obtain a place on a full-time secretarial course. A good working knowledge of the English language is essential. Additional qualifications are needed to specialise as a legal, medical or farm secretary. There are a number of postgraduate diploma courses for graduates wishing to train as bilingual secretaries.

## Personal Qualities and Skills

Good secretaries are judged by what they do, but qualities such as self-motivation, discretion, tact, loyalty, flexibility, excellent communication skills and smart appearance are expected.

## Salaries

Salaries start at £13,500 to £18,000 for jobs outside London, £19,000 to £25,000 in London. Jobs in not-for-profit sectors are at the lower end of the pay scale. Employment in banking, finance and law firms is at the upper end. With between 10 and 15 years' experience, salaries can rise to £30,000–£40,000.

**info**

Association of Medical Secretaries, Practice Managers, Administrators and Receptionists (AMSPAR), Tavistock House North, Tavistock Square, London WC1H 9LN; 020 7387 6005; www.amspar.co.uk

Council for Administration (CfA), 6 Graphite Square, Vauxhall Walk, London SE11 5EE; 020 7091 9620; www.cfa.uk.com

Institute of Chartered Secretaries and Administrators (ICSA), 16 Park Crescent, London W1B 1AH; 020 7580 4741; www.icsa.org.uk/

The Institute of Legal Secretaries and PAs, 9 Unity Street, Bristol BS1 5HH; 0117 927 7007; www.institutelegalsecretaries.com/

Institute of Qualified Professional Secretaries (IQPS) Limited, Suite 464, 24–28 St Leonards Road, Windsor, Berkshire SL4 3BB; 0844 8000 182; www.iqps.org

# C

## CABINET MAKER

### Qualifications and Training

You don't need any specific qualifications, but some employers might like you to have GCSEs, particularly in maths or a technical subject. If you are aged between 16 and 24, you could train through an apprenticeship. If you are over 24, you need to have some relevant skills, experience or qualifications.

There are several college based City & Guilds courses in furniture production – these courses are aimed at newcomers and current employees in the industry.

### Personal Qualities and Skills

You must be very practical and confident using machines and hand tools. You should be able to follow a technical drawing, adapt designs and do drawings of your own. You need good numeracy skills and if you become self-employed you also need some business awareness.

### Salaries

Expect around £11,500 when you start off, rising to £15,000 with three or four years' experience. Cabinet makers who become really skilled and get a good reputation can earn £35,000 plus.

info

Furniture Furnishing and Interiors National Training Organisation; 67 Wollaton Road, Beeston, Nottingham NG9 2NG; 0115 922 1200; www.ffinto.org

Skills Direct; 0870 850 5262

Construction Skills Certification Scheme; 0870 417 8777; www.cscs.uk.com

# CALL CENTRE OPERATOR

Call centre or contact centre operators work for a wide variety of companies and organisations dealing with customer queries on the telephone, by e-mail, text, fax or letter. Telephone work is the most likely and is what most people think of as call centre work. You might work for a mail order catalogue, a financial services advice line, a utilities provider, an IT support company or an organisation offering welfare, health or counselling advice of some kind. The type of employer you work for will determine the range of duties you undertake, but you are always likely to be involved in many of the following: answering queries, providing further information, referring callers to other agencies, updating computer records or selling products and services. As you gain experience, your work is likely to include supervising other staff and training new members of the team.

Many call/contact centres operate 24-hour services, so there are often opportunities to work as a shift supervisor and then to progress to a position with more management responsibility.

# Qualifications and Training

You don't always need formal qualifications – individual employers set their own entry requirements, which can include GCSEs grade A–C in maths and English. Job interviews for this work are likely to include practical tests to assess your telephone manner and how you deal with callers. You normally receive training from your employer both in call centre techniques and in any specialist knowledge that applies to its particular products or services. There are some college courses available in call centre techniques. These include City & Guilds in Contact Centre Skills and a BTEC introduction to Contact Centre Skills. These courses cover general topics such as telephone manner, confidentiality, data management and other communication skills. In some areas you may be able to take an apprenticeship in call/contact centre skills. Having built up some experience in this work, and if you gain promotion to supervisory or management level, there are several further qualifications towards which you could work. These include Telesales levels 2 and 3, Contact Centre Operations levels 1 and 2, and Contact Centre Professionals levels 3, 4 and 5. These NVQs cover areas such as developing customer relationships, IT skills, sales techniques, managing staff and resources, quality control and performance management.

There are sometimes openings for graduates to come into this work at management level.

## Personal Qualities and Skills

You must have excellent communication skills, primarily for speaking on the telephone. You may need to be persuasive, patient, sympathetic, thick-skinned, sensitive or calm. Clearly you need a different mix of skills to deal with someone who is placing a catalogue order, compared to someone who is anxious that they cannot pay a utility bill for example. You need good IT skills, the ability to work under pressure and to take responsibility if you want to progress to supervisory and management levels.

## Salaries

Salaries start at £12,000 to £15,000, rising to £15,000 to £19,000 with experience. Managers earn £20,000 to £25,000. With some call centre work there are opportunities to earn bonuses or commissions on sales made or customers signed up.

**info**

Customer Contact Association (CCA), Head Office, 20 Newton Place, Glasgow G3 7PY;
0141 564 9010; www.cca.org.uk

Institute of Customer Services, 2 Castle Court, St Peters' St, Colchester, Essex CO1 1EW;
01206 571716;
www.instituteofcustomerservice.com

e-skills UK, 1 Castle Lane, London SW1E 6DR; www.e-skills.com

# CAREERS ADVISER

Careers advisers or personal advisers/careers provide information, advice and guidance to school and college students and to adults in the community. They work both inside and outside education. In England, careers advisers work mainly for local authorities as personal advisers (PAs), helping young people aged 13–19 make choices about employment and further study, and helping them overcome any difficulties they face in this area. The work involves one-to-one interviews with clients, presentations to groups of clients or parents, and marketing work with local and national employers.

Outside England, careers advisers work in Careers Scotland, Careers Wales and the Training and Employment Agency in Northern Ireland. Some careers advisers also work in higher education and are employed by individual universities and colleges.

## Qualifications and Training

Most careers advisers have a degree or equivalent qualification. There are now foundation degrees available in work with young people and young people's services developed specifically for people who want to become careers personal advisers or youth workers. In addition, careers personal advisers must complete a qualification in careers guidance (CQG). This can be done either via a one-year full-time or two-year part-time course, or a work-based training course. Candidates also complete a portfolio of evidence that can be used for NVQ/SVQ level 4 in Advice and Guidance. Details of colleges and universities offering the CQG are listed on the Institute of Career Guidance (ICG) website. This site also lists employers who are registered to offer work-based training. Experience in other careers such as teaching, social work, commerce or industry is an advantage in this profession.

Experience of working with young people, in a paid or voluntary capacity is also beneficial. Everyone working in this field will have to undergo a full Criminal Records Bureau (CRB) check. You don't need a degree or foundation degree if you have NVQ level 3 qualifications in a relevant subject and relevant work experience.

To work in higher education, you do not necessarily have to have a CQG, though many applicants do. Universities and colleges set their own requirements. There are in-service certificate and diploma courses available in Careers Education, Information and Guidance in Higher Education.

## Personal Qualities and Skills

Excellent communication skills are essential. You are dealing with young people, their parents, teachers, employers and other professionals. You have to be well organised, good at disseminating information, able to present material to individuals and groups, and have reasonable IT skills. You should be confident, persuasive, assertive and tactful and you must be a good listener.

## Salaries

Salaries for trainees range from £20,000 to £22,000. Part-qualified advisers earn between £21,000 and £27,000. Since April 2008 Connexions services have been run by local authorities and at present there is no national agreed pay scale for careers or personal advisers. In the higher education sector, salaries used to be higher than for work with school leavers, but this is becoming less likely.

Department for Children, Schools and Families (DCSF), Sanctuary Buildings, Great Smith Street, London SW1P 3BT; 0870 000 2288; www.dcsf.gov.uk

Independent Schools Careers Organisation (ISCO), St George's House, Knoll Road, Camberley, Surrey GU15 3SY; 01276 687525; www.isco.org.uk/

Institute of Career Guidance (ICG), 3rd Floor, Copthall House, 1 New Road, Stourbridge, West Midlands

DY8 1PH; 01384 376 464; www.icg-uk.org

Association of Graduate Careers Advisory Services (AGCAS), Millennium House, 30 Junction Road, Sheffield S11 8XB; 0114 251 5750; www.agcas.org.uk/

National Association of Connexions Partners, Watsons Chambers, 5–15 Market Place, Castle Square, Sheffield S1 2GH; 0114 281 3418; www.nacp.co.uk

# CARPENTRY

(*see also* Cabinet Maker *and* Construction Trades)

# CARPET FITTER

Carpet retailers, furniture stores and department stores all employ their own trained personnel who deliver and fit carpets and other floor coverings to customers' homes, shops, offices or hotels. Many fitters are also self-employed.

## Qualifications and Training

GCSE English and maths or equivalents are usually required. Training is mainly given on the job, working with an experienced fitter, although in some firms there are possible opportunities for day-release courses leading to the examinations of the National Institute of Carpet and Floorlayers. Short one- to five-day and tailored courses are available through the Flooring Industry Training Association.

## Personal Qualities and Skills

Strength and fitness are important in order to handle heavy rolls of carpet. A good head for calculations and an eye for detail (such as matching patterns) are also essential. Generally, too, it is necessary to be able to drive.

## Salaries

Trainees earn between £12,000 and £14,000. Experienced carpet fitters earn between £15,000 and £21,000, and senior supervisors, who are fitters with other management and training roles, earn up to £25,000. Some carpet fitters become self-employed.

**info**

Construction Skills, Bircham Newton, King's Lynn, Norfolk PE31 6RH; 01485 577577; www.cskills.org

National Association of Carpet and Floor Layers, 4c St Mary's Place, The Lace Market, Nottingham NG1 1PH; 0115 958 3077; www.nacfl.org

# CARTOGRAPHY

Cartography embraces all aspects of map-making, including the making of charts, globes and models of the earth or heavenly bodies.

Working for government departments, map publishing companies and land and air survey companies, cartographers produce maps, charts, surveys and graphs. The information they produce is used in many ways. Cartographers produce the sort of everyday maps that anyone can buy, but they also produce highly specialised information for the Ministry of Defence and for industry. They update existing maps and charts and produce entirely new material.

Cartographers have to be able to collect and analyse data from satellites, and produce accurate maps and charts to a specified scale. The technology used for mapping has changed greatly in the last few years, so cartographers use highly specialised desktop publishing packages to aid them in their work.

## Qualifications and training

To train as a cartographer you normally need a degree in a relevant subject. These include geography, earth sciences, geographical information systems, mapping science and surveying. There are no degrees which cover only cartography, so you need to look carefully at course details to ensure that relevant cartography elements are included in the courses you are considering. The British Cartography Society's website includes useful information on appropriate courses. Training is on the job and covers surveying and the use of specialised computer packages. The Ordnance Survey and other government departments provide structured training programmes.

## Personal Qualities and Skills

You must be interested in geography and the environment. You need to be able to work accurately, paying attention to detail, and you should have good spatial awareness and a good sense of design. Excellent computer skills are very important. As you progress to more senior roles, you also need to be able to take responsibility for managing projects and staff.

## Salaries

Cartographers earn between £18,000 and £20,000; with experience salaries rise to between £25,000 and £35,000. You can earn more if you are a project leader or have other management responsibilities.

British Cartographic Society, 12 Elworthy Drive, Wellington, Somerset TA21 9AT; www.cartography.org.uk

Society of Cartographers; www.soc.org.uk

British Geological Survey (BGS), Kingsley Dunham Centre, Keyworth, Nottingham NG12 5GG; 0115 936 3100; www.bgs.ac.uk

Defence Geographic and Imagery Intelligence Agency Headquarters (DGIA), Watson Building, Elmwood Avenue, Feltham, Middlesex TW13 7AH; 020 8818 2422

Department for Environment, Food and Rural Affairs (DEFRA), Customer Contact Unit, Eastbury House, 30–34 Albert Embankment, London SE1 7TL; 020 7238 6951; www.defra.gov.uk

Department for Transport (DfT), Great Minster House, 76 Marsham Street, London SW1P 4DR; 020 7944 8300; www.dft.gov.uk

Lantra: The Sector Skills Council for the Environmental and Land-based Sector, Lantra House, Stoneleigh Park, Nr Coventry, Warwickshire CV8 2LG; 024 7669 6996; www.lantra.co.uk

Macaulay Land Use Research Institute, Craigiebuckler, Aberdeen AB15 8QH; 01224 498200; www.macaulay.ac.uk/

Met Office FitzRoy Road, Exeter, Devon EX1 3PB; 0870 900 0100; www.metoffice.com

info

**info**

Ordnance Survey (OS), Romsey Road, Southampton SO16 4GU; 08456 05 05 05; www.ordnancesurvey.co.uk

Ordnance Survey of Northern Ireland (OSNI), Colby House, Stranmillis Court, Malone Lower, Belfast BT9 5BJ; 028 9025 5755; www.osni.gov.uk/

Royal Institution of Chartered Surveyors (RICS), 12 Great George Street, Parliament Square, London SW1P 3AD; 0870 333 1600; www.rics.org

Scottish Executive Environmental and Rural Affairs Department

(SEERAD), Room 440, Pentland House, Edinburgh EH14 1TY; 08457 741741; www.scotland.gov.uk/About/Departments/ERAD

The Survey Association (TSA), Northgate Business Centre, 38 Northgate, Newark-on-Trent, Notts NG24 1EZ; 01636 642840; www.tsa-uk.org.uk

United Kingdom Hydrographic Office (UKHO), Admiralty Way, Taunton, Somerset TA1 2DN; 01823 337900; www.ukho.gov.uk

# CATERING

*see* Hospitality and Catering

# CHEMISTRY

Chemistry is the basis of a wide range of careers and is the science which deals with the composition, structure and uses of chemicals and substances.

## Analyst

Analysts work in industry, providing a service for research, development and production departments. They analyse the results of experiments and advise what a newly produced substance may be. An analyst may check the quality of raw materials bought in by a company and examine the quality of the company's own products. Public analysts are employed by local authorities to examine, for example, the state of the water supply; the adequacy of the sewage treatment system; toxic and suspect materials and leachate from landfill sites. They may also be asked to examine food from a suspect restaurant. Public analysts are frequently required to give witness on their findings in courts of law, and should be familiar with the law relating to goods and services.

# Chemist

Chemists study the structure and make-up of chemicals and other substances. They interpret the way substances interact and react under different physical conditions. They apply their knowledge in a variety of ways, eg to create new food products or materials such as plastics and artificial fibres. They work in many industries, developing new drugs for the pharmaceutical sector, analysing the impact of climate change on oceans, keeping water supplies safe and clean or developing products to improve the shelf life of food and drink. They may also work in forensics, examining the substances at the scene of a crime.

Some professional chemists are referred to as analytical chemists and their work focuses specifically on analysing chemicals and other materials, but they can still work across several different industries and sectors. Some chemists also work in academic research.

The chemist's work involves planning and conducting experiments, analysing results and writing up and/or presenting the results he or she produces. The work often involves the management and supervision of other laboratory staff.

## Qualifications and Training

To work as a chemist you need a degree in either chemistry or chemical science. Many employers prefer you to have a postgraduate qualification as well, or to have done a course which includes a placement in industry. Many graduate chemists may have to start work as a laboratory technician in a laboratory involved in the aspects of chemistry which interest them. Training is on the job, covering the use of technical equipment, computer packages, and health and safety. If you don't have a postgraduate qualification before you start work, you may be able to work towards this while you are employed.

## Personal Qualities and Skills

Of course you must be interested in chemistry and have an enquiring mind and a patient, persistent attitude to solving problems. You should be accurate and thorough in all your work and highly observant. You need to be good at handling delicate equipment and confident with IT. If you are supervising other staff you need good management and the ability to motivate colleagues.

## Salaries

New graduate chemists earn between £14,000 and £30,000, higher salaries being paid to entrants with PhDs and by pharmaceutical companies. With experience this range rises to £26,000 to £50,000.

## What is EYPS?

Early Years Professional Status (EYPS) is a Government status introduced in 2006 as recognition for Early Years practitioners with graduate level qualifications who have demonstrated that they meet a comprehensive set of national standards.

## Who can become an EYP?

Anglia Ruskin University is offering the fully-funded 12 month full-time training pathway at our Chelmsford and Cambridge Campuses for graduates wishing to work towards an inspiring new career in early years.

Graduates wishing to work as 'change agents' will raise the quality of early years provision and improve practice across the 0-5 age range.

At Anglia Ruskin University we combine University based training days alongside 'hands-on' practical 0-5 placement days, whilst equipping you with the skills and knowledge base to successfully meet the 39 national standards that form the EYPS assessment process.

## When does the training start?

Anglia Ruskin University is offering the fully-funded training programme in September 2010 at both our Chelmsford and Cambridge campuses.

## What is the financial cost?

All course fees are funded by the Children's Workforce Development Council (CWDC) and a candidate bursary of £5,000 is paid in instalments over the duration of the pathway.

**Graduate, Danielle Minahan gained EYP Status through the Full Training pathway with Anglia Ruskin University in 2009.**

"I attended a session to explore childcare training options. I found out about a new course called Early Years Professional Status which was aimed at raising the status of childcare by attracting leaders and raising the professionalism of the sector.

Anglia Ruskin University has a wealth of information and convinced me that there is a place for people with a professional background in childcare as leaders, motivators and, most importantly, visionaries who can see the path to raising the standards within the sector.

I was pleasantly surprised to find that the course wasn't all textbooks and lectures - the tutors had a fun and practical slant to the course. It was very demanding but was made manageable through the support and guidance offered by the tutors. Working in my placement was immensely satisfying and gave a taste of what was to come after completing the course.

I am now employed within a small nursery where I am leading the staff in implementing a range of initiatives aimed at improving the quality of provision offered.

EYPS is about being a leader, facilitator and support mechanism to bring about lasting positive change for the benefit of the children and families who rely on the services offered by the childcare sector."

For more information or to apply please see www.cwdcouncil.org or www.mpowernet.anglia.ac.uk or contact the EYPS team on 0845 196 4355 or eyps@anglia.ac.uk

cWdc

**info**

Analytical Science Network (ASN), c/o Royal Society of Chemistry, Burlington House, Piccadilly, London W1J 0BA; 020 7440 3326; www.chemsoc.org/networks/acn/asn.htm

Medicines and Healthcare Products Regulatory Agency (MHRA), 10–2 Market Towers, 1 Nine Elms Lane, London SW8 5NQ; 020 7084 2000; www.mhra.gov.uk

Royal Pharmaceutical Society of Great Britain (RPSGB), 1 Lambeth High Street, London SE1 7JN; 020 7735 9141; www.rpsgb.org.uk

Royal Society of Chemistry (RSC), Burlington House, Piccadilly, London W1J 0BA; 020 7437 8656; www.rsc.org

SEMTA: the Sector Skills Council for Science, Engineering and Manufacturing Technologies, Head Office, 14 Upton Road, Watford WD18 0JT; 01923 238 441; www.semta.org.uk

# CHILDCARE

This sector covers a range of occupations, but all involve the care of children, especially pre-school children.

## Childminder

A registered childminder looks after children and provides a caring environment along with stimulating play and learning activities. Childminders need to be responsible, trustworthy and affectionate. Childminders look after babies and children under five; there is a limit to the number of children of different age groups that can be cared for by a childminder.

A childminder's job needs careful planning and good organisation skills to arrange individual routines for children of different ages to include periods of play, exercise, naps and meals. It is important to keep records of payments, expenses and insurance. It is essential for the children's learning and development to include activities such as painting and drawing, reading stories and singing, and playing with natural materials and construction toys in- and outdoors.

A childminder is expected to provide food for the children, and with babies prepare bottles, feed the babies and change nappies. Older children will require physical care, such as washing hands and going to the toilet. It is important not to discriminate against children from different ethnic groups, religious backgrounds and family types.

### Qualifications and Training

While you do not need formal qualifications to work as a childminder, you must be aged over 18. If you are caring for children under the age of eight, you must be registered with the Office for Standards in Education, Children's Services and Skills (Ofsted).

In England your local authority's Children's Information Service (CIS) can provide you with information about how to register and send you an application pack. Ofsted is the registration body for England. You have to be interviewed and your home is also inspected. If you are approved, you must take a registered training course. The Council for Awards in Childcare and Education (CACHE) and the National Childminding Association has developed NVQ level 3 certificate and diploma courses in home-based childcare.

In Scotland you should contact the Care Commission, in Wales the Care Standards Inspectorate and in Northern Ireland your local Health and Social Care Services Trust.

## Personal Qualities and Skills

Of course you have to really enjoy working with children and to be prepared to share your home with them. You should have an open-minded attitude about different ways of bringing up children and you should be quite comfortable with both you and your home being scrutinised. You have to be extremely responsible, sensitive and patient. You need to be practical, with a sense of humour, and keep calm if problems arise. You have to be able to communicate well with parents as well as with their children. You need to be imaginative, sympathetic and sensible. You need to be very alert, especially on matters of health and safety.

## Salaries

Childminders charge between £3.50 and £6.00 per hour per child, more in some areas. What you earn therefore depends on hours worked and how many children you are looking after. As a childminder you are responsible for paying your own tax and insurance and you have to provide toys and the right environment for children from your earnings.

**info**

Skills for Care and Development, Albion Court, 5 Albion Place, Leeds LS1 6JL; 0113 245 1716; www.skillsforcareanddevelopment.org.uk

Scottish Childminding Association, Suite 2, 37 Melville Terrace, Stirling FK8 2ND; 01786 445377; www.childminding.org

Care Standards Inspectorate for Wales; 01443 848 450; www.csiw.wales.gov.uk

Office for Standards in Education (Ofsted), Royal Exchange Buildings, St Ann's Square, Manchester M2 7LA; 0845 640 4045; www.ofsted.gov.uk

Council for Awards in Childrens' Care and Education (CACHE), Beaufort House, Grosvenor Road, St Albans, Hertfordshire AL1 3AW; 0845 347 2123; www.cache.org.uk

Childcare Careers; www.childcarecareers.gov.uk

Childcarelink; 0800 2346 346; www.childcarelink.gov.uk

National Childminding Association, Royal Court, 81 Tweedy Road, Bromley, Kent BR1 1TG; 0845 880 0044; www.ncma.org.uk

# CACHE
## Qualifying the Care and Education Workforce since 1945

**Since its days as the NNEB, CACHE qualifications have enabled many to develop a successful career working with children and young people.**

So if you're interested in working in a nursery, a pre-school, a play centre or becoming a nanny, a childminder or a teaching assistant visit:

**www.cache.org.uk**

to learn about the qualifications that can take you there.

nurturing achievement

CACHE, Apex House 81 Camp Rd St Albans AL3 5GB

# Careers in Early Years Care and Education, and Playwork

For children to get a good start in life, they need to be looked after and educated by people with the right blend of skills and personal qualities. Working with children, especially young children, is demanding, but, also very rewarding. If you pursue a career in early years care and education and playwork you can make a real difference to children and their families.

Anyone with the right mix of skills and personal qualities can work with children and young people, and children benefit from being cared for by different members of society - women and men. However, employers prefer employees to be at least 17 before working with children.

## What Qualifications are Available?

There are a wide range of qualifications suitable for anyone wanting to work with children and young people. The qualifications are offered in Schools, Colleges and Training Centres. They are divided into two types: introductory level qualifications and more advanced qualifications, suitable for those with more experience.

For more information go to www.cache.org.uk

advertisement feature

## What are the Main Occupations?

People working in early years care and education and play have a number of different job titles and work in different types of organisations. The main occupations are set out below. Employers will generally look for qualified staff, so if you hold formal qualifications there will be more opportunities open to you.

### Childminders

Childminders usually work in their own home. If you want to be a childminder and look after children under the age of 8, you have to register with your local authority.

### Nanny

Nannies care for children of any age in the home of the child. They can be a live-in or a daily nanny.

### Crèche worker

Crèche workers may work in a variety of organisations that have attached crèches, for example: sports centres, universities, colleges and supermarkets.

### Nursery / Daycare / Pre-school Assistant

Assistants are involved with caring for babies, toddlers, pre-school children in a nursery or a children's centre, and work with the children under supervision.

### Nursery / Daycare / Pre-school Supervisor

Supervisors work in a nursery or childcare centre supervising the work of nursery assistants. Supervisors plan for the development of the children in their care.

### Nursery / Daycare / Pre-school Managers

Managers are trained to manage a team of staff in a nursery or children's centre and will be responsible for operational management including regulation procedures.

### Play workers

Play workers are employed in playgroups, out of school care groups, community centres or holiday clubs to name a few. They supervise play sessions for children aged 4 – 16 and support them in their play choices.

### Learning Support Assistants

Learning Support Assistants work in schools to assist teachers in the classroom. More senior workers will need some knowledge of curriculum and the development of children.

## Who are CACHE?

CACHE has been qualifying the Care and Education workforce since 1945 – when we were known as the NNEB. Our qualifications ensure that those who look after children and young people have the knowledge and practical training they need.

advertisement feature

# Nursery nurse

A nursery nurse works with babies and children under eight in the public, private and voluntary sectors. This can include schools, nurseries and hospitals. In schools, nursery nurses work in nursery, reception and infant classes alongside the teacher, providing and supervising educational and play activities. They may also be involved in providing out of school care at after-school clubs and on holiday schemes. Nursery nurses in hospitals can work in maternity and special care units, and on children's wards. Day nurseries, both private and local authority, employ nursery nurses to care for children under five whose parents are unable to care for them during the day. Nursery nurses can also be employed in clinics, residential homes, the community, family centres and private homes as nannies.

## Qualifications and Training

You don't necessarily need academic qualifications, but many employers and course providers expect you to have three to five GCSEs grades A–C. You can study for a two-year full-time NCQ level 3 award or you can work as a nursery assistant and study for qualifications part time. There are several different awards towards which you can work, including: CACHE Level 3 Diploma in Child Care and Education, the BTEC National Diploma in Children's Care, Learning and Development and NVQ level 3 in Children's Care, Learning and Development. The Government now expects all professionals to work towards early years professional status (EYPS). There are several ways to achieve this and how you do it will depend what qualifications you already have, how much experience you have and which particular pathway your employer supports and encourages. EYPS is an addition to, not an alternative to the qualifications listed above. Everyone working with young children also has to undergo a Criminal Records Bureau (CRB) check to ensure that they have no criminal convictions that would make them unsuitable for this work.

## Personal Qualities and Skills

You must really enjoy working with children. You have to be patient, calm, imaginative and practical. You need to be well organised and good at working as part of a team. You should be observant, safety conscious, sensitive and very good at communicating with children. You will also have to be able to build up good relationships with parents and other professionals.

## Salaries

During training salaries are rather low – £10,500 to £13,000. Qualified nursery nurses earn £14,000 to £17,000 and nursery managers of large nurseries may earn considerably more. Rates vary depending on whether you are working in the public or private sector. If you choose to work in someone's own home, you set your own fees.

info

Children's Workforce Development Council, 3rd Floor, Friends Provident House, 13–14 South Parade, Leeds LS1 5QS; 0113 244 6311; www.cwdcouncil.org.uk

Skills for Care, Children, Early Years and Young People's Workforces in the UK, 2nd Floor City Exchange, 11 Albion Street, Leeds LS1 5ER; 0113 390 7667; www.skillsforcareanddevelopment.org.uk

Scottish Childminding Association, Suite 2, 37 Melville Terrace, Stirling FK8 2ND; 01786 445377; www.childminding.org

Office for Standards in Education (Ofsted), Royal Exchange Buildings, St Ann's Square, Manchester M2 7LA; 0845 640 4045; www.ofsted.gov.uk

Council for Awards in Children's Care and Education (CACHE), Beaufort House, Grosvenor Road, St Albans, Hertfordshire AL1 3AW; 0845 347 2123; www.cache.org.uk

Childcare Careers; www.childcarecareers.gov.uk

Childcarelink; 0800 2346 346; www.childcarelink.gov.uk

National Childminding Association, Royal Court, 81 Tweedy Road, Bromley, Kent BR1 1TG; 0845 880 0044; www.ncma.org.uk

# Play worker

Play workers work with school-age children in many different settings, including breakfast clubs, after-school clubs, holiday play schemes, adventure playgrounds and play centres. What play workers actually do varies according to the age of the children they are working with and the ethos of the organisation which employs them. What all play work has in common is an emphasis on giving children and young people choices on how to use their leisure time and ideas on how to enjoy and be exposed to a wide range of activities. Play workers help children socialise and try out new activities. Play workers organise a wide range of activities including games, drama, sports, creative art, outings, storytelling and quiet time.

Play workers interact with children of different ages, abilities and backgrounds and they have to be able to engage effectively with all these children. Play workers also have to liaise with parents, keep records, come up with new ideas and take responsibility for health and safety.

Some play workers are based in hospitals, working with children who are sick or recovering from surgery. These play workers have to find activities that are suitable for each individual child's mental and physical condition. Play can have a significant effect on how well children recover or are able to cope with their illnesses, so hospital play work is highly specialised.

## Qualifications and Training

While no formal academic qualifications are required, some voluntary work with children will give you a real advantage. Local Authority Children's Information Services often run short courses on working with children. These only last one to three weeks; they are not a qualification, but an opportunity for you to get some idea about whether work with children would suit you. Current regulations mean than anyone working in play will now have to gain a formal qualification. Part-time accepted courses are run by the Council for Awards in Children's Care and Education (CACHE).

## Personal Qualities and Skills

Of course you must really enjoy working with children. You must be resilient, imaginative and patient. You should have good practical skills and be acutely aware of health and safety issues. You must be a good communicator: you will often be talking to parents as well as children. You need to be well organised, as you may have to do some paperwork.

## Salaries

Many people start as volunteers and the hours are not normal 9 to 5: they may be pre-school, or school holidays only. Pro rata play worker salaries are between £10,000 and £11,000. With management and planning responsibility you can earn £14,000 to £15,000.

Council for Awards in Child Care and Education (CACHE), Beaufort House, Grosvenor Road, St Albans, Hertfordshire AL1 3AW; 0845 347 2123; www.cache.org.uk

Children's Workforce Development Council, 3rd Floor, Friends Provident House, 13–14 South Parade, Leeds LS1 5US; 0113 244 6311; www.cwdcouncil.org.uk

Skills for Care and Development, Children, Early Years and Young People's Workforces in the UK,

2nd Floor, City Exchange, 11 Albion Street, Leeds LS1 5ER; 0113 390 7667; www. skillsforcareanddevelopment.org.uk

Scottish Childminding Association, Suite 2, 37 Melville Terrace, Stirling FK8 2ND; 01786 445377; www.childminding.org

National Association of Hospital Play Staff, Fladgate, Forty Green, Beaconsfield, Bucks HP9 1XS; www.nahps.org.uk

**info**

# CHIMNEY SWEEP

Chimney sweeps clean and remove soot and other debris from chimneys and flues of open fires, wood burning stoves and other oil, gas, coal or wood burning heating and cooking appliances. Cleaning chimneys reduces the risk of chimney fires and the levels of dangerous emissions. This work had gone into decline, but increasing numbers of people are installing wood burning stoves because they are considered a more environmentally friendly and economic form of heating. The work involves inspecting the job to be done and then removing soot and debris with special vacuum equipment and old fashioned brushes. As a chimney sweep you also remove the soot and dirt you have collected and leave the premises clean and tidy. You also advise customers on how to maintain or operate chimneys, flues and appliances safely.

## Qualifications and Training

Nearly all chimney sweeps are self-employed, so you have to fund your own training, purchase of equipment and insurance. No formal qualifications are necessary, but a background in practical, physical work is a useful start. The National Association of Chimney Sweeps (NACS) offers training and advice. Other than this, you may be able to find a local chimney sweep who is prepared to offer you some on the job training. A driving licence and vehicle are essential, as you will need to transport equipment and travel between customers.

## Personal Qualities and Skills

You have to be reasonably physically fit and be a good practical problem solver, with a systematic and tidy approach to your work. You also need to be good at talking to customers. Being self-employed you need to know how to market, promote and manage your business.

## Salaries

Since most sweeps are self-employed earnings depend on your number of customers and what you charge per job. Prices vary from £30.00 to £90.00 per chimney. The work is also seasonal – most people have their chimneys swept from early spring to late autumn, not mid-winter when they are using their fires and stoves.

info

National Association of Chimney Sweeps (NACS), Unit 15, Emerald Way, Stone Business Park, Stone, Staffordshire ST15 0SR; 01785 811732; www.chimneyworks.co.uk

Guild of Master Sweeps; www.guild-of-master-sweeps.co.uk

Construction Skills, Bircham Newton, King's Lynn, Norfolk PE31 6RH; 01485 577577; www.cskills.org

# CHIROPODIST (OR PODIATRIST)

Chiropodists are also known as podiatrists; the profession is in the process of changing its name. They are concerned with the health of feet. Those working in the NHS deal with problems caused by diabetes or arthritis and may work with those suffering from sports injuries. Ailments such as corns, bunions and malformed nails are more likely to be dealt with by those in private practice.

Chiropodists perform minor operations under local anaesthetic. They may work in the NHS in hospitals, clinics or health centres, or in private practice or large organisations. Many undertake postgraduate training to specialise in areas such as sports medicine, biomechanics and podiatric surgery.

## Qualifications and Training

To practise as a state registered chiropodist/podiatrist you must take a degree in podiatry approved by the Health Professionals Council (HPC). You then register with the HPC and The Society of Chiropodists and Podiatrists. To do a degree in podiatry you usually need five GCSEs grade A–C including maths, English and a biological science. You also need three A levels including one biological science. If you already have a degree in a biological science you can gain exemption from part of the degree course. Once you are in practice you must undertake annual continuing professional development activities monitored by the HPC.

If you do not wish to study for a degree, you can work in the private sector as a foot health practitioner and you can take a diploma in foot health care. Foot care practitioners can register with Foot Health Care Practitioners but you are not obliged to do so to practise. A similar role in the NHS is that of chiropody or podiatry assistant. Qualifications for these roles vary, but many employers and NHS Trusts require you to have three or four GCSEs grades A–C including a science subject. Some NHS areas offer cadet or apprenticeship schemes in this work.

## Personal Qualities and Skills

You have to be good with people, able to reassure and provide them with information. You need good practical skills with good manual dexterity. You should be able to work on your own, but also as part of a healthcare team. You need to be well organised and good at managing your own time. If you are in private practice you will also need good business skills.

## Salaries

Newly qualified chiropodists/podiatrists working for the NHS earn between £21,000 and just under £27,000. With specialist responsibilities chiropodists earn between £24,500 and £33,500. Consultant chiropodists earn up to £39,000. The NHS Careers website contains detailed information on salaries. Private practitioners set their own charges, but generally earn between £20,000 and £30,000. Assistants or foot health practitioners earn between £15,000 and £21,000.

Health Professionals Council (HPC), Park House, 184 Kennington Park Road, London SE11 4BU; 020 7582 0866; www.hpc-uk.org

NHS Careers, PO Box 376, Bristol BS99 3EY; 0845 606 0655; www.nhscareers.nhs.uk

Society of Chiropodists and Podiatrists, 1 Fellmonger's Path, Tower Bridge Road, London SE1 3LY; 020 7234 8620; www.feetforlife.org

info

# CIVIL AVIATION

The civil aviation sector relates to all the occupations within the world of civil aircraft flying, including passenger and goods transportation.

## Aeronautical engineer

(*see also* Engineering)

Air traffic engineers are responsible for the efficient operation of the wide range of sophisticated telecommunications, electronic systems and specialist equipment needed in air traffic control centres, airports and other specialist centres. This involves the installation, calibration and maintenance of radar, air-to-ground communication systems, navigational and landing aids, computer data and processing equipment, and visual display units. Opportunities may exist for engineers to look after day-to-day maintenance and, at graduate level, for field management, installation and development work.

## Air cabin crew

Flight attendants (air cabin crew) look after the safety, comfort and welfare of passengers. Before a flight they check stocks of equipment, welcome passengers on board and go through safety routines. During the flight they will serve ready-cooked meals and drinks, sell duty-free goods and deal with any problems passengers have. Flight reports are prepared by senior stewards, who also attend to first-class passengers and supervise junior staff.

## Aircraft maintenance engineer

(*see also* Engineering)

Aircraft maintenance engineers make sure that aircraft are airworthy. They maintain, service and overhaul the aircraft, their engines and equipment, working to very high standards set by the Civil Aviation Authority (CAA). Every part of every job is checked and certified. Engineers usually specialise in either mechanics or avionics, and work on major overhaul or in 'turnarounds' – the work carried out after each flight. Apart from working with the airlines, other opportunities are found with firms that specialise in aircraft maintenance. There are also a few openings for professional engineers in works management, production, planning, and research and development.

## Air traffic control

The safe and efficient movement of all aircraft through British air space and airports is the responsibility of National Air Traffic Service (NATS) air traffic control officers and assistants. With the aid of sophisticated radio, radar and computer systems and with visual checks on visibility and weather conditions made from the control tower, they ensure that aircraft are kept a safe distance apart and that pilots are well advised as to their position and prevailing conditions, give clearance to land and directions to loading bays. Air traffic controllers mainly work for NATS, although there may be limited opportunities with other employers, such as local authorities or aircraft manufacturers. All must hold a CAA licence stipulating the service they are qualified to give and where they can operate. Some of the more routine tasks, such as checking flight plans, updating weather information, logging aircraft movements and keeping runways clear, are carried out by the air traffic control assistants. Prospects for promotion to officer level are good, but air traffic control staff are employed to work at any location within the country.

# Airline customer service agent

Airline customer service agents work for individual airlines, handling companies, and airports and terminals. They deal with passengers from the moment they check in to when they board their flights. They are responsible for checking in luggage as well as customers. Customer service agents have to ensure that unaccompanied children or other passengers with special needs are safely escorted to their flights and they are also expected to calm nervous passengers before they board their planes.

# Pilot

Commercial pilots in the UK fly fixed-wing aircraft and helicopters. Before take-off the pilot must prepare a flight plan, study the weather, make sure that the craft is airworthy, check that the cargo and fuel are safely loaded and work out estimated arrival times. Little time is spent actually flying the aeroplane manually. The pilot spends most of the time carefully monitoring sophisticated computer-controlled automatic flying, navigational and communications systems. Pilots keep in touch with air traffic control and must be prepared to deal with sudden changes in weather and other conditions. Pilots work irregular hours but their actual flying time is strictly controlled.

Most UK pilots are employed by one of the major carriers of passengers and goods and when flying large aircraft they are part of a team. Opportunities for pilots of small aircraft and helicopters are to be found in flying executive jets, in the field of air taxiing, conducting aerial surveys, or as test pilots or flying instructors.

## Qualifications and Training

### Aeronautical engineer/Aircraft maintenance engineer

Entry to aircraft maintenance engineering is via craft, technician or student apprenticeships; entry qualifications depend upon the type of apprenticeship. The apprenticeships take the form of on-the-job training and part-time study at local colleges to prepare for aeronautical engineering/aircraft maintenance engineering qualifications offered by City & Guilds and Edexcel (BTEC)/ SQA or the CAA. Qualified aircraft engineers (including those from the armed forces) have to meet certain practical experience requirements before they can take examinations to become licensed aircraft maintenance engineers. There are some full-time courses in aeronautical engineering and aircraft maintenance, usually lasting two and a half years.

## Air cabin crew

Airlines usually train their own cabin crews at special centres on courses lasting four to six weeks. Applicants should be over 18, have a good level of general education to GCSE standard, preferably including English and maths, and have conversational fluency in at least one European language. Experience in a customer care setting can be helpful.

## Air traffic controller

You need five GCSEs grades A–C including maths and English, but 70 per cent of applicants have degrees, HNDs or other higher education qualifications. You must have good eyesight and colour vision and be physically fit. Most air traffic controllers train via the National Air Traffic Services (NATS) training scheme at Bournemouth Airport. You spend 13 weeks at the NATS college and after this your training lasts either six months, if you train as an aerodrome controller, or nine months if you train as an area controller. You have to pass exams at several stages and not all trainees make it. After this there is a further supervised training period of 18 months.

## Air traffic engineer

NATS runs a training scheme for graduate electrical/electronic engineers lasting a minimum of 15 months. The training is approved by the Institution of Engineering and Technology and will lead after approximately three years to chartered engineering status.

## Airline customer service agent

There are no standard entry requirements, but individual airlines and handling companies set their own requirements. They normally ask for a good standard of education and may require you to have GCSE grade A–C in English. A foreign language qualification can also be useful, as can previous experience in customer service work. You will need to live reasonably near an airport and you may well need your own transport because shift work could make reliance on public transport difficult. You will have to undergo security checks and many companies also ask you to have a medical examination.

## Pilot

UK pilots are required to hold a licence issued by the Joint Aviation Authorities (JAA) which represent the civil aviation departments of a group of European states that have collaborated to set common safety standards called Joint Aviation Requirements. Licence holders can work as pilots in any of the JAA member states. Full details of licensing requirements and organisations providing approved courses can be obtained from the CAA (see info box). Training to be a commercial pilot costs £50,000–£60,000 and may be integrated (*ab initio*) or modular. Helicopter courses tend to be more expensive. Most applicants wishing to undertake integrated courses are sponsored privately or by an airline. Such sponsorship is highly competitive and difficult to obtain. Trainees are generally expected to contribute to training costs either while training or by repaying some of the fees once in employment. An alternative entry route is via a short service flying commission with either the RAF or Royal Navy. All pilots are expected to attend retraining and refresher courses throughout their careers.

Entry requirements for sponsored pilot training vary between airlines, but most ask for a minimum of two/three A levels or equivalent, including maths and physics. Many airlines recruit graduates up to the age of 26. Eyesight must be of a very high standard. Normal colour vision and an excellent level of health and fitness are essential.

## Personal Qualities and Skills

### Aeronautical engineer/Aircraft maintenance engineer

Maintenance engineering requires a combination of practical interest, mechanical aptitude, accuracy and manual dexterity. Engineers must be willing to adapt and to retrain. Very high standards and a responsible attitude are also most important.

### Air cabin crew

Air cabin crew must be reassuring and approachable, smart, have lots of energy and stamina and have the confidence and the ability to act quickly and decisively in a firm but polite and tactful manner.

### Air traffic control officer

The work is stressful; officers need to be able to assimilate and interpret a great deal of information and instantly act upon it. They must be able to react quickly if conditions suddenly change, and be healthy, reliable and emotionally well balanced; good eyesight and colour vision are also important.

### Air traffic engineer

Normal colour vision, great care, accuracy and a basic understanding of the practical applications of electricity and magnetism are required.

### Airline customer service agent

You need excellent customer service skills. Delays and changes to flights mean customers are often stressed, anxious or angry. You need to keep calm and follow procedures quickly, but without cutting corners. You must be smart, tidy and presentable and reasonably physically fit.

### Pilot

Pilots must be very well balanced, physically fit, have stamina, be mentally and physically alert and ready to respond quickly to changing conditions. They must be unflappable, confident, self-assured leaders with considerable technical skill.

## Salaries

Many airlines have faced financial difficulties recently and this has held back wage rises. Every career in civil aviation offers different salaries: there is wide variation between what air cabin crew and airline customer service staff are paid compared to pilots or air traffic controllers. Different employers pay different rates, but as a general guide air cabin crew and customer service staff start on £11,000 to £14,000. Air traffic controllers earn £10,000 during training and £15,000 to £18,000 on being appointed. Once validated, after two years, salaries rise to £45,000 to £50,000. Pilots earn around £75,000 to £80,000 flying jet aircraft, much less for turboprops. They often have to pay a bond of £15,000 to the company that employs them and often have to pay for much of their own training.

**info**

Astac Ltd, Gloucestershire Airport, Cheltenham, Gloucestershire GL51 6SP; 01452 715 630; www.astac.co.uk/

BAE Systems Cwmbran Training College, Beacon House, William Brown Close, Llantarnam, Cwmbran, Gwent NP44 3AB; 01633 835 123; www.cwmbrancollege.com/

British Air Transport Association (BATA), Artillery House, 11–19 Artillery Row, London SW1P 1RT; 020 7222 9494; www.bata.uk.com

The British Air Line Pilots Association (BALPA), 81 New Road, Harlington, Hayes, Middlesex UB3 5BG; 020 8476 4000; www.balpa.org/

British Women Pilots' Association (BWPA), Brooklands Museum, Brooklands Road, Weybridge, Surrey KT13 0QN; www.bwpa.co.uk

Civil Aviation Authority (CAA), CAA House, 45–59 Kingsway, London WC2B 6TE; 020 7379 7311; www.caa.co.uk

Go Skills: The Sector Skills Council for Passenger Transport, Concorde House, Trinity Park, Solihull, West Midlands B37 7UQ; 0121 635 5520; www.goskills.org

Guild of Air Traffic Control Officers (GATCO), 4 St Mary's Road, Bingham, Nottinghamshire NG13 8DW; 01949 876405; www.gatco.org

International Air Transportation Association (IATA), Spencer House, 23 Sheen Road, Richmond upon Thames TW9 1BN; 020 7660 0068; www.iata.org

National Air Traffic Services (NATS), 4000 Parkway, Whiteley, Fareham, Hants PO15 7FL; 01489 616001; www.nats.co.uk

People 1st for Hospitality, Leisure, Travel and Tourism, 2nd Floor Armstrong House, 38 Market Square, Uxbridge, Middlesex UB8 1LH; 0870 060 2550; www.people1st.co.uk

# CIVIL SERVICE

The Civil Service is one of the UK's largest employers, with staff in a diverse range of occupations and professions. The Civil Service is made up of more than 170 departments and agencies all carrying out the work of government, from advising ministers on policies to dealing with daily enquiries about planning issues, benefits payments or education. While each department carries out its own recruiting and sets entrance requirements for specific jobs, there is an overall structure across most departments. This structure means you can decide at which level you would like to enter and what sort of work appeals to you.

# Careers in DWP

## Various locations across Great Britain

### Do you want to make a difference?

Every day, we make a real difference to millions of people in Great Britain, helping them to lead more rewarding lives, free from poverty.

### What we can offer

We want the best people working with us and offer a wide range of rewarding and challenging roles.

We offer a competitive salary complemented by an excellent pension scheme, and opportunities to receive bonus awards.

We want our people to reach their potential and offer focused training to support their career development.

It's important that our people achieve a strong work-life balance and we offer a variety of working patterns.

### How to apply

For more information about working for DWP, along with details of our current vacancies, go to our website at:

www.dwp.gov.uk/about-dwp/working-for-dwp/

POSITIVE ABOUT DISABLED PEOPLE

INVESTOR IN PEOPLE

**DWP** Department for Work and Pensions

# A Career in the Department for Work and Pensions

Have you ever thought about working for the Department for Work and Pensions?

We play a vital role in making a real difference to millions of people in Great Britain every day, helping them to lead more rewarding lives, free from poverty. Working with us you can contribute to helping the most vulnerable in society.

We are the largest government department serving over 20 million customers. Every working day we conduct 50,000 adviser interviews in our jobcentres, process over 3,000 applications to State Pension and receive over 85,000 calls to Jobcentre Plus Contact Centres.

We know this can only be achieved through the hard work and dedication of our people. They are our most valuable asset. Through a combination of teamwork and personal drive they help the Department to deliver results.

## Why join us?

You will have the opportunity to show us what you can do. We want you to reach your potential and we will provide access to a wide range of rewarding and challenging jobs where you can continue to learn and gain a broad range of experiences. You might be behind the scenes in a team formulating policy, or working in a local Jobcentre helping jobseekers prepare for work, or in a Regional Pension Centre providing customers with benefit and retirement information.

We offer a competitive salary complemented by an excellent pension scheme, and opportunities to receive bonus awards.

We want our people to reach their potential and offer focused training to support their career development.

It's important our people achieve a strong work-life balance. We offer a variety of working patterns to enable you to feel as fresh at home as you do at work

advertisement feature

## How to Apply

We use a competence based approach to fill most of our positions, meaning every applicant has an equal chance to demonstrate their skills and abilities by giving examples of tasks or experiences they may have gained in any area of their life.

The work we do can have a real positive impact on our customers. But don't take our word for it.....

"I work behind the scenes in DWP. It is a fast paced working environment and provides an interesting and varied workload - no two days are the same! I have been supported by my colleagues, received recognition for the success of my projects and feel valued as an employee. I have been able to utilise my skills and I feel there are plenty of opportunities throughout the Department for me to further my career."

*- DWP employee, Hull*

"My adviser did all he could to help with my return to work, I don't know how I would have coped without his help. He was there for me with any help and advice I needed. I would definitely recommend the Jobcentre and the services they have to offer"

*- Jobcentre Plus customer, Glasgow*

DWP is really committed to developing it's people. They've provided me with learning and development opportunities and breadth of experience which would have been difficult to achieve anywhere else. Influencing policies affecting over 100,000 employees and contributing to the Governments wider welfare reform agenda is both exciting and rewarding."

*- DWP HR Graduate, Sheffield*

If you are interested in working with us, go to our website for more information.

**www.dwp.gov.uk/about-dwp/working-for-dwp/**

advertisement feature

Work falls broadly into three groups: corporate services, which are concerned with finance, IT, human resources and communications; operation services, which is the day-to-day delivery of services through government offices, including all the face-to-face dealings with the public. Finally there is policy delivery, which is concerned with developing and implementing policies, working very closely with the government.

## Administrative officers and administrative assistants

Administrative officers and administrative assistants carry out the daily clerical and customer contact functions in every department and agency. Their work may involve dealing directly with the public, such as answering telephone enquiries, gathering information, processing documents, keeping records and entering data into computer systems.

## Junior managers/executive officers

Junior manager is the next step up the ladder after administrative officer. Junior managers are responsible for running small teams who carry out day-to-day functions for every department and agency. Tasks and responsibilities include motivating and training members of the team, carrying out annual appraisals and preparing and presenting reports on work progress to senior managers. They also have to deal with problems. If, for example, a client is unhappy with the service he or she has received, this will be referred to the junior manager in the first instance. After two years' successful work as a junior manager, it is possible to apply to join the Fast Stream management development programme.

## Fast Stream development programme trainees

The Civil Service offers a fast track accelerated training programme for recruits who want to get into senior management. Fast Stream entrants can be placed within many central government departments, and there is a special training route for anyone who wants to join the Diplomatic Service and a further pathway called the European Fast Stream. This places trainees in departments where there is a strong focus on European issues.

There are also some specific professional areas that have their own Fast Stream programmes. These include Fast Stream Economists, Fast Stream Statisticians and Fast Stream Technology in Business pathways. Government Communications Headquarters at Cheltenham also has its own Fast Stream training scheme.

## Qualifications and Training

At whatever level you enter, a great deal of your training will be on the job. All Civil Servants have to be either UK nationals or from a Commonwealth or EU country. For some posts, only UK nationals are accepted.

Each Department or Agency sets its own entry requirements, but there are some common guidelines. To become an administrative assistant or an administrative officer you do not need any formal qualifications. In practice, you often need five GCSEs grades A–C. Many applicants have A levels or are graduates. Many junior manager/executive officer posts ask that you have two A levels.

All Fast Stream applications must be made online. The schemes open for applicants in September each year and you have the option to express an interest in more than one scheme and department. Fast Stream graduate trainees need a good honours degree, a first or a 2.1, to be considered for the programme. Fast Stream Economists must have a 2.1 in economics. Fast Stream Statisticians must have at least a 2.2 in a numerate discipline. Fast Stream Technology in Business trainees must have a 2.1 in a business, engineering, technical, mathematical or scientific discipline.

Applicants to the Diplomatic Service must either have a degree or several years' work experience. They must pass a medical, undergo rigorous security checks and be prepared to work anywhere in the world. The Diplomatic Service also participates in the graduate Fast Stream programme.

For posts at all levels, departments often set aptitude tests of various kinds, which are designed to measure the kinds of skills that will be needed to do the job effectively. There is strong competition for Fast Stream posts in all areas.

For undergraduates considering a career in the Civil Service, there are a number of work experience and vacation work opportunities available. See the Civil Service Recruitment website.

Because the Civil Service has a structured route to development and promotion, it is possible to move into higher level jobs through experience and performance if you do not meet the initial selection criteria for those posts.

### Professional occupations

There are also many opportunities in the Civil Service and its agencies for people with a wide range of vocational and professional skills. There are posts for accountants, actuaries, architects, engineers, chemists, physicists, biologists, vets, lawyers, surveyors, IT specialists and many more. For many of these posts applicants need to have relevant professional and vocational qualifications in particular areas such as science, engineering, law or finance. See the Civil Service Recruitment website for more details.

## Personal Qualities and Skills

Of course, there is some variation in these according to the type of work you are involved in and the level of responsibility you have. All Civil Servants should have an interest in delivering high quality services and information to government, members of the general public and to other organizations. Civil Servants need to be flexible, able to cope with change, be good at working

# ✗ JOB HUNT

- ☑ Great challenge
- ☑ making a difference
- ☑ travel
- ☑ flexibility
- ☑ good salary

The EU needs Europe's brightest and best graduates to make a difference, for the issues of today and the challenges of the future. Our new recruitment competitions start in March 2010.

EU career – smart choice

## For more details check our website
### www.eu-careers.eu
Click on 'Discover EU Careers'

# ...for a career that ticks all the boxes

# EU Official

An EU Official is a member of the permanent staff of any of the European Institutions (European Commission, European Parliament, Council of the EU, Court of Justice, Court of Auditors, ...).

**What does a permanent official do?**

What don't we do? With its unique remit and multicultural working environment, the EU Institutions are unlike any other organisations in the world. Whatever your profile, the range of fields in which the EU Institutions operate is certain to contain just the right job for you.

EU officials do a wide range of tasks that are divided up into two categories: administrators (AD) and assistants (AST).

As an administrator you can find yourself playing a key role in the EU's legislative and budgetary processes, from coordinating the broad economic policies of the Member States, taking part in negotiations with non EU countries, helping run the common agricultural policy, or ensuring that Community law is uniformly interpreted and effectively applied. Whatever you do, the broad range of the EU's activities means that you can expect a high degree of responsibility from an early stage in your career.

As an assistant, you may play an important role in the internal management of the Institutions, notably in budgetary and financial affairs, personnel work, computing or librarianship. You may also assist in implementing policies in various areas of EU activities or be responsible for secretarial and clerical work and ensuring the efficient operation of an administrative unit.

advertisement feature

## What can we offer?

The EU Institutions offer a very attractive career package including these benefits:

1) Flexible but secure career progression- one employer, a lifetime of different jobs.
2) Being interested and challenged by work that actually makes a difference.
3) The opportunity to travel, and work with people from all over the world.
4) An environment where you are encouraged to learn new skills and languages.
5) A great package of benefits: excellent starting salary*, leave, career breaks and overall work/life balance.

*(Basic monthly salary for Administrator: 4200 € / Assistant: 2600 €)

## Where would you work?

Career opportunities with the EU span our representations and delegations within Member States and across the world.

But by far the majority of openings, about 80 %, are in Brussels, a modern, vibrant city with beautiful parks and great bars & restaurants.

Most of the remaining opportunities are in Luxembourg, a beautiful city in a beautiful little country, with excellent travel opportunities to France, Germany and Belgium.

## How do you apply?

Permanent officials are selected by open competitions organised by the European Personnel Selection Office (EPSO).

advertisement feature

In 2010, we will be changing the way in which permanent staff are selected for the EU institutions.

- Easier for you to plan your application: annual cycles of competitions for the most common job profiles such as administrators, assistants, interpreters and translators;
- Improved testing of your ability and potential: introduction of tests for core competencies;
- Better feedback: results with more detailed feedback.

In addition to specific professional skills and knowledge, the following core competencies will be assessed:

- analysis and problem solving
- communicating
- delivering quality and results
- learning and development
- prioritising and organising
- resilience
- working with others

Of course, in order to be considered for the selection process, you will first need to meet the eligibility criteria (qualifications, professional experience, etc.) of a given competition. For all competitions you must be a citizen of one of the EU countries and have at least two official EU languages - of which one is English, French or German.

More information on our new selection procedures, and announcements of the opening of competitions, can be found on our webpage:

**eu-careers.eu**

advertisement feature

under pressure and good at communicating in both written and spoken English. Beyond this, there are specific skills you will need to help you perform your own role effectively.

## Salaries

Salaries for Administrative Assistants range from £12,500 to £14,500. For Administrative Officers the range is £14,000 to £20,000. Junior Managers earn between £20,000 and £23,000. Fast Stream salaries start at around £26,500 and are around £37,500 at the end of a four- to five-year training period. There are small variations between different departments and agencies. Many posts attract performance-related pay bonuses and there are higher salaries for people working in London or Brussels.

**info**

Government Skills, Central Government, First Floor, Kingsgate House, 66–74 Victoria Street, London SW1E 6SW; 0203 300 8977; www.government-skills.gsi.gov.uk

Civil Service; www.civilservice.gov.uk/jobs. Administrative and executive level jobs are advertised locally and nationally in the press and through Jobcentre Plus. Many administrative assistant, administrative officer and junior manager posts are advertised in the local press and through Jobcentre Plus. You can also visit the Civil Service website to found out more about when and where vacancies are advertised.

# CLOTHING INDUSTRY

(*see also* Fashion)

The clothing industry is diverse and complex, with products ranging from off-the-peg garments that are turned out in thousands, to exclusive *haute couture* designs from top fashion houses. There are job opportunities in large factories, small workrooms, with large wholesaling firms, in small family businesses and on production lines. The largest sections of the industry are men's and boys' outerwear, women's and girls' outerwear, children's clothing, bespoke tailoring (made to measure) and dressmaking. More specialised areas such as millinery and glove making are relatively small. Skilled workers are generally in great demand in most areas.

## Pattern cutter

Pattern cutters work with clothing designers and clothing technologists. They produce the pattern templates from working drawings produced by fashion designers. They either cut patterns by draping material over dummies and cutting the pattern or they have standard cardboard patterns which they develop and alter to create different styles. Increasingly, pattern cutters use computers to help create their patterns.

## Qualifications and Training

Some fashion design companies and clothing manufacturers offer apprenticeships in pattern cutting. You must have four GCSEs grades A–C to apply
for these. Your GCSEs should include English, maths and a design subject.
Many trainee pattern cutters have a relevant foundation degree, degree or
diploma in clothing technology. Some fashion design degree and diploma
courses include relevant technical pattern cutting skills. The London College
of Fashion offers part-time and short, intensive pattern cutting courses.
Training is mostly on the job, but there are several NVQ and diploma courses
for which you can study while employed.

# Pattern grader

Pattern graders produce scaled-up and scaled-down versions of an original
pattern (made by a pattern cutter), so that manufacturers can make the same
garment in different sizes. Technology plays a key role in pattern grading.
Graders use scanning technology to produce extremely accurate patterns in
different sizes.

## Qualifications and Training

Most people start as pattern grading assistants and work their way up after a
period of about two years. It is also common to do an apprenticeship in
pattern grading with a clothing manufacturer or fashion design company.
You can also get into pattern grading or a similar technical role after a degree
or BTEC HND in clothing technology and production.

# Sample machinist

Sample machinists work to produce sample garments for customers and
designers. As a sample machinist, you may work on a number of different
product lines or concentrate on a particular style, for example sportswear or
evening wear. You also work with a variety of materials, including cotton,
wool, synthetics and leather. Sample machinists have to follow carefully the
instructions on colour and fabric given by the designer. They then stitch and
press the garment to give the designer a clear idea of what the finished item
will look like, what it will feel like and how it will hang. Experienced sample
machinists often take on a quality control role for other machinists.

## Qualifications and training

Sample machinists usually start as sewing machinists making up garments
once the samples and the design have all been completed. There is a wide
range of City & Guilds craft and design courses available in textile machining,
machine embroidery and pattern cutting. If you have four GCSEs you may
also be able to take an apprenticeship with a clothing manufacturer or fashion
design company. Training is on the job.

# Sewing machinist

Sewing machinists stitch garments together once the design has been finalised, the material cut and the sample garments completed. They normally work for clothing manufacturers and may be responsible for just one part of production, eg turning up hems, making buttonholes, stitching seams or fitting sleeves.

## Qualifications and Training

No formal qualifications are needed, but many companies will set a practical test to ensure you have appropriate manual dexterity skills. If you are interested in progressing to becoming a sample machinist or a pattern cutter, you may wish to take an apprenticeship. In this case you will need four GCSEs, usually including English, maths and a design subject.

## Personal Qualities and Skills

For all these roles you need an interest in clothing and textiles. For pattern cutting you should have good technical drawing and computer skills and the kind of numerate skills that mean you can take very precise measurements. You should have an eye for detail and design. Sample machinists need an understanding of fabrics, good hand and machine sewing skills and an understanding of the production process.

## Salaries

Sewing machinists start on between £11,000 and £13,000. Pattern graders earn between £11,000 and £16,000. Trainee pattern cutters and sample machinists start on between £12,000 and £19,500. The range is wide because fashion design companies tend to pay higher starting rates. Experienced pattern cutters and sample machinists can earn more than £20,000.

**info**

Confederation of British Wool Textiles Ltd, Merrydale House, Roydsdale Way, Bradford BD4 6SB; www.cbwt-learning.co.uk

Can U Cut It?; www.canucutit.co.uk

Skillfast-UK, Richmond House, Lawnswood House, Redvers Close, Leeds LS16 6RD; 0113 2399 600; www.skillfast-uk-org

Textile Institute, 1st Floor, St James's Buildings, Oxford Street, Manchester M1 6FQ; 0161 237 1188; www.textileinstitute.org

# COASTGUARD

HM Coastguard coordinates maritime search and rescue for the UK. Its area of responsibility, which covers approximately 10,500 miles of coastline and a million square miles of sea, is divided into four Search and Rescue Regions.

Each is headed by a Regional Inspector, and within each Region are Maritime Rescue Coordination Centres and Sub Centres from which searches and rescues are coordinated.

At these centres, a constant watch is kept on international distress frequencies, satellite, radio and telephone communications, all of which are responded to immediately. HM Coastguard can call upon a wide range of facilities for search and rescue, including lifeboats, helicopters, tugs and local rescue organisations for rescues at sea. On-shore rescues from cliffs and mud are carried out by teams of Auxiliary Coastguards.

## Qualifications and Training

Most entrants start as watch assistants. For this you need good basic literacy, numeracy and IT skills, and a strong interest in maritime affairs. Watch officers need good GCSEs grades A–C in English and maths, or their equivalent. For applicants without formal qualifications, the Maritime and Coastguard Agency can set competency tests. Watch officers must also have extensive experience of the sea. Many Watch officers have been in the Royal Navy or the Merchant Navy, or have had other first-hand experience of the sea. Auxiliary coastguards must be aged 16 or over. Posts are open to UK nationals and to EU and Commonwealth citizens. Applicants must be physically fit, with good hearing and eyesight.

All recruits attend a training course at the Maritime and Coastguard Agency's Training Centre in Dorset, after which training is a combination of classroom and practical-based assignments.

## Personal Qualities and Skills

As a coastguard you will have to take important decisions quickly and calmly. You need a clear speaking voice and the ability to work with modern communications equipment. You should have good leadership skills and work well as part of a team.

## Salaries

Salaries for trainees are between £13,500 and £15,400 – watch assistants earn around £16,750. Watch officers earn around £21,000. Coastguards may also earn additional money for working shifts.

info

Maritime and Coastguard Agency, Human Resources Recruitment Team, Bay 3/19 Spring Place, 105 Commercial Road, Southampton SO15 1EG; 023 8032 9308; www.mcga.gov.uk

# COLOUR SCIENCE AND TECHNOLOGY

Colour technologists are concerned with producing dyes and pigments that have a wide range of applications, including the textile, paint, rubber, plastics, paper, leather and foodstuffs industries. They must ensure that exact colours can be produced at an economic price and in the right quantities whenever they are needed. They are often involved in research and development projects. Technologists are also employed in sales, management, buying, development and research, quality control, customer liaison and technical services departments (depending on the industry involved and the expertise needed).

Textile technologists may work in the design, manufacture and operation of textile machinery, and in the design, production, coloration, finishing and manufacture of fibres, yarns and fabrics of all types.

## Qualifications and Training

You can get into this work as either a technical assistant, a technician or a graduate trainee. A significant majority of applicants are graduates, but if you have good A levels including chemistry you may well get in as a technician. This is an industry which supports graduate and non-graduate trainees in developing further skills. Larger companies often run formal training schemes of a year to 18 months. Preferred degree or HND subjects include analytical chemistry, applied chemistry, chemistry, colour science, maths, business studies and textiles technology. Some people also get into this work via an art-related subject such as art and design. Most training is on the job and usually includes frequent short courses to ensure that you remain up to date with all the latest technical developments.

## Personal Qualities and Skills

You need very good colour vision and technical ability, plus persistence in solving problems. You should be good at working as part of a team and also be able to develop a good sense of business awareness and the ability to work with and listen to customers or clients.

## Salaries

Salaries start at around £18,000 to £20,000 for technician roles and £21,000 to £27,000 for graduates, depending on the employer and the work experience you have had. Range of salaries at senior level is £28,000 to £40,000.

**info**

Oil and Colour Chemistry Association (OCCA), Priory House, 967 Harrow Road, Wembley HA0 2SF; 020 8908 1086; www.occa.org.uk

Science Engineering and Technology (SCENTA), 10 Maltravers Street, London WC2R 3ER; 020 7557 6411; www.scenta.co.uk

The Society of Dyers and Colourists (SDC), PO Box 244, Perkin House, 82 Gratton Road, Bradford BD1 2JB; 01274 725138; www.sdc.org.uk

The Textile Institute, 1st Floor, St James's Buildings, Oxford Street, Manchester M1 6FQ; 0161 237 1188; www.textileinstitute.org

# COMPLEMENTARY MEDICINE

The field of complementary medicine and treatments is growing, with new therapies and treatments being added continuously. Therefore the list of occupations shown here is not exhaustive, but gives a cross-section of the more established ones.

# Acupuncturist

Acupuncture is a system of treatment which involves the insertion of fine needles into one or more points of the body to restore the overall health of the person and help alleviate symptoms from which they may be suffering. Acupuncture can also be used for relieving pain, and in China is used to anaesthetise patients during operations. It has been practised in China and other Far Eastern countries for thousands of years and is a growing profession in the UK. Many health professionals, for example nurses and physiotherapists, train as acupuncturists.

## Qualifications and Training

To practise as an acupuncturist you must take an in-depth course (usually around three years full-time or the part-time equivalent). Acupuncture is currently unregulated, but you can work towards membership of a professional body, such as the British Acupuncture Council (BAcC) or the Acupuncture Society. The British Acupuncture Accreditation Board (BAAB) has approved several courses that lead to membership of the BAcC. To get on to a BAAB approved course you normally need at least five GCSEs grades A–C including a science. Some colleges may require two A levels, including a science subject. The BAcC website lists courses and their entry requirements. If you already have healthcare qualifications, these may gain you entry onto a course and you may be exempt from parts of the course. At present acupuncturists do not have to be registered with a professional body to practise, but the Health Professionals Council may develop a compulsory registration scheme in the near future.

## Personal Qualities and Skills

You must enjoy working with people and be good at putting them at ease – acupuncture is a treatment that makes many clients initially nervous. You need a real interest in biology, health and preventive care and you must have good, confident manual dexterity. You need a good business sense if you are self-employed and the ability to organise your own time and keep accurate records.

## Salaries

Most acupuncturists are self-employed and charge between £40.00 and £90.00 per session. An experienced practitioner, working full-time hours, would see about 30 clients a week. Annual earnings are between £19,000 and £35,000.

**info**

British Acupuncture Accreditation
Board; www.baab.org.uk

British Acupuncture Council (BAcC),
63 Jeddo Road, London W12 9HQ;
020 8735 0400;
www.acupuncture.org.uk

British Medical Acupuncture Society
(BMAS), BMAS House, 3 Winnington
Court, Northwich, Cheshire CW8
1AQ; 01606 786782;
www.medical-acupuncture.co.uk

Health Professionals Council;
www.hpc.uk.org

# Alexander technique practitioner

Alexander technique practitioners teach a form of physical and mental well-being known as the Alexander technique. Practitioners, usually working one-to-one with clients, teach them to develop better posture, poise, balance and coordination. They teach through demonstrating certain physical exercises and techniques, through manipulation, referred to as 're-coordinating', and through explaining and teaching relaxation techniques. Practitioners aim to teach a technique that can be applied to all aspects of daily life. Some clients may simply want to improve their sense of poise or wellbeing; others may wish to try the technique to help with emotional problems or physical aches and pains. Actors, musicians and other performers may employ Alexander technique practitioners to improve posture, presence and comportment.

## Qualifications and Training

There are no formal entry requirements, but you do need a good general education, and academic subjects that cover biology, physiology or anatomy are useful. A background in social care, social work, counselling or healthcare might also be useful. Most people who become practitioners have started as clients, found the technique useful and developed the desire to teach it to others. There are three separate training bodies: The Society of Teachers of the Alexander Technique (STAT), the Professional Association of Alexander Teachers (PAAT) and the Interactive Teaching Method (ITM); they have details of training opportunities at introductory/foundation and practitioner level. You will have to fund your own training. The training covers anatomy, physiology, biology and the science of movement. It also includes supervised practical sessions with clients.

## Personal Qualities and Skills

Practitioners must be good communicators able to explain things but also good at listening and being understanding. Practitioners also have to feel physically comfortable with other people and to promote that same sense of ease in their clients. They must have a genuine interest in physical and mental health issues and be able to develop a good grasp of scientific and practical matters. Usually self-employed, they also need appropriate financial and marketing skills.

## Salaries

Almost all Alexander technique teachers/practitioners are self-employed, charging anything from £20.00 to £50.00 per session – most sessions last about half an hour.

Professional Association of Alexander Teachers, Room 706, The Big Peg, 120 Vyse Street, Birmingham B18 6NF; 01746 761 024; www.paat.org.uk

Society of Teachers of the Alexander Technique (STAT), 1st Floor, Linton House, 39–51 Highgate Road, London NW5 1RS; 020 7482 5135; www.stat.org.uk

The Interactive Teaching Method (ITM);
www.alexandertechnique-itm.org

info

# Aromatherapist

Aromatherapists use the organic essential oils from aromatic plants to treat a whole range of physical and emotional symptoms. Based on discussing a client's symptoms, lifestyle, diet, overall state of health, etc, the aromatherapist prescribes a combination of essential oils to treat the person. This is done either by massage, or by giving a client oils to use in their baths, on their pillows, or to scent their rooms. While aromatherapists may work in beauty salons, they are also employed by healthcare organisations and often work closely with GPs, nurses and other healthcare professionals.

## Qualifications and Training

There are no specific academic qualifications but certificate and diploma courses are run at a number of state and private colleges. Some courses do set particular entry requirements such as a GCSE in biology and they may also set admissions tests. The length of courses varies from a weekend to an evening a week over one or two years. The longer courses offer a much greater depth of study.

## Personal Qualities and Skills

Aromatherapists must be very good at putting people at ease. They must be caring, patient and good listeners. They must be comfortable with close physical contact with other people.

## Salaries

Many aromatherapists are self-employed and charge between £20 and £40 an hour. Aromatherapists who are employed earn from £15,000 to £20,000 a year, though some earn much more than this.

**info**

Institute for Complementary Medicine, PO Box 194, London SE16 7QZ; 020 7237 5165; www.i-c-m.org.uk

Aromatherapy Consortium, PO Box 6522, Desborough, Kettering, Northants NN14 2YX; 0870 774 3477; www.aromatherapy-regulation.org.uk

International Federation of Aromatherapists (IFAS), 61–63 Churchfield Road, London W3 6AY; 020 8992 9605; www.ifaroma.org

# Chiropractor

Chiropractic is a healthcare profession concerned with, but not limited to, the diagnosis, treatment and prevention of structural and functional disorders affecting the musculo-skeletal system. Common complaints include low back and leg pain, headaches and neck and arm pain, as well as sports injuries. Working in a primary contact profession, a qualified chiropractor may be approached directly, without a medical referral, by patients seeking help.

Chiropractors are trained to utilise a wide variety of diagnostic techniques, including X-ray. Manual manipulation (adjustment) of spinal and extremity joints as well as soft-tissue structures is the most common treatment method employed. They will also offer advice on nutrition, rehabilitative exercises and modifications to activities of daily living. There is an increasing demand for chiropractic services and employment prospects are good both in the UK and in Europe.

## Qualifications and Training

Chiropractors are subject to statutory regulation by the General Chiropractic Council (GCC). It is illegal for anyone to describe themselves as a chiropractor if they are not registered with the GCC. Recognised courses are provided by the Anglo-European College of Chiropractic, McTimoney College of Chiropractic and the Universities of Glamorgan and Surrey. Entry requirements vary but normally include two science A levels or equivalent. Fees for courses vary considerably because some colleges are private.

## Personal Qualities and Skills

Manual dexterity and practical skills as well as a sound theoretical knowledge of the body are necessary. An ability to communicate with patients and inspire confidence is important.

## Salaries

Salaries vary according to number of patients and how well established the practice is. Patients are usually charged per session at £20 to £60 per hour. A new entrant earns up to £15,000 per year. With experience it is possible to earn £30,000; a large practice will pay an experienced person up to £40,000.

**info**

General Chiropractic Council, 44 Wicklow Street, London WC1X 9HL; 020 7713 5155; www. gcc-uk.org; e-mail: enquiries@gcc-uk.org

British Chiropractic Association, Blagrave House, 17 Blagrave Street, Reading, Berkshire RG1 1QB; 0118 950 5950; fax: 0118 958 8946; www.chiropractic-uk.co.uk; e-mail: enquiries@chiropractic-uk.co.uk

Anglo-European College of Chiropractic, 13–15 Parkwood Road, Bournemouth, Dorset BH5 2DF; 01202 436200; fax: 01202 436312; www.aecc.ac.uk

McTimoney College of Chiropractic, Kimber House, 1 Kimber Road, Abingdon, Oxfordshire OX14 1BZ; 01235 523336; www.mctimoney-college.ac.uk; e-mail: chiropractic@mctimoney-college.ac.uk

University of Glamorgan, Chiropractic Field, School of Applied Sciences, Pontypridd, Glamorgan, CF37 1DL; 01443 482287; www.glam.ac.uk

University of Surrey, European Institute of Health and Medical Sciences, Duke of Kent Building, Stag Hill, Guildford, Surrey GU2 7TE; 01483 686700; www.eihms.surrey.ac.uk

# Homeopath

Homeopathy is a system of healing which assists the natural tendency of the body to heal itself. There are three main principles of homeopathy. First is treating like with like – what produces the symptoms of a disease may also cure it; the patient is treated by a small amount of the substance causing the symptoms and the natural defences are stimulated. Second, the lower the dose the better the result. Third, the remedy should be unique to the particular patient at a particular time. Homeopathic remedies may be used to treat almost any reversible illness in adults, children or animals.

Many newly qualified homeopaths set up in partnership in a clinic with other homeopaths and some now work with GPs in fundholding practices. Homeopathic patients may come privately or be referred by GPs. Medical homeopaths (doctors who have trained in homeopathy) work as GPs, private practitioners or in one of the NHS homeopathic hospitals.

## Qualifications and Training

Medical doctors who have been qualified for a minimum of two and a half years may take a postgraduate course at one of the five teaching centres accredited by the Faculty of Homeopathy.

Non-medically qualified candidates have a choice of institutions and courses. Several organisations register homeopaths as professionally competent. The largest, the Society of Homeopaths, is involved in developing professional education and is currently establishing a formal procedure for accrediting courses in homeopathy. There is a database of recognised courses on its website.

## Personal Qualities and Skills

Homeopaths must have an interest in people, an ability to consider and interpret information and be good listeners and communicators.

## Salaries

Because most of the work is paid for on an hourly basis, salaries range from £5,000 to £30,000 pro rata. Homeopaths charge between £30 and £100 per hour, depending on their experience, their location and their clientele. £35 to £50 an hour is the most usual rate.

**info**

Skills for Health, Goldsmiths House, Broad Plain, Bristol BS2 0JP; 0117 922 1155; www.skillsforhealth.org.uk

Homeopathic Medical Association, 7 Darnley Road, Gravesend, Kent DA11 0RU; www.the-hma.org

Faculty of Homeopathy, Hahnemann House, 29 Park Street West, Luton LU1 3BE; 0870 444 3950; www.trusthomeopathy.org

Alliance of Registered Homeopaths, Millbrook, Millbrook Hill, Nutley, East Sussex TN22 3PJ; 08700 736339; www.a-r-h.org

Society of Homeopaths, 11 Brookfield, Duncan Close, Moulton Park, Northampton NN3 6WL; 0845 450 6611; www.homeopathy-soh.org

# Massage therapist

Massage therapists use several different techniques, but they all involve using their hands and fingers to manipulate soft tissue. Most massage therapists are self-employed, but they may work in beauty salons, sports centres and private health clinics, or occasionally for the NHS. Massage therapists work with people who are in pain or suffering stress. They work with sports men and women who have suffered injury and they may work with babies and their parents to help calm babies and improve the bond between parent and child. There are many different techniques and schools of massage; Indian head massage, sports massage and body massage are some of the key specialisms.

## Qualifications and Training

At present, this is an unregulated profession, so there are no agreed training routes, but the General Council for Massage Therapy (GCMT) recommends intending massage therapists to take an in-depth course. They have developed training guidelines and suggestions of what topics every course should cover and they should be able to give you useful guidance. Most massage therapy training is private, so you will have to pay for the training yourself. Entry requirements for training courses vary, but most will expect you to have five GCSEs grades A–C including English and a science subject.

## Personal Qualities and Skills

You must have excellent communication skills, able to reassure and put people at their ease. You will have to be a good listener too. You need to be physically fit with good stamina and an interest in science and health. If you are self-employed you will also have to have the right administrative and organisational skills to run your business. In many settings you will also have to work as part of a team.

## Salaries

Self-employed massage therapists charge between £25 and £70 an hour. If you work in a beauty salon you will probably earn between £14,000 and £16,000 a year. Many experienced massage therapists, who are skilled in a variety of massage techniques, may earn more than £30,000.

Massage Training Institute, PO Box 44603, London N16 0XQ; 020 7254 7227; www.massagetraining.co.uk

Guild of Infant and Child Massage, Fyfield, Greenhill Park Road, Evesham, Worcestershire WR11 4NL; 01889 564 555; www.gicm.org.uk

General Council for Massage Therapy; 0870 850 4452; www.gcmt.org.uk

Institute for Complementary Medicine, PO Box 194, London SE16 7QZ; 020 7231 5855; www.i-c-m.org.uk

International Therapy Examination Council (ITEC), 4 Heathfield Terrace, Chiswick, London W4 4JE; 020 8994 4141; www.itecworld.co.uk

Sports Massage Association, 1 Woodville Terrace, Lytham, Lancashire FY8 5QB; 0870 005 2678; www.sportsmassageassociation.org

**info**

# Naturopath

Naturopaths work in private practice since naturopathy is not offered by the NHS. They believe in treating the whole patient and in encouraging the body to cure itself, so do not generally give drugs which, they consider, often treat the symptoms without dealing with the actual cause of a problem. A naturopath uses treatments designed to correct total body chemistry; diet is seen as a major factor and patients are encouraged to eat more natural food. Hydrotherapy is often used to stimulate the blood to a specific area of the body or to draw it away from another (by applying cold packs to combat throbbing headaches, for example).

Naturopaths also need to be skilled in psychology since they recognise that physiological complaints may frequently be caused by psychological problems. Any remedies used tend to be nutritional, herbal or homeopathic, and naturopaths may also be trained in acupuncture or other systems of alternative or complementary medicine. In the UK, naturopathy is closely linked to osteopathy, and many naturopaths are qualified osteopaths using these skills in treating their patients.

## Qualifications and Training

Two graduate courses are offered by the British College of Osteopathic Medicine in London: a BSc (Honours) degree in Osteopathic Medicine combined with a Naturopathic Diploma and a BSc (Honours) degree in Naturopathic Medicine.

The usual minimum entry requirements are three good A levels or equivalent, one of which should be chemistry. Mature students may be considered on an individual basis, taking into account their academic and life experiences.

## Personal Qualities and Skills

Professional skills must be combined with a sympathetic and caring manner.

## Salaries

Salaries vary depending on hours worked, number of patients and fee scales. Fees range from £25 to £100 an hour.

info

British College of Osteopathic Medicine, Lief House, 120–122 Finchley Road, London NW3 5HR; 020 7435 6464; fax: 020 7431 3630; www.bcom.ac.uk; e-mail: info@bcom.ac.uk

General Council and Register of Naturopaths, Goswell House, 2 Goswell Road, Street, Somerset BA16 0JG; 08707 456984; fax: 08707 456985; www.naturopathy.org.uk; e-mail: admin@naturopathy.org.uk

# Osteopath

Osteopathy is a system of diagnosis and treatment where the main emphasis is on conditions affecting the musculo-skeletal system. Osteopaths use predominantly gentle manual and manipulative methods of treatment to restore and maintain proper body function. They work in private practice and are increasingly being asked to work as part of mainstream medicine. All osteopaths are required to register with the General Osteopathic Council (GOsC).

## Qualifications and Training

To practise as an osteopath, you need to take a degree approved by the General Osteopathic Council (GOsC). You then have to register with the GOsC. If you have other medical qualifications you may be able to take a shorter postgraduate course. You can find a list of all approved courses on the GOsC website. You normally need five GCSEs grades A–C and two or three A levels including at least one science. Osteopathy degree courses combine academic work and periods of practical placement. Before you can register with the Council you need to have a medical, character reference and a CRB check. You also need to take out your own liability insurance. Once you are working as an osteopath you have to complete 30 hours of continuing education each year, as part of your professional development.

## Personal Qualities and Skills

You have to be genuinely interested in working with people, able to put them at ease and gain their trust. You must have a keen interest in science and be physically fit. If you are self-employed, you must be good at managing and marketing your services.

## Salaries

Most osteopaths are self-employed and earnings are based on the rates they charge per treatment and consultation, usually between £25.00 and £75.00 per session. In your early career earnings will probably be around £20,000; later on, earnings can be up to £40,000.

General Osteopathic Council (GOsC), Osteopathy House, 176 Tower Bridge Road, London SE1 3LU; 020 7357 6655; www.osteopathy.org

**info**

# Reflexologist

A reflexologist applies pressure to the feet, or to the hands, to stimulate the reflexes, which acts as a treatment to release tensions in the body, improving circulation and stimulating the body's own natural healing processes. A usual session conducted with a client involves applying pressure to the hands and feet, to clear blockages and improve circulation, easing tension and restoring the body's natural balance to all organs and parts of the body.

## Qualifications and Training

Reflexology courses are available at colleges of further or higher education and private centres throughout the UK. The number of hours of study required by courses varies between 60 and 200. Most courses are private and there is a fee, but grants may be available.

## Personal Qualities and Skills

A reflexologist helps people and is sensitive and sympathetic to the client's needs and condition. It is essential to have good communication skills, including listening and understanding. The work involves solving problems. Reflexologists must be logical thinkers able to offer a solution to health problems and understand when to refer patients to suitable medical practitioners.

## Salaries

Newly qualified reflexologists earn £14,000 to £20,000. Experienced reflexologists with plenty of clients can earn around £30,000. Most reflexologists are self-employed so income is dependent on the number of clients seen and the geographical location. Some reflexologists may get contracts to work in hospitals, care homes, health clubs, etc.

**info**

Prince's Foundation for Integrated Health, 33–41 Dallington Street, London EC1V 0BB; 0203 1193 100; www.fih.org.uk/about_us

Association of Reflexologists, 27 Old Gloucester Street, London WC1N 3XX; 0870 5673320; www.aor.org.uk

Reflexology Forum; www.reflexologyforum.org

# Reiki healer

Reiki healing is a form of energy-based healing founded in Japan. Reiki healers endeavour to guide energies through the bodies of their clients, attempting to activate natural healing processes within the body. There are many systems of Reiki, but they all aim to help physical, emotional, mental or spiritual problems. Reiki is used to treat pain, stress and tiredness and it aims to induce calm and increase clients' energy levels. It is sometimes used in conjunction with traditional and other complementary therapies.

During a Reiki session, the client lies fully clothed on a bed or sits in a chair while the healer places his or her hands in a sequence of positions over the client's body. The whole body is treated rather than specific symptoms or areas. Treatment can take between one and two hours. Reiki is non-diagnostic, non-interventionist, non-manipulative and no pressure is applied.

## Qualifications and Training

There are no specific academic entry requirements, though many Reiki healers will have qualifications in other aspects of healthcare, counselling, or complementary therapies. You should have experience of working with people and you also need to undergo some Reiki healing yourself, to experience how it operates. Training is through one-to-one sessions with a Reiki master or teacher.

Training courses in Reiki are also offered at a number of colleges at introductory and advanced level. It is possible to gain a certificate or diploma awarded by an exam body such as the VTCT (Vocational Training Charitable Trust) or the OCN (Open College Network).

## Personal Qualities and Skills

You must have very good interpersonal skills. You need to be able to put people at ease, reassure them and listen to them. You need to have an open mind and a positive attitude about how Reiki healing works. You must be physically fit. If you are self-employed you need some business awareness, and financial and marketing skills.

## Salaries

Most Reiki healers are self-employed, charging for each individual healing session. Fees range from £20 to £70 an hour. What you can charge varies according to your geographical location and your level of experience.

The Reiki Federation, PO Box 1785, Andover, Hants SP11 0WB; 0870 850 2209; www.reikifed.co.uk

Reiki Association, 2 Spa Terrace, Fenay Bridge, Huddersfield HD8 0BD; www.reikiassociation.co.uk

info

# COMPUTING

*see* Information and Communication Technology

# CONSERVATION

Conservation falls broadly into two categories: environmental, and heritage and arts. They are each concerned with protecting and preserving – the former, the world in which we live, and the latter, our cultural history.

## Conservation/restoration art and heritage

Conservators and restorers look after historic buildings, paintings, pieces of sculpture, ancient books, historic tapestries, carvings, pieces of furniture and other objects. Conservators examine items for any signs of damage or deterioration. They do their best to ensure that objects are looked after properly, and protected and preserved in the most effective ways possible. Finally, they may take steps to restore them to something as close as possible to their original condition.

Conservators have to understand the effect of the environment on different materials, and to ensure that objects are not stored or displayed in harmful conditions. They have to be aware of and be able to control light, humidity, temperature and sources of pollution. They employ many different scientific techniques and they make photographic records of their work.

### Qualifications and Training

Most conservators have a degree. You need either a degree in art followed by a specialist postgraduate qualification in conservation, or a degree in a specific area of art, eg, ceramics and glass, or textiles. The Institute of Conservation lists relevant courses on its website. Highly skilled and experienced craftsmen and women who do not have a degree may also be able to get into conservation work if they can demonstrate their practical skills and knowledge of working with specific materials.

## Personal Qualities and Skills

Conservators must have a blend of interests in artistic, scientific and technical matters. They have to pay close attention to detail and be prepared to work patiently and extremely carefully. They also need to be good communicators, being able to explain their requirements and concerns convincingly.

## Salaries

New entrants earn between £18,500 and £22,000. This rises to around £20,000 to £24,000 after two or three years' experience. Senior conservators can earn between £27,000 and £35,000. If you develop a really good reputation and are able to work on really prestigious pieces, you may earn more than this.

# Environmental conservation

*see* Environment

**info**

British Antique Furniture Restorers' Association (BAFRA), BAFRA Head Office, The Old Rectory, Warmwell, Dorchester, Dorset DT2 8HQ; 01305 854 822; www.bafra.org.uk

Creative and Cultural Skills: the Sector Skills Council for Advertising, Crafts, Cultural Heritage, Design, Music, Performing, Literary & Visual Arts, 4th Floor Lafone House, The Leathermarket, Weston Street, London SE1 3HN; 020 7015 1800; www.ccskills.org.uk

Institute of Conservation, 3rd Floor, Downstream Building, 1 London Bridge, London SE1 9BG; 020 7785 3807; www.icon.org.uk

Museums, Libraries and Archives Council, Victoria House, Southampton Row, London WC1B 4EA; 020 7273 1444; www.mla.gov.uk

Museums Association, 24 Calvin St, London E1 6NW; www.museumsassociation.org

Guild of Master Craftsmen, 166 High Street, Lewes, East Sussex BN7 1XU; 01273 478449; www.thegmcgroup.com/theguild

The International Institute for Conservation of Historic and Artistic Works, 6 Buckingham Street, London WC2N 6BA; 020 7839 5975; www.iiconservation.org

# CONSTRUCTION

The construction industry is the overarching sector for any occupation that is involved in the building and decorating of new and existing buildings. Building work involves the construction and maintenance of any structure. It is allied to civil and structural engineering, building and environmental engineering, municipal engineering, and highway and transportation engineering. There is a huge range of career options within the industry for graduates, technicians and at craft level.

# Building control surveyor

Building control is undertaken by local authorities and Approved Inspectors. The main activities involve the examination and assessment of plans, site visits to inspect work, and liaison with designers, builders and other professionals within the construction team, and the fire authorities to ensure that new building construction and alterations to existing buildings conform to building regulations. A broad knowledge of the many areas of building work and skills in dealing with people need to be developed.

## Qualifications and Training

There are two components to qualifying as a Chartered Building Control Surveyor: successful completion of a Royal Institution of Chartered Surveyors (RICS) approved degree or diploma, followed by enrolment onto the Assessment of Professional Competence (APC) which is two years' practical training while in employment, concluding with an RICS professional assessment interview. Postgraduate conversion courses are also available.

## Personal Qualities and Skills

You have to be a good communicator, able to talk to property owners and builders, and you have to be firm and assertive when explaining, for example, why some work has to be redone. You have to have good technical knowledge and be able to convey this to other people. Maturity and common sense are vital.

## Salaries

Salaries start at between £16,000 and £21,000. If you have plenty of experience, qualifications, or are working towards qualifications, salaries can go up to £30,000. Like any job in the construction industry at present, job security is an issue and salaries are not likely to rise particularly fast.

# Want a degree – but don't want the debt?

**Want a degree, but don't want the debt? Earn while you learn with on-the-job training in the UK's largest single industry, with a leading UK construction company.**

Gain a BSc honours degree without the debt by studying one day a week at university. You will gain valuable construction experience four days a week, with the opportunity to gain additional qualifications and chartered status with one of the Built Environment Professional Institutions.

Balfour Beatty Construction offer positions in two main areas, engineering and commercial management. As a trainee engineer you will manage engineering aspects of a construction site including planning and supervising the work of subcontractors. As a commercial trainee you will look after the commercial and legal aspects of a construction site, ensuring costs are controlled and that clients are getting value for money.

There are exciting opportunities for individuals to work with an innovative and growing company. There is a competitive and rising salary, and you don't need to worry about paying fees.

You need a minimum of 260 UCAS points or equivalent to apply. To search for vacancies and apply, visit: **www.bbcl.co.uk**

**How big will you grow?**

**www.bbcl.co.uk**

INVESTOR IN PEOPLE

DNV

# Balfour Beatty
## Construction

**BUILDING PEOPLE**

# Balfour Beatty Construction Northern

## Case study –

### Adele Armitage
### Trainee Quantity Surveyor

I always wanted to work in a job that I could be constantly learning new things, meeting new people and challenging myself.

I have been very lucky in my role as a Trainee Quantity Surveyor with Balfour Beatty as the first project I am working on is the new acute Pinderfields Hospital in Wakefield with a project value of £200million. Working for Balfour Beatty on this project provides me with new, exciting and rewarding challenges everyday.

 My role involves preparing new Sub oontracts, measuring progress, reviewing and preparing payment certificates, making sure accurate and detailed records are kept as well as making regular visits on to the site to generally learn the construction process.

Balfour Beatty has given me the opportunity to combine my every day work with a day release programme at Sheffield Hallam University. The work is hard and sometimes it feels that there just aren't enough hours in the day, but with the support I have received from all my colleagues I am proud to say I have gained my HNC in Building Studies and this year I will be starting my degree in Quantity Surveying.

My ambition is to go on with Balfour Beatty get my degree and become a fully qualified Quantity Surveyor with RICS accreditation.

I really enjoy all aspects of my role and training and would recommend it to anyone.

### A Management Career in Construction

The construction industry is the UK's largest single industry, responsible for employing over 2 million people and producing about 10% of overall GDP.

Construction is very intellectually demanding as it is a complex process but the satisfaction of seeing your project completed and leaving your mark on the world is second to none.

Any construction project relies on a wide range of skilled people across several phases. The significant phases are as follows:

advertisement feature

144

**Concept and design** – this is undertaken by an Architect, usually assisted by a Structural Engineer, who works with the client to translate their aspiration into a design. Companies need to ensure that the design is practical to build and the costs and timescales are realistic.

**Selection of the construction team** – the client selects a team to build their project from a number of tenders, using criteria such as reputation, skills, creativity and price. They are assisted by a team of consultants, who help to determine the budget and the outline programme. Companies have teams of staff who work on tenders to ensure that they win plenty of projects for the future.

**Construction** – different parts of the project are built by specialist contractors – such as groundworkers, steel erectors, bricklayers, carpenters, electricians, decorators etc. The main contractor's job is to manage them through selecting the most appropriate contractor, plan the timescales involved, sequence them correctly, monitor their progress whilst on site and solve any problems. Throughout the project the main contractor must brief the client, stick to the budget, motivate the various teams and ensure that all activities are conducted safely.

**Ongoing maintenance and repair** – once a building is completed, specialist companies are responsible for ensuring that it works to its maximum efficiency throughout its lifecycle.

## Working for a main contractor

Balfour Beatty Construction is a main contractor which manages specialist contractors to ensure that a project is completed safely, on time, to budget and to the customer's quality standards.

As a UK-wide company we specialise in the construction of new buildings including hospitals, schools, offices and retail parks – ranging in value from half a million pounds to half a billion!

Examples of current projects include:

- The new Queen Elizabeth Hospital in Birmingham
- Northern Batch Hospitals'
- Manchester Schools

Most employees are based on construction sites across the UK, with some working from regional offices (Manchester, Newcastle, Leeds and Birmingham).

Balfour Beatty are at the forefront of the latest developments in construction – including safety, environment and sustainability, radical forms of project finance, innovative management techniques or new technology.

Overall turnover is around £450 million with 690 employees across the UK. Balfour Beatty Construction Northern are part of the Balfour Beatty

advertisement feature

Group, the UK's largest construction, engineering and services company with an overall turnover of £9.5 billion and 40,000 employees.

## The job roles

There are a number of different professional and managerial roles that you can aspire to become:

**Design Managers** manage the architects and ensure that their designs are safe and easy to build, meet the client's requirements in terms of user criteria, environmental performance, cost and timescale. They also act as a link between the architect and construction teams and ensure that everybody has the correct information in the right place at the right time.

**Engineers** are responsible for ensuring that the building is constructed with the correct level of dimensional accuracy and that specialist contractors are properly briefed and supervised.

**Estimators** work on tenders to predict the cost of the building that the client requires and discusses costs with potential specialist contractors.

**Planners** work out how long the different construction activities will take and so predict how long a project will take to complete and what resources will be required.

**Project Managers** are responsible for the project from start to finish and manage the site teams. They speak directly to the client throughout the project and ensure that the client is fully aware of the progress. The buck stops with the project manager!

**Site Managers** control the site itself, ensuring that the specialist contractors are co-ordinated, materials and plant are delivered and stored correctly, potential problems are solved in advance and that all activities are carried out safely.

For any of these roles a degree in a built environment subject is essential; this will give you not only the required underpinning knowledge but also provide you with the baseline for going on to become professionally qualified.

You can either go to university full-time and gain work experience during summer placements and a year out, alternatively you can study for the same degree on a part-time basis attending university one day a week.

## The debt-free degree

Want a degree but don't want the debt? Gain debt free degree and a well-paid and challenging job with excellent career development opportunities with Balfour Beatty.

It will take you five years to obtain your degree on a day release basis – only a year longer than a full time sandwich degree – and you will spend the other four days in the workplace, following a structured and accredited on-the-job training scheme.

These are permanent jobs with education and training attached so on completion of your degree you will continue your career by becoming chartered with one of the major construction industry professional bodies and moving up the management ladder.

## Training pathways

**Site Management** – you will start off in an engineering role, before moving into site supervision and then site management. Support will be given for a degree in Civil Engineering or Construction Management.

**Design Management** – you will assist the design managers in the flow of design information, as well as spending time on site in an engineering role and in an architects office understanding the design process. Support will be given for a degree in Architectural Technology or Construction Management.

**Commercial Management** – working as a junior quantity surveyor, you will select and monitor specialist contractors, control costs and ensure legal compliance. Support will be given for a degree in Quantity Surveying or Construction Management.

Whichever pathway you choose, as well as your degree you will receive intensive on the job training leading to NVQs at levels 3 and 4, technical and managerial training and regular safety training. Once you have finished your degree, your training will focus on becoming a Chartered Builder, Engineer or Surveyor.

## Entry requirements

You will need A-levels/Highers/AVCE with at least 260 UCAS points or an HNC/D in a built environment subject.

## Recruitment process

All applications must be made online. To see vacancies and apply, please visit the Balfour Beatty Construction Website: www.bbcl.co.uk

## Useful websites:

www.balfourbeatty.com – Balfour Beatty Group

www.bconstructive.co.uk – Careers in Construction

www.constructionskills.net – Sector Skills Council

www.cstt.org.uk – Chartered Surveyors Training Trust

www.ciob.org.uk – Chartered Institute of Building

www.ice.org.uk – Institute of Civil Engineers

www.rics.org.uk – Royal Institution of Chartered Surveyors

advertisement feature

Association of Building Engineers (ABE), Lutyens House, Billing Brook Road, Northampton NN3 8NW; 0845 126 1058; www.abe.org.uk

Construction Industry Training Board, CITB – Construction Skills, Bircham Newton, King's Lynn, Norfolk PE31 6RH; 01485 577577; www.citb.org.uk

Royal Institution of Chartered Surveyors (RICS), RICS Contact Centre, Surveyor Court, Westwood Way, Coventry CV4 8JE; 0870 333 1600; www.rics.org

## Clerk of works

The clerk of works undertakes independent inspection of the works in progress to ensure that they conform to the specification so that the client obtains value for money.

## Contract manager

The contract manager is the person responsible for the overall control of a building project. This means coordinating the subcontractors and specialist firms, the technical staff and the machine operatives and making sure that the whole project is completed within the specified time limit and to budget.

## CONSTRUCTION TRADES

There are many different construction trades: carpenters, painters and decorators, electricians, plasterers, plumbers and roofers. While they each have their own specialist knowledge and technical skills, much of the training and qualification route is similar for all of these trades. Have a look at the Qualifications and Training section at the end of this entry to see how to qualify and what kind of training to expect.

## Carpenter

There are several different jobs covered by the general term 'carpenter' – what they all have in common is that carpenters work with wood. They use wood to make doors, window frames, skirting boards, floorboards, cupboards and all the other woodwork you can think of in any domestic, public or commercial building. Some of the different roles include bench joiners, who prepare doors and window frames in a workshop ready for other workers to install them in properties; carpenters and joiners who work on site or inside or outside buildings, fitting cupboards, doors, window frames, etc; and wood machinists who prepare floorboards and skirting boards in the workshop ready for the carpenter and joiner to fix in place and finish.

# Demolition work

Demolishing a building properly and safely is one of the most highly skilled areas in construction.

## Demolition operative

Demolition operatives use heavy machinery to bring down walls, buildings and other structures. They have to be acutely aware of safety, calculating exactly how a building will collapse. They are also involved in clearance of the site once the building has been razed to the ground.

## Scaffolder

Scaffolders build scaffolding that might be used in demolition, but more significantly in construction. They build scaffolding from steel tubes and wooden platforms, and it is essential they build scaffolding that is safe for other construction workers to stand on and work from.

## Steeplejack

Steeplejacks work not just on steeples, but on any high structures, chimneys, clock towers, etc. They have not only to work at a great height, using special safety equipment, but also have to have a good working knowledge of many different trades because they are likely to have to carry out repairs to and with many different materials: glass, wood, paint, plaster, mortar, etc.

# Interior and finishing trades

Once a basic structure has been completed by bricklayers, carpenters, roofers, etc, there is still a great deal of work needed to make the building comfortable to live or work in and useful for the purpose for which it has been built. Ceiling fixers, floor layers, glaziers, painters and decorators, plasterers and plumbers are examples of some of the interior and finishing trades on offer.

## Ceiling fixer

Ceiling fixers and dry liners install ceilings, especially in large modern buildings with large expanses of high ceiling. They build structures to fit large sheets of plasterboard to, and cover the whole thing with a very thin layer of plaster.

# Electrician

This is a major construction industry career with many different options and pathways. You can see full details on page 182.

# Glazier

Glaziers work with glass, installing glass windows, doors and glass partitions. They have to be skilled in cutting and fixing glass, from basic double-glazing to more ornate glass effects.

# Painter and decorator

No building looks complete until the important finishing touches of painting, wood staining and papering have been applied. Interior decorators work inside and outside all kinds of buildings, from private houses to large warehouses, shops and offices.

# Plasterer

This is a highly skilled occupation, as plasterers have to line walls or ceilings with a layer of even, smooth and attractive plaster to act as a basis for painting, wallpaper or other finishes. They have to work quickly, achieving the desired finish before the plaster dries out. Some plasterers go on to develop skills in ornamental and decorative plasterwork.

# Plumber

Plumbers install and maintain all the necessary pipes, valves, tanks, boilers, etc that keep water and heating systems flowing through any building. They install and maintain drainage systems and repair flashing on roofs.

# Roofer

Roofs come in many different shapes and sizes and are made from many different materials. It is the job of roofers to fix roofs onto buildings and to ensure that these roofs are safe and weatherproof. Within roofing there are several different specialist trades: felt roofing, tiling and slating, lead roofing and many more. You may choose to work mainly with one of these materials, and become a specialist, or you may decide to work with all the different types of roofing material.

# Trowel trades

If you work with brick or stone you will learn one of these trades. Of the many construction occupations available, these offer you the chance to be creative as well as using practical skills.

## Bricklayer

Bricklayers build the external and internal walls of all kinds of buildings, from private houses to large hospitals, hotels and offices. They build garden walls and lay patios. They work mainly with ready-prepared bricks, building them up in layers, working to produce smooth and weatherproof results.

## Stonemason

Stonemasons have employed their skills for hundreds of years, using natural stone as their basic building material. Today stonemasons work both restoring historic buildings and building modern structures. This is highly skilled work and a flair for design as well as practical ability is very important.

# Supervisory roles

With so many different workers involved in building projects, both large and small, it is very important that there are people to take overall responsibility for employing workers, purchasing materials, health and safety, and day-to-day management.

## Site manager

Many site technicians become site managers, taking on more responsibility for larger projects and being in charge of everything that happens on the site.

## Site technician

Site technicians get involved with the general running and safety of the site. Your role would include hiring and buying materials and machinery, and organising people and equipment. It would be your responsibility to ensure budgets and plans are followed, and that everything meets technical requirements.

To become a site technician, you will need to have a strong knowledge of building methods and materials, and health and safety requirements, which you will have to teach workers on your site. You will need good communication and organisational skills, have a high level of competence in computing, and work well as part of a team.

There are no specific academic entry requirements to train as a site technician, though it is helpful to have GCSE/Standard Grade passes in science, maths and technology for the measurements and planning.

# Construction project manager

Construction project managers have overall responsibility for the planning, management, coordination and financial control of a construction project. It is their responsibility to see that the clients' wishes are adhered to and that the project is completed on time within the agreed budget.

## Qualifications and Training

While there appears to be a confusing array of construction qualifications, there are really three main routes into construction trades at craft and technical levels. These are through having relevant work experience, through an apprenticeship, or through a college course followed by training with an employer. If you already work on a building site as a labourer, your employer may be prepared to support you through training in one of the building trades.

If you would like to serve a traditional apprenticeship (TA) in a construction trade, you need to find an employer who will take you on and provide the work experience, while sending you on day release to college. During your apprenticeship you normally work towards NVQ levels 2 or 3. How many apprenticeships are on offer and in what trades varies throughout the country; Construction Skills has up-to-date information on availability. To do an apprenticeship you normally need three or four GCSEs grade A–C, including maths, English and a technical subject. These requirements do vary though, so check with local colleges and employers.

There are many full-time courses in construction available at local colleges. Entry requirements and exact qualifications vary widely. Many courses lead to an intermediate construction award (ICA) and if you achieve one of these, you may be able to progress to a shortened apprenticeship known as a programme-led apprenticeship (PLA).

If you are still at school and are thinking about careers in construction, a few schools have introduced a new diploma course for 14- to 19-year-olds. It only started in September 2008, so as yet there is no data on how employers will view it, but it may be an option you wish to discuss.

Many building contractors now insist that you have a Construction Skills Certification Scheme (CSCS) card to work on their sites. The card is proof of your skills and competence. To get your card you must pass a health and safety assessment and have an NVQ or equivalent qualification. The Construction Skills Certification Scheme helpline and website will provide you with further information.

## Personal Qualities and Skills

While a variety of trades have been described and each has its special require-ments, there are many skills and qualities that are important for all these occupations. You need to have a special interest in and feel for the particular material you are working with – wood, metal, plaster, stone, etc. You must be good at measuring and calculating, working out how much material you will need, and measuring exactly to ensure that something fits.

For all jobs you must be physically fit, though some work, such as bricklay-ing, is especially demanding. You may have to climb up and down scaffold-ing, work outside in unpleasant weather, or work in cramped spaces such as somebody's loft.

You need to get on with people. You often work as part of a team, and if you progress to supervisory or management roles you have to be organised and be good at motivating other people. If you are working in private houses, you must be polite, pleasant and trustworthy, and good at coming up with solutions to problems. If you become self-employed you must develop good business and financial skills.

## Salaries

Salaries for apprentices across the construction industry are agreed annually. First-year apprentices earn around £8,500, second-year apprentices earn around £10,600. Third-year apprentices earn around £12,800, more if they have achieved NVQ level 3, and on completion of apprenticeships salaries rise to around £18,000. With experience, all trades can earn between £19,000 and £23,000. There is considerable regional variation in salaries. There may also be opportunities to earn overtime payments, or bonuses on very busy projects. Many people with experience in one of the construction trades choose to become self-employed.

Salaries for management posts range from £21,000 to £33,000. Construction has been hit particularly hard by the recession and this has affected the amount of overtime, contract work and other benefits available.

**info**

Construction Confederation, 56–64 Leonard Street, London EC2A 4JX; 020 7608 5000; www.thecc.org.uk

Federation of Master Builders, FMB Head Office, Gordon Fisher House, 14–15 Great James Street, London WC1N 3DP; 020 7242 7583; www.fmb.org.uk

SkillsDirect; 0844 248 5262; www.citb-constructionskills.co.uk/cardschemes

Construction Skills Certification Scheme (CSCS); 0844 576 8777; www.cscs.uk.com

ConstructionSkills, Bircham Newton, King's Lynn, Norfolk PE31 6RH; 01485 577577; www.cskills.org

Summitskills. Vega House Opal Drive, Fox Milne, Milton Keynes, Bedfordshire MK15 0DF; 01908 303860; www.summitskills.org.uk

# CRAFTS

There are many occupations which can come under the banner of a 'craft' and listed below is a selection.

# Cabinet maker

*see* Carpentry

# Florist

The florist's job involves designing and creating flower arrangements and displays such as table decorations, bouquets, sprays and wreaths, as well as selling cut flowers and plants. Some florists buy from flower markets; others have stock delivered from wholesalers, local nurseries or overseas producers. The work can include providing office displays, making arrangements for banquets, functions and receptions, and decorating hotels and public buildings. Florists generally work a 40-hour week, including Saturdays.

## Qualifications and Training

You don't need formal qualifications to train as a florist and most florists train on the job while studying part-time for relevant NVQs in floristry at levels 2 and 3. Helping out in a florist's shop and joining a flower arranging group can strengthen your application. There are a range of other, more advanced part-time courses available, including BTEC National Diplomas in Floristry Design and Floristry Business.

## Personal Qualities and Skills

You must love working with flowers and plants and have an artistic flair for colour and design. You also need good customer skills, helping people plan flowers for weddings and funerals. You need good business skills if you wish to work for yourself, or manage a shop. You are often responsible for choosing and purchasing the flowers you use.

## Salaries

Trainees in floristry shops earn around £10,500. With experience you can earn £16,000 to £19,000. If you manage a shop you could earn £23,000 to £25,000. If you decide to become self-employed, earnings vary according to how much work you take on, but in some areas you can earn far more than you could working in a shop.

**info**

Society of Floristry; 0870 241 0432; www.societyoffloristry.org

National Association of Flower Arrangement Societies; www.nafas. org.uk

Lantra, Lantra House, Stoneleigh Park, Warwickshire CV8 2LG; 0845 707 8007; www.lantra.co.uk

# Jewellery trade

## Design

Jewellery designers craft a wide variety of items either by hand or using methods of large-scale production. These may be very expensive, traditionally styled pieces using gold or platinum, cheaper costume jewellery using synthetic stones and base metals, or fashion accessories made from beads, plastic or wood.

Although there are a few openings for designers of expensive jewellery, the more costly costume jewellery and mass-produced jewellery, there is more scope for original designers on either a freelance or artist/craftsperson basis, making fashionable ranges with semi-precious stones.

## Manufacture

The jewellery, silverware and allied industries encompass a vast range of specialist skills. Apart from mounting and silversmithing, other skills needed to support these occupations include gem setting, engraving (hand and machine), enamelling, chasing, engine turning, spinning, electroplating and polishing.

### Qualifications and Training

To work in a jeweller's shop you do not need any formal qualifications, but some employers do expect you to have GCSEs in maths and English. Training is usually with a more experienced jeweller and you can take NVQs levels 2 and 3 in retail sales and retail operations.

You can study for a Professional Jewellers' Diploma with the National Association of Goldsmiths (NAG). This covers introductions to precious metals, gemstones and to hallmarks (the marks which certify a precious metal's quality). This is a distance learning course which lasts about 18 months. NAG also runs a Professional Jewellers' Management Diploma designed for shop managers or people who would like to become shop managers. There are several independent training courses available for jewellers; the Jewellery and Allied Industries Training Council (JAITC) holds details of these (see the info panel for contact details).

In the jewellery manufacturing trades there are a number of apprenticeships available.

Most jewellery designers have a degree in three-dimensional design and have specialised in jewellery design within that course.

## Personal Qualities and Skills

For retail jewellery work, you have to have good communication and customer care skills and a real interest in the products you are selling. You should have an eye for detail and an awareness of colour and fashion. You need good numeracy skills and you should be highly dextrous, easily able to handle small and expensive items carefully. Anyone working in jewellery manufacture must be practical and careful, with an interest in scientific and technical processes as well as artistic effect.

Jewellery designers have to be artistic, imaginative, with a good understanding of the properties of different metals, gems and other materials. They also need to be good at promoting their products and have a sound understanding of business.

## Salaries

Starting salaries in jewellers' shops are between £12,000 and £16,000. Store managers earn between £17,000 and £25,000. Some own and run their own businesses and this may mean they can earn more. In manufacturing, salaries range from £14,000 to £18,000 depending on your level of skill and experience.

Jewellery designers earn between £15,000 and £25,000. Some designers with real flair and an eye to the changing world of fashion can earn far more than this, especially if they are designing jewellery for the rich and famous.

info

Creative and Cultural Skills, 4th Floor, Lafone House, The Leathermarket, Weston Street, London SE1 3HN; 020 70158100; www.ccskills.org.uk

Design Council, 34 Bow Street, London WC2E 7DL; 020 7420 5200; www.design-council.org.uk

Goldsmiths Company, Goldsmiths Hall, Foster Lane, London EC2V 6BN; 020 7606 7010; www.thegoldsmiths.co.uk

Goldsmiths Company Directory; www.whoswhoingoldandsilver.com

National Association of Goldsmiths, 78A Luke Street, London EC2A 4XG; 020 7613 4445; www.jewellers-online.org

Skillsmart Retail, Fourth Floor, 93 Newman Street, London W1T 3EZ; Tel: 0800 093 5001; www.skillsmartretail.com

Jewellery and Allied Industries Training Council (JAITC), British Jewellers' Association, 10 Vyse Street, Birmingham B18 6LT; www.jaitc.org.uk

# Leather craftworker

Leather craftworkers make and repair leather items. These include clothing, footwear, furnishings and accessories such as handbags and wallets. Some leather craftworkers specialise in products such as saddles and bridles for horses, book covers or weapons and armour for historic societies or theatre companies. The work involves cutting various types of leather from patterns, hand or machine stitching pieces of leather together, fitting fastenings such as buckles, adding linings of other materials and applying finishes such as wax or stains.

## Qualifications and Training

It is not straightforward to get into leather craftwork. You may be able to do an apprenticeship in textiles which includes leather work. Alternatively you may be able to do a college course in fashion and textiles which includes leather work, particularly all the practical skills you need to work with these materials.

If you are particularly interested in saddlery, the Worshipful Company of Saddlers and the Society of Master Saddlers run the Saddlery Apprenticeship Scheme which lasts for four years. You may need to relocate to take up training or employment, especially if you are thinking about rural leather crafts. The Leather Connection website includes useful information about relevant education and training. A lot of training is on the job, learning skills from more experienced craftworkers, but there are several NVQs you can work towards. These include Leather Production levels 2 and 3, Leather Goods level 2 and Footwear and Leather Products Manufacture level 3.

## Personal Qualities and Skills

You need good manual dexterity working with a range of highly specialised tools and equipment. You should have a real interest in the field in which you work, whether this is a rural craft like saddlery, or high fashion. You should be able to work accurately, taking measurements and adding fine detail. You may also need good customer skills.

## Salaries

New entrants to this work earn between £11,000 and £13,000 – possibly less during an apprenticeship. Experienced craftworkers can earn up to £19,000.

**info**

Leather Connection; www. theleatherconnection.com

Society of Master Saddlers, Green Lane Farm, Stonham, Stowmarket, Suffolk IP14 5DS; 01449 711 642; www.mastersaddlers.co.uk

Skillfast-UK, Richmond House, Lawnswood House, Redvers Close, Leeds LS16 6RD; 0113 239 9600; www.skillfast-uk-org

Worshipful Company of Saddlers, 40 Gutter Lane, London EC2V 6BR; 020 7726 8661; www. saddlersco.co.uk

# Potter/ceramic designer

Potters make and design objects from clay. They work with basic earthenware and fine porcelain, making everything from basic kitchen- and tableware to ornaments and individual pieces of art. They may design items for the mass market which will be made on a factory production line. At the other extreme they make expensive individual items to be sold through galleries and displayed at exhibitions. Designers working with mass market producers will have to liaise with buyers, production managers and other staff and will often play a quality control role in the whole process. Designers who are successful enough to work for themselves will work in a studio with their own wheel, kiln, etc.

## Qualifications and training

Most pottery/ceramics designers are graduates with a degree in ceramics or 3D design. If you are considering a course, it is worth checking what practical skills the course covers in addition to its artistic and creative content. To be taken on by a company or a design studio you will need to put together a portfolio of photographs of your work. If you are self-employed, there is a wide range of courses available through local Adult Education Institutes and short course details are also available from the Studio Pottery website. It is important if you are self-employed to keep up to date with new trends in design, new materials, glazes, techniques, etc.

If you wish to work in the more routine work on the manufacturing side, you will not need formal qualifications.

## Personal Qualities and Skills

You must love creating something with your hands and have a flair for design and good awareness of colour. You need to be imaginative, creative and practical. You need good people skills, being able to interpret design briefs given to you or for working with buyers from shops and galleries. If working for yourself, you need good business acumen.

## Salaries

If you are employed by a company or studio starting salaries are around £17,000, rising to £25,000. If you are self-employed salaries are much more difficult to predict and can be much lower than those for employed designers. Like many art and craft careers, potters may have to boost their artistic earnings by taking on other, more routine work. Many potters increase their income by teaching on pottery courses.

**info**

a-n The Artists Information Company, First Floor, 7–15 Pink Lane, Newcastle Upon Tyne NE1 5DW; 0191 241 8000; www.a-n.co.uk

Association for Ceramic Training and Development (ACTD), St James House, Webberley Lane, Longton, Stoke on Trent ST3 1RJ; 01782 597016; www.actd.co.uk/

Crafts Council, 44a Pentonville Road, London N1 9BY; 020 7278 7700; www.craftscouncil.org.uk

Crafts Potters Association of Great Britain (CPA), 7 Marshall Street, London W1F 7EH; 020 7437 7605; www.cpaceramics.com/cpa.html

Creative and Cultural Skills, 4th Floor, Lafone House, The Leathermarket, Weston Street, London SE1 3HN; 020 7015 1800; www.ccskills.org.uk

The Design Council, 34 Bow Street, London WC2E 7DL; 020 7420 5200; www.designcouncil.org.uk

Studio Pottery; www.studiopottery.co.uk

# Thatcher

Thatchers are self-employed craftspeople who roof, re-roof or repair thatched buildings with long straw, combed wheat straw, reed and other materials. The materials and methods they use have to preserve the building in its original form. A thatched roof gives good insulation against heat and cold and lasts 20 to 50 years. A roof is thatched by taking off the old thatch and then pegging down layers of new straw or reed.

## Qualifications and Training

Academic qualifications are not essential. Thatching can be learned on the job as an apprentice to a Master Thatcher. Training takes four to five years. The Countryside Agency runs a training scheme for people of all ages, leading to NVQ level 2 in Thatching.

## Personal Qualities and Skills

Thatchers need to be robust, good with their hands and not mind bad weather or heights. They also need common sense, and the ability to make decisions and to deal with customers.

## Salaries

Salaries start at between £13,000 and £16,000, rising to £22,000 with two or three years' experience. In some regions it is possible to earn more than this because there is a high demand for thatches.

New Entrants Training Scheme,
Herefordshire College of Technology,
Folly Lane, Hereford HR1 1LS;
01432 365314;
www.hereford-tech.ac.uk

Thatching Information Service,
Thatcher's Rest, Levens Green,

Great Munden, Nr Ware,
Hertfordshire SG11 1HD;
01920 438710

National Society of Master
Thatchers, c/o The Secretary, 15
High Street, Steventon, Abingdon,
Oxfordshire OX13 5RZ

**info**

# CUSTOMS AND EXCISE

There is far more to this work than high-profile drugs or arms seizures. Customs and excise officers carry out three main types of work. They check passengers, luggage, freight and mail at ports and airports, ensuring that people are not carrying or importing illegal goods or items upon which appropriate tax has not been paid. They visit distilleries and oil refineries, ensuring that appropriate excise duty has been paid on these items. They visit and inspect businesses to ensure that their VAT records are correct and up to date.

## Qualifications and Training

There are several entry levels for this work. To start on Band 2 you must have two GCSEs grades A–C. To start on Band 3/4 you must have five GCSEs grades A–C. You can start as a junior manager (Band 5) and you will need five GCSEs grades A–C and two A levels or their equivalent. At all levels one of the GCSEs must be English language. Many successful Band 5 applicants are graduates. All the above levels are recruited directly by HM Revenue & Customs. If you apply for Fast Stream entry, you apply to Central Civil Service Recruitment; then, if you join HM Revenue & Customs you become a customs officer straight away. For the Fast Stream you must have a good honours degree, either a First or an upper second. Most of the training is on the job and includes appropriate short courses and sometimes opportunities to take professional qualifications.

## Personal Qualities and Skills

You must be able to get on with people, being polite, tactful and able to question and listen carefully. You should be honest and fair and be able to analyse complex information. For much of the work on the excise and VAT side you must have good numeracy skills.

## Salaries

Assistant customs officers earn around £15,500 and customs officers earn between £19,500 and £26,000.

Administrative grade salaries are between £12,759 and £19,500. Junior managers earn between £20,000 and £25,000. Senior managers can earn more than £40,000. Like other government departments, there are some opportunities to earn performance-related pay.

**info**

HM Revenue & Customs;
www.hmrc.gov.uk

www.civilservice.gov.uk/jobs

Government Skills, Central

Government, First Floor, Kingsgate House, 66–74 Victoria Street, London SW1E 6SW; 0203 300 8977; www. government-skills.gsi.gov.uk

# D

## DENTISTRY

All professionals in dentistry in the UK must be registered with the General Dental Council. This includes dentists, dental hygienists, dental therapists, dental nurses and dental technicians.

## Dentist

Dentists aim to prevent tooth decay and gum disease and to identify and treat such diseases. This involves filling, crowning and extracting teeth, scaling, and cleaning teeth and gums. They design and fit dentures and plates and take corrective measures for teeth growing abnormally. They are also involved with the rectification of fractured jaws and surgery of the mouth. Much of the dentist's work today is highly technical and requires a lot of manual dexterity. There is growing emphasis on preventive work, and the dentist is expected to counsel and educate.

Opportunities exist both in the UK and abroad. In general dental practice dentists work on contract to the NHS, but growing numbers work in private clinics. Some work in hospitals, community services, school services or the armed forces. There are also opportunities for dentists to work in university dental teaching and research.

Specialist areas of dentistry include paediatric dentistry and oral and maxillofacial surgery. A number of large companies also provide dental treatment facilities for staff at work and there are some openings within occupational dentistry. The armed services also provide short service commissions or permanent careers for medical and dental staff.

Dentists need to have confidence and the ability to reassure patients as many are apprehensive about dental treatment. Team work is important as working closely with the surgery assistant and any specialists the practice employs is essential.

### Qualifications and Training

To practise as a dentist you must have completed a five-year degree in dentistry at one of the UK's 14 dental schools. To get a place on one of these courses you must have three A levels (grade requirements vary from AAA to ABB), which must include chemistry and either maths or physics. Graduates with science degrees can also get into dental school: some courses are specifically designed for graduates. Some dental schools offer a pre-dental foundation year in science for graduates without suitable science qualifications.

All entrants are assessed at the interview stage on a clearly defined list of skills. These are: strong academic ability, self-discipline, commitment to completing this long and demanding degree course, manual dexterity and technical dental skills, plus the ability to maintain intense concentration for prolonged periods, the ability to build relationships with patients and colleagues, high level communication and interpersonal skills for interaction with patients of all ages and backgrounds, an interest in the welfare of others and a sympathetic manner, good administrative and managerial abilities, information technology skills due to the increasing use of computers for keeping records and accounts, and for digital imaging of radiographs and intra-oral photography. After completing your degree you have to do a period of vocational training with an approved dental practitioner.

When you have graduated from dental school you begin a period of work-based vocational training, working under supervision in an approved dental practice. Many graduate dentists undertake the recently introduced General Professional Training (GPT), which offers structured training in hospital and general practice settings.

As a qualified dentist, you can specialise by doing further postgraduate training in a specific area of interest, for example orthodontics (straightening or moving teeth).

## Personal Qualities and Skills

As is clear from the skills required by dental schools, you have to be strong academically, with excellent manual dexterity and a real ability to work well with people. You have to be very resilient: most patients are stressed and/or uncomfortable when they visit a dentist, so your people skills contribute enormously to your potential success.

## Salaries

Dentists' earnings are affected by the type of work they do and the balance of NHS and private work they undertake. Trainees during their period of vocational training earn around £30,000. Dentists who have completed their training earn between £55,000 and £80,000. Some work, such as private, cosmetic dentistry can be very lucrative and take earnings to more than £150,000. The most senior consultant dentists in the NHS earn £170,000.

**info**

British Dental Association, 64 Wimpole Street, London W1G 8YS; 020 7935 0875; www.bda-dentistry.org.uk

NHS Careers, PO Box 376, Bristol BS99 3EY; 0845 606 0655; www.nhscareers.nhs.uk

Health Learning and Skills Advice Line; 0800 015 0850; www.learndirect-advice.co.uk/campaigns/nhs/

General Dental Council, 37 Wimpole Street, London W1G 8DQ; 020 7887 3800; www.gdc-uk.org

# Dental hygienist

Dental hygienists clean, polish and scale teeth and in some cases prepare patients for oral operations. Through lectures and practical experience they also endeavour to educate children and adults on the importance of proper dental care. Dental hygienists work to the written prescription of a dentist.

## Qualifications and Training

Applicants for the Diploma in Dental Hygiene must be over 18 with five GCSE passes, including biology and English. They also need two years' experience as a dental nurse or two A levels or equivalent. Manchester University offers a three-year BSc in oral health science. Graduates work as oral health therapists which combines the skills of a hygienist and therapist.

## Personal Qualities and Skills

Manual and visual dexterity. Candidates should have an ability to communicate in order to educate patients in good dental hygiene practice. The ability to work in a team is important.

## Salaries

Salaries vary from region to region and between NHS and private practices. Newly qualified dental hygienists earn between £21,000 and £26,000; experienced hygienists earn between £32,000 and £36,000. In some fashionable private practices, earnings can be higher than this.

# Dental nurse

Dental nurses prepare the surgery and get the appropriate instruments ready. During treatment, they assist the dentist by passing instruments, mixing materials, taking notes from the dentist's dictation for records and making sure the patient is comfortable at all times. Once the patient has left, the dental nurse tidies the surgery and sterilises all the instruments. Sometimes, particularly in general practice, dental nurses also help with reception work – making appointments, taking payments, dealing with the paperwork, meeting and reassuring patients.

## Qualifications and Training

Many dentists like to train their own assistants and expect applicants to be educated to GCSE standard. In 2004 it became necessary for dental nurses to have obtained NVQ level 3 in Oral Healthcare or passed the National Certificate of the Examining Board for Dental Nurses. Preparation for this exam can be obtained either at evening or day-release classes or via full-time attendance on a course lasting between one and two years. A certificate is awarded on passing the exam and completing 24 months' practical experience. Courses are offered by colleges of further education and dental hospitals. Courses offered by dental hospitals usually require four GCSE passes, including English and biology.

## Personal Qualities and Skills

Candidates should be equable, sympathetic and have an agreeable nature and an ability to communicate. Good administrative and managerial skills and the ability to work in a team are important.

## Salaries

Salaries for dental nurses vary greatly depending on the type of practice and its location. Some employers pay around the national minimum wage; others pay more and include additional benefits. Average salaries are between £9,000 and £12,000.

# Dental technician

Dental technicians design and fabricate a wide variety of different materials and equipment to make crowns, dentures, metal plates, bridges, orthodontic braces and other appliances prescribed by a dentist.

## Qualifications and Training

The usual entry requirements for courses are five GCSEs or equivalents (including English, maths, physics and chemistry). The Edexcel (BTEC) diploma in dental technology is a full-time three-year course but can also be studied part-time.

## Personal Qualities and Skills

Good technical skills and the ability to work in a team.

## Salaries

Dental technicians earn £7,500–£9,000 while training, rising to £10,000–£18,000 when qualified.

# Dental therapist

Dental therapists work in local authority clinics and hospitals, assisting dentists by carrying out simpler forms of treatment such as fillings and the extraction of first teeth. They also give guidance on general dental care. Dental therapists must always work to the written prescription of a dentist.

## Qualifications and Training

To become a dental therapist you must take either a diploma in dental therapy or a degree in oral health sciences including modules on dental therapy and hygiene. The British Association of Dental Therapists (BADT) can provide details of relevant dental schools; diplomas last two years, degree courses three years.

To get onto either course you need five GCSEs grades A–C, including human biology, plus two A levels. If you are already a qualified and experienced dental nurse, you may be able to do a course without meeting the usual academic requirements.

## Personal Qualities and Skills

You must be very good at working with people, able to reassure, be calm, encourage and teach. You should have an interest in science and healthcare and you should also be practical, with good manual dexterity and good eyesight. You must be physically fit and resilient.

## Salaries

Salaries range from £15,000 to £22,000. With experience, and working in private practice, you can earn considerably more than this.

British Association of Dental Nurses, 11 Pharos Street, Fleetwood, Lancashire FY7 6BG; 01253 778631; www.badn.org.uk; e-mail: admin@badn.org.uk

British Dental Association, 64 Wimpole Street, London W1G 8YS; 020 7935 0875; www.bda-dentistry.org.uk

National Examining Board for Dental Nurses, 110 London Road, Fleetwood F17 6EU; 01253 778417

British Dental Hygienists' Association, 13 The Ridge, Yatton, Bristol BS19 4DD; 01934 876389; www.bdha.org.uk

Dental Technicians' Education and Training Advisory Board (DTETAB), 64 Wimpole St, London W1M 8AL

General Dental Council, 37 Wimpole Street, London W1G 8DQ; 020 7887 3800; www.gdc-uk.org

British Orthodontic Society, BOS Office, 291 Gray's Inn Road, London WC1X 8QJ; 020 7837 2193; www.bos.org.uk

**info**

# DIETICIAN

A dietitian is an authority on diet and the application of the principles of nutrition. Dietitians working in hospitals collaborate with medical staff, other healthcare professionals and catering staff in planning the correct balance of foods for all the patients, depending on their general state of health and medical requirements. Dietitians are also employed by local health authorities to work with general practitioners, in health centres and clinics dealing with infant welfare and antenatal treatment. Some dietitians may now be employed directly by fundholding GPs. They are also called upon to educate other healthcare professionals in nutrition. Other opportunities for dietitians exist in education, research, the food industry and the media. Increasingly, dietitians work in a freelance capacity.

## Qualifications and Training

To work as a dietician in the NHS you need either a degree in dietetics and human nutrition or a postgraduate qualification in dietetics. If you choose to do a degree, then your must have three A levels grades A–C including chemistry and one other science. If you opt for the postgraduate route, then you need a good honours degree in a life science, medicine or nutrition. You should check with the British Dietetic Association (BDA) to ensure that the course you are considering meets the approved professional standards.

If you do not want to go through higher education, you may be able to start work as a dietetic assistant in the NHS and train to NVQ level 3 in Allied Health Professions (Support) Dietetics. Applicants for assistants' posts need to have four GCSEs grades A–C usually including maths, English and a science.

## Personal Qualities and Skills

You have to be extremely good at talking to people, listening to them and explaining complex information in a way that can be easily understood. You also have to be able to tell people things they would rather not hear. You have to have an aptitude for and an interest in scientific and medical concepts. You have to be able to work well as part of a health professional's team. You may also need presentation skills to explain ideas to groups of people rather than always working one-to-one.

## Salaries

Dieticians start on between just under £23,000 and £27,500. Experienced dieticians can earn £31,000 to £33,500 and team leaders can earn close to £40,000. Some dieticians are self-employed and their earnings are based on the fees they charge clients. Others work in private clinics specialising in advice on weight loss or coping with allergies, for example, and here earnings may be higher than in the NHS.

**info**

British Dietetic Association (BDA), Charles House, 148/9 Charles Street, Queensway, Birmingham B3 3HT; 0121 200 8080; www.bda.uk.com

NHS Careers, PO Box 376, Bristol BS99 3EY; 0845 606 0655; www.nhscareers.nhs.uk

Health Professions Council (HPC), Park House, 184 Kennington Park Road, London SE11 4BU; 020 7582 0866; www.hpc-uk.org

# DISC JOCKEY

Disc jockeys provide music and entertainment at a range of venues such as clubs, private parties and radio stations. They use a variety of high-tech equipment for mixing, pitch control and cross-fading, and may also be responsible for lighting and multimedia effects.

## Qualifications and Training

A strong interest and enjoyment of different music styles is essential, and it is useful to have an interest in technology and electronics. Some DJs specialise in specific music genres such as soul, funk, hip-hop and pop. Most are self-taught and usually begin their career by volunteering their services at clubs, radio stations or to friends. It is useful to send a tape demonstrating DJ skills when asking for work.

## Personal Qualities and Skills

DJs must have a lively personality, a sense of fun and natural creativity. They need to have a good knowledge of and genuine interest in music and be able to interact effectively with an audience.

## Salaries

Sometimes you have to start off doing unpaid work. Very often you are paid by the session, anything from £50 to £300, most sessions lasting a few hours. Really experienced club and radio DJs with an established reputation can earn up to £1,000 per session.

Skillset, Focus Point, 21 Caledonian Road, London N1 9GB; 08080 300 900 for England, Wales and Northern Ireland; www.skillset.org

Radio Academy, 5 Market Place, London W1W 8AE; 020 7255 2010; www.radioacademy.org

Hospital Broadcasting Association; www.hbauk.com

Community Media Association, The Workstation, 15 Paternoster Row, Sheffield S1 2BX; 0114 279 5219; www.commedia.org.uk

Commercial Radio Companies Association, The Radiocentre, 77 Shaftesbury Avenue London W1D 5DU; 020 7306 2603; www.crca.co.uk

**info**

# DIVING

## Diver

Divers work for many different employers. Some work in the oil and gas industry, surveying, checking and building rigs and pipelines. They work for the police, searching and retrieving evidence or attempting rescues, for the media in underwater filming, and for fish farms, checking stock and equipment. They may also work for surveying companies or for archaeological research. Divers work in the sea, in rivers, in lakes, canals and reservoirs. Divers also work as instructors, either training others to become professional divers or working in outdoor education and leisure, teaching people who are interested in recreational diving. They normally specialise in a particular type of diving and this is

# THE WORLD'S LEADING
## SUBSEA TRAINING CENTRE

The Underwater Centre in Fort William is the ideal place to train for a career which offers excellent earning potential and world-wide travel:

- Industry tailored commercial diving courses
- Specialist career packages with tools training
- Experienced instructors respected world-wide who will prepare you for employment and advancement in the industry
- Unique, practical training
- Excellent deep-water training site simulating offshore environment
- Custom built on-shore facilities

For more information contact us on: **+44 (0)1397 703786**
info@theunderwatercentre.co.uk  www.theunderwatercentre.com

THE
**UNDERWATER CENTRE**
F O R T   W I L L I A M

**BAC** ACCREDITED    SQA Approved Centre

---

## The World's Leading Subsea Training Centre
## – The Underwater Centre, Fort William

The Underwater Centre was set up in the early 1970s by the British Government to enable divers to be trained in the skills required to service the booming North Sea oil and civil engineering diving industries, safely. They chose Loch Linnhe, Fort William, as the location for their school thanks to its sheltered, inland location and water depths of 50m very close by and 150m within a mile of its very large pier, which is the hub of the Centre's operations. The Underwater Centre is uniquely blessed with a subsea geography other diving establishments can only dream of. The combination of a sheltered, seawater site which provides direct access to a range of water depths makes it an ideal

advertisement feature

location, not just for learning to dive, but for ROV training and, increasingly, technology testing.

The courses offered by The Underwater Centre are designed to provide suitable training so that students meet the internationally recognised HSE standards for SCUBA, surface supplied, surface supplied top-up (known as 'wet bell') and closed bell diving. Vocational skills such as non-destructive testing, subsea welding and tools skills are provided as part of the Centre's training packages. As well as the varied diving courses, The Underwater Centre offers courses for prospective dive supervisors and assistant life support technicians too. When you combine the range of courses with the infrastructure and geographical suitability of the Centre, it's easy to see why it is one of the most popular choices amongst people seeking a career in commercial diving.

The Underwater Centre trains divers who, once they have successfully completed a course, are qualified under U.K. Health and Safety Executive (HSE) certification. The HSE diving 'ticket' is internationally recognised and is generally viewed as the benchmark, allowing a diver to work almost anywhere in the world. There are four component parts of the HSE's diver legislation which cover the key skills of SCUBA diving, surface supplied diving, surface supplied top-up diving and closed bell diving (also known as 'saturation' and 'mixed gas'). These certificates allow you to work legally as a diver. However, like all jobs, you don't get paid for travelling to work. This is where the additional training in the various vocational skills comes in. Students on The Underwater Centre's Premium Career Course will also learn how to weld and burn underwater, operate power tools and pneumatic equipment and inspect underwater.

Accredited by the British Accreditation Council, which oversees the quality of independent, further and higher education in the UK, The Underwater Centre is the first provider of subsea training to be given this prestigious seal of approval.

For potential students, The Underwater Centre offers the opportunity to try diving in full commercial diving equipment. On the Centre's 'familiarisation' day prospective students can tour the Centre and its facilities and dive in the Centre's purpose-built 1.5M litre, indoor tank. This is a great opportunity for potential students to get the feel for commercial diving equipment, ask any questions about commercial diving as a career and also meet the instructors and staff. The familiarisation day gives a close-up view of what to expect whilst training and working as a commercial diver. The familiarisation days take place regularly throughout the year.

advertisement feature

determined by how deep they have to dive and by what kind of breathing apparatus they use.

## Qualifications and Training

You must be extremely physically fit to train as a diver. You must pass a strict medical before you can start to train and you have to pass annual medicals throughout your diving career. Both the medical and the diving training course you complete have to be approved by the Health and Safety Executive (HSE) before you can work as a commercial diver.

While you don't need academic qualifications for the actual diving, you may well need qualifications relevant to the industry in which you are working. Scientific divers often have a degree in oceanography. Others may have a degree in surveying. For work in the offshore oil and gas industry, you may need welding or other construction qualifications.

The police and the Royal Navy train their own divers, so you will have to pass their selection procedures.

## Personal Qualities and Skills

As well as physical fitness, you must be able to work in hazardous and frightening conditions. You should have a great awareness of safety issues at all times, and you must be very thorough in checking equipment and following procedures.

## Salaries

Divers are usually paid by the day. Rates vary enormously from £120 a day for inshore work for a surveying or civil engineering company, to as much as £1,000 a day for some offshore work in the oil and gas industry. You need to bear in mind that most divers will probably only complete 200 dives a year.

**info**

The Underwater Centre, An Aird, Fort William, Invernesshire PH33 6AN; 01397 703786; www.theunderwatercentre.co.uk

Professional Association of Diving Instructors (PADI), Unit 7, St Philips Central, Albert Road, St Philips, Bristol BS2 0PD; 0117 300 7234; www.padi.com

Nautical Archaeology Society, Fort Cumberland, Forth Cumberland Road, Eastney, Portsmouth PO4 9LD; 023 9281 8419; www.nasportsmouth.org.uk

Cogent, Unit 5, Mandarin Court, Centre Park, Warrington, Cheshire WA1 1GG; 01925 515200; www.cogent-ssc.com

Health and Safety Executive, Rose Court, 2 Southwark Bridge, London SE1 9HS; 0845 345 0055; www.hse.gov.uk

International Marine Contractors Association, 5 Lower Belgrave Street, London SW1W 0NR; 020 7824 5520; www.imca-int.com

# DOMESTIC APPLIANCE SERVICE ENGINEER

Domestic appliance service engineers service and repair all kinds of household goods including washing machines, fridges, televisions, DVD players – in fact all kinds of electrical and gas appliances. Service engineers work for retailers, for manufacturers, for servicing companies and some are self-employed. As well as replacing worn or damaged parts in appliances, they may offer routine servicing, checking that everything is running smoothly and removing dust, limescale or other debris from appliances. They also advise customers on the best way to care for their appliances.

## Qualifications and Training

While no formal qualifications are necessary, in practice most organisations will expect you to have qualifications and background experience in at least two of the following areas: electrics, electronics, gas fitting, mechanics, plumbing and refrigeration. There are several relevant Edexcel BTEC and City & Guilds courses at levels 2 and 3. Look for courses with units in consumer goods or specialist options on TV, DVD and PC repair and maintenance. People aged 16 to 24 who are interested in this work could consider an apprenticeship in electrics, gas fitting or plumbing. Training is usually provided by the employer and consists of new trainees assisting and learning from a more experienced engineer until they are able to take on more complex jobs or work on their own.

## Personal Qualities and Skills

As well as good practical skills and knowledge of a wide range of appliances, you must have good problem-solving ability and you must be good at dealing with people. You must be polite and friendly to customers, good at explaining problems, and able to listen to their concerns.

## Salaries

Salaries start at between £12,000 and £16,000. With a few years' experience this rises to £16,000 to £22,000. Anyone with highly specialised skills, such as gas servicing, may earn £25,000 or more.

SEMTA, 14 Upton Road, Watford, Hertfordshire WD18 0JT; 0808 100 3682; www.semta.org.uk

Domestic Appliance Service Association, 69 The Maltings, Stanstead Abbotts, Hertfordshire SG12 8HG; www.dasa.org.uk

Gas Safe Register, PO Box 6804, Basingstoke, Hants RG24 4NB; 0800 4085 500; www.gassaferegister.co.uk

info

# DOMESTIC SERVICE

*see also* Chauffeur/chauffeuse, Chef/cook, Childminder, Gardener

Domestic service is not one career. It covers a whole range of jobs which you might carry out in someone else's home to help with the running of the house, cleaning, cooking, gardening, childcare, etc. This work has several links with other careers such as chef, nanny, au pair or gardener. It may involve driving as a chauffeur/chauffeuse, working as a bodyguard or working as a personal assistant, proving secretarial as well as other support. Some positions may simply involve being a 'live-in' companion to someone.

Some domestic service jobs could include such roles as butler, housekeeper, maid, valet, footman, etc, which are not part of most people's everyday lives. These people work in palaces, grand houses and private estates, corporate headquarters, and the homes of the very rich and the famous or infamous.

At the other end of the scale, domestic work could include going round to someone else's house to do a few hours' cleaning, ironing or cooking each week.

## Qualifications and Training

Encompassing such a variety of jobs, there is no one typical entry route or set of requirements that covers all these roles. Very often, you will be expected to have those qualifications which are relevant for your particular responsibilities, eg catering qualifications if you work as a chef, secretarial qualifications if you work as a PA. For some jobs such as maid/PA a hairdressing or beauty therapy qualification could also be an advantage. Many positions will require you to have a good general standard of education with four or five GCSEs at grades A–C. Some specialist recruitment agencies (mostly in London) can offer training courses. Many jobs at what might be thought of as the glamorous end of the market tend to be filled through personal recommendation.

## Personal Qualities and Skills

While these vary very much according to what you are doing, there are some things which apply to almost all jobs in domestic service. You must be trustworthy and honest, and have a mature attitude. You should be extremely discreet and tactful. You should be able to work as part of a team and be able to remain calm in busy or stressful situations. You should have good communication skills and you should present a smart, clean and tidy appearance.

## Salaries

Salaries vary enormously – some work would be paid at minimum wages, or just a little above this level. In other instances, your job may include accommodation, meals, clothing and travel allowances and other benefits.

**info**

If you are looking for work in large houses, private estates, etc, then appropriate recruitment agencies are your best starting points. For local jobs, cleaning or ironing, you will find adverts in local shops and the local press. Jobcentre Plus and Connexions/careers offices may also be able to advise you.

# DRESSER

*see* Broadcasting

# DRESSMAKER

*see* Fashion

# DRIVING

Although many jobs require the ability to drive a vehicle, the occupations in this section refer to those which require professional driving skills.

## Chauffeur/chauffeuse

Chauffeurs are skilled car drivers who are employed either by one person or by companies or organisations where senior personnel need personal transport on hand at all times. Private chauffeurs may live in accommodation provided and have various other duties. Apart from the actual driving, the job will also involve making sure the cars are well maintained and clean. Some chauffeurs have a security role and may also act as bodyguards.

### Qualifications and Training

No formal academic qualifications are required, but you must have several years' driving experience and a full, clean UK driving licence. Some employers like you to have an Advanced Driving Certificate from the Institute of Advanced Motorists. For some posts you will need a foreign language and perhaps other skills such as car maintenance or gardening, if your time spent actually chauffeuring is likely to be fairly limited. Many chauffeurs have worked as taxi drivers or have been in the police force or armed services.

### Personal Qualities and Skills

You must have excellent driving skills, and be careful, confident and sensible. You need to be polite, smart and tactful and able to respect people's privacy and use your discretion. You must be flexible, calm and reasonably physically fit.

### Salaries

Starting salaries are between £12,500 and £17,000. With experience these rise to around £25,000. Some posts bring other benefits such as accommodation or a lot of foreign travel.

**info**

Institute of Advanced Motorists, IAM House, 510 Chiswick High Road, London W4 5RG; 020 8996 9600; www.iam.org.uk

GoSkills, Concorde House, Trinity Park, Solihull, Birmingham

B37 7UQ; 0121 635 5520; www.goskills.org

British Chauffeurs Guild Ltd, 13 Stonecot Hill, Sutton, Surrey SM3 9HB; 020 8544 9777; www.britishchauffeursguild.co.uk

# Courier

Couriers deliver and collect parcels, generally in larger towns and cities. Around 10,000 couriers work in Central London. Mostly the delivery or collection is in the same city, sometimes in a different one and very occasionally in another country. Most couriers use a motorbike, which they may be required to buy. Couriers carrying packages abroad travel by air.

In large and congested cities, there is an increasing trend for couriers to travel by pushbike, and some couriers use small vans.

## Qualifications and Training

Couriers don't need formal qualifications, but good literacy skills are important. You must be aged 17 or over and have a driving licence appropriate to the vehicle you are to drive, eg motorcycle, car or van. A basic knowledge of motor vehicle maintenance can be valuable and motorcycle couriers usually have to provide their own vehicle, plus its road tax and insurance. Once you are employed you can work towards NVQs levels 2 and 3 in Carry and Deliver Goods. Units include road safety and customer care.

## Personal Qualities and Skills

Good, safe driving skills and an ability to deal with people are both important. You are often under a great deal of pressure to be quick, so you must be able to cope with this and not compromise safety. Sometimes knowledge of foreign languages can be useful.

## Salaries

Couriers start on between £11,500 and £13,500 a year and with experience they can earn £15,000 to £20,000. Motorcycle couriers in London can earn £24,000. Remember that out of these earnings, you may have to pay for fuel, insurance and the maintenance of your vehicle. Many couriers are self-employed. Some employers pay bonuses for good attendance, reliability and punctuality. Remember that most work is likely to be in large cities.

**info**

Skills for Logistics, 14 Warren Yard, Warren Farm Office Village, Stratford Road, Milton Keynes MK12 5NW; 0870 242 7314; www.skillsforlogistics.org

# Driving examiner

Driving examiners must ensure that candidates are competent to drive without endangering other road users and demonstrate due consideration for other drivers and pedestrians. The examiner directs learner drivers over an approved route and asks them to carry out various exercises. While doing this, the examiner must take notes without distracting the candidate's concentration and must make a fair assessment of the learner's ability.

## Qualifications and Training

Driving examiners are required to complete a strict selection process, followed by four weeks' training. They must have detailed knowledge of the Highway Code and road and traffic safety problems, some mechanical understanding, have held positions of responsibility and dealt with the public. Driving examiners must be over 25 and have had extensive experience of a variety of different vehicle types. Vacancies are advertised both locally and nationally by the Driving Standards Agency. Selection is dependent upon passing a special driving test and interview. For those who are successful, there are continuous checks by a supervising examiner to ensure the maintenance of a high standard.

## Personal Qualities and Skills

Examiners should be fair, sympathetic, friendly, clearly spoken and have a calm, unflappable nature. The ability to work to a strict timetable is important.

## Salaries

Varies depending on hours worked. Examiners generally have annualised hours contracts and minimum working hours are guaranteed on entry into employment.

Private Hire, Hackney Carriage and Chauffeur Industry Training Organisation, 14 Widdrington Terrace, North Shields NE29 0BZ; 0191 258 1955

GoSkills, Concorde House, Trinity Park, Solihull, Birmingham B37 7UQ, 0121 635 5520; www.goskills.org

info

# Driving instructor

Driving instructors teach clients how to drive in preparation for all categories of the Driving Standards Agency's theory and practical driving tests. Instructors can also provide post-test training for the Pass Plus scheme as well as prepare clients for advanced driving tests, such as the DIAmond Advanced Motorists test.

The industry is now very much structured to self-employment, with instructors either having their own business or existing as an independent operation within a franchise agreement.

## Qualifications and Training

All driving instructors must be registered with the Driving Standards Agency (DSA). To register to train you must have held a full UK/EU driving licence for four years and you must not have been disqualified from driving at any time in the last four years. You will have to pass criminal record checks and a series of tests. You can get a starter pack containing all the information you need from the DSA and they also provide information on approved training courses. Driving schools and other specialist training schools run the training courses and the length and cost of training varies.

You take your theory test first and you can attempt this as many times as you like. Once you have passed this, you have to pass a special driving test and a test of your ability to teach. You must do all three tests within a two-year period. When you have passed you can join the Driving Instructors' Association (DIA) register of approved instructors. The DIA offer the chance for continuing professional development and advanced training and you can take an NVQ level 3 in Driving Instruction.

## Personal Qualities and Skills

As well as excellent, safe driving skills you need an ability to work really well with your students. People learning to drive may be nervous, anxious and lacking in confidence, or alternatively they may be careless and over-confident. You have to be able to work flexible hours and if you become self-employed you have to have good organisational and business skills.

## Salaries

When you first qualify you will probably earn between £15,000 and £16,000 in your first year. With experience £23,000 to £25,000 is more likely. Good, experienced instructors who have built up a reputation could earn £30,000 plus.

info

Driving Instructors' Association (DIA), Safety House, Beddington Farm Road, Croydon CR0 4XZ; 020 8665 5151; www.driving.org

Driving Standards Agency (DSA) – ADI Branch, Stanley House, 56 Talbot Street, Nottingham NG1 5GU; 0115 901 2618; Starter Pack Orders: 0870 121 4202; www.dsa.gov.uk

GoSkills, Concorde House, Trinity Park, Solihull B37 7UQ; 0121 635 5520; www.goskills.org

# Heavy goods vehicle driver

This work ranges from driving conventional flat-bodied lorries that can carry a variety of loads to driving lorries designed for one purpose, such as car and animal transporters and milk tankers. Drivers often take a load from A to B and then carry one back from B to A in the UK or across Europe. As well as driving, lorry drivers may have to help with the loading and unloading of goods. Drivers of potentially dangerous products must know how to handle them safely and certification is required.

## Qualifications and Training

There are no formal academic entry requirements for driving work, but you must be able to read maps, handle documents and deal with people, as well as enjoy driving and already have a normal full, clean, driving licence. To drive vehicles of 7.5 tonnes you need a class C licence and you cannot normally apply for this until you are aged 21. To drive an articulated vehicle you need a C + E licence, which you cannot normally obtain until you are 25. Skills for Logistics, the Sector Skills Council for the Freight and Logistics Industry, has developed a range of specific qualifications. You can take NVQ level 2 in Carrying and Delivering Goods and in Goods Vehicle Driving. These NVQs are employment based, with some college or off-site training. You can also serve apprenticeships in goods vehicle driving. The Young Drivers Scheme (YDS), operated by Skills for Logistics, allows you to obtain a full C class driving licence at age 18 and a C + E licence at age 21.

For older entrants it is difficult to get your training funded by an employer, so you may have to consider paying for this yourself; it costs more than £2,000.

## Personal Qualities and Skills

You must be a good driver with a thorough understanding of road safety, and the patience to tolerate long drives and heavy traffic. You must be happy spending many hours on your own, but also be able to work with warehouse employees and customers and remain pleasant and friendly.

## Salaries

When you qualify you are likely to earn between £16,000 and £18,000 in your first year. With experience, £24,000 to £26,000 is more likely. Good, experienced instructors who have built up a reputation could earn £30,000 plus.

**info**

Skills for Logistics: The Sector Skills Council for Freight and Logistics, 14 Warren Yard, Warren Farm Office Village, Milton Keynes MK12 5NW; 0870 242 7314; www.skillsforlogistics.org

Local Job Centre Plus offices

*The LGV Learner Driver's Guide* (Kogan Page)

*Professional LGV Driver's Handbook* (Kogan Page)

# Passenger transport

*see also* Engineering, Railway Work *and* Logistics

As well as drivers, there are many other jobs involved in passenger transport, including customer services, engineering and maintenance, information technology, logistics and marketing.

# Bus/coach driver

Bus and coach drivers transport passengers either on local or long journeys. Bus drivers work mainly on shorter routes in particular towns or cities, or between a small number of these. Their work involves taking fares, checking passes, giving information about timetables and assisting passengers who may have difficulties, such as a disability or bulky luggage. Coach drivers tend to take people on longer journeys, say between cities or even countries. They may also take people on tours to see sites of special interest or to view impressive scenery. While their work is similar to that of bus drivers, they may also have to load luggage, give information about the sites or country-side through which they are driving and check that all passengers who should be on board are on the coach. Some bus and coach drivers may also be involved in community transport driving school buses for example.

## Qualifications and Training

Your essential qualification for this work is a Passenger Carrying Vehicle (PCV) licence. To drive a bus or a coach you must be aged 21, or 18 to drive a minibus. Many bus and coach companies will take you on and train you to gain your PCV, so long as you already have a full, clean EU driving licence. You can train independently through a driving school; you need to check with local driving schools whether they offer this training option. A recent EU Directive requires PCV drivers to obtain a Certificate of Professional Competence (CPC). You can get this through periodic short training courses and your employer company should be able to help with this. The Transport Office website carries more details about this. Some employers will give you the opportunity to train to NVQ level 2 in Passenger Transport.

Companies set their own entry standards, but many will expect you to have three or four GCSEs and you will have to meet their medical requirements.

## Personal Qualities and Skills

Safety awareness is paramount. It is the responsibility of any driver to be ever conscious of the safety of his or her passengers. You need to be calm and patient in congested traffic, and with difficult passengers. Your people skills are very important; you need to be polite, helpful and good at giving informa-tion. You may also need to be firm and assertive in some situations.

## Salaries

New drivers earn between £12,000 and £14,000 – with experience drivers earn up to £19,000. Some coach drivers may also earn additional money in tips.

| | |
|---|---|
| GoSkills, Concorde House, Trinity Park, Solihull, Birmingham B37 7UQ; 0121 635 5520; www.goskills.org | Transport Office; www. transportoffice.gov.uk |

**info**

# Taxi driver

A 'taxi' is a traditional hackney carriage (like the black London taxis). The hackney carriage driver is allowed to 'ply for hire' – drive around the streets looking for passengers – and can be flagged down by a 'fare' (passenger). They may also operate from taxi ranks (known as 'standing for hire') in the streets. A private hire vehicle, on the other hand, has to be booked over the telephone or in person at the office from which it operates. Drivers therefore spend a good proportion of their time waiting around for passengers. Hours for both types of driver are generally long and unsocial (since there is a good deal of evening or night work, as well as weekend and public holiday work). Drivers may be owner-drivers or work for a company.

## Qualifications and Training

Taxi drivers must be at least 21 years of age to be granted a licence, although in practice, because of insurance requirements, most are over 25. A valid Group A driving licence and relevant driving experience are also necessary. Hackney carriage drivers are legally bound to take the shortest or quickest route to a passenger's destination. Trainee drivers usually have to pass special tests, known as 'knowledge tests', to prove that they know their way about sufficiently well. These tests are generally oral, the most demanding being the Knowledge of London Test, which is required before drivers may operate in the capital. This usually takes some 18 months to two years to complete. Specialised training schools exist and there are also special training schemes for the disabled and for people who have been in the forces. In London, too, an additional driving test must be passed before a licence is granted.

## Personal Qualities and Skills

Driving in traffic demands a calm, unflappable personality, with lots of patience. Drivers also need to have a good memory. In addition, a taxi driver must be 'of good character', as a licence will not be granted to anyone who has committed certain offences.

## Salaries

Almost all taxi drivers are self-employed and have to pay tax and National Insurance out of their earnings. Owner-drivers generally earn more than drivers employed by a company (who are often on a fixed rate), although they must also finance the repairs and servicing costs incurred by their own vehicles. Average earnings are around £14,000.

**info**

GoSkills, Concorde House, Trinity Park, Solihull, Birmingham B37 7UQ; 0121 635 5520; www.goskills.org

National Private Hire Association, 8 Silver Street, Bury, Lancashire BL9 0EX; 0161 280 2800; www.phtm.co.uk

Transport Office; www.transportoffice.gov.uk

# E

## ECONOMIST

Economists are employed by central and local government, by regional development bodies, higher education institutions, banks, insurance companies, trade unions and international organisations. They apply economic theory and knowledge and give advice on a whole range of topics related to the economy and finance. They study statistical data and trends to try to interpret and predict how the economy will perform. Their work may cover interest rates, taxation, employment policies, trends in consumer behaviour, what we buy and what we spend. Economists devise methods for sampling data, determine how to analyse data and how to translate them into information that can be used to inform policy decisions, solve problems or plan strategies.

### Qualifications and Training

Economics is a graduate profession. You need either a degree in economics or in economics in combination with business, finance or law. In these cases the majority of your modules should still be in economics, and must cover micro and macro economics. You need a 2.1 or better and many employers look for high A level grades too. If you have a degree in another subject you may get into economics, but only by completing a postgraduate course in economics. Competition for posts is fierce and you can improve your chances by joining your student industrial society or something similar, to demonstrate your interest in business and economics. The Civil Service runs an annual recruitment scheme for graduate economists. Most training is on the job, where you might be sent on several short courses as well as being supervised and guided by senior staff.

### Personal Qualities and Skills

Economists need excellent written and spoken communication skills, and to be good at translating technical and mathematical concepts into everyday language. They need good research skills, and be able to analyse and interpret a wide variety of data. They need good judgement and must be able to work with great accuracy. They have to be able to work under pressure and manage their own workloads effectively. IT skills are also important.

## Salaries

New entrants to the profession earn between £27,000 and £35,000. After three to five years' experience salaries rise to between £40,000 and £50,000. Many salary packages include other benefits such as private health insurance.

Government Economic Service (GES), HM Treasury, 1 Horse Guards Road, London SW1A 2HQ; 020 7270 4835; www.ges.gov.uk/

Royal Statistical Society (RSS), 12 Errol Street, London EC1Y 8LX; 020 7638 8998; www.rss.org.uk

Society of Business Economists, Dean House, Vernham Dean, Andover, Hants SP11 0JZ; 01264 737552; www.sbe.co.uk

# ELECTRICIAN

Electricians work in domestic houses, factories and commercial buildings and on road systems, railways and vehicles. They install, service and repair every kind of electrical system, from wiring to individual pieces of equipment.

## Auto electrician

*see* Motor Industry

## Highway electrician

These electricians install, maintain and replace the electrical and electronic systems that operate street lighting and road traffic management systems. They work from high, mobile platforms.

## Installation electrician

Installation electricians install, inspect and test wiring systems in every kind of building. They either strip out old wiring systems and replace them, or work with other members of the construction team on new buildings, installing new wiring systems.

## Instrumentation electrician

Instrumentation electricians work mainly in the manufacturing industry, installing and maintaining the electrical and electronic systems that run the manufacturing process, whether this is a conveyor belt to fill bottles of drink, build cars, or pack frozen vegetables. They are involved in measuring how efficiently electrical and electronic operations are working.

## Maintenance electrician

Maintenance electricians work mainly in manufacturing, maintaining and testing electrical and electronic equipment.

## Panel building electrician

Panel building electricians work from diagrams, putting together complex electrical and electronic control panels. An office building could have a central panel that controls heating and air conditioning, and this is an example of the kind of panel that these electricians build.

## Repair and rewind electrician

When components in pumps, compressors or transformers go wrong, repair and rewind electricians analyse what the problem is and either repair or replace various components. They work both in industry and in domestic properties, repairing goods such as washing machines and fridges.

## Service electrician

The dividing line between repair and servicing is not always distinct. Service engineers check equipment and make minor adjustments, to minimise the risk of things going wrong. These electricians also work in industry and private homes.

## Theatre electrician

Away from the world of manufacturing or faulty TV sets, theatre electricians maintain and repair all the systems that operate lighting, sound and other specialist theatrical equipment. They need to be extremely good all-rounders.

### Qualifications and Training

To qualify as an electrician you must achieve an electrotechnical NVQ level 3. There are various routes to achieving this, but the most common, provided you are between the ages of 16 and 24, is to do a three- to four-year apprenticeship. These are mainly employer-based, but include some college work and practical and written assessments. Though it is not always essential, many employers require you to have GCSEs grades A–C in English, maths, technology and a science subject. If you are not eligible for an apprenticeship you can do college-based City & Guilds courses at GNVQ levels 2 and 3.

Electrotechnical NVQ level 3 offers several different pathways, including electrical installation, electrical maintenance, electrical instrumentation and

Friday : 3.49pm : 39°46.0'N 86°9.4'W

# Making it faster

At Rolls-Royce, you can look forward to achieving your ambitions sooner rather than later. Because, around here, we don't believe in standing still. As the world's leading provider of power systems for use on land, at sea and in the air, we are perpetually in motion – constantly thinking, dreaming, planning, exploring and innovating.

Building on a century's worth of forward momentum to deliver excellence – everywhere, every day, and for everyone. Don't stop moving. Find out more about our graduate programmes and apply by visiting www.rolls-royce.com/careers

**Trusted to deliver excellence**

Engineering, Commercial, Customer Management, Finance, HR, Manufacturing Leadership, Project Management, Purchasing, Supply Chain

www.rolls-royce.com/careers

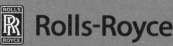

# Graduate Training at Rolls-Royce

When you join the graduate training programme at Rolls-Royce, you have access to all the training, guidance and support you need to develop valuable skills and establish yourself in your chosen career. You'll also work with some of the world's leading engineers, helping to develop technological solutions to help power the world around us.

To find out more, come to our open day or visit
**www.rolls-royce.com/careers/graduate_progs/**

## 'The graduate programme is number one of its type.'

Unlike many of his fellow graduates, Andrew Powell's degree isn't in engineering, it's in chemistry. But at Rolls-Royce, this hasn't hindered his progress – far from it. The company are keen to recruit from a wide range of disciplines, and Andrew's knowledge and skills have already been put to good use.

'The Rolls-Royce graduate programme has been voted the most popular training scheme in the engineering, design and manufacturing sectors, and it's not difficult to see why,' he says. 'The programme is extremely varied and challenging, and offers a great combination of training and experience. All new recruits enjoy between four to six three month placements. I chose to apply to the recently formed Civil Nuclear business unit as I believe that nuclear power will play a key role in the future provision of low carbon energy in a diversifying national portfolio.

'Other graduates are working within the four other sectors: Civil and Defence Aerospace, Marine, and Energy and we've all been involved in important projects. For me, it's exciting to realise that my work will play a part in Rolls-Royce's plans for the growing domestic market for nuclear power.

'I'm based in Derby, and have been fortunate to work with some incredibly skilled and innovative engineers. I'm not sure yet where my long term future in the company lies, but that's one of the real strengths of the graduate scheme, there are so many opportunities. I could decide to move into project management or I may choose to focus on a more specialist engineering role. But whatever direction I take, I'm proud to be able to say that I'm working with one of the world's leading companies, and a firm that's dedicated to finding solutions to complex engineering challenges within power systems.'

advertisement feature

associated equipment, installing highway electrical systems, electrical panel building and electrical machine rewind and repair. A great deal of training takes place on the job.

Recent changes to the Building Regulations have meant that many types of household electrical work must be approved either by a buildings inspector or by an electrician who has acquired an appropriate certificate. Electricians can take part in a short scheme to allow them to self-certify their work.

## Personal Qualities and Skills

You must have good practical and technical skills and be able to follow technical drawings and diagrams. You should be reasonably fit, and for some jobs you need to be able to cope with heights or working in confined spaces. You should have good colour vision. You need to be able to work on your own, or as part of a team, and you must have good communication skills, and be able to talk to people without using a lot of technical jargon.

## Salaries

At the start of an apprenticeship you will earn around £12,500 rising to £18,000 at the end of your training. Newly qualified electricians earn around £19,000 to £24,000, but experienced electricians can earn much more than this. Many electricians are self-employed, which means earnings are related to how much work they can get, and what they charge.

**info**

Engineering Council UK (ECUK), 246 High Holborn, London WC1V 7EX; 020 3206 0500; www.engc.org.uk

SEMTA, 14 Upton Road, Watford, Hertfordshire WD18 0JT; 01923 238 441; www.semta.orf.uk

Women into Science Engineering and Construction, 2nd Floor, Weston House, 246 High Holborn, London WC1B 7EX; 020 3206 0408; www.wisecampaign.org.uk

www.apprenticeships.org.uk

# ENGINEERING

The British engineering industry is a major wealth producer, and almost every other industry depends upon engineering in some way. Engineering provides a challenging career for men and women, with employment offered by industry, universities and colleges, consulting engineers, contractors, local authorities and the armed forces. The Engineering Council gives a simple definition of engineering, saying that it involves 'the application of science and maths to the solving of practical problems and the making of useful things'. The variety of specialisations are covered by over 20 professional institutions. A selection is described below.

# Aerospace engineering

Aerospace engineering is one of the most technically advanced areas of engineering. It is both exciting and rewarding, involving leading-edge technology, variety, skill and innovation. This diversity means that career opportunities can be found across the entire global aerospace spectrum, from research, design, manufacture and maintenance, through to operation and support. However, the dramatic downturn in the aerospace industry in 2001 significantly reduced opportunities, and it may be some time before the good employment prospects once offered by the industry return.

# Agricultural engineering

The main areas in which agricultural engineers are involved are: design and production of agricultural machinery; planning, design and construction of farm buildings and associated equipment; field engineering – irrigation, drainage and land resource planning; and service engineering, involving the sale, servicing, repairing and installation of farm machinery. They are also involved in forestry engineering, amenity and ecological engineering, and precision farming using satellite positioning systems.

# Automotive engineering

In the vehicle manufacturing industry engineers may be employed in design, development, production, operations management and maintenance activities. In motor vehicle servicing, the work tends to be at craft level, with some engineers using their technical base to develop into motor vehicle engineering management. Currently, NVQs in Vehicle Mechanical and Electronic Systems Maintenance and Repair are offered at levels 2 and 3.

# Biochemical engineering

This involves the application of engineering principles to industrial processing. Biochemical engineers are involved in the research, design, construction and operation of plant used for the processing of biochemicals such as those used in effluent treatment, fermentation and the production of drugs.

# Biomedical engineering

Biomedical engineers, also referred to as clinical engineers or bioengineers, work on the research, design, development and maintenance of technology and equipment used to meet patients' clinical needs both during and after medical treatment. They work in the fields of instrumentation, rehabilitation and biomaterials. They build and test prototypes, run clinical trials and evaluate the performance of equipment and materials. Examples of their work include new heart valves, replacement joints and new types of hearing device.

## Building services engineering

(*see also* Construction)

Building services engineers are concerned with heating and ventilation, refrigeration, lighting, air conditioning, electrical services, internal water supply, waste disposal, fire protection, lifts, and acoustic and communication systems. The work involves the planning and design of engineering systems, and supervision of contracts, working in collaboration with architects, surveyors, structural engineers and builders.

## Chemical engineering

Chemical engineers are concerned with large-scale processes, not always in the chemical industry. The term 'process engineering' is often used to describe their work, as they are more interested in the physical factors involved in a process than in the chemical reaction itself. Chemical engineers are employed in the oil, chemical, pharmaceutical, food, brewing and process industries.

## Civil engineering

Civil engineering plays an important part in everyday life. Civil engineers devise, plan and manage development in vital areas – the design and construction of state-of-the-art roads, dams, harbours, railroad systems, bridges and airports. Civil engineers also play an important part in the provision of electricity and water supplies, and in managing traffic and transport. Every project is unique and involves the expertise of a team of people who plan, design, build and maintain these essential assets.

## Communications engineering

Communications engineers work for large telecommunications organisations, government departments and small companies specialising in communications technology. They are responsible for overseeing the developing, installation and day-to-day management of communications projects of many kinds. Their work involves discussing project briefs, sourcing appropriate materials and products, conducting site surveys, managing staff and finding solutions to technical problems. Communications engineers are usually graduates in a telecommunications engineering, physics or computer science-based degree.

# The Royal Academy of Engineering
## Best Programme

# Engineering your Career

During university, if you are studying Engineering, the Royal Academy of Engineering is here to help you.

The Engineering Leadership Scheme has two awards to help undergraduate engineering students. The Standard Award enables you to take short courses to enhance your engineering knowledge and personal skills, and the Advanced Award enables you to enhance your studies and personal development throughout your degree after the first year

After university, the Executive Engineers Programme exists to support top graduates wanting to fast-track to Chartered status and the Sainsbury Management Fellowship Scheme funds MBAs for qualified engineers wanting to go into the business world, with a similar scheme running for life scientists.

The Academy also has a funding programme for full and part-time engineering Masters students and for postgraduates wanting to attend foreign conferences, the International Travel Grants Scheme could help with expenses.

For information about all the Academy's schemes, visit:
**www.raeng.org.uk**

## The Royal Academy of Engineering

# Recession-busting – a job for engineers

Engineering innovation is the key both to lifting the country out of recession and to solving the toughest challenges facing the world – tackling climate change, developing clean renewable energy to power the world, eradicating poverty through sustainable development and creating new technologies to fight disease. Engineering will play a central role in tackling these global challenges and creating a thriving low-carbon, hi-tech economy.

The UK is the world's sixth biggest manufacturer and a leader in fields such as small satellites, biological sciences, and structural design. However, there are also exciting prospects for developing new forms of renewable energy and upgrading the country's infrastructure to cope the predicted effects of climate change. Large-scale projects like managing distributed electricity general through a 'smart grid', energy storage schemes and a charging network for electric vehicles offer endless possibilities for innovative engineering. The race is already on to offer new engineering services and low-carbon solutions on a world scale.

There are many other avenues for ambitious engineers in managing rivers. The proposed London Tideway Tunnels will be an enormous challenge, but essential to reduce the level of untreated sewage overflowing from London's Victorian sewers into the Thames. The recent disastrous floods in Cumbria showed the need for managing waterways, inspecting and redesigning bridges to cope with the increased incidence of extreme rainfall predicted for the UK. Larger storm drains, porous pavements and measures to divert and store flood water until it can be safely released into rivers may all be needed in the future.

## A diverse engineering workforce

Inspiring people to become engineers and maximising their potential is vital to renewing the health of the UK economy. If the UK is to remain competitive we must use the full talents of potential engineers from all backgrounds. Diverse teams produce better results in engineering, where different experiences and ways of thinking often lead to innovative outcomes. The business benefits of diversity are well established and, with an engineering skills shortage facing the UK, it is more important than ever to attract engineers from diverse backgrounds.

advertisement feature

Women now form over 45 per cent of the UK labour market but only 13 per cent of engineering undergraduates are women. However, more women and people from under represented groups are now entering the profession as engineering companies realise the numerous benefits of improving equality and diversity in terms of retaining intellectual capital, for example by offering career breaks and flexible working options to all employees, regardless of gender.

The Royal Academy of Engineering is keen to promote diversity in all its schemes, working in close collaboration with the UK Resource Centre for Women in SET, the Athena Forum and the WISE (Women in Science, Engineering and Construction) Campaign. We are widening access to the engineering profession for women, ethic minorities and late entrants through the London Engineering Project, which is now being rolled out across the country through the National Engineering Programme.

### Engineering in the field

**Name:** Tabindah Akhtar
**Occupation:** Senior Engineer, London Tideways Tunnel
**Employer:** Halcrow Group Ltd

Tabindah graduated with a degree in Environmental Engineering from The University of Southampton. She has been with the Halcrow Group since 2002 working on a number of large scale projects that have involved managing multi-disciplinary teams, contract management and the procurement of architects.

She is currently working on the complex London Tideway Tunnels project, a Thames Water scheme which will intercept up to 34 combined sewer overflows to substantially reduce discharge into the River Thames and provide a cleaner river Thames.

*Comment:*

"The highlights in my career have been working as project manager on the £20 million Three Mills Lock & Water Control Structures, the British Waterways scheme to restore navigation to the Bow Back Rivers in East London, which also creates the waterway network for London 2012 and its legacy. Most recently, I was lucky enough to work as Halcrow project manager on the Thames Barrier Gates – a project with a 100 year life where Halcrow are working for the Environment Agency to extend the design life of the gates out to 2100, reducing the risk of flooding to the nation's capital.

advertisement feature

192

"Throughout my career, I have received a great deal of encouragement and support from my peers, and I am constantly learning from the many talented engineers with whom I work. Although a career in civil engineering may not traditionally have the same financial incentives as other professions, for me, the satisfaction of working on projects that make a major contribution to society far outweigh any financial reward."

**Name:**       John Armstrong

**Occupation:**  Engineering Manager, Enfield Power Station

**Employer:**    E.ON UK Ltd

With a career in engineering firmly in mind, John enrolled at The University of Birmingham on a four-year Masters degree course in mechanical engineering with business that included a final year project on combustion engine optimization. He spent his third year at the University of Melbourne, Australia, and went on to gain a first class degree.

John joined E.ON in 2005 as a member of the Asset Engineering team, primarily supporting two combined heat and power stations in the North of England. His current role as Engineering Manager at Enfield Power Station involves responsibility for all maintenance and engineering aspects of a 408MW Combined Cycle Gas Turbine power station and associated 14km high pressure gas pipeline.

*Comment:*

"A career in engineering has given me an opportunity to travel widely and work with lots of great people. Engineering has given me the opportunity to take great pride in the exciting projects and places I have been part of and to take on more responsibility and challenge as my career has progressed."

**Name:**       Sharan Gill

**Occupation:**  Engineer – Structures

**Employer:**    Transport for London

Sharan chose science-based GCSEs and A-Levels then went to University to do an Engineering Science degree. Following that she received a place on the TfL Civil Engineering Graduate Scheme which allowed her the opportunity to do short placements around the company. She is currently working towards chartership with the Institution of Civil Engineers.

advertisement feature

Sharan works in the Highway Structures Team, with responsibility for maintaining structures (bridges, subways, retaining walls, culverts) that support the Red Routes in London.

*Comment:*

"A career in engineering is not all about design and calculations. Common sense and communication are big parts of the job too; being able to explain not just what, but also why we are doing the things we do is very useful. It's also the knowledge that the work I do really helps people who work, live and travel in London, even though most people have no idea of all the work going on behind the scenes."

**Name:**       Carolyn Lawlor

**Occupation:**  Customer Service Engineer

**Employer:**   Openreach (BT)

At the age of 39, Carolyn was a late-comer to the world of engineering. The BT call centre she had worked at part-time for ten years was closing, but she was offered a transfer into engineering. She trained on the job with the benefit of several courses and was the only female telephone engineer on a team of 20, but earned respect and proved herself equal to the job.

*Comment:*

"Retraining was a difficult decision that affected the whole family – my children were aged 15, 13 and 3 years at the time. The job meant several weeks away training, and working full-time, but it was without doubt the best decision I could ever have made, and one I am very proud of. The world of telecommunications is ever-changing, so there is always something new to learn and experience. Every day is different and challenging, and there is no opportunity to be bored!

"Being a telecommunications engineer is a great job for a nosey person! I have worked in so many different places, from convents to country houses - I've provided lifelines for the elderly and tagging lines for law breakers. There is real job satisfaction in knowing that you have reconnected someone with the outside world, whether they are a vulnerable person, or a business."

## Control engineering

This is a multidisciplinary field involving electrical and electronic engineering, maths, computer science, instrument engineering and mechanical engineering. Specialisation in control engineering often follows the study of another branch of engineering.

## Electrical and electronic engineering

The technology of electrical engineering deals with heavy current, while electronic engineering deals with light current. Applications of heavy current include electrical machinery of all kinds, generating stations and distribution systems. Light current is used for such products as transistors, microprocessors and telecommunications equipment. The two fields are often interdependent and training is closely related. Electronics is a rapidly developing field and offers excellent opportunities, as do the allied disciplines of computer and software engineering.

## Energy engineering

This branch of engineering is concerned with the use, production, distribution, conversion and conservation of energy, with due regard to the environment. Energy engineers are employed across the whole spectrum of industry, as energy management and control are essential elements in containing costs, reducing pollution and addressing environmental concerns. The majority of openings are in major fuel industries (including renewables), consultancy and research.

## Environmental engineering

Environmental engineering is a developing and increasingly important profession. Environmental engineers work for local authorities and private companies large and small. Their work is concerned with assessing the impact of human activity on the environment. The three main areas in which they work are waste management, land reclamation and pollution control. Their work involves visiting many different kinds of site, liaising with surveyors, engineers, scientists and other organisations. They may use computer models to simulate the environmental impact of particular activities.

## Fire engineering

This involves the application of engineering principles to the assessment, prevention and inhibition of fire risk within buildings, manufacturing plant and industrial processes. The various stages include the use of mathematical principles in the assessment of fire risk, the application of scientific principles to fire safety practices and the use of management techniques for the inhibition and prevention of the onset and spread of fire.

Fire engineers are employed in the fire services, architectural and building design, project management, insurance assessment, industrial processing, the aircraft industry, environmental health and any area of safety where the possibility of fire or combustion represents a hazard.

# Gas engineering

Gas engineering involves specialisation in the use, transmission and distribution of gas (natural or manufactured), or in the production of gas, or in related fields such as exploration.

# Geotechnical engineering

Geotechnical engineers often have a background in civil engineering or geological science. Applying the science of rock and earth mechanics, they work out how the ground will behave if tunnels are bored into it or buildings and other structures built into and onto it. They also work on civil engineering and construction projects to help ensure that the environment of the ground around the project is preserved. They can tell where flooding or erosion, for example, might cause problems.

# Instrument engineering

(*see also* Control engineering)

Instrument engineers are concerned with the measurement of pressure, temperature, and so on, designing, installing and maintaining instrument systems.

# Manufacturing systems engineering

This branch of engineering deals with the skills required to operate new manufacturing systems: computerised production, computer-controlled assembly, robotic systems and flexible manufacturing systems.

# Marine engineering

This discipline is related to offshore engineering under the general title of 'maritime engineering', which involves engineering systems and equipment in a maritime environment. Both marine and offshore engineers are involved in design, research, consultancy, survey, manufacture, installation and maintenance activities, the former with vessels of all sizes and types, the

AMEC has aligned itself, and formed strong relationships with, the appropriate Institutions associated within the field of operation of its business. These Institutions include the: ICE; IChemE; IMechE; IET; CIBSE; CIOB; RSC and RICS.

**amec**

As a Graduate Trainee you will be registered on the appropriate Institution's Monitored Development Scheme to enable you to obtain chartered status at the earliest opportunity.

We will pay for your institution fees throughout your employment with us.

Our Graduates must be eligible to work in the UK without a work permit and must be mobile. We have HQ offices at Knutsford and Darlington, with offices at Warrington, Cumbria, Gloucester, Berkshire and Swindon.

Check out our careers by going to www.amec.com and navigating to the careers page.

## Company profile:

AMEC is a focused supplier of high-value consultancy, engineering and project management services to the world's energy, power and process industries. With annual revenues of over £2.6 billion, AMEC designs, delivers and maintains strategic and complex assets for its customers, making AMEC the natural partner for the new energy challenge.

AMEC's Natural Resources, Power & Process and Earth & Environmental businesses employ 22,000 people in more the 40 countries globally.

Our Power & Process Europe business supports all of the key mechanical, nuclear, engineering licensees and the industries regulators. So join our team and you'll enjoy all the variety and high-level technical and business challenges you'd expect from a FTSE 100 company. We can offer you an unrivalled opportunity to make a real difference to our business and that of our clients, right at the forefront of this exciting and expanding industry.

Our credited graduate development schemes offer a fast track to Chartered status and training includes:- Strong mentoring culture; On-the-job training; Technical Lectures; Courses and conferences.

You will be assigned a Mentor for the duration of your development scheme, and beyond and our training will comprise of a combination of on-the-job, formal courses and lectures and following formal graduate training we will continue to support your career development via in-house, external or further education opportunities to help you maintain your professional competence.

latter with offshore platforms, sub-sea installations and under-sea vehicles. Employment opportunities exist within firms offering design and research activities, engine- and shipbuilding firms, classification societies, government bodies, the Merchant Navy and the Royal Navy.

# Materials engineering

Materials engineers work in a diverse range of industries, working on the research and development of new materials to advance technologies; innovating and modifying materials to improve the performance and efficiency of existing products; and investigating the failure of products or structures. They work with all types of materials including plastics, metals, alloys, glass, ceramics and composites. Some of the industries they work in include telecommunications, power generation, sport and medicine. Materials engineers have developed materials used in modern tennis rackets, replacement hip joints and internet broadband connections; these are just a few examples. Most materials engineers have a degree in materials engineering or materials science, or a degree in applied physics or chemistry.

# Mechanical engineering

Mechanical engineering is the biggest branch of the engineering industry. It involves the skills of designing, developing, producing, installing and operating machinery and mechanical products of many types. The field is enormous in scope, and most engineers specialise in a particular area. Other branches of engineering, such as electrical and civil engineering, overlap with mechanical engineering to a certain extent.

Mechanical engineers are employed in almost every sector of industry. Some of the largest areas of employment are machine tools, railway engineering, aerospace and the automobile industry.

# Mining engineering

In Britain, most mining engineers are employed by companies in mining areas, working for consultants who monitor mining activity and subsidence. They need some knowledge of related disciplines such as mechanical, electrical and civil engineering, and to understand geology and surveying in relation to mining. The majority of openings in metal mining are overseas.

# Nuclear engineering

Nuclear engineering involves the applications of nuclear energy and associated research and development. The work of designing and constructing nuclear reactors and the management of nuclear power stations through waste management and storage and decommissioning of plant is carried out by nuclear engineers.

## Offshore engineering

Offshore engineers are concerned with the construction and operation of drilling platforms and wellheads, and other engineering problems related to the exploitation of offshore oil and gas.

## Operations engineering

Operations engineers are concerned with specifying, evaluation, acquisition, commissioning, inspection, maintenance, asset management and disposal of facilities, systems, vehicles and equipment. Career opportunities exist at craft and technician level in the servicing and maintenance of a wide variety of industries, of which transport is the largest. Chartered and incorporated engineers may be engaged in asset or fleet engineering management, requiring multidisciplinary engineering, commercial and legal knowledge and encompassing health and safety, reliability, environmental and economic factors, or in specialised inspection roles. Many technicians build on their practical skills by further career development to aspire to these more senior positions.

## Petroleum engineering

Petroleum engineers are concerned with exploration and drilling for oil. They obtain and interpret information – for example, the quantities and quality of oil discovered.

## Process engineering

Process engineers work in large and small companies manufacturing all kind of products. They develop efficient industrial processes to make the huge range of products on which modern society depends, including: food and drink, fuel, artificial fibres, pharmaceuticals, chemicals, plastics, cosmetics, cleaning products, energy, and clean water. Their role can be similar to that of chemical engineers.

## Production engineering

Production engineers develop and improve manufacturing techniques. They are responsible for designing production systems to ensure that products can be manufactured to the specified design, in the right quantities, at the right price and by the required date. Their work overlaps with production management.

# Recording engineering

*See* Broadcasting.

# Structural engineering

Structural engineers are concerned with the design and maintenance of the framework and fabric of large structures such as bridges, motorways and office blocks.

# Transport engineering

Transportation (or traffic) engineers are concerned with managing the best use of roads and related facilities, and work mainly with road traffic. Transportation planners, who are not necessarily engineers, are concerned with the provision of all types of transport. The current priority is to provide an integrated transport system.

# Water engineering

Water engineers mostly work for water companies and river authorities, ensuring the supply of fresh water, and dealing with the reclamation and disposal of water which has been used.

## Qualifications and Training

Since this section of the guide describes so many different careers, this outline of qualifications and training is a very general guide. Each of the different specific professional engineering bodies and the sector skills councils will be able to provide you with much more detailed information.

An important starting point is to realise that you cannot normally cross over from one area of engineering to another. If you train within agricultural engineering, civil or electrical engineering, for example, the knowledge, skills and experience you develop will relate very particularly to that type of engineering. There may be exceptions, but you really need to consider what type of engineering appeals to you before you start your engineering studies or training.

### Graduate engineers

Most professional engineers are graduates who have completed a degree in just one type of engineering. There are degrees available in all the types of engineering described in the previous paragraphs. For most degrees in technical subjects you will need three A levels, although grade and subject requirements vary between institutions and subjects. Physics, maths, chemistry and other science subjects are often required. Many engineering degree courses offer the option to spend a year out in industry. Once you have completed your degree and are in employment, you are likely to work towards becoming a chartered engineer, working towards professional examinations through the relevant engineering organisation, eg the Institute of Mechanical Engineers.

Professional engineers are likely to have responsibility to research and development, problem solving, managing work teams and projects and bringing creative ideas to the whole engineering process.

## Technician engineers

For many types of engineering, if you do not wish to study for a degree, you may be able to get in at technician level. This usually means you should have five GCSEs grades A–C including English, maths and a science subject. Your employer may give you the opportunity to train to NVQ level 3 in a relevant subject. You can also consider college courses offering City & Guilds or BTEC qualifications. Cogent, SEMTA and Summitskills websites offer plenty of information. You may also be able to train through an Apprenticeship. Check your local Jobcentre Plus and Connexions careers office for details of what is on offer locally.

Every engineering production line, construction site, processing plan or scientific laboratory will also employ a number of staff to handle the day-to-day processes, quality testing, looking after equipment, and doing all the routine work to keep systems running. For these jobs, entry requirements vary greatly, but many will not require formal academic qualifications.

**info**

Institute of Engineering Technology, Savoy Place, London WC2R 0BL; 020 7240 1871; www.theiet.org

Engineering Council, 10 Maltravers Street, London WC2R 3ER; 020 7240 7891; www.engtech.co.uk

Engineering Training Council in Northern Ireland, Interpoint, 20–24 York Street, Belfast BT15 1AQ; 028 9032 9878; www.etcni.org.uk

Automotive Skills, 93 Newman Street, London W1T 3DT; 0800 093 1777; www.automotiveskills.org.uk

Cogent, Minerva House, Bruntland Road, Portlethen, Aberdeen AB12 4QL; 01224 787800; www.cogent-ssc.com

SEMTA, 14 Upton Road, Watford, Hertfordshire WD18 0JT; 0808 100 3682; www.semta.org.uk

Summit Skills, Vega House, Opal Drive, Fox Milne, Milton Keynes MK15 0DF; 01908 303969; www.summitskills.org.uk

UK Standards for Professional Engineering Competence (UK-SPEC); www.uk-spec.org.uk

Women into Science and Engineering, 22 Old Queen Street, London SW1H 9HP; 020 7227 8421; www.wisecampaign.org.uk

The Women's Engineering Society (WES), Michael Faraday House, Six Hills Way, Stevenage, Herts SG1 2AY; 01438 765506; www.wes.org.uk

Auto Industry, DTI Automotive Regional Unit, 5 St Philips Place, Birmingham B3 2PW; 0121 352 5231; www.autoindustry.co.uk

# ww.energyzone.net

e most comprehensive online guide to UK energy education and ning from the Energy Institute.

**About energy**

**Towards a career in energy**

**Advancing your career in energy**

professional development, teachers' resources, ining, careers, students' zone, events, projects, mpetitions, awards, job profiles, fact sheets, ancial support, job search, key employers, mentoring…

*formation for students, teachers, people working the energy sector and those looking to join the ergy industry.*

e Energy Institute is the leading chartered professional mbership body for those working in energy.

ergy Institute, 61 New Cavendish Street, London W1G 7AR,
t: +44 (0)20 7467 7100 f: +44 (0)20 7255 1472
nfo@energyinst.org www.energyinst.org

www.energyzone.net

# Careers in the energy industry

Energy is an extremely diverse field offering many job opportunities in an industry that is constantly evolving. It is a critical factor in the economy and for society as a whole, and the need for energy professionals is increasing as energy issues move to the forefront of the economic and social agendas. To respond to the current challenges, the industry seeks professionals with ideas and ingenuity in addition to personal qualities and the right skills.

### What careers are available in the energy industry?

Energy professionals are found in a wide range of careers, from engineers, environmental scientists and geologists to public servants, consultants and economists.

The main energy sectors cover exploration and production (E&P), distribution and demand-side management. The E&P sector employs engineers, geologists, physicists and even mathematicians in developing new sources of energy, such as wind power, as well as working to improve efficiency in the recovery of existing ones, such as oil. The distribution sector employs engineers, marketers, traders and economists whilst the demand-side employs those who regulate the industry, set energy and environmental policy as well as energy consultants.

### What qualifications are needed?

Energy is a subject that features highly in a range of educational and vocational programmes. It has always formed a large part of the engineering disciplines. Increasingly energy engineering, environmental engineering and sustainable development are emerging as subjects in their own right.

There is no unique path of study to become an energy professional, but the Energy Institute (EI), as the professional body for the energy sector, accredits over 100 courses in energy – many at Masters level which provide a variety of routes into the industry.

Full-time students on energy-related courses can get free membership of the EI which includes a membership magazine, *Petroleum Review* or *Energy World*, free membership of their local branch, as well as discounts on other learning and networking opportunities. Graduates get a reduced rate membership with additional benefits to assist in developing their career in energy.

*The Energy Institute supports over 13,000 professionals around the world. Its purpose is to promote the safe, environmentally responsible and efficient supply and use of energy in all its forms and applications. It is licensed by the Engineering Council (UK) to offer Chartered, Incorporated and Engineering Technician status to engineers and by the Science Council to award Chartered Scientist status.*

*Join the Energy Institute today by visiting*

**www.energyinst.org**

energy
INSTITUTE

advertisement feature

**info**

Institute of Agricultural Engineers, Barton Road, Silsoe, Bedfordshire MK45 4FH; 01525 861096; www.iagre.org

Institution of Chemical Engineers (IChemE), Davis Building, 165–189 Railway Terrace, Rugby CV21 3HQ; 01788 578214; www.icheme.org

Chartered Institute of Building Services Engineers, 222 Balham High Road, Balham, London SW12 9BS; 020 8675 5211; www.cibse.org

Institution of Civil Engineers (ICE), 1 Great George Street, Westminster, London SW1P 3AA; 020 7222 7722; www.ice.org.uk

British Computer Society (BCS) (relevant for electronics engineers), 1st Floor, Block D, North Star House, North Star Avenue, Swindon SN2 1FA; 0845 300 4417; www.bcs.org

Energy Institute, 61 New Cavendish Street, London W1G 7AR; www.energyinst.org.uk

Institute of Materials, Minerals and Mining (IOM3), 1 Carlton House Terrace, London SW1Y 5DB; 020 7451 7300; www.iom3.org

Institution of Mechanical Engineers (IMechE), 1 Birdcage Walk, Westminster, London SW1H 9JJ; 020 7222 7899; www.imeche.org.uk

Institute of Nanotechnology, 6 The Alpha Centre, University of Stirling Innovation Park, Stirling FK9 4NF; 01786 447520; www.nano.org.uk

Institution of Nuclear Engineers, Allan House, 1 Penerley Road, London SE6 2LQ; www.inuce.org.uk

Institute of Physics, 76 Portland Place, London W1B 1NT; 020 7470 4800; www.iop.org

Institute of Physics and Engineering, Fairmount House, 230 Tadcaster Road, York YO24 1ES; 01904 610821; www.ipem.ac.uk

NHS Careers, PO Box 376, Bristol BS99 3EY; 0845 606 0655; www.nhscareers.nhs.uk

Royal Aeronautical Society, 4 Hamilton Place, London W1J 7BQ; 020 7670 4300; www.aerosociety.com

Energy Institute, 61 New Cavendish Street, London W1 7AR; 0207 467 7100; www.energyinst.org

## Personal Qualities and Skills

Professional engineers, in whatever discipline they choose to specialise, require excellent problem solving, scientific and technical skills. They need to be imaginative in finding solutions to difficulties and they need to have a rigorous and thorough approach to research and testing. They also need good teamwork skills and good project management and human resource management skills. Working at technician or more junior levels, you may need good numeracy skills and good manual dexterity.

## Salaries

Salaries for graduate entrants vary widely across the many fields of engineering. Starting salaries around £20,000 to £23,000 cover most branches and these rise to £27,000 to £50,000 with experience. Some engineers become senior project managers with higher salary potential. Technician engineers earn between £16,000 and £28,000.

# ENVIRONMENT

Occupations in the environment sector are concerned with the protection and preservation of the natural world in which we live.

# Energy manager

Energy managers are responsible for making sure that companies or domestic properties are as efficient as possible in the way they use energy. Their primary duties are to save expenditure on energy and reduce carbon emissions. Energy managers are also responsible for ensuring the compliance with all relevant government standards and legislation. They develop strategies and policies to reduce energy consumption and carry out site inspections and energy surveys. They may manage projects to make changes within their organisation and be responsible for managing a budget. They may also have an awareness-raising role, promoting more efficient use of energy and alternative energy sources. The increasing government legislation, public awareness and rising energy costs are all ensuring the importance of efficient energy usage and the staff to manage this.

## Qualifications and Training

A degree in engineering, building services or environmental science may be useful in gaining employment in this area. There are also an increasing number of degrees specifically in energy engineering or sustainable energy that would be relevant to the role. An HND or Foundation degree in engineering; building/construction or architectural technology; business studies; environmental studies or management would also be a possible entry route. A postgraduate qualification may be useful for more senior positions. There are some qualifications that focus specifically on energy management such as the Training in Energy Management through Open Learning (TEMOL) course run by the Energy Institute.

## Personal Qualities and Skills

Energy managers should be good communicators, able to negotiate and influence others. They should be able to manage projects and stimulate change. They need good numeracy skills for managing budgets and making calculations. They should also have an enthusiasm for energy issues.

## Salaries

Starting salaries range from £20,000 to £34,000 – the wide variation reflects the sector you work in and higher salaries being paid to energy managers with postgraduate qualifications. Salaries after a few years' experience are between £30,000 and £60,000.

| The Energy Institute, 61 New Cavendish Street, London, W1G 7AR; www.energyzone.net | Energy and Utility Skills, Friars Gate, 1011 Stratford Road, Solihull, West Midlands, B90 4BN; www. euskills.co.uk |
|---|---|

*info*

# ENVIRONMENTAL CONSERVATION

Environmental conservation covers a range of activities from recycling waste to habitat management. It does not just involve green issues but is about making the best use of scientific knowledge to produce solutions for a sustainable environment. Conservation includes the protection of rural and urban landscapes, plants and animals and countryside recreation. This includes protection and management of rivers, coastal zones and waterways, together with their fisheries and fish stocks.

There are opportunities in a range of organisations from government departments to the voluntary sector. Competition for jobs is high but there can be a lack of applicants with experience, which often needs to be gained through voluntary work. A large proportion of those working for conservation organisations do so on a voluntary, casual or part-time basis. It is estimated that 47,000 paid employees work in this sector alongside 200,000 volunteers. The majority of those in permanent jobs have higher education qualifications. Many of the permanent jobs are with government agencies, which include the following.

## Countryside conservation officer

Countryside conservation officers are involved in the protection and appropriate development of all types of countryside and rural environment. Their work is varied. They may be involved in implementing schemes to protect or improve landscape, or they may advise on the environmental impact of proposed developments. They may put into practice schemes to protect particular plants, birds, insects and animals, or in creating new habitats for these plants and animals. The work may also involve educating the public about how to use the countryside appropriately and negotiating with other land users, or preparing reports for planning committees and other formal bodies. Conservation officers are employed by local government, government agencies, charitable trusts such as the National Trust and the Woodland Trust, and environmental consultancies.

### Qualifications and Training

For most jobs you need a degree, preferably in a subject such as ecology, geography or environmental conservation. This is a very competitive field, so you also need some good practical skills. The majority of people who get full-time paid work of this sort have done some voluntary work first for one of the countryside organisations. Check the info panel for the major countryside organisations in the UK. Once you are employed there are plenty of courses you can do to increase your knowledge and skills in specific areas, eg woodland, birdlife, or coastal erosion.

### Personal Qualities and Skills

These vary according to your particular responsibilities and tasks, but a love of the countryside is always essential. Interest in geography, botany and zoology may be important. You should be good at keeping records and measuring scientific data of various kinds. You should be prepared to work outside, but also be able to communicate effectively at meetings or in an educative role.

### Salaries

Salaries tend to be fairly low, starting at £14,000 to £16,000. At management level salaries can be £20,000 to £30,000. Many of the employing organisations are charities operating on tight budgets. Salaries can be higher working for consultancies.

## Countryside ranger/warden

Countryside rangers are responsible for the day-to-day management of areas of countryside such as common land, heaths, woodland or wetlands. They undertake practical work such as tree planting or carrying out field surveys to determine how prevalent particular species are in a specified area. Rangers patrol sites, making sure that footpaths, bridges and gates are in good order. They can also provide advice and help to members of the public, keeping an overall eye on safety. They may also have responsibility for managing budgets and for organising exhibitions, or conducting educational tours of sites.

### Qualifications and Training

You do not need any formal qualifications to do this work, but you will almost certainly have to do some voluntary work. Some conservation organisations offer a range of short training courses to volunteers in subjects such as species identification, hedge layering, coppicing and risk management. You can also do City & Guilds courses in environmental conservation, for which you do not need any formal qualifications.

## Personal Qualities and Skills

As well as a passion for the countryside you should be very practical and confident in using tools and equipment. You need good communication skills and for many posts you also have to have reasonable office and IT skills.

## Salaries

Starting salaries vary considerably according to the type of organisation you are employed by. Local authority salaries for rangers are around £17,000.

info

Natural England, 1 East Parade, Sheffield S1 2ET; 0114 241 8920; www.naturalengland.org.uk

Lantra, Lantra House, Stoneleigh Park, Nr Coventry, Warwickshire CV8 2LG; 0845 707 8007; www.lantra.co.uk

Countryside Management Association, Writtle College, Lordship Road, Writtle, Chelmsford, Essex CM1 3RR; 01245 424116; www.countrysidemanagement.org.uk

Institute of Ecology and Environmental Management (IEEM), 45 Southgate Street, Winchester, Hampshire SO23 9EH; 01962 868626; www.ieem.org.uk

LG Careers (Local Government), www.lgcareers.com

Groundwork UK, www.groundwork.org.uk

Field Studies Council, Montford Bridge, Preston Montford, Shrewsbury, Shropshire SY4 1HW; 0845 345 4071; www.field-studies-council.org

Conservation Volunteers Northern Ireland, Beech House, 159 Ravenhill Road, Belfast BT6 0BP; 028 9064 5169; www.cvni.org.uk

British Trust for Conservation Volunteers (BTCV), Sedum House, Mallard Way, Potteric Carr, Doncaster DN4 8DB; 01302 388888; www.btcv.org.uk

National Trust, PO Box 39, Warrington WA5 7WD; 0870 458 4000; www.nationaltrust.org.uk

National Trust for Scotland, Wemyss House, 28 Charlotte Square, Edinburgh EH2 4ET; 0131 243 9300; www.nts.org.uk

# Recycling officer

Recycling officers work mainly for local councils, planning and developing policies to help local people recycle as much waste material as they can. Recycling officers organise schemes to recycle glass, paper, cans and plastic. They may also organise and manage schemes to encourage residents to make compost, either on their own properties or at central points set up by the local authority. Reducing waste is an important and very topical area of local authority work, so the significance of this area of work has increased. Recycling officers are also involved in organising publicity about recycling. They often attend meetings of both formal bodies such as parish councils, and informal societies such as gardening clubs.

## Qualifications and Training

While there are no formal academic entry requirements, most successful applicants have either a degree or a Higher National Diploma. The most useful subjects include environmental science, earth studies, geography, or any science subject. If you don't have a degree, then plenty of useful paid or voluntary work on recycling projects strengthens your application. If you can offer relevant NVQs at levels 2 and 3 this also helps. NVQs at levels 2 and 3 are available in Recycling Operations, Waste Management and Environmental Conservation. Much of the training is on the job. You are likely to need to do frequent short updating courses, because technology and knowledge are changing rapidly in this field.

## Personal Qualities and Skills

You must be a good communicator, able to present written information and oral reports. You should be well organised, good at prioritising, and you need reasonable IT skills. Being able to manage teams of people is very important.

## Salaries

New entrants start on between £20,000 and £25,000. Salaries may be less than this if you work for a community organisation. With experience and considerable management responsibility salaries rise to £30,000 to £40,000.

**info**

Waste and Resource Action Plan (WRAP), The Old Academy, 21 Horse Fair, Banbury, Oxon OX16 0AH; 0808 100 2040; www.wrap.org.uk

LG Careers (Local Government); www.lgcareers.com

Chartered Institution of Wastes Management, 9 Saxon Court, St Peter's Gardens, Marefair, Northampton NN1 1SX; 01604 620426; www.ciwm.co.uk

Waste Management Industry Training and Advisory Board, Peterbridge House, 3 The Lakes, Northampton NN4 7HE; 01604 231950; www.wamitab.org.uk

Energy and Utility Skills, Friars Gate Two, 1011 Stratford Road, Shirley, Solihull B90 4BN; 0845 077 9922; www.euskills.co.uk

# ENVIRONMENTAL HEALTH

Environmental health workers' aim is to protect the public from environmental health risks.

# Environmental health officer/practitioner

Environmental health officers (EHOs) are enforcers, educators and advisers, and are employed in both the public and private sectors. Their responsibilities include pollution control, including noise control, environmental protection, the inspection of food and food premises, health and safety in workplaces and in the leisure industry, and the control of housing standards, particularly in the private rented sector. Much of their time is spent out of the office, dealing with the public and visiting premises of all types.

## Qualifications and Training

The usual route to becoming an environmental health officer/practitioner is through a degree in environmental health. You can either do a three-year degree, followed by a one-year work placement, or a four-year degree that includes a third year work-based training placement. If you have a science degree, you can also enter the profession by doing a postgraduate course in environmental health. In all cases, your course should be accredited by the Chartered Institute of Environmental Health (CIEH) in England, Wales and Northern Ireland, or the Royal Environmental Health Institute of Scotland in Scotland. Alternatively, if you have an HNC, HND or foundation degree in science, you may be able to enter directly into the second year of a degree. If you have A levels or an HND you may prefer to work as an environmental health technician for a local authority. From this point, with your employer's support, you can do the environmental health degree on a part-time basis while continuing to work in an environmental health department. As a trainee environmental health officer you have to keep a detailed portfolio of your work and also pass the professional qualifying exams of the CIEH.

## Personal Qualities and Skills

EHOs need a broad mix of skills. They have to be able to deal with complex legal and scientific information. They must be able to explain the law to members of the public or other non-lawyers. They should be diplomatic and calm, but at other times they will also have to be assertive and determined.

Chartered Institute of Environmental Health (CIEH), Chadwick Court, 15 Hatfields, London SE1 8DJ; 020 7928 6006; www.cieh.org

Environment Agency (EA); visit the EA website to check for details of regional offices; 08708 506 506; www.environment-agency.gov.uk

Food Standards Agency, Aviation House, 125 Kingsway, London WC2B 6NH; 020 7276 8000; www.food.gov.uk

Royal Environmental Health Institute of Scotland (REHIS), 3 Manor Place, Edinburgh EH3 7DH; 0131 225 5444; www.rehis.org

info

## Salaries

Starting salaries for environmental health officers/practitioners are between £27,000 and £33,000. Salaries in and around London tend to be the highest. There is some weekend and late evening work involved and this may attract additional payments. At management level environmental health practitioners earn £35,000 to £60,000.

# Health and safety adviser

*see* Health and Safety

# Pest control technician

Pest controllers control not only mice, rats, cockroaches and ants that may be damaging foodstuffs in a factory, hotel or private home, but also rabbits, moles, birds and foxes that attack farmers' crops. They work for local authorities and private firms. Service staff are employed to lay traps and set poison. There are also opportunities for graduates in research and management.

## Qualifications and Training

Qualifications in pest control are usually preferred, although at assistant level full training is provided on the job, including day or block release to achieve a recognised qualification, such as British Pest Control Association courses. The British Pest Control Association and the Royal Society for the Promotion of Health have merged their basic pest control qualification – BPC Diploma Part 1 and RSPH Certificate in Pest Control. The examination was assessed and piloted between Autumn 2003 and Spring 2004. As part of this partnership other BPCA examinations, including the advanced level certificate (BPC Diploma Part 2), the fumigation certification scheme and the newly introduced Certificate for Surveyors – Pest Control (CSPC) will ultimately be brought under the joint BPCA/RSPH umbrella.

## Personal Qualities and Skills

This is not a job for the squeamish and the work demands a mature outlook, an ability to get on with many kinds of people, to work in varying conditions and to work alone. The ability to drive is important.

**info**

Asset Skills, 2 The Courtyard, 48 New North Road, Exeter, Devon EX4 4EP; 08000 567160; www.assetskills.org

Royal Society for Public Health, 3rd Floor, Market Towers, 1 Nine Elms Lane, London SW8 5NG; 020 3177 1600; www.rsph.org.uk

British Pest Control Association (BPCA), Ground Floor, Gleneagles House, Vernongate, Derby DE1 1UP; 0870 609 2687; www.bpca.org.uk

National Pest Technicians Association (NPTA), NPTA House, Hall Lane, Kinoulton, Nottingham NG12 3EF; 01949 81133; www.npta.org.uk

## Salaries

Starting salaries are between £14,000 and £16,000. With experience and qualifications you can earn £25,000 to £27,000. Many pest control technicians set up their own small businesses.

# EVENTS ORGANISATION

Many organisations and businesses hold both internal and public events. The role of conference and events organisers is one of project management, ensuring that the event runs smoothly and efficiently.

# Events organiser

'Events organiser' is a job title which covers many extremely similar work roles. These jobs include conference or exhibition organiser and events, conference or exhibition manager or coordinator. What all these jobs have in common is that the events organiser/manager is involved at every stage of organisation, right through from the first planning meeting to being there at the event, to ensure that everything runs smoothly and successfully. Events include trade fairs, exhibitions, festivals, fund raising events, product launches, training events and social occasions. Events can be small and local, or large and international. They may last for one evening or as long as a week. What the different job titles denote is the specific types of events for which you are responsible. These might be exhibitions, conferences or social events such as parties or weddings.

The work involves meeting clients to discuss what they want from the event, agreeing budgets and researching and booking appropriate venues, catering and entertainment. The work also involves checking health and safety issues and logistical planning. The events organiser also attends the event itself to solve any problems that arise on the spot.

## Qualifications and Training

People move into events organisations and management from a variety of backgrounds. You don't necessarily need any formal qualifications, as relevant experience and the right blend of skills are often more important. There are, however, a growing number of events management courses at degree, foundation degree and HND level. The Association of Events Organisers website carries details of these courses. Other useful degree subjects include business, marketing, public relations and hospitality.

Having practical experience in organising events is really important. If you have worked in hospitality, organising conferences and banquets at hotels, for example, this gives you a real advantage. Organising social events on a voluntary basis can also be valuable.

Training is very much on the job, as you normally begin as an assistant to a more experienced organiser/manager. There are a range of relevant NVQs towards which your employer may want you to work. Professional organisations such as the Association of Exhibition Organisers (AEO) or the Association for Conferences and Events (ACE) offer training and networking opportunities.

## Exhibition designer

Exhibition designers are responsible for designing the displays and stands that form part of all kinds of exhibition. They may be working on large public exhibitions, trade fairs, or small temporary exhibitions set up by a business or a charity. The work involves discussing briefs with clients, producing sketches of ideas. These might be drawn by hand or computer-generated. Designers also have to liaise with suppliers and technical staff to ensure that the finished display matches the agreed brief.

### Qualifications and Training

Employers prefer you to have formal qualifications in display design. It is sometimes possible to acquire these while working as an assistant designer. The British Display Society (BDS) provides details of relevant certificate and diploma courses. It is also possible to get into this work with a degree in a design-related subject such as three-dimensional design or interior design. There are now a small number of degree courses in exhibition design being offered. Check with the BDS for details.

### Personal Qualities and Skills

You have to have really excellent organisational and communication skills to succeed in this work. You must be a good administrator, keeping clear records and keeping track of the progress of any event. You must be able to establish relationships with new people very quickly and be able to lead teams of people who may not have worked together before. You must be creative, imaginative and calm in the face of crises.

For exhibition design you need good practical, technical and creative skills, as well as all the people skills required for other aspects of events organising.

### Salaries

Salaries for new entrants to both events organisation and exhibition design are between £19,000 and £25,000. Senior managers earn between £35,000 and £45,000; some employers pay staff bonuses if events are successful. Some organisers, especially those dealing with social events such as weddings and parties, are self-employed and charge a fee according to the scale of the work involved. Exhibition designers start on around £16,000. With a few years' experience this rises to £25,000 to £35,000.

**info**

Chartered Institute of Marketing (CIM), Moor Hall, Cookham, Maidenhead, Berkshire SL6 9QH; 01628 427500; www.cim.co.uk

People 1st, 2nd Floor, Armstrong House, 38 Market Square, Uxbridge, Middlesex UB8 1LH; 0870 060 2550; www.people1st.co.uk

Association of Exhibition Organisers, 119 High Street, Berkhamstead, Hertfordshire HP4

2DJ; 01442 285810; www.aeo.org.uk

Association for Conferences and Events (ACE), ACE International, Riverside House, High Street, Huntingdon, Cambridgeshire PE18 6SG; 01480 457595; www. aceinternational.org

Association of British Professional Conference Organisers (ABPCO), Wellington Park, Belfast BT9 6DJ; 028 9038 7475; www.abpco.org.uk

# FARMING

(*see also* Agriculture)

In recent years, economic conditions and animal health crises have had significant effects on jobs in this sector. Incomes have fallen and opportunities become more limited. There is increasing mechanisation and a tendency towards greater specialisation and larger farms. Mixed farms are now in a minority, and most farmers choose to specialise in one or two areas of production. The most common of these are milk, cereals, poultry, sheep, pigs or beef. In order to survive, many farmers have to consider other activities such as leisure and recreation, niche markets, or crops for energy and raw materials. To make a farm profitable, the modern farmer needs a thorough working knowledge of the type of farming to be undertaken, an understanding of general agricultural science, and years of practical experience as well as an aptitude for farming and farm management.

Opportunities are few, land and equipment are expensive. Land prices have made the chances of a beginner becoming a tenant farmer almost impossible. Most of those who go into farming come from farming families.

## Farm manager

Farm managers are employed by the landowner and are responsible for all aspects of the day-to-day working of the farm. They must plan ahead, organise the staff and work schedules, decide which crops to plant or which animals to rear, and keep a check on buildings and machinery. In addition, they must deal with the office work and accounts.

## Farm worker

Farm workers are employed by farmers, who may well be big businesses, and by landowners to carry out practical and manual tasks on farms. The work could involve working with livestock, with crops or with a combination of these two. Your work could involve milking cows, feeding and checking sheep, cattle, pigs and poultry. It could involve preparing the ground to plant crops, harvesting those crops, or maintaining farm machinery. You could also work repairing and maintaining farm buildings. Most farms in the UK are large, and each farm employs few workers; nevertheless you are likely to become a specialist in particular work such as dairy cows, arable crops or crops for energy generation. Many farms have to diversify to generate income, so the farm on which you work may have a farm shop, horses kept at livery or a local pheasant or partridge shoot on the land. Your work may involve helping with any of these or similar enterprises.

## Qualifications and Training

When recruiting farm managers, most employers look for candidates who have hands-on experience of farming, but most farm managers now will also have a degree in agriculture or a closely related subject. Farm workers don't necessarily need any formal qualifications, though it may be an advantage if you have GCSEs in maths, English and a technical subject. There are many full- and part-time college courses in all the specialist areas of farm work.

## Personal Qualities and Skills

At whatever level you are working you must have a commitment to farming and a willingness to work in all weathers at any time of the year and to put in some unsocial hours. Farm workers need good practical skills and must be able to work alone, unsupervised or as part of a team. If you look after livestock you need a highly responsible attitude. Farm managers must be well organised, with good numerate and communication skills. They also need to be imaginative and good at marketing. A great awareness of health and safety and potential risks is important at all levels in farming.

## Salaries

Many farm salaries are set annually by the Agricultural Wages Board, but this does not apply to all management jobs. New entrant farm managers earn around £21,000 to £27,000. Managers with a lot of responsibility managing large farms can earn £30,000 to £50,000. Farm workers earn close to the minimum wage, but there may be plenty of opportunities to work overtime at certain times of year. Average salaries for farm workers are between £11,500 and £18,000 at the start of your career, £19,000 to £22,000 with experience.

**info**

Lantra House, Stoneleigh Park, Nr Coventry, Warwickshire CV8 2LG; 0845 707 8007; www.lantra.co.uk

# FASHION

(*see also* Clothing Industry)

Clothing is one of the UK's largest manufacturing industries and employs over 145,000 individuals. The fashion industry covers all aspects of clothing and accessories for men, women and children, and falls into three main sectors: *haute couture* houses, where original model garments are made for individual customers; wholesale *couture*, where trends set by the *haute couture* houses are closely followed, and limited numbers of model garments in stock sizes are made for retail; and wholesale manufacture, which occupies the largest sector of the fashion industry. Here, the latest trends are adapted to styles that are attractive to the main market, and mass produced at acceptable prices.

# Designer

Fashion designers design garments for all levels of the fashion market. The majority work for high street stores, or their suppliers, designing garments which will be manufactured in their thousands. Some fashion designers work for more upmarket labels designing products which are still for a mass market, but which are produced in much smaller quantities. A few designers work in *haute couture*, designing individual one-off items. Fashion designers may specialise in particular types of clothing such as baby wear, evening wear, hats or sports wear. Some choose to specialise in designing accessories or footwear. Most fashion designers start by designing garments to someone else's brief, but a small number will design original items – this is probably the ultimate goal of most people who go into fashion design. Fashion designers start by making a sketch, often used computer aided design, and work from this to the finished product. The work also involves liaising closely with buyers, sales managers and marketing professionals.

## Qualifications and Training

It is increasingly difficult to get into this work without a degree, and preferably a relevant one in fashion, clothing technology, knitwear, embroidery, graphic design or art and design. If you have a degree in another subject, or you have not gone on to higher education, you really need to have worked in the fashion industry and have an impressive portfolio of your design ideas to show to a prospective employer. Training is rarely formal and is very much a case of 'pick it up as you go along'. Sometimes there are opportunities to undertake short training courses in new techniques or associated with new technology.

## Personal Qualities and Skills

Of course a passionate interest in clothing, colour, design and fabrics is essential. In addition you need to be good at analysing trends and almost being able to second-guess what will happen next. You have to be able to work as part of a team, cope under pressure, solve problems and have good drawing skills, both freehand and with computer software. You need to have a lot of self-confidence, and be good at promoting your ideas to others.

## Salaries

In London salaries start between £17,000 and £23,000. Outside London, it will be much less than this, but there are only a few opportunities outside London. Good junior designers who have worked for three or four years in design can earn £30,000 to £42,000.

**info**

The Chartered Society of Designers (CSD), 1 Cedar Court, Royal Oak Yard, Bermondsey Street, London SE1 3GA; 020 7357 8088; www.csd.org.uk

Clerkenwell Green Association, 33–35 St John's Square, London EC1M; 020 7251 0276; www.cga.org.uk

Crafts Council, 44a Pentonville Road, Islington, London N1 9BY; 020 7806 2500; www.craftscouncil.org.uk

The Design Council, 34 Bow Street, London WC2E 7DL; 020 7420 5200; www.designcouncil.org.uk

Hidden Art, Mazorca Projects, Shoreditch Stables, Ground Floor Rear, 138 Kingsland Road, London E2 8DY; 020 7729 3800; www.hiddenart.com

Skillfast-UK, Richmond House, Lawnswood House, Redvers Close, Leeds LS16 6RD; 0113 2399 600; www.skillfast-uk-org

UK Fashion Exports, 5 Portland Place, London W1B 1PW; 020 7636 5577; www.ukfashionexports.com

# Dressmaker

Opportunities for dressmakers occur in *couture* houses which make specially designed costumes for a particular collection or customer, in wholesale fashion houses making mass-produced garments, and in theatres both making and adapting costumes. Dressmakers may also be employed by large stores to carry out alterations, or they may be self-employed making clothes either from home or from a workshop. Teachers of dressmaking are employed in schools, colleges and by adult education centres.

## Qualifications and Training

No formal qualifications are necessary, but City & Guilds qualifications and NVQs are available. Some degrees and HNDs in clothing design or fashion have a dressmaking option.

## Personal Qualities and Skills

Dressmakers need to combine artistic and practical skills with an ability to follow instructions and to recognise problems as they arise and make the necessary adaptations. They may have to deal with temperamental designers and their customers.

## Salaries

Salaries vary, but trainees earn between £11,000 and £13,000, and with experience dressmakers can earn £17,000 to £20,000. Many dressmakers are self-employed and can earn quite large amounts of money, especially if they are making items like wedding dresses or other special-occasion wear.

| | |
|---|---|
| Skillfast UK: The Sector Skills Council for Apparel, Footwear, Textiles and Related Businesses, Richmond House, Lawnswood Business Park, | Redvers Close, Leeds LS16 6RD; 0113 239 9600; www.skillfast-uk.org<br><br>Local Job Centre Plus and Connexions/Careers Centres |

info

# Model

Models work as 'live' or photographic models, generally showing clothes or accessories. Photographic and advertising models rely on an agent to get them work and handle the fees. Competition is intense and very few models get to the top of the profession.

Fashion models are employed full-time by couturiers, wholesalers or fashion stores as 'live' models. They have the garments draped and pinned on them during the design stages, and show them to the public. Live models must be tall, at least 1.72 m (5 ft 8 in). Photographic modelling involves posing in garments chosen to be illustrated in magazines, newspapers, catalogues or on advertising posters. This work is often out of season for the type of garments being modelled and some of the work is done abroad. Expenses include the provision of accessories, a good basic wardrobe and hairdressing.

## Qualifications and Training

Private model schools run training courses for live and photographic modelling. Reputable schools will only take entrants whom they think will succeed, and will introduce them to agencies at the end of the training period. The London College of Fashion, a non-commercial college, offers a one-year full-time course leading to a certificate in fashion modelling. Students should have three GCSEs grades A–C or equivalent.

## Personal Qualities and Skills

A model must be able to work hard, be punctual and reliable, get on well with people, and have a great deal of common sense. Competition is intense and only those who can interpret what the stylist and photographer want will get to the top. A female model should be at least 1.72 m (5 ft 8 in) tall and have body statistics of about 86–61–86 cm (34–24–34 in). A male model should be at least 1.83 m (6 ft) tall. Models should have clear skin, good hands, nails and teeth, healthy hair and attractive features.

## Salaries

Models normally work freelance and are paid per day or per job. Rates vary enormously depending on how well established you are and what kind of modelling you do. Routine modelling for clothing catalogues may pay £50 to £60 per day. At the top end of the profession these rates are between £600 and £1,000 per day. Working for a fashion house, rates vary from £10,000 to £40,000 per year. Remember that your agent may charge up to 20 per cent of your fee.

**info**

Association of Model Agents,
122 Brompton Road, London
SW3 1JD; 020 7584 6466
(send sae for information)

London College of Fashion,
20 John Princes Street, London
W1M 0BJ; 020 7514 7400; www.
input.demon.co.uk/careers-
modelling.html

Alba Model Information,
31 The High Street, Durrington,
Salisbury, Wiltshire SP4 8AE;
0871 717 7170 (calls from a UK
landline cost 10p per minute); www.
albamodel.info; www.
albamodelinformation.com

# FILM AND TELEVISION PRODUCTION

Opportunities to work in film production arise in television, film companies and advertising. Most people who work in this area are self-employed free-lancers. Film production involves both studio and location work. Jobs within film production are much sought after, vacancies are few and competition is consequently fierce. Individuals who are serious about working in this area will need to develop personal marketing skills in addition to their creative craft skills.

# Animation

Animation involves the design, creation and operation of animated production and effects. Much of the work is done using computer animation techniques, though there are still opportunities for traditional 'cell' animation.

# Announcer

Announcers work to detailed and carefully timed scripts, communicating information to the viewer from a soundproof 'behind the scenes' office. They sometimes write or adapt their own material and need to be able to work on their own.

## Archivist/librarian

(*see also* Archivist)

Archivists and librarians collect, collate, preserve and make available collections of recorded visual, sound, written and other materials for use by various productions. Archives are valuable business resources, and some archivists are now involved in selling and marketing materials.

## Art and design

(*see also* Art and Design)

The art and design function is to create a visual effect to meet the needs of the production, creating manual or computer-generated graphics.

## Camerawork

Workers in this area operate and assist with still, film and video cameras to record images as directed, using different techniques.

## Costume/wardrobe

The wardrobe department interprets the production requirements in terms of costumes and accessories to ensure historical accuracy and an accurate portrayal of the style and ethos of the period.

## Direction

The director is responsible for achieving the creative, visual and auditory effect of a production and, equally importantly, motivating a team.

## Engineering

Engineers provide a design, maintenance and installation service to the production site and equipment. Research specialists are usually employed by the equipment manufacturers or design consultancies.

## Film, video and audio tape editing

Raw tape or film is shaped to interpret the requirements of the director, either by physical cutting (film) or by selecting sequences and re-recording onto a master tape using sophisticated computer equipment.

## IT specialist

IT specialists support many aspects of broadcasting, film and video, either within the companies or as consultants, providing and maintaining relevant systems and software.

## Journalist

(*see also* Journalism)

Journalists generate and report on local, national or international stories, and research relevant background information. Bi-media (radio and television) contracts are increasing. Some journalists present their own work.

## Laboratory technician

Lab technicians develop and process film, and duplicate and check video tapes, ensuring high technical quality.

## Lighting

Lighting specialists ensure that the stage or set is correctly lit to meet the needs of the production.

## Make-up and hairdressing

(*see also* Beauty *and* Hair)

Make-up and hairdressing professionals interpret the requirements of the production and research to ensure accurate representation of the historical or design concept. They maintain a continuity of approach throughout the production in studio or on location.

## Management

Management directs and coordinates the different elements of the industry to ensure their efficient function – ranging from commissioning a production to negotiating international rights. Specialists work in a full range of business areas.

## Marketing and sales

Marketing and sales staff work in an international market place to raise revenue for broadcasters or film makers. Airtime is sold, sponsorship and co-production rights are negotiated and spin-off products, such as books, toys and DVDs, are developed.

# Model maker/prop maker

Model makers and prop makers work not only in film and TV, but in the theatre too. They make all kinds of props from moving models to fake jewellery, replica weapons and even fake food. Model makers and prop makers use a wide range of skills including carpentry, sculpting, casting, sewing, painting, welding and computer aided design (CAD). It may well be that some prop makers develop experience and a reputation for being especially skilled in one or two of these areas.

# Producer

Producers perform a variety of management and operational roles to bring together the many elements of a production, either in a studio or on location. Often responsible both for the initial concept and raising the essential finance, they are the team leaders.

# Production assistant

Production assistants provide high-quality administrative and secretarial support to the producer and director at every stage of production, coordinating all activities and preparing schedules and scripts.

# Production manager

Production managers organise all essential support facilities for the team, from accommodation and transport to on-set catering. They will also roster crews and arrange payments.

# Production operative

Production operatives perform the operational duties of the production such as vision mixing and autocue operations.

# Researcher

Researchers support the producer, helping to turn ideas into reality – providing and following up ideas, contacting and interviewing people, acquiring relevant factual material, and writing briefings for presenters.

# Runner/gofer

This job is the traditional entry-level job for the industry. Bright, highly moti-vated – often highly qualified – people act as general assistants, taking messages, making deliveries, being indispensable, and learning the basics of the commercial business.

# Setcraft/props

People working in this area construct the scenery, sets and backdrops to meet the production brief, reflecting both historical accuracy and required design and style. They also maintain sets during a production, and operate any mechanical features as directed. Props (hired or made) are used to dress the set.

# Sound

Sound craftspeople interpret the requirements of a production in terms of sound collection. During post-production they may be involved in recording, editing and dubbing, using a range of sophisticated equipment.

# Special effects

Special effects designers create and operate effects for a production, within technical limitations and budget, and operate the necessary machines.

# Support staff

Many people working in film, video, television and radio fulfil essential support roles, including administration, catering, driving and cleaning.

# Transmission

Technicians and engineers work to exhibit the production in a high-quality form, which can involve projecting images or operating transmission equip-ment linking electronic signals from the studios to a transmitter.

# Writer

*(see also* Writer on page 495)

Writers work to produce or edit scripts for a variety of radio, television, DVD or film productions.

## Qualifications and Training

The film and television industry has changed rapidly over the last decade and one of the results of this has been that at all levels and whatever your specific job, you need to be multi-skilled and flexible. While formal academic qualifications are not essential, this is an exceedingly competitive field, the result being that many entrants to all jobs within the film, TV and video industry are graduates. Degrees in communications, multimedia, photography, media studies, film and television are particularly useful. These courses are also extremely popular and thus entry is competitive. Look for courses where you get the chance to use state of the art technology and where there may be opportunities for work placements or at least contacts with the industry.

If you wish to get into production/direction you may have to start in research or marketing, or as a production assistant – whichever, most careers in this sector require you to work your way up from the bottom, or be prepared to make sideways transfers.

Skillset, the sector Skills council for the audio-visual industries, provides a range of free and subsidised training courses and works closely with the industry to try to ensure that employees are training in appropriate skills. FT2 Film and Television Freelance Training offer training to people who want to establish freelance careers in production and other technical areas. Some television companies offer graduate training schemes, but unsurprisingly, these are massively over-subscribed.

## Personal Qualities and Skills

You either need to have creative flair and imagination, or be able to see the value of these and support them. For many roles you need good technical skills and the ability to work carefully and patiently maintaining good powers of concentration. You need excellent people skills, you are often working in situations where the whole team is under pressure and you have to be able to keep calm. In many situations, you need to be good at promoting yourself and your ideas.

## Salaries

With so many different jobs in this industry, here are just a few salary examples to give a flavour of the range of possible earnings. Runners are paid between £12,500 and £14,000, but the experience is extremely useful. Trainee production assistants earn between £12,000 and £14,000. Experienced production staff earn between £19,000 and £25,000. Technicians earn between £15,000 and £26,000. Directors' salaries are not necessarily high, if they are working for small companies on low budget productions.

Many staff work freelance and are paid on a daily basis or a fee per contract. BECTU sets rates in the industry. Your own fee negotiating skills are often important in this field.

**info**

BBC, Television Centre W12 7RJ;
020 8752 5942; www.bbc.co.uk

British Film Institute (BFI),
21 Stephen Street, London W1T 1LN;
020 7255 1444; www.bfi.org.uk

Broadcasting Entertainment
Cinematographic and Theatre Union
(BECTU), 373–377 Clapham Road,
London SW9 9BT; www.bectu.org.uk

Skillset, Focus Point, 21 Caledonian
Road, London N1 9GB;
0207 7139800; www.skillset.org

British Film Institute (BFI),
21 Stephen Street, London W1T 1LN;
020 7255 1444; www.bfi.org.uk

FT2 – Film & Television Freelance
Training, Third Floor,
18–20 Southwark Street,
London SE1 1TJ; 020 7407 0344;
www.ft2.org.uk

New Producers Alliance (NPA),
NPA Film Centre, 1.07 Tea Building,
56 Shoreditch High Street,
London E1 6JJ; 020 7613 0440;
www.npa.org.uk

# FIRE SERVICE

Firefighters save and rescue life and property in emergencies. Fighting fires is only one aspect of their work; other emergencies they deal with are tanker spillages, car, train and aeroplane crashes, flooding, building collapse, and explosions where people and animals may have to be rescued. Some firefighters specialise in particular areas such as training or communications. The Fire Service also promotes fire safety through education programmes, and advice on fire protection and prevention for existing properties and new buildings. In addition it enforces legal regulations to reduce risks of injury by fire, such as the provision of secure escape routes.

The Fire Service is administered by local authorities in the UK. Recruitment is undertaken by each local brigade, which is responsible for its own recruitment procedures. The Ministry of Defence, Army, Royal Air Force, Royal Navy and the British Airports Authority all have their own brigades.

## Qualifications and Training

No formal qualifications are necessary, but GCSEs in maths, English and science are useful. You must be aged 18 or over to train as a firefighter. In order to pass the National Firefighter Selection Tests you have to fill in a detailed application form and pass a physical fitness test, a medical and a range of aptitude tests. The training is on the job, with frequent courses on new risks, better procedures, etc.

## Personal Qualities and Skills

As a firefighter you have to be calm and courageous, prepared to go into dangerous situations, but sensible enough to tackle things calmly. You must be good at reassuring frightened or injured people and you must be good at working as part of a team. You may also be involved in teaching about fire prevention and safety, so you must enjoy dealing with people.

## Salaries

Salaries for trainee firefighters start at around £22,500. On achieving full competence, the rate for a firefighter is between £28,000 and £29,500. Firefighters working in London earn an additional £4,500. Crew managers earn £35,000 plus, and a station manager earns around £38,000.

www.fireservice.co.uk; gives detailed information on recruitment

Skills for Justice, Centre Court, Atlas Way, Sheffield S4 7QQ; www.skillsforjustice.com

**info**

# FISH FARMER

In Britain around 500 fish farms produce fish, mainly rainbow trout and Atlantic salmon, for consumption and sport. Pacific oysters, mussels and scallops are also farmed. This is a growing activity and although most farms are owner-run, there are opportunities for farm managers and workers. Scientists also work in the industry, testing new methods for improving conditions, stocks and disease control. Bailiffs are employed to look after the general welfare of the fish from hatchery to harvesting. As more food manufacturers move into fish farming, there is a need for marketing staff.

## Qualifications and Training

What qualifications you need to get into fish farming depends on whether you wish to go straight into management, or whether you prefer to start at technician level. To become a manager or assistant manager, you normally need a relevant degree. There are a small number of fisheries degrees available in the UK. You may also be able to get into management with a degree in another subject such as agriculture or environmental management. If you wish to start at technician level, you may not necessarily need formal qualifications, though you could consider a part-time BTEC first diploma in Fisheries Husbandry or a two-year full-time BTEC National Diploma in Fisheries Management.

Once you are working in fish farming, you may want to consider taking Institute of Fisheries Management part-time certificate and diploma courses in fisheries management.

## Personal Qualities and Skills

You need to have a real interest in the scientific aspects of what you are doing. You have to enjoy working with living organisms. You have to be prepared to work in all weathers and conditions. You may have to work as part of a team, but you also have to be happy and confident in working on your own.

## Salaries

Fish farm technicians earn between £14,000 and £18,000. Assistant managers earn around £25,000 and managers of large fish farms can earn up to £38,000. For some posts accommodation may be provided, though occasionally this may only be a caravan.

**info**

British Trout Association, The Rural Centre, West Mains, Ingliston EH28 8NZ; 0131 472 4080; www.britishtrout.co.uk; e-mail: mail@britishtrout.co.uk

Institute of Fisheries Management (IFM), 22 Rushworth Avenue, West Bridgford, Nottingham NG2 7LF; 0115 982 2317; fax: 0115 945 5722; www.ifm.org.uk; e-mail: admin@ifm.org.uk

Lantra Connect, Lantra House, Stoneleigh, Kenilworth, Warwickshire CV8 2LG; 0845 707 8007 (Lantra Connect – Helpline); www.lantra.co.uk; e-mail: connect@lantra.co.uk

Vacancies are generally advertised in local newspapers and in the specialist magazines such as *Fish Farmer* and *Fish Farming International*.

# FISHING

Fishing covers work on many kinds of commercial boats from single-handed vessels to large factory ships employing crews of 15 to 20. The usual progression for fishermen and women is to start as deckhands, work up to mate and finally to fishing vessel skipper. Fishermen and women work on inshore vessels which stay close to the shore and on vessels which go limited distances out to sea. They also work on vessels which go far out into the ocean.

## Fishing vessel deckhand

Deckhands help with everything from gutting and cleaning the fish caught to preparing food for other crew members and keeping the boat clean and orderly. They repair nets and also help set up trawling and hauling equipment.

## Fishing vessel skipper

Skippers are responsible for the management of every voyage. They have to plan where to fish and take the responsibility for navigation and for health and safety aboard the vessel. They oversee the use of the vessel's fishing gear and other technical equipment. They manage the workload of the crew and deal with any problems which arise.

## Qualifications and Training

To become a deckhand you don't need any formal qualifications, though previous experience of the sea and boating or sailing of some kind is useful. Most people train through training schemes organised around the UK. Contact the Sea Fish Industry Authority for details. If you have had some useful experience, it may be worth approaching a skipper directly to see if he or she will take you on. Training is on the job, but if you progress to become a mate or a skipper you can take NVQ level 3 in Marine Vessel Operations (mate) or Marine Vessel Operations (skipper).

### Personal Qualities and Skills

As either a deckhand or a skipper you must have good eyesight and hearing and be physically fit and have a lot of physical courage. The work is often dangerous as you have to deal with wind, storms and cold seas. You must be able to tolerate working with a small group of people, often in cramped, uncomfortable conditions. You need to be able to tolerate long periods away from home, family and friends.

### Salaries

There are wide variations in salaries for deckhands and skippers. Earnings are based on the size of the catch and the value of the fish caught. Salaries for deckhands and skippers are between £11,000 and £26,000. Skippers on large commercial vessels can earn considerably more than this. Income is also affected by legal restrictions on size of catch and the number of days on which a vessel is permitted to leave port to fish.

Seafish Industry Authority, Origin Way, Europarc, Grimsby DN3 9TZ; 01472 252300; www.seafish.org

Lantra, Lantra House, Stoneleigh Park, Nr Coventry, Warwickshire CV8 2LG; 0845 707 8007; www.lantra.co.uk

**info**

# FLORISTRY

*see* Crafts

# FOOD SCIENCE AND TECHNOLOGY

Food scientists study the properties and behaviour of foods from raw materials through processing to the final product, using a variety of scientific disciplines, notably chemistry and biology, but also physics and nutrition. Food technologists use food science and other technological know-how to turn raw materials into finished products for the consumer in an industry that is becoming increasingly sophisticated.

The majority of those qualifying in food science or technology will readily find employment in a variety of positions in the food industry, which covers not only the manufacture of food but its ingredients, food packaging and the manufacture of food-processing machinery. Positions exist in production, quality assurance or in product or process development. The growth of 'own label' products has led to additional opportunities in the food retailing sector, where technologists are responsible for developing new products, identifying suppliers, and ensuring the quality of the product from manufacture, through distribution to the store and, ultimately, to the consumer's table. Those keen to secure a career in research will find opportunities in government service, in research associations, as well as in commercial organisations and the universities. There are additional opportunities in environmental health, education, consultancy, public health laboratories and in technical publishing and journalism.

## Qualifications and Training

There are several routes into this work. You can start as a lab technician with a food or drinks manufacturer. For this you normally need four GCSEs including maths and a science. If you are successful, you can then study part-time for higher qualifications and progress to technologist-level jobs. You could study a degree in food technology; you normally need two or three A levels including biology or chemistry to do this. If you have one A level there is a range of BTEC HNC and HND full- and part-time courses for which you could apply. Exact course requirements vary so check with colleges. If you have a degree in an unrelated subject, there are some postgraduate courses in food safety and food quality management that could gain you entry. The Institute of Food Science and Technology careers website provides information on all these options.

## Personal Qualities and Skills

You need a real interest in food and food preparation, combined with an aptitude for and interest in science. You should be a good communicator, able to share ideas or enforce legislation if necessary. You must be careful and methodical and acutely aware of food safety and hygiene issues. You should be able to work well in a team, but able to work on your own too. If you are involved in recipe development you should be creative. If you are involved in research, you need an enquiring mind.

## Salaries

Working at technician level, salaries start at around £20,000. Graduate food technologists earn between £22,000 and £25,000. If you have five to ten years' experience and management responsibility, salaries range from £30,000 to £45,000.

**info**

Improve – The Food and Drink Sector Skills Council, Ground Floor, Providence House, 2 Innovation Close, Heslington, York YO10 5ZF; 0845 644 0448; www.improveltd.co.uk/

Institute of Food Science and Technology (IFST), 5 Cambridge Court, 210 Shepherd's Bush Road, London W6 7NJ; 020 7603 6316; www.ifst.org; www.ifstcareers.org

# FORENSIC SCIENTIST

The Forensic Science Service (FSS), an agency of the Home Office, employs scientists for both research and operational forensic science. Forensic scientists examine and try to identify, by means of analytical chemistry, molecular biology and microscopic analysis, samples of materials such as clothing, hair, blood, glass, paint and handwriting, in order to provide evidence to expose criminals, the location of a crime, the weapons used, and other relevant details.

## Qualifications and Training

This is a highly competitive graduate entry profession. The most relevant degrees are biology, chemistry, biochemistry, crop and soil science, materials science, pharmacology and physiology. While there are many undergraduate degrees in forensic science, not all of these qualify you as a forensic scientist. You should check individual course details very carefully. Most forensic scientists also have relevant postgraduate qualifications and some laboratory work experience. Most training is on the job, but you are also likely to have to attend several short courses to improve your knowledge and skills.

## Personal Qualities and Skills

You must have an enquiring and logical mind. You should be patient and able to pay attention to really small details. You should have good scientific skills and knowledge and you must be persistent. Excellent written and oral communication skills are also vital.

Defence Science and Technology Laboratory (DSTL), Porton Down, Salisbury, Wiltshire SP4 0JQ; 01980 613121; www.dstl.gov.uk/about_us/index.htm

Forensic Alliance, Headquarters and Culham Laboratory, F5 Culham Science Centre, Abingdon, Oxfordshire OX14 3ED; 01235 551800; www.forensicalliance.com

Forensic Science Northern Ireland (FSNI), 151 Belfast Rd, Carrickfergus, County Antrim BT38 8PL; 028 9036 1888; www.fsni.gov.uk/

Forensic Science Service (FSS), Trident Court, 2920 Solihull Parkway, Birmingham B37 7YN; 0121 329 5200; www.forensic.gov.uk

Forensic Science Society, Clarke House, 18a Mount Parade, Harrogate, North Yorkshire HG1 1BX; 01423 506068; www.forensic-science-society.org.uk

Home Office, Direct Communications Unit, 2 Marsham Street, London SW1P 4DF; 0870 000 1585; www.homeoffice.gov.uk

LGC, Queens Road, Teddington, Middlesex TW11 0LY; 020 8943 7000; www.lgc.co.uk/

SEMTA: The Sector Skills Council for Science, Engineering and Manufacturing Technologies, Head Office, 14 Upton Road, Watford WD18 0JT; 01923 238441; www.semta.org

info

## Salaries

Starting salaries for trainee forensic scientists typically range from £15,000 to £18,000. You may start higher up the scale if you have a postgraduate qualification. After around two years salaries are £25,000 to £35,000. Senior forensic scientists can earn £50,000.

# FORESTRY

Trees, woodlands and forests cover some 13 per cent of the land area of Britain. The job of the forester is to manage this resource to achieve multiple objectives, balancing competing factors. Forests and woodlands give society many things: they create employment, give space for recreation ranging from rallying to solitary strolls in ancient woodlands, while providing a home for a vast array of plants, birds and animals and producing timber for construction, paper and a multitude of other uses.

Forestry needs people with a vast range of skills and abilities ranging from manual workers who tend and manage forests by planting, fencing and felling, to machine operators who drive very sophisticated machines that fell and extract timber from woodlands. These operations are managed by supervisors and foresters who plan and oversee forests and woodlands. Their work is very varied and includes tasks such as managing habitats for bio-diversity, and planning the felling and planting of forests, along with the management of staff and supervision of large contracts.

## Qualifications and Training

What qualifications you need depends on whether you are hoping to start as a forest worker or to get into forestry management. In either cases some voluntary work with a woodland or forestry-based organisation is a very good starting point. The Woodland Trust is one such organisation, but there are others. Check the Volunteering England website to find out about local opportunities.

To become a forest worker you do not need any formal qualifications. You could choose to study full-time or part-time at an agricultural college where you could complete a BTEC National Diploma in Forestry and Arboriculture. If you are already employed in forestry, your employer may be happy for you to do a course part-time. Whether the course is full- or part-time, you should check with the college as they may have formal entry requirements including GCSEs including maths and science. Passing one of these courses will enable you to progress to skilled worker level and then on to management. If your work involves using a chainsaw or applying pesticides you will have to pass proficiency tests before you are allowed to do this. The National Proficiency Test Council provides information about these tests, but your employer can also help you arrange to take these.

If you prefer to go straight into forestry management, then you will need to do a degree or HND course in forestry or a related subject such as country-side management.

Forestry Commission, Personnel Division, 231 Corstorphine Road, Edinburgh EH12 7AT; 0131 334 0303; www.forestry.gov.uk; e-mail: enquiries@forestry.gsi.gov.uk

Institute of Chartered Foresters, 7a St Colme Street, Edinburgh EH3 6AA; 0131 225 2705; www.charteredforesters.org; e-mail: membership@charteredforesters.org

Royal Forestry Society of England, Wales and Northern Ireland, 102 High Street, Tring, Hertfordshire HP23 4AF; 01442 822028; www.rfs.org.uk; e-mail: rfshq@rts.org.uk

Arboricultural Association, Ampfield House, Ampfield, Nr Romsey, Hampshire SO51 9PA; 01794 368717; fax: 01794 368978; www.trees.org.uk; e-mail: treehouse@dialpipex.com

Royal Scottish Forestry Society, Hagg-on-Esk, Canonbie, Dumfriesshire DG14 0XE; 01387 371518; fax: 01387 371418; www.rsfs.org; e-mail: rsfs@ednet.co.uk

National Proficiency Tests Council (NPTC), Avenue 'J' , National Agricultural Centre, Stoneleigh, Warwickshire CV8 2LG; 02476 696553; www.nptc.org.uk; e-mail: information@nptc.org.uk

Lantra Connect, Lantra House, Stoneleigh, Kenilworth, Warwickshire CV8 2LG; 0845 707 8007 (Lantra Connect – Helpline); www.lantra.co.uk; e-mail: connect@lantra.co.uk

Forestry Contracting Association, Dalfling, Blairdaff, Inverurie, Aberdeenshire AB51 5LA; 01467 651368; www.fcauk.com

## Personal Qualities and Skills

You have to be extremely practical and very safety conscious. You must have a real love of woodlands, forests and trees and an interest in nature. You should be very happy to work outdoors in all sorts of weather conditions. You will often be working on your own and unsupervised, so you have to be comfortable with this, but also good at working as part of a team.

## Salaries

Forest workers start on around £12,000, while skilled workers earn between £14,500 and £17,500. Supervisors earn around £20,000 and forestry managers may earn up to £25,000. Occasionally accommodation is provided, but this is by no means standard practice.

# FOUNDRY WORK

Foundry work is craft-based. The industry provides for a wide range of industries, metal-cast components such as propellers, turbines, crankshafts, all types of machinery, and domestic items such as fireplaces.

Craftspeople are employed in foundry work as pattern, mould and model makers and to maintain the equipment. The introduction of computerised processes means foundries also employ machine operators with a range of different skills. Technical engineering staff are concerned with estimating, inspection and laboratory work. There are many opportunities for operatives in foundry work as die casters, dressers, finishers, moulders, coremakers and in metal melting.

There are also limited openings for foundry technologists, metallurgists, chemists and engineers in research and development. Graduate trainees are recruited to production and administrative management posts.

## Qualifications and Training

While you don't need formal qualifications it may help if you have already worked in another area of engineering, manufacturing or production and/or if you have a forklift licence. There may be opportunities to do an apprenticeship in foundry work; what is available varies from region to region. If you want to do an apprenticeship you may need three GCSEs including one technical subject. Much of your training will be on the job, but your employer may give you opportunities to study for engineering qualifications. If you cannot get in through an apprenticeship and do not have previous experience, a college BTEC or City & Guilds course in engineering could improve your prospects. Vocational diplomas for 14–19-year-olds have recently been introduced in the manufacturing sector. These combine school or college study with work experience and may provide a further route into foundry work. You need to be physically fit to do foundry work and some employers may require you to pass a medical as part of the selection process.

## Personal Qualities and Skills

You must be physically fit with good stamina. You have to be extremely safety conscious at all times. You must be able to follow instructions and work as part of a team. You may have to work on several different projects and you need a high level of concentration.

## Salaries

Salaries for trainee foundry operatives are between £13,000 and £16,000. With some experience salaries rise to £20,000 to £22,000. You may earn more if you have additional supervisory or other responsibilities.

**info**

Institute of Cast Metal Engineers, National Metalforming Centre, 47 Birmingham Road, West Bromwich, West Midlands B70 6PY; www.icme.org.uk

SEMTA (Science, Engineering and Manufacturing Technologies Alliance), 14 Upton Road, Watford, Hertfordshire WD18 0JT; 0800 282167; www.semta.org.uk

www.apprenticeships.org.uk

# FUNDRAISING

Fundraising managers work mainly for charities, but sometimes for pressure groups, community projects and other organisations. They are responsible for overseeing all those activities that help their organisations to generate income. Their varied activities include working with advertisers and marketing specialists to decide how to target a particular audience; working with businesses to obtain corporate funding such as the sponsoring of a project; and organising special fundraising events. They are also responsible for managing trading through charity shops or mail order catalogues; keeping in touch with donors; and organising and supervising the work of volunteers. The particular mix of tasks varies greatly. Large charities may employ fundraising managers who specialise in just one of the above areas. Working for a small charity, you may have to turn your hand to anything and everything.

## Qualifications and Training

While there may be no specific entry qualifications, many fundraisers are graduates with a degree in business studies or marketing. This work is now highly competitive and organisations have to consider who will really be able to help them generate income. A background in advertising, public relations, finance or marketing is ideal. Having done some voluntary work for your chosen charity, or for something similar, can also strengthen your application.

The Institute of Fundraising offers a part-time foundation course in the basics of fundraising, for people who have just embarked on this career. They also offer a certificate in fundraising management, which is equivalent to NVQ level 4. A great deal of training is informal and on the job.

## Personal Qualities and Skills

A full range of excellent interpersonal skills is essential. You must be persuasive, good at negotiating and able to speak confidently to groups of people. You need good business sense, IT skills and numeracy, and the knack of spotting an imaginative solution or coming up with an appealing idea.

## Salaries

Fundraising managers earn between £17,000 and £25,000. With experience and working for a large organisation it is possible to earn far more than this. Some vacancies with small organisations or community groups will be less well paid and many may be part-time with pro rata pay for hours worked.

Institute of Fundraising, Park Place, 12 Lawn Lane, London SW8 1UD; 020 7840 1000; www.institute-of-fundraising.org.uk

Working for a Charity, NCVO, Regent's Wharf, 8 All Saints Street, London NW1 2DP; 020 7250 2512; www.workingforacharity.org.uk

info

# FUNERAL DIRECTOR

Funeral directors collect the deceased from hospital or their residence and prepare them for burial or cremation, which may include embalming. Most funeral premises include private viewing rooms for family visitations. The funeral director often makes all the funeral arrangements on behalf of the family, such as the date, time and place of any ceremony and interment or cremation. The funeral director places the relevant notice of death and acknowledgement of thanks for sympathy in newspapers, pays all the fees, arranges flowers, transports the coffin and mourners to and from church, and will act as a collection point for flowers, or donations in lieu, if desired.

Funeral directors may be employed by large firms such as cooperative societies, or by small family-run concerns. In remote rural areas, a local carpenter or other craftsperson may also work as a funeral director.

## Qualifications and Training

Those wishing to obtain the Diploma in Funeral Directing must register with the National Association of Funeral Directors (NAFD) and will also have student membership of the British Institute of Funeral Directors (BIFD). Full details of the diploma course are forwarded to each student. Every student must follow the foundation module – there are no exceptions.

A satisfactory standard must be reached in the foundation module before proceeding to the diploma. A student will be required to have 24 months' experience and have arranged 25 funerals before the diploma is awarded. NVQs levels 2 and 3 in Funeral Services are available for those employed within the profession.

## Personal Qualities and Skills

Tact, sympathy and a reassuring, helpful nature are essential to funeral directors when they are advising the bereaved. They also need to combine administrative ability with technical expertise in the varied preparations of funeral arrangements. On-call and out-of-hours work is an integral part of the job and an ability to adapt to irregular hours is essential.

## Salaries

Salaries vary greatly depending on size of firm, many of which are family concerns. Average earnings are between £15,000 and £25,000.

**info**

British Institute of Embalmers, Anubis House, 21c Station Road, Knowle, Solihull, West Midlands B93 0HL; 01564 778991; www.bioe.co.uk; e-mail: enquiry@bioe.org.uk

National Association of Funeral Directors, 618 Warwick Road, Solihull, West Midlands B91 1AA; 0845 230 1343; www.nafd.org.uk; e-mail: info@nafd.org.uk

Institute of Burial and Cremation Administration, 107 Parlaunt Road, Langley, Slough, Berks SL3 8BE; 01753 771518; fax: 01753 770518

# FURNITURE AND FURNISHING

## Furniture manufacture

Modern furniture production for the mass market employs a wide range of people. In factories, staff work on production lines, cutting, joining, finishing and assembling complete items or flat-packed products. Staff employed in purchasing departments source suitable materials while sales and marketing staff with wholesalers and retailers promote and sell furniture products. In addition to these roles, whose equivalents may be found in other industries and businesses, there are a number of specific jobs associated with furniture production.

## Furniture designer

As a furniture designer you could be designing furniture for the mass market, to be made in very small quantities, or one-off items. You could be designing furniture made from a range of materials, wood, MDF, even metal or plastics – think of garden and conservatory furniture for example. You might be designing office furniture or an expensive individual item commissioned by a customer.

If you work for the mass market, and the majority of designers do, your role will mainly involve drawing and designing the specifications for an item and perhaps being involved in making a prototype. If you are designing individual items, you may make the whole item yourself from start to finish.

### Qualifications and Training

Most designers have a relevant degree, or HND; most appropriate subjects include furniture design, 3D design, and furniture technology and product design. Some skilled craftsman who get into the bespoke market, making individually commissioned items, may not have formal academic qualifications but may simply have built up a reputation through work they have already completed.

### Personal Qualities and Skills

Wherever you aim to place yourself in the furniture design market, you will have to have creative flair, imagination and a range of practical skills. For the mass market you will need good drawing and computer-aided design skills. You will need to understand the properties of various materials and be aware of costing and budgets for these materials. You will also have to be able to work as part of a design and production team. If you are working in more of a niche market, you may be self-employed and have to have all the appropriate self-marketing and business skills.

# Furniture restorer

Furniture restorers repair, restore and preserve antique furniture. They have to use techniques from woodwork, metalwork, cabinet making, conservation and French polishing. Restorers often need to use modern materials such as resins to repair old pieces of furniture. The work can involve anything from a minor repair, putting a handle back in place, to completely rebuilding an impressive dining room suite. One important aspect of the work is to be able to agree with a client what is realistically achievable with a particular piece of work.

## Qualifications and Training

The British Association of Antique Furniture Restorers (BAFRA) can give advice on how to train to do this work. While there are not necessarily any formal entry qualifications, many furniture restorers do have degrees in furniture design, or other art or conservation related subjects. BAFRA has lists of recommended courses. If you do not wish to go through a degree course, there are City & Guilds courses in furniture construction offered at a small number of colleges.

## Personal Qualities and Skills

Patience and the ability to pay meticulous attention to fine detail are very important. You have to have good practical and technical skills and a good eye for understanding what a particular piece of furniture would have looked like in its original state. A genuine interest in antiques and history will also make the work more enjoyable. On large projects, say in a stately home, you may be working as part of a large conservation and restoration team.

# Upholsterer

Upholsterers make the padding and soft coverings for furniture such as chairs, sofas, stools and mattresses and headboards for beds. They work with a range of materials from natural fibres such as woollen cloth cotton, leather or suede, to modern, synthetic materials. Upholsterers work in two distinct areas – mass manufacturing or individually crafted pieces of work. The work involves planning the work, advising on fabrics and estimating costs, preparing patterns and templates, cutting out fabric, fixing webbing and springs, covering frames with padding and fabric using stitching, staples, tacks or glue, making cushions and adding finishing decorations and trimmings.

## Qualifications and Training

You don't necessarily need formal qualifications, but if you choose to work in mass production, your employer may encourage you to work towards an NVQ level 1 in supporting furniture production. If you wish to work for yourself or in a small craft centre or workshop then a City & Guilds qualification in furniture production could be very useful for you. Building up experience via short courses run by local colleges can be a very useful starting point.

## Personal Qualities and Skills

You need a good eye for design, especially an awareness of colour, texture and the impact created by different fabrics. You have to have good practical skills and good drawing skills, either free hand or computer aided. If you work for yourself, you need appropriate business and self-marketing skills.

## Salaries

New designers working for the mass market start on between £15,500 and £19,000. With experience this rises to £25,000 and £50,000 – although only a few people reach the top end. In niche markets the salary range is enormous, and is based very much on experience and reputation. Restorers earn between £20,000 and £40,000. Upholsterers working for the mass market earn £12,500 to £16,000. Working as an individual craftsperson you could earn around £17,000, but earnings can be much higher than this if you make it into expensive niche markets such as individually designed and produced one-offs in expensive and luxurious fabrics.

Arts Council England,
14 Great Peter Street,
London SW1P 3NQ;
0845 300 6200; www.artscouncil.org.uk

British Design Innovation (BDI),
9 Pavilion Parade, Brighton BN2 1RA; 01273 621378; www.britishdesign.co.uk/

The Chartered Society of Designers (CSD), 1 Cedar Court, Royal Oak Yard, Bermondsey Street, London SE1 3GA; 020 7357 8088; www.csd.org.uk

British Antique Furniture Restorers Association (BAFRA), BAFRA Head Office, The Old Rectory, Warmwell, Dorchester, Dorset DT2 8HQ; 01305 854822; www.bafra.org.uk

Crafts Council, 44a Pentonville Road, Islington, London N1 9BY; 020 7806 2500; www.craftscouncil.org.uk

Creative and Cultural Skills: the Sector Skills Council for Advertising, Crafts, Cultural Heritage, Design, Music, Performing, Literary & Visual Arts, 4th Floor Lafone House, The Leathermarket, Weston Street, London SE1 3HN; 020 7015 1800; www.ccskills.org.uk

The Design Council, 34 Bow Street, London WC2E 7DL; 020 7420 5200; www.designcouncil.org.uk

The Guild of Master Craftsmen, 100 High Street, Lewes, East Sussex BN7 1XU; 01273 478449; www.thegmcgroup.com/theguild

Skillfast-UK (relevant for upholsterers), Richmond House, Lawnswood House, Redvers Close, Leeds LS16 6RD; 0113 2399 600; www.skillfast-uk-org

info

# GARDENING

Gardening, also known as amenity horticulture, involves not only planting and caring for flowers, trees and shrubs, but also the routine jobs of cleaning out flower beds, sweeping leaves and, in the winter, shovelling snow.

## Gardener

(*see also* Landscape Architect)

Gardeners may be employed by local authorities to care for parks or school and hospital grounds, work for a garden centre or landscape contractor, or be self-employed. Heritage gardening is a growth area and involves working for organisations such as the National Trust, English Heritage, and other private gardens.

### Qualifications and Training

It is desirable but not always necessary to have formal qualifications to become a gardener. Training is given on the job, often as part of an apprenticeship; NVQ levels 1–3 are available. Full-time training courses in horticulture are available at colleges throughout the country, from first diploma level. The Royal Horticultural Society offers a limited number of opportunities for practical training and plantsmanship at its gardens at Wisley, Rosemoor and Hyde Hall. Voluntary Internships for four or more weeks are available for those studying horticulture at college, and at a number of schools work experience placements are available for secondary pupils.

### Personal Qualities and Skills

You must have a real interest in the plants you work with, whether they are commercial fruit and vegetables or ornamental flowers and shrubs. You should be very practical and happy to work in all weathers and you must be patient – some of your work takes a long time to come to fruition. For some gardening jobs you need an eye for design and colour. You should be comfortable working on your own, but able to talk to people about their gardens, their crops and their ideas.

## Salaries

Most people employed in commercial horticulture are paid on a nationally agreed scale which is revised annually for agricultural workers. The scale is graded and you are paid according to your levels of experience and the work you do. At the start of your career this rate is around minimum wage and annual income is about £11,000. With experience and training this rises to £18,000. Many gardeners are self-employed, charging an hourly rate of anything from £7.00 to £20.00 an hour.

Lantra, Lantra House, Stoneleigh Park, Nr Coventry, Warwickshire CV8 2LG; 0845 707 8007; www.lantra.co.uk

Royal Botanic Gardens Kew, Richmond, Surrey TW9 3AB; www.rbgkew.org.uk

Horticultural Correspondence College, Freepost, Notton, Chippenham, Wiltshire SN15 2BR; 01249 730326; www.hccollege.co.uk

National Proficiency Tests Council (NPTC), Stoneleigh Park, Stoneleigh, Warwickshire CV8 2LG; 024 7685 7300; www.nptc.org.uk

Royal Horticultural Society (RHS); www.rhs.org.uk

LGcareers; www.lgcareers.com

**info**

# GAS SERVICE ENGINEER

Gas service engineers, also known as gas service technicians or gas service fitters, work in people's homes and on business premises, installing, servicing and repairing appliances and systems such as cookers, boilers and central heating systems. They test controls and safety devices to ensure that they are working and they locate and repair gas leaks. Often they specialise in installation, servicing or repair, but some gas service engineers will work in all three areas.

## Qualifications and Training

The usual route to qualification is through a technician-level apprenticeship lasting between three and four years. You need four GCSEs grades A–C including English, maths and science, and you must have perfect colour vision. Most apprentices start at age 16, but you can start up to the age of 24. Successful completion of the apprenticeship also leads to an NVQ level 3 award.

To work as a gas fitter, installer or service engineer, you must register with the Gas Safe Register, which will check your qualifications and ascertain that you have had suitable training and work experience before allowing you to register.

## Personal Qualities and Skills

You must be practical, able to handle tools and instruments, and you must be able to apply technical knowledge to practical problems. You have to be able to work on your own or as part of a team, and it is important that you are polite and friendly and enjoy meeting and dealing with people. Having an acute awareness of safety issues is essential.

## Salaries

Trainees earn between £12,000 and £15,000, and newly qualified technicians earn between £17,000 and £20,000. With several years' experience you can earn up to £26,000.

# Gas network engineer

Gas network engineers lay and service the gas pipelines that supply domestic and commercial premises. The work involves digging holes using mechanical digging equipment, using maps and plans to trace where you need to dig, laying and repairing pipes, connecting homes and businesses to the gas network and dealing with emergency leaks.

## Qualifications and Training

You do not need formal qualifications to work as a gas network engineer, but if you train through an apprenticeship you will normally need four GCSEs grades A–C including maths, English and a technical subject. If you are not joining through an apprenticeship, you will have an advantage if you have experience and/or qualifications in engineering or building services. You will also need a driving licence.

## Personal Qualities and Skills

You need to be physically fit and you must be able to follow plans and instructions accurately. You need to have a keen awareness of safety issues and you should be good at working as part of a team. As you progress, you may need to develop supervisory responsibilities too.

## Salaries

Apprentices and new entrants to the work earn £11,000 to £14,000. Once you have completed your apprenticeship or built up some experience salaries rise to £18,000 to £25,000. With supervisory responsibilities earnings can be £32,000 plus.

British Gas Recruitment, Harrow Way, Basingstoke, Hampshire RG22 4AR; www.britishgasacademy.co.uk

Energy and Utility Skills, Friars Gate Two, 1011 Stratford Road, Shirley, Solihull B90 4BN; 0845 077 9922; www.euskills.co.uk

Engineering and Construction Industry Training Board, Blue Court, Church Lane, Kings Langley, Hertfordshire WD4 8JP; 01923 260000; www.ecitb.org.uk

Gas Safe Register, PO Box 6804, Basingstoke, Hampshire RG24 4NB; 0800 408 5500; gassaferegister.co.uk

info

# GEOLOGY

Geology, often referred to as geoscience, really encompasses a range of careers. Geoscience is concerned with the understanding of the earth, its rocks, minerals, fossils, the dynamics of how the continents move, why earthquakes occur and what its 460-million-year history can tell us. There are highly academic fields of geology, the discovery, collection, classification and analysis of fossil remains of flora and fauna from millions of years ago. Geoscience is also concerned with very practical and current questions, advising on whether a particular site is suitable for the building of a bridge, a dam or a tunnel, working out where natural resources like oil, gas and metals can be found and how safely they can be extracted.

Some geologists work as lecturers in higher education, others who are interested in some of the scientific rather than the scientific/commercial applications work in some of the following.

## Paleontologist
Paleontologists study fossils and all the layers of rock that make up the earth's crust to try to find out more about the physical history of the planet, the pattern of past climate changes, or the movements of whole land masses for example.

## Seismologist
These are the scientists we hear from when earthquakes and tsunamis are being reported on – why they have occurred, how powerful they were and what we might do to predict where these dangerous phenomena are next likely to occur.

## Volcanologist
Volcanologists make a close study of active volcanoes and the area that surrounds them. They also look at extinct and dormant volcanoes to try to better predict when and where the next eruptions are likely to occur. They spend time actually working in and around craters as well as based in laboratories.

What comes out of volcanoes gives them a chance to study the structure of the core of the planet.

Geologists who work mainly in the extraction industries locating and extracting oil, gas, metals, minerals and soil fulfil some of the following roles.

## Engineering geologist

Engineering geologists analyse the underlying structure of major construction sites before tunnels, pipelines, bridges, harbours, docks and buildings. They identify potential problems and advise on best materials and construction methods to be used. They analyse and assess soil, rocks, water courses and other ground conditions. They take into account environmental conditions and they work to ensure that construction projects will be safe in the short and long term.

## Mining geologist

Whether companies are extracting rock and stone, minerals, metals, coal or precious metals and gemstones, mine geologists provide advice and expertise on the geological aspects of development and production in mine, pit and quarry sites. In overseeing drilling and surface exploration programmes, they help to determine likely directions for future development.

## Seismic interpreter

Seismic interpreters use data generated by movements in the rocks below the earth's surface, to work out exactly what quantities of oil and gas are stored beneath the surface. They use complex computer software and data from satellite stations to help them in their work.

## Geotechnician

Geotechnicians support the work of geoscientists. They are based mainly in laboratories and their work involves preparing and analysing rock samples to discover their chemical make-up. Some geotechnicians work at drilling sites, logging data and monitoring activity.

## Qualifications and Training

Geoscience, except for technicians, is a graduate profession. Degrees in geology, geophysics, geo-engineering, geochemistry, earth sciences or similar subjects may all be acceptable. Many geologists also have a postgraduate qualification. To get onto one of these degree courses you normally need A levels including maths and one science. While this is a competitive area of work in some ways, geologists with good qualifications are likely to be in considerable demand because resources are getting harder to locate and more difficult to extract. You may be able to get a job as a junior geotechnician if you have five GCSEs grades A–C, including English, science and maths, but some employers prefer you to have A levels, an HND or a degree. There are only a few science-based HNDs which specialise in geology and geoscience.

## Personal Qualities and Skills

You need a strong interest in the area of geoscience in which you want to work. You have to have a rigorous scientific approach to your work, be able to construct surveys, analyse and interpret data. You have to be good at working as part of a team, but also able to work independently. You need good powers of observation – to be quick to spot any changes in data. For some jobs you have to be able to work in physically hard conditions, on oil rigs, up a volcano, etc.

## Salaries

Geoscientists earn between £30,000 and £45,000. Project leaders and other senior geologists can earn £50,000 to £60,000. Salaries are highest in the oil and gas industry; this is also the work where you may have to spend long periods away from home. Geotechnicians earn between £18,000 and £29,000. The higher salaries are, once again, paid in the oil and gas industries.

Natural Environment Research Council, Polaris House, North Star Avenue, Swindon, Wiltshire SN2 1EU; 01793 411500; www.nerc.ac.uk

Geological Society, Burlington House, Piccadilly, London W1J 0BG; 020 7434 9944; www.geolsoc.org.uk

British Geological Survey, Kingsley Dunham Centre, Keyworth, Nottingham NG12 5GG; 0115 936 3143; www.bgs.ac.uk

info

# H

## HAIR

## Hairdresser

Hairdressers offer a variety of services involving hair, such as cutting, styling, perming and colouring. Salons or individual stylists may specialise in male or female hairdressing, or a niche market such as specialist colouring, Afro-Caribbean or ethnic hairstyles. Hairdressers may also be responsible for answering the telephone, making appointments, serving drinks to clients, cleaning and stock control. They work in salons, hotels, airports, cruise liners, hospitals and prisons. Some hairdressers work as freelances. There are over 170,000 hairdressers in the UK.

### Qualifications and Training

You don't always need formal qualifications to become a hairdresser. You can either train at a salon, where you may go on day release to a college or to the salon's own training centre. Alternatively you can do a full- or part-time college course in hairdressing or barbering. NVQ levels 1, 2 and 3 are available in hairdressing. Salon and college entry requirements vary, but you may need four GCSEs grades A–C including English, maths and an arts subject. There may be apprenticeship schemes in hairdressing available, but this varies across local areas. Where there are apprenticeships available you are again likely to need four GCSEs. Vocational diplomas for 14–19-year-olds have recently been introduced in hairdressing; these combine school or college study with work placement, but are not available in every area.

### Personal Qualities and Skills

Hairdressers should have a genuine interest in people, a natural friendliness, the ability to stay calm under pressure, creative ability and an eye for detail. A presentable personal appearance is also essential. Hairdressers must not have skin conditions that can be affected by chemicals.

## Salaries

Trainees earn around £11,000 to £13,000. Stylists earn £16,000 to £21,000. There is a lot of regional variation and salaries also depend on how fashionable the salon is deemed to be. Top stylists can earn more than £30,000. This is work where you can sometimes make additional money from tips. It is also possible to become self-employed, visiting people in their homes to cut, colour, perm and style their hair. In this case, what you earn depends on what you charge.

Hairdressing and Beauty Industry Authority (HABIA), Oxford House, Sixth Avenue, Sky Business Park, Robin Hood Airport, Doncaster DN9 3GG; www. habia.org

**info**

# HEALTH AND SAFETY

## Health and safety adviser

Health and safety advisers work for every kind of organisation, from multinationals and government agencies to small businesses. Advisers work in partnership with employers, employees, directors and trade unions, and are responsible for ensuring that all safety legislation is adhered to and that suitable policies and practices are put in place. They help organisations minimise safety risks and they are often involved in staff training.

## Health and safety inspector

Health and safety inspectors work to assess and improve every kind of work practice and the health and safety applications attached to it. In the UK one person is killed every day at work, and inspectors working for the Health and Safety Executive (HSE), which is a government agency, are constantly working to try to reduce this statistic. Inspectors check work premises, from building sites to farms and factories, and they have legal powers to demand changes. They are also called in to investigate when accidents do occur.

### Qualifications and Training

It is possible to become an adviser without a degree, if you have plenty of work experience in management, engineering, science or health, but there is a move towards making this a graduate entry profession. Degrees in occupational health, engineering, health science and management are the most favoured, and these each have their own entry requirements. Graduates or HND holders of any subject can become health and safety inspectors, but again there is a preference for subjects such as engineering, environmental health and physics.

If you are accepted by the Health and Safety Executive you undergo a two-year structured training programme. This involves a combination of short courses and on-the-job training.

## Personal Qualities and Skills

To become a health and safety inspector you have to be extremely observant and thorough in your approach to what you see and what you are told. You have to be an excellent communicator, able to explain to someone why a work station or a production line may be unsafe. You need to persuade people to do the right thing, but be firm enough to take action if they do not. You need to be a well-organised administrator.

## Salaries

Health and safety advisers earn between £18,000 and £24,000. Trainee health and safety inspectors earn around £26,000 with a rise of around 10 per cent on successful completion of the two-year training period. Senior health and safety inspectors can earn around £40,000.

info

British Safety Council, National Safety Centre, 70 Chancellor's Road, London W6 9RS; 020 8741 1231; www.britishsafetycouncil.co.uk

Chartered Institute of Environmental Health (CIEH), Chadwick Court, 15 Hatfields, London SE1 8DJ; 020 7928 6006; www.cieh.org

Department for Work and Pensions (DWP), Room 112, The Adelphi, 1–11 John Adam Street, London WC2N 6HT; 020 7712 2171; www.dwp.gov.uk/

The Health and Safety Executive (HSE), Headquarters, Rose Court, 2 Southwark Bridge, London SE1 9HS; 0845 345 0055; www.hse.gov.uk

Health and Safety Executive for Northern Ireland (HSENI),

83 Ladas Drive, Belfast BT6 9FR; 0800 0320 121; www.hseni.gov.uk

Institution of Occupational Safety and Health (IOSH), Membership Department, The Grange, Highfield Drive, Wigston, Leicestershire LE18 1NN; 0116 257 3100; www.iosh.co.uk

National Examination Board for Occupational Safety and Health (NEBOSH), Dominus Way, Meridian Business Park, Leicester LE19 1QW; 0116 263 4700; www.nebosh.org.uk

Royal Society for the Prevention of Accidents (RoSPA), Head Office, Edgbaston Park, 353 Bristol Road, Edgbaston, Birmingham B5 7ST; 0121 248 2000; www.rospa.com/

# HEALTH SERVICE (NON-MEDICAL)

There are plenty of non-medical jobs and career paths open to people in healthcare. Some of these services are provided by the National Health Service (NHS), others such as catering, cleaning or laundry are often provided by companies that are contracted to do this work on behalf of the NHS.

## Catering staff

Cooks, housekeepers and kitchen assistants working either for the NHS or for catering companies provide a range of hospital meals. They have to cater for special diets and try to provide a range of tempting food. Working within a tight budget is a key skill in this work.

## Clerical staff

The NHS employs large numbers of clerks, secretaries, telephonists, receptionists and other administrative workers. Some of this work involves patient contact, eg receptionists at clinics, or ward clerks. Other work is more behind the scenes, ordering supplies, booking appointments and updating records.

## Domestic services staff

Domestic services staff are either employed by the NHS or by private companies that have contracts to clean health service premises and also laundering all the sheets, pillow cases, towels, etc.

## Estates staff

Hospitals, clinics and other NHS premises need building services engineers to ensure that lighting, heating, air conditioning and other environmental management systems work at all times. Architects and surveyors are needed to design new premises or plan refurbishment of existing older properties.

## Information science and technology

Computer systems of many kinds are important for keeping records, monitoring care and sharing information. All kinds of IT staff are employed, from data input clerks to systems development.

## Manager

This is a very broad term. The NHS employs managers in finance, human resources, strategic planning, performance monitoring and the day-to-day running of every kind of health service establishment.

## Porter and messenger

Porters move patients and equipment from one part of a hospital or other healthcare centre to another. Messengers take important messages from one department to another. Even in these days of electronic communications urgent messages are delivered by messengers.

## Scientist

*see* Medical and Healthcare Science

## Sterile services staff

Sterile services staff clean and sterilise all medical equipment. Some of this equipment is highly technical, so disinfecting it and preparing it for use is a painstaking and complex task. Applicants for this work usually need GCSEs in English, maths and a science.

### Qualifications and Training

These vary considerably for different jobs. It is worth consulting specific career areas such as Accountancy, Biomedical Engineering, Hospitality, Human Resource Management, Information Technology and Secretarial work. For some work, such as being a porter or a kitchen assistant, you may not need any formal academic qualifications. For most management posts you need either a degree or professional qualifications in a relevant area such as accountancy or management studies. Posts in science, engineering or information technology will require relevant qualifications from GCSE to postgraduate level.

### Personal Qualities and Skills

The common thread for all these jobs is a genuine commitment to working within and for healthcare and wanting to deliver a good service to patients. For any work involving patient contact, being sensitive and caring is important. All jobs require you to be a good communicator and to be able to work very well as part of a team. Particular jobs require specific practical skills such as cooking, IT skills or being good with technical equipment.

## Salaries

Apart from doctors and the most senior managers, all NHS staff are paid on a clearly defined scale known as Agenda for Change (AfC). New entrants to junior posts such as kitchen assistant, porter or junior administrative assistant are paid between £13,000 and £17,000. Once you have supervisory functions and/or additional responsibilities, salaries rise to £17,000 to £20,000. Jobs in IT, human resources and management start at £20,000 rising to £37,000; senior managers in all functions can earn far more than this. This salary information is a guide only, because there are so many different points on the scale. The NHS Careers website sets out detailed information.

NHS Careers, PO Box 376, Bristol BS99 3EY; 0845 606 0655; www.nhscareers.nhs.uk

NHS Learning and Development Service; 08000 150 850; e-mail: learning@nhscareers.nhs.uk

NHS Education for Scotland, Careers Information Service, 66 Rose Street, Edinburgh EH2 2NN; 0131 225 4365; www.nes.scot.nhs.uk

*info*

# HEALTH VISITOR

*see* Nursing Professions

# HEALTHCARE ASSISTANT

*see* Nursing Professions

# HORTICULTURE

Horticulture refers to the commercial cultivation of flowering plants, shrubs, ornamental trees, soft fruit such as raspberries and strawberries, fruit trees, vegetables and herbs. Horticultural work occurs in a range of settings including garden centres, plant nurseries, parks and formal gardens, market gardens, community horticulture projects and large farms. The main horticultural jobs are described below, but in addition horticultural specialists may work in teaching at agricultural colleges, in advisory work on new projects, or in areas such as marketing. Currently research on more sustainable methods of horticulture that use less water or fewer pesticides is a significant area of research and development.

# Arboriculturist

Arboriculturists are tree specialists who develop expertise in the planting, care, management and production of trees of every kind, from orchard fruits and native English woodland trees to exotic varieties. They study sites to assess their suitability for particular trees and carry out surveys of tree populations and attempt to analyse and solve any problems that stop the trees thriving. They often work for formal gardens, parks, local authorities and conservation bodies. Their role may cover supervising other manual workers carrying out activities like pruning or planting. They may also help to resolve disputes over trees on boundaries, or decisions on whether a particular tree should be preserved.

## Qualifications and Training

You can either enter this work with a degree in arboriculture or forestry management, or you can work towards appropriate professional qualifications once you have had some work experience with a forestry or woodland management organisation. If you take this second route, you may not need any formal qualifications. Professional qualifications include the Arboricultural Association Technician's Certificate in Arboriculture, the Royal Forestry Society's Professional Diploma in Arboriculture (DipArb (RFS)) or the Institute of Chartered Foresters' Professional Examination (with arboriculture options).

## Personal Qualities and Skills

You need a genuine interest in trees and conservation. You must also have a scientific and logical approach to your work. You must be a good communicator, able to supervise others and put across your ideas to groups or individuals. You should be physically fit and happy working in all weathers.

## Salaries

Salaries start at around £17,000, but with either a degree and/or considerable experience, salaries rise to £20,000 to £27,000.

# Horticultural manager

As a horticultural manager you will be responsible for the day-to-day care of plants and the supervision of staff. Your exact tasks will vary enormously, depending where you are working, for example in a garden centre, a market garden or a commercial nursery. You may be involved in a lot of hands-on work, watering, feeding, pruning and planting. You may also be involved in working out costs, developing new products and markets, managing and training staff and negotiating with suppliers or dealing with queries from customers.

## Qualifications and Training

You may not need formal qualifications to get into this work; many managers have worked their way up from more basic jobs. Individual employers set their own entry requirements and some will expect you to have three to four GCSEs including maths, English and a science. Some managers have a degree in horticulture or a related subject.

## Personal Qualities and Skills

You need a blend of good practical and interpersonal skills. You should have a real interest in plants and be prepared to develop highly specialised knowledge. You must be able to motivate other people and ensure that work is carried out carefully. You should also be able to deal well with customers, being helpful and informative, or with suppliers, using good negotiating skills.

## Salaries

Because of the many different types of employer, salaries vary from £16,000 to £40,000. Most people doing this work earn between £20,000 and £25,000.

# Horticultural worker

Horticultural workers carry out all the daily tasks associated with planting, growing, caring for, propagating and harvesting flowers, shrubs, vegetables, fruit and trees grown for commercial or amenity purposes. Your day-to-day tasks could include sowing seeds, taking cuttings, checking plants for signs of pests and diseases, and pruning, tidying and moving plants. Your job could include some landscaping work and you may also deal with customer queries if you are working in a garden centre or nursery.

## Qualifications and Training

You don't need formal qualifications to get into this work, though some employers will expect you to have GCSEs in maths, English and science. There are several part-time qualifications at NVQ levels 1 and 2 towards which you can work once you are in employment.

## Personal Qualities and Skills

You have to have a real interest in plants of all kinds and enjoy growing them and making them thrive. You need good practical skills and you must be physically fit with good manual dexterity. You should be able to follow instructions and then work on your own. You should also be able to work as part of a team. You may also have to work directly advising members of the public.

## Salaries

Salaries start at £12,000 to £13,000 rising to £15,000 to £17,000. You may earn more as you take on supervisory or other responsibilities.

**info**

Lantra – The Sector Skills Council for the Environmental and Land-based Sector, Lantra House, Stoneleigh Park, Coventry, Warwickshire CV8 2LG;
0845 707 8007; www.lantra.co.uk

Institute of Horticulture (IoH), 14/15 Belgrave Square, London SW1X 8PS; 020 7245 6943; www.horticulture.org.uk

Royal Botanic Garden Edinburgh, 20A Inverleith Row, Edinburgh EH3 5LR; 0131 552 7171; www.rbge.org.uk

Royal Botanic Gardens Kew, Richmond, Surrey TW9 3AB; 020 8332 5000; www.kew.org

Royal Horticultural Society (RHS), 80 Vincent Square, London SW1P 2PE; 0845 260 5000; www.rhs.org.uk

LGcareers; www.lgcareers.com

Institute of Chartered Foresters, 59 George Street, Edinburgh EH2 2JG; 0131 240 1425; www.charteredforesters.org

Arboricultural Association, Ullenwood Court, Ullenwood, Cheltenham, Gloucestershire GL53 9QS; 01242 522152; www.trees.org.uk

Grow careers; Advice Line: 0845 707 8007; www.growcareers.org.uk

# HOSPITALITY AND CATERING

There is a wide variety of job opportunities in this category at all levels, from managers and supervisors to craft workers. Sometimes the dividing lines are not clear-cut, and it is quite usual for individuals to move up from one to another.

# Chef/cook

In addition to creating and supervising the preparation of all kinds of different dishes, a head chef/cook has to be trained in the management of a kitchen, being responsible for the staff and the organisation of their workload, planning the menus, budgeting, ordering and approving the necessary ingredients, and maintaining high standards of efficiency and hygiene. Chefs are employed in hotels, restaurants, industrial organisations (such as offices or factories), institutions (such as hospitals, schools and universities or colleges) and in the armed forces. In large establishments the chef de cuisine is in overall charge, while there may be a number of chefs de partie (in charge of their part of the kitchen) and a number of commis chefs (still learning the trade).

## Qualifications and Training

No formal qualifications are necessary, but depending on what training route your employer wishes to put you through, you may need four GCSEs including English and maths. If you want to study full- or part-time at college before you start training with an employer, you can study for BTEC National

**AWARDING QUALIFICATIONS *for* LICENSED RETAIL**

**RAISING STANDARDS IN LICENSED RETAIL**

The licensed retail sector (pubs, bars, restaurants, hotels and other licensed premises) offers great career choices

BII, the professional body for the sector, offers information, help, support and qualifications for every stage of your licensed retail career.

## BIIAB:

- part of BII

- the industry's dedicated awarding body - with over 25 years of experience

- the leading provider of sector-specific qualifications

- offers a wide portfolio of qualifications for every step of your career.

**For more information**

**01276 684449**

**info@bii.org**

www.biiab.org

www.bii.org

## Professional Alcohol Retailing

BII is the professional body for the licensed retail industry. We're here to support high standards, social responsibility and training and development of those who enjoy a career in our dynamic industry – be it for a couple of years or a lifetime.

**Think you want to run a pub, or a restaurant?**

Then you'll need a licence to sell alcohol and you'll need a National Certificate for personal Licence Holders (NCPLH) before you even apply to your local council for one.

The NCPLH from BII's awarding body, BIIAB, is the market leading qualification of its kind. You'll also need to know the law, of course, and the BIIAB NCPLH will teach you everything you need to know.

Just as important as your licence will be top class training in every aspect of the business – from customer service and basic kitchen skills to cellar techniques and staff management. BIIAB has a qualification to support you every step of the way.

**Why not start today with the entry level Award in Responsible Alcohol Retailing, or the Introduction to Licensed Retail Operations?**

Visit www.bii.org or call 01276 684449 for more information.

With over 1,000 titles in printed and digital format, **Kogan Page** offers affordable, sound business advice

## www.koganpage.com

You are reading one of the thousands of books published by **Kogan Page**. As Europe's leading independent business book publishers **Kogan Page** has always sought to provide up-to-the-minute books that offer practical guidance at affordable prices.

Certificates and Diplomas in hospitality and catering; you need four GCSEs grades A–C to get a place on one of these courses. You can study for NVQ courses to levels 1, 2 and 3, either full-time before you start work or part-time while you are training in a kitchen. There are also apprenticeships (leading to NVQ level 2) and Advanced Apprenticeships (leading to NVQ level 3) available in food preparation and cookery. These last 12 and 24 months respectively. There are also some NVQ level 4 courses available in kitchen and larder, confectionery and patisserie.

If you have five GCSEs and two A levels, there are several foundation degree courses available in food preparation, including professional cookery, professional patisserie, culinary arts, culinary creativity and hospitality. Vocational diplomas for 14–19-year-olds have recently been introduced in the hospitality sector, combining school or college study with work experience. At present there are only a few of these available.

## Personal Qualities and Skills

Chefs need a real passion for food and a creative attitude to making the best use of ingredients, whether they work in a top restaurant, a country pub or a hospital canteen. Despite the public image seen on TV, being able to keep calm under pressure is a great asset. Chefs must be good team leaders and motivators, able to get people to work well together.

## Salaries

Trainee chefs earn between £12,500 and £15,000. Chefs in charge of a section of the kitchen earn between £16,000 and £20,000. Head chefs earn up to £30,000. A head chef in a large, high quality hotel running a large kitchen can earn £40,000 to £50,000. The hospitality industry has been hit by the recession, which has held back some salaries.

# Fast food/restaurant manager

The responsibilities of fast food and restaurant managers vary very much according to the kinds of outlet in which they work. Fast food managers work mainly for chains that operate burger, pizza and fried chicken eateries, for example. As a fast food outlet manager your responsibilities are mainly for organising the work of the staff team, making sure that everyone works quickly and efficiently and solving problems if they arise. You are likely to be responsible for the food preparation area, as well as the customer service and eating areas. You have a major role in training new staff. As a restaurant manager you might be working in a large hotel, a small independent restaurant, a national chain of eateries or a fast food outlet. Restaurant managers tend to work front of house, welcoming guests, and ensuring that service is good and customers are satisfied. You will certainly be liaising with kitchen staff, but management of that area is likely to be the chef's domain.

## Qualifications and training

You don't necessarily need formal qualifications to become a fast food manager. Many managers begin as counter service staff, then become shift supervisors and from there progress to management. A few companies do offer graduate training schemes and accept graduates from any discipline. If you are interested in food and catering there are degrees in hospitality management, culinary arts management and hotel and catering management available at several universities. In all cases a great deal of training is on the job, but your employer may send you on short courses at college or run in-house, and there is a wide variety of catering and management qualifications you could consider.

## Personal qualities and skills

You have to have excellent interpersonal skills. The balance of how much time you spend with customers or managing your staff team depends very much on the kind of establishment for which you are working. In all instances you need to be polite, friendly, calm if problems arise or under pressure. In fast food management you need to be very aware of health and safety and food hygiene issues.

## Salaries

Assistant managers earn between £18,000 and £22,000 and managers earn £20,000 to £26,000. At the luxury end of the restaurant business, a manager may earn up to £40,000. Working for fast food chains it may be possible to move into area or head office management roles with salaries of around £30,000.

# Food service assistant

Waiters and waitresses, as well as serving, may cook special dishes at table or specialise in particular skills such as wine-waiting. As well as serving food and drink, they have to maintain contact with their customers; unfriendly staff may ruin the reputation of a restaurant. Promotion is to head waiter/waitress.

# Hotel housekeeping

Room staff, cleaners and other support staff keep the hotel clean and comfortable. The head housekeeper is in charge of this aspect of hotel life.

# Hotel reception

Receptionists receive guests, handle reservations and perform bookkeeping duties, so it is important to be good at figures, able to handle cash and use computers. Languages are an advantage. Working hours are arranged to deal with early and late arrivals and departures, so may entail shift and weekend work.

# Kitchen staff

In the kitchen there are opportunities at all levels, from the chef in charge of a select restaurant to the dishwasher in a snack bar. There are also opportunities for freelance work – catering for directors' dining rooms, private parties and business lunches, for instance. It is demanding work, often in 'unsocial hours', when most people are out enjoying themselves. Some cooking can be repetitious (such as take-away menus), some creatively satisfying.

# Management

Catering management can cover work in a roadside or motorway restaurant, a luxury restaurant, a hospital meals service, a snack bar, a take-away service, university and college restaurants, the armed forces, outdoor events or contract catering (providing meals and snacks to the management and staff of the contractor, for example a bank or insurance company). The manager in charge is normally responsible for budgeting, menu planning, stock monitoring, seeing that good food is served as and when it is required, often round the clock, keeping customers satisfied and supervising staff.

Large hotels have a general manager, food and beverage manager, personnel and training manager and house manager, and there may also be heads of departments or sections. There are specialised opportunities in the fields of finance, administration, food and beverage operations, accommodation services, sales and marketing, product development, public relations, personnel and training.

Accommodation management is concerned with the domestic side of colleges and universities (where managers are sometimes known as bursars), hospitals, local authority day centres and residential homes, for the aged or disabled, for instance. The demanding duties of such managers include responsibility for accommodation and catering, particularly in halls of residence, which may be used as conference centres during the vacation. The work can involve personal contact with the residents (in homes, for instance, where the population is fairly permanent), or be more in the nature of house-keeping, as in hospitals where the patients are constantly changing and are not the direct concern of the domestic staff.

## Qualifications and Training

There are two main routes to qualification: attending a college or university as a full-time student, or joining a training programme operated by an employer or an organisation that works with employers to provide training, such as the Hotel and Catering Training Company (HCTC). In the latter case, entrants learn on the job and attend college or a training centre on a short-course or day-release basis. Recruits on the work-based training programme will generally acquire NVQ awards. An increasing number of employers are offering Modern Apprenticeships, which provide a route to higher-level technical or supervisory posts, and NVQs at level 3.

Full-time courses are available in hospitality-related subjects, including HNDs, foundation degrees and degree courses.

## Personal Qualities and Skills

Catering workers usually need physical fitness and stamina as well as high standards of personal hygiene. Skin complaints may disqualify entrants. Managers need to be well motivated with good interpersonal and team skills. All staff have to be prepared to work split shifts and antisocial hours.

## Salaries

Salaries for kitchen and domestic staff start at around minimum wage: £10,500 to £12,000. New managers earn around £16,000 in small hotels. In medium-sized hotels earnings are between £20,000 and £30,000. A manager of a large, successful hotel, or working for a chain of hotels in a head office management job, can earn up to £60,000.

**info**

People 1st: The Sector Skills Council for the Hospitality, Leisure, Travel and Tourism Industries, 2nd Floor, Armstrong House, 38 Market Square, Uxbridge, Middlesex UB8 1LH; 0870 060 2550; www.people1st.co.uk

# Publican/licensee

Publicans manage licensed premises, mainly pubs and bars. They work for breweries, pub chains or for themselves running a free house. The publican/manager runs the premises which may include a restaurant, fruit machines and overnight accommodation, and is responsible for stock control, staff management and the overall standards of drink, food and customer service. Pubs and bars vary enormously, from lively late-night city centre bars providing music and other entertainment to quiet rural pubs serving a local village clientele. The demands that these different settings make on their managers will vary considerably.

## Qualifications and Training

Many publicans/licensees work their way up to this position by starting work as a bar person and gradually taking on more responsibility. Alternatively, pub chains and breweries may take people onto management training schemes and give them appropriate training and experience to take on a pub or bar of their own. Each employer sets its own selection criteria, but some will expect applicants to have HNDs, a foundation degree or a degree in a relevant subject such as business studies, marketing or hospitality. A good track record in work which involves customer service and taking on considerable responsibility is also a big advantage. Licensees must be aged 18 or over, have no criminal convictions and be able to satisfy the local authority that they are a suitable person to hold such a licence.

## Personal Qualities and Skills

You have to have excellent organisational and budgeting skills. You must be good at leading and motivating other people. You should enjoy working with members of the public, being able to provide a listening ear or a firm instruction as the need arises. You must be calm but able to react quickly in any potentially difficult situations, such as when dealing with customers who have drunk too much.

## Salaries

Trainee and assistant managers earn between £15,000 and £20,000. Experienced managers generally earn between £25,000 and £30,000. Income may be related to turnover or to brewery and pub chain bonus schemes. If you are running your own establishment, your income will depend on how well that business does. In all cases, you are likely to have to work long hours to earn your living.

British Franchise Association, Thames View, Newtown Rd, Henley-on-Thames, Oxon RG9 1HG; 01491 578050; www.thebfa.org

Food and Drink Federation, 6 Catherine Street, London WC2B 5JJ; 020 7836 2460; www.fdf.org.uk

Institute of Hospitality (formerly HCIMA), Trinity Court, 34 West Street, Sutton, Surrey SM1 1SH; 020 8661 4900; www.instituteofhospitality.org

Improve – The Food and Drink Sector Skills Council, Ground Floor, Providence House, 2 Innovation Close, Heslington, York YO10 5ZF; 0845 644 0448; www.improveltd.co.uk

Scottish Food and Drink Federation (SFDF), 4a Torphichen Street, Edinburgh EH3 8JQ; 0131 229 9415; www.sfdf.org.uk

Skillsmart Retail: The Sector Skills Council for Retail, 4th Floor, 93 Newman Street, London W1T 3EZ; 020 740 5060; www.skillsmartretail.com

*info*

# Barperson

Bar staff work in pubs, bars, restaurants and hotels, selling and serving alcoholic and non-alcoholic drinks to customers. In some cases they may also be responsible for taking food orders, selling snacks, etc. In some bars they will also have to know how to mix an extensive range of cocktails.

## Qualifications and Training

You don't need formal qualifications to do this work. You must be aged 18 or over and you must have very good people skills. Some experience in retail or other customer care work is valuable.

### Personal Qualities and Skills

You should be friendly and helpful. You must be able to keep calm in what is often a very hectic, crowded and noisy environment. You should be able to use your initiative and work well as part of a team.

### Salaries

Much of the work is part-time and many bar staff are paid the minimum wage, though this can be increased through tips. Annual income works out at between £12,000 and £15,000.

**info**

British Institute of Innkeeping (BII), Wessex House, 80 Park Street, Camberley, Surrey GU15 3PT; 01276 684449; www.bii.org

Wine and Spirit Educational Trust (WSET), International Wine and Spirit Centre, 39–45 Bermondsey Street, London SE1 3XF; 020 7089 3800; www.wset.co.uk

People 1st, 2nd Floor, Armstrong House, 38 Market Square, Uxbridge, Middlesex UB8 1LH; 0870 060 2550; www.people1st.co.uk

# HOUSING OFFICER/MANAGER

Housing officers work mainly for local authorities and housing associations, but there are also opportunities in voluntary and private housing concerns. The work covers a broad range of areas that will vary by organisation and sector. In catering for the demand for rented accommodation, the housing officer will manage and maintain properties, which includes dealing with rent arrears, reporting repairs, applications, allocations and arranging property exchanges and transfers. Housing officers often work with social and welfare agencies, and need to have a basic understanding of the different welfare benefits.

### Qualifications and Training

The basic qualifications needed for professional training in housing are three GCSEs and one A level or equivalent. Students over the age of 21 who do not meet these requirements but have relevant work experience may be considered as exceptional entrants. Contact local colleges to discuss this in more detail.

Those employed in housing follow a day-release or distance-learning course to study for the Chartered Institute of Housing's professional qualification (PQ). NVQ levels 2, 3 and 4 in Housing are available, and anyone working in housing is eligible to do these; NVQ level 4 allows candidates to proceed to stage 2 of the Chartered Institute of Housing's PQ.

In addition to the course, candidates also need to do the work-based Test of Professional Practice (TPP), normally completed within two years. The PQ can take three or four years to complete, depending on whether the graduate or non-graduate route is taken.

Graduates or mature entrant candidates are required to study a one-year graduate foundation course followed by a two-year professional diploma. Non-graduates are required to complete an Edexcel (BTEC)/SQA HNC in housing studies followed by a two-year professional diploma. There are also full-time degree courses and full- and part-time postgraduate diplomas. The Test of Professional Practice will still need to be undertaken with these alternative routes.

## Personal Qualities and Skills

An interest in improving people's living conditions, good interpersonal skills, effective organisation skills, sensitivity to an individual's needs and flexibility are all important.

## Salaries

As a trainee, or working mainly in customer service dealing with telephone, e-mail and personal enquiries, salaries range from £15,000 to £17,000. As a more experienced housing officer having a caseload and dealing with more challenging problems, salaries range from £20,000 to £28,000. Senior housing managers earn £30,000 to £45,000. There is regional variation and salaries are also affected by whether you work for a local authority or a housing association.

Asset Skills, 2 The Courtyard, 48 New North Road, Exeter EX4 4EP; 01392 423399; www.assetskills.org

Chartered Institute of Housing (CIH), Octavia House, Westwood Business Park, Westwood Way, Coventry CV4 8JP; 024 7685 1700; www.cih.org

Defence Estates Housing Directorate, Defence Estates Head Office, Kingston Road, Sutton Coldfield, West Midlands B75 7RL; 0121 311 2140; www.defence-estates.mod.uk

Housing Corporation, Maple House, 149 Tottenham Court Road, London W1T 7BN 0845 230 7000; www.housingcorp.gov.uk/

National Housing Federation (NHF), Lion Court, 25 Procter Street, London WC1V 6NY; 020 7067 1010; www.housing.org.uk/

Royal Institution of Chartered Surveyors (RICS), Surveyor Court, Westwood Way, Coventry CV4 8JE; 0870 333 1600; www.rics.org

info

# HUMAN RESOURCES

The field of human resources (HR) deals with all the functions in a business or organisation that relate to staff issues, such as recruitment, training and development, and employment. In some businesses the term 'personnel' is used, although human resources is more commonly used now.

# Human resources officer/manager

The role of an HR professional can vary and is largely dependent on the individual organisation's needs and the value that the organisation's senior managers place on the HR function. It can include working at a strategic level on a range of HR policies, processes and practices in relation to the business needs of the organisation. More commonly, however, HR advisers work on day-to-day issues such as recruitment, contracts of employment, payroll, training, induction, disciplinary and grievance procedures, redundancy programmes, equal opportunities policies and setting up staff support systems. In large organisations, individuals may specialise in one of these areas, but in smaller companies they will deal with all aspects of the job.

## Qualifications and Training

This is a mostly graduate profession, unless you have a great deal of relevant experience. Any degree subject is usually acceptable, but business, psychology and human resource management could give you an advantage. You can also take postgraduate qualifications in human resource management. To do this, you normally need a degree, but other applicants with HNDs and/or relevant work experience might also be successful. Some people get into HR having worked in other areas of management, or having done administrative jobs in HR departments. The Chartered Institute of Personnel and Development (CIPD) offers a range of professional qualifications for which you can study while working. Check their website for further details.

## Personal Qualities and Skills

You have to have a broad range of management skills for this work. You should be highly organised with good administrative and basic IT skills. You need to be good at building relationships with people; you must have integrity and sensitivity, but also be assertive. You need to be able to interpret and explain legal and statistical information.

## Salaries

Typical starting salaries for graduates range from £21,000 to £26,000. At senior levels salaries range from £35,000 to £80,000. This wide variation is accounted for by the range of size and type of companies and organisations who employ human resources managers. Location, type of industry and number of staff employed are all important factors in determining pay.

**info**

Chartered Institute of Personnel and Development (CIPD), 151 The Broadway, London SW19 1JQ; 020 8612 6200; www.cipd.co.uk

# Training officer/manager

Training officers work in medium-sized and large firms and organisations, national and local government, emergency services and voluntary organisations. They are responsible for identifying training requirements, designing training programmes, delivering training to individuals or groups and evaluating the success of training.

## Qualifications and Training

This is an area of work that people move into after gaining experience in other posts or following general HR experience. A professional qualification is advisable. The Chartered Institute of Personnel and Development (CIPD) offers a certificate in training practice for those new to the profession or with limited experience. NVQs in training and development at levels 3–5 are available.

## Personal Qualities and Skills

You need to be happy and confident presenting to or facilitating groups of people. You need to be a good problem solver able to get people to change their attitudes. You must also be well organised, positive and enthusiastic. Sometimes you will have to be creative and imaginative, developing your own training materials.

## Salaries

Salaries start at between £18,000 and £22,000, sometimes a little more in London.

5th Floor, St Andrew's House, 18–20 St Andrew Street, London EC4A 3AY; 020 7936 5798; www.lifelonglearninguk.org

Chartered Institute of Personnel and Development (CIPD),

151 The Broadway, London SW19 1JQ; 020 8612 6200; www.cipd.co.uk

ENTO, Kimberley House, 47 Vaughan Way, Leicester LE1 4SG; 0116 251 7979; www.ento.co.uk

info

# HYPNOTHERAPIST

Hypnotherapists help people deal with a whole range of problems from stress and anxiety to giving up smoking, losing weight or increasing self-confidence. They work by putting their clients in a deeply relaxed state where they can then absorb positive ideas that will help them deal with difficulties or to change their behaviour in some way.

## Qualifications and Training

While there are no specific academic entry qualifications to become a hypno-therapist, the three main hypnotherapy organisations are working towards regulating the profession. The three main certificate awarding and training bodies are the National Council for Hypnotherapy (NCH), the Hypnotherapy Society and the General Hypnotherapy Register (GHR). You need to contact these organisations to obtain course details. There are some postgraduate courses in hypnotherapy. To do one of these, you must already have a degree; psychology or healthcare subjects would again be particularly useful, though not essential. A background in healthcare, counselling or psychology would also be very useful. The courses provide training in the theory and practice of hypnotherapy. If the profession becomes regulated, then more clearly supervised training is likely to result.

## Personal Qualities and Skills

You must have very good communication skills, be able to talk to people, listen to them and put them at ease. You have to have an extremely responsi-ble and mature attitude to your work. A pleasant, calm voice is also an asset. Since you are likely to be self-employed, you need good organisational and financial skills too.

## Salaries

The majority of hypnotherapists are self-employed and charge per session. Charges for one session vary from £40 to £150, depending on whether you are seeing someone just once for a specific issue, or whether you are offering a series of weekly sessions. Newly qualified hypnotherapists earn between £15,000 and £21,000 if they work hours that equate to a full-time job.

**info**

The General Hypnotherapy Register, PO Box 204, Lymington SO41 6WP; 01590 683770; www.general-hypnotherapy-register.com

Hypnotherapy Society; 0845 602 4585; www.hypnotherapysociety.com

National Council for Hypnotherapy (NCH), PO Box 421, Charwelton, Daventry, Northants NN11 1AS; 0800 952 0545; www.hypnotherapists.org.uk

Skills for Health, Goldsmiths House, Broad Plain, Bristol BS2 0JP; 0117 922 1155; www.skillsforhealth.org.uk

# I

# ILLUSTRATION

*see* Art and Design

## Medical illustrator

*see* Medical and Healthcare Science

# IMMIGRATION OFFICER

Immigration officers and assistant immigration officers work for the UK Border Agency, which is part of the Home Office. They work at the nearly 50 air and seaports checking passports, visas and work permits and interviewing any travellers who are non-EU or non-British citizens entering the United Kingdom. Immigration officers have to try to establish why people are visiting the UK and check that the reasons given are really the case. They may be involved in surveillance work and in arranging to remove people from the United Kingdom who do not have the right to remain.

## Qualifications and Training

You may not need formal entry qualifications, though a good general education is an advantage. The Border Agency sets its own selection tests, which are designed to assess your powers of written and spoken communication and your ability to take responsibility. You must be aged between 18 and 64. Having a foreign language can also be an advantage. For many roles you need a driving licence and for most posts you must be a British citizen. Training is on the job and there is a clear career development and promotion structure in the Border Agency.

## Personal Qualities and Skills

You need good powers of observation, a calm but firm manner and the ability to work closely as part of a team. You may need to take quick decisions and you must be able to take responsibility.

## Salaries

New entrants earn close to £20,000, rising to £32,000 with supervisory responsibility.

■ info

UK Border Agency; www.ind. homeoffice.gov.uk

Civil Service Jobs online; www. civilservice.gov.uk/jobs

Jobs are also advertised in local and national press and at Job Centres.

# INFORMATION SCIENCE

Information science is the collection, classification, storage and retrieval of information and knowledge, and the main occupations relating to this are outlined below.

## Information scientist

Rather like librarians, information scientists organise, manage and develop information systems. Working with IT and paper-based systems, they store, analyse and retrieve information and distribute it to interested clients. They work for many types of organisation and with all kinds of information, including scientific, technical, legal, commercial, financial and economic. As well as cataloguing and indexing information and dealing with enquiries, information scientists often have to analyse statistics or write reports summarising highly technical or specialised information.

### Qualifications and Training

This is a graduate profession and unless your degree is in librarianship or information science/management, you also have to do a one-year postgraduate qualification. Competition for places on these courses is fierce, and you need a year's experience in a library or information centre of some kind before you start your course.

### Personal Qualities and Skills

You must be able to get on well with people and enjoy dealing with enquiries. It is important for you to have good IT skills: experience of handling databases is particularly useful. You should have a good memory and either a breadth of knowledge or highly specialist knowledge in a particular field such as law or science.

### Salaries

Trainees earn between £16,000 and £20,000. Newly qualified professionals earn £20,000 to £28,000. With further professional experience information scientists earn between £28,000 and £40,000.

# Librarian/information manager

Librarians and information managers anticipate the information needs of their clients, acquire that information by the most efficient means possible on behalf of their clients, and may well analyse it and repackage it for the client. Information may come in the form of a book or journal, or may be extracted from databases in-house, on CD ROM or online. Librarians and information managers need to be able to use the internet themselves and show others how to do so.

Information needs to be organised to make it accessible to users by indexing, cataloguing and classifying. Librarians and information managers promote and exploit the library's collection to the library or information source users and assist them with any enquiries. They work in public libraries and schools, universities and colleges, in government, in the law, in hospitals, business and industry, and also in accountancy, engineering, professional and learned societies and in virtually all areas of economic activity.

## Qualifications and Training

Library assistants are usually required to have four to five GCSEs or equivalent, to include English language; training is on the job. Part-time or distance-learning vocational courses leading to City & Guilds and SQA qualifications are available to library assistants in post. NVQs levels 2–4 in Information and Library Services are also available. To qualify as a professional librarian or information officer and gain Chartered Membership of the Library Association, a degree or postgraduate qualification accredited by the association is necessary.

First degree courses, postgraduate diplomas and Master's are jointly accredited by the Library Association and the Institute of Information Scientists. A full list of the courses offered by 17 universities is available through the Library Association website. The Library Association and Institute of Information Scientists have joined together to create a new organisation, the Chartered Institute of Library and Information Professionals.

## Personal Qualities and Skills

Librarians and information managers need to be well educated, with an outgoing personality, and able to communicate with people at all levels with clarity, accuracy and tact. They need intellectual curiosity, breadth of knowledge and a logical and methodical approach to seeking out, organising and presenting information. A good memory is also useful. Management skills and an interest in working with computers are important assets.

## Salaries

Library assistants earn from £15,000 to £18,000. Newly qualified librarians earn £18,500 to £23,500. Chartered librarians earn between £23,000 and £28,000. The Chartered Institute of Library and Information Professionals produces annual salary guidelines.

**info**

The Association for Information Management (Aslib), Holywell Centre, 1 Phipp Street, London EC2A 4PS; 020 7613 3031; www.aslib.co.uk

Chartered Institute of Library and Information Professionals (CILIP), 7 Ridgmount Street, London WC1E 7AE; 020 7255 0500; www.cilip.org.uk

Chartered Institute of Library and Information Professionals in Ireland, BELB, 40 Academy Street, Belfast, Northern Ireland BT1 2NQ; 028 9056 4011; www.cilip.org.uk/ireland

Chartered Institute of Library and Information Professionals in Wales, c/o Department of Information and Library Studies, University of Wales Aberystwyth, Llanbadarn Fawr, Aberystwyth, Ceredigon SY23 3AS; 01970 622 174; www.dis.aber.ac.uk/cilip_w/index. htm

Chartered Institute of Library and Information Professionals in Scotland (CILIPS), 1st floor Building C, Brandon Gate, Leechlee Road, Hamilton ML3 6AU; 01698 458888; www.slainte.org.uk/CILIPS/

# INFORMATION AND COMMUNICATION TECHNOLOGY

Information and communication technology (ICT) has an effect on all aspects of our lives. Almost all businesses and services make use of ICT to reach more customers, offer better services, reduce costs and improve efficiency. In the airline industry, for example, ICT underpins everything from selling and allocating seats to calculating fuel and filing flight plans. In the UK alone, 1 million people work as ICT professionals: 45 per cent in the ICT industry itself, and 55 per cent in an ICT role in other industries. The e-skills National Training Organisation (NTO) estimates that around 150,000 to 200,000 additional ICT professionals are needed every year. A career in ICT can mean working in any industry – from the media to healthcare, education to financial services. Most jobs need a combination of technical, business and personal skills and can be divided into the categories that follow.

This is such a significant, growing and developing employment sector, that it is only possible to cover some of the major job titles and work areas in the following sections. When looking for work in this field it is important to read job specs and adverts carefully and to avoid a narrow approach to looking for highly specific job titles.

## Applications developer

Applications developers (sometimes referred to as applications program-mers), translate software requirements into concise and precise program-ming code. Most applications developers specialise in a specific development environment, such as e-commerce, e-learning or computer games commerce.

They develop detailed knowledge of particular computer languages. Their main activities involve writing specifications and designing, building, testing, implementing and sometimes supporting applications using computer languages and development tools.

# Computer games developer

Computer games developers design interactive games for PCs and for games consoles. They design new games and develop and update existing ones. Development of games is very much a team effort, where professionals with different areas of expertise, eg animation, design, graphics and sound engineering all have to work together. The starting point is the original idea or concept, with all these aspects of the technology contributing to a successful finished title. There are now some degree courses available in computer games development.

# Computer service technician

Technicians are employed by retailers, manufacturers and organisations that make extensive use of computers in their business. Regular upgrading of office systems means a substantial amount of time is spent on installing and checking new systems, the rest being spent on diagnosing and correcting faults.

# Database administration

Organisations obtain and store information about their customers, accounts, orders or stock levels on computers. The database manager takes responsibility for maintaining these and for security, access and the legal use of information held.

# Forensic computer analyst

This is a relatively small but growing area of IT specialist work. Forensic computer analysts work for the police and various government agencies helping to tackle IT crime. Your work may involve investigating computer hacking, internet fraud, the downloading of pornography, terrorist networks and industrial, commercial and political espionage. You are likely to need a relevant IT degree or industry qualification to get into this work.

# Hardware engineer

Engineers design, develop and undertake research into computers and the computerised components of cars and appliances. They are involved in

# The sharpest minds need the finest advice. **Kogan Page** creates success.

## www.koganpage.com

You are reading one of the thousands of books published by **Kogan Page**. As Europe's leading independent business book publishers **Kogan Page** has always sought to provide up-to-the-minute books that offer practical guidance at affordable prices.

**KoganPage**

## Make a smart move

IT Sales Executives and
Microsoft Business Account Managers

Basic between 16k and 22k,
OTE  c 30k year 1, c45k year 2 and c80k year 3

Softcat aims to be the leading quality provider of software licensing, hardware, security solutions and associated IT services to the corporate sector.

Our mission is simple: "to demonstrate unrivalled levels of customer service and employee satisfaction."

You do not need many years of sales experience, a proven sales ability and good communication skills are the key to securing this role. We are looking for talented closers who can capitalise on the opportunities provided. You do not have to come from an IT background as full training and lots of support and development will be provided.

For this opportunity we are looking for people with a flair and passion for sales.

Our reward structure is simple: the more you achieve, the faster you progress and the more you earn!

positions based in Marlow and Manchester

**THE SUNDAY TIMES**
**100**
BEST
COMPANIES
TO WORK FOR **2009**

Visit www.softcat.com/careers for more info, email your CV to jobs@softcat.com or call 01628 403408
Softcat, Thames Industrial Estate, Fieldhouse Lane, Marlow, Bucks, SL7 1TB

## Who Are We?

Softcat Limited was established in 1993 by our Chairman Peter Kelly, an entrepreneur who believes in the ethos of 'work hard, play hard'. With his business ethics and understanding of how to support his staff, he has created the unique culture that is Softcat today.

Softcat aims to be the leading quality provider of software licensing, hardware, security solutions and associated IT services to the corporate sector.

Our mission is simple: "to demonstrate unrivalled levels of customer service and employee satisfaction."

## What makes us distinctive?

Voted 3rd Best Company to work for by The Sunday Times 2009, an achievement received as a result of what our employee's have to say about their career prospects, salary, rewards, recognition and the leaders of the organisation.

## Let's talk perks:

New sales employees can expect to earn on average: 30k OTE in year 1, 40k in year 2 and a staggering 80k in year 3! At Softcat we have in place one of the best commission structures within the IT industry, where you truly are rewarded for your efforts.

Within a sales role everyone knows the focus is the commission payments at the end of each month but what about a little extra reward too...... Trips to places like Fiji, Rio and the Galapagos Islands are just some of the destinations that are in store for someone with the right drive and determination.

Contribution payments to your student loan, healthcare, Denplan and a company contributory pension are all our standard perks but with the added bonus of tea and toast delivered to your desk, a shirt ironing service and a whole host of parties for you to enjoy.

## The role:

As an IT Sales Executive you will be responsible for selling the company's products and services. Your role will initially involve business development and you will get the opportunity to visit clients as and when you feel appropriate.

advertisement feature

Day to day, your role will involve generating new accounts by targeted activity, contacting prospects and following up on marketing activity. You will also manage your accounts, taking responsibility for developing an understanding of client needs and introducing new products – whilst making sure you deliver the first class service the company is reputable for.

## How we can develop your career:

The Training and Development manager is there to support you from day 1! A structured training programme already in place to ensure you are given the best start for a successful career with us. Future managers play a big part in your induction so you can later assess which sales team you would like to join.

At Softcat your career path is down to you, we just provide all the tools to get you there!

## Location:

Marlow, Bucks and Manchester

## We are looking for people who have:

- Drive
- Determination
- The will to succeed
- Intelligence
- Focus
- Passion to excel

---

*Graduate Name:* Lynette Wilkins
*Graduate Job Title:* Deputy Sales Team Leader

*Graduate Quote:*
Since I graduated from Nottingham Trent University with a 2:1 BA in Business Economics in June 2007 I wasn't really sure what I wanted to do. After seeing the job advert for Softcat in a local paper I decided to apply. I wasn't sure I wanted to go into a sales role but after attending an assessment day I knew it was somewhere I wanted to work. Everyone was so friendly and helpful and it's a place where working hard gives great rewards with good commission and loads of incentives.

Having very little IT knowledge was not a problem when I started as we had a couple of weeks of intense training on everything you needed to know. Once you join a team you have plenty of support and direction in how to be successful at Softcat.

---

advertisement feature

manufacture, installation and testing. As well as dealing with engineering issues they need to be aware of safety, efficiency and environmental factors.

## Help desk adviser

Help desk advisers give advice to customers by telephone, by e-mail and by online diagnosis. They are the first line of support for customers who are experiencing difficulties with hardware and software. They work with their customers to identify faults and suggest solutions. If they cannot help the customer to solve the problem, they may refer them to a second line of support. They work for retailers, manufacturers, broadband providers and in-house for all kinds of large organisations.

## IT research and development

Those who work in this sector create new technologies or new products. This could mean researching new approaches to mobile communications, or developing software packages. Job titles in this area include software developer, product tester and technical author.

## IT sales and marketing

This covers promoting or selling products, services and IT solutions. You may be assigned to a particular customer or group of customers, or specialise in particular products or services.

## IT services

This covers a range of customer-facing roles and could include developing websites, designing and installing IT systems for customers, supporting customers with software or hardware problems, and managing projects. Job titles include software support professional, technical architect and hardware engineer.

## Multimedia programmer

The key to being a successful multimedia programmer is that you have to have both creative and imaginative skills and good technical IT skills. Multimedia programmers add all those functions that make a product multimedia. They write computer programs or create websites which draw together multimedia features such as text, sound, graphics, digital photography, 2D/3D modelling, animation and video, working to a designer's specification. Multimedia products work on particular 'platforms', predominantly the internet, as well as interactive television, information kiosks, DVDs, CD ROMS, computer games consoles and mobile phones.

## Network engineer

A network is a system of computers and other communication equipment linked to exchange information. This could be used to enable staff to share information through a company intranet or for global communication via the internet. Network engineers advise clients on options and benefits, as well as installing and testing equipment. They also diagnose faults and maintain the hardware, software and cabling systems.

## Software engineer

They have a similar role to that of programmers but use this in technical and engineering settings. They may, for example, work on systems for contact centres or air traffic control. Most have a degree in software engineering or a related computer science. Many universities ask for maths A level or equivalent for entry to such courses. As most commercial and manufacturing functions now have established IT systems, the work undertaken by software engineers has shifted emphasis from creating new systems to using existing software and devising appropriate interfaces to integrate it with new products.

## Systems analyst

Systems analysts work on delivering the best IT solutions for an organisation's needs. They examine how and where computerised systems would be of benefit, assess the hardware needed and look at the most cost-effective solutions. Systems analysts then work with programmers and supervise software production.

## Systems support staff

Systems support staff work for suppliers of software and hardware, internet service providers or the computer departments of large companies. They provide technical support to users, often via the phone or e-mail. The work involves establishing what the problem is, helping the client put things right or deciding to refer the problem to other specialists. It requires detailed product knowledge as well as extreme patience and excellent communication skills. Training is often on the job, with entrants coming from a variety of backgrounds in which they have been able to demonstrate high levels of computer literacy.

# Trainer

Software packages are increasingly complex and users require training to get the best out of them. Trainers are employed by software vendors, training consultancies and user companies for their own staff. Trainers need to be familiar with the packages at all levels, and have excellent communication and teaching skills. They may also be required to develop and write materials.

# Web designer

(*see also* Art and Design)

Web designers design and plan websites either for their own company or for clients. The complexity of the task varies according to the nature of the site, and can include extensive use of multimedia or implementing secure systems for financial transactions. A considerable amount of time is spent testing sites and checking they are user-friendly. Once the site is working properly, designers upload It to a server and may be responsible for registering it with search engines in terms of both content and design.

Designers need an in-depth knowledge of the internet and must be up to date with technological developments. Many designers work on a freelance basis. The availability of jobs in this area is decreasing as increasingly sophisticated software packages are making web design less of a specialist area.

## Qualifications and Training

Many employers set their own entry requirements, but are increasingly asking for academic or vocational qualifications from NVQs to degrees. Applicants for posts may be asked to take aptitude tests to assess their numeracy, logic, accuracy, thinking speed and verbal reasoning. Systems analysts and programmers are generally expected to be graduates. Entry to computer science degrees is normally with two or three A levels or equivalent, including maths. Web designers need knowledge of HTML and Java as well as familiarity with web design software such as Dreamweaver and Flash. Technicians and network engineers usually have a related National Diploma or vendor qualifications.

There are a large number of computer-related courses, and entry requirements vary according to the nature of the course. A growing number of foundation degrees with flexible entry requirements are becoming available. Product-specific and professional qualifications are offered by companies such as Microsoft, Cisco and Novell and by professional bodies such as the British Computer Society, the Help Desk Institute and the Institute for the Management of Information Systems.

Employment-based training opportunities include Modern Apprenticeships for school leavers and Graduate Apprenticeships for those from non-IT disciplines. Many companies run their own programmes as well as sending trainees on relevant external courses.

## Personal Qualities and Skills

The balance of skills that are most important varies between some of the above roles, but excellent problem solving, analytical and technical expertise and the willingness to develop with technological advances are all essential, though to different degrees. Being able to work under pressure, being part of a team and communicating well, especially to less technically trained colleagues, are equally important.

## Salaries

This work covers an extensive range of types of career, types of employer and entry levels for different jobs. Consequently the salary variation is very wide, and the salaries given are just a few typical examples. Location, size of industry and the general economic picture influence this sector greatly. Help desk advisers start on between £15,000 and £17,000. Network engineers start on between £18,000 and £24,000. Web developers start between £16,000 and £23,000. Jobs which involve management or sensitive areas such as computer security will pay much higher salaries – £30,000 to £50,000.

**info**

British Computer Society (BCS), 1st Floor, Block D, North Star House, North Star Avenue, Swindon SN2 1FA; 0845 300 4417; www.bcs. org

British Film Institute (BFI), 21 Stephen Street, London W1T 1LN; 020 7255 1444; www.bfi.org.uk

British Interactive Media Association (BIMA), Briarlea House, Southend Road, Billericay, Essex CM11 2PR; 01277 658107; www.bima.co.uk

e-skills UK – The Sector Skills Council for IT and Telecoms, 1 Castle Lane, London SW1E 6DR; 020 7963 8920; www.e-skills.com

Institution of Analysts and Programmers (IAP), Charles House, 36 Culmington Road,

London W13 9NH; 020 8567 2118; www.iap.org.uk

Institute for the Management of Information Systems (IMIS), 5 Kingfisher House, New Mill Road, Orpington, Kent BR5 3QG; 0700 002 3456; www.imis.org.uk

Intellect UK, Russell Square House, 10–12 Russell Square, London WC1B 5EE; 020 7331 2000; www.intellectuk.org

National Computing Centre (NCC), Oxford House, Oxford Road, Manchester M1 7ED; 0161 228 6333; www.ncc.co.uk

Skillset (Sector Skills Council for the Audio Visual Industries), Focus Point, 21 Caledonian Road, London N1 9GB; 020 7713 9800; www.skillset.org

# INSURANCE

Insurance is a very significant employer in the UK. Many large insurance companies, providing insurance cover for every kind of item, situation and mishap, are based in the UK or have large operations here. There are many

Have you got the GIFT OF THE GAB?

Determined to talk yourself up the career ladder?

Or are you more of a people person?

Talented people are always in demand in the insurance profession.

Big on opportunity. Big on reward.

It's a surprising little secret you'll quickly want to tell everyone about.

discover risk .co.uk

different career pathways open to people who have an interest in working with people and with financial information.

## Agent

An agent is really a salesperson, working for an insurance company. The agent explains and tries to sell insurance products of all kinds to customers, both private individuals and large and small businesses.

## Broker

Insurance brokers are the link between customers and insurance providers. They have a detailed knowledge of insurance products, whether this is life assurance, motor insurance, buildings insurance or any other specific field. They do not work for one insurance company – they work for customers trying to find the most appropriate insurance cover at the best possible price.

## Claims administrator

Claims administrators, sometimes known as claims settlers or claims technicians, deal with policy holders who are making claims. Administrators issue forms, explain procedures to customers, gather further information and issue payments where claims are simple. If there is some dispute or the claim is very complex, they may have to refer it to their managers. Claims administrators work for brokers or for insurance companies. They normally specialise in a particular type of insurance, eg motor or household.

## Claims inspector

When anyone makes a claim on their insurance, the claims inspector assesses the claim to ensure that it is truthful and also to check that the insurance company is liable for payment. Inspectors carry out detailed inspections of damaged goods or property and their work often involves interviewing claimants either in person or by telephone.

## Loss adjuster

Loss adjusters carry out very similar work to that of the claims inspector – the key difference is that they are independent. They investigate claims on behalf of insurance companies. They assess the causes of loss or damage, and make sure that the insurance claim is valid and covered by the policy. They can deal with all kinds of insurance claim, including damage by fire, flooding, theft or accident.

# Risk surveyor/analyst

Insurance risk surveyors, also known as insurance risk analysts, work for general insurance companies, brokers, or firms of specialist surveyors. Their main role is to advise about risk, based on technical knowledge, experience and good practice. They visit sites such as commercial premises or engineering works and produce detailed reports on any particular risks associated with the site. They can also advise people on how to reduce the impact of these risks.

# Technician

Insurance technicians provide all the day-to-day administrative and clerical back-up that keeps the insurance industry going. In fact, they are often referred to as insurance clerks or insurance administrators. The work includes sending out routine correspondence such as policy renewal reminders, entering data onto computer systems or sending out marketing information. Exact tasks and responsibilities vary according to what kind of insurance organisation and for what department they are working.

# Underwriter

Underwriters assess the financial risk involved in insuring particular items, premises or projects. They calculate the prices for insurance premiums, aiming to fix on a price that will be profitable for the insurer but also competitive for potential customers.

## Qualifications and Training

Insurance claims administrators and technicians usually need four or five GCSEs grades A–C, including English and maths. Exact requirements vary from firm to firm. For brokers and underwriters, different firms set their own entry requirements. These vary from five GCSEs grades A–C to two A levels or a degree in a mathematical subject. Many firms like you to have had some experience in insurance or other financial work. Study for examinations from the Chartered Insurance Institute while working is usual and takes two to five years depending on the level you are working towards.

Brokers are regulated by the Financial Services Authority (FSA) and need to meet the FSA's training and competency standards. Brokers who deal in long-term investments such as pensions and life assurance need an approved qualification from the FSA.

Loss adjusters normally have several years' experience in the insurance industry or in other professional fields such as accountancy, law or surveying.

## Personal Qualities and Skills

People working in insurance must have excellent written and spoken English, be able to talk to people and write concise accurate reports. Some roles require good negotiating skills and the ability to deal with sensitive situations. Some degree of numeracy skill is important for all jobs. To be an underwriter, you need to be able to analyse complex statistical information.

## Salaries

New entrants to the industry earn £15,000 to £18,000 – some larger firms or firms offering graduate traineeships pay more. After a few years' experience, and after obtaining professional qualifications, salaries rise to £25,000 to £45,000. In jobs that involve the sale of insurance products, some earnings are made up by commission or bonuses.

**info**

Ifs School of Finance, IFS House, 4–9 Burgate Lane, Canterbury, Kent CT1 2XJ; 01227 818609; www.ifslearning.ac.uk

Financial Services Skills Council, 51 Gresham Street, London EC2V 7HQ; 0845 257 3772; www.fssc.org.uk

Chartered Insurance Institute, 42–48 High Road, South Woodford, London E18 2JP; 020 8989 8464; www.cii.co.uk

British Insurance Brokers Association (BIBA), 14 Bevis Marks, London EC3A 7NT; 0870 950 1790; www.biba.org.uk

Insurance Careers; www. insurancecareers.cii.co.uk

# INTERIOR DECORATOR

*see* Construction Trades

# INTERIOR DESIGNER/ INSCAPE DESIGNER

Interior designers work for commercial organisations as well as undertaking private commissions. They are responsible for the interiors of buildings (whereas an architect is responsible for its shell). Interior design can cover materials for floors and ceilings, fitments and fittings, and colour schemes, along with electrical and spatial planning. The commercial organisations may be offices, hotels, pubs, stores or banks. Interior designers may work with architects, have their own consultancies, or work in design units within large organisations.

## Qualifications and Training

Most interior designers have a degree in one of the following subjects: fine art, fashion and textile design, product design, interior design or graphic design. It is possible to get into this work without a degree if you have really demonstrable creative flair or a lot of relevant experience. Most training is on the job, working closely with more experienced and established designers. It can be valuable to do short courses on photography, desktop publishing and new product knowledge, in order to remain current.

## Personal Qualities and Skills

As well as an eye for colour and a feel for fabric, you need considerable technical and product knowledge and technical drawing skills, either on paper or with computer aided design (CAD). You need to be able to work closely with other people and, if you work freelance, you should be confident enough to promote your own work.

## Salaries

Salaries start at between £16,000 and £21,000, but can go much higher if you have established your reputation. If you work freelance you can charge £30 or more an hour. What you can charge depends upon geographical location and upon personal recommendations of your work.

The Chartered Society of Designers (CSD), 5 Bermondsey Exchange, 179–181 Bermondsey Street, London SE1 3UW; 020 7357 8088; www.csd. org.uk

Crafts Council, 44a Pentonville Road, Islington, London N1 9BY; 020 7278 7700; www.craftscouncil. org.uk

The Design Trust, 9 Burgess Hill, London NW2 2BY; 020 7435 4348; www.thedesigntrust.co.uk

The British Interior Design Association (BIDA), 3/18 Chelsea Harbour Design Centre, Lots Road, London SW10 0XE; www. bida.org

info

# J

## JEWELLERY

*see* Crafts

## JOURNALISM

Journalism is the profession that writes and produces material for print, broadcast and digital media. Newspapers, magazines, television, radio and the internet offer myriad opportunities for journalists. Journalists can develop specialist fields or work in a general capacity. They can work as salaried employees or as freelances, for national or local press.

## Editor

The editor of a publication is responsible for its policy, content and the appointment and organisation of staff. An editor will prepare schedules for content and will build up key relationships with external bodies. An editor of a publication will become the spokesperson for the title and will be expected to speak at conferences and to comment publicly on issues of importance. The editor works closely with the different groups within the team, including writers, production staff, advertising sales team, marketing and the publisher (*see also* Publishing). The editor will hold regular editorial meetings to discuss current work and to plan forthcoming features. The editor will also oversee the editorial budget. Section editors (newspapers and magazines) specialise in specific areas and run their own teams of journalists and commission articles for their sections. Typical newspaper sections include home affairs, foreign affairs, health, media, education and travel.

### Qualifications and Training

Most editors have come from a background in journalism and have worked their way up to the job, and so may have journalism qualifications.

## Personal Qualities and Skills

Editors coordinate the editorial team and need to have good leadership and managerial skills. Financial planning is also a key element to the job and being able to manage financial resources is important. The editor's role as a spokesperson for the publication requires confident communication skills and the ability to speak in public and in the media.

## Salaries

Salaries vary widely according to whether you edit a trade magazine, a local free newspaper, a paid-for regional paper, a popular weekly or monthly magazine, or a national daily newspaper. At the lower end, editors of trade magazines or free local newspapers earn between £25,000 and £35,000. At the top end, editors of national daily papers may earn £80,000 to £90,000. Editors of regional newspapers and well known magazines earn between £40,000 and £60,000 – more for some magazine titles.

# Journalist

Reporters find, research and write news articles and features for newspapers, magazines, special-interest periodicals, news agencies, radio, television and the internet (*see* Broadcast Journalist). Most reporters start out on local papers, where they cover a mix of stories from weddings to council meetings. Local reporters are generally expected to multi-skill and might be expected to write the local news or features, sub-edit or take photographs. They work irregular hours and must be able to produce accurate, interesting and readable copy quickly, often in noisy offices or even public places. Editors look for trainees with an interest in current affairs and events, an accessible writing style and a good use of grammar, and an understanding of the role of the local newspaper within its community. Good time management and being able to work under pressure are also important qualities as journalists have to work to strict deadlines.

Inexperienced journalists are expected to work their way up, starting with more routine jobs. Regional and local newspapers recruit trainee reporters and photographers under a training contract and some newspaper groups run trainee schemes. These schemes are open to school or college leavers who have not taken a specialist university or college course. Applications should be made direct to the editor for traineeships. Direct entrants to these schemes will be expected to attend block release or day release courses and to sit the National Council for the Training of Journalists (NCTJ) National Certificate or a National (Scottish) Vocational Qualification.

National papers generally employ reporters with some experience, and will look to journalists who have had experience on local newspapers. Trade magazine experience, where a knowledge of a specialist area has been developed, is also a route to entry in the national press. Occasionally national newspapers do advertise for trainee recruits but these opportunities are rare.

Trade magazines are also a route into the industry. Many magazines are produced on a monthly or fortnightly basis and specialise in particular subjects.

Reporters on trade magazines are able to develop a specialist subject that can then be used to transfer to writing for national newspapers or to develop into a freelance career.

Experienced journalists have the opportunity to become feature writers or columnists for national newspapers. Feature writers suggest subjects for research, and produce longer than average articles dealing with topics not necessarily of current news value but of general interest. Feature writers will have developed an expertise or specialism within the subject they write about, and may have come originally not from a journalistic background but from the specialist area on which they write. Columnists often write about subjects from a personal point of view. Feature writers and columnists tend to be freelance writers working for a number of different newspapers, magazines and publishers, and will also work in broadcast media.

## Qualifications and Training

You can either train with a newspaper (known as direct entry), or take a course at college or university (known as pre-entry). If you opt for a course you need to check that it is accredited by the National Council for the Training of Journalists (NCTJ). To get onto most courses you will need five GCSEs grades A–C including English, and two A levels. If you already have a degree you may be able to take an 18-week fast track course in journalism. Whether you train via work or through a course, competition for entry is extremely fierce. You need to do as much as you can to strengthen your application. Write articles for local newspapers or student magazines and try to get some voluntary work experience on a local newspaper. Journalism courses allow you to take the NCTJ preliminary certificate as part of your studies. Whether you enter journalism through a course or as a direct entrant, much of your training will be on the job, learning from more experienced colleagues.

**info**

National Council for the Training of Journalists (NCTJ), The New Granary, Station Road, Newport, Saffron Walden, Essex CB11 3PL; 01799 544014; www.nctj.com

National Union of Journalists (NUJ), Headland House, 308 Gray's Inn Road, London WC1X 8DP; 020 7278 7916; www.nuj.org.uk

Newspaper Society, St Andrews House, 18–20 St Andrews Street, London EC4A 3AY; 020 7632 7400; www.newspapersoc.org.uk

The Periodical Publishers Association (PPA), Queens House, 28 Kingsway, London WC2B 6JR; 020 7404 4166; www.periodicalstrainingcouncil.org/

Periodicals Training Council (PTC), Queens House, 28 Kingsway, London WC2B 6JR; 020 7404 4166; www.periodicalstrainingcouncil.org/

Scottish Newspaper Publishers Association, 48 Palmerston Place, Edinburgh EH12 5DE; 0131 220 4353; www.snpa.org.uk

## Personal Qualities and Skills

To be a good journalist you must have excellent writing skills and be able to adapt these to suit your particular audience. You should be good at researching information, talking to people, listening and encouraging them to talk to you. You need very good IT skills and you must be able to meet a deadline without fail.

## Salaries

Trainees earn £15,000 to £20,000. Once you have completed your training, earnings are between £20,000 and £40,000, depending on whether you work for a magazine, a local or regional newspaper or a national daily. The most successful journalists can earn £100,000, but few reach this level.

# Broadcast journalist

Broadcast journalists work in radio, television and online. Unlike print journalists, almost all broadcast journalists take a postgraduate pre-entry course. Some journalists still make the transition to broadcasting from newspapers, but it is increasingly regarded as a specialist branch of the profession in its own right. As in print, broadcast journalists will need to have good communication skills, an enquiring mind, a knowledge of current events and a sense of what makes a news story. The ability to speak clear, standard English is important. Both the BBC and ITN run traineeships for entrants into broadcast journalism.

Experience in radio journalism can be found in hospital, community and college radio. This can be used as evidence of interest and experience when applying to courses – many postgraduate courses will require a recorded news story as part of their application procedure.

## Qualifications and Training

You can move into broadcast journalism from newspaper or magazine journalism and join a new entrant training scheme with a TV or radio broadcaster – this is referred to as direct entry. You can complete a degree or postgraduate qualification in broadcast journalism – this is known as the pre-entry route. You can also get details of courses from the Broadcast Journalism Training Council. If you have a degree in journalism, media studies or politics this may strengthen your application for a training position. This is a fiercely competitive field and any voluntary work for community radio could be helpful.

## Personal Qualities and Skills

You have to be an excellent communicator, able to speak clearly and with confidence. You need to be able to listen and to question and to be sensitive or persistent as required. You also need good writing and research skills. You have to be able to work under pressure and to meet deadlines.

## Salaries

Salaries on training schemes are between £16,000 and £19,000. Once you are qualified, these rise to £25,000 to £40,000. Top broadcast journalists who are household names can earn far more than this – some in the region of £100,000 plus.

**info**

Broadcast Journalism Training Council, 18 Miller's Close, Rippingale, near Bourne, Lincolnshire PE10 0TH; 01778 440025; www.bjtc.org.uk

Radio Academy, 5 Market Place, London W1W 8AE; 020 7927 9920; www.radioacademy.org

The RadioCentre, 77 Shaftsbury Avenue, London W1D 5DU; 020 7306 2603; www.radiocentre.org

National Council for the Training of Journalists (NCTJ), The New Granary, Station Road, Saffron Walden, Essex CB11 3PL; 01799 544014; www.nctj.com

Skillset, Focus Point, 21 Caledonian Road, London N1 9GB; www.skillset.org

# Press photographer

A small number of trainee photographers are recruited into the press each year. Press photographers work in newspapers, magazines and online, although many now work in a freelance capacity. Press photographers can specialise in areas such as sport or fashion. News photographers will work closely with journalists and editors.

## Qualifications and Training

Trainee photographers are expected to gain a National or Scottish Vocational Qualification or National Certificate in Press Photography during work experience. Direct entrants are expected to have two years' relevant experience or to have taken an education course in photography.

## Personal Qualities and Skills

Press photographers work under pressure and independently. They need good physical health and the ability to work unsocial hours, as well as technical and creative skills.

## Salaries

£12,000, rising to £40,000+ for experienced photographers.

info

Association of Photographers (AOP), 81 Leonard Street, London EC2A 4QS; 020 7739 6669; www.the-aop.org

British Association of Picture Libraries and Agencies (BAPLA), 18 Vine Hill, London EC1R 5DZ; 020 7713 1780; www.bapla.org.uk

British Association of Professional Photography (BIPP), Prebendal Court, Oxford Road, Aylesbury, Buckinghamshire HP19 8EY; 01296 336367; www.bipp.com

Bureau of Freelance Photographers, Focus House, 497 Green Lanes, London N13 4BP; 020 8882 3315; www.thebfp.com

Master Photographers Association (MPA), Jubilee House, 1a Chancery Lane, Darlington, Co. Durham DL1 5QP; 01325 356555; www.thempa.com

National Council for the Training of Journalists (NCTJ), The New Granary, Station Road, Newport, Saffron Walden, Essex CB11 3PL; 01799 544014; www.nctj.com

National Union of Journalists (NUJ), Headland House, 308 Gray's Inn Road, London WC1X 8DP; 020 7278 7916; www.nuj.org.uk

Photo Imaging Council, Orbital House, 85 Croydon Road, Caterham, Surrey CR3 6PD; 01883 334497; www.pic.uk.net

Skillset (Sector Skills Council for the Audio Visual Industries), Focus Point, 21 Caledonian Road, London N1 9GB; 020 7713 9800; www.skillset.org

Society of Wedding and Portrait Photographers, 6 Bath Street, Rhyl LL18 3EB; 01745 356935

# Sub-editor

Sub-editors are journalists who work for national daily or weekly newspapers, local and regional newspapers and magazines of every kind. They process all the copy that will appear in their publication to ensure that it is accurate, free of typographical errors and spelling mistakes, makes sense and reads well. Sub-editors take the stories written by journalists and reporters and rewrite the copy to make it fit the 'house-style', adhere to word counts and remain within the law. The sub-editor is responsible for putting the story on the page and is often responsible for designing and laying out pages. Sub-editors write headlines, picture captions and summaries.

## Qualifications and Training

Many sub-editors will have been trained as journalists and then specialised. The NCTJ runs short courses and distance learning qualifications for sub-editors. The Periodical Publishers Association also runs courses for sub-editors.

## Personal Qualities and Skills

Sub-editors must be meticulous in their work. They are required to make quick decisions and to have the confidence to rewrite or cut the work of others. They must be able to work under pressure and to meet deadlines.

## Salaries

Starting salaries are between £18,000 and £24,000, depending whether you work for a local paper or a regional or national title. Salaries may sometimes be lower than this, because it is such a competitive field. Senior sub-editors earn from £25,000 to £52,000. Top salaries are only paid to chief sub-editors on national newspapers.

# Web content editor

Web content editors research, write, edit, proof and update material on websites. This material includes images as well as text. Just like any magazine or newspaper journalist or editor, web content editors try to ensure that what they produce is appropriate to their target readership. Web content might include local and national news, opinion, information about products and services, factual information or entertainment. Editors work closely with technical staff who develop and design websites. Web content editors also liaise closely with the clients for whom they are writing, editing and updating material.

## Qualifications and Training

There is no one route for entry into this work. Many web content editors have worked as journalists. Some have worked in IT or marketing, and many have considerable experience in the profession or subject with which they are going to work. Knowledge of desktop publishing and photo imaging packages can greatly increase your employability.

## Personal Qualities and Skills

You need excellent writing skills, with a good grasp of English grammar. You should be creative, but not lose sight of the importance of detail and accuracy. You should be able to write to very specific word counts or house styles and you should be able to communicate really well with other members of your team.

## Salaries

New entrants earn between £18,000 and £23,000. With three or four years' experience, and depending on the size of the organisation you work for and where you live, this can rise to well over £30,000.

**info**

National Council for the Training of Journalists, Latton Bush Centre, Southern Way, Harlow, Essex CM18 7BL; 01279 430009; www.nctj.com; e-mail: info@nctj.com

National Union of Journalists, Headland House, 308–312 Gray's Inn Road, London WC1X 8DP; 020 7278 7916; www.nujtraining.org.uk

Periodicals Training Council, Periodical Publishers Association, Queens House, 28 Kingsway, London WC2B 6JR; 020 7404 4166; fax: 020 7404 4167; www.ppa.co.uk; e-mail: info@ppa.co.uk

Society for Editors and Proofreaders, Riverbank House, 1 Putney Bridge Approach, Fulham, London SW6 3JD; 020 7736 3278; fax: 020 7736 3318; www.sfep.org.uk; e-mail: administration@sfep.org.uk

*Careers and Jobs in the Media* (Kogan Page)

# L

## LABORATORY TECHNICIAN

Assisting with research, helping to diagnose diseases, measuring pollution levels and developing new products – these are some of the tasks laboratory technicians help to undertake. Laboratory assistants ensure that equipment is clean and in working order. They set up experiments and investigations and record data. They may also be involved in stock control, monitoring and ordering chemicals, equipment and other supplies. Laboratory technicians working in education help school and college students to use equipment safely and record results correctly, and they may be involved in demonstrating how to conduct experiments. Laboratory technicians work in education, in medicine, in the pharmaceutical industry, in food science and in research laboratories of every kind.

### Qualifications and Training

You can get into laboratory technician work with four GCSEs grades A–C, so long as you have maths and one science. However, many employers now expect applicants to have GTEC, HNC or HND qualifications, a foundation degree, or a degree in a science subject, eg biotechnology or chemistry. It is also possible to start as a laboratory assistant and work towards qualifications on a part-time basis. There are several qualifications to choose from: NVQ levels 2, 3 and 4 in Laboratory and Associated Activities or NVQ levels in clinical laboratory support. You could also study part-time for a BTEC HND/ HNC or foundation degree, while working, rather than before joining this profession. If you work in a school science laboratory, CLEAPSS, the School Science Service, offers several professional development courses. Because technology is changing fast, your employer, whether you work in healthcare, education or research and development, is likely to send you on short courses to keep you up to date with changes and developments.

### Personal Qualities and Skills

You need a genuine interest in science and in the kinds of projects on which you are working. You need to have a very thorough and careful approach to all your work, able to follow procedures and record results accurately. You will need a range of technical and IT skills, though the precise nature of these varies from job to job. You have to be good at working as part of a team. If you are working in schools or colleges, you may have to explain and demonstrate experiments and procedures to students and assist them in their work, so good training and information giving skills are important.

## Salaries

Laboratory assistants earn £13,000 to £15,000. Starting salaries for technicians are between £14,500 and £21,000. Senior technicians earn £20,000 to £27,000. A highly skilled technician with considerable professional experience and qualifications could earn more than this. Private sector laboratories tend to pay the highest salaries, especially in 'cutting edge' fields of biotechnology.

Association for Science Education (ASE), College Lane, Hatfield, Hertfordshire AL10 9AA; 01707 283000; www.ase.org.uk

SEMTA (Science, Engineering and Manufacturing Technologies Alliance), 14 Upton Road, Watford, Hertfordshire WD18 0JT; 0800 282167; www.semta.org.uk

CLEAPSS Schools Science Service, Brunel University, Uxbridge UB8 3PQ; 01895 251496; www.cleapss.org.uk

NHS Careers, PO Box 376, Bristol BS99 3EY; 0845 606 0655; www.nhscareers.nhs.uk

# LAND AND PROPERTY

The land and property sector covers a wide range of occupations all to do with the management, sale and purchase of land and buildings.

## Estate agent

Estate agents are responsible for the sale, letting and management of any kind of property – factories, shops, offices and farms as well as residential property. In many cases, they also deal with valuation and survey work, and offer other services such as auctioneering and financial services advice. Large firms provide a wide range of these services through specialist departments employing qualified professionals, particularly in the area of surveying and valuation. Dedicated sales staff fulfil the role of property negotiators, and in the majority of smaller firms with just one or two branches, a combination of these functions will be found.

### Qualifications and Training

You don't necessarily need formal qualifications to become an estate agent. Relevant experience and the right skills are extremely important. At the moment there are not many graduates in this profession, but some large estate agent chains do run graduate training schemes. Where this is the case, a degree in a relevant subject such as surveying or business may put you at an advantage. Many people start work in an administrative role with an estate agent and work their way up. In this case, each agent sets its own entry requirements, but many expect you to have GCSEs in English and maths.

You normally start as a trainee sales negotiator and receive on-the-job training from more experienced agents. The National Association of Estate Agents (NAEA) offers a range of distance-learning professional qualifications for estate agents. Qualifications cover residential property agency, commercial property agency, property letting and management, and property auctions.

## Personal Qualities and Skills

You must be outgoing with very good people skills. You should be a good negotiator. You should be well organised, able to keep track of several things at the same time. You should have good written as well as spoken English and you should have a genuine interest in property.

## Salaries

Trainees earn between £13,000 and £20,000, and once you handle sales you earn commission on properties sold. This can take earnings to £20,000 to £50,000. Estate agency is in the frontline when there are fluctuations in the property market, so you can easily lose commission-based earnings. There is also wide regional variation in earnings, because of the wide range of property values.

Asset Skills, 2 The Courtyard,
48 New North Road, Exeter, Devon
EX4 4EP; helpline: 0800 056 7160;
www.assetskills.org

Royal Institute of Chartered
Surveyors, Surveyor Court,
Westwood Way, Coventry CV4 8JE;
0870 333 1600; www.rics.org

National Association of Estate Agents
(NAEA), Arbon House, 6 Tournament
Court, Edgehill Drive, Warwick
CV34 6LG; www.naea.co.uk

# Gamekeeper

Gamekeepers work on large country estates for private landlords, management firms and private syndicates who wish to organise a shoot. They rear the game birds and fish, and protect them from poachers and predators. They must ensure that the proper environment for the game is maintained, and on shooting days, organise the beaters.

## Qualifications and Training

There are no formal entry qualifications, but gamekeepers must have a driving licence, be good at handling a dog, and be suitable to apply for a shotgun licence. There are part-time and full-time City & Guilds and BTEC courses in gamekeeping, and gamekeeping and countryside management. Some of these courses may set specific entry requirements. The training is on the job and most gamekeepers start as an assistant or under keeper.

## Personal Qualities and Skills

You have to love being outside in all weathers and have a real interest in nature. You need to be very practical, good with your hands and physically fit. It is important that you are very observant, both of animal and plant life and of safety issues. You are on your own for a great deal of the time, but you must be able to communicate well with other people when shoots or other events are taking place.

## Salaries

Salaries start at between £13,000 and £16,500. Many jobs include free or subsidised accommodation, and clothing allowances or other benefits.

Lantra, Lantra House, Stoneleigh Park, Nr Coventry, Warwickshire, CV8 2LG; 0845 707 8007; www. lantra.co.uk

National Gamekeepers' Organisation, PO Box 107, Bishop

Auckland DL14 9YW; 01388 665899; www.nationalgamekeepers.org.uk

Scottish Gamekeepers Association; 01738 587515; www. scottishgamekeepers.co.uk

**info**

# Home inspector

Everyone selling his or her home on the open market in England or Wales has to produce a special home information pack. As a result of this legislation, a new career for home inspectors has been created. Home inspectors are trained and qualified to produce energy rating certificates and general home condition reports, which are essential parts of these home information packs. Home inspectors will visit homes to carry out their inspections and then write up appropriate reports.

The whole introduction of home inspection packs has proved controversial, and on top of this, home inspectors are completely reliant on plenty of property transactions taking place to keep them in employment. This means that at present, this is a comparatively insecure career.

## Qualifications and Training

There are no set academic entry requirements, though many home inspectors will come from a background in estate agency, building surveying or similar. Candidates with A levels or equivalent may be at an advantage. To practise as a home inspector you do have to pass a professional diploma in home inspection (DipHI) offered by City & Guilds and the Awarding Body for the Built Environment (ABBE). If you already have relevant professional experience this is likely to count towards your diploma.

### Personal Qualities and Skills

Home inspectors must be good at dealing with people, tactful and truthful. They need good practical skills in taking measurements and a real understanding of construction, with the ability to assess the significance of defects and problems. They will have to be able to write clear, concise and truthful reports.

### Salaries

There is still very little salary data for this work, but given that for most people home inspection will be a second career, salaries are likely to be in the region of £20,000 to £30,000. If home inspectors are self-employed, their income will depend on how much work they can get, and in the current climate, making a good living from home inspection alone may prove rather difficult.

Asset Skills, 2 The Courtyard,
48 New North Road, Exeter,
Devon EX4 4EP; 08000 567160;
www.assetskills.org

Awarding Body for the Built
Environment; 0121 331 5174; www.
abbeqa.co.uk

Chartered Institute of Building
(CIOB), Englemere, Kings Ride,
Ascot, Berkshire SL5 7TB; 01344 630
700; www.ciob.org.uk

Royal Institution of Chartered
Surveyors (RICS), Surveyor Court,
Westwood Way, Coventry CV4 8JE;
0870 333 1600; www.rics.org

## Land agent

*see* Rural Practice Surveyor

## LANDSCAPE MANAGEMENT AND DESIGN

*see* Gardening

## LANDSCAPE ARCHITECT

Landscape architecture as a profession covers the three divisions of design, management and science.

# Landscape designer

Designers are trained in the planning and design of all types of outdoor spaces. They use design techniques based on their knowledge of the functional and aesthetic characteristics of landscape materials, and of the organisation of landscape elements, external spaces and activities. Their work ranges from large-scale landscape planning to the preparation of schemes for the short- and long-term development of individual sites. It also includes preparing detailed designs, specifications, contract drawings and letting and supervising contracts. Some practitioners are also qualified in other disciplines such as planning and architecture, and the landscape designer draws on many fields in order to promote new landscapes, and sustain existing ones.

# Landscape manager

Landscape managers employ management techniques in the long-term care and development of new and existing landscapes, and also in determining policy and planning for future landscape management and use. They have particular expertise in the management and maintenance of landscape materials, both hard and soft, based on established principles of construction, horticulture and ecology. In addition, the landscape manager will have a thorough knowledge of budgetary control procedures, property and resource management, especially related to labour requirements and machinery, and the letting and administration of contracts.

# Landscape scientist

Landscape scientists explore and investigate the flora, fauna and geology of an area to be landscaped or which has already been landscaped. They survey areas to find out what impact landscape projects will have on wildlife. They suggest strategies to encourage new wildlife into an area. They are involved at all stages of a project, from initial planning through to monitoring wildlife and other natural phenomena in an area once a project has been completed.

## Qualifications and Training

The recognised professional qualification for those working in all aspects of landscape architecture is Member of the Landscape Institute (MLI), which entitles the use of the title Chartered Landscape Architect. There are three divisions: Design, Management and Science. Associate Membership, the first step towards achieving this, is gained after completing an accredited degree. Two years' relevant work is required as an Associate Member before taking the Institute's Professional Practice Examination and progressing to full Professional Membership. A list of accredited courses is available from the Landscape Institute.

## Personal Qualities and Skills

Those working in design need creativity, imagination, a practical outlook, interest in the landscape and an enthusiasm for working outdoors. Those in management require good organisational and interpersonal skills, consistent application and a practical outlook. Scientists need enthusiasm for the subject, technical commitment and good communication skills.

## Salaries

Salaries for new graduate landscape architects and scientists are around £22,000. For fully qualified and chartered landscape architects, salaries range from £25,000 to £45,000. Some landscape specialists earn £50,000 plus. There is much variation according to whether you are working for a corporate development company landscaping gardens of expensive commercial premises, or working on a project funded by a voluntary body, for example.

**info**

Lantra, Lantra House, Stoneleigh Park, Warwickshire CV8 2LG; 0845 707 8007; www.lantra.co.uk

Landscape Institute, 33 Great Portland Street, London WIW 8QG; 020 7299 4500; www.landscapeinstitute.org

Institute of Ecology and Environmental Management (IEEM), 45 Southgate Street, Winchester, Hampshire SO23 9EH; 01962 868626; www.ieem.org.uk

# LAW

The legal profession has many occupations within it, but all are based on upholding the laws of the land and dealing with those who contravene the laws. The word 'lawyer' is a blanket term that covers both solicitors and barristers. Solicitors advise clients and operate in the lower courts. Barristers are instructed by solicitors to act for clients, and work in the higher courts. Opportunities for lawyers can be found in the public and private sector as well as within the legal system. The legal profession also offers careers for those who have not trained as lawyers, such as legal clerks and executives.

# Advocate/barrister

The services of a barrister are required by solicitors (*see also* Solicitor), who deal with the clients and then 'brief' the barrister. Barristers give specialised advice on the law and plead counsel in the higher courts. They may also appear in the lower courts, where they usually begin their careers. Some are employed in the Army Legal Services, giving advice on all aspects of service and civil law that may affect the Army.

# The Law Society

# Supporting LPC students

Questions about finding a training contract?
Don't know which firms to apply to?
The Junior Lawyers Division (JLD) of the Law Society is here to help.

### A new source of information and advice

A dedicated section of our website tells you all
you need to know about becoming a solicitor.
It includes information and advice about:

- legal career paths
- getting a training contract
- accessing mentoring schemes
- national and regional skills events
- student forum events
- free, confidential helpline
- membership benefits and discounts
- our junior lawyer webinars and 'top tips' series

For professional advice visit www.lawsociety.org.uk/students

### Representing junior lawyers

The JLD represents LPC students, trainees and solicitors with up to five
years' active post qualification experience.

### Campaigning for LPC students

The JLD campaigns on issues that affect you and your future as a
solicitor, including the cost of academic training, training contract
reform and access to the profession.

*professional*
**advice**

www.lawsociety.org.uk/students

# The Law Society

## Becoming a solicitor

A career as a solicitor can be incredibly rewarding, providing many exciting challenges and opportunities. More than 130,000 solicitors work in England and Wales with approximately 6,000 qualifying each year in a wide range of areas of law. In recent years more women than men have qualified and at least 22% of people qualifying have been from minority ethnic groups. Qualification does require considerable academic and financial commitment and competition for training contracts is fierce.

## A wide range of career options

A solicitor is a confidential adviser who has direct contact with clients, combining legal expertise and people skills to provide expert legal advice and assistance.

There are a variety of different career options available.

- 83,000 solicitors work in private practice, ranging from sole practitioners to multinational firms
- 11,000 solicitors are employed by commercial and industrial organisations dealing with their legal business in-house
- 4,000 solicitors are employed in local government, advising on the services the authority provides to the community
- 2,300 solicitors work for the Crown Prosecution Service, prosecuting most criminal cases in England and Wales and advising the police on prosecutions

Other opportunities are available in the Magistrates' Court Service, in law centres, teaching institutions, charities and the armed forces.

## Routes into the profession

The three main routes are outlined below.

1. A qualifying law degree, followed by the Legal Practice Course and a training contract
2. A degree in any subject, followed by the Common Professional Examination or the Graduate Diploma in Law, the Legal Practice Course and a training contract. Find out more at www.sra.org.uk
3. The ILEX routes. Qualification by ILEX routes is longer than by other routes and is designed to enable individuals to study while working. Find out more at www.ilex.org.uk

advertisement feature

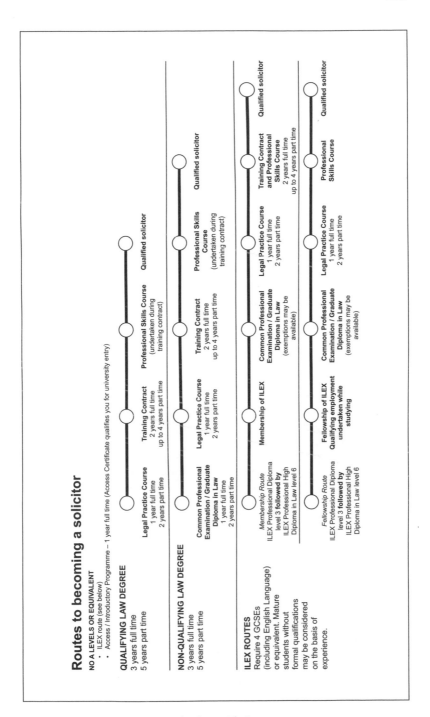

advertisement feature

300

## Competing for a training contract

There is immense competition for training contracts and it is recommended that applications are made in the second year of undergraduate studies. The two year training contract enables individuals to apply, under supervision, the skills and knowledge acquired during the academic and vocational stages.

Most trainees undertake their training contracts in private practice, but training contracts are also offered within local and central government, commerce and industry, the Crown Prosecution Service, the Magistrates' Court Service and other approved organisations. Details of firms and organisations authorised to take on trainee solicitors can be found at www.lawsociety.org.uk under 'Find a solicitor'.

## The Law Society – supporting solicitors

The Law Society represents solicitors in England and Wales. It supports junior lawyers while they are training and qualifying and throughout their careers by helping, protecting and promoting solicitors.

## The Junior Lawyers Division

The Junior Lawyers Division (JLD) of the Law Society represents and campaigns for students and paralegals enrolled with the Solicitors Regulation Authority (SRA), trainee solicitors, and solicitors with up to five years' active post-qualification experience. Membership of the JLD is free and automatic upon enrolment with the SRA.

## How can the JLD help?

The JLD recognises that throughout a member's legal career there will be times when specific support and guidance is required.

The **JLD Helpline** is staffed by qualified helpline volunteers who are able to provide help and assistance on a range of issues affecting the membership. The JLD Helpline is free and available between 9:00am and 9:00pm, Monday to Friday. The JLD Helpline number is **08000 856 131**.

Other benefits include:

- an exclusive web area to support junior lawyers through the early career stages, from getting a training contract to providing advice on redundancies
- career advice and planning services
- regional and national social and networking events
- competitively priced and accredited CPD training
- discounts on products and services, including membership of Law Society groups
- international connections and information to assist in qualifying abroad

For more information on all of the above, and to register for regular updates, visit www.lawsociety.org.uk/juniorlawyers

# Testimonial from trainee solicitor Nicole Baygan

**What inspired you to begin a career in the law?**

I have always found the law fascinating due to its complexity and continual evolvement. A law degree is highly regarded, even if you end up deciding to pursue another career. I have always enjoyed legal research and wanted a job which involved a lot of client contact and a career in law was therefore perfect for me.

**What approach did you take when applying for training contracts?**

I understood that attaining a training contract would be challenging. Competition for training contracts is tough and always has been. My approach was to gain as much experience as possible. I began by securing a summer placement after the completion of my law degree which led to a paralegal job. I worked as a paralegal for two years before I started applying for training contracts. Due to my previous experience in the profession, I felt more confident about my ability and believe this was apparent in the interviews. I also realised that law is a business and networking and business skill development is crucial. After I graduated I was elected to the committee of the Merseyside Trainee Solicitors Group and subsequently the Merseyside JLD. I have been on the MJLD committee for two consecutive years now and have also recently been elected to the JLD executive committee. I believe that my involvement on these committees has definitely improved my CV and helped in obtaining a training contract.

**What has been the most interesting aspect of your training contract so far?**

Every day of my training contract is different. I enjoy the fact that the job is varied and there is never a dull day. I am currently undertaking a seat in family law. I have had days when a client has turned up resulting in me having to attend an urgent injunction hearing before a Judge a few hours later. I have also had the opportunity to visit a client in prison. I relish the challenges involved in this unpredictable area of law and look forward to going to work every day.

**What advice would you give to anyone considering a career in the law?**

Be prepared to work hard! Not just academically but in practice as well. It is becoming increasingly difficult to obtain a training contract and you must not be under any illusion that this will just be given to you. Competition is fierce and it is therefore crucial that if you decide to commence a career in law you are realistic about your career prospects. If you are passionate about the law and willing to work hard then do pursue it as it is an incredibly interesting, enjoyable and rewarding career.

advertisement feature

In Scotland, an advocate is the equivalent of a barrister. Advocates may not select their clients. Provided that a reasonable fee is tendered they may not, without good cause, refuse instructions to act in litigation. Advocates also work in the public sector, Crown Prosecution Service, the legal section of a government department or as Parliamentary drafters.

Barristers specialise in arguing a case in court and offer a legal opinion for solicitors when asked to consider a particular question of law. Barristers are instructed by solicitors on behalf of clients and never directly employed by clients.

The majority of barristers work independently through sets of 'chambers' (which are a collective organisation of barristers), and tend to be self-employed. Once established within chambers, barristers can advertise for work.

## Qualifications and Training

This is a highly competitive, almost exclusively graduate profession. In England and Wales you will either need a good law degree (2.1) or a good degree in another traditional academic subject. If your degree is not in law, you must take a one-year full-time or two-year part-time course – the Common Professional exam (CPE) or Graduate Diploma in Law (GDL). After this, the route is the same for everyone. You must get a place on the Bar Vocational Course (BVC). This is also offered as one-year full-time or two-years part-time and there is a central clearing system for applications. Applicants for the BVC also have to join one of the four Inns of Court before starting the course. At the end of the BVC, hopeful barristers apply for a pupillage in a set of barristers' chambers (their word for offices). After completing a pupillage, the next stage is to get a tenancy to practice in a set of chambers. All stages are exceedingly competitive.

In Scotland advocates need to pass a postgraduate diploma in law and spend two years practising as a solicitor before being called to the bar.

## Personal Qualities and Skills

As it will be necessary to understand and interpret complex legal wording into clear basic English, barristers must have an excellent command of the English language and a meticulous understanding of the use of words. Barristers must understand and talk knowledgeably about technical matters in order to be able to cross-examine the most expert witness, for example, on complex aspects of technology. It is also useful if barristers present a highly confident and self-assured manner and can put on a 'good performance' in court. Since the work is confidential, a barrister needs to be trustworthy and discreet.

## Salaries

Most barristers' earnings come from the fees they charge to clients, so what you can earn varies enormously from being a newly qualified barrister scratching around for cases, to an established barrister with a strong reputation. Salaries in the first year range from £10,000 to £90,000 and after a few years' experience the range is £40,000 to £200,000.

General Council of the Bar,
2/3 Cursitor Street, London EC4A
1NE; 020 7440 4000; www.
barcouncil.org.uk

Details of education and training at
the Bar: www.legaleducation.org.uk

Faculty of Advocates,
Advocates Library, Parliament
House,
11 Parliament Square, Edinburgh
EH1 1RF; 0131 226 5071; www.
advocates.org.uk

info

# Barrister's clerk/advocate's clerk

The barrister's clerk is the administrator or manager of the business chambers, deciding which briefs to accept, which of the barristers in the chamber to give them to, and negotiating the fees with the solicitor. The accounts, the barristers' appointment books and the efficient day-to-day running of the office are all part of the job of an experienced clerk.

## Qualifications and Training

The minimum qualification is four GCSE pass grades at A, B or C in academic subjects. Training is on the job and juniors can apply through the Institute of Barristers' Clerks to attend a two-year part-time Edexcel (BTEC) national certificate course studying organisation, finance, management, law, marketing and chambers administration. On obtaining the certificate, juniors may apply, after five years' service, for qualified Membership of the Institute of Barristers' Clerks.

The Bar in Scotland is divided into 10 'stables', each of which is served by an advocate's clerk and a deputy clerk employed by Faculty Services Ltd. Training is provided in service. The job of advocate's clerk is very similar to that of barrister's clerk in England and Wales. Their rates of pay are linked to the Civil Service scale on a level that roughly relates to a comparable post within the courts' administration. The 10 advocate clerks have clerical and secretarial staff to provide them with administrative support.

## Personal Qualities and Skills

In order to manage efficient chambers and the barristers who work from them, a barrister's clerk needs good organisational skills, the ability to lead a team as well as be part of a team, and to get on with the general public. A good command of written and spoken English and an appreciation of the necessity for absolute confidentiality at all times are vital to success in this career.

## Salaries

Starting salaries are in the region of £10,000. Junior clerks with two or three years' experience receive £13,500–£18,000, going up to £28,000 for very experienced juniors. Senior clerks may earn £60,000–£75,000 plus a performance-related bonus. Senior clerks were traditionally paid a fee which was a percentage of the barrister's own earnings. Some are still paid in this way, and the fee is usually around 5 per cent.

The Bar Council, 289–293 High
Holborn, London WC1V 7HZ; 020
7242 0082; www.barcouncil.org.uk/

Institute of Barristers' Clerks (IBC),
289–293 High Holborn, London
WC1 7HZ; 020 7831 7144; www.
barristersclerks.com

# Court staff

## Court administrative officer

Court administrative officers and court administrative assistants ensure the smooth day-to-day running of the courts. They book cases, allocate cases to courtrooms, prepare lists of the day's cases and send out correspondence. They may also be involved in the collection of fines and providing information to members of the public. More senior administrative officers lead teams of assistants, ensuring that all the tasks listed above are carried out efficiently.

### Qualifications and Training

To work as an administrative assistant you require two GCSEs grades A–C and to be an administrative officer you need five GCSEs grades A–C. If you have other useful administrative experience, you may be considered without these formal qualifications.

### Personal Qualities and Skills

You must be able to deal calmly and politely with people. You should have good organisational skills and be able to stay calm in a busy environment. You should be able to pay attention to detail and work well as part of a team.

## Court clerk

Court clerks are legal advisers who give advice to unpaid (non-stipendiary) magistrates who are trying cases in the magistrates' courts. They are qualified lawyers, but they do not take part in the decision making about judgments and sentencing. As magistrates do not have to be legally qualified, it is the court clerks who ensure that magistrates interpret and apply the law correctly.

### Qualifications and Training

Court clerks have to be either qualified solicitors or barristers, who themselves must have either a law degree or an approved postgraduate legal qualification. Court clerks follow a set training programme and also learn by working with more experienced clerks, finding out about the many different areas of work – road traffic, licensing, fines enforcement, sentencing, etc.

### Personal Qualities and Skills

As well as a real interest in and broad knowledge of the law, court clerks must be logical thinkers, capable of undertaking fairly detailed research. They must be discreet, sensitive and calm, but also able to remain detached when dealing with stressful and upsetting situations.

# Weightmans

Weightmans is a friendly and inspiring top 60 law firm with offices in Birmingham, Leicester, Liverpool, London and Manchester.

Our aim is to be both the law firm and employer of choice.

With a reputation built on an excellent service to clients, an open culture, trust and reliability, Weightmans recognises the importance of a happy and well motivated workforce and the worth of promoting diversity in order to achieve this.

However you don't have to take just our word for it. Weightmans has been repeatedly recognised as a Top Legal Employer.

We are currently recruiting for various positions across the Practice.

**If you are interested in Weightmans and share our values, please visit www.weightmans.com or contact Sarah O'Hanlon, Recruitment Co-ordinator on 0151 243 9887.**

**www.weightmans.com**
Birmingham Leicester Liverpool London Manchester
Weightmans LLP is an equal opportunities employer
Weightmans LLP is a limited liability partnership

# Who are we?

Weightmans is a friendly and inspiring top 60 law firm with offices in Birmingham, Leicester, Liverpool, London and Manchester.

Our practice is structured along three business lines: Commercial, Public Sector and Insurance. We have a formidable reputation and heritage in insurance in which the firm is a leading national player. We have a growing reputation in the public sector market, acting for many local, police and fire authorities, and many NHS trusts. In addition, we also have a commercial business line which accounts for over 20% of our turnover.

## Why work for Weightmans?

At Weightmans, we aim to be an employer of choice and we prize highly the success of our people. Success at Weightmans includes both achieving the best result for our clients but also achieving and being recognised for our true potential. We value:

- Teamwork and respect
- A commercial approach
- Clear decision making
- Constant improvement

We work hard to put these ideals into practice and to ensure that our people are involved in interesting work and enjoy the opportunity to progress and develop their careers.

We have been recognised as a Top Legal Employer for our culture and employment practices. We are also highly ranked in the Diversity League Table.

## What are the benefits?

Weightmans has a firm-wide salary review every September. Prior to the review, we undertake extensive internal and external research and benchmarking exercises to ensure that not only our pay structures remain competitive but equally our people are rewarded for their contribution.

Weightmans realises though that it is not just salary that keep people happy, Weightmans provide a range of benefits which include: 25 days holiday, matched contribution pension, life assurance, private medical insurance, a health scheme, corporate gym membership, and childcare vouchers.

Our firm is committed to equal opportunities and the promotion of diversity. Weightmans treats all members of the practice fairly and creates a positive working environment to enable everyone to contribute their best.

## Corporate Social Responsibility

Weightmans' CSR Programme supports a wide range of environmental and ethical approaches to doing business, as well as encouraging continued support for local communities and charities. Weightmans offer every employee two days paid leave to participate in voluntary and community activities outside of working hours. In addition we encourage staff to participate in all charitable and pro bono initiatives we may offer through our own working environment.

We also work with the Charities Trust to set up a tax efficient way for staff to make donations directly through their payroll.

## How to find out more about us...

**If you are interested in Weightmans and you share our values, you can find out more about our current vacancies on our website www.weightmans.com or contact Sarah O'Hanlon, Recruitment Co-ordinator on 0151 243 9887.**

**Weightmans promotes equal opportunities and diversity.**

**Weightmans**

**www.weightmans.com**
Birmingham Leicester Liverpool London Manchester

Weightmans LLP is an equal opportunities employer
Weightmans LLP is a limited liability partnership

## Court usher

Whether you are a defendant, a witness, a jury member or a lawyer, it is the responsibility of the court usher to ensure that you know where you should be, what you should do and how you should do it. Ushers ensure that the court room is prepared and that everyone is present. They call witnesses and defendants, label evidence and administer the taking of oaths. At Crown Court, where a jury trial is taking place, court ushers escort members of the jury to and from the courtroom. They remain on duty outside the jury room while the jury is in discussion and they take messages between the jury and the judge.

## Qualifications and Training

You do not necessarily need any formal qualifications to become a court usher, though you would be expected to have a good general level of education. Previous work experience of dealing with the public and handling difficult situations are more important than professional qualifications. Your training will be on the job and you start by shadowing another usher. You will probably be sent on several short in-house courses. Skills for Justice have recently introduced NVQ levels 2 and 3 qualifications in court operations, so you may have the opportunity to work towards one of these.

## Personal Qualities and Skills

These are really important. You have to be trustworthy and truthful and you must have excellent people skills, be able to calm, reassure and explain, but be able to remain confident if people are hostile or difficult. You have to be well organised and pay attention to detail.

## Salaries

Court administrative assistants and ushers are paid between £14,000 and £15,000, while court administrative officers earn between £16,000 and £21,000. Trainee court clerks start on £19,000 to £21,500, rising to £26,000 on completion of training.

**info**

HM Courts Services, Clive House, Petty France, London SW1H 9HD; 020 7189 2000; www.hmcourts-service.gov.uk

Skills for Justice, Centre Court, Atlas Way, Sheffield S4 7QQ; www.skillsforjustice.com

## Court reporter

Court reporters attend court sittings and take down a complete report of all the evidence, the summing-up or judgment and, on occasions, the speeches of counsel in the various cases. Formerly, the proceedings were taken down in shorthand; now a palantype or stenograph is used. This is a typewriter-like machine that enables the reporter to achieve 200 words per minute. In addition, computers may be used to prepare transcripts, with all the advantages of on-screen editing and speed of preparation. The work sometimes involves travelling to a number of different courts. The majority of verbatim reporters begin their careers in the courts but can also work for Hansard, producing reports of proceedings in the House of Commons and the House of Lords. Television subtitlers also use the skills of verbatim reporting.

## Qualifications and Training

No specific academic qualifications are demanded for court reporters, although GCSE and A level passes can be an advantage. Applicants need to have proven ability in shorthand or stenotyping (usually over 150 words per minute), good typing speeds, and a thorough knowledge of grammar and punctuation. Legal experience can also be an asset. Details of full-time, part-time and distance-learning courses are available from the British Institute of Verbatim Reporters. In Scotland, there are no college courses but training is provided on the job by working alongside an experienced reporter.

Administrative officers need five GCSE passes (grade C or above), one of which must be English. The Scottish Court Service looks for applicants with Highers. Training lasts for two to three years, during which time trainees work and undertake courses run by the Court Service.

## Personal Qualities and Skills

Anyone concerned with the courts must be discreet, honest and trustworthy, as most of the work is confidential. Reporters must show a high degree of accuracy.

## Salaries

Salaries are between £16,000 and £20,000. Many court reporters work free-lance and can earn anything from £60 to £320 a day. What you earn depends very much on how complex and demanding your work is.

HM Courts Service, Clive House, Petty France, London SW1H 9HD; 020 7189 2000; www.hmcourts-service.gov.uk

Ministry of Justice, Selbourne House, 54 Victoria Street, London SW1E 6QW; 020 7210 8500; www.justice.gov.uk

British Institute of Verbatim Reporters (BIVR), Cliffords Inn, Fetter Lane, London EC4A 1LD; 020 8907 8249; www.bivr.org.uk

info

# Paralegal

Paralegals work for firms of solicitors, commercial companies and public sector bodies. They are not qualified solicitors or legal executives, but they develop considerable specialist knowledge. They normally specialise in a specific area of the law such as conveyancing, probate or family law. Their work involves researching information, drafting and managing documents, attending client meetings and some general clerical work. Paralegals also have to keep up to date with legal developments in their specialist field.

## Qualifications and Training

While there are no specific entry qualifications for paralegals, many hope to become solicitors, barristers or legal executives. This means that many applicants for these posts have a law degree. In any case, some firms ask for four or five GCSEs grades A–C or two A levels. Training is on the job and there are City & Guilds courses leading to a certificate level 2 and diploma level 3 available in paralegal studies. The Institute of Legal Executives (ILEX) also offers part-time and distance-learning courses for paralegals.

## Personal Qualities and Skills

You must be very well organised, able to manage your own workload and pay attention to detail. You should have good spoken and written English skills and be interested in legal matters.

## Salaries

Salaries for paralegals are between £16,000 and £25,000. For large city law firms salaries can be much higher than this, and some firms pay substantial annual bonuses.

The Institute of Paralegals, 2nd Floor, Berkeley Square House, Berkeley Square, London W1J 6BD; 0870 243 2308; www.instituteofparalegals.org

Institute of Legal Executives (ILEX), Kempston Manor, Kempston, Bedfordshire MK42 7AB; 01234 841000; www.ilex.org.uk

National Association of Licensed Paralegals, 73 Shenley Road, Lambeth, London SE5 8NE; 020 7252 7545; www.nationalparalegals.com

# Legal executive

A legal executive is a professional lawyer employed in a solicitor's office or in the legal departments of commerce and central and local government. The training and academic requirements in a specified area of law are at the same level as those required of a solicitor. Consequently, with few exceptions, a legal executive is able to carry out tasks that are similar to those undertaken by solicitors. The main areas of specialisation are conveyancing, civil litigation, criminal law, family law and probate. In addition to providing a worthwhile career in its own right, the legal executive qualification provides access to those wishing to qualify as solicitors via the Institute route. In Scotland, the term 'legal executive' is not used, but solicitors engage assistants to do similar work.

## Qualifications and Training

The minimum entry requirement is four GCSEs to include English, but A level students and graduates are welcome. As an alternative, the Institute accepts a qualification in vocational legal studies, and has special arrangements for

**The City Law School**
CITY UNIVERSITY LONDON

World-class legal education
in the heart of London

# Mastering the Law

# Your career,
# Your course,
# Your way

Apply to The City Law School, London and take the next step in your professional development. Our carefully created postgraduate courses offer a valuable blend of realistic practical experience and in-depth legal theory to both law and non-law graduates.

Each course is taught by student focused specialists with considerable professional and teaching experience, giving you personalised access to some of the best legal and academic minds available today.

**Conversion courses:**
> Graduate Diploma in Law
> Graduate Entry LLB

**Professional courses:**
> Bar Professional Training Course
> Legal Practice Course
> Legal Practice Course and Bar Professional Training Course Conversion to an LLM

**Masters in Law (LLM):**
> LLM International Commercial Law
> M.Jur International Commercial Law
> LLM Maritime Law
> LLM Criminal Litigation
> LLM Civil Litigation and Dispute Resolution
> PhD, MPhil or LLM by Research

For more information and to apply online, visit **www.city.ac.uk/law**

Alternatively, please email **law@city.ac.uk** or call us now on **+44 (0)20 7040 3309**. Please quote the following reference when contacting us: **Times2010**

www.city.ac.uk/law

# The City Law School, City University London

Located in the heart of legal London, The City Law School is one of London's major law schools offering an impressive range of academic and professional courses. We're the first law school in London to educate students and practitioners at all stages of legal education.

With three levels of study: undergraduate, postgraduate and professional, we offer courses suitable for everyone interested in following a career in law, no matter what stage they are at in their study or where they come from. The school takes a personalised approach to your learning experience and aims to develop you into the professional, dynamic, highly motivated, "practice-ready" lawyers of the future.

## Undergraduate Law at City

Each year around 130 students enrol on our undergraduate courses here at The City Law School. Our LLB (Hons) provides you with the essential legal and academic skills to be successful in law. Whilst our LLB in Law and Property Valuation (Hons) is the perfect pathway to start a career in either law, property development or management. Both courses qualify you to go on to the Legal Practice Course if you're an aspiring solicitor or the Bar Professional Training Course (BPTC) if you wish to practice at the Bar. Our LLB in Law and Property Valuation (Hons) is also accredited by the Royal Institute of Chartered Surveyors, so upon successful completion of the course you can apply for the Assessment of Professional Competence.

## Postgraduate Law at City

Our postgraduate courses are suitable for both law and non-law graduates. Our nationally renowned Graduate Diploma in Law and Graduate Entry LLB (Hons) allow non-law graduates to qualify to progress to the professional legal skills courses all UK lawyers are required to take, the LPC for solicitors and the BPTC for barristers.

First developed in 1976, our **Graduate Diploma in Law** was one of the first of the Common Professional Examination courses for non-law graduates wishing to start training for a career in law. On the course, you will study the seven core foundation subjects that you would normally cover during an undergraduate law degree in just one year.

Our **Graduate Entry LLB (Hons)** provides accelerated learning for non-law graduates, allowing you to achieve a LLB Law degree in just two years rather than the usual three. The course allows you to study the seven core foundations subjects that you would normally learn in an undergraduate degree as well as a range of specialist elective subjects.

Our **LLM Programmes** give you the opportunity to develop your understanding and expertise in a number of distinct areas of law. Our masters include: LLM International Commercial Law; M.Jur International Commercial Law; LLM in Maritime Law (UK); LLM Maritime Law (Greece); LLM Criminal Litigation; and LLM Civil Litigation and Dispute Resolution.

## Professional Law at City

Our professional legal courses are fully accredited by the relevant professional body and are developed and delivered by our team of highly respected practitioners and academics.

Our world renowned **Bar Professional Training Course (BPTC)** is designed to meet every demand of the modern Bar. We are extremely proud of our reputation, the strength of our links with the Bar, the quality of our training, the expert support we provide to help students secure pupillages, and the work done by our Pro Bono Advice unit.

On successful completion of the course, you will receive the City University London Postgraduate Diploma in Professional Legal Skills, which will enable you to be called to the Bar and take your first steps into profession legal practice.

Our **Legal Practice Course (LPC)** is dynamic and transaction-based and has been designed to ensure that you are fully prepared for the demands of the modern legal profession. With a heavy focus on practical skills focus, this course will show you what it is really like to be a practising solicitor and will help you develop the skills and confidence required to join the legal profession and practice successfully.

The quality of our LPC has been recognised consistently by the Solicitors Regulation Authority (SRA), who have repeatedly awarded us the highest grading in all areas of the course.

### Contact

**The City Law School**
Admissions Team
City University London
Northampton Square,
London, EC1V 0HB

T: +44 (0)207 040 3309
E: law@city.ac.uk

www.city.ac.uk/law

advertisement feature

students who are over 21. In the main, training is on a part-time basis so that there is potential for trainees to 'learn while they earn'. For those already working in a legal environment, but with no formal legal qualifications, an NVQ (level 4) in Legal Practice is available, and the Institute of Legal Executives (ILEX) is the awarding body.

## Personal Qualities and Skills

An ability to communicate, both verbally and in writing, with people at all levels, absolute discretion and trustworthiness, together with meticulous attention to detail, are essential.

## Salaries

Salaries for trainees are between £15,000 and £20,000. Qualified legal executives earn between £25,000 and £50,000. Geographical location and the kinds of work in which your firm specialise affect your salary.

**info**

Institute of Legal Executives, Kempston Manor, Kempston, Bedfordshire MK42 7AB; 01234 841000; www.ilex.org.uk; e-mail: info@ilex.org.uk

# Solicitor

The role of the solicitor is to provide clients with skilled legal representation and advice. The clients can be individual people or companies, or any type of organisation or group. A solicitor may work on all kinds of legal matters, from house purchases to defence of people accused of crimes; from selling a corporation to drafting a complicated will or trust. Solicitors may also represent clients in all courts, but will often brief a barrister (see Barrister) to represent the client, and then act as a liaison between them.

Scottish solicitors can appear in all courts and tribunals in Scotland up to and including the Sheriff Court. They can also gain rights of audience, enabling them to appear in the higher courts by becoming a solicitor-advocate, or may brief an advocate to represent their clients.

While some solicitors may deal with a variety of legal problems, others specialise in a particular area such as shipping, planning and construction, financial services or social security. Specialisation within the profession is increasing. The majority of solicitors work in private practice, with firms made up of several partners. Many others work as employed solicitors in commerce, industry, local and central government and other organisations.

Solicitors are instructed directly by clients and have a lot of contact with them. They have rights of audience in the magistrates' court and the county court. Unlike barristers, solicitors do not wear wigs but do wear gowns if they appear in county court. Solicitors are governed by a professional body called the Law Society.

## Qualifications and Training

England and Wales: the Law Society governs the training of solicitors in England and Wales, which takes place in two stages – the academic and the professional. Most, but not all, entrants to the profession are graduates. Fellows of the Institute of Legal Executives over the age of 25 with five years' qualifying experience do not need to complete the academic stage. Non-law graduates take the Common Professional Examination (CPE) or a Postgraduate Diploma in Law; those with the qualifying law degrees are exempt from this. The next stage, the vocational stage, is taken via the legal practice course, available at a number of colleges or universities. It is a one-year full-time or two-year part-time course. The trainee solicitor then has to undertake a two-year training contract with an authorised firm or organisation. During the course of this, a 20-day professional skills course is undertaken, usually on a modular basis.

Scotland: the Law Society of Scotland governs the training of solicitors in Scotland. It is possible to study for a Bachelor of Laws degree at five Scottish universities: Aberdeen, Dundee, Edinburgh, Glasgow and Strathclyde. Alternatively, it is possible to take the Law Society's own examinations by finding employment as a pre-diploma trainee. After completion of the LLB degree or professional examinations, all graduates who would like to become solicitors must take the diploma in legal practice – a 26-week postgraduate course, which also offers training in office and business skills. After successful completion of the degree and the diploma, those who wish to become solicitors then serve a two-year training contract with a Scottish solicitor. Trainees must undertake a further two-week course of study, keep training records, which will be examined and monitored by the Society, and take a test of professional competence. The trainees can then apply to the Law Society of Scotland for a practising certificate. All Scottish solicitors must hold a Law Society of Scotland practising certificate.

## Personal Qualities and Skills

A high level of academic achievement, integrity, good communication skills, patience, discretion, a good command of language and problem-solving skills are all required.

Law Society, 113 Chancery Lane, London WC2A 1PL; 020 7242 1222; fax: 020 7831 0344; Legal Education Line: 0870 606 2555; www.lawsociety.org.uk; e-mail: legaled@lawsociety.org.uk

Law Society of Scotland, 26 Drumsheugh Gardens, Edinburgh EH3 7YR; 0131 226 7411; fax: 0131 225 2934; www.lawscot.org.uk; e-mail: legaleduc@lawscot.org.uk

*So... you want to be a lawyer?* (Kogan Page)

*Careers in the Law* (Kogan Page)

info

### Salaries

There is wide variation. The Solicitors Regulation Authority makes recommendations on starting salaries, suggesting £17,000 in the regions and £19,000 in London. Many commercial city firms pay far more than this: £30,000 to £32,000. After completing training, salaries are higher if you specialise in commercial law – £60,000 to £150,000. In non-commercial law, salaries are between £40,000 and £80,000.

# LEISURE AND AMENITY MANAGEMENT

People employed in this field may work in leisure centres, Outward Bound centres, theatres and arts centres, historic houses and ancient monuments, country areas offering nature trails, fishing and camping facilities to the public, or even be in charge of bingo or dance halls. Managers, as well as being interested in their particular leisure activity, are responsible for the administrative and financial running of the enterprise. Many in this field are employed in local government, but there are also opportunities in private sports centres, health and fitness clubs and tourist attractions.

### Qualifications and Training

There are two ways to qualify in leisure management, by starting as either an assistant manager or a management trainee. Each employer sets its own entry requirements, but a good standard of education including GCSEs in English, maths and a science are usually necessary. A strong interest in sport and leisure and a track record of working with people are also important. While working as an assistant or trainee, the Institute of Sport and Recreation Management offers a number of qualifications for which you can work on a part-time basis.

Alternatively you can take a degree in sports and leisure management, sports science, sports studies or similar and start work as a graduate manager or management trainee. Degrees in business, psychology or tourism may also be useful entry qualifications.

### Personal Qualities and Skills

You should have a genuine interest in sport and fitness. You need excellent interpersonal skills and be good at motivating other people. You should be very well organised and have a flair for marketing and publicity. You should have some grasp of financial management and reasonable IT skills.

### Salaries

Salaries range from £18,000 to £24,000 for assistant or trainee managers. Managers earn between £21,000 and £26,000, and senior managers running large facilities can earn £35,000 to £38,000.

Institute of Sport and Recreation Management (ISRM), Sir John Beckwith Centre for Sport, Loughborough University, Loughborough, Leics LE11 3TU; 01509 226 474; www.isrm.co.uk

SkillsActive – The Sector Skills Council for Active Leisure and Learning, Castlewood House, 77–91 New Oxford Street, London WC1A 1PX; 020 7632 2000; www.skillsactive.com

info

# LINGUISTICS, LANGUAGES AND TRANSLATION

## Interpreter

Interpreters communicate between people who do not share a common language. They use two main techniques: simultaneous and consecutive interpreting. Conference interpreters usually work using the simultaneous method in a booth with headphones and communicative technology, allowing them to hear the speaker and interpret to their audience.

Very few openings are available for interpreters, even worldwide. Conference interpreters work at international conferences such as the United Nations or the European Commission and at the International Court of Justice, using simultaneous or consecutive interpreting. Some work for international agencies; others are freelance. Demand for conference interpreters in particular languages may fluctuate depending on the political and economic requirements of the day. Interpreters with specialist knowledge, such as engineering or economics, may have the chance to work at conferences on their subject. Interpreters may also work as guides in tourist centres, and to do this they must usually be accredited and trained as guides.

Demand for interpreting in the public services (police, courts, public health and local government) has led to the creation of the National Register of Public Service Interpreters, which covers a wide range of African, Asian, European and Far Eastern languages. This register is supported by the Home Office and the UK legal agencies. The Institute of Translation and Interpreting (ITI) can also help source qualified public service interpreters from its membership, as can numerous other commercial agencies.

### Qualifications and Training

To take a degree course, two A levels or equivalent, including a foreign language, are normally required. At the newer universities and colleges, training in interpreting and translating is offered, combined with regional studies or technological or business studies, aimed at industry, commerce and international organisations. A list of these courses is offered by the Institute of Linguists and the Institute of Translation and Interpreting (ITI). Such degree courses usually involve work or study abroad. The Institute of Linguists Educational Trust also offers the only qualification in public service interpreting – the Diploma in Public Service Interpreting, which is mapped at between NVQ levels 4 and 5.

## Personal Qualities and Skills

Fluency in two or more languages should be allied with a natural feeling for words and phrases and a good ear. It is necessary to be able to think quickly, to remain alert for long periods, and to be socially confident. Subject knowledge is essential, especially for simultaneous interpreting, which requires a degree of understanding and anticipation of subject matter and context.

## Salaries

Interpreters new to the profession earn between £18,500 and £21,000. The majority of interpreters work freelance and daily earnings vary from £200 to £700 a day. This wide variation is based on geographical location, the setting you work in and the complexity of what you are translating – more difficult languages also command a higher rate. Experienced interpreters can earn £30,000 to £50,000 a year.

**info**

Association Internationale des Interprètes de Conférence (AIIC), 10 Avenue de Sécheron, CH – 1202, Geneva, Switzerland; 41 22 908 15 40; www.aiic.net

Chartered Institute of Linguists (IoL), Saxon House, 48 Southwark Street, London SE1 1UN; 020 7940 3100; www.iol.org.uk

The European Commission (Representation in the UK), 8 Storey's Gate, London SW1P 3AT; 020 7973 1992; ec.europa.eu/unitedkingdom/

Home Office, Direct Communications Unit, 2 Marsham Street,

London SW1P 4DF; 020 7035 4848; www.homeoffice.gov.uk

Institute of Translation and Interpreting (ITI), Fortuna House, South Fifth Street, Milton Keynes MK9 2EU; 01908 325 250; www.iti.org.uk

The National Centre for Languages (CILT), 3rd Floor, 111 Westminster Bridge Road, London SE1 7HR; 020 7379 5101; www.cilt.org.uk

National Register of Public Service Interpreters (NRPSI), Saxon House, 48 Southwark Street, London SE1 1UN; 020 7940 3166; www.nrpsi.co.uk

# Translator

Translators work freelance from home or as staff translators, within a commercial organisation whose main business is not translation, or within a translation agency. Normally, they only translate from another language into their mother tongue. The work translated varies from whole books to business letters and documents. Translators, especially those who specialise in work for publication, must be able to express themselves very well. In areas where the subject matter of the text is specialised, for example computing, maths or mountaineering, expert knowledge is required of the translator. A broad-based general knowledge is always an advantage. Translators may be responsible for finding their own work but may also be registered with a translation company or agency.

## Qualifications and Training

Proficiency in a foreign language is obviously necessary, as is the ability to write well in the target language. An understanding of the culture of the relevant countries is important. Increasingly, there is a need to be computer-literate. Most translators have a postgraduate qualification or a diploma in translation. First degree courses in translation are available at a number of universities and diplomas are available via the Institute of Linguists.

## Personal Qualities and Skills

Translators must be meticulous, conscientious, creative and persistent. The ability to carry out research as and when necessary, and good interpersonal skills are also required.

Association of Translation Companies (ATC), 5th Floor, Greener House, 66–68 Haymarket, London SW1Y 4RF; 020 7930 2200; www.atc.org.uk

Chartered Institute of Linguists (IoL), Saxon House, 48 Southwark Street, London SE1 1UN; 020 7940 3100; www.iol.org.uk

Institute of Translation and Interpreting (ITI), Fortuna House, South Fifth Street, Milton Keynes MK9 2EU; 01908 325 250; www.iti.org.uk

International Federation of Translators, 2021 Union Avenue, Suite 1108, Montreal (Quebec), H3A 2S9, Canada; 1 514 845 0413; www.fit-ift.org

The National Centre for Languages (CILT), 3rd Floor, 111 Westminster Bridge Road, London 3E1 7HR, 020 7379 5101; www.cilt.org.uk

info

## Salaries

Starting salaries are between £18,000 and £21,000 – £25,000 to £30,000 for experienced translators. Many translators work freelance, in which case they are usually paid a fee per thousand words translated. This fee ranges from £80 to £220. The rate depends on the language(s) being translated. Translating Chinese characters commands the highest fees.

# LITERARY AGENT

Literary agents act as negotiators between authors and publishers, film producers and theatre managements. Initially they read authors' manuscripts and decide whether or not to accept an author as a client. Once accepted, an author may be guided by an agent about ideas for books and changes to existing manuscripts. The agent then finds a publisher or producer for the author's work and negotiates the best possible terms. The agent deals with the publisher on all matters that will affect the client, including the contract, manuscript delivery, follow-up titles, advertising, publicity, paperback, television and film rights, and obtaining payments when due.

Some literary agents also act for foreign publishers attempting to find British publishers who will bring out an English edition of a book already published abroad. Like publishers, agents tend to specialise in areas such as fiction, general non-fiction and specialist publishing.

## Qualifications and Training

No particular educational qualifications are necessary. Experience of the book trade is the most important factor, and most literary agents have gained this by working in a publishing house. Foreign languages are an asset, particularly in the international field.

## Personal Qualities and Skills

Agents need shrewd literary judgement and a knowledge of worldwide market conditions, negotiating and legal skills, business and financial ability. They must be hard working, persistent, adaptable and sympathetic towards their authors.

## Salaries

Agencies receive a percentage of the money earned by the author – usually 10–20 per cent. Literary agents working for these companies would receive a salary plus annual bonuses related to the level of commission they bring in.

info

Association of Authors' Agents;
www.agentsassoc.co.uk

*The Writers' and Artists' Yearbook,*
A&C Black (annual publication)

# LOCAL GOVERNMENT

Local government is responsible for developing local policies and delivering local services. In addition to the specific local government roles described below, local government provides education, social care, environmental health, leisure facilities and public protection. These departments employ appropriately qualified professionals including teachers, social workers, lawyers, architects, trading standards officers, housing officers, engineers, environmental health officers and many more. Local authorities also employ specialists in finance, human resources and business management, and some specialised administrators eg, registrars of births, deaths and marriages, and clerks to council committees. The lgcareers website gives details of the range of jobs on offer.

local government jobs:
# www.LGjobs.com

## let the job find you
sign up for jobs
by email now

visit: www.LGjobs.com

---

### Local government – a career serving your local community

Local government provides many of our most essential services – care for the vulnerable members of our society, education in schools, collection and recycling of our household waste, protection of our consumer rights, inspection of our shops, pubs and restaurants to ensure they meet health and safety standards, plus many more. All of these services support the communities we live in and enable people to have a better quality of life in a pleasant environment.

Wherever you are in the country, there are local councils – more than 400 in the UK – so working for local government offers the opportunity to work for and with local people making a difference where you live.

### What kind of careers are there in my local council?

Considering the range of services your council provides, you realise how many different types of career there are too – there are over 600 occupational areas. Here are some examples of jobs you might come across:

advertisement feature

- Accountant
- Environmental health practitioner
- Legal executive
- Leisure attendant
- Library assistant
- Occupational therapist
- Planner
- Social worker
- Teaching assistant
- Trading standards officer

## What kind of qualifications do I need?

There are opportunities for everyone in councils, whether you have GCSEs, A-Levels, a degree, NVQs, previous work experience, or no formal qualifications. The kind of qualifications and experience you need for a particular job depends on the kind of job, for which you are applying. For example, if you want to be a planner, you will need a relevant degree and professional qualifications. If you want to apply for a housing officer post, you might find that some previous experience would be necessary. Requirements for a position as a customer service assistant might rely more on personal qualities than on formal qualifications.

## Earning and learning in local government

There are now increasing numbers of Apprenticeship opportunities in councils, which offer the chance to earn money, gain on-the-job training and study for a qualification. Apprenticeships cover all sorts of occupations from customer service to childcare and ICT to health and social care.

## Why would I want to work for my local council?

- You can contribute to your local community, help people and improve their lives.
- There are loads of different types of jobs.
- You get a good salary.
- Councils are equal opportunities employers and value diversity.
- There are opportunities to study and train while you work.
- You can benefit from flexible working arrangements.
- There may be a range of other benefits, such as generous annual leave, reduced rate membership at leisure facilities and reduced fares on public transport.

## Find out more – visit www.LGcareers.com

# Local government administrative assistant

Local government administrative assistants provide support in all council departments, eg, housing, social services or planning. Your work will vary depending on where you work and what your specific role is, but many tasks are common to most administrative assistant posts. As an administrative assistant your work could include processing forms, answering queries on the telephone or at a help desk, sorting mail, filing, photo copying, inputting and updating information on computers, finding information and taking notes at meetings.

# Local government officer

Local government officers are responsible for putting council policy into practice. Your day-to-day tasks will vary according to your particular role and responsibilities, but are likely to include supervising and training administrative staff, keeping records, dealing with enquiries, presenting and preparing information for committees or other meetings, monitoring performance, overseeing projects and managing budgets.

## Qualifications and Training

Entry requirements vary between councils. For some administrative assistant posts you may need GCSEs including maths and English; formal qualifications are often not required. Administrative officers usually need four or five GCSEs including maths and English. Entry requirements for local government officers vary widely, depending on the job, and can be anything from four GCSEs including maths and English to a degree or equivalent qualification. Local authorities provide training on the job and support for part-time study for relevant professional qualifications.

## Personal Qualities and Skills

While every role demands particular knowledge and skills, there are some common threads that are essential for all employees. You must have a genuine interest in and commitment to serving your local community. Most jobs require a good level of communication skills, as they involve direct contact with members of the public. You should be flexible and able to work well as part of a team. You should also be prepared to take on responsibilities. Some jobs require good IT or numeracy skills.

## Salaries

Administrative assistants are paid between £14,000 and £19,000, and local government officers are paid from £18,000 to £39,000 – more if you move into senior management. Salaries are higher in London than elsewhere and many councils pay performance-related bonuses.

**info**

Local Government Careers;
www.lgcareers.com

# LOGISTICS

(*see also* Road Transport)

Logistics is the management of the moving of goods or materials from one place to another.

# Freight forwarder

A freight forwarding firm will arrange for the most efficient means of the international transport of goods, and will ensure that all documentation, legal and insurance requirements are met, and customs duties paid. Freight forwarders may be individuals or firms; they may specialise in a particular method of transportation, certain goods or countries. They may arrange for a number of different shipments to be grouped together for more economical transport. Some very large organisations have their own freight forwarding department or a subsidiary company.

Freight forwarders are usually located near ports or airports and in provincial centres. They employ people to deal with a wide range of clerical and administrative tasks such as sales, personnel, timetabling, accounting and computer work.

## Qualifications and Training

School leavers can enter the industry through the Modern Apprenticeship route. NVQs are available in International Trade and Services, Distribution and Warehousing Operations, and Organising Road Transport. There are several degree courses in international trade, logistics, supply chain management, transport, export studies and overseas business. Large companies may offer graduate training schemes for those with relevant degrees.

The Institute of Freight Forwarders offers an Advanced Certificate in International Trade that can be studied full- or part-time or by correspondence. The Institute of Logistics and Transport offers a range of professional qualifications from introductory to MSc level which can be studied by distance learning.

## Personal Qualities and Skills

People working in freight forwarding need excellent problem-solving and communication skills. Accuracy and clarity are essential, as misunderstandings can cause major problems. IT skills are essential with a growth in internet trading and greater use of technology such as global position satellite systems to plan and manage journeys. Geographical, cultural and religious awareness are also important.

# Creating an interactive logistics career development framework

## Skills for Logistics

Skills for Logistics, the Sector Skills Council for the Freight Logistics Industries has developed Stairway Interactive. Based on the Professional Development Stairway, Stairway Interactive provides the logistics industry with a career development framework that enables employers and employees to plan and map career progression and provides the foundation on which to base structured Continuous Professional Development (CPD) programmes. Stairway Interactive, is an online toolkit that has been developed to provide you with the opportunity of managing your team's and your own CPD

Underpinning Stairway Interactive is a series of Sector Approved Profiles (SAPs) covering most jobs found in logistics. These SAPs have been developed in careful consultation with practitioners from companies of all sizes across the sector and are based on the National Occupational Standards which support qualifications.

Once the appropriate SAP has been selected for either your role or for those in your team, you can start to enjoy the benefits of clear and comprehensive support for all of your skills development needs:

- Logging current and previous qualifications and experience

- Highlighting skills gaps and signposting associated learning needs and solutions

- Planning their career development

- Managing succession planning

- Managing recruitment

- Managing induction processes

- Administering your appraisal system

- Appraising the benefits of investment in training

- Benchmarking the competences of your staff

---

## Developing your career in Freight & Logistics

If you are looking for a career in the freight & logistics sector, you can now plan your personal development using the Stairway Interactive.

Stairway Interactive offers a comprehensive Continuous Professional Development solution to the logistics industry. It provides the ability to map job functions to the Sector Approved Profiles which are underpinned by National Occupational Standards.

Regardless of whether you are using The Stairway for your own individual purposes or as a line manager, it provides a foundation to support all your requirements including:

- Career mapping
- Training Needs Analysis
- Staff Appraisals
- Succession Planning
- Job Descriptions

**www.skillsforlogistics.org**

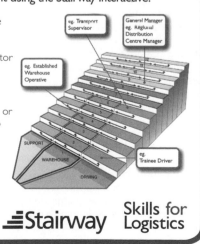

≡Stairway  Skills for Logistics

## Salaries

Salaries for school leaver trainees are between £14,000 and £17,000. Graduate trainees working for larger companies start on between £19,000 and £23,000. Senior managers in freight forwarding departments can earn £30,000 to £40,000.

**info**

British International Freight Association (BIFA), Redfern House, Browells Lane, Feltham, Middlesex TW13 7EP; 020 8844 2266; www.bifa. org

The Chartered Institute of Logistics and Transport (CILT) UK, Earlstrees Court, Earlstrees Road, Corby, Northants NN7 4AX; 01536 740104; www.ciltuk.org.uk

Freight Transport Association (FTA), Hermes House, St John's Road,

Tunbridge Wells, Kent TN4 9UZ; 01892 526 171; www.fta.co.uk

Institute of Export, Export House, Minerva Business Park, Lynch Wood, Peterborough PE2 6FT; 01733 404400; www.export.org.uk

Skills for Logistics, 14 Warren Yard, Warren Farm Office Village, Stratford Road, Milton Keynes MK12 5NW; 0870 242 7314; www. skillsforlogistics.org

# Supply chain manager

Supply chain managers (also known as logistics or distribution managers) are the ones who ensure that food, drink, clothing, electrical equipment, in fact anything that you can buy from a retail outlet, arrives where it should when it should. The manager has to ensure that supplies neither run out nor build up in over-large quantities in warehouses, shops or anywhere along the supply chain. You can work either for a large retailer which has its own logistics department or for a logistics contractor which organises all the transport and distribution on behalf of retailers and wholesalers. Your responsibilities are likely to include planning delivery timetables, monitoring stock levels using computer databases, tracking the movement of goods through depots, overseeing the ordering and packaging process ready for dispatch. You also have to monitor performance, and try to come up with ways of making the whole process more efficient and cost-effective, and you are also responsible for recruiting and managing staff in the distribution department. Your work would involve close liaison with purchasing officers, warehouse managers and transport staff.

## Qualifications and Training

There are two ways to get into supply chain management. Some people take a foundation degree, HNC, HND or degree in a relevant subject such as transport management, supply chain management or international transport. Other subjects such as geography and business subjects might also include relevant modules. Some large companies do prefer to recruit graduates for their management training programmes. However, it is possible to join a company in its distribution or logistics department and work your way up into a management role. You may also choose to take some relevant qualifications on a part-time basis if you choose this second route.

## Personal Qualities and Skills

You need good planning skills and you must also be able to pay attention to detail. You need to be numerate with good IT skills too. You have to be able to work under pressure and solve problems quickly and calmly. You must have a good range of people skills, be excellent at leading and motivating, good at soothing ruffled and agitated managers somewhere else along the supply chain and able to liaise effectively with others.

## Salaries

Graduate trainees earn between £18,000 and £22,000. If you start by working your way up, your salary will depend very much on what job you are doing, but once you get into supply chain management your earnings are similar to those of a graduate trainee. In either case, once you have completed some training and built up a year or two of experience, salaries rise to £25,000 to £30,000. For very large operations, the most senior managers can earn £40,000 to £50,000.

Chartered Institute of Logistics and Transport (CILTUK), Logistics and Transport Centre, Earlstrees Court, Earlstrees Road, Corby, Northants NN17 4AX; 01536 740100; www.ciltuk.org.uk

Skills for Logistics, 14 Warren Yard, Warren Farm Office Village, Stratford Road, Milton Keynes MK12 5NW; 0870 242 7314; www. skillsforlogistics.org

info

# M

## MANAGEMENT CONSULTANT

Management has been defined as the art of getting results through other people, and consultancy as giving professional advice. Management consultants are employed to provide a higher degree of expertise than is available in a particular company; to recommend business solutions and assist in their implementation; to assist in cultural change and to provide expertise to solve specific business issues.

Firms of management consultants specialise, tending to divide their activities into the following areas: organisation, development and policy formation – long-range planning and reorganisation of a company's structure; production management – production control arrangements; marketing, sales and distribution; finance and administration – installation of budgetary control systems; personnel management selection; management of information systems – the provision of software, systems analysis; economic and environmental studies – urban and regional development planning, work for overseas organisations. With the growth in e-commerce many consultancies are providing advice on e-business solutions.

## Management coach

This is a relatively new career and management coaches work far more with individuals than with whole organisations or departments. They work mostly with managers at a senior level in all kinds of organisation, helping them to work more efficiently and effectively and working on any problem areas, for example presenting in public, interpreting data, and team leadership.

### Qualifications and Training

Management consultancy is a graduate-only profession and preferred degree subjects include business, management, IT, economics and psychology. If you specialise in a particular area of consultancy such as marketing or human resources, a relevant degree is helpful. You should have a 2.1 and an A level tariff of 320 points. Training is on the job, but many consulting firms provide extensive in-house courses. After about two years in the profession you are likely to have the option either to take a Master's in Business Administration (MBA) or a professional qualification linked to your area of expertise, for example finance, marketing or human resources. Management coaches have often worked as management consultants and developed a special interest in personal coaching and one-to-one work.

## Personal Qualities and Skills

You need to be an excellent communicator, one-to-one, with groups and on paper. You should have good IT and numerical skills and the ability to analyse problems and suggest solutions. You should have a broad knowledge of business issues. If you are working as a management coach, you need to be very good at working one-to-one, good at motivating people and accurate in analysing their problems.

## Salaries

Starting salaries are between £27,000 and £37,000, depending on location and the type of consulting. Experienced consultants can expect to earn between £35,000 and £55,000. This is a field of employment that can offer extremely high salaries for very successful consultants – £50,000 to £125,000.

Chartered Institute of Personnel and Development (CIPD), 151 The Broadway, London SW19 1JQ; 020 8612 6200; www.cipd.co.uk

Chartered Management Institute (CMI), Management House, Cottingham Road, Corby, Northants NN17 1TT; 01536 204222; www.managers.org.uk

Institute of Management Consultancy (IMC), 3rd Floor, 17–18 Hayward's Place, London EC1R 0EQ; 020 7566 5220; www.imc.co.uk

Management Consultancies Association (MCA), 49 Whitehall, London SW1A 2BX; 020 7321 3990; www.mca.org.uk/

# MANUFACTURING

Manufacturing encompasses many occupations, all of which are concerned with the large-scale production of goods and packaging.

# Factory worker

Factory work is all about the manufacturing of products of every kind: food, furniture, cars, clothing, electronic equipment, etc, in fact, everything that we use. A whole range of jobs support any manufacturing process: administration, research, engineering and marketing, but they are covered elsewhere.

The term 'factory worker' refers to workers who are involved in the production process – and specific tasks and duties vary depending on what is being

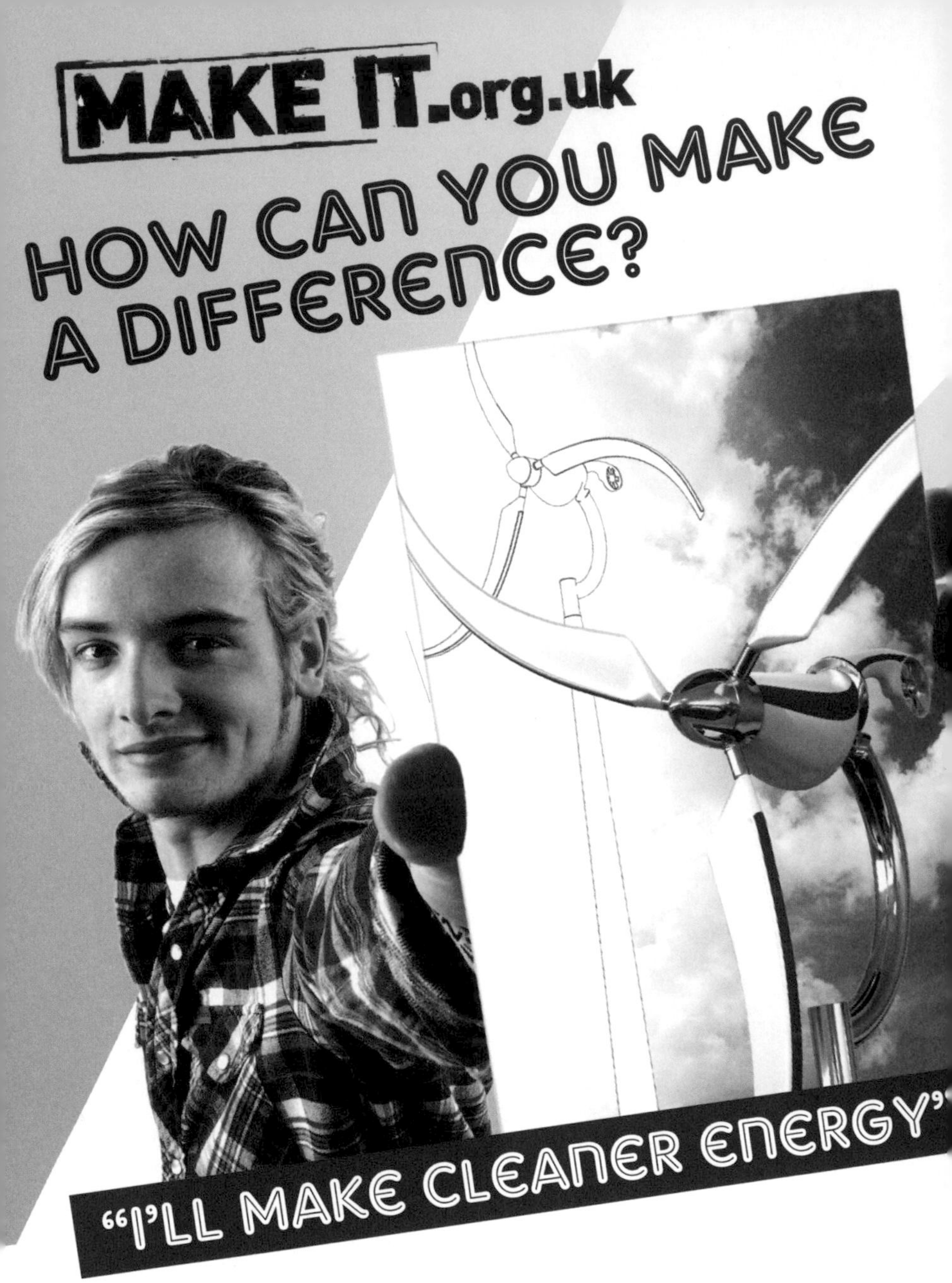
MAKE IT.org.uk
HOW CAN YOU MAKE A DIFFERENCE?
"I'LL MAKE CLEANER ENERGY"

Manufacturers are the people behind tomorrow's solutions, like clean ene technologies; lifesaving drugs; eco friendly aircraft; electronic cars; smart mob and high performance trainers.

If you want to make a real contribution to your world, you can play an impor role – from hands-on production and engineering - to design and researc through to HR, marketing, sales and admin.

Make your career matter **www.makeit.org.uk**

# MAKE IT.org.uk

## Make It in Manufacturing

If you think today's manufacturing is about standing on a production line sticking cherries on bakewells, or mindlessly processing widgets ... you're about 30 years out of date.

The days of dark satanic mills are long gone: modern manufacturing is a global enterprise competing on innovation, creativity and all-round smart thinking.

### What is manufacturing?

Manufacturing covers a huge range of things, starting with innovation – maybe somebody coming up with an idea for a new pair of trainers or a component for a fuel efficient aircraft. As well as the production side, there are many other steps involved in getting a product to market, including research, design, costing, sourcing and purchasing raw materials, marketing, selling and transporting.

It means there are literally thousands of different career opportunities – from designers to scientists - to engineers to managers - to sales and marketing.

There's so much choice creating today's 'must have' products - like iPods, trainers or medicines. Perhaps more critical are the jobs developing tomorrow's inventions - carbon-free cars, robotics or cures for disease.

### Become a top earner

It's challenging, enjoyable and rewarding - what's more, the salaries are attractive. Manufacturing can offer better pay and a more worthwhile career than many other sectors. A production manager, for example, earns the same as an architect which is more than either a finance or retail manager. On average, professional engineers - whether they're electronic, mechanical, chemical,

advertisement feature

aeronautical, or any other sort - can expect to earn at least £10,000 above the national average salary.

## Broaden your horizons

Manufacturing is a global enterprise – often involving multiple sites and suppliers and customers across the globe, so travel is a big part, and many jobs provide a chance to see the world and to use your talent for languages.

It's also important to work with people you get on with. Fortunately, manufacturing attracts a great breadth of people and there's a tremendous sense of teamwork and friendship.

## Manufacturing is going places

One of the many myths surrounding manufacturing is that it's died out in the UK and has all gone to China. True, some of the mass produced manufacturing has been outsourced to lower cost economies, but the UK remains the sixth largest manufacturing industry in the world. It accounts for around one seventh of our national wealth, contributing £150 billion to national output, generating more than half of our exports and employing close to five million people – directly or indirectly.

The government predicts that manufacturing will be one of the top jobs of the future – stating that in the new world economy quality jobs will come from a renaissance in manufacturing and the expansion of knowledge-based industries, such as engineering.

## Are you the brightest and the best?

Because modern manufacturing has become much more technologically advanced in recent years, many of the jobs within the sector are highly skilled and it's necessary to recruit the brightest and best young people.

Manufacturers are the people who invent the future and if you would like to find out more about how you can shape the world around you through an interesting and rewarding career then visit our website at **www.makeit.org.uk**

advertisement feature

produced. Workers may operate special machinery for building cars, work on a conveyor belt filling cans of drink, wash and grade raw fruit and vegetables to be processed, assemble complete items by putting components together, or monitor the quality and consistency of any product. The range is really very wide.

## Qualifications and Training

For most jobs there are no specific academic requirements, although some employers may like you to have GCSEs in maths, English and technology. Many employers set their own entry tests to measure how well you are likely to perform the tasks you will be expected to do. There are now some GNVQs level 2 available in Performing Manufacturing Operations, and if you are under 24 years old there may be opportunities to do an apprenticeship in electrical, electronic or mechanical engineering.

## Personal Qualities and Skills

You need to be good at practical work and quick with your hands. It is important that you don't mind carrying out repetitive tasks and that you can keep your concentration while doing this. You must be able to follow instructions, pay close attention to safety and work well as part of a team.

## Salaries

Starting salaries range from £12,000 to £16,000, and if you take on some supervisory responsibility they can rise to £20,000. Many jobs include shift work allowances.

Local Job Centre Plus and Careers/Connexions Centres

SEMTA (Science Engineering and Manufacturing Technologies Alliance), 14 Upton Road, Watford, Hertfordshire WD18 0JT; 0808 100 3682; www.semta.org.uk

Improve (Food and Drink Sector Skills Council), 1 Green Street, London W1K 6RG; 020 7355 0830; www.improvefdssc.org

Cogent (Sector Skills Council for the Oil and Gas Extraction, Chemicals Manufacturing and Petroleum Industries), Minerva House, Bruntland Road, Portlethen, Aberdeen AB12 4QL; 01224 787800; www.cogent-ssc.com

info

# Packaging technologist

The purpose of packaging is to protect, preserve, contain and present its contents. It also has a vital function in branding and brand awareness. Opportunities for work exist with manufacturers of raw packaging materials, with companies that produce packaging and companies that have a product to be packed. Many small firms do not have their own packaging adviser/technologist, and hire a consultant when the need arises.

Work opportunities exist in developing materials for packaging purposes, for designing equipment to manufacture or fill packaging, for structural design of parts, for graphic design on packs, for physical and chemical testing, and for quality assurance.

## Qualifications and Training

Packaging modules are available in some first degree courses, and two universities offer an MSc in Packaging Technology. The Diploma in Packaging Technology from the Institute of Packaging is internally recognised as a qualification of excellence. It can be studied in three ways: residential, part-time and by distance learning.

## Personal Qualities and Skills

Technologists and scientists must be able to look at problems in a practical way and have the ability to communicate their ideas to others both verbally and on paper.

## Salaries

New entrants earn between £15,000 and £20,000, senior technologists can earn £25,000 to £30,000, with research and development work attracting the higher salaries.

**info**

IoP the Packaging Society, c/o Institute of Materials, Minerals and Mining, 1 Carlton House Terrace, London SW1Y 5DB; 020 7451 7300; www.iom3.org/packaging
www.packagingfutures.com

# Sheet-metal worker/plater

Sheet-metal workers/platers are engaged in shaping, cutting and joining together pieces of metal. Sheet-metal workers work with thin metal sheet up to 3 mm thick, using a wide range of hand and power tools. They make such items as aircraft sections and car prototypes. Platers work with metal plates from 3 mm thick upwards. As well as hand and power tools, heavy presses are needed to bend the plate. Products include ship and submarine parts and industrial boilers.

## Qualifications and Training

If you are between 16 and 24 years old and want to join a National Apprenticeship Scheme for Engineering Construction (NASEC), you need GCSEs (A–C)/S grades (1–3) in maths, English and a science. If you have engineering drawing, metalwork or other practical subjects as well you may have an advantage. Applicants without the required entry grades may also be considered. These apprenticeships take up to three years and you train on the job, working along-side experienced sheet-metal workers. This apprenticeship leads to an NVQ level 3 award in engineering production. Older applicants can get into this work without GCSEs, but won't get the opportunity to do a full apprenticeship.

## Personal Qualities and Skills

You must have good manual dexterity and be able to concentrate for long periods of time. You should be good at following instructions, but able to work without direct supervision. Normal eyesight is essential and good colour vision is important.

## Salaries

Starting salaries range from £14,500 to £16,000. With experience you can earn between £17,000 and £25,000.

**info**

Engineering Construction Industry Training Board (ECITB), Blue Court, Church Lane, Kings Langley, Hertfordshire WD4 8JP; 01923 260000; www.ecitb.org.uk

SEMTA (Science, Engineering and Manufacturing Technologies Alliance), 14 Upton Road, Watford, Hertfordshire WD18 0JT; 0800 282167; www.semta.org.uk

The Welding Institute, Granta Park, Great Abington, Cambridge CB21 6AL; 01223 899000; www.twi.co.uk

Local press and Job Centre Plus

# Toolmaker

Toolmakers work in engineering, making a wide range of jigs, used to guide cutting tools and to hold the work in position; fixtures, to hold metal for bending or welding or to hold parts together; press tools in different shapes and sizes for cutting parts; mould tools to make items such as fridge interiors or mobile phone cases and measuring gauges. Toolmakers are often involved in making small quantities of a new product when it is at the design and development stage. Toolmaker machinists make the tools, often specialising in just one kind. Toolmaker fitters work on large structures that are constructed from many parts. They check all the parts, number them and then fit them together.

## Qualifications and Training

If you are between 16 and 24 years old and want to do a National Apprenticeship Scheme for Engineering Construction (NASEC) apprentice-ship, you need GCSEs (A–C)/S grades in maths, English and a science. If you have engineering drawing, metalwork or other practical subjects as well you may have an advantage. Applicants without the required entry grades may also be considered. These apprenticeships take up to three years and you train on the job, working alongside experienced toolmakers. This apprenticeship leads to an NVQ level 3 award in engineering production. Older applicants can do BTEC Certificates in manufacturing engineering.

## Personal Qualities and Skills

You must have good manual dexterity and be able to understand engineering drawings. You should be good at following instructions, but able to work without direct supervision. Normal eyesight is essential and good colour vision is important.

## Salaries

Starting salaries range from £15,000 to £17,000. With experience you can earn between £19,000 and £25,000.

**info**

Engineering Construction Industry Training Board (ECITB), Blue Court, Church Lane, Kings Langley, Hertfordshire WD4 8JP; 01923 260000; www.ecitb.org.uk

SEMTA (Science, Engineering and Manufacturing Technologies

Alliance), 14 Upton Road, Watford, Hertfordshire WD18 0JT; 0800 282167; www.semta.org.uk

The Welding Institute, Granta Park, Great Abington, Cambridge CB21 6AL; 01223 899000; www.twi.co.uk

Local press and Job Centre Plus

# Welder

Welders join pieces of metal together by applying intense heat and melting the edges so that two pieces become one. The sorts of items welded are metal sections of aeroplanes, ships, oil rigs, cars and power turbines. Welders work in light and heavy engineering firms, in foundry work and in shipbuilding. Some plastics are also welded.

Welders work on all types of fabrication from the manufacture of metal-frame chairs, to high-quality, complex applications such as building a submarine.

## Qualifications and Training

If you are aged between 16 and 24 you can do an Engineering Apprenticeship. There are no set entry qualifications for this, but many employers do prefer you to have GCSEs in English, maths, technology and a science subject. If you have these GCSEs, this also offers a wider range of further qualifications you can take part-time or full-time at college. These qualifications are also open to people of any age. There are several different NVQ awards related to welding, including fabrication and welding, performing engineering operations and welding with pipe work.

## Personal Qualities and Skills

You must have good practical and technical skills and be able to concentrate for long periods of time. You should be good at following instructions, but able to work without direct supervision. Normal eyesight is essential and good near vision is important.

## Salaries

Salaries start at between £14,000 and £17,000, and with experience you can earn £20,000 to £26,000, Highly skilled specialist welders may earn up to £30,000.

Engineering Construction Industry Training Board (ECITB), Blue Court, Church Lane, Kings Langley, Hertfordshire WD4 8JP; 01923 260000; www.ecitb.org.uk

SEMTA (Science, Engineering and Manufacturing Technologies

Alliance), 14 Upton Road, Watford, Hertfordshire WD18 0JT; 0800 282167; www.semta.org.uk

The Welding Institute, Granta Park, Great Abington, Cambridge CB21 6AL; 01223 899000; www.twi.co.uk

Local press and Job Centre Plus

# MARINE SCIENTIST

Marine scientists are drawn from various academic disciplines, mainly biology, geology and oceanography. This is a small but developing profession concerned with a detailed study of plant and animal life in the oceans and along coastlines. Its main purpose, as well as expanding our knowledge and understanding, is to research the food chains and levels of fish stocks in the oceans and to analyse the impact of pollution and other human activity on the ecology of the water. Marine scientists are employed by governments, research organisations, pressure groups and the marine laboratories of private organisations.

## Qualifications and Training

Two or three A levels or equivalents in biology, chemistry and maths or another science, plus GCSE level or equivalent in maths and physics are necessary for entry to a first degree course in biology. Some universities offer degrees in marine biology, but it may be advisable to take a broader degree in applied biology first.

## Personal Qualities and Skills

Biologists need the same characteristics as all scientists: patience and the willingness to repeat experimental work and measurements to check results, a methodical way of working, good observation and accuracy.

## Salaries

For entrants with degrees or HNDs, starting salaries range from £17,000 to £27,000, depending on your job title, role and what type of organisation you work for – public, private or voluntary body. If you have a PhD, your starting salary will be between £23,000 and £34,000.

**info**

The Centre for Environment, Fisheries and Aquaculture Science (CEFAS) CEFAS Lowestoft Laboratory, Pakefield Road, Lowestoft, Suffolk NR33 OHT; 01502 562244; www.cefas.co.uk

Challenger Society for Marine Science, Room 251/20, National Oceanography Centre Southampton, University of Southampton, Waterfront Campus, Southampton SO14 3ZH; www.soc.soton.ac.uk/OTHERS/CSMS

Institute of Marine Engineering, Science and Technology (ImarEST), 80 Coleman Street, London EC2R 5BJ; 020 7382 2600; www.imarest.org

Lantra: The Sector Skills Council for the Environmental and Land-based Sector, Lantra House, Stoneleigh Park, Coventry, Warwickshire CV8 2LG; 0845 707 8007; www.lantra.co.uk

The Marine Biological Association (MBA), The Laboratory, Citadel Hill, Plymouth, Devon PL1 2PB; 01752 633 207; www.mba.ac.uk

Marine Conservation Society, Unit 3, Wolf Business Park, Alton Road, Ross-on-Wye, Herefordshire HR9 5NB; 01989 566 017; www.mcsuk.org

Natural Environment Research Council (NERC), Polaris House, North Star Avenue, Swindon SN2 1EU; 01793 411500; www.nerc.ac.uk

Plymouth Marine Laboratory, Prospect Place, The Hoe, Plymouth PL1 3DH; 01752 633 100; www.pml.ac.uk

SEMTA: the Sector Skills Council for Science, Engineering and Manufacturing Technologies, 14 Upton Road, Watford WD18 0JT; 01923 238 441; www.semta.org.uk

Scottish Association for Marine Science (SAMS), Dunstaffnage Marine Laboratory, PO Box 3, Oban, Argyll PA37 1QA; 01631 559 000; www.sams.ac.uk

# MARKETING EXECUTIVE

Marketing is the process of persuading us to buy or of raising the profile of products, services or causes. The role of marketing executive can be varied and demanding, since marketing covers many activities including advertising, promotion, sponsorship, public relations, media relations and research. As an executive you could be involved in planning, developing and managing any of these activities. Marketing executives work either for specialist marketing consultancies or for in-house marketing departments working to sell, promote or increase market share of that business's products or services. Day-to-day tasks can include writing press releases, planning campaigns, liaising with customers, training sales staff, writing brochures or website entries, attending meetings, building up and maintaining good contacts in the media and, more illusively but very importantly, coming up with new ideas.

# Get Noticed

**You are your own campaign**
Give yourself an edge with The Chartered Institute of Marketing

Continuing professional development
(CPD) is the key to your ongoing
success. Take control of your
learning and rise above the rest in
today's competitive climate.

Let us help you to Get Noticed.

**Find out more**
**call** +44 (0)1626 427120
**visit** www.cim.co.uk/pack

**For more information
about CPD visit**
www.cim.co.uk/charteredcpd

 The Chartered
Institute of Marketing

cpd
Chartered CPD Programme

## Marketing

If you are considering a career in marketing you are not alone. Marketing
is more popular than ever, with 1 in 7 UK students now hoping to
become a marketer (Source: HESA -Higher Education Standards
Agency). So why is marketing such a popular career choice? Although it
has a reputation for being glamorous and at the more creative end of the
business spectrum, it actually encompasses a wide range of skills – from
copywriting and PR through to market research and data analysis.

A commonly used explanation of marketing is that it's all about "getting
the right goods and services to the right people, at the right time, at the
right price with the right communications and promotion". That's a lot of
things to get right, so you can see that marketing is a complex process
involving much more than just the highly visible advertising and
promotion side we encounter in our day to day lives.

advertisement feature

Some marketing jobs primarily involve research skills or data analysis, whilst others demand creativity and interpersonal skills. Most require a mix of logic and meticulous planning, drive, tenacity and excellent communication skills – an exciting blend of left and right-sided thinking. What other profession can combine creativity, strategic thinking and being at the heart of the business decision-making process?

Marketing roles do vary enormously: from marketing to consumers, marketing to other businesses, or on another level, working either client-side or agency-side (marketing agencies are often used to support businesses with their creative and often strategic needs).

Marketing is a hard working but well rewarded profession, with typical salaries for Marketing Assistants or Junior Account Executives around £18k-£22k. Working as an Assistant Brand Manager, Marketing Executive or Junior Account Manager, would typically take your salary to about £25k-£30k. As a full Product, Brand or Marketing Manager you can expect to earn around £30k or more. Senior level marketers, working at a strategic level as a Marketing Director or Brand Planner, can expect to earn upwards of £40k.

One of the best ways to kick-start your marketing career is to study one of The Chartered Institute of Marketing's (CIM's) professional qualifications; a blend of marketing knowledge and practical application that is highly regarded by employers.

In your career you will almost certainly have opportunities for training and **continuing professional development (CPD)**. CPD helps ensure your knowledge and skills stay up to date throughout your career – vitally important in such a fast-moving profession as marketing, and something employers are keen to see.

Whatever stage you are at in your marketing career, CIM, the largest community of marketing professionals in the world, offers you a structured framework in which to monitor, manage and plan your development. Our Chartered CPD Programme enables you to work towards Chartered Marketer status, the ultimate accolade for a marketer.

Visit **www.getin2marketing.co.uk** for more information about a career in marketing or **www.cim.co.uk** for a world of marketing resources.

advertisement feature

## Qualifications and Training

There are two main routes into marketing. You either need a degree in a relevant subject such as marketing or a business-related subject, or you can get into marketing if you already have relevant experience in sales or customer services. The Chartered Institute of Marketing offers several professional qualifications towards which you can work while employed. These courses cover all aspects of marketing and are pitched at several levels, from introductory to postgraduate diplomas.

## Personal Qualities and Skills

You must be an enthusiastic and energetic communicator, able to motivate staff and persuade customers and clients. You also need to be a good team member, able to listen to the ideas of others. You have to be a good organiser and great planner. You have to be a creative thinker, imaginative and able to come up with something new.

## Salaries

Starting salaries are between £20,000 and £28,000 – geographical location and the sector you work in affect salaries. Senior marketing managers earn between £25,000 and £55,000. Some senior marketing executives can earn £100,000.

The Chartered Institute of Marketing (CIM), Moor Hall, Cookham, Maidenhead, Berks SL6 9QH; 01628 427500; www.cim.co.uk

The Communication Advertising and Marketing Education Foundation (CAM), Moor Hall, Cookham, Maidenhead, Berkshire SL6 9QH; 01628 427120; www.camfoundation.com

The Institute of Direct Marketing (IDM), 1 Park Road, Teddington, Middlesex TW11 0AR; 020 8977 5705; www.theidm.co.uk

*How to get on in Marketing, Advertising and Public Relations* (Kogan Page)

**info**

# MARKET RESEARCHER

Market research is the collection and analysis of information about markets, organisations and people to support better business decisions. It is used to discover gaps in the market, to ensure customer satisfaction and to plan effective marketing campaigns. In a competitive environment, the more knowledge a business has about its customers, the more likely it is to succeed.

Over the past few decades, market research techniques have developed significantly, making it a more precise science. Methods used depend on the requirements of the business and the budget available, and include interviews with individuals, surveys by telephone, post and via the internet, and increasingly using mobile phone text messaging. These are used to gather quantitative (numerical) data. Qualitative research by face-to-face interviews with individuals or groups is geared to providing insight into why people hold the views they do, and provides greater understanding of customers. Interviewers are known as field workers, and their work, and that of the analysis personnel, is organised by the research executive, who is in overall charge of the project for a marketing executive or client, and is responsible for interpreting the results.

Every year, the Market Research Society (MRS) publishes the *Research Buyer's Guide*, which lists the majority of market research agencies in the UK and outlines the size of each agency, together with their areas of specialisation. The guide also details other organisations that can offer advice on getting started in market research; the online version of the guide is free at www.rbg.org.uk.

## Qualifications and Training

Field workers do not need qualifications but must be articulate, persuasive and presentable. Applicants for research and executive positions will be expected to hold a degree. The majority of market research graduates are drawn from disciplines that require strong communication or analytical skills, such as languages, English literature, maths, psychology, geography, history, politics, science and IT. However, graduates with degrees as contrasting as zoology and theatre studies are also welcomed by the industry.

The Market Research Society offers a range of qualifications that are linked to the UK's National Qualifications Framework and are designed to suit a wide range of candidates, from those with no experience to practitioners seeking continuous professional development.

## Personal Qualities and Skills

Excellent communication skills and ability to get on with people of all types. Analytical skills, numeracy and data interpretation are important.

**info**

Association for Qualitative Research (AQR), Davey House, 31 St Neots Rd, Eaton Ford, St Neots, Cambs PE19 7BA; 01480 407227; www.aqr.org.uk

BMRB (British Market Research Bureau), Ealing Gateway, 26–30 Uxbridge Road, Ealing, London W5 2BP; 020 8433 4000; www.bmrb.co.uk

Chartered Institute of Marketing (CIM), Moor Hall, Cookham, Maidenhead, Berks SL6 9QH; 01628 427500; www.cim.co.uk

Direct Marketing Association, DMA House, 70 Margaret Street, London W1W 8SS; 020 7291 3300; www.dma.org.uk

The Institute of Direct Marketing (IDM), 1 Park Rd, Teddington, Middlesex TW11 0AR; 020 8977 5705; www.theidm.co.uk

Ipsos MORI; 79–81 Borough Road, London SE1 1FY; 44 (0)20 7347 3018

Market Research Society (MRS), 15 Northburgh Street, London EC1V 0JR; 020 7490 4911; www.mrs.org.uk/

Social Research Association (SRA), 24–32 Stephenson Way, London NW1 2HX; 020 7388 2391; www.the-sra.org.uk

## Salaries

Market research analysts who interpret the data and results, or managers who plan and develop research, start on salaries of £21,000 to £26,000. Experienced research executives earn between £30,000 and £45,000. Market research interviewers working on a casual basis earn £50 to £80 per day. Interviewers who are permanent employees earn between £12,000 and £16,000.

# MEAT INDUSTRY

As well as retail and supermarket work as a butcher, or working for large organisations such as hotels, there are other openings in the meat industry. Some wholesale establishments selling pre-packed meat need teams of butchers for boning, cutting and packing the meat, or processing it into pies. Wholesale butchers do not meet the general public but deal with other butchers and retailers. Workers are also needed in abattoirs, to handle and kill the animals, and to inspect and deal with the meat.

# Butcher

Career prospects are varied in the meat industry, extending from work in a small retail shop through to supermarkets; from meat buying for large organisations such as hotels and caterers, to the manufacture of meat and poultry products.

### Qualifications and Training

A good general education is necessary but there are no formal educational requirements. Training is on the job and courses are available at further education establishments and technical colleges, leading to examinations of the Meat Training Council. NVQs are available at levels 1–4, and Higher National diploma/certificate qualifications. Modern Apprenticeships are available. Further training, appropriate to the relevant sector of the industry, in management, meat technology, or small business ownership, may follow an apprenticeship.

### Personal Qualities and Skills

Butchers need to be very practical, with good manual dexterity, and not squeamish. They must ensure that they and their work environments are really clean and hygienic and they must enjoy talking to people and giving advice. A good business sense is also useful.

### Salaries

Trainee butchers earn £12,000 to £12,500. Skilled butchers earn between £14,000 and £19,000. Skilled butchers who are also section managers and who have responsibilities for sourcing and buying produce can earn £25,000 or more. In some geographical areas there is a shortage of skilled butchers.

**info**

Meat Training Council, PO Box 141, Winterhill House, Snowdon Drive, Milton Keynes MK6 1YY; 01908 231062; www.meattraining. org.uk

Scottish Meat Training, 8–10 Needless Road, Perth PH2 0JW; 01738 637785; www.foodtraining.net

Improve Ltd, Sector Skills Council for Food and Drink Manufacturing and Processing, Providence House, 2 Innovation Lane, Heslington, York YO10 52F; 0845 644 0448; www. improveltd.co.uk

# MEDICAL AND HEALTHCARE SCIENCE

Many scientific disciplines play a key part in medicine – in the development and testing of drugs and the monitoring of the performance of these drugs. Scientists contribute to the understanding of the processes of disease and damage to tissue, organs and systems, as well as to the development of equipment and techniques to improve diagnosis and treatment. There are very many jobs in medical and healthcare science, and those described here are examples from some of the different areas of science in medicine.

## Life scientists and pathologists

Life scientists work in hospital laboratories, in community health and for other national agencies concerned with blood, health protection and organ transplant. Life scientists work in three broad areas: pathology, investigating causes and development of diseases; genetics, looking at genetic components of illness; and embryology, investigating the development of life and treatments for infertility. Some examples of these scientific roles are shown below.

### Clinical embryologist
This is a rapidly developing field. Clinical embryologists are involved in research and investigation of various aspects of IVF treatment and other programmes of assisted reproduction. This work involves the collection of eggs from patients for examination, checking fertility levels of individuals and the application of 'cutting edge' and sometimes controversial technologies.

### Clinical immunologist
Clinical immunologists use sophisticated laboratory techniques to examine the effects on the immune system of syndromes such as AIDS and allergic conditions such as hay fever or asthma. They apply the knowledge they acquire to developing better treatments of these conditions. This is a fast moving and developing area of medical science.

## Clinical microbiologist

Clinical microbiologists work to diagnose all kinds of infections – bacterial, viral, fungal or parasitic. What they discover about the infections a patient has plays an important role in how that patient is treated: what antibiotics are given, for example. They also work for the Health Protection Agency helping prevent the spread of diseases.

## Phlebotomist

Phlebotomists take blood samples from patients, so that these samples can be analysed to diagnose diseases and other disorders. They have to take great care when collecting blood to disturb the patient as little as possible, to label the blood taken correctly and to ensure that it is taken to the correct laboratory. Phlebotomists also work for the blood donor agency, collecting healthy blood from volunteers.

# Physiological scientists

Physiological scientists monitor the body's systems, breathing, hearing, sight, heart, liver, kidneys, brain, etc. They help investigate problems and produce information that will assist doctors making diagnoses. In some roles they work to maintain many of the body's systems and functions during surgery. Many physiological scientists work directly with patients in outpatient clinics and on hospital wards.

## Cardiographer

Cardiographers work in hospitals, operating the electrocardiograph (ECG) machines that monitor the functioning of the heart. They reassure patients and explain the procedure to them, before fitting electrodes to the patient's body, ensuring they are correctly connected to the machine, and take readings that a doctor uses to make decisions about diagnosis and treatment.

## Neurophysiology technologist

Neurophysiology technologists, also referred to as clinical physiologists (neurophysiology), work in hospital outpatient departments, in intensive care units and in operating theatres. Their work is concerned with monitoring and measuring activities in the central and peripheral nervous systems. They use highly sophisticated equipment to obtain their readings. They work closely with patients of all ages – a child who has suffered a brain injury, or an older person who has had a stroke, for example. They also work closely with other members of the healthcare team.

## Perfusionist

Perfusionists (or perfusion scientists) work in operating theatres where patients are undergoing open heart surgery. The term 'perfusion' refers to the movement of liquid through tissue. The perfusionist ensures that oxygen is circulated through the patient's blood even when the action of the heart and lungs is temporarily stopped in order to carry out the surgery.

Perfusionists use a range of complex machinery and monitoring equipment to carry out their work. They must alert fellow members of the operating team if they have any causes for concern.

# Physical scientists and biomedical engineers

Physical scientists working in medicine develop ways to measure what is happening in the body, to develop new ways of diagnosing and treating diseases and to develop new equipment to aid in treatment. They also have to ensure that such equipment works safely.

## Medical physicist

Medical physicists are involved in developing highly sophisticated equipment for measuring the effects of illnesses and disabilities. Medical physicists have developed X-ray and ultrasound scanning equipment and they use their research skills to refine and improve these techniques and technologies. They often work closely with radiographers in the field of nuclear medicine, treating cancer cells with the correct dose of radiation.

## Clinical engineer

Clinical or bio-engineers design equipment for monitoring, diagnosis, treatment and rehabilitation or research. They may design laser equipment or electronic aids for patients with disabilities. They examine the mechanics of the human body to see how to replicate the functions of particular organs or systems. They develop a detailed knowledge of materials and of engineering processes, and apply this technical knowledge in a medical environment.

## Medical laboratory technician

All the scientific research and development work that goes on throughout the health service and in medical schools needs the support of medical laboratory technicians and assistants. Laboratory technicians work in all aspects of medical and clinical sciences, whether it is testing blood, screening cells for disease, or developing a new material to treat burns or wounds. Medical laboratory technicians assist scientists in setting up experiments, monitoring these experiments and recording the results.

## Qualifications and Training

With so many career options, there are several different entry levels. What follows is a guide to the main points to consider.

To work as a scientist involved in research and development in such fields as pathology, microbiology or biochemistry you need a relevant degree in that subject, normally at least a 2.1. Many applicants have postgraduate degrees as well. In some instances you need to ensure that your degree is accredited by the appropriate professional body – the Institute of Biomedical Science, for example. Relevant degrees include biology, microbiology, biochemistry, chemistry, physics, physiology and medicine.

Many more patient-focused roles in life science and physiological science require you to have two or three A levels, including sciences. It is important to check the particular requirements for the jobs that interest you.

Laboratory technicians usually need five GCSEs grades A–C including English, maths and at least one science subject. Assistant laboratory technicians may be able to get into laboratory work without formal qualifications and work towards relevant NVQs while employed.

All roles include training on the job and often provide opportunities to work towards appropriate professional qualifications.

## Personal Qualities and Skills

If you are engaged in research and development you must have a rigorous and questioning scientific approach to your work – be good at problem solving and coming up with imaginative solutions. If your work involves contact with patients, you must have an understanding and reassuring manner, but you must also be able to avoid becoming too emotionally involved in your work. Many roles require you to have good practical skills, manual dexterity and the ability to be meticulous and highly observant. Many roles will also require you to use complex instruments and take careful recordings of results.

## Salaries

Most NHS jobs are on a graded, structured pay scale, Medical laboratory technicians earn from £14,000 to £19,000. Most scientists start on the scale between £21,000 and £27,000, though senior scientists earn between £36,000 and £55,000.

NHS Careers, PO Box 376, Bristol BS99 3EY; 0845 606 0655; www.nhscareers.nhs.uk

Health Professions Council, Park House, 184 Kennington Park Road, London SE11 4BU; 020 7582 0866; www.hpc-uk.org

Institute of Biomedical Science, 12 Coldbath Square, London EC1R 5HL; 020 7713 0214; www.ibms.org

Association of Clinical Scientists, c/o Association of Clinical Biochemists, 130–132 Tooley Street, London SE1 2TU; 020 7940 8960; www.assclinsci.org

Health Learning and Skills Advice Line; 0800 015 0850; www.learndirect-advice.co.uk/campaigns/nhs/

Institute of Physics and Engineering in Medicine (IPEM), Fairmount House, 230 Tadcaster Road, York YO24 1ES; 01904 610821; www.ipem.ac.uk

Association of Clinical Biochemists, 130–132 Tooley Street, London SE1 2TU; 020 7403 8001; www.acb.org.uk

Association of Clinical Cytogeneticists; www.cytogenetics.org.uk

info

**info**

Society for General Microbiology;
www.socgenmicrobiol.org.uk

British Society for Immunology;
www.immunology.org

Association of Clinical Embryologists;
www.ivf.net/ace

Recruitment Centre for Clinical
Scientists; 020 7582 0866; www.
nhsclinicalscientists.info

Association for Science Education
(ASE), College Lane, Hatfield,
Hertfordshire AL10 9AA;
01707 283000; www.ase.org.uk

CLEAPSS Schools Science Service,
Brunel University, Uxbridge UB8 3PH;
01895 251496; www.cleapss.org.uk

SEMTA (Science, Engineering and
Manufacturing Technologies
Alliance), 14 Upton Road, Watford,
Hertfordshire WD18 0JT;
0800 282167; www.semta.org.uk

Association of Medical Laboratory
Assistants, 12 Coldbath Square,
London EC1R 5HL; 020 7713 8050;
www.amlauk.org

# Medical illustrator

Medical illustrators employ a range of artistic and technical skills to produce photographs, drawings, videos and other digital images in healthcare settings. They produce material to help assess the effectiveness of treatment regimes by photographing patients at different stages of their treatment. They may produce material for medical textbooks, websites, lectures and other training and teaching activities. Some specialise in forensic work, taking pictures of non-accidental injuries or copying evidence from X-rays and slides.

Because medical illustrators use a combination of photography, video and drawing skills, there may be some opportunities to take work which allows you to develop special expertise in one or other of these areas. You are likely to spend your time working in hospital wards, operating theatres and clinics, as well as studios and technical laboratories.

## Qualifications and Training

While it is not always necessary to have formal qualifications, it is now very difficult to get into this work without a foundation degree, HND or degree in a relevant subject. The most useful subjects are graphic design and photography. It is likely that in the near future medical illustrators will only be able to practise if they are state registered. The exact date for this has not been finalised. However, when this does happen all new entrants to this profession will have to have a relevant degree which meets the standards for registration. It is very useful if you can gain some relevant work experience with an NHS trust medical photography department. You should also be able to produce a portfolio of your work at interview.

## Personal Qualities and Skills

This work demands a wide range of qualities and skills. You should have artistic and photographic ability and be competent working with technical equipment. You must have an interest in and some knowledge of biology, physiology and diseases and medical conditions. You have to have excellent interpersonal skills, and be sensitive and empathic when dealing with people who are anxious or vulnerable. You should be good at working as part of a team, but be able to get on with your own work unsupervised.

## Salaries

Salaries start at between £21,000 and £27,000. Senior medical illustrators earn between £25,000 and £34,000. Large teaching hospitals have much bigger medical illustration departments so these offer more scope for management jobs, which pay up to £39,000.

British Institute of Professional Photography, Fox Talbot House, 2 Amwell End, Ware, Hertfordshire SG12 9HN; 01920 464011; www.bipp.com

Health Learning and Skills Advice Line; 0800 015 0850; www.learndirect-advice.co.uk/campaigns/nhs

Medical Artists' Association; www.maa.org.uk

Institute of Medical Illustrators, 29 Arboretum Street, Nottingham NG1 4JA; www.imi.org.uk

NHS Careers, PO Box 376, Bristol BS99 3EY; 0845 606 0655; www.nhscareers.nhs.uk

info

# MEDICINE

Doctors work in many healthcare settings in both the NHS and in private clinics and hospitals. For the NHS they work in general practice in local medical centres, polyclinics and in hospitals. In hospitals there are many different medical specialisms doctors can follow. In private practice doctors work in hospitals, clinics and medical centres.

# General practitioner

Family doctors, or GPs, may form long-standing relationships with their patients. They must be able to diagnose and deal with a broad spectrum of illnesses and disorders, mainly those common within the community, but also to recognise those that are rare. Increasingly, doctors are asked to help their patients to cope with personal and emotional problems. They have to be aware of and take into account physical, psychological and social factors when looking after their patients. About 90 per cent of GPs now work together in group practices, allowing some specialisation.

For doctors who work in the community, people are of prime importance. GPs are involved with individuals' problems, whether personal, social, organisational or environmental. General practice is the most personalised of all the health services, based close to patients' homes and with opportunities for long-term relationships between doctor and patient. Within this context, it is the doctor's job to give early treatment and continuing care for the great variety of problems and disorders presented by patients. GPs have to deal with many moral decisions, and much of the work is challenging because of its unpredictability.

General practice differs from all other areas of medicine in that it is not salaried and GPs are technically self-employed. The government sets an average amount that GPs are supposed to earn, and basic pay is based on the number of patients on a GP's list.

# Hospital doctor

Hospital doctors treat hospital inpatients and patients who come to the hospital through outpatient clinics. Hospital doctors work in one of 50 different specialist areas within medicine, treating illness, disease and infection. The specialisms fall into three main groups: medicine, surgery and psychiatry. During training, they will learn about every aspect of health and with more experience choose a specialist area which interests them. Doctors choosing to work in medical areas can specialise in such fields as cardiology or paediatrics. They prescribe treatments or organise further investigations, and they monitor patients' progress. Surgeons perform operations of many kinds. They can choose to specialise in such areas as orthopaedics, repairing damaged and broken bones. Psychiatrists treat patients with mental illnesses such as anxiety or depression, prescribing drugs, or behavioural or talking therapies.

# Research and teaching

Research work is carried out in universities, hospitals, public health laboratories, and other research establishments and pharmaceutical manufacturing companies. There are opportunities too for teaching in universities. Teaching may involve very little or no contact with patients, or it may be similar in content to hospital doctors' work. An academic career in medicine either through teaching or research is possible in practically all hospital specialities, general practice and public health medicine.

## Qualifications and Training

To become a doctor in the UK you must take a five-year degree course in medicine recognised by the General Medical Council (GMC). To be accepted onto one of these courses you must have three A levels, normally an A and two Bs including maths and two sciences. In Scotland you need five H grades and two Advanced Science Highers, one of which must be chemistry.

The GMC also approves some six-year degree courses in medicine designed for applicants who do not have the appropriate science grades. The additional year is a pre-medical course in science. In some cases, an Access to Higher Education course may be accepted. It is important to check carefully with the GMC, to ensure that you embark on an approved course.

As part of the selection process for a degree you may be asked to take a UK Clinical Aptitude Test (UKCAT). This test assesses behavioural and mental attributes relevant to people working in medicine. Check the UKCAT website to find out about participating universities and how to apply to take the test. All medical degrees combine practical training and clinical experience with academic learning. Having completed your medical degree you then undertake a two-year foundation programme gaining further experience and consolidating your learning.

## Personal Qualities and Skills

All doctors must have excellent interpersonal skills – these qualities have become increasingly important in selecting appropriate students for medical school.

## Salaries

Junior doctors in postgraduate foundation training earn £33,000. Doctors in specialist training earn between £33,000 and £44,000. Hospital doctors earn from £45,000 and specialists earn £70,000. Senior consultants earn more than £150,000. GPs earn from £44,000 on qualifying to £80,000 plus.

info

NHS Careers, PO Box 376, Bristol BS99 3EY; 0845 606 0655; www.nhscareers.nhs.uk

Royal College of Surgeons of England, 35–43 Lincoln's Inn Fields, London WC2A 3PE; 020 7405 3474; www.rcseng.ac.uk

General Medical Council (GMC), Regent's Place, 350 Euston Road, London NW1 3JN; 0845 357 3456; www.gmc-uk.org

UK Clinical Aptitude Test; www.ukcat.ac.uk

Royal College of General Practitioners, 14 Princes Gate, London SW7 1PU, 020 7344 3051, www.rcgp.org.uk

Health Learning and Skills Advice Line; 0800 015 0850

# MERCHANT NAVY

The Merchant Navy refers to all non-military shipping and comprises cargo ships, tankers, ferries and cruise ships. The Royal Fleet Auxiliary also employs civilian crew. While different ships will carry different ranges of personnel, eg more engineers on a tanker, more cooks and hospitality staff on a passenger cruise liner – there is still a clear staffing structure on every ship and below are the main job titles and the work associated with them. In addition to the jobs outlined, ships employ catering staff and administrative staff. Cruise liners employ a whole range of additional personnel including medical staff, hairdressers, activities coordinators and entertainers of many kinds.

# Deck officer

Deck officers are responsible for every aspect of the ship, from its navigation to the management of the crew and the safety of passengers and crew. There are four grades of deck officer: captain or master, chief officer, second officer and third officer. The captain is in overall charge of the ship. The other three levels of officer share a range of responsibilities for navigation, cargo handling, safety of crew and passengers, supervision of crew, and management of overall maintenance. The levels of responsibility become greater for each deck officer grade.

## Qualifications and Training

You can join as an officer cadet or marine apprentice if you have four GCSEs grades A–C including English, maths and physics or combined science. You must also be sponsored by a shipping company or another training provider. There are also some opportunities to be sponsored through a foundation degree or degree programme in science. These industry-sponsored courses include practical training onboard ships as well as your academic studies.

## Personal Qualities and Skills

You must have good leadership skills and be able to motivate people and work as part of a team. You should have good technical ability and enjoy learning about equipment and systems. You have to be able to tolerate long periods away from home and sometimes work in rough and uncomfortable conditions.

## Salaries

Officer cadets are paid between £5,500 and £8,500. Once you are qualified as a junior officer you are paid between £20,000 and £22,000. Senior officers, ie chief officers and captains on large ships, earn between £25,000 and £30,000.

# Merchant Navy rating

Merchant Navy ratings are the crew members who work on the decks, in the engine room, handling the cargo and providing catering services onboard ships. Exact duties vary according to the size and type of vessel and depending on what special skills or training you have. Work might include loading and unloading cargo, cleaning every part of the vessel and routine maintenance jobs.

## Qualifications and training

To train as a Merchant Navy rating you have to be taken on and sponsored for training by a shipping company or by the Royal Fleet Auxiliary. You need to apply directly to these. Each company sets its own entry requirements, but three or four GCSEs are a good guide. These should include English, maths and a science subject. If you have previous experience in engineering or in catering, this can give you a real advantage. Training is through a combination of college-based training and experience on board. You can work towards NVQs in marine support. You then have to make a choice between deck work, catering or engineering. If you continue with your studies you can go on to train as an officer.

## Personal Qualities and Skills

All ratings have to have a real interest in shipping vessels and in being at sea. You need to be physically fit and comfortable working in harsh conditions. The atmosphere is very different on a large tanker compared to an upmarket cruise liner – so you need to consider this when you decide what jobs to apply for. Teamwork is very important indeed. You need to be practical for all Merchant Navy work, but you will also need particular skills depending on whether you specialise in catering, engineering or deck management.

## Salaries

Merchant Navy ratings earn very small salaries during training, though their college fees and all living expenses onboard ship are paid by the employer. Experienced ratings earn between £17,000 and £23,000.

Royal Fleet Auxiliary Service (RFA), CNR RFA Recruitment, Room G-13, Building 1/080, Jago Road, Portsmouth PO1 3LU; 0045 604 0520; www.royalnavy.mod.uk/operations-and-support/royal-fleet-auxiliary

Marine Society & Sea Cadets, 202 Lambeth Road, London SE1 7JW; 020 7654 7000; www.ms sc.org

A Career at Sea; www.gotosea.org.uk

# METALLURGIST

Metallurgists are involved with the extraction of metals from ores, their purification, and with reclaiming them from scrap. They are also concerned with developing new alloys and processing metals during manufacture.

## Qualifications and Training

GCSE passes in a science subject, maths and English or equivalent are required for entry to Edexcel (BTEC) and SQA two-year courses for a certificate or diploma in metallurgical studies. Candidates who have successfully completed the two-year course and those with A levels or equivalent in maths, physics or chemistry may study for the Edexcel (BTEC)/SQA Higher Certificates and diplomas, or qualify for entry to full-time, sandwich or part-time courses leading to degrees in metallurgy.

## Personal Qualities and Skills

Metallurgy demands an interest in scientific and technological subjects, an ability to solve practical problems and work with other people on specific projects.

## Salaries

New graduates earn between £18,000 and £27,000. With a few years' experience earnings rise to between £30,000 and £37,000.

**info**

Institute of Cast Metal Engineers (ICME), National Metalforming Centre, 47 Birmingham Road, West Bromwich, West Midlands B70 6PY; 0121 601 6979; www.icme.org.uk

Institute of Materials, Minerals and Mining (IOM3), 1 Carlton House Terrace, London SW1Y 5DB; 020 7451 7300; www.iom3.org

Metals Industry Skills and Performance, 5/6 Meadowcourt, Amos Road, Sheffield S9 1BX; 0114 244 6833; www.metskill.org.uk

Proskills UK, Centurion Court, 85b Milton Park, Abingdon, Oxfordshire OX14 4RY; 01235 833844; www.proskills.co.uk

# METEOROLOGIST

Meteorologists are the people who tell us what the weather is going to do. While we are all aware of weather forecasting on television and radio, meteorologists provide information for many other clients too. People who want accurate weather forecasts include organisations involved in air transport, shipping, public service, the media, the armed forces and retail businesses. Individuals involved in air travel or water sports or outdoor pursuits like climbing, farmers or sporting organisations – all of these can plan more effectively if they know what the weather is likely to do. Meteorologists collect data from satellites all over the world. They use computerised and mathematical models designed to make short- and long-range forecasts concerning weather and climate patterns. They also study the impact of weather on the environment, taking measurements, recording results and looking at patterns over time. The study of meteorology is one of the sciences most frequently used in the study of climate change.

The largest employer of meteorologists in the UK is the Met Office, but meteorologists are also employed by agriculture and fisheries organisations, the oil and gas industry, research organisations and the Environment Agency. Some work for small consultancies contracted to provide information for the kinds of organisations just listed.

## Qualifications and training

Meteorology is a graduate profession – many meteorologists also have post-graduate qualifications. The most useful degree subjects include maths, physics, meteorology, environmental science and oceanography. The Met Office usually takes entrants with a First or 2.1 degree. It is very unusual to get in with a HND or a foundation degree. The Met Office does have a Mobile Met unit (MMU) and it is possible to apply to be a forecaster for this unit if you have good A levels in maths and physics. Technical support staff and administrative staff employed by the Met Office do not need degrees, but from these roles it is not possible to become a meteorologist. The Met Office provides a structured training scheme for new entrants.

The Met Office offers a small number of highly sought after summer placements which can provide really useful experience. Experience of computer modelling, even if it is not weather related, is also extremely useful.

## Personal Qualities and Skills

Of course you must be interested in the weather – who isn't? In addition you have to have very good observational skills and the ability to generate and interpret highly complex data. You must be able to work as part of a team, and be able to communicate scientific information in such a way that it can be easily understood by the non-scientist.

## Salaries

Graduate trainees in the Met Office earn just under £19,000 and just under £25,000 once they have completed their training. Private weather consultancies may pay higher salaries, but they do not usually provide the training.

British Antarctic Survey (BAS), High Cross, Madingley Road, Cambridge CB3 0ET; 01223 221400; www.antarctica.ac.uk/

Environment Agency (EA); 08708 506 506; www.environment-agency.gov.uk

Institute of Physics, 76 Portland Place, London W1B 1NT; 020 7470 4800; www.iop.org

Met Office, FitzRoy Road, Exeter, Devon EX1 3PB; 0870 900 0100; www.metoffice.com

Natural Environment Research Council (NERC), Polaris House, North Star Avenue, Swindon SN2 1EU; 01793 411500; www.nerc.ac.uk

Royal Meteorological Society, 104 Oxford Road, Reading, Berkshire RG1 7LL; 0118 956 8500; www.rmets.org

SEMTA: the Sector Skills Council for Science, Engineering and Manufacturing Technologies; 14 Upton Road, Watford WD18 0JT; 01923 238 441; www.semta.org.uk

info

# MICROBIOLOGIST

Microbiology is the study of tiny living organisms (bacteria, viruses, fungi, protozoa and algae) and the massive impact they have on almost every aspect of our lives. There are good job opportunities for microbiologists in the human and animal healthcare sector, medical research, and the food production and agricultural industries. Microbiologists are employed in hospitals, research institutes, industrial research and development and manufacturing sites, universities and environmental companies. Their skills and knowledge are vital to the rapidly growing biotechnology industry, where gene technology, fermentation and bioprocessing play an important part in developing products of the future.

## Qualifications and Training

Minimum requirements for entry to a full-time first degree course are five GCSE passes (grades A–C) and two A level science passes. Some courses concentrate on specific areas of microbiology, others are more general and allow specialisation at a later stage. Some courses offer a period of industrial training. It is also possible to obtain qualifications via part-time study while working in a laboratory.

## Personal Qualities and Skills

Microbiologists have enquiring minds, are good problem solvers and can work accurately. Good communication skills are vital as microbiologists have to describe their work to other people. Most scientists work in a multidisciplinary group, so it helps to be a good team worker.

## Salaries

Junior research posts earn between £21,000 and £27,000. Salaries in the food and drink industry start at between £24,000 and £30,000 – in pharmaceuticals starting salaries are around £30,000. Senior microbiologists earn £40,000 to £50,000.

info

Society for General Microbiology, Marlborough House, Basingstoke Road, Spencers Wood, Reading RG7 1AG; 0118 988 1800; fax: 0118 988 5656; www. socgenmicrobiol.org.uk; e-mail: careers@sgm.ac.uk

www.microbiologyonline.org.uk

'Microbiologists make a difference' (free leaflet from the above)

'Your career in microbiology' (free booklet from the above)

# MILK ROUNDSPERSON

*see* Roundsperson

# MODELMAKER

Models can be made to represent almost anything: towns, office blocks, oil terminals, shopping centres, motorways, houses, cars and planes. They are often scaled-down versions of the real thing, but sometimes they can be enlargements. They are used to show what the real thing will look like, and if they are working models, they may be used as testers. Models are often used too in television and films. Modelmakers work for firms specialising in such work, or sometimes branch out on their own.

## Qualifications and Training

Formal academic qualifications are not necessary. Modelmakers may teach themselves or learn at evening class; some large firms offer apprenticeships. Edexcel (BTEC) courses in modelmaking are available at some FE colleges and some art colleges.

## Personal Qualities and Skills

Patience, manual dexterity, and a good sense of design, shape and colour are necessary. Modelmakers must be prepared to do one job for a considerable length of time; a project such as a model town could take up to a year to complete.

## Salaries

Salaries start at between £16,000 and £19,000, though experienced model makers can earn up to £30,000.

Creative and Cultural Skills, 4th Floor, Lafone House, The Leathermarket, Weston Street, London SE1 3HN; 020 7015 1800; www.ccskills.org.uk

DD&D, 9 Graphite Square, Vauxhall Walk, London SE11 5EE;

020 7840 1111; www.dandad.org

Skillset, Focus Point, 21 Caledonian Road, London N1 9GB; 08080 300 900 for England, Wales and Northern Ireland; 0808 100 8094 for Scotland; www.skillset.org

info

# MOTOR INDUSTRY

The motor industry provides a range of job opportunities, from technical to sales and management roles. A common theme for all these jobs is that you have to have a real interest in motor vehicles. The following section gives details of the most commonly found job titles and training routes within this industry.

# Auto electrician

Auto electricians are motor vehicle technicians who have highly specialised knowledge of and skill in the complex electrical and electronic systems that are part of modern motor vehicles.

### Qualifications and Training

To be an auto electrician, you need to do an apprenticeship. To start an apprenticeship you must have five GCSEs grades A–C, including maths and English. The apprenticeship combines on-the-job training with your employer and college-based learning. Through your apprenticeship you can gain an NVQ certificate.

### Personal Qualities and Skills

You must be good at working with your hands and able to solve problems. You must be good at working as part of a team.

## Automotive engineer

*see* Engineering

## Body repairer and refinisher

Body repairers and refinishers restore cars, vans, trucks and motorcycles to their original condition after accidents, damage or other wear and tear. This includes replacing windscreens and other glass, hammering out dents and rubbing away patches of rust. Repair and refinishing covers several different roles including body repair, electrical, mechanical and trim repair, and vehicle valeting.

### Qualifications and Training

For any job in body repair and refinishing, apart from car valeting, you need to do an apprenticeship. To be accepted for an apprenticeship you must have five GCSEs grades A–C, including maths and English. The apprenticeship combines on-the-job training with your employer and college-based learning. Through your apprenticeship you can gain relevant NVQ certificates.

### Personal Qualities and Skills

These vary according to exactly which aspect of body repair and refinishing you have chosen, but they all demand that you pay great attention to fine detail, that you can find ways to solve problems and that you are able to work as part of a team.

## Roadside assistance and recovery technician

Roadside assistance and recovery workers are called to the scene of vehicle breakdowns. They have to make quick, accurate assessments as to whether they can repair the vehicle on the spot or whether it will have to be towed away. They also have to reassure vehicle drivers and passengers and explain to them clearly what the best course of action is.

## Qualifications and Training

For this work you must be 21 years old and hold a full clean driving licence. Most successful applicants will already have worked for three years or more with motor vehicles, usually as a vehicle technician. Most technicians qualify through an apprenticeship.

## Personal Qualities and Skills

You need to be extremely responsible, with good technical skills and knowledge. You must be able to take decisions on your own and to solve problems. You must have good people skills, be polite, friendly and reassuring, and good at explaining technical problems.

# Vehicle parts operative

Vehicle parts operatives deal with the ordering and management of the hundreds of separate parts that need to be replaced in every type of vehicle. Vehicle parts operatives have to be able to recognise any vehicle part and know that part's place in a vehicle. They have to liaise with customers, with technicians, with manufacturers and with distributors. The work involves ordering and finding stock, controlling stock levels and advising customers.

## Qualifications and Training

To work as a parts operative, you need to do an apprenticeship. To be accepted on an apprenticeship you must have five GCSEs grades A–C, including maths and English. The apprenticeship combines on-the-job training with your employer and college-based learning. Through your apprenticeship you can gain relevant NVQ certificates.

## Personal Qualities and Skills

You must be really interested in vehicles, be very well organised, able to work under pressure and good at dealing with people. You must be good at handling a lot of detailed information.

# Vehicle salesperson

People working in vehicle sales, often described as sales executives, sell cars and other vehicles to private and business customers. They have to know a great deal about cars, not just those they are trying to sell, but those they may be purchasing or taking in part exchange.

## Qualifications and Training

There are no formal entry qualifications for this job. Many vehicle salespeople have worked as vehicle technicians or in other roles in the automotive industry. Some have come from a selling background in other sectors.

Tuesday : 4.13pm : 60°23.3'N 5°19.9'E

# In full flow

As an MBA, you know that success is not about resting on your laurels. It's about maintaining forward momentum. That's why you're looking to join a company that's as dynamic as you are. A company that knows what it means to be a leader – never standing still, always pushing boundaries, constantly developing. That's why you're looking for an employer that will make the most your abilities, offering genuine opportunities grow into a senior global management role with five years. That's why you should be looking join Rolls-Royce. Keep moving.
Visit www.rolls-royce.com/careers/mbas

**Trusted to deliver excellen**

Engineering, Business Development, Business Improvement, Commercial Sales and Marketing, Finance, Human Resources, Information Technology, Operations Management, Purcha

www.rolls-royce.com/careers

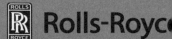

# MBA opportunities at Rolls-Royce

When you work as an MBA at Rolls-Royce, you have access to all the training, guidance and support you need to develop valuable skills and establish yourself in your chosen career. You'll also work with some of the world's leading engineers, helping to deliver technologies that help power the world around us.

To find out more, come to our open day or visit
**www.rolls-royce.com/careers/mbas**

---

### 'My colleagues are full of drive, and come from a huge range of cultures.'

With an MBA from INSEAD, Chim Yuen Chong chose to work at Rolls-Royce because he wanted to develop his business acumen and industry knowledge while contributing to the success of a major global company. He currently works in Marine Services, and focuses on strategic business development initiatives. These include mergers and acquisitions, business analysis, market intelligence and key development projects.

'I feel an enormous sense of pride working for Rolls-Royce,' he says, 'and it's thrilling to be associated with a company that is one of industry's genuine movers and shakers. My colleagues are full of zest and drive, and have a real desire to make a difference. I work with people from a huge range of cultures and backgrounds, and this helps both my personal and professional development.'

'My work is incredibly varied. I might be focusing on a specific business case, or I could be involved in sizing up an acquisition or joint venture initiative. I also work with senior executives in establishing strategic development plans for a business segment.'

'I've gained a solid understanding of this industry, and this will put me in good stead as I move towards more senior roles. Looking forward, I think I'd like to take on a functional role within a regional business management group. But I know whatever the future holds, Rolls-Royce will provide me with fantastic opportunities and important challenges.'

advertisement feature

### Personal Qualities and Skills

Sales executives have to combine good technical knowledge with excellent people skills. You must be polite, friendly, prepared to answer detailed questions and able to offer clear explanations.

## Vehicle technician

Vehicle technicians work to repair and maintain cars, vans, trucks and motorcycles. It is usual for technicians to specialise in just one of these groups of vehicles. Vehicle technicians also work at the many fast-fit centres which fit tyres, exhausts or other parts and systems. Some technicians specialise in MOT testing or in converting petrol cars to run on liquid petroleum gas (LPG).

### Qualifications and Training

To become a motor vehicle technician (with the exception of fast tyre fitting) you need to do an apprenticeship. To start an apprenticeship you must have five GCSEs grades A–C, including maths and English. The apprenticeship combines on-the-job training with college-based learning. Through your apprenticeship you can gain relevant NVQ certificates.

### Personal Qualities and Skills

All motor vehicle technicians have to have a real interest in working with vehicles and be good at working with their hands. You often need to be a good problem solver and patient too – sometimes why something won't work is not obvious.

## Vehicle valeter

Vehicle valeters clean and polish vehicles for individual customers and for car showrooms, and vehicle leasing and rental companies. Valeters clean the inside and the outside of vehicles. They may have to vacuum, clean windows and other glass, steam clean, wash, use high pressure hoses and wax and polish vehicles. Some vehicle valeters combine vehicle pickup and delivery with their valeting work.

### Qualifications and Training

There are no formal entry qualifications for this work, but if your job involves driving, you must have a full, clean driving licence. A mature attitude is important, and some experience in customer care work can be an advantage.

### Personal Qualities and Skills

You must be very thorough, good at paying attention to detail and you should be reasonably physically fit. You should be polite, friendly and trustworthy.

## Salaries

Apprentices earn £11,000 to £14,000, rising to £16,000 to £20,000 on completing training. Experienced technicians can earn £25,000 plus. Car valeters earn between £12,000 and £15,000. Sales people normally earn a basic salary plus commission on each vehicle they sell; the basic salaries start at around £15,000 with a possible £5,000 in commission and bonuses. Many people with technical qualifications and experience go self-employed.

Vehicle Operating Services Agency (VOSA), Training Services, Berkeley House, Croydon Street, Bristol BS5 0DA; 0870 606 0440; www.vosa.gov.uk

Institute of the Motor Industry, Fanshaws, Brickendon, Hertford SG13 8PQ; 01992 511521; www.motor.org.uk

**info**

# MUSIC

(*see also* Performing Arts)

Music covers a wide range of careers and yet there are only limited openings in each of these. Music includes people who make, repair and tune instruments, composers and arrangers, lyricists and performers. In addition, there are many behind-the-scenes jobs in marketing, promotions, finance and management in this diverse industry.

## Composer

Composers and song writers either write original pieces or devise new arrangements for pieces that have already been written, orchestral arrangements of piano pieces, instrumental versions of songs, jazz arrangements of classics, etc. It is very hard to make a living purely from composition, unless you have a really well-established reputation, or can get a position as composer in residence – and there certainly aren't many of these. Once established, you may be commissioned to write pieces, film scores for example. The nature of composition has changed with the impact of powerful software, which enables you to cut out some of the basics of writing out music or structuring chords. No software, however, can replace flair, talent and imagination.

## Musical instrument maker/repairer

Musical instrument makers and/or repairers build, repair, restore and maintain musical instruments of all kinds, from modern electric guitars to ancient pianos. Most repairers specialise in a particular instrument or family of instruments, such as woodwind, string, brass or pianos. Some develop special skills in restoring very old instruments, others make and build instruments using modern materials such as plastics and carbon fibres. One specialised field in musical instrument repair is piano tuning.

## Qualifications and Training

You do not need specific qualifications to get into this work, but you do need careful training. You should certainly have excellent manual dexterity and a good ear. There are a few courses in musical instrument making and repair. These include the ASET Certificate in Classical Musical Instrument Technology at levels 2 and 3 and BTEC HNC/HND in Instrument Technology. London Metropolitan University offers foundation degree and degree courses in musical instrument technology. You can find out about short courses in instrument repair from the National Association of Musical Instrument Repairers website. If you are interested in piano tuning, the Association of Piano Tuners provides details of training courses.

## Personal Qualities and Skills

As well as manual dexterity and a love of the instrument or instruments on which you wish to work, you need a range of people and business skills. Many instrument makers and repairers are self-employed, so you must be able to market your services and deal with potential customers.

**info**

www.cukas.ac.uk
A new website for central applications to the UK's major music conservatoires.

The Associated Board of the Royal Schools of Music (ABRSM), 24 Portland Place, London WC1B 1LU; 020 7636 5400; www. abrsm.ac.uk

Association of British Orchestras, 20 Rupert Street, London W1D 6DF; 020 7287 0333; www.abo.org.uk

Conservatoires UK Admissions Service (CUKAS), Rosehill, New Barn Lane, Cheltenham GL52 3LZ; 0871 468 0470; www.cukas.ac.uk/

Corps of Army Music, HQ Army Music, Royal Military School of Music, Kneller Hall, Twickenham, Middlesex TW2 7DU; 020 8744 8650; www.army.mod.uk/music/

Incorporated Society of Musicians (ISM), 10 Stratford Place, London W1C 1AA; 020 7629 4413; www.ism. org

Jazz Services, First Floor, 132 Southwark Street, London SE1 0SW; 020 7928 9089; www. jazzservices.org.uk

MCPS-PRS Alliance, Copyright House, 29–33 Berners St, London W1T 3AB; 020 7580 5544; www.mcps-prs-alliance.co.uk

Musicians' Union (MU), 33 Palfrey Place, London SW8 1PE; 020 7582 5566; www. musiciansunion.org.uk

Trinity College London, 89 Albert Embankment, London SE1 7TP; 020 7820 6100; www. trinitycollege.co.uk

## Salaries

Starting salaries are between £13,000 and £17,000. Instrument repairers and makers with experience and a good reputation can earn more than £30,000. If you are self-employed, you will set an appropriate fee for the level of work involved and the length of time the job is likely to take.

# Musician

*see* Performing Arts

# Music teacher

With music now placed as one of the foundation subjects in the National Curriculum there is an increasing demand for music teachers. Opportunities range from private instrumental teaching to class teaching at primary, secondary and tertiary levels. Class teachers and some visiting instrumental teachers working in state schools require Qualified Teacher status.

Private teachers set up and develop their own independent, studio-based business. The Incorporated Society of Musicians (ISM) sets professional standards for members who are listed in their Register of Professional Private Music Teachers. They set minimum hourly tuition fees, so that a reasonable income can be assured, and advise on business matters such as tuition contracts.

## Qualifications and Training

Entry to undergraduate courses of study usually requires a minimum of five GCSEs and one or more A levels, preferably including music. Full-time courses of study over three or four years, usually leading to a degree, are available at conservatoires (performance-based), universities (more academic) and colleges of higher education (more broad spectrum). Singers require a longer training, often over six years. Conservatoires and universities also offer a range of postgraduate courses. Teachers require an appropriate teaching qualification, such as a PGCE (Postgraduate Certificate in Education). Details of courses in performance, composition, musicology and teaching are available from the Incorporated Society of Musicians' website. The government has introduced a training scheme for the music industry under the 'New Deal' initiative; details are available from Job Centre Plus centres.

## Personal Qualities and Skills

A love of music, a positive and persuasive personality, robust physical and mental health, stamina, patience and excellent communication skills are essential for any career in music. Competition is fierce for performers, and only a very few talented musicians can establish a successful solo career. The ability to get on well with others helps to ensure good relationships with colleagues, managers and promoters to support career development.

## Salaries

Salaries vary enormously. Guidance on rates of pay is available from the Incorporated Society of Musicians. Hourly rates of £16–£20 are usual.

# Music therapist

*see* Therapy

# Piano tuner

*see* Musical Instrument Maker/Repairer

# N

## NAVAL ARCHITECT

Naval architects are professional engineers who play a key role as project loaders and specialists in the design, building and marketing of all systems that have to move just above, on or under the sea, including merchant ships, warships, offshore structures, submarines, hovercraft, yachts and other small craft. They also have to ensure that a safe, economic and seaworthy design is produced. The workplace may be a large company, a small group, a consultancy or a government department.

### Qualifications and Training

The usual way to become a naval architect is with a degree or diploma accredited by the Royal Institute of Naval Architects (RINA). Approved subjects include naval architecture, marine engineering and ocean engineering. You need A levels in maths, physics and one other subject to study any of these accredited courses. Anyone with a qualification in another engineering discipline should check with the RINA to see whether it is acceptable, or what further qualifications and training they need to undertake. Without a degree or diploma it may be possible to take equivalent Engineering Council qualifications. Several companies are accredited to provide training. This training covers three areas: design, engineering practice and management services. After a minimum of two years' work experience you can apply to become a chartered or incorporated engineer with the RINA.

### Personal Qualities and Skills

A genuine interest in ships, boats and other vessels is a good starting point. You must have good technical engineering knowledge and a creative attitude to problem solving. Naval architects need good report-writing skills and the confidence and clarity to explain technical problems to non-technical people.

### Salaries

Trainees start on between £22,000 and £25,000. Qualified and experienced naval architects earn around £40,000 to £50,000. Experienced and senior naval architects can earn £75,000.

**info**

Institute of Marine Engineering, Science and Technology, 80 Coleman Street, London EC2R 5BJ; www.imarest.org.uk

The Royal Institution of Naval Architects (RINA), 10 Upper Belgrave Street, London SW1X 8BQ; 020 7235 4622; www.rina.org.uk

SEMTA: the Sector Skills Council for Science, Engineering and Manufacturing Technologies; Head Office, 14 Upton Road, Watford WD18 0JT; 01923 238 441; www.semta.org.uk

# NURSING PROFESSIONS

Nurses, health care assistants, midwives and health visitors work in many different settings including hospitals, health clinics, GP practices and the wider community. They work in the NHS, the independent healthcare sector, charities and voluntary organisations.

# Healthcare assistant

Also known as health support workers, healthcare assistants work alongside nurses and provide basic care for patients. They help with treatments, keep wards tidy and complete basic paperwork. They work on general hospital wards, in clinics and outpatient departments, psychiatric hospitals, hospices and in care homes. There are also opportunities for community-based work, providing physical care to individuals who might otherwise have needed to go into hospital or a residential care home.

### Qualifications and Training

No prior qualifications are needed to start work as a healthcare assistant, but hospitals, care homes and other organisations do provide training and there is currently a drive to ensure that everyone doing this work will achieve at least NVQ level 2.

### Personal Qualities and Skills

Like qualified nurses, healthcare assistants must have patience, tact, tolerance and an ability to communicate with the patients in their charge. Physical fitness is essential as the job sometimes involves heavy work (such as lifting and turning patients).

### Salaries

Newly qualified healthcare assistants earn from £13,500 to £17,000, more in London. Experienced healthcare assistants who have taken additional qualifications earn up to £18,500. Some healthcare assistants working in specialised areas such as maternity earn up to £21,500.

# Health visitor

Health visitors promote health and contribute to the prevention of mental, physical and social ill health in the community. This involves educating people in ways of healthy living and making positive changes in the environment. Education may be achieved by teaching individuals or families in their own homes, in health centres, clinics, in informal groups, or through campaigns for the promotion of good health practices through local or national mass media.

The health visitor may work with people who are registered with a GP or who live within a defined geographical area. The work includes collaboration with a wide range of voluntary and statutory organisations.

## Qualifications and Training

Applicants must hold a first-level nurse or midwifery qualification with post-registration experience. One-year health visitor courses are provided at institutions of higher education.

All approved programmes now lead to the award of Specialist Practitioner (Public Health Visiting/Health Visiting). These programmes are at a minimum of first degree level.

## Personal Qualities and Skills

Health visitors must be excellent communicators, able to convey information to all types of people without being patronising. They must have self-confidence, tact and a lot of common sense. They must be able to work alone, yet know when to seek advice. They should be confident, articulate public speakers.

## Salaries

Newly qualified health visitors are paid £29,000 to £33,500. Team leaders and manager health visitors are paid £30,000 to just under £39,000.

| | |
|---|---|
| NHS Careers; Careers Helpline: 0845 606 0655; www.nhscareers.nhs. uk<br><br>Community Practitioners and Health Visitors Association, | 40 Bermondsey Street, London SE1 3UD; 020 7939 7000; fax: 020 7403 2976; www.msfcphva. org; e-mail: infocphva@ amicustheunion.org |

*info*

# Midwife

Midwives (who may be female or male) provide care and advice to mothers and fathers before, during and after birth; they are either employed by the NHS in hospital and/or community settings, including home births, by private hospitals, or work independently. The midwife provides care during normal pregnancy and birth, and up to 28 days following the birth. The midwife will also care for women who have complications. The midwife is an integral part of the multidisciplinary team responsible for delivering care, working closely with obstetricians and other health professionals in ensuring the well-being of mothers and babies.

## Qualifications and Training

To qualify as a midwife you need to complete a degree or diploma course in midwifery that is approved by the Nursing and Midwifery Council (NMC). Institutions running courses can set their own academic entry requirements, but there are broad general guidelines. For nursing diploma courses you need five GCSEs grades A–C, including English, maths and a biological science. For degree courses the same GCSE requirements apply, but you also need two A levels. Applicants must be aged 17.5 in England and Wales, 17 in Scotland and 18 in Northern Ireland. In England you must apply through the Nursing and Midwifery Admissions Service (NMAS) – the contacts for Scotland, Wales and Ireland are listed in the info panel. Applicants who do not meet these entry requirements may be successful if they can demonstrate literacy and numeracy skills and provide some evidence that they have recently undertaken successful study of some kind. If you have a nursing degree or diploma (adult branch) you can do a 12 to 18 month midwifery diploma.

## Personal Qualities and Skills

Midwives must have extremely good interpersonal skills, and be caring, practical, friendly and encouraging. They must be able to work as part of a team, but also to take responsible decisions on their own.

## Salaries

Newly qualified midwives earn between £21,000 and £27,000. Community midwives earn £25,000 to £34,000. Senior midwives and those involved in research and management earn £30,000 to £38,000.

# Nurse

Nurses care for people of all ages who are ill, injured or suffering from mental, emotional or physical disabilities. They are based in hospitals, in clinics, in local GP practices, in schools, in the community and in industry. While there are many settings in which nurses work, there are four main branches that determine your career path, namely, adult nurse, children's nurse, mental health nurse and learning disabilities nurse.

Adult nurses care for patients aged 18 and over in hospitals, clinics and other settings. They work with people who have long-term illnesses, who are recovering from surgery or who have suffered injury and trauma. Your daily tasks could include checking temperatures, blood pressure and respiratory rate, giving drugs and injections, cleaning and dressing wounds, administering blood transfusions and drips and using hi-tech equipment. Once qualified adult nurses may choose to specialise in fields such as operating theatre work, accident and emergency, coronary care and many more.

Children's nurses undertake the same variety of work as adult nurses, but their patients are all aged under 18 years. The work might involve caring for premature or newborn babies, or nursing older children who have long-term or terminal illnesses. Babies and young children may not be able to explain what is wrong, so children's nurses must develop good powers of observation.

Learning disabilities nurses work with people of all ages who need help with aspects of everyday living. These nurses may work in hospitals, in day care or residential settings, special schools and the community. The work normally involves assessing clients to see what they can do and where they need help, and then teaching, advising and developing programmes that help those people to reach their potential.

Mental health nurses work in hospitals, psychiatric units and the community. They work to support people who experience difficulties caused by conditions such as depression or anxiety. They work with people who have phobias, or who have suffered traumas through accidents or illnesses. Mental health nurses also work with people who have become dependent on alcohol or other substances. The work involves helping people to live and cope more effectively, whether this is through medication, talking problems through, or developing programmes of beneficial activities.

## Qualifications and Training

You have to choose which of the branches of nursing interests you most since the courses are each tailored to one of these branches. Having made this choice, the entry route for each branch is very similar. To become a nurse you must complete either a degree or diploma course approved by the Nursing and Midwifery Council (NMC). To get onto a diploma course you need five GCSEs grades A–C including maths, English and one science. For a degree course you need the same GCSEs plus two A levels. Some institutions run Advanced Diplomas, which are pitched between the diploma and the degree-level course. There are other routes in. If you have graduated in another subject you may be able to do a two-year fast track course. All courses combine academic learning with practical experience. If you are a healthcare assistant and have NVQ level 3 qualifications you may be able to get full nursing qualifications on a part-time basis. All applicants for courses must have a Criminal Records Bureau (CRB) check. Once qualified, there are many opportunities for further training and developing specialist skills and knowledge in particular fields of nursing.

## Personal Qualities and Skills

While the balance of required skills and qualities may vary between the different branches of nursing, there are many requirements common to all. Nurses must be caring and compassionate and enjoy working with people. They have to be emotionally resilient, often dealing with distressing situations. Nurses must be practical and have good manual dexterity and confidence in handling specialised equipment. They need an interest in the science, anatomy and physiology that underpins health and illness. They must be very observant and also good at working as part of a healthcare team. In senior roles they must also be able to motivate, train, supervise and monitor the work of others.

## Salaries

Newly qualified nurses earn between £21,000 and £27,000. With experience, specialist knowledge and management responsibilities, salaries are between £27,000 and £39,000. There are opportunities to work overtime, which is paid at time and a half. These figures are based on working for the NHS. Some private sector salaries are higher, and some charity sector salaries are lower.

**info**

Nursing and Midwifery Council (NMC), 23 Portland Place, London W1B 1PZ; 020 7637 7181; registration contacts: overseas 020 7333 6600, general 020 7333 9333; www.nmc-uk.org

Nursing and Midwifery Admissions System, Rosehill, New Barn Lane, Cheltenham, Gloucestershire GL52 3LZ; 0870 112 2206 for general enquiries, 0870 112 2200 for application packs; www.nmas.ac.uk

NHS Careers, PO Box 376, Bristol BS99 3EY; 0845 606 0655; www.nhscareers.nhs.uk

NHS Education for Scotland, Careers Information Service, 66 Rose Street, Edinburgh EH2 2NN; 0131 225 4365; www.nes.scot.nhs.uk

National Leadership and Innovation Agency for Healthcare (Wales), Innovation House, Bridgend Road, Llanharan CF72 9RP; 01443 233333; www.wales.nhs.uk/sites3/home. cfm?OrgID-484

Northern Ireland Practice & Education Council for Nursing & Midwifery, Centre House, 79 Chichester Street, Belfast BT1 4JE; 028 9023 8152; www.n-i.nhs.uk/nipec/index.htm

Nursing Careers Centre (NCC), 31/32 Fitzwilliam Square, Dublin 2; 01 639 8500; www.nursingcareers.ie

## OIL/GAS RIG WORK

There are various openings for personnel working on oil or gas drilling rigs, both onshore (on land) and offshore (such as in the North Sea). Opportunities in all fields are generally limited to experienced and/or highly qualified applicants. An offshore rig has to be self-sufficient and is a combination of a factory, hotel and heliport. The catering and accommodation are similar to the provision onshore. Many of the routine factory tasks (such as cleaning and maintenance) are carried out by outside contractors and service companies.

## Diver

(*see also* Diving)

Divers are employed in exploration and production work, as well as underwater repair work such as welding.

## Drilling crew

The drilling crew is responsible for the drilling of wells, and the operation and maintenance of a variety of heavy machinery. The crew consists of a toolpusher who manages the team and is responsible for the safety and integrity of the operation, and a team of people including a driller, assistant driller, derrickman, roughnecks and roustabouts. A typical drill crew will number around 10 people. Progression to the role of driller is hierarchical, with people working through general labouring jobs (roustabouts), working on the drill floor (roughnecks) or at the top of the derrick (derrickman). The work is physical, from the operation of the drilling equipment to the cleaning and maintenance of pumps and equipment. A graduate drilling engineer and a range of other specialists such as logging engineers, directional drilling specialists and mudloggers will also work with the drill crew.

# Engineer

(*see also* Engineering)

A production engineer supervises activities ranging from production and storage, gas compression and injection (to assist in the recovery of the oil), to tanker loading. The reservoir engineer is concerned with the behaviour of the oil accumulation or reservoir, and has to attempt to discover how much oil remains below ground and what are the most effective methods of recovery. Economics plays an important role. The maintenance engineer must ensure that all equipment is functioning properly, selecting and monitoring the companies under contract.

# Geologist

(*see also* Geology)

The oil companies employ technical experts such as geologists, geophysicists and drilling and petroleum engineers. Geologists collect and analyse data from a variety of sources to determine whether drilling might prove successful at a particular site, and to optimise production from existing oilfields. There are opportunities around the world.

## Salaries

The harsh nature of this work leads to relatively high salaries. Roughnecks and derrickmen earn around £27,000. Drillers and assistant drillers earn from £32,000 to £40,000. Drilling engineers start on between £28,000 and £35,000, increasing to £35,000 to £45,000. Geologists and geophysicists are paid similar salaries to those earned by engineers. Annual leave is usually very generous if your job involves a lot of time working offshore.

info

Cogent, Unit 5, Mandarin Court, Centre Park, Warrington, Cheshire WA1 1GG; 01925 515200; www.cogent-ssc.com

Engineering Construction Industry Training Board (ECITB), Blue Court, Church Lane, Kings Langley, Hertfordshire WD4 8JP; 01923 260000; www.ecitb.org.uk

Institute of Materials, Minerals and Mining (IOM3), 1 Carlton House Terrace, London SW1Y 5DB; 020 7451 7300; www.iom3.org

Oil and Gas UK, 2nd Floor, 232–242 Vauxhall Bridge Road, London SW1V 1AU; 020 7802 2400; www.oilandgasuk.co.uk

SEMTA: the Sector Skills Council for Science, Engineering and Manufacturing Technologies, Head Office, 14 Upton Road, Watford WD18 0JT; 01923 238 441; www.semta.org.uk

Society of Petroleum Engineers, Part Third Floor East, Portland House, 4 Great Portland Street, London W1W 8QJ; 020 7299 3300; www.spe.org

Oilcareers; www.oilcareers.com

# OPTOMETRY

## Dispensing optician

Dispensing opticians do not examine eyes or test sight, but supply and fit spectacles and other aids prescribed by an optometrist. They usually work in general practice, including independent businesses, partnership, as an employee of corporate bodies or as a franchisee. There are also job opportunities in hospitals and clinics. Once registered, dispensing opticians can undertake further training to enable them to fit contact lenses.

### Qualifications and Training

To practise as a dispensing optician, you must complete a training course approved by the General Optical Council (GOC) and pass a professional examination administered by the Association of British Dispensing Opticians (ABDO). There is a choice of four methods to achieve this: a two-year full-time diploma; a three-year day-release course; a three-year distance-learning course; or a three-year full-time degree course in dispensing optics or ophthalmic dispensing management. Degree courses require you to have five GCSEs and two A levels, but entry requirements are a little more flexible if you choose the other routes. Dispensing opticians have to demonstrate to the ABDO that they have undertaken appropriate continuing education and have to register annually. There is a lot of on-the-job training, academic study and practical placements involved in qualifying for this profession.

### Personal Qualities and Skills

You must be pleasant, friendly, approachable and patient. You must also be good at handling delicate equipment and have reasonable mathematical skills for taking measurements and making calculations. It is also useful to have a grasp of fashion and style, since this is very important to many of your clients when they choose spectacles or lenses.

### Salaries

Trainees and assistants without full qualifications earn £17,000 to £21,000. Qualified opticians earn £23,000 to £30,000. Many opticians run their own businesses, in which cases earnings may be higher than this, but it is a very competitive market.

Association of British Dispensing Opticians, Godmersham Park, Godmersham, Kent CT4 7DT; 01227 738 829; www.abdo.org.uk

General Optical Council, 41 Harley Street, London W1G 8DJ; 020 7580 3898; www.optical.org/

# Optometrist

Optometrists are trained to examine eyes and test sight, detect and measure defects in healthy eyes and prescribe spectacles, contact lenses or other appliances to correct or improve vision. They must carry out whatever tests are clinically necessary to detect signs of injury or disease to the eye or elsewhere, and must refer these patients to a medical practitioner. Most optometrists work in general practice in a variety of arrangements, including independent businesses, partnership, as an employee of corporate bodies, as a franchisee or in the hospital eye service. There are also job opportunities in research organisations, academic departments, ophthalmic hospitals and clinics.

## Qualifications and Training

Optometrists must be registered with the General Optical Council before being permitted to practise in the UK. To obtain registration they must pass the professional qualifying exam run by the College of Optometrists. The exam is in two parts. For Part I the candidate must gain a BSc honours degree in optometry after three years of study at an accredited institution (or four years in Scotland). Part II is taken after the candidate has completed a pre-registration year of supervised practice. The professional qualifying exam combines practical and oral assessment of the candidate's ability to manage patients and practise safely as an independent optometrist.

For acceptance onto a university course students normally need three A levels, two of which must be maths or science. GCSEs should include English and physics if not gained at A level. Average entry grades vary but are usually 320 A level points.

## Personal Qualities and Skills

Opticians need mathematical and scientific skills to make accurate observations and calculations. They also need an ability to get on with and communicate effectively with patients of all ages and backgrounds and to be able to put them at their ease.

## Salaries

In the pre-registration year, most optometrists in private practice earn around £18,000. If you do your pre-registration year in an NHS hospital the salary is close to £19,000. Hospital optometrists tend to be paid slightly more than their private practice colleagues once qualified – £27,000 to £33,000 in the NHS and £22,500 to £28,000 in private practice.

info

College of Optometrists, 42 Craven Street, London WC2N 5NG; 020 7839 6000; fax: 020 7839 6800; www.college-optometrists.org

General Optical Council, 41 Harley Street, London W1G 8DJ; 020 7580 3898; www.optical.org

The Association of Optometrists; www.assoc-optometrists.org/hospital/hospitals.html

Careers information can be found at the College of Optometrists: www.college-optometrists.org/index.aspx/pcms/site.education.careers.look/

# Orthoptist

Orthoptists diagnose and treat various abnormalities and weaknesses in the eye, such as a squint or double vision. Many patients are children, and special equipment and exercises are used to help correct any defects while they are still young. They work closely with medical eye specialists and, where operations are necessary, with ophthalmic surgeons. Most orthoptists work within the NHS, in hospitals and clinics (including school clinics). There are also opportunities in private practice and teaching.

## Qualifications and Training

To practise as an orthoptist you must pass a degree approved by the Health Professionals Council (HPC). Details of approved degree courses are available from the HPC and also from the British and Irish Orthoptic Society. For these degree programmes you normally require five GCSEs grades A–C including English, maths and two sciences. You also need two or three A levels, one of which must be biology.

## Personal Qualities and Skills

You need to enjoy working with people, be good at putting them at ease, and be patient and reassuring, especially when working with children. You need good powers of observation, good manual dexterity and good numeracy skills.

## Salaries

Newly qualified orthoptists earn between £21,000 and £27,000. With experience you can earn more than £38,000. These figures are based on working for the NHS. In private practice, initial salaries may be lower than NHS, but this gap is likely to close with experience.

NHS Careers, PO Box 376, Bristol BS99 3EY; 0845 606 0655; www.nhscareers.nhs.uk

Health Professionals Council, Park House, 184 Kennington Park Road, London SE11 4BU; 020 7582 0866; www.hpc-uk.org

British and Irish Orthoptic Society, Tavistock House North, Tavistock Square, London WC1H 9HX; 020 7387 7992; www.orthoptics.org.uk

info

# PAINTER AND DECORATOR

*see* Construction Trades

# PATENTS

A patent is a legal document that gives an inventor the right to claim an invention as his or her own work and to produce, sell or make the invention. It also protects the inventor from having his or her work and/or ideas copied by others.

## Patent agent/patent attorney

Patent agents/patent attorneys (these terms are interchangeable) have expertise in the area of intellectual property, advise individual clients and companies on matters relating to patent law, and act on their behalf if they wish to patent an invention, or to register a trademark or a design in the UK or abroad. First, records are searched to gauge the likelihood of a patent being granted. The patent agent then draws up the particulars of the client's invention clearly and concisely, ensuring it neither infringes another patent nor is liable to be copied without infringing its own patent. In cases where a client's patent has been infringed, the agent advises as to the best course of action. Patent agents are employed by private practice firms of patent agencies, industrial companies with a patent department and the government.

## Patent examiner

These are civil servants who examine the applications for patents submitted by patent agents and others. The principal task is to establish the originality or otherwise of the invention and whether or not the applicant is entitled to the protection claimed. There is some opportunity to work abroad in the European Patent Office.

# Patent officer

These are civil servants employed in protecting Crown rights in new inventions and developments, compensating the owners of patents used by the Crown and generally advising government departments on matters relating to patents.

## Qualifications and Training

The minimum educational requirement for an agent is a degree in a science or a technology-related subject. It is usually necessary to register as a patent agent in the European Patent Office. This involves taking the European qualifying exams, for which a degree is necessary.

Patent examiners and officers need a first- or second-class honours degree in engineering, physics, chemistry, maths or an equivalent professional qualification.

## Personal Qualities and Skills

Curiosity, the ability to assimilate new ideas, good analytical and critical skills, clear and concise thinking and the capacity for logical and clear expression both in speech and writing are all essential.

## Salaries

Trainee patent attorneys earn between £25,000 and £33,000. Once qualified, salaries are between £50,000 and £70,000. Experienced patent attorneys can earn up to £95,000. Patent examiners start on between £23,000 and £27,500, rising to £32,000 to £35,000.

Chartered Institute of Patent Agents, 95 Chancery Lane, London WC2A 1DT; 020 7405 9450; www cipa.org.uk; e-mail: mail@cipa.org.uk

Patent Office, Concept House, Cardiff Road, Newport, South Wales NP10 8QQ; 0845 950 0505; fax: 01633 813600; www.patent.gov.uk

Inside Careers, Unit 3, The Quadrangle, 49 Atalanta Street, London SW6 6TR; 020 7565 7900; fax: 020 7565 7938; www. insidecareers.co.uk – downloadable guide to becoming a patent attorney

# PERFORMING ARTS

Performing arts cover the range of occupations in the world of entertainment.

# Actor

Acting mainly involves the interpretation of someone else's work and the communication of it to an audience, although there are opportunities for actors to write their own material. Actors are employed in various types of theatre (commercial, subsidised, community, fringe and theatre-in-education), and also in television, film, radio, and television and radio commercials. Competition is keen and, because it is such a precarious profession, those entering it must be prepared for long periods of unemployment.

## Qualifications and Training

Most potential actors attend drama school. The National Council for Drama Training is a useful source for information on accredited courses. A good general education is important, and some schools require GCSEs and A levels or equivalent. Training courses at established schools usually last two or three years. Entrance is by audition and is competitive. Further experience may be gained from working in a repertory company or in fringe theatre. This may be an alternative way of entering the profession, but it is becoming increasingly difficult to enter solely by this method.

## Personal Qualities and Skills

Acting requires a combination of intelligence, sensitivity and imagination, together with a good memory, determination and physical stamina.

**info**

The Conference of Drama Schools, CDS Ltd, PO Box 34252, London NW5 1XJ; 020 7692 0032; www.drama.ac.uk

Conservatoire for Dance and Drama, 1–7 Woburn Walk, London WC1H 0JJ; 020 7387 5101; www.cdd.ac.uk/

Creative and Cultural Skills: the Sector Skills Council for Advertising, Crafts, Cultural Heritage, Design, Music, Performing, Literary & Visual Arts, 4th Floor Lafone House, The Leathermarket, Weston Street, London SE1 3HN; 020 7015 1800; www.ccskills.org.uk

Equity, Guild House, Upper St Martins Lane, London WC2H 9EG; 020 7379 6000; www.equity.org.uk

The Independent Theatre Council, 12 The Leathermarket, Weston Street, London SE1 3ER; 020 7403 1727; www.itc-arts.org

London Academy of Music and Dramatic Art (LAMDA), 155 Talgarth Road, London W14 9DA; 020 8834 0500; www.lamda.org.uk

National Association of Youth Theatres, Arts Centre, Vane Terrace, Darlington DL3 7AX; 01325 363330; www.nayt.org.uk

National Council for Drama Training, 1–7 Woburn Walk, Bloomsbury, London WC 1H 0JJ; 020 7387 3650; www.ncdt.co.uk

Skillset (Sector Skills Council for the Audio Visual Industries), Focus Point, 21 Caledonian Road, London N1 9GB; 020 7713 9800; www.skillset.org

## Salaries

Many actors struggle to make a living through acting, especially in their early careers. Often they take on other casual work to supplement their incomes. Equity, the actors union, sets minimum rates for its members. These rates vary according to the type of work, geographical location and number of performances being given. Many actors earn £6,000 a year from acting, but salaries range from this low rate to £30,000. Household names on TV and in films, etc, can command extremely high salaries, but these people only make up a small percentage of the profession. Equity can advise members on minimum rates.

# Dancing

Dance can be divided into the two main categories of theatre dance (ballet, modern and contemporary dance, jazz and tap) and social dance (ballroom, folk dance and disco). However, there are no hard and fast divisions between the different forms. The profession of dancing consists of two main areas: performing and teaching. Choreography, notation, dance animation and dance therapy are related areas of work.

### Choreographer

Choreographers create and plan dance routines and oversee the execution of their plans by the dancers. Choreographers are often former dancers.

### Dance animateur

Dance animateurs work in the community or education to encourage participation and involvement and to raise the profile of dance activity locally. Their precise role is dependent on the funding organisation and the needs of the community in which they work. Animateurs are often qualified dance teachers.

### Dance notator

Notators are employed by dance companies to record their repertoire, and assist choreographers and rehearsal staff in the revival of choreographic works. Most notators are graduates of vocational dance schools or ex-professional dancers, as the work involves close and informed observation of the choreography, the ability to demonstrate the movement accurately and the ability to work effectively with professional dancers.

### Dance performer

Many of those who wish to perform have had early training in ballet and/or other forms of theatre dance. Opportunities in ballet and contemporary companies are limited, and many dancers find their first employment in companies abroad. Dancers also work in pantomimes, shows and musicals, and on cruise ships. Professional performers find it useful to be members of Equity, the British actors' union.

## Dance teacher

Teachers of dance can specialise in one area of dance teaching or teach in a variety of areas. The demand for teachers is high, especially as dance is now seen as a form of recreation. Teachers may work in commercial dance studios and professional dance schools both in the UK and abroad.

## Qualifications and Training

Ideally, ballet students should attend a recognised residential establishment such as the Royal Ballet School from the age of 11 to 18. Means-tested financial assistance may be available to UK students. Dancers who want to become teachers must obtain the relevant qualifications, for which full-time and part-time courses are available. These generally have an entry requirement of four or five GCSEs at grade C and above. The Royal Academy of Dancing offers certificates, diplomas and degrees in classical ballet teaching. The courses are available on a part-time and full-time basis.

## Personal Qualities and Skills

Dancers need to be hard working, self-disciplined both physically and mentally, dedicated and determined. They must be imaginative, able to express themselves artistically, and have a good sense of timing and an ear for music.

info

British Association of Teachers of Dancing, 23 Marywood Square, Glasgow G41 2BP; 0141 423 4029; www.batd.co.uk

British Dance Council, Terpsichore House, 240 Merton Road, South Wimbledon, London SW19 1EQ; 020 8545 0085; www.british-dance-council.org

Council for Dance Education & Training (CDET), Old Brewer's Yard, 17–19 Neal Street, London WC2H 9UY; 020 7240 5703; www.cdet.org.uk

Equity, Guild House, Upper St Martins Lane, London WC2H 9EG; 020 7379 6000; www.equity.org.uk

Foundation for Community Dance, LCB Depot, 31 Rutland Street, Leicester LE1 1RE; 0116 253 3453; www.communitydance.org.uk

The Independent Theatre Council, 12 The Leathermarket, Weston Street, London SE1 3ER; 020 7403 1727; www.itc-arts.org

National Dance Teachers' Association, PO Box 4099, Lichfield WS13 6WX; 01543 308 618; www.ndta.org.uk

National Resource Centre for Dance, University of Surrey, Guildford, Surrey GU2 7XH; 01483 689 316; www.surrey.ac.uk/NRCD

Royal Academy of Dance, 36 Battersea Square, London SW11 3RA; 020 7326 8000; www.rad.org.uk

## Salaries

Equity, the trade union for actors and performers, negotiates minimum rates for dancers and these are currently £350 per week. Non Equity members are often paid less than this, but dancers often accept these lower rates while they are trying to establish their careers. Experienced dancers can earn £500 a week and in London's West End rates are often closer to £700 to £750 a week.

# Musician

(*see also* Music)

A musical training, leading to a degree or equivalent qualification, opens the door to a wide range of careers in music, including performing, teaching, administration, management, broadcasting, recording, journalism, publishing, promotion, librarianship and the retail trade.

Many professional musicians work on a freelance basis as soloists, orchestral players, commercial session musicians and in a variety of chamber music ensembles including classical, rock, dance and jazz groups. A performer's working life often includes some teaching, master classes or community education work alongside regular and vital practice.

Some musicians arrange their own engagements, others have an agent or use a diary service to find work. For all performers, membership of a professional association or union is desirable.

There are opportunities, particularly for those who already play an instrument, to join the Army, the RAF or Royal Marines as a bandsman.

## Qualifications and Training

Entry to undergraduate courses of study usually requires a minimum of five GCSEs and one or more A levels, preferably including music. Full-time courses of study over three or four years, usually leading to a degree, are available at conservatoires (performance-based), universities (more academic) and colleges of higher education (more broad spectrum). Singers require a longer training, often over six years. Conservatoires and universities also offer a range of postgraduate courses. Details of courses in performance, composition, musicology and teaching are available from the Incorporated Society of Musicians' website. The government has introduced a training scheme for the music industry under the 'New Deal' initiative; details are available from Job Centre Plus.

## Personal Qualities and Skills

A love of music, a positive and persuasive personality, robust physical and mental health, stamina, patience and excellent communication skills are essential for any career in music. Competition is fierce for performers, and only a very few talented musicians can establish a successful solo career. The ability to get on well with others helps to ensure good relationships with colleagues, managers and promoters to support career development.

## Salaries

There is wide variation in earnings. Most musicians are self-employed and either have short contracts or are simply paid for individual jobs. There are some permanent salaried posts in orchestras, but many members of orchestras and bands of all types, as well as session musicians working in recording studios, are self-employed. What you earn depends on how much work you get, how good you are and how much your particular instrument or style is in demand. The Musicians' Union (MU) can offer detailed guidance on what you might expect to be paid for work at your level and your instrument.

**info**

The Associated Board of the Royal Schools of Music (ABRSM), 24 Portland Place, London WC1B 1LU; 020 7636 5400; www. abrsm.ac.uk

Association of British Orchestras, 20 Rupert Street, London W1D 6DF; 020 7287 0333; www.abo.org.uk

Conservatoires UK Admissions Service (CUKAS), Rosehill, New Barn Lane, Cheltenham GL52 3LZ; 0871 468 0470; www. cukas.ac.uk/

Corps of Army Music, HQ Army Music, Royal Military School of Music, Kneller Hall, Twickenham, Middlesex TW2 7DU; 020 8744 8650; www.army.mod.uk/music/

Incorporated Society of Musicians (ISM), 10 Stratford Place,

London W1C 1AA; 020 7629 4413; www.ism.org

Jazz Services, First Floor, 132 Southwark Street, London SE1 0SW; 020 7928 9089; www.jazzservices.org.uk

MCPS-PRS Alliance, Copyright House, 29–33 Berners St, London W1T 3AB; 020 7580 5544; www.mcps-prs-alliance.co.uk

Musicians' Union (MU), 33 Palfrey Place, London SW8 1PE; 020 7582 5566; www. musiciansunion.org.uk

Trinity College London, 89 Albert Embankment, London SE1 7TP; 020 7820 6100; www.trinitycollege.co.uk

# Singer

Singers are performers who use certain styles of music, such as pop, rock, jazz, folk, country and western, world or 'easy listening' music. Singers sometimes play musical instruments, record music in a studio, for albums or 'session' work, work as a solo artist or as part of a duo or group, and write songs for themselves or other musical artists.

Singers need to practise for many hours at a time and attend regular rehearsals. They enjoy listening to as much varied music as possible, at gigs, concerts and clubs, and on the radio, internet and on CD.

Some singers include dance and movement as part of their performance. If a singer is successful, it is possible to appear in videos or on television. To be a successful singer really depends on an individual's talent, determination and hard work.

## Qualifications and Training

The more experience of performing the better; a singer can start at parties and public events. If a singer is then spotted by a recording company it could be possible to get a recording contract. Alternatively, singers can contact record and music publishing companies directly by sending them a 'demo' tape recording. BTEC and SNCC courses in music are available, as are degrees in popular music. In addition, HND and HNC courses are also available in a wide range of relevant subjects. Entry requirements usually start with one A level/H grade or equivalent. Strong evidence of ability and interest in music are normally required.

There are many other full-time and part-time courses, both privately and state funded, and popular music courses offered by adult education institutes and local community organisations.

## Personal Qualities and Skills

Success depends largely on musical talent and individuality. A passion for music and the ability to perform to an audience are good qualities for a singer. A certain level of discipline, focus and determination is required.

## Salaries

Only a small minority of singers earn high incomes. Many singers supplement their earnings with full-time work because they often earn less than the national average wage. The Musicians' Union sets minimum rates for musicians. Singers performing live often earn the national minimum rate of £47.50 for up to two hours before midnight. A very experienced singer making backing tracks on an album might earn about £350 per three-hour session.

A solo musician on tour could earn between £500 and £2,000 per week, depending on experience. Equity (the performers' union) sets minimum rates for singers appearing in stage or television productions. The minimum rate for performances in London's West End is £320 per week for eight shows.

**info**

Brit School for Performing Arts and Technology, 60 The Crescent, Croydon CR0 2HN; 020 8665 5242; fax: 020 8665 5197; www.brit.croydon.sch.uk

British Phonographic Institute (BPI), Riverside Building, County Hall, Westminster Bridge Road, London SE1 7JA; 020 7803 1300; fax: 020 7803 1310; www.bpi.co.uk

Equity, Guild House, Upper St Martins Lane, London WC2H 9EG; 020 7379 6000; fax: 020 7379 7001; www.equity.org.uk; e-mail: info@equity.org.uk

Incorporated Society of Musicians, 10 Stratford Place, London W1C 1AA; 0207 629 4413; fax: 020 7408 1538; www.ism.org; e-mail: membership@ism.org

Musicians' Union, 60/62 Clapham Road, London SW9 0JJ; 020 7582 5566; fax: 020 7582 9805; www.musiciansunion.org.uk

Rockschool, 245 Sandycombe Road, Kew TW9 2EW; 020 8332 6303; fax: 020 8332 6297; www.rockschool.co.uk

Scottish Arts Council, 12 Manor Place, Edinburgh EH3 7DD; 0131 226 6051; fax: 0131 225 9833; www.scottisharts.org.uk

# PHARMACY

Pharmacists are involved in the dispensing of medicinal drugs, usually prescribed by doctors. There are three branches of the profession: community pharmacists, hospital pharmacists, and industrial and research pharmacists.

## Community pharmacist

Community pharmacists work from the high street, health centre and rural pharmacies as part of the NHS. They dispense prescriptions and ensure that medicines ordered on prescription or bought over the counter are correctly and safely supplied, with all necessary advice on their use. They keep a poisons register, and act as a link between the doctor and the pharmaceutical manufacturer, being prepared to discuss developments with both. They are readily accessible health advisers to the public. In addition, they sell a wide range of non-pharmaceutical articles.

## Hospital pharmacist

They dispense drugs for hospital in- and outpatients and work side by side with nurses, doctors and other health professionals to ensure NHS patients receive the most appropriate medicines in the most effective way. In addition, in some hospitals, pharmacists manufacture their own products, take part in research work and come into direct contact with in-patients by accompanying medical staff on their ward rounds.

## Industrial and research pharmacist

They work as part of a team of scientists researching diseases, developing new drugs and carrying out clinical trials. Industrial pharmacists are also recruited to work in the areas of manufacturing, regulatory and medical affairs, sales and marketing, and computer science/information technology.

### Qualifications and Training

Pharmacists must complete a four-year Master of Pharmacy degree, followed by one year's paid competency-based training and a registration examination. Entry to degree courses is with A level chemistry plus two other A levels or equivalent; maths and biology are preferred.

### Personal Qualities and Skills

On top of excellent relevant medical knowledge and the need to be very careful and accurate, it is also important that you get on well with people and can be patient and understanding. Pharmacists already have responsibility for handling dangerous drugs, and it seems likely that they will be given greater prescribing rights in the near future, when responsibility and decision making will be extremely important aspects of their skills mix.

## Salaries

In the NHS newly qualified pharmacists earn from around £21,000 to nearly £27,000. Senior pharmacists and pharmacists with special responsibilities are paid from £33,000 to £44,000. Salaries for retail pharmacists are between £23,000 and £30,000.

Association of the British Pharmaceutical Industry, 12 Whitehall, London SW1A 2DY; 020 7930 3477; fax: 020 7747 1414; www.abpi.org.uk; www.abpi-careers.org.uk

Guild of Healthcare Pharmacists, 40 Bermondsey Street, London SE1 3UD; 020 7939 7042; www.ghp. org.uk

National Pharmaceutical Association (trade association for community pharmacists), Mallinson House, 38–42 St Peter's Street, St Albans, Hertfordshire AL1 3NP; 01727 832161; fax: 01727 840858; www.npa.co.uk; e-mail: npa@npa.co.uk

Royal Pharmaceutical Society of Great Britain, 1 Lambeth High Street, London SE1 7JN; 020 7735 9141; fax: 020 7735 7629; www.rpsgb.org. uk; e-mail: careers@rpsgb.org.uk; Scottish Department: 36 York Place, Edinburgh EH1 3HU; www.rpsgb. org.uk/scotland/ index.html; e-mail: info@rpsis.com

NHS Careers, 0845 606 0655; www. nhscareers.nhs.uk

*A Future in Pharmacy* (Royal Pharmaceutical Society of Great Britain)

info

# Pharmacy technician

Pharmacy technicians work as part of the pharmacy team and are supervised by a pharmacist. Their duties can include the dispensing of medicines from prescriptions, preparing sterile medicines, assessing stocks of drugs, patient counselling, advising on health promotion issues and collecting and collating information on drugs from a variety of sources. Pharmacy technicians can work in chemists, hospitals, the armed forces, the prison service, or within the pharmaceutical industry.

## Qualifications and Training

A nationally recognised qualification is the NVQ Pharmacy Services at level 3 which is available from approved centres. Entry requirements for this are generally four GCSEs at grade C or above, including English, mathematics and chemistry plus one other science. Mature applicants are welcome, and previous education and work experience are considered.

## Personal Qualities and Skills

As a pharmacy technician you should have a real interest in science and the ability to be accurate and careful. You should be able to deal sensitively and tactfully with people, be good at working as part of a team, and in some posts you may have to use sales skills as well.

## Salaries

In the NHS pharmacy technicians earn £21,000 to £27,000. The NHS also employs pharmacy support workers, who earn £15,200 to £17,000. In the private sector pharmacy technicians can earn up to £30,000.

NHS Careers, PO Box 376, Bristol BS99 3EY; 0845 606 0655; www.nhscareers.nhs.uk

National Pharmaceutical Association (NPA), Training Dept, Mallinson House, 38–42 St Peters Street, St Albans, Hertfordshire AL1 3NP; 01727 832161; www.npa.co.uk

Royal Pharmaceutical Society of Great Britain, 1 Lambeth High Street, London SE1 7JN; 020 7735 9141; www.rpsgb.org.uk

# PHOTOGRAPHY

Photographers produce visual images of many different kinds, either working to a brief given them by a client, or exploring subject matter they have chosen themselves. Photographers use a range of photographic equipment, including conventional and digital cameras, lighting systems and computer programs developed to manipulate photographs. Some photographers also develop their own work, using either traditional darkroom methods or digital processing. The subject matter you work with is determined by the field of photography in which you work. Typical aspects of the job include choosing locations and subjects, selecting appropriate cameras and accessories, and setting up lighting and background. Photographers also have to compose the picture, whether this is discussing a pose with a model or arranging still life objects.

## Advertising/editorial photographer

Advertising photographers take pictures for magazines and brochures. These pictures either advertise a product or illustrate a story. Many advertising photographers specialise in particular subjects such as food, cars, portraiture or landscapes.

## Corporate photographer

Corporate photographers work for large businesses and other organisations taking pictures for annual reports, promotional brochures or in-house journals.

Some people working in this field become specialist industrial photographers, taking pictures of the manufacturing process as well as finished products.

## Fashion photographer

Fashion photographers take pictures of models promoting clothes, shoes, jewellery, cosmetics and hairstyles. At the top end of the market they work for well-known magazines, taking pictures of models whom people have heard of. At the other end of this market, photographers take hundreds of pictures for mail-order catalogues.

## General practice photographer

General photographers take pictures for a range of clients in their local community. A great deal of the work involves wedding photography, but these photographers often cover community events and family occasions. Many do some work for local newspapers that don't employ in-house press photographers. Those photographers who do specialise mainly in weddings or other special occasions are sometimes described as social photographers rather than general practice photographers.

## Medical photographer

*see* Medical and Healthcare Science

## Scientific/technical photographer

Some photographers specialise in taking pictures for scientific journals and research papers. They may have to work with microscope slides as well as living subjects. The work of the wildlife photographer is a highly specialised aspect of this type of photography.

### Qualifications and Training

While there are no formal entry requirements, this is a very competitive field. There are several courses you can do, and being able to combine a course with a good portfolio of your work and some relevant work experience is the best way to improve your chances of success. Courses are available at many levels, including City & Guilds, BTEC Certificates and Diplomas, A levels and degree courses. Many people start work as a photographer's assistant to gain basic skills and knowledge. The British Institute of Professional Photography (BIPP) awards the Professional Qualifying Examination (PQE) to photographers – the award is based on assessing a photographer's portfolio to ensure that it is of a good professional standard.

## Personal Qualities and Skills

These vary according to your chosen specialism, but all photographers must have the ability to perceive and recreate visual impact in a creative way. They must all be competent with technical equipment and normally need great patience. For most jobs, photographers must be able to work well with people, whether it is as subjects, or as fellow members of a work team. They also need good business management skills.

## Salaries

Starting salaries are between £11,000 and £21,000. Many photographers have to start as photographer's assistants and may earn less than this to begin with. Successful photographers earn between £20,000 and £30,000; a few may earn up to £60,000. Many photographers work freelance or are self-employed, where annual earnings range from £14,000 to £45,000.

**info**

Association of Photographers (AOP), 81 Leonard Street, London EC2A 4QS; 020 7739 6669; www.the-aop.org

British Institute of Professional Photography (BIPP), Prebendal Court, Oxford Road, Aylesbury, Buckinghamshire HP19 8EY; 01296 336367; www.bipp.com

Creative and Cultural Skills: the Sector Skills Council for Advertising, Crafts, Cultural Heritage, Design, Music, Performing, Literary & Visual Arts, 4th Floor, Lafone House, The Leathermarket, Weston Street, London SE1 3HN; 020 7015 1800; www.ccskills.org.uk

Master Photographers Association (MPA), Jubilee House, 1a Chancery Lane, Darlington, Co Durham DL1 5QP; 01325 356555; www.thempa.com

Photo Imaging Council, Orbital House, 85 Croydon Road, Caterham, Surrey CR3 6PD; 01883 334497; www.pic.uk.net

Skillset – Sector Skills Council for the Audio Visual Industries, Focus Point, 21 Caledonian Road, London N1 9GB; 020 7713 9800; www.skillset.org

# Photographic technician

Photographic technicians work either in large photographic laboratories or in mini labs in high street stores. If you work in a professional laboratory, you may use traditional darkroom techniques developing films. Much of the work now on the high street and in traditional laboratories involves using computerised equipment producing prints or CDs from images taken on digital cameras. In both cases the work involves producing pictures of the best possible quality. Technicians check for quality, analyse problems and may give feedback to customers on what could have gone wrong. Based in high street stores, the work also involves dealing directly with customers, packaging pictures, and taking orders and payments.

# Digital imaging technician

Digital imaging technicians work for professional photo finishing laboratories and picture libraries. The work usually involves discussing the format and finish of an image with a client, scanning images into a computer, using specialised software to manipulate the images, change colour, resize or crop a picture where appropriate, print the finished image onto paper, save it on CD or upload it onto a website. Digital imaging technicians are often responsible for building up banks of images that can then be purchased by clients.

## Qualifications and Training

You may not need formal qualifications to work in a high street mini lab, though some employers may ask for GCSEs including maths and a science. To work in a professional laboratory you are far more likely to need qualifications in photography, such as an HND, a foundation degree, or a degree. If you do want to work in digital imaging, it may also be helpful to build up a portfolio of images on which you have worked; you also need to be competent with relevant computer software packages such as Photoshop.

## Personal Qualities and Skills

In all cases you need a genuine interest in photography. For all positions you need good basic IT skills. To work for a professional digital imaging lab you need a high level of desktop publishing skill. You need good communication skills, be able to explain problems to customers, or clarify a brief from a client. You have to be good at working as part of a team.

## Salaries

For photographic technicians starting salaries are between £12,000 and £15,000 on the high street, possibly more in professional laboratories. Digital imaging technicians earn from £20,000 to £35,000.

British Institute of Professional Photography (BIPP), Prebendal Court, Oxford Road, Aylesbury, Buckinghamshire HP19 8EY; 01296 336367; www.bipp.com

Skillset, Focus Point, 21 Caledonian Road, London N1 9GB; 08080 300 900 (England and Northern Ireland); www.skillset.org

Association of Photographers, 81 Leonard Street, London EC2A 4QS; 020 7739 6669; www.the-aop.org

info

# PHYSICIST

Physicists study the world around us; they try to understand and explain why objects exist and behave in the way they do. As well as tackling these profound questions physicists apply their knowledge in many practical ways – anything from the development of the next generation of mobile phones to the forecasting of climate change. Using mathematical techniques and computer modelling they can have useful input into many industries. Physicists could be involved in the development of new medical instruments, the exploration of new methods of power generation or the investigation of artificial intelligence and robotics. Physicists work closely with many other scientists and engineers including materials engineers, biomedical engineers, astronomers and information technologists. Physicists also work in teaching, academic research and scientific publishing.

## Qualifications and Training

This is a complex and intellectually challenging profession. Employers normally require at least a good honours degree in physics, applied physics or engineering, but many applicants will also have a Master's degree or a PhD. To gain a place on a physics degree course you need five GCSEs and A levels in maths and physics. If you do not have these A levels you may be able to do a bridging course or a foundation degree in science to meet these requirements.

## Personal Qualities and Skills

Above all, you need an enquiring mind and the ability to think in new directions and find imaginative ways of tackling problems. You also have to be logical and methodical in your thinking and you must be a good communicator. You have to be patient – you may be working on something for a long time before you get any answers, or the answers you would like. You have to be able to work successfully on your own, or as part of a team.

## Salaries

New entrants earn £21,000 to £25,000. Research physicists who have just completed PhDs earn around £26,000. In industry, physicists earn from £30,000 to £50,000 plus. Senior researchers and project leaders in academia earn £35,000 to £45,000.

**info**

SEMTA, 14 Upton Road, Watford, Hertfordshire WD18 0JT; 0800 282167; www.semta.org.uk

Science Council, 210 Euston Road, London NW1 2BE; 020 7611 8754; www.sciencecouncil.org

Institute of Physics, 76 Portland Place, London W1B 1NT; www.iop.org

# PHYSIOTHERAPIST

Physiotherapists treat patients suffering from a wide variety of diseases, conditions or injuries by physical means. They help people who have had a stroke to regain the use of lost functions, treat sports injuries and people with arthritis, and help children with cerebral palsy to learn to walk. The techniques used include massage and manipulation, exercise, electrotherapy and hydrotherapy. Most physiotherapists work in the NHS but there are many opportunities now for employment in industry, sports clinics, schools and private practice.

## Sports physiotherapist

The increasing number of opportunities to work with sportsmen and women, both professional and amateur, has become a rather specialised and growing area within physiotherapy. Sports physiotherapists must hold a first aid certificate and be a chartered physiotherapist. There is a special interest group within the Chartered Society of Physiotherapy (CSP) for therapists who specialise in treating sporting injuries. There are also several postgraduate diplomas and Master's courses available in sports physiotherapy.

### Qualifications and Training

To be registered with the Health Professionals Council and the Chartered Society of Physiotherapy you must complete an approved degree in physiotherapy.

Entry requirements for these degrees in England, Wales and Northern Ireland usually include four AS levels at grade B, followed by three A levels at grade C or above, including a biological science. You also need five GCSEs grades A–C including maths, English and a range of science subjects. In Scotland, you need five H grades (AABBB) with at least two science subjects. Appropriate access to higher education courses may also be accepted.

### Personal Qualities and Skills

You must enjoy working with people, putting them at ease, explaining treatments and teaching exercises. You must have a good grasp of physiology and have good manual dexterity. You should be good at observing people and you also need to be able to work well as part of a team.

### Salaries

Newly qualified physiotherapists in the NHS start on salaries between £21,000 and just under £27,000. Senior physiotherapists earn £25,000 to £34,000. Physiotherapists with management responsibility earn up to £38,000. Some physiotherapists work in private practice, where salaries may be a little higher, but where there are fewer management posts. Many physiotherapists are self-employed, and earn £30,000 to £75,000.

**info**

Chartered Society of Physiotherapy,
14 Bedford Row, London WC1R 4ED;
020 7306 6666; www.csp.org.uk

Association of Chartered
Physiotherapists in Sports Medicine;
www.acpsm.org

NHS Careers, PO Box 376, Bristol
BS99 3EY; 0845 606 0655; www.
nhscareers.nhs.uk

Health Professionals Council,
Park House, 184 Kennington Park
Road, London SE11 4BU; 020 7582
0866; www.hpc-uk.org

# PLUMBER

*see* Construction Trades

# POLICE SERVICE

## Police community support officer

Police community support officers (PCSOs) are a recent introduction to the police service. This work is done by civilians, rather than serving police officers, but they support and report to local police. They patrol public areas, providing a visible presence to reassure the public. In some areas they have powers to direct traffic or issue arrest warrants, and they often work at events such as football matches or public demonstrations.

### Qualifications and Training

There are no formal academic requirements or age restrictions for applying to become a PCSO. Applicants must be UK, EU or Commonwealth citizens. Foreign nationals who have indefinite leave to remain in the UK and the right to work here are also eligible. While each police force sets its own entry requirements for PCSOs, they all tend to use similar selection criteria. You apply via an application form and after an initial screening of these forms you will be invited to an interview. You will also have to sit a written test and take part in role-play exercises to assess how you would cope with the range of situations the job throws up. Many forces set fitness tests, because you may have to undertake long foot patrols. Thorough background and security checks are made on all successful applicants. Having a criminal record does not necessarily exclude you from applying, but any convictions for violent or public order offences will certainly disqualify an applicant. Training takes between three weeks and three months, and is mainly classroom-based; it covers many aspects of the work, including using computer systems, first aid, radio communications and patrolling.

## Personal Qualities and Skills

You need very good people skills, and to be confident dealing with difficult or sensitive situations. You need to be able to work on your own or as part of a team, to take decisions or seek support as appropriate. You must be able to keep calm in pressured situations and you should be able to remain alert and observant.

## Salaries

Salaries start at £16,000 to £17,000, rising to £19,000 to £21,000 with experience. In some geographical locations salaries are higher – up to £26,000.

# Police officer

Police officers are recruited as trainee police constables (PCs). PCs work in all aspects of policing, including preventing and investigating crime, maintaining public order and protecting people and property. PCs work from police stations or out on the beat, either on foot or in patrol cars. There are many opportunities to specialise in particular areas of police work once you have completed your probationary period.

There is a separate British Transport Police Force, which operates on passenger transport services to prevent crime, protect public safety and maintain public order.

## Qualifications and Training

Each police force does its own recruiting, but they all work to a nationally agreed competency framework. While there are no formal educational requirements for joining the police service, there is a demanding selection procedure. Joining the police service is open to British or Commonwealth nationals and also to other foreign nationals who have no restrictions on their right to work in the UK. Applicants must be aged 18 or over. The first stage is to complete an application form and a medical questionnaire. If you are successful at this stage, you are invited to a selection centre to sit a variety of physical and psychometric tests. The physical fitness tests relate to tasks you would have to perform as a serving police officer. Sessions to help you prepare for these tests and to know what to expect are run throughout the UK several times a year.

The psychometric tests include written numeracy, literacy, information handling and reasoning tests, plus personality tests to assess your suitability for the demands of the job. The selection procedure also includes an interview and a full medical, with eyesight and hearing tests. You must have good vision and colour vision and be physically fit. If you pass the selection procedure, references are followed up and security checks including your financial status are made. Minor convictions or cautions do not necessarily preclude you from joining the police, but you must declare these.

There is an accelerated training scheme for graduates, the Graduate Development Programme (GDP). This is extremely competitive and many graduates wishing to join the police do so through the ordinary route.

New recruits work a probationary period of two years. During this time, training is a mixture of on-the-job training with the local police service and college-based learning. Everyone goes through the Initial Police Learning and Development Programme. During this period trainees work towards the NVQ level 3 in Policing and either during or shortly after this two-year period they are also expected to complete the NVQ level 4 in Policing. All policemen and women will undergo a wide variety of training throughout their career, enabling them to cope with changes in the law, social policy, information management and technology.

## Personal Qualities and Skills

You need a mature attitude and the ability to assess and weigh up situations quickly and then take appropriate action. You must be able to follow orders and have the confidence to instruct others. You must be able to stay calm in difficult situations and you must be emotionally resilient. You need excellent and varied people skills, able to be confident, assertive, diplomatic, reassuring, patient or firm as the occasion demands. You must be effective as part of a team, but also capable of working on your own.

## Salaries

Salaries are set by individual police forces – the average starting salary is between £22,000 and £24,500, with incremental rises for each year of service. Sergeants earn around £40,000 and inspectors earn up to £50,000.

**info**

Skills for Justice, Centre Court, Atlas Way, Sheffield S4 7QQ; www.skillsforjustice.com

Police Service Recruitment; www.policecouldyou.co.uk

Scottish Police Force; www.scottish.police.uk

Consensia Partnership; www.selectnip.org

British Transport Police, Force Headquarters, 25 Camden Road, London NW1 9LN; 0800 40 50 40; www.btp.police.uk

Police Service of Northern Ireland, Headquarters, Brooklyn, 65 Knock Road, Belfast BT5 6LE; 028 9065 0222; www.psni.police.uk

# POLITICAL WORK

Though politics offers relatively few career opportunities, there are a number of jobs in politics associated with supporting political parties, undertaking political research and lobbying political bodies on behalf of interest groups.

# Politician

Politicians for the House of Commons, the Scottish Parliament, the Welsh Assembly and the European Parliament are all elected, so they don't 'apply' for their jobs in the traditional sense. Their work involves representing the concerns of their constituents and contributing to the process of decision making by joining in debates, asking questions and voting.

# Political party agent

Only large political parties employ full-time agents. The agents are responsible for organising and motivating party activity at a local level, whether this is training volunteers, organising meetings or maintaining contact between local party members and their MP.

# Political researcher

Many different kinds of organisations employ political researchers; MPs, political parties, trade unions, public relations consultancies and non-government organisations are the most likely employers. The work involves detailed research, by monitoring the media, the daily work of both Houses of Parliament and the institutions of the European Union. Researchers also provide detailed answers to questions on almost every topic imaginable.

# Public affairs consultant/lobbyist

This very specialised field of public relations employs researchers and lobbyists to monitor political information and to lobby government on behalf of their clients. Clients may be businesses, trade unions or pressure groups, or any organisations that wish to influence the decision-making processes of government.

## Qualifications and Training

Politicians do not need specific qualifications and come from many different career backgrounds; law is one of the more common. Other political jobs require at least a good 2.1 degree in a relevant subject, such as economics, law, politics or social policy. Many successful applicants also have postgraduate qualifications.

## Personal Qualities and Skills

Politicians have to be good communicators who are well organised and able to balance the needs of their constituency work with demands in Westminster, or wherever they are based. Good organisational and interpersonal skills as well as a rigorous attitude to information research are essential for other political jobs.

## Salaries

Junior research staff earn between £14,000 and £18,000; up to £20,000 in London. If you work for a politician, there are no general guidelines on what you should be paid. Senior researchers earn from £20,000 to £35,000. Public affairs consultants start on around £25,000 rising to £35,000. MPs earn more than £60,000 plus a range of additional allowances. This system is currently under discussion and may change in the near future.

**info**

Local constituency parties

Conservative Central Office, 32 Smith Square, London SW1P 3HH; 020 7222 9000; www. conservatives.com

Labour Party, Millbank Tower, Millbank, London SW1P 4GT; 0870 590 0200; www.labour.org.uk

Liberal Democrats, 4 Cowley Street, London SW1P 3NB; 020 7222 7999; www.libdems.org.uk; e-mail: info@libdems.org.uk

A list of all other UK political parties is available from http://bubl.ac.uk/uk/parties.htm

Association of Professional Political Consultants (APPC), c/o Citigate Public Affairs, 26 Grosvenor Gardens, London SW1Y 0GT; 020 7838 4883; www. appc.org.uk

Parli-training, Suite 49, 34 Buckingham Palace Road, Belgravia, London SW1W 0RD; 020 7898 1103; www.parli-training.co.uk; e-mail: enquiries@parli-training. co.uk

Parliamentary Communications Ltd, 14 Great George Street, Westminster, London SW1P 3RX; 020 7878 1576

# POSTMAN/WOMAN

Postmen and women deliver mail to private and business addresses. They each have a round including several hundred addresses which they visit on foot, by bicycle or by van. Postmen and women also sort the mail for their own rounds and some mail is still sorted by hand. Postmen and women may also be responsible for collecting mail from post boxes, local post offices and from business addresses.

Some postmen and women work at district or central offices, sorting mail to be sent to other areas of the UK or overseas.

There are many other delivery and administrative opportunities within the Post Office, including work for Parcelforce and work behind post office counters.

## Qualifications and Training

There are no formal entry qualifications, but applicants have to pass an aptitude test which assesses their suitability for postal work. Once employed it is possible to work towards NVQ level 2 in Mail Delivery Services. This covers mail sorting, mail handling and working with automated systems. Apprenticeships are available for applicants aged 16–18, but many postmen and women are taken on at age 18 or over. If your job involves driving, you must have a full, clean driving licence.

## Personal Qualities and Skills

You need good basic literacy and numeracy skills and you must not mind doing repetitive tasks. It is essential to be physically fit, reliable and honest. You need to be polite and friendly, but not mind working on your own.

## Salaries

New postmen and women earn £15,000; this rises to around £17,000 after one year of service. It is also possible to earn more through working unsocial hours, taking on driving duties, or other responsibilities. With junior management responsibilities salaries rise to £18,000 to £21,000.

Royal Mail Group plc, 148 Old Street, London EC1V 9HQ; www. royalmailgroup.com

For local vacancies contact your nearest Royal Mail Delivery Office or check the Royal Mail website.

info

# PRINTING

The purpose of printing is communication, whether the printed matter is books, magazines, newspapers, security documents or bank cards. Printers are also involved in other products, from wallpaper and floor coverings to advertising slogans on milk cartons. The printing industry covers a wide range of jobs in both factories and offices. It employs 200,000 people in 12,000 companies.

## Camera/scanner operator

The reproduction of colour photographs is largely done by electronic scanners, requiring technical ability rather than the craft skills of the past.

## Finishing department

Printed products are usually produced in large flat sheets or reels. To convert and finish sheets or reels into books, brochures or magazines, the material must be folded, stitched, sewn and trimmed. A range of specialised machinery is used to produce the finished product at high speed. Great care is needed at this stage to avoid faults, which could result in scrapping the product and financial loss to the company.

# Graphic design

(*see also* Art and Design)

This is the most artistic job in the printing industry. Designers liaise with clients, understand their needs and transform ideas into high-quality printed products. A mastery of computers, complete understanding of processes, techniques, typography and colour is required. Applicants normally enter the industry after a National Certificate diploma or higher-level course in graphic design.

# Office jobs

Account executives look after individual printing jobs; they write instructions for each department and check the product's arrival into and departure from each section. Estimators work out how much a job will cost. Cost clerks go through the costs item by item and discover where and why the money was spent. Sales staff find customers.

In large companies production controllers manage a team of estimators and production control staff. They interpret sales orders, estimate costs, plan materials purchase, arrange time on appropriate machines, set priorities and advise customers on the progress of their order.

# Pre-press department

Most setting is via electronic transfer or CD. The pre-press operator uses a computer keyboard and mouse to set type and arrange the page, which is output to film or direct to the printing plate. An error in the pre-press department could result in the scrapping of thousands of books or products.

# Printing department

This is where ink is applied to paper or other materials, by a variety of large and small printing machines. Such machines are complex and often computer controlled. They are managed by one or more craftspeople who control the physics and chemistry of the press to ensure that each copy produced is perfect.

# Proofreader

Proofreaders check customers' proofs for spelling mistakes and incorrect typefaces before returning them. When setting to disk, proofreading is done automatically.

## Qualifications and Training

While you don't always need academic qualifications to get into printing, most companies do ask for GCSEs grades A–C in English, maths, science and IT. The range of qualifications acceptable for office and management jobs is wide. Some jobs require GCSEs; others are open to applicants with A levels or a degree. Training is mostly on the job, and the British Printing Industry Federation runs a number of short courses, and also provides information on companies offering training. You can work towards a range of different NVQs, depending on what work you do and what is of special interest. Possibilities include Machine Printing levels 2 and 3, offering several options, such as lithography, web offset and screen printing; Digital Print Production levels 2 and 3, with units on machine operation, digital artwork and pre-press work; and Mechanised Print Finishing and Binding, covering finishing methods in general print and newspapers.

## Personal Qualities and Skills

For many roles in print you need good colour vision and excellent manual dexterity. You need to have a real interest in the finished product and how it looks. You should be keen to learn new skills and able to adapt quickly as technology changes fast in this field. You should be able to work well as part of a team, but able to take responsibility for your own work.

## Salaries

The variety of jobs results in a wide range of salaries. On the machine operating and finishing side, salaries start at £16,000 to £20,000. Where jobs are more technically demanding, earnings can reach £40,000. Managers earn £18,000 to £40,000. Many posts include shift-work allowances and opportunities to earn overtime.

British Printing Industries Federation (BPIF), Farringdon Point, 29–35 Farringdon Road, London EC1M 3JF; 0870 240 4085; www.britishprint.com

Proskills UK Ltd, Centurion House, 85B Milton Park, Abingdon, Oxon OX14 4RY; 01235 833844; www.proskills.co.uk

Scottish Print Employers' Federation, 48 Palmerston Place, Edinburgh EH12 5DE; www.spef.org.uk

Get into Print; www.getintoprint.org

# PRISON OFFICER

Prison officers are employed in prisons, detention centres, young offender institutions and remand centres. The work involves supervising prisoners inside the place of detention, escorting them to courts and other prisons and, if relevant, teaching a skill or trade. Officers also deliver programmes that help prisoners address their offending behaviour. Some specialist prison officers are employed as hospital officers, dog handlers, security experts and caterers.

## Qualifications and Training

Five GCSEs, including maths and English, are required and applicants must pass an aptitude test and an interview. Training is a mixture of time spent at a local prison and residential courses at an officers' training school. In Scotland, the requirement is five standard grades (1, 2 or 3) or equivalent (including maths and English) or three years' experience managing people. A good level of physical fitness is required. NVQs in Custodial Care are available at levels 2 and 3, as is Custodial Healthcare level 3 and Youth Justice levels 3 and 4. There is special training for caterers, dog handlers, physical education instructors and medical staff. An accelerated promotions scheme exists for graduate entrants.

## Personal Qualities and Skills

Officers should be positive thinkers with humanity and common sense; they must be good listeners, assertive, have excellent communication skills and the ability to mix with a wide range of people.

## Salaries

In England and Wales new prison officers start on a range from £18,000 to nearly £28,000. Pay in inner and outer London includes additional allowances. With experience this rises to £29,000. Senior officers earn £31,000 to £33,000. In Scotland, new officers start on £17,000, rising to £23,000 with a few years' experience.

**info**

Skills for Justice, Centre Court, Atlas Way, Sheffield S4 7QQ; www.skillsforjustice.com

HM Prison Service, Recruitment Section, Cleland House, Page Street, London SW1P 4LN; www.hmprisonservice.gov.uk

Scottish Prison Service, Calton House, 5 Redheughs Rigg, Edinburgh EH12 9HW; 0131 244 8745; www.sps.gov.uk

# PRIVATE INVESTIGATOR

Private investigators work with individuals, businesses, insurance companies, solicitors and other organisations. They are often self-employed, but may be employed by organisations such as law firms or insurance companies. The work is very varied, including tracing missing persons, investigating insurance claims and presenting legal or financial documents to private individuals and to businesses. Private investigators also investigate commercial piracy and fraudulent activities. Work activities are varied, including interviewing people, carrying out detailed research and surveillance operations.

## Qualifications and Training

There are no formal entry qualifications, but many private investigators have worked in other security roles – it is normally a second career. A good standard of general education is important. All private investigators must be licensed by the Security Industry Authority (SIA) and the SIA is in the process of developing both the licensing system and appropriate qualifications. The Academy of Professional Investigation runs a level 3 advanced diploma in private investigation. The Academy also offers advice on where you might obtain some training.

## Personal Qualities and Skills

You must have excellent powers of observation and concentration. You need good people skills to be able to talk to people and encourage people to share information with you. You need good research and information gathering abilities and some knowledge of IT. You should be self-confident with good business awareness.

## Salaries

New entrants earn around £13,000. Private investigators on regular salaries earn between £15,000 and £25,000. It is harder to predict incomes for those who are self-employed, but £20,000 to £25,000 is a reasonable estimate.

Academy of Professional
Investigation, Clair House,
3–5 Clair Road, Haywards Heath,
West Sussex RH16 3DP;
01444 441111;
www.becomeadetective.oom

Association of British Investigators
(ABI), 27 Old Gloucester Street,
London WC1N 3XX; 0871 474 0006;
www.theabi.org.uk

Institute of Professional
Investigators, 83 Guildford Street,
Chertsey,
Surrey KT16 9JL; 0870 330 8622;
www.ipi.org.uk

Security Industry Authority (SIA),
PO Box 9, Newcastle Upon Tyne
NE82 6YX; 0870 243 0100;
www.the-sia.org.uk

# PROBATION OFFICER

Probation officers work with people who have committed criminal offences. They work with prisoners both while they are serving sentences and after release, to try to ensure that they do not re-offend. They supervise offenders who have community rather than custodial sentences. They interview offenders and try to help them understand the impact and consequences of what they have done. They supervise group activities of various kinds and they prepare reports for courts, magistrates and prison officials.

## Qualifications and Training

The training of probation officers is currently under review and the present training programme has been suspended until final decisions are made about the structure of the new arrangements. Your local Probation Training Consortium will not have any further information. Once the decision has been made about the future of training, details will appear on the Probation Home Office website and passed on to local Probation Service Consortia.

## Personal Qualities and Skills

You need a mature and calm approach to your work. You must have excellent written and spoken communication skills. You must have an understanding approach to people and their problems, but you also need firm confidence to challenge and question behaviour. You must be caring, but also emotionally resilient. You need to be able to work well as part of a team and you must have excellent organisational skills. You have to develop a good understanding of the law and legal processes.

## Salaries

Trainee probation officers earn £18,000 to £19,000 while they are working towards the Diploma in Probation Studies. Trainees in London get an additional allowance. Qualified officers earn £27,500 to £33,000. Senior probation officers with management responsibility earn more than £40,000.

**info**

National Probation Service, 1st Floor Abell House, John Islip Street, London SW1P 4LH; www.probation.homeoffice.gov.uk

Skills for Justice, Centre Court, Atlas Way, Sheffield S4 7QQ; www.skillsforjustice.com

Probation Board for Northern Ireland, 80–90 North Street, Belfast BT1 1LD; 028 9026 2400; www.pbni.org.uk

Scottish Social Services Council, Compass House, 11 Riverside Drive, Dundee DD1 4NY; 0845 60 30 891; www.sssc.uk.com

# PSYCHOLOGY

Psychologists work in many different settings, in hospitals and healthcare, in schools and for local education authorities, in industry, in marketing and business, for the police and criminal justice system, and in sport. While these settings may be very different, all psychologists work to measure, understand, predict and assess human behaviour.

## Qualifications and Training

For most branches of psychology, you must obtain Graduate Basis for Registration (GBR) with the British Psychological Society (BPS). This means completing a three- or four-year degree in psychology, accredited by the BPS, and it is important to check the status of any psychology degree before you begin your studies, if you think you may wish to register as a chartered psychologist. If your undergraduate degree is not in psychology you can start by doing a BPS approved Conversion Course and sitting a qualifying examination. Consult the BPS website for details of these courses. Further detail on specific qualifications for the different branches of psychology is given in the following sections.

# Clinical psychologist

Clinical psychologists work mainly in health and social care settings with clients of all ages who are facing a variety of mental health and emotional problems. Clinical psychologists work as part of a multidisciplinary team devising programmes to help people who are suffering from such conditions as severe anxiety or phobias, depression, addictive behaviour, or behaviours resulting from neurological or physical injury. They assess their client's mental and emotional states and may offer advice, counselling or therapy.

## Qualifications and Training

In addition to a BPS accredited degree, clinical psychologists must complete a three-year NHS-funded doctorate programme in clinical psychology. Places on these programmes are highly sought after, so you normally need a First or 2.1 degree plus some relevant work experience. Work as an assistant in a clinical psychology department is most useful, but course providers will give you advice on what work experience is suitable.

# Consumer psychologist

Consumer psychologists do not have to be chartered with the BPS. They work in marketing in commercial businesses and other organisations, trying to understand and make use of the psychological basis of the choices that consumers make and why they choose to buy a certain product or service. Much of their work involves interviewing people or organising focus groups. They interpret the results of these interviews and discussions to help marketers understand and exploit trends in consumer behaviour.

## Qualifications and Training

Most consumer psychologists have a degree either in psychology or in a marketing discipline where the course has covered consumer psychology in some depth. Some consumer psychologists start their career in other roles in marketing departments.

## Counselling psychologist

Counselling psychologists work with children and adults of all ages, helping them to deal with difficulties of many kinds. These could include psychological conditions such as anxiety or depression. Problems may be associated with life situations such as domestic violence or bereavement. Sometimes the problems are associated with substance abuse or eating disorders. Counselling psychologists advise their clients on ways of coping with situations and moving on.

### Qualifications and Training

In addition to the BPS accredited degree, counselling psychologists need to complete a postgraduate qualification in counselling psychology, also approved by the BPS. There is an alternative 'independent route' into this field of psychology. This entails the equivalent of three years' full-time study, supervised work, the submission of a portfolio and an oral examination by the BPS.

## Educational psychologist

Educational psychologists work with school students and other young people who are experiencing difficulties in learning and making progress with their education. Students may encounter difficulties because they have a learning disability, a sensory impairment or some emotional problem which is getting in the way. Educational psychologists work with individual students, with parents, teachers and other professionals, to try to find ways round the problem. They may advise students on new ways to learn, encourage them to talk about problems or set up particular programmes of study and activities.

### Qualifications and Training

In addition to a BPS accredited degree, educational psychologists in England, Wales and Northern Ireland must complete a three-year doctorate in Educational Psychology; in Scotland they must complete a two-year Master's in Educational Psychology plus one year of supervised practice.

## Forensic psychologist

Forensic psychologists work mainly in the prison and probation services. The aim of their work is to try to develop interventions that stop offenders from re-offending and help them find ways to change their behaviours. Work may be one-to-one or in groups. They also advise prison governors and other prison and probation staff on what treatment programmes and institutional policies might be most effective in helping reduce offending. They work closely with the court system, with victims and with witnesses. They have to evaluate the programmes they have set up to measure their effectiveness.

## Qualifications and Training

In addition to a BPS accredited degree, forensic psychologists must complete a Master's degree in forensic psychology (one year full-time, two years part-time) and then undergo two years' supervised practice.

# Health psychologist

This is a new and evolving area, and is the practice and application of psychological methods to the study of behaviour relevant to illness and healthcare. Health psychologists work in community, social care and healthcare settings examining the psychological aspects of illness. They help people implement programmes of behaviour that might prevent health problems and they also work with people learning to cope with various aspects of chronic and acute illnesses. At present, only a small number of health psychologists are employed by the NHS.

## Qualifications and Training

In addition to a BPS accredited degree in psychology, health psychologists must complete a Master's degree in health psychology and two years' supervised work experience.

# Occupational psychologist

Occupational psychologists work in organisations of many kinds or for private consultants. They examine how particular work tasks affect the well-being or performance of workers and they also determine which personal characteristics allow someone to perform tasks well. A major part of their work is in designing recruitment tests that will help employers select the most likely candidates to succeed in particular work roles. Occupational psychologists also work with organisations to solve issues of conflict within a work team, or to identify possible new management strategies.

## Qualifications and Training

In addition to a BPS accredited degree in psychology, occupational psychologists need to complete a Master's degree in occupational psychology plus two years' supervised practice. An alternative route is to undertake three years' supervised practice and study for the BPS Certificate in Occupational Psychology.

# Sports and exercise psychologist

Sports psychologists work with sportsmen and women, helping them to improve their performance by examining the psychological aspects of their games and strategies. Sports psychologists teach techniques like relaxation and visualisation, which should help people to perform better. They also undertake research on the general effects of taking part in sport and physical exercise. Sports psychologists are often self-employed, though some are employed by sports teams or by umbrella organisations for particular sports.

## Qualifications and Training

This is a very new branch of psychology, so there is no formal training route in place yet. Most entrants will have a degree in psychology or in sports science, followed by a Master's degree in sports psychology. This is followed by a period of supervised work experience.

## Personal Qualities and Skills

Psychologists have to have excellent interpersonal skills, and be easily able to work with and listen to people who may be very distressed. They have to be good at observing and highly perceptive. In many roles they need good numeracy skills and the ability to write good reports.

## Salaries

In the NHS clinical psychologists and counselling psychologists start on around £21,000 to £27,000. Outside the NHS salaries vary. Some counselling psychologists are self-employed. Educational psychologists earn £22,000 to £29,000 during training and £31,000 to £42,000 on qualifying. Trainee forensic psychologists start on £18,000 rising to £23,000 after completing training. Occupational psychologists earn between £25,000 and £42,000. Many sport and exercise psychologists are self-employed; earnings to start with are normally £22,000 to £27,000, but much higher with experience and a good reputation. Most experienced psychologists in all branches of the profession earn between £25,000 and £50,000.

**info**

British Psychological Society (BPS), St Andrews House, 48 Princess Road East, Leicester LE1 7DR; 0116 254 9568; www.bps.org.uk. The BPS has divisions for each of the separate branches of psychology.

NHS Careers, PO Box 376, Bristol BS99 3EY; 0845 606 0655; www. nhscareers.nhs.uk

# PSYCHOTHERAPIST

Psychotherapy is a generic term, within which there are many specialist disciplines. People may practise as psychoanalytic psychotherapists, as cognitive or behavioural psychotherapists, or as counsellors, with varying degrees of training and experience; however, there are plans to introduce greater regulation.

Psychotherapists may work with individuals of any age, couples and families, or groups, resolving problems such as over-shyness, over-aggression, sleeping disorders, separation difficulties, behavioural problems, eating difficulties, self-harm and depression. They work in hospitals, in- and out-patient clinics, child and family consultation centres, GPs' surgeries, special schools for disturbed children, and in private practice.

## Qualifications and Training

The picture is very different depending on whether you want to go into private practice or work for a recognised public body such as the NHS or HM Prison Service. At present, for private practice there are no specific entry requirements and a wide range of courses of varying quality is available. If you are aiming for salaried employment with a public institution the situation is very different. You must have a degree, preferably in psychology or a healthcare subject. Training that conforms to standards set by the UK Council for Psychotherapy (UKCP) or the British Psychoanalytic Council is normally required. To complicate matters, prospective employers often state which of these they require, so it may well be worth perusing job adverts before you embark on training. The British Association of Counselling and Psychotherapy produces a directory of approved training courses. Approved training courses usually require you to undergo personal therapy as part of your training, and this can prove expensive. Many psychotherapists have worked in other social service, social care or medical professions and take on psychotherapy as a second career.

## Personal Qualities and Skills

You must be a really good listener, able to encourage someone else to talk. You have to be sensitive, patient and calm; able to cope with your clients showing signs of distress. You need to be able to offer understanding and encouragement without becoming overly emotionally involved in your clients' problems. The training and the work can be personally very challenging, so you need emotional resilience. You also need to be well organised and good at working as part of a team.

The Association of Independent Psychotherapists, PO Box 1194, London N6 5PW; 020 7700 1911; www.aip.org.uk

British Association for Counselling and Psychotherapy (BACP), BACP House, 15 St John's Business Park, Lutterworth LE17 4HB; 01455 883300; www.bacp.co.uk

British Association of Psychotherapists (BAP), 37 Mapesbury Road, London NW2 4HJ; 020 8452 9823; www.bap-psychotherapy.org

British Psychoanalytic Council, West Hill House, 6 Swains Lane, London N6 6QS; 020 7267 3626; www.psychoanalytic-council.org

The Guild of Psychotherapists, 47 Nelson Square, Blackfriars Road, London SE1 0QA; 0207 401 3260; www.guildofpsychotherapists.org.uk

Skills for Care and Development, Albion Court, 5 Albion Place, Leeds LS1 6JL; 0113 245 1716; www.skillsforcare.org.uk

Skills for Health, 2nd Floor, Goldsmiths House, Broad Plain, Bristol BS2 0JP; 0117 922 1155; www.skillsforhealth.org.uk

UK Council for Psychotherapy (UKCP), 2nd Floor, Edward House, 2 Wakley Street, London EC1V 7LT; 020 7014 9955; www.psychotherapy.org.uk

info

## Salaries

Some psychotherapists are employed by the NHS and they start on a range of £22,000 to £26,000, rising to £32,000 with experience. Many psychotherapists work in private practice and their earnings are linked to what they charge – anything from £30 to £120 per hour; £45 to £60 is the most likely.

# PUBLIC RELATIONS OFFICER

As a public relations (PR) officer/executive/consultant, your main role is to maintain and improve your employer or client's image with customers, or with the general public. Some public relations officers work in-house for a particular company or organisation. Many companies are not large enough or do not choose to employ in-house PR specialists, so many PR professionals work for specialist public relations consultancies providing services for a range of clients. Wherever you work, your responsibilities are likely to include a mix of the following: writing brochures, leaflets, press releases, speeches and articles for websites; monitoring the public and media perception of a person, organisation, service or product; organising publicity campaigns and press launches; making presentations; developing and maintaining good relations with the media; and representing your client/company at a wide range of events.

## Qualifications and Training

This is a very competitive industry and while not absolutely essential, most entrants are graduates. Degrees in advertising, business, marketing, journalism or public relations are all relevant. The Chartered Institute of Public Relations (CIPR) provides a list of approved degrees. It is possible to join a PR company or department as an administrative assistant and work your way up. Many PR professionals move into a career in PR following on from work in advertising, marketing or journalism. Most of the training is on the job or through a variety of short courses, many run by the CIPR.

## Personal Qualities and Skills

You must be excellent at all aspects of communication, able to write fluently and at the correct level. You must be confident at speaking in public, dealing with awkward questions, and building good one-to-one relationships. You have to be a good problem solver and an excellent organiser. You must be able to work as part of a team and to cope with pressure.

**info**

Public Relations Consultants Association, Willow House, Willow Place, London SW1P 1JH; 020 7233 6026; www.prca.org.uk

Chartered Institute of Public Relations (CIPR), 32 St James's Square, London SW1Y 4JR; 020 7766 3333; www.cipr.co.uk

## Salaries

Trainees earn between £17,000 and £20,000. Experienced PR executives earn between £25,000 and £40,000. Someone running a PR consultancy can earn up to £80,000 to £100,000.

# PUBLISHING

Publishing houses differ in their structure, but most have three main departments: editorial, production/design, and sales and marketing. Additionally, there are the service departments found in most commercial offices: accounts, reception, personnel, warehousing and distribution.

## Book publishing: editorial

This is the department which attracts the most applicants, although editors are a very small percentage of the total publishing labour force. Editors liaise with those involved in the design, planning and production of each book. They read and edit the manuscript, prepare it for the typesetter, check the proofs and are responsible for assembling all the various parts, paginated in the correct order, for the printer. There is no automatic promotion system or salary structure. In a small company the only way to move up may be to move out.

The editorial director or managing editor runs a centralised copy-editing department, and commissions and supervises freelance editorial workers.

## Commissioning editor

Commissioning editors are responsible for both identifying new authors and new titles likely to be successful and for monitoring the performance of the current titles being published by their company. A commissioning editor's work can include identifying possible future market trends, setting out proposals and costings for new book titles, deciding whether to accept manuscripts and proposals submitted by hopeful authors and overseeing the progress of any book, from the initial idea to the finished product being on sale.

## Copy-editor

Copy-editors check the manuscripts submitted by authors and prepare this material for publication. They have to ensure that the text makes sense and that it is in the right 'house style'. Copy-editors work closely with authors, discussing and agreeing necessary changes. Copy-editors need to be alert to any possible legal questions which the text may raise. They also keep commissioning editors informed of progress and problems.

# Editorial assistant

Editorial assistants support the whole publishing process in many ways. They often act as personal assistants to commissioning editors or senior copy-editors. They carry out general office duties, such as maintaining databases or filing systems. They are often the contact point on any project for authors, editors, design and production staff, and marketing and sales departments.

## Qualifications and Training

The most usual career route is to work your way up from editorial assistant through copy-editor and then commissioning editor. It is sometimes possible to join a publisher as a commissioning editor in academic or professional publishing, if you have highly relevant knowledge of particular topics. There is fierce competition for entry level editorial jobs, so you may well find it useful to do some work shadowing or voluntary work. This also helps you build up a network of contacts. Editorial work is almost exclusively a graduate career. Degrees in English or publishing are especially useful. If you are interested in a specific area such as scientific publishing, then a degree in a subject relevant to this may also be helpful.

## Personal Qualities and Skills

All editorial staff need excellent written and spoken communication skills. To be successful you must be able to work to strict deadlines and work well as part of a team. You have to pay close attention to detail and have an eye for good presentation. Commissioning editors must be good negotiators, planners and project managers.

## Salaries

Commissioning editors earn between £18,000 and £20,000 to begin with, rising to £30,000 with a few years' experience. Senior commissioning editors earn £45,000 plus. Copy-editors earn between £16,000 and £35,000 if they work in-house. Freelance copy-editors negotiate a fee per contract, often based on an hourly rate. This is around £20 to £30 an hour, but some publishers pay less, or more, than this. Editorial assistants usually start on between £16,500 and £22,000.

# Production controller: books

The production controller draws up an accurate specification for the book and invites tenders from typesetters, printers, paper suppliers and binders. When all the estimates have been received, the production controller places orders and ensures that all the production stages are carried out to the required standard, and on schedule. Undemanding production work on, for example, leaflets or reprints, is often given to a production assistant, who is regarded as a trainee.

# Designer: books

(*see also* Art and Design)

Designers prepare layouts, sketches, specimen pages and dummies, and mark up the manuscripts for the typesetter after they have been edited. All the activities of the design department are managed by the design director. Directors discuss illustrated or complicated technical books with the author and the editor, commission freelance artwork, arrange the in-house preparation of artwork and impose a visual style on the company product.

## Training and Qualifications

Production and design staff tend to be graduates and will be expected to have a vocational diploma or relevant qualification.

## Personal Qualities and Skills

Production and design professionals will need to be able to work under pressure and to tight deadlines. Being able to work well in a team and to interpret editorial briefs is also a quality expected in this area. Good planning skills are also essential. Production staff will also be expected to negotiate with printers and freelance designers for good deals.

## Salaries

For production assistants starting salaries range from £15,000 to £20,000, rising to an average of around £26,000 after a few years' experience. Senior production staff earn around £30,000. With the impact of technology the demarcation lines between editorial and production assistants are not always clear.

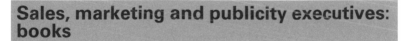

# Sales, marketing and publicity executives: books

(*see also* Marketing, Public Relations Officer *and* Sales Representative)

Depending on the size of the company, there will be one, two or three departments working on the promotion and selling of the books. Applicants are usually graduates and should be creative and write lively and informative copy.

Sales representatives will spend a considerable amount of time travelling to booksellers both in the UK and abroad. They will present details of new publications in order to secure orders for the books, and continue to present the back catalogue to potential purchasers.

## Training and Qualifications

Marketing and publicity executives are expected to have good literacy skills and are normally graduates. A postgraduate marketing qualification is also expected in more experienced marketing professionals. Sales representatives are also expected to have had experience within the book trade, and international sales representatives are expected to have a language degree or equivalent qualification.

### Personal Qualities and Skills

Staff in this field need to be able to work in a team, and to develop and stick to marketing plans and budgets. They should have an interest in the field and the ability to pick up leads, and require good communication and literacy skills.

### Salaries

Sales and marketing assistants earn between £16,000 and £18,000. Marketing executives earn between £20,000 and £30,000, with similar rates for publicity managers. A marketing manager for a large publisher can earn more than £40,000.

## Indexer: books

Indexers provide a systematic arrangement of the terms appearing in a book, journal or other publication, which could be electronic or paper-based. They also work with page numbers or other locators in order to ensure the information can be easily found. Indexers are generally employed by publishers or authors. Most are freelances working from home.

### Qualifications and Training

No formal qualifications are required but a good education, normally to degree level, is necessary plus subject knowledge in the case of specialist books. Training is by open-learning course leading to accreditation. Registered indexers prove their experience and competence through an assessment procedure and admission to the Register of Indexers.

### Personal Qualities and Skills

An ability to analyse a text and meticulous attention to detail are essential, plus the ability to work to set requirements and time limits.

### Salaries

Indexers are usually self-employed and charge either by the hour or a fixed rate for a particular contract. The Society of Indexers can give you advice on what you should charge. They recommend a basic hourly rate of £19.50 per hour for straightforward work, but for more complex indexing work you may well be able to negotiate a much better rate.

## Magazines and newspapers

(*see also* Journalism)

The organisation of periodical publishing differs from that of book publishing and has much in common with newspapers. The main areas of activity outside the service departments are editorial, advertisement sales and circulation. Editorial jobs within the magazine and newspaper industry are covered in 'Journalism'.

However, in addition to editorial opportunities a number of alternative career paths can be found in magazine and newspaper publishing. Advertising sales are crucial to the majority of magazines and newspapers, and represent just one of the opportunities available to those who wish to work in these fields of publishing but are not seeking a job as a journalist.

## Advertisement sales representative: magazines

Commercial magazines depend on advertising revenue for survival. Graduates are often recruited straight from university to sales posts and are trained on the job. Sales staff must know the magazine's readership and build up advantageous contacts with potential advertisers. They spend a lot of time researching, analysing and planning, and need a persuasive manner and numerical skills.

### Qualifications and Training
Requirements for trainees vary and many sales reps learn through work experience.

### Personal Qualities and Skills
Sales staff need an outgoing personality and good communication skills, the ability to work under pressure and to meet deadlines.

### Salaries
Many advertising reps earn a basic salary of approximately £14,000 and then are expected to earn the rest on commission. Successful advertising sales reps can earn £40,000+.

## Design: magazines

(*see also* Art and Design)

The range of work includes cover design, typographical design, layout, design of advertisements and direct mail material. Entrants will need a design qualification. Entrants need to have a good working knowledge of current design software used within the industry.

# Production manager: magazines

Production staff are trained in the printing trade. It is their responsibility to see that the magazine is available at point of sale on publication day, and this involves meticulous planning and a tolerance of stress.

## Training and Qualifications

Production and design staff tend to be graduates and are expected to have a vocational diploma or relevant qualification.

## Personal Qualities and Skills

Production and design professionals need to be able to work under pressure and to tight deadlines. Being able to work well in a team and to interpret editorial briefs is also a quality expected in this area. Good planning skills are also essential.

**info**

Association of Learned and Professional Society Publishers, 51 Middletons Road, Yaxley, Peterborough, Cambridgeshire PE7 3NU; 01733 247 178; www.alpsp.org

Book Indexing Postal Tutorials; Contact: Ann Hall; 07708 571548; alanindex@tiscali.co.uk

The Booksellers Association of the United Kingdom and Ireland Ltd (BA), Minster House, 272 Vauxhall Bridge Road, London SW1V 1BA; 020 7802 0802; www.booksellers.org.uk

Data Publishers Association (DPA), Queens House, 28 Kingsway, London WC2B 6JR; 020 7405 0836; www.dpa.org.uk/

The Periodical Publishers Association (PPA), Queens House, 28 Kingsway, London WC2B 6JR; 020 7404 4166; www.periodicalstrainingcouncil.org/

Periodicals Training Council (PTC), Queens House, 28 Kingsway, London WC2B 6JR; 020 7404 4166; www.periodicalstrainingcouncil.org/

Publishers Association (PA), 29b Montague Street, London WC1B 5BW; 020 7691 9191; www.publishers.org.uk

Publishing Training Centre, Book House, 45 East Hill, Wandsworth, London SW18 2QZ; 020 8874 2718; www.train4publishing.co.uk

Skillset, Focus Point, 21 Caledonian Road, London N1 9GB; www.skillset.org

The Society for Editors and Proofreaders (SfEP), Erico House, 93–99 Upper Richmond Road, Putney, London SW15 2TG; 020 8785 5617; www.sfep.org.uk

Society of Indexers (SI), Woodbourn Business Centre, 10 Jessell Street, Sheffield S9 3HY; www.indexers.org.uk

The Society of Young Publishers, c/o The Bookseller, Endeavour House, 189 Shaftesbury Avenue, London WC2H 8TJ; www.thesyp.org.uk

## Salaries

Salaries for new entrants range from £14,500 to £18,000. In London salaries are a little higher and this is where many jobs are based. Production managers' salaries vary very much according to the range they are producing and how large a team they have to manage, but a general guide is £22,000 to £34,000.

# PURCHASING OFFICER/INDUSTRIAL BUYER

Purchasing careers exist in all large organisations, whether profit-making or not. Essentially, purchasing and supply management involves identifying the requirements of the company's internal customers and then obtaining the necessary products and services by negotiation and agreement with suppliers. The primary objective is to obtain value for money. This does not always mean achieving the very lowest price – sometimes other commercial considerations are more important. For example, the flexibility and speed of response of the supplier might be the deciding factor, or the need to minimise risk by choosing a vendor with a good business record.

In a manufacturing environment such as a car plant, the purchaser is directly involved in buying components such as wheels, lights and shock absorbers for the production line. In a financial services company, purchases might well be for telecommunications systems, catering services and marketing services, including advertising and design. In retail purchasing the role is slightly different as buyers are more involved in merchandising, selecting product lines which appeal to the consumer and sell quickly.

### Qualifications and Training

Most companies require a minimum of four or five GCSE passes. Graduates or individuals with A levels usually enter as trainee buyers, working with experienced personnel and continuing their training in the workplace. The minimum requirement for individuals wishing to study for the Foundation Stage of the CIPS Graduate Diploma is two A levels and three GCSEs (or equivalent). The Certificate in Purchasing and Supply Management is offered to those with no A levels.

### Personal Qualities and Skills

You need good written and spoken communication skills and a high level of numeracy. You have to have the confidence to negotiate firmly and the temperament to take risks at times. You should be able to build good relationships with people and you need a good all-round business awareness.

### Salaries

Salaries for new entrants are between £19,000 and £26,000. With a few years' experience this range increases to £25,000 to £35,000. Senior purchasing managers with large organisations can earn £60,000.

**info**

Chartered Institute of Purchasing and Supply (CIPS), Easton House, Easton on the Hill, Stamford, Lincs PE9 3NZ; 01780 756777; www.cips.org

# QUARRYING

Quarrying is opencast mining for clay, sand, limestone, slate and other materials that are just below the layer of topsoil. Quarry workers or quarry operatives are involved in the operations connected with this extraction process. Modern quarrying involves using very heavy machinery to excavate, transport, cut and crush the different products, and quarry workers operate this machinery.

## Qualifications and Training

There are no specific academic entry qualifications, but you must be fit, and having an LGV (light goods vehicle) driving licence or experience of using heavy plant and machinery can be an advantage. If you are between 16 and 24 years old, you may be able to do an apprenticeship; availability of these varies according to locality. Some employers will expect you to have four GCSEs to do an apprenticeship; these should include, English, maths and technology. The industry offers the chance to do NVQs at levels 2 and 3 in Drilling Operations, Plant Operations and Process Operations. There is also an NVQ level 3 in Working with Explosives, and there are higher-level courses in Sampling. The majority of training is on the job.

## Personal Qualities and Skills

You need to be physically fit and confident in handling highly specialised technical equipment. You should have good numeracy skills for calculating quantities and you must be able to work as part of a team. You should have an acute awareness of health and safety issues.

## Salaries

New entrants start on around £12,000; this rises to £17,000 after two or three years' experience. Senior quarry workers earn between £20,000 and £25,000. There are often opportunities to increase earnings with overtime and shift-work payments.

EPIC Training Ltd, Alban Row, 27–31 Verulam Road, St Albans, Herts AL3 4DG; 01727 869008; www. epicltd.com

www.careersinquarrying.co.uk

info

# R

## RADIOGRAPHER

Radiography is a caring profession which calls for considerable technological expertise. There are two branches: diagnostic radiography and therapeutic radiography. Diagnostic radiographers are responsible for producing high-quality images on film and other recording materials which help doctors to diagnose disease and the extent of injuries. Therapeutic radiographers help to treat patients, many of whom have cancer, using X-rays, ionising radiation and sometimes drugs.

### Qualifications and Training

All radiography qualifying courses are now at degree level. Courses are normally based in a university or higher education institution affiliated to a university, with half the time spent on clinical education in hospital departments associated with the university.

On graduation, entrants are eligible for State Registration by the Radiographers Board of the Council for Professions Supplementary to Medicine, which is an essential requirement for employment in the National Health Service. The requirements for entry to radiography courses are two A levels and three GCSEs at grade C or above, or equivalent. Entry is also possible through validated access courses, and applications from mature candidates are welcomed by many radiography education centres.

### Personal Qualities and Skills

As well as having an interest in science, radiographers should be caring and compassionate but sufficiently level-headed not to get upset when dealing with sick people. They need to be patient and calm when faced with patients who may be frightened or difficult. Good health and reasonable strength are needed for lifting people and heavy equipment. In addition, radiographers should be good humoured, and able to work well in a team and assume responsibility.

### Salaries

Newly qualified radiographers are paid between £21,000 and £27,000 (NHS salaries Band 5). Specialist radiographers are paid between £24,000 and £29,000 and senior radiographers (described as advanced in the NHS pay scales) are paid £30,000 to £39,000.

Society and College of
Radiographers,
207 Providence Square, Mill Street,
London SE1 2EW; 020 7740 7200;
fax: 020 7740 7204; www.sor.org

NHS Careers, PO Box 376, Bristol
BS99 3EY; careers helpline:
0845 606 0655;
www.nhscareers.nhs.uk/index.html

A Factsheet 'What is a radiographer?'
is available from NHS Careers

info

# RAILWAY WORK

The rail industry employs a vast number of people: drivers, revenue protection inspectors, customer service assistants, signal operators, engineers,
fitters, clerical workers, technicians and managers. The last are responsible
for the day-to-day running of the railways or are in charge of departments
such as planning, engineering, marketing and accounts.

## Qualifications and Training

Train drivers must be aged 21 with a good general education. Train companies set their own entrance requirements, but often use aptitude tests including tests on train cab simulators. Training takes between 9 and 18 months
and includes work towards NVQ level 2 in Rail Transport Operations (Driving).
It is likely that a licensing system for train drivers will be introduced in the
near future.

Electricians, fitters and mechanics often have experience as technicians or
electricians in other sectors before they join the railway. Apprenticeships
may be an option for school leavers; those with four or five GCSEs grades
A–C including maths, English and a science are able to join. All technicians
and engineers are put through Personal Track Safety (PTS) training by their
employers before they are allowed to work on railway tracks.

Station assistants, booking clerks and other customer service staff need no
formal entry qualifications. Engineers and managers normally have a degree
in a relevant subject: electrical or mechanical engineering, or business
subjects respectively.

## Personal Qualities and Skills

An interest in railways is a good starting point. Roles such as driving and
signal work require good concentration, and safety awareness at all times is
essential. Many positions entail a great deal of customer contact or team
work, so good interpersonal skills are extremely important.

## Salaries

Trainee drivers earn around £15,000–£25,000, and up to £35,000 once training
is completed. Trainee fitters/electricians start on £13,000, less for apprentices.
After training, earnings are between £17,000 and £20,000.

**info**

Network Rail, 40 Melton Street,
London NW1 2EE; 020 7557 8000;
www.networkrail.co.uk

GoSkills, Concorde House, Trinity
Park, Solihull, Birmingham B37 7UQ;
0121 635 5520; www.goskills.org

# RECEPTIONIST

*see* Hospitality and Catering, *and* Business Administration

# RECRUITMENT CONSULTANT

The aim of recruitment/employment consultants is to fit people to jobs. Agencies deal with all types of staff, from office and secretarial to highly complex and specialist technical roles. Much of the work involves selling to potential users and matching clients' demands. This includes interviewing prospective job candidates, keeping records of their details and matching them to employers' requirements.

## Qualifications and Training

Many recruitment consultants have come into the industry after some experience of another job, for example sales, personnel or office work. They are trained either in-house or on courses run by the Recruitment and Employment Confederation (REC). The REC offers two levels of qualification: the Foundation Award, suitable for those in their first year in the industry, and the Certificate in Recruitment Practice for those with more than one year's experience. Both qualifications can be studied by distance learning or at an evening class.

## Personal Qualities and Skills

Recruitment consultants must be able to relate to people at different organisational levels, have good communication skills, work quickly and calmly under pressure and be organised and resilient.

**info**

Chartered Institute of Personnel and
Development (CIPD), 151 The
Broadway, London SW19 1JQ;
020 8612 6200; www.cipd.co.uk

ENTO (Employment National
Training Organisation), Head Office,
4th Floor, Kimberley House, 47
Vaughan Way, Leicester LE1 4SG;
0116 251 7979; www.ento.co.uk

Recruitment and Employment
Confederation (REC), 15 Welbeck
Street, London W1G 9XT; 020 7009
2100; www.rec.uk.com

## Salaries

Salaries for trainees consist of a basic salary of around £16,000 plus commission for successful placing. After three years or so, consultants earn between £30,000 and £50,000. In a slow job market it is much harder to achieve the commission part of earnings.

# RELIGIOUS LEADER

Religious leaders work with faith communities and with people who do not subscribe to any religious belief system. As a religious leader your role includes offering spiritual and moral leadership to your followers. Your work encompasses leading groups of people in acts of worship or in specific ceremonies. These might include religious festivals or significant occasions for individuals and families, births, deaths, marriages, or ceremonies for new members who join a particular faith. The Church of England is the established church in the UK, but as well as other Christian faith groups, there are significant numbers of members of other faiths – Buddhism, Islam, Hinduism, Judaism and Sikhism are the largest groups. Your work normally involves pastoral care, visiting people who are sick, have been bereaved, or who have relationship problems. Religious leaders also talk to those who are having a crisis of faith, or those who want to find out more about a particular belief system. Some faith groups would expect their leaders to go out and actively try to recruit new members, but this would not always be the case. For many religious leaders, part of their work would also include taking part in interfaith discussions or giving advice to government departments, charities and voluntary organisations. Many religious leaders work full- or part-time in hospitals, universities, prisons or for charities, voluntary or faith-based organisations.

## Qualifications and Training

Each faith has its own particular entry qualifications, but these are usually based on a commitment to and understanding of a particular faith rather than purely academic qualifications. Your best starting point is to check with your own religious leader about how to begin to work towards becoming one yourself. Do remember that religious groups do not have to comply with all the normal equal opportunities legislation, so in some instances it is not possible, for example, for women to become religious leaders. There may be other restrictions. There are many degree courses available in theology, religion and comparative religion, and if this career really interests you, taking such a course could be a useful way for you to explore the subject more deeply.

## Personal Qualities and Skills

A commitment to your own faith and an understanding of the problems that people encounter are essential. The skills mix you might need would vary somewhat not just between different faiths, but between different jobs within that faith. The work of a prison chaplain is quite different to that of someone working in a rural parish, or an inner city area, for example.

## Salaries

Pay varies greatly. Some religious leaders are paid a full-time salary and/or are provided with accommodation and other benefits. Many religious leaders have other jobs and do their religious work on a voluntary basis. You need to check with the faith group which interests you, exactly what financial benefits may be available.

**info**

The Board of Deputies of British Jews, 6 Bloomsbury Square, London WC1A 2LP; 020 7543 5400; www.bod.org.uk

The Buddhist Society, 58 Eccleston Square, London SW1V 1PH; 020 7834 5858; www.thebuddhistsociety.org

Churches Together in Britain and Ireland, 3rd Floor, Bastille Court, 2 Paris Garden, London SE1 8ND; 020 7654 7254; www.ctbi.org.uk

Hindu Council UK, Boardman House, 64 Broadway, Stratford, London E15 1NT; 020 8432 0400; www.hinducounciluk.org

Inter Faith Network for the United Kingdom, 8a Lower Grosvenor Place, London SW1W 0EN; 020 7931 7766; www.interfaith.co.uk

Ministry in the Church of England; www.cofe-ministry.org.uk

The Muslim Council of Britain, PO Box 57330, London E1 2WJ; 0845 262 6786; www.mcb.org.uk

Network of Sikh Organisations UK, Suite 405, Highland House, 165 The Broadway, Wimbledon, London SW19 1NE; 020 8544 8037; www.nsouk.co.uk

# REMOVALS

Removers play a key role in the chain of events leading up to departure from one home and arrival in another – which can be around the corner or on the other side of the world. It is the remover's job to see that all the customer's belongings are professionally packed and transported to their destination. The work may involve packing fragile objects quickly and efficiently, as well as travelling long distances. Some large companies have their own storage facilities, so employees may be involved in ensuring that furniture is stored safely.

Estimators are the technical salespeople in a removals company. They visit customers' homes and estimate the amount of packing space needed, the time it will take and the price.

## Qualifications and Training

Employees can work towards NVQs for the removals and storage industry. Progression is also possible to supervisory level. An LGV (large goods vehicle) licence would be beneficial, but is not essential when starting out. Estimators should have a good standard of education with good passes preferably in English, maths, geography and modern languages, hold a full car driving licence and be able to express themselves clearly and persuasively. Training is on the job.

## Personal Qualities and Skills

Removers should be fit and strong. They must be honest and have a sense of responsibility towards other people's possessions. Common sense and the ability to work in a team are important.

## Salaries

Earnings and job security in this sector are highly dependent on an active property market. Generally, starting salaries are fairly low, £12,000 to £14,000, rising to £16,000 to £19,000 for more experienced staff. Drivers may earn up to £21,000. All employees may earn more for shift work, weekend work, etc.

Skills for Logistics, 14 Warren Yard, Warren Farm Office Village, Stratford Road, Milton Keynes MK12 5NW; 0870 242 7314; www.skillsforlogistics.org

British Association of Removers, Tangent House, 62 Exchange Road, Watford, Hertfordshire WD18 0TG; 01923 699480; www.bar.co.uk

# RETAILING

Retailing is a sector offering many different career opportunities. As well as the careers outlined in this section, retailing offers opportunities in distribution management and warehouse work, in finance, in marketing and in human resource management. There are openings at school leaver level through to graduate and senior management opportunities. Retail outlets include small shops, specialising in a particular type of product: shoes, car spares or quality foods, for example. Supermarkets, department stores and discount stores are just some of the other examples of retail outlets.

# Checkout operator

Checkout operators work at the tills in supermarkets and other large retail stores. They scan the prices of all the items customers have purchased, process payments whether by cash, cheque or card, and they may also offer some assistance with packing, eg wrapping delicate items or putting frozen foods into separate bags.

## Qualifications and Training

No specific qualifications are necessary, though individual stores may request a good standard of education. Training is provided on the job and it is possible to obtain NVQ level 1 in Checkout Operations and NVQ levels 2 and 3 in Customer Service and Sales. Career progression is to supervisory roles.

## Personal Qualities and Skills

You must be polite and friendly and able to talk to people without losing your concentration or slowing down. You need good numeracy skills in order to spot errors. You must have good stamina and be able to work under pressure in a hectic environment.

## Salaries

New checkout staff earn around £11,500, rising to £13,000 to £14,000 with some experience. Supervisors earn around £17,000 to £19,000. A few stores include all staff members in profit-sharing schemes.

Skillsmart Retail, Fourth Floor, 93 Newman Street, London W1T 3EZ; 0800 093 5001; www. skillsmartretail.com

Wholesale and Retail Training Council (WRTC), 10 Hydepark Road, Mallusk, Newtonabbey BT36 4PY; 028 9084 5830; www.wrtc.co.uk

# Display designer/visual merchandiser

Display designers are responsible for shop windows and displays inside stores. These may be to attract customers into a shop, promote a new product or reinforce a company image. Displays are often seasonal or themed. Some designers work to instructions from head office, others create their own designs. The work may include making props, arranging lighting and general care of the display areas. Some shops also employ visual merchandisers who arrange products according to an organisation's display policy.

## Qualifications and Training

While there are no standard, formal entry qualifications, in practice most entrants have a relevant qualification. There are several three- or four-year degree courses in Design Merchandising Management and Exhibition and Retail Design. There are also some two-year foundation degrees available in display design or visual merchandising. Other art-based qualifications may be accepted by some employers. A great deal of training is on the job.

## Personal Qualities and Skills

You need real artistic flair and to be good at working with colour and with three-dimensional design. You should be imaginative and practical, able to work as part of a team and able to relate design ideas to commercial impact. You also need good IT skills and preferably be able to use CAD (computer assisted design).

## Salaries

Trainees earn between £11,000 and £14,000, while experienced display designers earn up to £22,000. It is possible for a display manager with a large store to earn more than £35,000.

British Display Society,
146 Welling Way, Welling,
Kent DA16 2RS; 020 8856 2030;
www.britishdisplaysociety.co.uk

Skillsmart Retail, Fourth Floor,
93 Newman Street, London
W1T 3EZ; 0800 093 5001; www.
skillsmartretail.com

**info**

# Retail store manager

Retail store managers work in department stores, in supermarkets and in small, individually owned stores. In a small store they will run the whole operation. In a supermarket they may be responsible for one area, fresh produce or the checkouts, for example. In a department store they may run one or several departments. Managers are responsible for ensuring that everything runs smoothly. They have to organise work rosters, ensure that sales targets are met, that customer service is of a high standard and that sales staff are fully trained.

## Qualifications and Training

There are several ways to become a retail store manager. Large stores or chains may run graduate management training programmes or programmes open to school leavers with two or three A levels. Experience, however, is often as important as qualifications, and many managers start out as sales assistants and work their way up to management positions.

# Sales assistant

There are many opportunities for sales staff in retailing. Your responsibilities and tasks depend on what kind of retail outlet you are working in, as well as your level of experience. In general, sales staff are expected to sort stock, sell goods, ensure these goods are attractively displayed and deal with payments for goods. They also answer customers' queries, give information about products and offer advice. Some sales staff process orders for new stock.

## Qualifications and Training

While no formal academic qualifications are necessarily needed, GCSEs grades A–C in English and maths are a help as is some experience of working with people. Training is on the job, and large stores or chain stores may offer some structured training programmes. It is possible to work towards several NVQs at levels 2 and 3 in retail, including Sales, Retail Operations and Customer Service. Many people who start as sales assistants become supervisors for a section of a store, or progress to become store managers.

## Personal Qualities and Skills

You must be polite and friendly and enjoy working with people. You need good basic literacy and numeracy skills and must be reasonably physically fit. Being smart and tidy is important, especially in fashion retailing. For anyone interested in supervisory and management responsibility, you have to be very well organised, good at taking decisions and good at leading and motivating other people.

## Salaries

Trainee store managers on graduate training schemes start on between £18,500 to £25,000; sometimes starting salaries are a little less than this if you are not on a graduate scheme. As your career progresses there is a huge variation in salary, so managers can earn anything from £23,000 to £60,000. The variation is due mainly to the size and type of store and also whether bonus schemes increase pay. Sales assistants earn between £12,000 and £15,000, but there are often opportunities to move into supervisory or management roles.

**info**

The Retail Academy, PO Box 296, York YO1 6WA; 01904 658 856; www.retailacademy.org

Skillsmart Retail: The Sector Skills Council for Retail, 4th Floor, 93 Newman Street, London W1T 3EZ; 020 746 5060; www. skillsmartretail.com

# ROAD TRANSPORT

(*see also* Bus/coach driver, Heavy goods vehicle driver *and* Logistics)

Road transport includes passenger transport and road haulage. Passenger transport covers bus and coach travel. Haulage is the transportation and distribution of all goods that are carried by road – food and drink, cars, household electrical goods, building materials and much more. While many functions, eg, administration, financial management, human resources, information technology and marketing are not specific to road transport, there are some particular roles involved. In addition to those described below, passenger transport and haulage firms employ drivers and customer service staff on the passenger side, and drivers and warehouse staff in haulage.

## Road haulage load planner

Load planners work to ensure that goods transported throughout the country and to overseas destinations are moved in the most efficient and cost-effective way possible. Load planners decide on the size, type and number of vehicles to be used for any job. They monitor progress as loads are moved, and work out back-up plans in case anything goes wrong, such as traffic hold ups or breakdown of refrigeration equipment. They discuss plans with clients and they may be involved in working out costs. Load planners often use specialised computer software to aid planning, but may have to resort to pen and paper.

## Qualifications and Training

To start as a trainee, you don't always need formal qualifications, though many employers do ask for GCSEs grades A–C including maths and English. There are sometimes opportunities to do an apprenticeship, in which case you are likely to need three or four GCSEs. A background in transport and distribution is also useful. Most of your training is on the job, and you may be able to work towards NVQ levels 2 and 3 in distribution and warehouse operations.

## Road transport manager

Managers work in passenger and goods transport, planning routes, organising schedules, managing staff, liaising with customers and calculating costs. It is the manager's job to ensure that whatever is transported, goods or people, are carried in the safest, most efficient and most cost-effective way. Managers have to ensure that all operations comply with UK and EU legislation on health and safety and employment. They have to know about transporting particular types of load such as dangerous chemicals, live animals or perishable foods. They are also likely to be involved in training and recruitment of staff.

## Qualifications and Training

Many managers work their way up from administrative, driving, or ware-house posts. Some companies run management training schemes and entry requirements vary, but may be an HND, foundation degree or degree in a relevant subject. Acceptable subjects include business, logistics, supply chain management and transport. Most training is on the job. Every transport operator has to have at least one employee who has achieved the Certificate of Professional Competence, so as a trainee manager, you would be expected to work towards this.

## Personal Qualities and Skills

Planners and managers need to be logical, well organised and careful in their work. Good IT and numeracy skills are important. You also have to be a good communicator, able to manage staff and deal with clients. Managers have to be able to understand and apply relevant legislation. Planners and managers have to be good problem solvers.

## Salaries

Trainee planners earn £15,000 to £19,000, rising to £20,000 to £24,000 with experience. Managers earn £20,000 to £24,000 when they are training; £25,000 to £35,000 with experience. In large passenger transport organisations salaries for senior managers can be £50,000 to £70,000.

GoSkills, Concorde House, Trinity Park, Solihull, Birmingham B37 7UQ; 0121 635 5520; www.goskills.org

Skills for Logistics, 14 Warren Yard, Warren Farm Office Village, Stratford Road, Milton Keynes MK12 5NW; 0870 242 7314; www.skillsforlogistics.org

Chartered Institute of Logistics and Transport (CILT UK), Logistics and Transport Centre, Earlstrees Court, Earlstrees Road, Corby, Northants NN17 4AX; 01536 740100; www.ciltuk.org.uk

info

# ROOFER

*see* Construction Trades

# ROUNDSPERSON

The roundsperson we are all most familiar with is probably the person who delivers milk and other dairy products to people's doorsteps on a daily basis.

In fact, working as a roundsperson can involve delivering and selling goods and services of many kinds to private homes and business premises. Examples include doing a sandwich round to businesses, selling ice cream or fast food and running mobile shops, selling many different kinds of goods. Usually, you work for yourself or you operate a franchise for a franchising company.

## Qualifications and Training

You do not need any formal qualifications to do this work, but some companies set their own entry tests, and you need good basic maths skills for calculating prices and making out bills. You need a full driving licence and many companies prefer applicants to be over 21 years old. If you are selling fast food, you will need a licence to trade from your local Environmental Health Department. You could do a number of relevant NVQs in customer service and sales. If you are employed by a retailer or a franchising company, it usually provides specific training about its own products and services.

## Personal Qualities and Skills

For most of the time you are working on your own, but you have to enjoy and be good at dealing with customers. You must be well organised with good numeracy skills and usually some computer skills these days. You have to be highly motivated and not mind working some antisocial hours or being out in all weathers.

## Salaries

When you start off it is hard to earn more than about £10,000, though with experience this can rise to £15,000 to £20,000; there are only a few types of round (milk and sandwiches, for example) where you are likely to receive seasonal tips.

**info**

British Franchise Association, Thames View, Newtown Road, Henley-on-Thames, Oxfordshire RG9 1HG; 01491 578050; www.british-franchise.org.uk

Improve: The Food and Drink Manufacturing and Processing Sector Skills Council, Providence House, 2 Innovation Close, Heslington, York YO10 52F; 0845 644 0448; www.improveltd.co.uk

Dairy Training and Development Council, 19 Cornwall Terrace, London NW1 4QP; 020 7486 7244; www.dairytraining.org.uk

Local Job Centre Plus and Connexions/Careers Centres

## ROYAL AIR FORCE

(*see* Armed Forces)

## ROYAL MARINES

(*see* Armed Forces)

## ROYAL NAVY

(*see* Armed Forces)

# S

## SALES REPRESENTATIVE

A sales representative may work for a manufacturer, wholesale distributor or service industry, persuading potential customers to buy the firm's products and also looking after the needs of existing customers. The representative is usually assigned a geographical area and travels around it on the firm's behalf. It is possible to be a representative for any number of products, from soap powder to pharmaceutical supplies to office equipment, machine tools and beauty products.

### Qualifications and Training

Requirements for trainees vary, but most firms look for four GCSEs grades A–C or equivalent and in some companies recruitment is at graduate level. Sales reps may study for examinations set by such bodies as the Chartered Institute of Marketing or the Managing and Marketing Sales Association. Diplomas and certificates are also issued by various trade associations representing particular types of product. Technical sales representatives usually have a degree or equivalent in the relevant subject.

### Personal Qualities and Skills

An outgoing, friendly personality, a manner that inspires confidence and the ability to speak forcefully and persuasively, plus persistence and stamina, are all important.

### Salaries

Salaries for new sales representatives vary depending on location and the product(s) or service(s) they are selling – £20,000 to £26,000, rising to £27,000 to £40,000 with experience. In most cases, salary comprises a basic rate of pay plus on-target earnings (OTE), in other words you have to achieve the sales targets your employer set. Some of the highest salaries are paid in the pharmaceuticals sector.

Association of the British
Pharmaceutical Industry (ABPI),
12 Whitehall, London SW1A 2DY;
0870 890 4333; www.abpi.org.uk

Chartered Institute of Marketing
(CIM), Moor Hall, Cookham,
Maidenhead, Berks SL6 9QH;
01628 427500; www.cim.co.uk

Institute of Sales & Marketing
Management (ISMM), Harrier Court,
Lower Woodside, Bedfordshire
LU1 4DQ; 01582 840001; www.ismm.
co.uk

info

# SCIENTIFIC RESEARCH

Research scientists work in medicine, in physics and in life sciences. They are employed in industry and in academia. The topics and issues they research are extremely wide ranging and are of course determined by the particular field of science in which they work. They may be involved in developing new products, materials or medicines, examining the effects of chemicals on behaviour, or of climate upon plants. Research scientists may be involved in the development of drugs, the study of genetics or stem cell research. In astrophysics they may be tackling questions about the nature of the universe or the structure of asteroids. In whichever scientific specialism researchers work, their main role is to design, carry out and analyse the results of scientific experiments.

## Qualifications and Training

Scientific research is a graduate entry profession. While job titles vary, there are basically three levels at which you can get into research. Technician level posts require an undergraduate degree in a science discipline relevant to the field of research. Research assistants usually need to have a Master's degree in the appropriate area of science, and research associates have usually completed a PhD.

## Personal Qualities and Skills

Regardless of which field of science you enter, you must have a rigorous and questioning approach to whatever you do. You need good numeracy skills and the ability to interpret data accurately. Many posts require good IT skills and/or the ability to work with highly specialised equipment. You need to be able to work on your own and as part of a team. You may well have to negotiate for funds and you have to be an imaginative problem solver with a real fascination for your subject.

## Salaries

Typical starting salaries: £16,000–£20,000 at technician level; £20,000–£25,000 for research assistant level (usually with an MSc or MPhil); £25,000–£33,000 at postdoctoral research associate level. Research scientists working in industry or leading a research project or team may earn considerably more than this – in the region of £45,000 to £60,000.

Biotechnology and Biological
Sciences Research Council (BBSRC),
Polaris House, North Star Avenue,
Swindon SN2 1UH; 01793 413200;
www.bbsrc.ac.uk/

Institute of Biology (IOB);
9 Red Lion Court, London EC4A 3EF;
020 7936 5900; www.iob.org/

Engineering and Physical Sciences
Research Council (EPSRC),
Polaris House, North Star Avenue,
Swindon SN2 1ET; 01793 444000;
www.epsrc.ac.uk

Institute of Mathematics and its
Applications, Catherine Richards
House, 16 Nelson Street,
Southend-on-Sea, Essex SS1 1EF;
01702 354020; www.ima.org.uk

Medical Research Council (MRC),
20 Park Crescent, London W1B 1AL;
020 7636 5422; www.mrc.ac.uk

Science and Technology Facilities
Council (STFC), Polaris House,
North Star Avenue, Swindon
SN2 1SZ; 01793 442000; www.pparc.
ac.uk

# SECURITY WORK

Security guards and security officers work for all kinds of organisations and businesses, where buildings, property and people need protection. They work to prevent theft and other criminal activities and to alert the police when the need arises. Typical tasks for security guards and officers include door supervision, checking people who enter a premises to confirm identity, patrolling buildings on foot or monitoring them from a control room, guarding cash and other valuables as they are delivered or removed or when they are in transit, and checking individuals and observing behaviour at airports or other public places. Many security staff begin as security guards and then progress to becoming security officers or supervisors with responsibility for coordinating security arrangements and training other security staff.

## Qualifications and training

You don't need formal qualifications, but many employers do ask for a good standard of education including GCSEs in English and maths. You have to pass security checks and your work and personal history is checked for the previous 10 years prior to your seeking employment. Whether you need to be licensed by the Security Industry Authority (SIA) depends on whether you work in-house or for a security contractor. If you work in-house, in other words, as an employee of the company for whom you are providing security services, you don't need a licence. If you are employed by an agency or contract company, you do. The training to obtain a licence takes about four days. The SIA is currently looking into licensing all security staff, including in-house employees. Whoever employs you, you may be expected to do training courses in dog handling, first aid, or other specialist skills.

## Personal Qualities and Skills

You need to be polite and helpful, but also able to challenge people assertively when this is appropriate. You should be able to write clear, short reports detailing an incident. You might have to handle technical equipment of various kinds. You should be confident, with a mature attitude to your work and you must be able to use your initiative. You must be reasonably fit and in many instances you will have to work shifts or do night work.

## Salaries

New security staff earn between £12,000 and £16,000 a year. With experience you can earn £21,000 to £23,000.

Skills for Security, Security House, Barbourne Road, Worcester WR1 1RS; 0845 075 0111; www.skillsforsecurity.org.uk

Security Industry Authority (SIA), PO Box 1293; Liverpool L69 1AX; 0844 892 1025; www.the-sia.org.uk

British Security Industry Association (BSIA), Kirkam House, John Comyn Drive, Worcester WR3 7NS; 0845 389 3889; www.bsia.co.uk

info

# SHEET-METAL WORKER

*see* Manufacturing

# SHIPBROKER

Shipbrokers act as go-betweens for ship owners, looking for cargo to fill their vessels, and charterers, seeking to ship their dry cargo and tanker requirements. Sale and purchase of vessels is also an important service offered to clients. Brokers are paid commission on the contracts arranged. The Baltic Exchange in London is the centre of the chartering market. It is a self-regulated market and the Exchange maintains a register of those seeking employment, which its member companies may consult. Vacancies are also advertised on the website. Additionally, shipbrokers/ship's agents in ports make arrangements when a ship calls for customs clearance – loading and discharging cargoes, meeting crew requirements and so on. Port agents who attend to cargo liners may also be involved in marketing and documenting cargo. In order to maintain contact with the international scene, shipbrokers tend to work long hours and to travel abroad frequently.

## Qualifications and Training

There are no fixed entry requirements to get into shipbroking, but different companies set their own entry criteria. A few will accept you with GCSEs grades A–C, but it is common for companies to recruit applicants who have at least A levels, or their equivalent. Some employers prefer you to have a degree. Any subjects are acceptable, but business studies, modern languages and courses that include modules on transport and/or logistics will be particularly appreciated. A background in administrative work of any kind can also be very useful. There are sometimes opportunities to do an apprenticeship in International Trade and Service (ITAS) and you may also be able to study to NVQ levels 2 and 3 in this subject. You can also work through e-learning and distance learning courses towards membership of the Institute of Chartered Shipbrokers. The majority of training, however, is provided on the job.

## Personal Qualities and Skills

You have to be very well organised and pay especial interest to being very clear and accurate in what you write and what you say. You should be a good communicator, able to talk to customers, importers and exporters and good at communicating with people whose first language is not English. You must have good IT skills, and command of any modern language can be really useful. You have to have a good knowledge of geography and be sensitive when working with people of other cultures.

## Salaries

Salaries for new entrants are between £18,000 and £23,000. With a year or two's experience this rises to £26,000 to £35,000. Senior shipbrokers can earn £35,000 to £50,000.

**info**

Institute of Chartered Shipbrokers; 0207 623 1111; www.ics.org.uk

British International Freight Association (BIFA), Redfern House, Browells Lane, Feltham, Middlesex TW13 7EP; 020 8844 2266; www.bifa.org

The Chartered Institute of Logistics and Transport (CILT) UK, Earlstrees Court, Earlstrees Road, Corby, Northants NN7 4AX; 01536 740104; www.ciltuk.org.uk

Freight Transport Association (FTA), Hermes House, St John's Road, Tunbridge Wells, Kent TN4 9UZ; 01892 526 171; www.fta.co.uk

Institute of Export, Export House, Minerva Business Park, Lynch Wood, Peterborough PE2 6FT; 01733 404400; www.export.org.uk

# SIGNWRITER

*see* Art and Design

# SOCIAL CARE AND SOCIAL WORK

Social care and social work cover a variety of roles and professions, all concerned with working with people who need some kind of support. In this work you might be working with families under stress, older people who have become ill, young adults involved in substance abuse, children at risk or people with mental health problems.

# Care assistant

Care assistants, also called care workers or social care workers, are employed in many settings with various service users (formerly referred to as 'clients'). The overall job of a care assistant is to help and support people in their daily lives with tasks such as getting up in the morning, bathing and showering, getting dressed, preparing and eating meals, or going out shopping. Some care workers work with clients in their own homes, visiting frail elderly people each day to help them get up and dressed or to go to bed in the evenings. Care assistants also work in residential homes for elderly people or for people who have learning disabilities, physical impairments or mental health problems. The work can involve helping people with personal care, such as washing and dressing, helping them to eat, or to take part in activities. An important part of the work is also simply to talk to and reassure people.

## Qualifications and Training

You don't necessarily need formal qualifications, though experience of working with people is a big advantage, especially work in a caring role. Once you are employed, you will receive training on the job, including taking part in a 12-week induction programme. There are also several relevant NVQ awards towards which you can work. Before you can work as a care assistant you will have to undergo a Criminal Records Bureau (CRB) check. If you are providing care to people in their own homes you are likely to need a driving licence.

## Personal Qualities and Skills

You need to be caring, compassionate and patient. You need very good communication skills, be able to listen and to encourage people to communicate with you. You need to be practical and physically fit. You need to be a good problem solver and you must be able to work as part of a team.

## Salaries

Salaries start at little more than minimum wage, around £12,000. Salaries can rise to £15,000 to £17,000 and there may be some opportunities to earn overtime payments.

General Social Care Council, 2 Hay's Lane, London SE1 2HB; 020 7397 5800; www.gscc.org.uk

Skills for Care (England), Albion Court, 5 Albion Place, Leeds LS1 6JL; 0113 245 1716; www.skillsforcare.org.uk

info

It's not just a lump of Plasticine

It's a laugh

It's what shall we make?

It's a rocket

It's a dinosaur

It's watching an 8-year-old boy with his new foster family

It's noticing how he shares a joke with his foster brother

It's laughing when the dinosaur looks more like a horse

It's seeing that everything's alright

It's knowing he's happy with his new family

It's a relief

It's the result of two years' hard work

It's not just a lump of Plasticine

It's one of the most important tools we use

*Social work with children & families* is changing

We can train you to use tools like these

And give you support as you progress through your training and career

Call 0300 123 1220 or search **Be the differen**

cWdc

Children's Workforce
Development Counci

# Be the difference
## Consider a career in social work

Imagine having a job where no day is the same, where you can draw on your observation and investigative skills to help protect vulnerable children while doing your best to keep families together. This is the life of a social worker with children and families.

Whether you are about to graduate, have recently left university or are looking for a fresh challenge, you are probably at a cross roads, trying to decide your next move while looking for a career that will motivate and inspire. The current economic climate may be making you assess what you really want out of a job – career progression, financial rewards, high-quality support and training. Social work is a challenging and rewarding profession and offers all of these.

As a social worker, you'll develop the ability to assess and evaluate situations intelligently, whilst using empathy and patience to create personal connections with some of the most at-risk children and young people in our society.

Leo Dufficey has seen the positive impact of these personal connections. Leo works as a front-line social worker and believes his role allows him to help families in a unique way. "One day you're out dealing with a crisis situation – you've got somebody's entire family around and you've got this privileged position that nobody outside of this family ever sees. You see the dynamics, the interactions between people," says Leo. "You get to help them to make decisions and they look to you for guidance and there's a feeling of value within that. You get a eureka moment at the end of it and you start to see a plan to help people out of things. Suddenly they're not stuck anymore."

It takes a special kind of person to help families in this way. As a social worker for children and families you are an advisor, an advocate, a counsellor and a listener. We need bright and committed people from a wide range of backgrounds to join the profession, people who can demonstrate understanding while being highly analytical and good at problem solving.

advertisement feature

Laura Bleaney wanted to make practical use of the analytical skills she picked up whilst undertaking her history degree at Kings College, Cambridge. After a few years working, she  returned to university to study a Masters in social work. "When I graduated I worked in international development, but after spending two years there I realised I wanted to work more directly with children and families in a hands-on way," says Laura, who now works as a front-line children's social worker for Hackney Council in London. "As a social worker, every day throws up a different challenge and the breadth of the job means there are so many ways to help protect vulnerable children. There are also opportunities for me to progress within my department and on to management if I want, which means there are several long term possibilities for me to explore."

As well as offering clear career progression and being personally satisfying, social work is also financially rewarding. As a newly qualified social worker you can expect to start on a salary of approximately £18,000 (more in London), increasing to around £30,000 as your career progresses and you gain more experience and responsibility.

It is also a diverse career. Social workers can be employed by a local authority or work for a charity such as the NSPCC or for an independent organisation such as a fostering agency. The role is varied and could range from working in children's homes or managing adoption and foster care processes, through to helping children who have problems at school or are facing difficulties brought on by illness in the family.

Social workers are highly qualified professionals and it takes the right training to help you get there. Every social worker needs to hold a professional qualification in social work; either a three-year degree or a two-year Masters. There are several initiatives to support those wanting to make social work their career.

advertisement feature

If you're a social work graduate about to enter your first role, there is the opportunity to participate in the Newly Qualified Social Worker (NQSW) pilot programme. This provides a structured and managed induction year with reduced caseload and guaranteed employer support and supervision.

Ngozi Palmer is a deputy team manager who oversees four social workers. She has some words of advice for people coming into the profession: "You need emotional intelligence; to be able to empathise and respond appropriately, and you need to be resilient. But it's also stimulating and exciting - genuinely no two days are the same. Building relationships and gaining the trust of vulnerable children takes a lot of skill and patience; but when it finally does happen, it's one of the most rewarding moments there is to experience."

If you believe you can be the difference in a child's life, social work with children and families is for you. To learn more please search online for 'Be the difference' or call 0300 123 1220.

The Children's Workforce Development Council leads change so that the thousands of people working with children and young people across England are able to do the best job they possibly can.

CWDC has launched a national marketing campaign to attract, recruit and retain high calibre social workers to work in social work with children, young people and families.

To learn more about how you can *Be the difference* in a child's life, please search 'Be the Difference' or call 0300 123 1220.

advertisement feature

# Care home managers

Care home managers manage care homes that are registered to provide care. The majority of homes provide care for elderly people who are too unwell or too frail to continue living in their own homes. There are also care homes for adults with learning and physical disabilities. The majority of care homes are in the independent (private) sector, but some are run by local authorities, and many are run by not-for-profit organisations. Care home managers are responsible for all the day-to-day running of the home – everything from seeing that appropriate nursing care is delivered to ensuring that catering and laundry services run well. Care home managers also look at ways to make care more effective, for example introducing programmes of activities that could help people with dementia to enjoy a better quality of life. Managers also have to respond to complaints and concerns raised by residents, or their relatives. They also have to ensure that the home complies with all appropriate legislation and standards. They also have to be business managers – homes are businesses and have to be financially viable – so it is the manager's job to ensure that rooms are occupied and that the home is well marketed and builds links with its local community.

## Qualifications and Training

This work has become increasingly professionalised in recent years and there are national minimum standards set for qualifications for care home managers. Most care home managers move into this work as a second career. They have either come from a background in nursing or other areas of health care, or else they have backgrounds in businesses such as hospitality. Care home managers need to have a relevant degree, healthcare or business qualification. In all cases they should be qualified to NVQ level 4. Exact requirements depend on the type of clients and the level of care a home is registered to provide, eg, nursing as well as general daily care. You will have to undergo a Criminal Records Bureau (CRB) check to enter this profession.

## Personal Qualities and Skills

You need a wide range of skills, though the balance of these depends on the size and type of home you manage. You need to be caring and compassionate. You also need to be a good team leader and able to motivate staff. You need good business skills, be able to handle budgets and market the home. You need excellent communication skills, be able to listen sympathetically to a resident and to deal effectively with other healthcare professionals, the media or the wider community.

## Salaries

Salaries depend not only on your level of experience, but on the size and type of home you manage and whether your employer is in the independent, public or not-for-profit sector. Generally salaries start at between £20,000 and £30,000, but can reach £40,000 if you work for one of the larger care provider organisations.

Care Quality Commission; www.cqc.org.uk/

Skills for Care, Albion Court, 5 Albion Place, Leeds LS1 6JL; 0113 245 1716; www.skillsforcare.org.uk

info

# Social work assistant

Social work assistants are part of the social work team. They support qualified social workers who are involved in helping and advising many different clients in the community, in day care establishments, residential homes, hospitals, schools and their own homes. The work can be varied but might include making contact with clients, booking appointments and following up on enquiries, making routine visits to people to monitor situations, advising clients on what services and resources could be available to them, and conducting routine interviews. A key part of the role is to refer situations to qualified social workers if you have any concerns about a client you have spoken to or visited. Your work is also likely to involve keeping records, attending meetings and updating yourself on changes in social care legislation.

## Qualifications and Training

While you don't necessarily need formal academic qualifications, many employers expect you to have two or three GCSEs grades A–C. What is most important to employers is whether you have had experience of working with vulnerable people. You may find your application is strengthened by doing some voluntary work. There are also several full- and part-time BTEC certificate and diploma courses in health and social care. These normally include work placements, so this could also be a way of strengthening your application. You will have to pass a Criminal Records Bureau (CRB) check to do this type of work. Once you have started work, your employer has to provide induction training to approved national standards, and you may also be able to study part-time for further qualifications such as a foundation degree in health and social care.

## Personal Qualities and Skills

You need excellent communication skills, to be able to listen to and explain things to people who may be coping with high levels of stress. You have to be highly observant, too. You must be calm in tense situations and while you have to take responsibility, you must be very clear about when to refer a situation to other professionals. You must be well organised, a good administrator and excellent at working as part of a team.

## Salaries

Starting salaries are between £16,000 and £17,000, more in London. With experience and if you take further qualifications you can earn £18,000 to £23,000.

# Social worker

Social workers are qualified professionals who work in the same settings as social work assistants – a service user's home, schools, hospitals, day centres, residential homes, and specialist units such as drug dependency centres. They work within a framework of relevant legislation and increasingly they work as part of multidisciplinary teams with healthcare workers. Each social worker has an allocated caseload to deal with. More than half of qualified social workers work with children and young people. This can include working with young offenders, pupils who have poor school attendance records, or children whose families are in a crisis of some kind. Much of a social worker's job is to carry out assessments of any service user's situation to see what kind of support they might need, or whether some intervention is required. Can an elderly person continue to cope living in his or her own home, or might they be better off in a residential home? Is it appropriate to leave a child with its family, or should he or she be placed in care? What treatment programme might help an adult with mental health problems to cope more easily with daily life? These are just a few examples of the kinds of questions that social workers tackle. They have to attend meetings, prepare reports, conduct interviews, monitor progress and review cases on a regular basis. The majority of social workers are employed by local authorities, but some voluntary and not-for-profit organisations employ their own social workers. Senior social workers are also involved in the purchasing of care packages, the training of staff and the development of strategy.

## Qualifications and Training

To qualify as a social worker in England you need either a three-year undergraduate or a two-year postgraduate qualification in social work accredited by the General Social Care Council (GSCC). To do an undergraduate degree you normally require three GCSEs and two A levels. It is worth checking with individual course providers because some will accept you without this if you have alternative qualifications or substantial relevant work experience. If you already have a degree then you can apply for a two-year postgraduate Master's course in social work. In all cases your course combines academic study with periods of work placement. If you are interested in social work with children, families and young people, some new initiatives are being developed – a pilot Graduate Recruitment Scheme, aiming to attract high-achieving graduates onto postgraduate social work courses and a new employment-based training programme for graduates are starting in 2011.

Once qualified, social workers must register with the GSCC and they must re-register after three years, during which time they must continue learning and professional development. The GSCC has developed three post-qualifying awards towards which social workers can work. These are certificates in specialist and advanced social work. There are five possible areas of study that link into these awards, focusing on mental health, adult social care, children, young people and their families, education practice and management and leadership.

## Personal Qualities and Skills

Social workers must be patient, understanding and able to empathise with people. They must also have the emotional resilience to cope with distressing situations and clients who are angry, upset or frightened. They must be able to keep calm and assertive when taking decisions that service users may strongly disagree with. They have to be able to take difficult decisions and be responsible for these decisions. Social workers must be able to work alone, but also as part of a social and healthcare team. They must be good organisers and able to manage a demanding caseload.

## Salaries

On qualifying salaries are between £18,000 and £25,000. Once you have had a few years' experience salaries range from £26,000 to £40,000.

General Social Care Council, 2 Hay's Lane, London SE1 2HB; 020 7397 5800; Registration helpline: 0845 070 0630; www.gscc.org.uk

Skills for Care (England), Albion Court, 5 Albion Place, Leeds LS1 6JL; 0113 245 1716; www.skillsforcare.org.uk

Care Council for Wales (CCW); www.ccwales.org.uk

Northern Ireland Social Care Council (NISCC); www.niscc.info

Scottish Social Services Council (SSSC); www.sssc.uk.com

Social Work and Care Careers; 0300 123 1100; www.socialworkandcare.co.uk

NHS Business Services, Social Work Bursary; 0845 610 1122; www.nhsbsa.nhs.uk/Students

# SPORT

While relatively few earn a significant living from being a professional sportsperson, there are many other occupations within the sports sector.

# Coach

Coaches help individuals and teams identify areas for improvement in physical fitness levels and for specific sports skills. They also plan and implement training programmes in a wide variety of sports provided by sports centres, clubs, schools, hotels and swimming baths.

Much coaching is done on a voluntary basis; however, there are opportunities for paid work, and many coaches work in a self-employed capacity. Some local authorities employ coaches to offer facilities for local schools at one or more centres in the authority. Such coaches are expected to be able to coach in most of the following sports: badminton, basketball, climbing (on indoor walls), ice skating, squash, swimming, tennis, trampolining and weight training. Increasingly, there is a need for coaches in the summer months to work in outdoor activity centres.

## Qualifications and Training

Formal academic qualifications are not necessary in order for you to become a coach. You need to check the qualifying route with the national governing body for your chosen sport. They will all have their own approved coaching schemes. These vary in length and some are full-time, some part-time, while others can be done via distance learning. The key to qualifying for any of these is to have demonstrable skill in your chosen sport and be able to show you have the ability to teach others. There are several degrees available in sports science or sport and exercise. While a degree is not necessary to become a coach, these courses may provide useful background on the psychology of performance. Some of them also offer the opportunity to work towards coaching qualifications in conjunction with studying the academic programme. The various sporting governing bodies have designed qualifications equivalent to NVQs levels 1 to 4. You cannot become an assistant coach until you are aged 16, but beginning as soon as you are able to do so, in the sixth form, for example, can be very beneficial.

## Personal Qualities and Skills

In addition to a passion for, and understanding of your own sport, you must have excellent communication skills. You must be able to motivate an individual or help a group of players function effectively as a team. You have to be physically fit yourself and aware of the rules and regulations governing your sport. You need lots of enthusiasm, but you must be sensitive enough to work with people of different abilities.

**info**

Department for Culture, Media and Sport (DCMS), 2–4 Cockspur Street, London SW1Y 5DH; 020 7211 6200; www.culture.gov.uk

English Federation of Disability Sport (EFDS)

SkillsActive – The Sector Skills Council for Active Leisure and Learning, Castlewood House, 77–91 New Oxford Street, London WC1A 1PX; 020 7632 2000; www.skillsactive.com

Sport England, 3rd Floor, Victoria House, Bloomsbury Square, London WC1B 4SE; 020 7273 1551; www.sportengland.org

Sport Northern Ireland, House of Sport, Upper Malone Road, Belfast BT9 5LA; 028 90 381222; www.sportni.net

Sports Coach UK, 114 Cardigan Road, Headingley, Leeds LS6 3BJ; 0113 274 4802; www.sportscoachuk. org

Sport Scotland, Caledonia House, South Gyle, Edinburgh EH12 9DQ; 0131 317 7200; www.sportscotland. org.uk

Sports Council for Wales, Sophia Gardens, Cardiff CF11 9SW; 0845 045 0904; www.sports-council-wales.org.uk

UK Sport, 40 Bernard Street, London WC1N 1ST; 020 7211 5100; www.uksport.gov.uk

## Salaries

Many coaches work part-time and earn £10 to £12 an hour. Full-time work at a basic level pays around £15,000 to £16,000 a year. Senior and experienced coaches may earn £25,000 to £35,000. In professional sport, coaches working with national teams or individuals may earn considerably more than this. They may also be paid bonuses for success in competitions or prizes won.

# Physiotherapist

*see* Physiotherapy

# Teacher

*see* Teaching

# Sportsperson

There are opportunities in sport for professional sportspeople and for careers in coaching. Not all sports allow players to be professionals, and there are some, such as snooker, where there is room for only a very few professionals. Sports attracting professionals in relatively large numbers are football, cricket, golf, horse racing, rugby (league and union) and tennis.

Sportspeople's careers are generally short, but if, during their careers, they have made a name for themselves, there may be opportunities in journalism, broadcasting or consultancy.

## Qualifications and Training

Professional sportspeople naturally need to be excellent at their sport. Those in team games generally begin by playing for their school, town or county side. In this context, a young player may be noticed by professional selectors. In the case of football, it is not necessary to join a local football league club; apprentices are taken on from all over the country. Because a club apprentice has no guarantee that he will ever play for the first side, some clubs allow apprentices time off to obtain academic qualifications.

## Personal Qualities and Skills

As well as talent, professional sportspeople must possess dedication, perseverance, commitment and be highly competitive.

## Salaries

Salaries for professionals are often low initially, but the rewards for top performers may be very high. The amount of money earned varies enormously depending upon the sport. Coaches' salaries vary according to whether the work is full- or part-time, what type of work they are doing and the number of hours.

**info**

SkillsActive, Castlewood House, 77–91 New Oxford Street, London WC1A 1PX; 020 7632 2000; www. skillsactive.com

Sport England, 3rd Floor, Victoria House, Bloomsbury Square, London WC1B 4SE; 0845 850 8508; www.sportengland.org

Sport Scotland, Caledonia House, South Gyle, Edinburgh EH12 9DQ; 0131 317 7200; www.sportscotland. org.uk

Sports Council for Northern Ireland, House of Sport, Upper Malone Road, Belfast BT9 5LA; 028 9038 1222; www.sportni.net/

Sports Council for Wales, The National Sports Centre, Sophia Gardens, Cardiff CF1 9SW; 029 2030 0500; www.sports-council-wales.co.uk

## SPORTS AND RECREATION FACILITY MANAGEMENT

Sports and recreation facility managers are responsible for the efficient running of leisure centres, swimming pools, sports halls and associated facilities. Managers usually start their career as a recreation assistant and progress through supervisory and assistant manager positions via on-the-job training and professional development.

### Qualifications and Training

There are two routes into this career. You can either start as a junior or management trainee and work for professional qualifications, or you can do a BTEC qualification, foundation degree or degree course. The Institute of Sport and Recreation Management (ISRM) and the Institute of Leisure and Amenity Management (ILAM) run relevant certificate and diploma courses that can be studied on a part-time basis. There is also a wide choice of BTEC, foundation degree and degree courses available in sports and leisure management, leisure studies, sports science and recreation management. Whether you work your way up or join as a graduate trainee, there is a lot of on-the-job training.

### Personal Qualities and Skills

You need excellent interpersonal skills, to be able to motivate staff and to work well with members of the public. You must be well organised, energetic and able to take responsibility.

## Salaries

Trainee and assistant managers earn between £14,000 and £17,000. Newly qualified managers earn between £18,000 and £25,000. An experienced manager of a large facility can earn more than £35,000.

SkillsActive, Castlewood House, 77–91 New Oxford Street, London WC1A 1PX; 0800 093 3300; www.skillsactive.com

Institute of Sport and Recreation Management (ISRM), Sir John Beckwith Centre for Sport, Loughborough University, Loughborough, Leics LE11 3TU; 01509 226474; www.isrm.co.uk

Institute of Leisure and Amenity Management (ILAM), ILAM House, Lower Basildon, Reading, Berks RG8 9NE; 01491 874800; www.ilam.co.uk

**info**

# Swimming pool attendant/lifeguard

Swimming pool attendants and lifeguards work at swimming pools in hotels with leisure facilities, private sports clubs, public swimming pools and local authority leisure centres. Their key responsibility is to ensure the safety of everyone in the pool, watching to make sure no one is getting into difficulty and rescuing and providing first aid to anyone who needs assistance. They also make sure that people are behaving safely and sensibly in the pool. This is very much the lifeguard side of the work. Some swimming pool attendants are also responsible for monitoring the water quality in the pool and checking for levels of chemicals or bacteria. At some facilities, pool attendants may also supervise dry activities such as a gym and fitness suite.

Lifeguards also work as teachers, ensuring that people adhere to safe bathing areas and other rules, monitoring the water for incidents, taking part in rescues, giving first aid and liaising with other authorities such as the police or local coastguard.

## Qualifications and training

Formal academic qualifications are not essential for this work. To be a swimming pool attendant or lifeguard you must be aged 16 and to work as a beach lifeguard you must be aged 18. In both cases you must be physically fit and be a good swimmer. To work at a swimming pool you have to have one of the Royal Lifesaving Society (RLSS) lifesaving qualifications – see their website for details. They also offer national qualifications for beach lifeguarding work. All qualifications have to be reviewed every two years, when you must have both your swimming and your first aid skills checked. Local swimming pools and swimming clubs can provide a lot of helpful information on qualifying.

## Personal Qualities and Skills

Apart from your swimming skills, you must have excellent 'people' skills, be friendly and approachable but also calm, confident and authoritative at times. You should be very observant and good at making quick and very important judgements.

## Salaries

Salaries are around £12,000 to £14,000 a year, but in fact many lifeguards and pool attendants work part-time and are paid an hourly rate. Full-time work is more common in large leisure centres, where pool attendants have a wider range of responsibilities and duties.

**info**

SkillsActive, Castlewood House, 77–91 New Oxford Street, London WC1A 1PX; Advice line: 08000 933300; www.skillsactive.com

Swimming Teachers Association (STA), Anchor House, Birch Street, Walsall, West Midlands WS2 8HZ; 01922 645097; www.sta.co.uk

Royal National Lifeboat Institute (RNLI), West Quay Road, Poole, Dorset BH15 1HZ; 01202 663553; www.rnli.org.uk/lifeguards

Surf Life Saving Association of Great Britain (SLSA GB), 1st Floor, 19 Southernhay West, Exeter EX1 1PJ; 01392 218007; www.surflifesaving.org.uk

Lifesavers, The Royal Lifesaving Society UK (RLSS), River House, High Street, Broom, Warwickshire B50 4HN; 01789 773994; www.lifesavers.org.uk

# STATISTICIAN

Statisticians design experiments and surveys. They analyse the results of these and use their findings in many different ways. They work for all kinds of organisations, from central and local government, local authorities and the NHS to private industry and commerce in many sectors. Their work varies according to the sector in which they work, but it can include designing experiments to monitor the effectiveness of a new drug, measuring trends in air pollution, predicting the performance of pension plans, or analysing the results of consumer surveys for predicting the future demand for particular products and services. Their work can be concerned with scientific, psychological, social or commercial issues and questions.

## Qualifications and Training

For most trainee positions you need a good honours degree in a highly numerate discipline, eg maths or economics. If you are working in medical statistics you will probably need a degree or postgraduate qualification in medical or life science. The Civil Service offers a range of training schemes for statisticians with a good honours degree in a numerate subject. Some employers consider applicants with a degree in social science and psychology, particularly if that degree has covered statistical methods in some detail and if work is going to be linked to these specific areas. Training is on the job, though many statisticians work for postgraduate qualifications on a part-time basis.

## Personal Qualities and Skills

In addition to having proven ability with numerical and scientific data, statisticians have to be creative thinkers, good problem solvers and excellent communicators. As a statistician you often need to report your findings and analysis in clear, everyday language to non-mathematical colleagues or clients. You also have to be a good team worker.

## Salaries

Salaries for trainees are between £18,000 and £30,000. With a few years' experience salaries rise to £30,000 to £53,000. In general, business and industry pay higher salaries than central and local government and science and medicine.

Association of Clinical Data Management, 105 St Peter's Street, St Albans, Herts AL1 3EJ; 01727 896080 www.acdm.org.uk

Higher Education Statistics Agency (HESA), 95 Promenade, Cheltenham GL50 1HZ; 01242 255577; www.hesa. ac.uk

Institute of Clinical Research (ICR), Institute House, Boston Drive, Bourne End, Buckinghamshire SL8 5YS; 0845 521 0056; www.icr global.org

Medical Research Council (MRC), 20 Park Crescent, London W1B 1AL; 020 7636 5422; www.mrc.ac.uk

Medicines and Healthcare Products Regulatory Agency (MHRA), 10–12 Market Towers, 1 Nine Elms Lane, London SW8 5NQ; 020 7084 2000; www.mhra.gov.uk

Royal Statistical Society (RSS), 12 Errol Street, London EC1Y 8LX; 020 7638 8998; www.rss.org.uk

Scottish Executive, St Andrew's House, Regent Road, Edinburgh EH1 3DG; 0131 556 8400; www. scotland.gov.uk

Statisticians in the Pharmaceutical Industry (PSI), PSI Executive Office, Resources for Business, Association House, South Park Road, Macclesfield SK11 6SH; 01625 267882; www.psiweb.org

# SURVEYING

Surveying covers a wide variety of work within one profession, and a number of professional bodies offer qualifications in the different areas (see below). There are also technician qualifications. Surveying technicians work in all the same fields as surveyors but without being professionally qualified.

## Aerial surveying

A specialisation of land surveying (see below), aerial surveying involves photogrammetry – the use of aerial photographs as a basis for calculations. Qualifications are offered by the Architecture and Surveying Institute (ASI) and the Institute of Civil Engineering Surveyors.

## Archaeological surveying

This relatively new specialisation involves working on an archaeological dig, making plans, maps and cross-sections of the excavations. It requires the skill of a cartographer as well as that of a land surveyor. The Architects' and Surveyors' Institute (ASI) has members in this discipline.

## Building surveying

The structural surveying of properties and reporting on their condition and valuation is carried out by building surveyors/building engineers. They advise on necessary repairs and maintenance, and prepare plans and specifications for alterations and improvements. Local and central government employ a large proportion of qualified building surveyors, although many are in private practice. Qualifications in this area are available from the Association of Building Engineers (ABE), the ASI and the Royal Institution of Chartered Surveyors (RICS).

## General practice

This includes auctioneering, estate agency, valuation and estate management. People working in this area are responsible for the selling or letting, surveying, valuation and management of both urban and rural property. Qualifications in general practice are offered by the ABE, the ASI and the RICS.

## Hydrographic surveying

The hydrographer surveys and charts underwater areas, such as ports and harbours and offshore areas where drilling for oil takes place. Hydrographic surveying qualifications are offered by the ASI and the RICS.

## Land surveying

The land surveyor measures and charts the earth's physical features so that maps can be drawn. The scale of the work can range from a one-house building site to a whole region of Africa, and there are opportunities in public services (the Ordnance Survey and the Ministry of Defence, for example), as well as in private practice or large commercial organisations. Qualifications are offered by the ASI and the RICS.

# Minerals surveying

Minerals surveyors assist in the design, development and surveying of quarries and underground mines, ensuring safety for the workers as well as optimum profitability for the company extracting the minerals. They also value mineral workings for rating and taxation, and therefore need to be all-rounders with knowledge of geology, the management of mineral workings, taxation and planning legislation. This area of surveying is unique in having its qualifications and duties laid down by law. Minerals surveyors must hold the surveyor's certificate granted on behalf of the Secretary of State for Industry by the Mining Qualifications Board. They must be at least 21 and have at least four years' practical experience (including 2,000 hours underground) in order to sit the exam for this certificate. Further qualifications are provided by the RICS and the ASI.

# Planning and development surveying

Surveyors specialising in this area work on a range of projects connected with development, redevelopment and regeneration. They oversee projects such as regenerating a rundown housing area, new developments on brownfield sites or the conservation of rural properties. Their work involves looking at the viability of planning proposals, considering different planning options and monitoring developments that are agreed to ensure that they are adhering to the original proposals and plans.

# Quantity surveying

In private practice, quantity surveyors work with an architect to draw up design specifications in line with the client's budget. When the finished design is agreed, the quantity surveyor draws up a bill of quantities, detailing the materials and labour that will be needed. Building contractors work on this bill of quantities in preparing their tender for the job; they will use their own quantity surveyors to estimate their costs. Quantity surveyors also monitor costs as the work progresses and is completed. If they train for this work while employed by construction contractors, they usually take the qualification of the RICS. Professional qualifications are also offered by the ASI.

# Rural practice

This is often combined with land agency, and concerns the use and development of agricultural land. The qualifying bodies in this area are the ASI and the RICS.

## Qualifications and Training

The RICS offers a range of qualifications in the different areas of surveying. Normally entrants need three A levels or equivalent for entry into an RICS-approved degree or diploma course. An alternative is undertaking an HND or HNC in a related surveying discipline, which can give advanced entry to those courses. On successful completion of an RICS-approved degree or diploma, graduates enrol onto the Assessment of Professional Competence (APC), which is two years' practical training while in employment, concluding with an RICS professional assessment interview. Various degree backgrounds are valuable for surveying; one-year full-time and two-year part-time postgraduate conversion courses are available.

Technicians need a relevant HNC/HND or NVQ level 4 followed by the Assessment of Technical Competence. This is two years' RICS structured training while working, which concludes with the RICS technical assessment interview. Those who have gained technical membership of the RICS can take a bridging course to become a Chartered Surveyor.

## Personal Qualities and Skills

Logical and orderly thinking, ability in figure work and detailed drawings are called for in this precision work. Communication skills and business acumen are essential. Good oral and written English is an asset, and some areas may require specialised mathematical ability.

## Salaries

Newly qualified surveyors earn between £21,000 and £26,000. Experienced surveyors earn between £27,000 and £43,000. Senior chartered surveyors working for large companies can earn more than £50,000. Some surveying work, especially general practice, building or quantity surveying, is sensitive to the general economic climate. Salaries may not rise so fast when the property market is sluggish.

**info**

Asset Skills, 2 The Courtyard, 48 New North Road, Exeter, Devon EX4 4 4EP; 01392 423399; www.assetskills.org

College of Estate Management, Whiteknights, Reading, Berkshire RG6 6AW; 0800 019 9697; www.cem.ac.uk

Chartered Institute of Building, Englemere, Kings Ride, Ascot, Berkshire SL5 7TB; 01344 630700; www.ciob.org.uk

Royal Institution of Chartered Surveyors (RICS), Surveyor Court, Westwood Way, Coventry CV4 8JE; 0870 333 1600; www.rics.org

Royal Institution of Chartered Surveyors (RICS) Wales, 7 St Andrews Place, Cardiff CF10 3BE; 029 2022 4414; www.rics.org

Royal Institution of Chartered Surveyors (RICS) Scotland, 9 Manor Place, Edinburgh EH3 7DN; 0131 225 7078; www.rics.org

Royal Institution of Chartered Surveyors (RICS) Northern Ireland, 9–11 Corporation Square, Belfast BT1 3AJ; 028 9032 2877; www.rics.org.uk

# T

## TAXATION

Those who work in the area of taxation deal with the payment of taxes, which is a source of revenue for public expenditure.

## Tax adviser/technician

Tax advisers/technicians work for private firms or independently, offering assistance to other firms/individuals who need guidance through the complications of the tax laws. A tax adviser is able to advise clients on how to plan and present their taxable income so that they legally pay the least tax possible.

Tax technicians work for firms of accountants or solicitors, in clearing banks and for consultancy firms that offer a complete tax service to their clients. However, the largest area of work involves corporate tax in organisations that have their own tax department to prepare corporate tax and VAT returns on behalf of the company.

### Qualifications and Training

There are two main ways into this profession. If you choose direct entry then you apply to become a taxation trainee with a firm of accountants or the tax department of an industrial or commercial or other large organisation. You can then take the Association of Taxation Technicians (ATT) examination. If you pass this you are eligible to take the Chartered Tax Adviser (CTA) examination and become a member of the Chartered Institute of Taxation. You do not need a degree for direct entry, but some applicants do have degrees in business studies, accountancy or mathematics. Accountancy firms and other employers set their own entry requirement, but you must have good numeracy skills. The alternative route into this profession is to qualify first as an accountant, solicitor or barrister and then apply to take the CTA examination. This route is quite popular with graduates.

### Personal Qualities and Skills

You have to be a logical thinker and a good communicator. You need the ability to translate complex financial information into something that is

# Next Step?

Looking to further your tax knowledge or progress your career in tax?

The ATT has the answer with its new exam structure offering a choice of seven subjects.

Gain a Certificate of Competency or continue to full membership of the leading professional body dealing with UK tax compliance.

**The choice is yours!**

For further details please visit the ATT website at www.att.org.uk or call the Association of Taxation Technicians on 020 7235 2544

The Association of Taxation Technicians

# The Association of Taxation Technicians' Modular, Flexible Qualification

## THE BEGINNINGS

The ATT was created in 1989 to recognise the increasing demand for tax services and the need for a qualification appropriate to individuals working in tax departments. Those needs are even more valid today and the ATT now has over 10,000 members, affiliates and registered students. It offers a formal qualification from a highly-respected body, with a range of associated membership benefits.

## THE PAST

Originally, there were two compulsory tax papers, plus 'hurdle' papers in principles of law and accounting. However, this did not suit all who were providing tax services so the exam was revised in 2007 to make it broader and more flexible.

## THE PRESENT

Now, there are seven free-standing papers that candidates can sit pretty much as and when they want. For each paper passed, you can apply for a certificate of competency in that subject – a strong, formal qualification in its own right. This looks great on the CV, and offers the option, once all criteria are satisfied, to progress to membership of the ATT.

To gain membership of the ATT you need to pass four papers which are:

- personal taxation (paper 1);
- business taxation and accounting principles (paper 2);
- practice administration and ethics (paper 7); and
- one voluntary certificate paper from the following list: business taxation; higher skills; IHT, trusts and estates; VAT; business compliance.

You can sit the papers all at the same time, or at your own pace – you retain the credit for a paper for at least three years. Students use home-study manuals and a range of 'distance learning' resources from various training providers; including practice exams, tuition and revision courses

## ....AND THE FUTURE

The new structure opens the doors to an ATT qualification much wider, making it more accessible, achievable and affordable. For prospective candidates, it is less daunting to acquire a qualification in 'bite sized' chunks. For those funding the qualification themselves, the credit system of the certificates of competence reduce the cost and risk factor associated with the rigid two-paper format. For full details and to download the full ATT prospectus, please visit **www.att.org.uk**

advertisement feature

readily understood by someone without a financial background. You also have to be an imaginative problem solver with good business and commercial awareness.

## Salaries

Newly qualified tax technicians earn between £27,000 and £37,000. During training salaries are between £21,000 and £27,000. Tax advisers with a few years' experience or in senior positions can earn £40,000 to £60,000.

**info**

Association of Taxation Technicians, 12 Upper Belgrave Street; London SW1X 8BB; 020 7235 2544; www.att.org.uk

Chartered Institute of Taxation, 12 Upper Belgrave Street, London SW1X 8BB; 020 7235 9381; www.tax.org.uk

Financial Services Skills Council, 51 Gresham Street, London EC2V 7HQ; 0845 257 3772; www.fssc.org.uk

# Tax inspector

Tax inspectors work for HM Revenue & Customs (HMRC), formed from the merger of the Inland Revenue and HM Customs & Excise departments. It is the government department responsible under the direction of the Treasury for the efficient administration of income tax, tax credits, corporation tax, capital gains tax, petroleum revenue tax, inheritance tax, National Insurance contributions and stamp duties. Inspectors are responsible for the tax affairs of businesses and individuals, ensuring they pay the right amount at the right time, and helping them to obtain their entitlements and meet their obligations. Inspectors detect and deter non-compliance and encourage voluntary compliance by carrying out enquiry work.

## Qualifications and Training

If you wish to join HMRC as a trainee tax inspector you need either a good degree (at least 2.1) in any subject, or a professional accountancy qualification. With either of these you can apply to join HMRC's Tax Professionals Development Programme. Competition for places on this scheme is fierce. If you do not have the appropriate qualifications, you can join HMRC as an administrative assistant (GCSEs grades A–C in maths and English), or an administrative officer (five GCSEs grades A–C). HMRC may be prepared to offer you an administrative job without the appropriate GCSEs if you pass an aptitude test. After some experience you can then apply to join the Tax Professionals Development Programme, which lasts four years and includes on the job training and further examinations.

## Personal Qualities and Skills

You must be very good at analysing large quantities of information and data. You must be a creative problem solver with an open, enquiring mind. Good written and spoken English, numeracy and IT skills are also essential. You must be a good communicator, calm, fair and able to interpret and apply rules.

## Salaries

Graduate trainees on the Tax Professionals Development Programme earn £25,500 with an additional £2,000 for working in London. Having completed the programme, salaries start at £31,000 rising to £44,000 plus with appropriate experience and responsibilities.

HM Revenue & Customs; www.
hmrc.gov.uk

Civil Service Careers;
www.careers.civil-service.gov.uk

Financial Services Skills Council,
51 Gresham Street, London EC2V 7HQ;
020 7216 7366; www.fssc.org.uk

Tax Working; www.taxworking.org.
uk

**info**

# TEACHING

Most formal teaching is done in schools, while lecturing is carried out in universities and other further and higher education establishments.

# Lecturer

### Further education

Lecturers in this field may teach anyone over the age of 16. The range of subjects taught in further education is diverse and growing rapidly. Most lecturers have a particular expertise but are increasingly expected to teach outside their specialist area. They may work on vocational and/or academic courses. In order to meet the demands of their clients, further education colleges offer courses on a full- or part-time basis. These include evening courses and short courses.

### Higher education

Lecturers in universities and other higher education institutions (HEIs) teach mainly undergraduates. As well as teaching, many carry out research, write articles and books, and give outside lectures and broadcasts. Competition is fierce and it is unlikely that a new graduate would be able to enter higher education as a first job.

## Qualifications and Training

Qualifications for those wishing to teach in further education have recently been revised by Lifelong Learning UK, and the new qualifications system replaces all previous qualifications. To start with you must have either A levels or NVQ level 3 qualifications in the subject(s) you want to teach. When you start teaching you have to take a short introductory course – the Aware in Preparing to teach in the Lifelong Learning Sector. After this, you can work part-time towards level 3 and 4 certificate courses or a level 5 diploma. The level 5 diploma confers full teacher status on you. If you plan to teach on vocational courses, relevant experience in that field is also extremely useful.

To lecture in higher education you normally need a degree and often a postgraduate degree related to the subject(s) you wish to teach. Sometimes it is possible to do some part-time teaching, while you are studying for a postgraduate qualification. On more vocational courses it may be possible to lecture without these qualifications if you have plenty of experience in an appropriate area of business or technology. Many higher education (HE) institutions also expect you to study part-time for formal qualifications in HE lecturing. Institutions often provide many in-house courses on management, curriculum development, IT and administration.

## Personal Qualities and Skills

At all levels you need a compelling and communicable interest in the subject you are teaching. You also need an in-depth knowledge of that subject. You need to be able to plan and develop materials and be a well-organised administrator. You need excellent communication skills, and to be confident when delivering a lecture in a large lecture theatre, but equally good working one to one or with small groups of students. If you are working in higher education, you may also need good research skills.

## Salaries

In further education lecturers/teachers are paid between £23,000 and £33,000. Teachers who take on leadership and management roles can earn £40,000 to £50,000 or more. Higher education lecturers on full-time contracts earn between £33,000 and £43,000. Lecturers with considerable management responsibility or other special roles earn £43,000 to £52,000.

**info**

Lifelong Learning, 5th Floor, St Andrew's House, 18–20 St Andrew Street, London EC4A 3AY; Information and Advice Service: 020 7936 5798; www.lluk.org

Higher Education Academy; www.heacademy.ac.uk

Institute for Learning; www.ifl.org.uk

University and College Union (UCU); www.ucu.org.uk

# Teacher

Teachers work in all schools in the state and independent sectors – the state sector is by far the larger. The teacher's role is to help pupils acquire particular knowledge and understanding of a subject. Teachers plan lessons, set and mark assignments, help pupils who are having difficulty and maintain a good working atmosphere in the classroom. Whether teachers cover one or several subjects depends on the age range they train and qualify to teach.

The different options are: nursery or early years, teaching pupils aged three to five; primary, teaching pupils aged 5 to 11; secondary, teaching pupils aged 11 to 18; and special educational needs teaching, working with pupils of all ages who have special needs associated with disability, psychological or behavioural issues.

Other work can include supervising pupils in various activities, attending parents' evenings and other functions, and doing all the administrative work and record keeping associated with pupils' assessments and progress.

## Qualifications and Training

To teach in state schools, you must attain Qualified Teacher Status (QTS) by undertaking a course of Initial Teacher Training (ITT). This is not essential to work in the independent sector, but many schools prefer it. There are several types of ITT, but there are certain criteria which you must meet for all of them. You must have GCSEs grade A–C in English and maths. If you are teaching beyond key stages 2/3 your GCSEs must also include a science at grade A–C. You must pass QTS skills tests in English, maths and information and communications technology (ICT). These tests are computerised and run at more than 40 centres throughout England. In Wales, you do not have to take these. You must have a satisfactory Criminal Records Bureau (CRB) check and some experience of working with children and young people is a great advantage

The first routes to Qualified Teacher Status are to gain a degree in the subject you want to teach at secondary level or in a subject related to the core curriculum at primary level, followed by a Postgraduate Certificate in Education (PGCE). A PGCE can be one year full-time college-based, two years part-time college-based or one year full-time school-based. If you already have some relevant teaching experience there is an option to do a flexible tailor-made PGCE programme by distance learning. The Graduate Teacher Training Registry (GTTR) provides details of courses and an online applications system.

Alternatively, you can do a three- or four-year BEd (Bachelor of Education) or a BA or BSc which awards QTS. Most of these degree courses are for primary teachers, but a few are available at secondary level.

A third method is to undertake a School Centred Initial Teacher Training (SCITT) – these are considered to be at PGCE level. Schools run Graduate Teacher Programmes (GTPs) where graduates work as unqualified teachers while undergoing training. You can find details of course providers on the Training and Development Agency for Schools website. On this website you can also find details of other employer based schemes for people with HNDs, two years of degree level study, or overseas qualifications.

Teach First is a special scheme operating in London and Manchester for graduates with a 2.1 in a curriculum subject who are prepared to work in challenging schools and take part in special leadership training courses.

## Personal Qualities and Skills

Teachers must enjoy working with the age group they teach. They must be excellent communicators, able to motivate and encourage their students. They have to have great self-confidence, be able to handle difficult situations and discuss issues with parents as well as students. They must be able to work under considerable pressure, be well organised administrators and come up with imaginative solutions to problems.

## Salaries

New entrants in England and Wales are paid on a scale ranging from just under £21,000 to just over £30,000. Incremental points are awarded for taking on particular responsibilities or for working in challenging schools. Pay in and around London is a little higher. Rates in Scotland and Northern Ireland are similar to those in England and Wales. Senior teachers are paid on a scale of £30,000 to £49,000.

**info**

Department for Children, Schools and Families (DCSF), Sanctuary Buildings, Great Smith Street, London SW1P 3BT; 0870 000 2288; www.dcsf.gov.uk

General Teaching Council for England (GTC), Whittington House, Alfred Place, London WC1E 7EA; 0870 001 0308; www.gtce.org.uk

The General Teaching Council for Northern Ireland (GTCNI), 4th Floor, Albany House, 73–75 Great Victoria Street, Belfast BT2 7AF; 028 9033 3390; www.gtcni.org.uk

General Teaching Council for Scotland (GTCS), Clerwood House,

96 Clermiston Road, Edinburgh EH12 6UT; 0131 314 6000; www.gtcs.org.uk

General Teaching Council for Wales (GTCW), 4th Floor, Southgate House, Wood Street, Cardiff CF10 1EW; 029 20550350; www.gtcw.org.uk

GTTR (Graduate Teacher Training Registry), Rose Hill, New Barn Lane, Cheltenham, Glos GL52 3LZ; 0871 468 0469; www.gttr.ac.uk

Training and Development Agency for Schools (TDA), 151 Buckingham Palace Road SW1W 9SZ; 020 7023 8000; www.tda.gov.uk

# Teacher – English as a Foreign Language (EFL teacher)

Teaching English to people from all over the world and in many different countries is referred to as Teaching English as a Foreign Language (TEFL) teaching. Adults and children undertake short English language courses for many reasons – to improve business communications, to increase educational opportunities, to prepare for study in the UK or other English-speaking countries, or simply for social and leisure reasons. There are language centres and schools throughout the UK and in many other countries employing TEFL teachers.

## Qualifications and Training

You do not need to be a qualified teacher to train as an EFL teacher. While this work may be open to anyone with a good level of education and an excellent command of English, it is increasingly becoming a graduate entry career. A degree in English, a modern language or education is particularly useful. You then study for an appropriate certificated course; this usually amounts to 100 hours, including teaching practice. Suitable courses include the CELTA (Certificate in English Language Teaching to Adults) run by Cambridge University Examinations and the CertTESOL (Trinity College London Certificate in Teaching English to Speakers of Other Languages). Note that to work in some countries you will need qualified teacher status (see Teacher) and you may also need a work permit.

## Personal Qualities and Skills

You need to be confident, imaginative, lively and highly communicative. You have to be able to work with groups of people of all ages from teenagers upwards and you also have to have the understanding and patience to work with people of different abilities and varying prior levels of knowledge of English. You have to be able to make classes fun and clear and have the organisational skills to plan your workload. You need to be able to maintain order in a classroom, especially if working with excitable teenagers on their first trip abroad.

info

The British Council, Bridgewater House, 58 Whitworth Street, Manchester M1 6BB; 0161 957 7000; www.britishcouncil.org

International Association of Teachers of English as a Foreign Language (IATEFL), Darwin College, University of Kent, Canterbury, Kent CT2 7NY; 01227 824430; www.iatefl.org

League for the Exchange of Commonwealth Teachers (LECT), 7 Lion Yard, Tremadoc Road, Clapham, London SW4 7NQ; 0870 770 2636; www.lect.org.uk

National Association for the Teaching of English and Other Community Languages to Adults (NATECLA), National Centre, South Birmingham College, Room HB110, Hall Green Campus, Cole Bank Road, Hall Green, Birmingham B28 8ES; 0121 688 8121; www.natecla.org.uk

Trinity College London, 89 Albert Embankment, London SE1 7TP; 020 7820 6100; www.trinitycollege.co.uk

University of Cambridge ESOL Exams, 1 Hills Road, Cambridge CB1 2EU; www.cambridge-efl.org

## Salaries

Based on working full-time in the UK salaries are between £14,000 and £19,000 a year. However, many jobs are not full-time – you are often paid an hourly or monthly rate which equates to the figures above. Much of the work is seasonal too. Working abroad there is an enormous range in salaries, but often accommodation is provided in addition to your salary.

# Teaching assistant

Teaching assistants or classroom assistants provide help and support for qualified teachers in the classroom. They can work in any school, but most are employed at primary school level helping younger children with reading, writing and mathematics. They often provide particular support to children with special needs or whose first language is not English. They also help prepare lesson materials.

If a job ad describes the post as 'Learning Support Assistant' rather than a classroom or teaching assistant, the work involves supporting an individual child who has particular special needs, such as a sensory impairment, or a physical or psychological disability.

## Qualifications and Training

At present, this varies from LEA (local education authority) to LEA, though the government does plan to introduce a standard training model. Many LEAs do not ask for any formal qualifications, but some ask for GCSEs in English and mathematics.

## Personal Qualities and Skills

Teaching assistants must be able to build good relationships with children and have a lot of common sense. They should be able to work well as part of a team, and being imaginative and creative is also useful.

## Salaries

Teaching assistants are often paid on an hourly rate and this is sometimes close to the minimum wage, though it can be £6.50 to £8 an hour. A lot of the work is part-time and available only during term time.

# TELECOMMUNICATIONS

(*see* Communications Engineering)

# THEATRE

(*see also* Performing Arts for Actor, Dancing, Musician and Singer; *see* Film and Television Production for Lighting, Make-up and hairdressing)

Many jobs such as director, producer, lighting technician, prop maker, make-up artist and wardrobe manager are common to television, film and in some instances (for example, sound technician) radio as well as theatre. There are also jobs in administration, front of house, taking bookings and selling programmes. There are jobs in marketing, advertising a theatre's activities or looking for sponsorship. There are practical opportunities such as carpentry. There are, however, some jobs that are specific to live theatre.

# Actor

(*see* Performing Arts)

# Stage hand

Stage hands, also referred to as stage technicians or crew, play an essential role behind the scenes, helping to ensure that props, scenery and special effects are exactly where they should be at just the right moment. Daily tasks vary, but can include helping carpenters to build, erect and paint scenery; moving scenery and furniture during a performance, either manually or with automated equipment; opening and closing stage curtains; and clearing and tidying the stage, studio or back-stage area after a performance. Stage hands also have to attend rehearsals to become familiar with a performance, so that they know exactly what they have to do and can time it perfectly.

## Qualifications and Training

You do not need formal qualifications – practical experience is more important. Many stage hands start as casual workers helping with large productions before they are able to get full-time work. Having experience of back-stage work through school, college, university or other amateur dramatics is extremely helpful. Having practical woodwork skills can also give you a good start. It is often worth approaching local theatre stage managers direct to see if they can offer you casual work. After this, training is very much on the job.

## Personal Qualities and Skills

You must be physically fit and happy to work at evenings and weekends. You must be able to maintain a good level of concentration, and work quickly, quietly and calmly during a performance. You should have a real interest in theatre and you must be able to work as part of a team.

## Salaries

Full-time stage hands earn between £11,000 and £15,000, but there is not always full-time work available. Experienced theatre technicians with large companies can earn up to £20,000.

# Stage manager

Stage managers are responsible for ensuring that all the technical and practical sides of rehearsals and live performances run smoothly. The stage manager is in charge of all stage hands and technicians and he or she has to ensure that everyone, including the performers, is in the right place at the right time. Typical activities for a stage manager include organising rehearsals, managing the props budget and the props themselves. Liaising with other departments, eg, lighting, set designers and wardrobe, cueing performers to go on stage, cueing sound and lighting staff, working closely with front of house staff and keeping the 'prompt copy' of the script (which details the performers' positions on stage, script changes, and the props, lighting and sound needed for each scene).

## Qualifications and Training

Most new entrants to stage management have degrees or professional diplomas in stage management and technical theatre. You can take a degree or diploma in this subject at drama school. Alternatively, you could take a degree in drama, stage management or practical theatre at a college or university. Some people who have worked as actors move into the stage management side of the profession. It is also possible to work your way up from a behind the scenes job such as a stage hand, but this route is becoming increasingly difficult. Practical experience is as important as formal qualifications. You must have had some experience of stage management through amateur dramatics, school, college, or university drama groups.

## Personal Qualities and Skills

You must be an excellent communicator with outstanding organisational skills. You should be able to liaise with people at every level in theatre. You need to be calm, quick at solving problems, able to take responsibility, good at motivating or pacifying others and easily able to think about several different things at once – a true multi-tasker.

## Salaries

Salaries for assistant stage managers are from £16,000 to £24,000. Stage managers earn £21,000 to £40,000 or more. High salaries are few and far between because theatres often work on very tight budgets.

**info**

National Council for Drama Training (NCDT), 1–7 Woburn Walk, London WC1H 0JJ; 020 7387 3650; www.ncdt.co.uk

Stage Management Association, 55 Farringdon Road, London EC1M 3JB; 020 7242 9250; www.stagemanagementassociation. co.uk

Creative and Cultural Skills, Lafone House, The Leathermarket, Weston

Street, London SE1 3HN; www.creative-choices.co.uk

Equity, Guild House, Upper St Martin's Lane, London WC2H 9EG; 020 7379 6000; www.equity.org.uk

Association of British Theatre Technicians, 55 Farringdon Road, London EC1M 3JB; 020 7242 9200; www.abtt.co.uk

# THERAPY

There are many different therapists working in the NHS and the independent healthcare sector. They are referred to as 'Allied health professionals' and form part of the healthcare team. The range they cover includes many art-based therapies, such as art, music and drama, but also covers occupational and speech and language therapy. The salaries for all these professionals are very similar, so refer to the 'Salaries' section under 'Speech and language therapy' for information.

# Art therapy

Art therapy is used as a treatment for psychological and emotional disorders. Drawing, painting, modelling and sculpture are among the creative activities employed. Art therapy is a State Registered profession. All training courses need to be approved by the Council for Professions Supplementary to Medicine (CPSM) and the British Association of Art Therapists. Details are on the Health Professionals Council website.

Most art therapists work in hospitals, some in special schools and child guidance clinics, and some in prisons, detention centres and community homes. As posts are often part-time, therapists usually work for more than one institution within an area.

### Qualifications and Training

You normally need a degree in art and design to be eligible to do a postgraduate diploma or Master's in art therapy approved by the British Association of Art Therapists. If you have a degree in psychology or social work, you may be accepted onto one of these postgraduate diplomas. Courses last two years full-time or three years part-time, and once you have completed the course you must register with the Health Professionals Council (HPC) if you wish to work for the NHS or in social services.

## Personal Qualities and Skills

A real ability to communicate and to encourage others to do so has to be combined with imaginative, artistic and creative ability. Your clients may be distressed, confused and anxious and you have to be patient, sensitive and calm. You need to be good at working as part of a team and capable of managing your workload effectively.

**info**

British Association of Art Therapists (BAAT), 24–27 White Lion Street, London N1 9PD; 020 7686 4216; www.baat.org

Health Professionals Council (HPC), Park House, 184 Kennington Park Road, London SE11 4BU; 020 7582 0866; www.hpc-uk.org

NHS Careers, PO Box 376, Bristol BS99 3EY; 0845 606 0655; www.nhscareers.nhs.uk

# Dance/movement therapy

This form of therapy uses movement and dance as a medium through which the individual can engage creatively in a process of growth and personal integration. Dance movement therapists work with individuals and groups in health, education and social service settings. Their clients include people who are emotionally disturbed or have learning difficulties, and those who want to use this therapy for personal growth.

## Qualifications and Training

A postgraduate qualification in dance movement therapy is required. The University of Roehampton and Goldsmiths College both offer this qualification.

## Personal Qualities and Skills

A good understanding of dance and movement and communication skills are needed, as is an understanding of the clinical environment.

**info**

Association of Dance and Movement Therapists (ADMT), 32 Meadfoot Lane, Torquay TQ1 2BW; www.admt.org.uk

Health Professionals Council (HPC), Park House, 184 Kennington Park Road, London SE11 4BU; 020 7582 0866; www.hpc-uk.org

# Drama therapy

Drama therapists work with people of all ages who are experiencing emotional or psychological problems, especially in communicating and understanding their own feelings. Drama therapists help people to express their feelings through role play and other drama-based exercises. They encourage clients to be creative and to use their imaginations. Drama therapists work closely with psychologists, social workers and other members of the social and healthcare team.

## Qualifications and Training

Drama therapists must be graduates with a degree in drama or theatre studies. Occasionally people with degrees in psychology or social work experience are also able to enter this profession. The main qualification is a postgraduate diploma or Master's course approved by the British Association of Drama Therapists (BADth). Having completed this diploma, if you wish to work in the NHS or for social services you must register with the Health Professionals Council.

## Personal Qualities and Skills

Excellent interpersonal skills are essential. You must be sensitive, understanding and yet positive, encouraging and confident. The clients you work with have probably experienced great difficulty or very stressful situations, so they will require a lot of patience. You must be imaginative and creative. You should work well as part of a team, but be able to take responsibility for your own caseload.

British Association of Drama Therapists (BADth), 41 Broomhouse Lane, London SW6 3DP; 020 7731 0160; www.badth.org.uk

Health Professionals Council (HPC), Park House,184 Kennington Park Road, London SE11 4BU; 020 7582 0866; www.hpc-uk.org

NHS Careers, PO Box 376, Bristol BS99 3EY; 0845 606 0655; www.nhscareers.nhs.uk

# Music therapy

Music therapy is an interactive, primarily non-verbal intervention. It provides a process through which clients can express themselves, become aware of their feelings and interact more easily. The therapist uses live, improvised music to draw the client into an interactive musical relationship. Therapists work with people of all ages, in a wide variety of settings, including special schools, psychiatric hospitals, hospices and day centres. Music therapy is used in many clinical areas, including communication disorders, developmental delay, learning disabilities, mental health problems, physical difficulties, emotional problems, challenging behaviour and terminal illness.

## Qualifications and Training

Music therapy is a State Registered profession and the Council for Professions Supplementary to Medicine recommends that postgraduate students should be at least 23 years old. The training is a postgraduate diploma course lasting between one and two years. Some courses offer a part-time option. Before training as a music therapist, students need to have completed a three-year musical training leading to a diploma or degree. People from related disciplines, such as psychology or education, may also sometimes be accepted onto a training course if they have sufficient practical musical skills.

## Personal Qualities and Skills

Music therapists need to be highly skilled musicians, and be able to use music creatively. Therapists also need to develop an understanding of their own reactions and responses. For this reason, student therapists are required to have their own personal therapy during training. Training courses generally prefer students to be over 25 when they begin training.

**info**

Association of Professional Music Therapists (APMT), 61 Church Hill Road, East Barnet, Hertfordshire EN4 8SY; 020 8440 4153; www.apmt.org

Health Professionals Council (HPC), Park House, 184 Kennington Park Road, London SE11 4BU; 020 7582 0866; www.hpc-uk.org

NHS Careers, PO Box 376, Bristol BS99 3EY; 0845 606 0655; www. nhscareers.nhs.uk

# Occupational therapy

Occupational therapists work with people who have physical, mental or social problems, either from birth or as the result of accident, illness or ageing. Their aim is to enable people to achieve as much as they can for themselves. They start with a thorough assessment of each client and his or her lifestyle, in order to establish what the person wants to achieve. Treatment can involve adapting living and working environments, teaching coping strategies and discovering the most beneficial therapeutic activities.

Although occupational therapists often work as part of a team, they have more autonomy than other healthcare workers in the way they apply their knowledge and expertise. They work in hospitals, social service departments, individuals' homes, residential and nursing homes, schools, universities, charities and prisons. They may also work in private practice.

Employment and promotional opportunities are excellent and all UK-educated occupational therapists receive a qualification that is recognised by the World Federation of Occupational Therapists, giving them opportunities to work abroad.

## Qualifications and Training

Entry to the profession is normally on completion of a full- or part-time degree in occupational therapy. Most courses require three A levels or equivalent; mature students will be considered without these academic requirements. Accelerated two-year full-time courses are also available to graduates of other disciplines. Part-time in-service programmes are also available for those employed as occupational therapy support workers or technical instructors. Some part-time courses can be studied irrespective of employment status. Although courses vary, all include the principles and practice of occupational therapy, behavioural, biological and medical sciences, and periods of clinical practice in a variety of hospital and community settings.

## Personal Qualities and Skills

In addition to academic ability, potential occupational therapists require sensitivity, tolerance, problem-solving skills and the ability to work as part of a team. Reliability, honesty and patience are also important, as well as enthusiasm, dedication and the desire to help and care for others.

British Association of Occupational Therapists, 106–114 Borough High Street, Southwark, London SE1 1LB; 020 7357 6480; www.baot.org.uk

Health Professionals Council (HPC), Park House, 184 Kennington Park Road, London SE11 4BU; 020 7582 0866; www.hpc-uk.org

# Speech and language therapy

Speech and language therapists (SLTs) identify, assess and treat people who have communication and/or swallowing disorders. A large proportion of these will be children but SLTs also help adults who may have communication or swallowing problems caused by disease, accident or psychological trauma. Some SLTs specialise in a particular patient group, for example in the area of severe learning difficulties, hearing impairment or neurological disorders, while others choose more general, broad-based practice. The NHS is the largest employer of SLTs, working in community clinics, hospitals, special schools and homes for the mentally or physically disabled. Some of the larger voluntary organisations also employ SLTs. Often the SLT works closely in a team which may include members of the medical, teaching, therapeutic, psychological and other caring professions.

## Qualifications and Training

Speech and language therapy is a degree-entry profession. Courses leading to professional qualifications are offered at 15 universities and colleges of higher education throughout the UK. There are a number of two-year postgraduate diploma and Master's courses available to candidates with a relevant degree.

Entry qualifications for courses vary from one institution to another, but the minimum is five GCSEs and two A levels or equivalent. A good balance of language and science is expected. Other equivalent qualifications are considered on merit. All courses will consider applications from mature students (over 21), who are encouraged to apply in the normal way.

Students who successfully pass all academic and clinical components of an accredited course are eligible to obtain a certificate to practise and to enter the professional register of the Royal College of Speech and Language Therapists as full professional members.

Opportunities also exist to work as a speech therapist's assistant. An NVQ in care at level 3 is available.

## Personal Qualities and Skills

It is essential that speech therapists themselves should have clear speech and be able to listen actively. In addition, they must have an interest in people as individuals, as well as an enquiring mind, initiative, patience, imagination and a willingness to take responsibility.

## Salaries

In the NHS all the various therapy professionals are paid on the same scale. The differences in pay relate to how long you have worked, your level of experience and your responsibilities rather than to the particular therapy specialism in which you practise. Newly qualified therapists are paid on band 5 of the NHS pay scales, which range from just under £21,000 to a little under £27,000. Senior therapists are paid on band 6, from £25,000 to £33,000. Therapists with more management or other special responsibilities are paid on band 7, from just under £30,000 to £38,000. In the independent healthcare sector salaries for new entrants may be a little higher than those in the NHS, but the gap closes at management level. Working for charitable organizations, as many art therapy professionals do, salaries can be a little lower than in the NHS.

**info**

Royal College of Speech and Language Therapists (RCSLT), 2 White Hart Yard, London SE1 1NX; 020 7378 1200; www.rcslt.org; e-mail: postmaster@rcslt.org

NHS Careers, PO Box 376, Bristol BS99 3EY; Careers helpline: 0845 606 0655; www.nhscareers. nhs.uk

# Therapy support worker

Therapy support workers, sometimes referred to as assistants, work across the many different health professions allied to medicine. They assist therapists in their work with patients and help patients to carry out the activities which therapists have designed for them. What you might actually be doing varies according to your particular role. With an art therapist, you might be helping prepare materials and equipment as well as working with patients. If you are working with an occupational therapist you might accompany him or her and a patient on a home visit to see what adaptations to the home might be necessary. If you are working with a physiotherapist, perhaps you will be supervising some exercises, helping a patient get ready for a session in the hydrotherapy pool, or taking a patient's blood pressure. In whatever role you are working, you are likely to have a great deal of contact with patients and work closely with other members of the healthcare team.

## Qualifications and Training

There are no standard entry requirements, but each hospital and each therapy specialism may set its own requirements. Most will want a minimum of four GCSEs grades A–C; sometimes one of these will need to be a science, for physiotherapy for example, whereas for art therapy an art and design subject would be more usual. Often the most important thing is to have had some experience of working with people. Training is provided on the job, but you may have opportunities to attend short courses, work towards NVQs.

## Personal Qualities and Skills

While some of these may vary according to which healthcare profession you are supporting, there are many skills and qualities that apply in all situations. You will have to be very good at working with people, understanding, sensitive and good at explaining procedures or treatments. You will need to be good at working as part of a team and you may need to have practical, IT or administrative skills as well.

## Salaries

There is considerable variation, but many support staff are paid on NHS Bands 3 and 4. This range is from around £15,000 to £18,000 for Band 3 posts and £17,500 to £21,000 to Band 4 support workers. The NHS Careers website gives more detail on exact salaries.

Local Primary Care Trusts and hospitals do their own recruiting.

Skills for Health, Goldsmiths House, Broad Plain, Bristol BS2 0JP; 0117 922 1155; www.skillsforhealth.org.uk

NHS Careers, PO Box 376, Bristol BS99 3EY; 0845 606 0655; www. nhscareers,org,uk

info

# TOWN AND COUNTRY PLANNER

Planners are concerned with reconciling the needs of the population for buildings, shopping centres, schools and leisure centres with the necessity of preserving and enhancing the natural and built environment. They collect information about the present use of land, and the position of roads and other features, as well as drawing up plans for new schemes. Planners in development control ensure that buildings or developments intended for a particular area are suitable and do not conflict with existing buildings or the surrounding environment. Planners work for local and central government, environmental agencies, and to an increasing extent in private practice. There are also varied opportunities for planning support staff.

## Qualifications and Training

To enter a degree or diploma course in town planning, five GCSE passes and two A levels are desirable. Useful subjects include maths, English language, geography and history or a foreign language. Those with a Royal Town Planning Institute (RTPI)-accredited degree or diploma in town planning have satisfied the academic requirement for election to corporate membership of the Institute. To achieve membership, these candidates also need to be able to demonstrate two years' experience in town and country planning. Planning courses are available at undergraduate and postgraduate levels, full- and part-time and on a distance-learning basis.

Planning support staff are normally expected to have good GCSE grades in English, maths and other appropriate subjects, but relevant experience might be a deciding factor for more mature candidates. There are colleges that offer courses for support staff on a part-time or block-release basis. Qualifications gained are the Edexcel (BTEC) certificate, higher certificate or higher diploma in planning or the SQA certificate or higher certificate in planning. An NVQ at level 3 in Town Planning Support is also available for support staff.

## Personal Qualities and Skills

Town planners and support staff need to have a knowledge of many subjects: economics, sociology, architecture and geography. Planners must be able to work in a team and cooperate with experts in other subjects. Planners need to take advice and opinions from many different people, and therefore need to be able to reconcile the conflicting views of various interest groups. They must be good communicators and have imagination, and an interest in, and understanding of, both people and the environment.

## Salaries

Assistants earn around £15,000 while newly qualified planners earn between £20,000 and £27,000. Senior planners earn between £25,000 and £35,000. Team leaders and managers earn between £30,000 and £40,000.

**info**

Local Government Careers; www. lgcareers.com

Asset Skills, 2 The Courtyard, 48 New North Road, Exeter EX4 4EP; 01392 423399; www. assetskills.org

Royal Town Planning Institute, 41 Botolph Lane, London EC3R 8DL; 020 7929 9494; www.rtpi.org.uk

Royal Town Planning Institute in Scotland, 57 Melville Street, Edinburgh EH3 7HL; 0131 226 1959; www.scotland.rtpi.org.uk

# TRADING STANDARDS OFFICER

Trading standards officers are employed by local authorities and are responsible for enforcing a very wide range of legislation aimed at protecting consumers and traders. Laws relate to food and consumer product safety, credit, descriptions of goods and services, prices, animal health and welfare. While most operations are carried out through random inspections, officers are also required to investigate complaints and, where appropriate, take matters to court.

## Qualifications and Training

The essential qualification for trading standards officers is the Diploma in Consumer Affairs and Trading Standards (DCATS). The usual way to obtain this qualification is to take a degree in consumer protection or a postgraduate qualification approved by the Trading Standards Institute (TSI); people then apply for trainee trading standards officer posts with a local authority. If you have a lot of previous experience in consumer affairs you may not have to have a degree or postgraduate qualification. Some local authorities may offer sponsorship to applicants interested in doing a degree in consumer protection. Without a degree or relevant experience you can apply for posts as an enforcement officer or consumer adviser in trading standards departments and study for the Foundation Certificate in Consumer Affairs and Trading Standards. The TSI has developed a range of modular courses for trading standards workers at all levels. For all of these you must undergo on the job training and submit a portfolio of your work activities.

## Personal Qualities and Skills

You need a broad mix of skills to work in trading standards. You must be a good communicator, confident and persistent, but also patient and tactful at times. You should be able to handle technical equipment and complex technical information. Good IT and numeracy skills and an interest in the law are also important. You should be happy working as an effective member of a team, but also able to work on your own.

## Salaries

Salaries for trainees are between £17,500 and £23,500; once qualified, salaries range from £25,000 to £35,000, £40,000 to £45,000 for management roles. Many trading standards officers move to work with private sector employers or with organisations that look after consumer interests in relation to utilities or the communications industry. These posts are normally paid at equivalent to or higher than management roles in local government trading standards departments.

Local Government Jobs;
www.lgjobs.com

Food Standards Agency, Aviation House, 125 Kingsway, London WC2B 6NH; 020 7276 8000; www.food.gov.uk

Trading Standards Institute (TSI), First Floor, 1 Sylvan Court, Sylvan Way, Southfields Business Park, Basildon SS15 6TH; 0845 608 9400; www.tsi.org.uk

info

# TRAFFIC WARDEN

Traffic wardens are civilians who work in conjunction with local police forces. They check parking meters and penalise drivers parking on double yellow lines or in other illegal places. They may also be required to do school crossing patrols or traffic control duty, as well as receiving vehicles towed into the police pound and looking out for out-of-date car licences.

## Qualifications and Training

Each Police Authority sets its own entry requirements, but there is usually no need to have formal educational qualifications; instead you have to pass a written test, which includes maths and English. Training is on the job, sometimes being supervised by a police officer, and many areas send you on a short, introductory course.

## Personal Qualities and Skills

You need to be calm, confident and possess a degree of common sense to do this work. You should be a good communicator, able to deal with aggression without becoming aggressive yourself.

## Salaries

There is some variation between localities, but generally starting salaries are between £19,000 and £23,000, more in London. In most cases, you can earn more through shift allowances.

**info**

Police Service Recruitment; www.policecouldyou.co.uk

# TRAVEL AND TOURISM

(*see also* Civil Aviation)

Travel and tourism covers a wide range of jobs connected with transport, hospitality, recreation management, marketing and administration. There has also been a growth in IT-related jobs linked to travel and tourism as the numbers of people making their own travel and holiday arrangements via the internet has increased.

Below are some of the key jobs which are very specific to the tourism and travel industry.

# Tour manager

Tour managers (sometimes referred to as tour directors) organise and accompany parties of holidaymakers on a wide variety of tours and excursions. They are often involved in the planning and the marketing of these tours. Another key part of their role is to deal with any problems which holidaymakers have, from losing a passport to being taken ill or simply wanting further information about a particular activity or destination.

# Tourist guide

Tourist guides or couriers accompany groups of tourists on visits to places of interest. These could be castles, museums, art galleries, city centres or places of natural wonder. Your main role as a tour guide is to give detailed and interesting information about these sites of interest. In some cases you will need to have a really good knowledge of your area, as with special interest tours, where your customers have real knowledge and enthusiasm for art, or history, for example.

# Resort representative

The role of a resort representative is often very similar to that of a tourism manager, but resort representatives are usually based around one centre and work for one tour operator. They have to receive each party of holidaymakers as they arrive at airports and seaports. They accompany them to hotels and run welcome meetings to tell them about tours and activities on offer. They make sure they are available at regular times to deal with queries and in many cases they also accompany parties on tours and trips, or at least take the bookings for these events.

## Qualifications and Training

To work as a tourism manager, tourist guide or resort representative you do not need formal academic qualifications. Many applicants do have good GCSE results, A levels and a degree in a subject such as education, tourism, geography, history or marketing. Being able to speak the language in the country in which you work is a big advantage. A background in customer care, hospitality or other work in travel and tourism is a big plus for all these jobs.

## Personal Qualities and Skills

You need to have excellent interpersonal skills, being friendly, helpful and calm. You also need excellent organisational skills and to be a tour manager or resort rep you often need good marketing skills too. Tourist guides need to have a genuine interest in the sites and objects they are describing and a flair for conveying information in a lively and informative way.

## Salaries

Resort representatives and tour managers earn £10,000 to £15,000, but they get board and lodging in addition to a salary. Some tour managers are self-employed, even though they are allocated work by tour operators. Tourist guides are mostly self-employed and the work is often seasonal or part-time. The Association of Professional Tourist Guides can offer guidance on what fees you should charge.

**info**

People 1st, 2nd Floor, Armstrong House, 38 Market Square, Uxbridge, Middlesex UB8 1LH; 0870 060 2550; www.people1st.co.uk

Guild of Registered Tourist Guides, The Guild House, 52d Borough High Street, London SE1 1XN; 020 7403 1115; www.blue-badge.org.uk

Institute of Tourist Guiding, Lloyd's Court, 1 Goodman's Yard, London E1 8AT; 020 7953 1257; www.itg.org.uk

Association of Professional Tourist Guides, 33–37 Moreland Street, London EC1V 8HA; 020 7780 4060; www.aptg.org.uk

Institute of Travel and Tourism, PO Box 217, Ware, Hertfordshire SG12 8WY; 0870 770 7960; www.itt.co.uk

GoSkills, Concorde House, Trinity Park, Solihull B37 7UQ; 0121 635 5520; www.goskills.org

International Association of Tour Managers (IATM), 397 Walworth Road, London SE17 2AW; 020 7703 9154; www.iatm.co.uk

Association of Independent Tour Operators; www.aito.co.uk

# Tourism officer

Tourism officers work for national or regional tourist boards and local authorities with the aim of attracting visitors to Britain or to a particular region. The work includes promoting attractions, working with press and public relations agencies, designers and photographers to advertise local features, researching local history to develop new attractions, and participating in exhibitions both nationally and overseas to promote the area. They work closely with businesses in attracting holidaymakers, tour operators, exhibitions and conferences to the area, and research future trends and needs. They are also responsible for overseeing the council's tourist information offices.

## Qualifications and Training

Having a degree or HND in a business- or tourism-related subject can be an advantage, but personal qualities and proven business skills are just as important. NVQs in tourist information at levels 2–3 are available.

Previous tourist information centre experience, paid or voluntary, is invaluable. Marketing, travel agency or other retail experience is advantageous.

## Personal Qualities and Skills

Good communication skills are essential, as are marketing and promotional experience and skills, including the ability to be creative, and write snappy copy to promote the area and various events. Excellent organisational skills and the ability to get on with a wide cross-section of people, from business leaders and councillors to residents and visitors, are important. A knowledge of languages, geography, history or archaeology can be an advantage for some posts.

## Salaries

Assistants in tourist information centres earn between £10,000 and £14,000, while managers of these centres earn £17,000 to £20,000. Managers of large centres in prime locations may earn up to £30,000.

Local Government Careers; www. lgcareers.com – for further careers information; www.lgjobs.com – for current job vacancy adverts in local councils all over the country

National and local tourist boards

Institute of Travel and Tourism, Studio 3, Mill Studio, Crane Mead, Ware, Herts SG12 9PY; 0870 770 7960; fax: 0870 770 7961; www.itt.co.uk; e-mail: enquiries@itt.co.uk

TTC Training, The Cornerstone, The Broadway, Woking, Surrey GU21 5AR; 01483 727321; fax: 01483 756698; www.ttctraining. co.uk; e-mail: info@ttctraining.co.uk

*Careers and Jobs in Travel and Tourism* (Kogan Page)

**info**

# Tourist information assistant/manager

Tourist information assistants and managers provide information and advice to members of the public about accommodation, leisure activities, amenities, visitor attractions, special events and transport in a particular location and also nationwide. Most tourist information centre staff are employed by local authorities, but some private visitor attractions and organisations such as national parks employ people in this role. Much of the day-to-day work as an assistant is answering questions from visitors to the centres, on the telephone or by e-mail, on all the subjects just listed. Your work is also likely to involve booking events, journeys or accommodation for visitors. Tourist information officers also have many items for sale – books, postcards and gifts – so you will also be selling these items. Part of the job includes collecting appropriate brochures, leaflets and display information for the centre and making sure they are well displayed and that all information is up to date. As a manager of a centre you have responsibility for choosing and purchasing items to be sold, training and recruiting staff, and ensuring that the centre is presentable, welcoming and efficient.

## Qualifications and Training

There are no specific entry requirements for this work, though a good standard of education is important. Many local authorities and other employers expect you to have three or four GCSEs including maths and English. To join directly as a manager, it may be useful if you have a qualification in marketing, travel and tourism, or business, but these are not essential. Having some background experience in retailing or other jobs working directly with the public is a big advantage for both assistant and manager posts.

## Personal Qualities and Skills

You need to be very good at dealing with people – friendly, approachable and able to give information in a clear and precise way. You should be well organised, and good at sorting and updating information. You need basic computer skills, and some creative flair is useful for organising window or other displays. Working as a manager, you have to be good at motivating people, and good at guessing what products and ideas are likely to do well. All staff must be good at working as part of a team.

## Salaries

Starting salaries for assistants are £17,000 to £19,000; managers earn £20,000 to £30,000, though the latter is only likely in the larger tourist information centres.

**info**

Local Government Jobs; www. localgovernmentjobs.com

Institute of Travel and Tourism, PO Box 217, Ware, Hertfordshire SG12 8WY; 0844 4995 653; www.itt.co.uk

People 1st, 2nd Floor, Armstrong House, 38 Market Square, Uxbridge, Middlesex UB8 1LH; 0870 060 2550; www.people1st.co.uk

# Travel agent

Travel agents sell tickets for travel by air, land and sea on behalf of transport organisations. They make hotel bookings for individual travellers, business people and holidaymakers. Some travel companies deal only with business travel, and are also involved in arranging conferences and trade fairs. However, travel agents are best known for selling package holidays on behalf of tour operators. Many travel agents will also advise travellers on visas, foreign currency and necessary injections.

## Qualifications and Training

Modern Apprenticeships and NVQ qualifications are available. No specific qualifications are asked for but GCSEs in maths, English and geography are an advantage. Computer literacy is becoming increasingly important.

## Personal Qualities and Skills

Travel agents must enjoy dealing with the general public, and have a responsible attitude regarding the accuracy of information given, and good administrative and ICT skills.

## Salaries

Working mainly on the administrative side your earnings start at between £13,000 and £16,000. Once you start taking on more sales work, salaries go up to £15,000 to £25,000. Many sales consultants are also paid commission on holidays or other products sold. Travel agency staff may also get discounts on holidays or flights.

---

Local Job Centre Plus and Careers/Connexions Centres

Institute of Travel and Tourism, Studio 3, Mill Studio, Crane Mead, Ware, Herts SG12 9PY;
0870 770 7960; fax: 0870 770 7961;
www.itt.co.uk;
e-mail: enquiries@itt.co.uk

TTC Training, The Cornerstone, The Broadway, Woking, Surrey GU21 5AR; 01483 727321; fax: 01483 756698; www.ttctraining.co.uk;
e-mail: info@ttctraining.co.uk

*Careers and Jobs in Travel and Tourism* (Kogan Page)

info

## UNDERTAKER

*see* Funeral Director

## UNDERWRITER

*see* Insurance

# VETERINARY SCIENCE

(*see also* Animals)

Veterinary science is concerned with the care of animals, including both farm animals and domestic pets.

# Veterinary nurse

Veterinary nurses (VNs) assist vets during operations and X-rays, sterilise instruments, look after animals recovering from surgery, and keep the animals and their cages clean. After qualification, the work of a veterinary nurse can include practice management, staff supervision, teaching and training other nurses or support staff. Some VNs choose to work outside veterinary practice in research establishments, colleges, zoos and breeding or boarding kennels.

## Qualifications and Training

A nationally recognised Veterinary Nursing Scheme (VNS) is administered by the Royal College of Veterinary Surgeons (RCVS), which keeps a register of veterinary practices able to offer training. To train as a veterinary nurse you must be aged 17 or over and have five GCSEs grades A–C including English, maths and two science subjects. You must also be employed by a practice registered to offer training. You can get details of practices approved to provide training from the RCVS website or from the British Veterinary Nursing Association (BVNA). If you particularly want to work with horses you can do specialised training as part of your qualification, but you must be working for a practice that takes on equine work.

If you do not have the required GCSEs, and are working for an approved practice, you can take a day release or distance learning level 2 Certificate for Animal Nursing Assistants. As an alternative to the Veterinary Nursing Scheme there are several degree and HND courses available in veterinary nursing. If you consider this route, ensure that the course you choose is approved by the RCVS.

# TOGETHER
## WE **CAN** MAKE
## A DIFFERENCE

The IAT's purpose is *to advance knowledge and promote excellence in the care and welfare of animals in science* and to enhance the standards and status of those professionally engaged in the care, welfare and use of animals in science.

Job satisfaction in helping to discover new medical drugs and therapies to treat illness, including cancer, diabetes and asthma, and protect the health of people and animals.

Animal technologists work in universities, veterinary colleges, pharmaceutical companies, specialist research organisations and animal breeding companies.

During your career as an animal technologist you will be given:

- Accredited Training and Education

- Continued Professional Development

- Career Pathway and Support

Institute of
Animal Technology

Visit our website **www.iat.org.uk** for further information

# ANIMAL TECHNOLOGY

Animal technology is the specialist profession for those who are responsible for the care and welfare of animals in science (ranging from rats and mice to marmosets, farm animals and fish).

Animal technology is a career that involves caring for animals within the exciting and rapidly evolving scientific environment of a UK bio-medical research centre.

Animal technologists work in universities, veterinary colleges, pharmaceutical companies, specialist research organisations and animal breeding companies.

Animal technologists enjoy the satisfaction of helping to discover new medical drugs and therapies to help understand and treat illness, including cancer, diabetes and asthma, and protect the health of people and animals. We operate to high professional standards, caring for laboratory animals in an expert manner while maintaining the highest scientific and welfare standards.

Working in close knit teams, with colleagues who share our professional dedication to excellence in the ethical care of laboratory animals.

Our work requires life-long learning to update our knowledge and skills. We study for formal IAT qualifications through workplace training, day release and distance learning.

A structured career path starts with the First Certificate in Animal Husbandry and we have the opportunity to pursue qualifications through to MSc and PhD level. There are many opportunities for specialisation, promotion and career development.

advertisement feature

# INDIVIDUAL NARRATIVE

Sally now aged 36, began her career as a trainee animal technologist in 1997 whilst also performing laboratory analysis work. After working in a number of different types of animal research facilities, including academic, government and pharmaceutical organisations, Sally now works as a Supervisor managing 25 staff for a charity funded research body, committed to releasing all research data and models information to the global community.

Sally explains: "My interest in caring for animals has been lifelong and I have taken every opportunity to experience it by working as a volunteer at local vets and stables. I was surprised and pleased to discover a career existed where I could care for animals directly and contribute to discovering information for human and animal health. Animals are fascinating and rewarding to work with on a daily basis. Since I have become a manager I have really enjoyed training new staff because I recognise I can develop someone else's interest and passion for caring for animals. The reward is being able to coach people to have the right approach and I can watch someone handle a rat with kindness and confidence and know I taught them how".

Sally was delighted to find animal technology is a well structured career. "I like to learn new information and approaches and do the best I can. Passing my exams to become a RAnTech (Registered Animal Technologist) was an important step in my career because it recognises my commitment to the animals and their standards of care".

Sally believes animal technology is a good career option for young scientists: "We can specialise if we wish – one of my team is very interested in breeding and another in immunology. I personally enjoy management and training. We are relatively well paid compared to many other animal care jobs but then we are scientifically trained. Medical studies take a long time but it is wonderful knowing that work you are doing now might prove to be an important turning point in treating a disease".

Sally concludes: "The work can be tiring and sometimes repetitive but every job is made more enjoyable by the interaction with the animals. What matters is that we do our job of caring for the animals and working to high scientific standards – the benefits to medical research follow from this".

advertisement feature

# INTRODUCING THE INSTITUTE OF ANIMAL TECHNOLOGY

The IAT's purpose **is to advance knowledge and promote excellence in the care and welfare of animals in science** and to enhance the standards and status of those professionally engaged in the care, welfare and use of animals in science.

Representing animal technologists both within the UK and Europe, the IAT has over 2000 members made up of individuals and 60 corporate organisations, including the vast majority of the UK's Named Animal Care and

Welfare Officers (NACWOs). NACWOs have a legal obligation to be **'actively involved, on a day to day basis, in safeguarding the welfare of the protected animals bred, kept and used at designated establishments'.**

Recognising the importance of learning, both academic and skills based, plus personal development throughout the careers of animal technologists, the IAT supports animal technologists to achieve their full potential. This enables our members to contribute fully to the field of laboratory animal science and technology, animal welfare and UK biomedical science and drug development.

For over sixty years the IAT has awarded qualifications in animal technology and accredited Continuing Professional Development (CPD) for animal technologists and other professionals involved in the care and welfare of laboratory animals.

Education and qualification is a key role of the IAT. The IAT is recognised by the Qualifications and Curriculum Authority (QCA) as a formal Awarding Body, for its Further Education qualifications in animal technology, leading to Membership (MIAT) of the Institute.

The IAT is currently developing a Graduate Programme, leading to degree level qualifications and Fellowship (FIAT) of the IAT.

In addition to formal education, the IAT actively and enthusiastically promotes Continuing Professional Development (CPD), enabling animal technologists to keep up to date with the latest in animal husbandry and related scientific advances.

We invite you to view **www.iat.org.uk** to find out more about the IAT's actitivies and the roles of animal technologists in Biomedical research.

advertisement feature

## Personal Qualities and Skills

You have to love animals and be calm, kind and patient when handling them. You have to be able to deal with sad or distressing situations and you must be able to communicate with people as well as their pets. You need to be practical, with an interest in science, and you can't be the least bit squeamish.

## Salaries

Salaries for trainees range from £13,000 to £15,000. Qualified veterinary nurses earn £17,000 to £22,000. Senior veterinary nurses in large practices may earn £25,000. There are sometimes opportunities for overtime through working weekends or evening and night shifts, or for being on-call supporting on-call vets.

# Veterinary surgeon

Most vets work in private practice, usually starting out as a veterinary assist-

**info**

Lantra, Lantra House, Stoneleigh Park, Nr Coventry, Warwickshire CV8 2LG; 0845 707 8007; www.lantra.co.uk

Royal College of Veterinary Surgeons (RCVS), Belgravia House, 62–64 Horseferry Road, London SW1P 2AF; 020 7222 2001; www.rcvs.org.uk

British Veterinary Nursing Association (BVNA), 82 Greenway Business Centre, Harlow Business Park, Harlow, Essex CM19 5QE; 01279 408644; www.bvna.org.uk

ant and working their way up into a partnership or into their own business. Some specialise in small-animal treatment, including pets such as dogs, cats and birds, while others work with particular kinds of animals such as farm animals, racehorses or the more exotic zoo animals. Other vets go into research or industry. The Department of Environment, Food and Rural Affairs, for instance, employs a substantial number to work on disease control, monitoring such epidemics as foot and mouth or swine vesicular disease. Others are employed by animal welfare organisations, such as the PDSA, in animal hospitals. Vets are also needed in the food-processing industries, where their job is concerned with checking that conditions are humane and hygienic.

## Qualifications and Training

A veterinary surgeon must hold a degree from one of the six veterinary schools in the UK. The six universities offering the course set their own entrance requirements but all demand an extremely high standard of A level passes or equivalent. Chemistry is essential, and other useful subjects are physics, maths, biology and zoology. The course lasts five years (six at

Cambridge), and covers a formidable amount of academic and practical work, comparable to that needed to be a doctor.

## Personal Qualities and Skills

Vets need to be sympathetic but detached. They must be excellent communicators, explaining to and reassuring pet owners and farmers. Patience, calmness and, later on, a good business sense and problem-solving skills are also important.

## Salaries

Newly qualified vets earn around £30,000, but with a few years' experience this rises to £45,000 to £50,000. Senior vets in large practices can earn far more than this – £60,000 to £80,000.

British Equine Veterinary Association, Mulberry House, 31 Market Street, Fordham, Ely, Cambridgeshire CB7 5LQ; 01638 723555; www.beva.org.uk

Royal College of Veterinary Surgeons (RCVS), Belgravia House, 62–64 Horseferry Road, London SW1P 2AF; 020 7222 2001; www.rcvs.org.uk

info

# W

## WATCH AND CLOCK MAKER/REPAIRER

Watch and clock makers make timepieces by hand, sometimes to a design of their own.

Repairers receive watches and clocks from customers for servicing and repair. They must be able to examine a timepiece thoroughly for worn-out parts, clean and regulate a watch or clock, and repair or replace faulty parts. The work involves the use of precision tools and electronic equipment. Restoration is carried out on antique clocks and watches.

### Qualifications and Training

You may be able to get a trainee position without qualifications and gain qualifications part time. There are also several courses accredited by the British Horological Institute (BHI), including certificates at preliminary, intermediate and final level. You can study for these at the University of Central England in Birmingham and through distance learning modules. The University of Central England also offers an HND in clock and watch servicing. You may be able to complete courses specialising in restoring and conserving antique clocks and watches. Some local colleges offer part-time courses in clock and watch servicing and repair, and this could also be a useful way to get started.

### Personal Qualities and Skills

A real interest in watches, clocks and mechanical devices is a good starting point. You need excellent manual dexterity, be able to work on intricate, delicate and detailed devices and to maintain a level of careful concentration. You need mathematical skills and you may also need drawing skills. You must be able to deal with clients and customers and if you work for yourself, you need all the skills of running a business – bookkeeping, marketing your services, managing your own time, etc.

### Salaries

Salaries for new entrants are around £15,000. Experienced repairers can earn £25,000 to £30,000 – some of the highest salaries may be paid in restoration and conservation work. If you are self-employed, there is a lot of variation in earnings, depending on how much work you do, but £20,000 may be a reasonable average.

British Horological Institute, Upton Hall, Upton, Newark, Nottinghamshire NG23 5TE; 01636 813795; fax: 01636 812258; www.bhi.co.uk; e-mail: info@bhi.co.uk

# WATER QUALITY SCIENTIST

Water quality scientists test, analyse, monitor and maintain the quality of drinking water. They also analyse and monitor the water in lakes and rivers and in the ground. They have to ensure that water quality complies with rigorous standards set by legislation. They deal with complaints about quality of drinking water and investigate possible sources of contamination. They also work closely with businesses and other organisations, looking at possible implications for water supply of particular types of development, eg potential sources of pollution, increased demand on supply. They conduct research on water quality and they may be called upon to deal with any emergency such as a total breakdown of supply.

## Qualifications and Training

You normally need a science degree to do this work. Preferred subjects include chemistry, biology, microbiology and environmental science. It may be possible to get into water science with an HND in a relevant science. Competition is strong in this field, because of its link to the environment. Any voluntary work you have done in an environmental science setting will be highly valued, as will any relevant paid work experience in a laboratory. In fact, many people aiming to be water quality scientists do work their way up from more junior positions in the industry.

## Personal Qualities and Skills

You need a rigorous and meticulous approach when collecting and analysing samples. You must be a good communicator as you may be dealing with customers, other businesses or representatives of the legislative authorities. You have to be a good problem solver and you should be able to work well as part of a team. You need a genuine interest in the environment.

## Salaries

Salaries for trainee scientists are between £15,500 and £22,000. Senior water quality scientists earn £28,000 to £40,000. Technician level salaries are around £13,000 to £15,000.

**info**

Chartered Institution of Water and
Environmental Management
(CIWEM), 15 John Street,
London WC1N 2EB; 020 7831 3110;
www.ciwem.org

Drinking Water Inspectorate (DWI),
Ashdown House, 123 Victoria Street,
London SW1E 6DE; 020 7944 5956;
www.dwi.gov.uk

Environment Agency (EA): Visit the
EA website to check for details of
regional offices; 0870 850 6506;
www.environment-agency.gov.uk

# WELFARE ADVICE WORK

## Welfare advice worker

Welfare advice workers are employed by local authorities, by the Citizens
Advice Bureau (CAB) and by a wide range of charities and voluntary organisations. Advice workers answer questions and offer confidential advice and
practical help (eg help with filling in a form), to members of the public. Some
work with specific client groups, rather than the general public, eg students at
a college, or tenants of a housing association. The work often involves advocacy work, taking up an issue on behalf of a client or dealing with bureauc-
racy on their behalf. Some advice workers are generalists, offering advice on
many different problems; working for the CAB is a good example of this.
Other welfare advisers specialise in issues such as debt management,
housing questions, consumer concerns, education and career decisions or
discrimination of some kind.

### Qualifications and Training

While there are no formal entry qualifications many advice workers are graduates in sociology, psychology or similar subjects. They have often had experience of working with people and many advice workers begin their advice
careers in a voluntary capacity. There is a variety of part-time courses available at NVQ levels 2, 3 and 4 in advice and guidance work – many people
undertake these once they are working in this field.

### Personal Qualities and Skills

You must be very good at listening to people and at explaining documents or
rules patiently and carefully. You need good information research skills and
good powers of persuasion if your role involves advocacy work of any kind. You
need to be well organised, and flexible with good written communication skills.

### Salaries

Starting salaries range from £14,000 to £24,000 – though few posts pay at the
top of this range. If you work for a local authority, or an academic institution,

your starting salary is likely to be higher than if you work for a voluntary body or charity. Salaries can be as high as £30,000, but this is usually only the case if your work involves management, bidding for funds, staff training, etc, not simply the advice-giving role.

Advice UK, 12th Floor, New London Bridge House, 25 London Bridge Street, London SE1 9ST; 020 7407 4070; www. adviceuk.org.uk

National Association of Citizens Advice Bureaux (NACAB), Myddelton House, 115–123 Pentonville Road, London N1 9LZ; www.citizensadvice.org.uk

info

# WINE TRADE

(*see also* Publican/licensee *and* Retailing)

The wine trade has grown and changed significantly in the past two decades, increasing opportunities in wine retailing, buying, importing and marketing. Wine specialists work for supermarkets, for off-licence chains, for specialist wine traders and for the expanding home delivery market. Opportunities exist in retail management, marketing and importing. To work as a wine buyer, you need extensive experience and knowledge. Wine merchants who do not employ their own buyers may use wine brokers who work with growers and select the kinds of wine in which a particular merchant is interested. There are now many English vineyards springing up, creating some further marketing opportunities.

## Qualifications and Training

On the retail management side, entry requirements vary – some ask for A levels, some prefer graduates. To get into wine brokerage or wine buying, you normally have to have worked in the trade and also completed wine tasting courses. The Wine and Spirits Education Trust (WSET) runs a wide range of courses for professionals as well as amateurs; check the website for further details.

## Personal Qualities and Skills

You need good people skills, whether dealing directly with customers or working with growers from all parts of the world. You need to have a flair for business, good organisational skills and the ability to work as part of a team and to motivate others.

## Salaries

As a junior retail manager your salary is likely to be between £15,000 and £19,000. Managers of larger wine and spirit retailers may earn £25,000. Sales staff marketing home delivery wine services earn between £15,000 and £20,000, with possibilities to earn more through commissions on sales. Experienced wine buyers may earn £35,000.

# WSET®

The largest global provider of education and qualifications in
## *wines & spirits*

**Level 1 Foundation Certificate in Wines**
**Level 1 Foundation Certificate in Spirits**
**Level 2 Intermediate Certificate in Wines & Spirits**
**Level 2 Professional Certificate in Spirits**
**Level 3 Advanced Certificate in Wines & Spirits**
**Level 3 International Higher Certificate in Wines & Spirits**
**Level 4 Diploma in Wines & Spirits**
**Level 5 Honours Diploma in Wines & Spirits**

There are over **360** Approved Programme Providers in **50** countries
around the globe delivering WSET qualifications.
To find out more about our courses including where you can study, visit…

# www.wsetglobal.com

The WSET is approved in the UK by the Qualification and Curriculum Authority (Ofqual). The WSET has been developing
the trade professional for 40 years and in the academic year 2008/2009 over 25,000 candidates sat a WSET examination.

The WSET® was founded in 1969 to promote, provide and develop high-quality education and training in wines and spirits for those in the UK wine and spirit industry. Since then, WSET has grown into the foremost international awarding body in the field of wines and spirits with a suite of sought-after qualifications.

We design courses, produce teaching and learning materials and set examinations, working through a network of Approved Programme Providers (APPs) around the world. These external Providers are rigorously checked to ensure that they deliver the high standard of teaching required to enable students to pass their WSET qualification, so you can be sure of a consistent level of quality and integrity, which will make your learning experience both rewarding and enjoyable.

Wine & Spirit Education Trust, International Wine & Spirit Centre,
39-45 Bermondsey Street, London SE1 3XF, UK
Tel: +44(0) 20 7089 3815 • Email: wset@wset.co.uk • Web: www.wsetglobal.com

advertisement feature

**info**

Skillsmart Retail: The Sector Skills
Council for Retail, 4th Floor,
93 Newman Street,
London W1T 3EZ; 020 746 5060;
www.skillsmartretail.com

Wine & Spirit Education Trust
(WSET), International Wine & Spirit
Centre, 39–45 Bermondsey Street,
London SE1 3XF; 020 7089 3800;
www.wset.co.uk

# WRITER

For writers other than journalists, making a living purely from writing can be very difficult, so many writers, especially before they are established, have other careers as well. There are only a handful of people who become successful fiction writers or writers of really popular non-fiction such as biographies. There are some jobs for writers in residence with theatre companies and regional arts organisations, prisons or university departments, but many of these posts are temporary contracts.

Technical authors write user manuals and instruction books for anything from washing machines to computer software, and there are writers who specialise in writing textbooks and other teaching materials. Technical authors are often on permanent, or at least more secure contracts. Many writers of textbooks have other jobs in education.

## Qualifications and Training

There are no formal entry qualifications, though most writers have a good level of education, especially in English or other subjects where a good command of the language is important. There are many creative writing courses which can teach the technical aspects of writing, but creativity is not something you can learn. If your goal is to work in film, radio or television, it might be worth considering a script-writing course.

Technical authors come from a wide range of academic disciplines, but science, technology and engineering are particularly useful backgrounds. While there are no specific entry requirements for this work, it is very much a graduate profession.

## Personal Qualities and Skills

Being a brilliant communicator of the written word is the key to your success. While creative writers have to have imagination, flair and a way of drawing the reader in, technical authors must be able to make complex material accessible. All writers have to be determined, self-disciplined, highly motivated and able to cope with rejection. Technical authors have to have a very thorough and careful approach to their work.

## Salaries

For creative writers the average income is only around £5,000 a year and more than half of all creative writers have additional jobs, many in teaching or lecturing. Technical authors earn between £18,000 and £30,000.

**info**

Association of British Science Writers, Wellcome Wolfson Building, 165 Queen's Gate, London SW7 5HD; 0870 770 3361; www.absw.org.uk

British Association of Communicators in Business (CIB), Suite GA2, Oak House, Woodlands Business Park, Linford Wood, Milton Keynes MK14 6EY; 01908 313755; www.cib.uk.com

Creative and Cultural Skills: the Sector Skills Council for Advertising, Crafts, Cultural Heritage, Design, Music, Performing, Literary & Visual Arts, 4th Floor Lafone House, The Leathermarket, Weston Street, London SE1 3HN; 020 7015 1800; www.ccskills.org.uk

Masterclass, Theatre Royal Haymarket, London SW1Y 4HT; 020 7389 9660; www.trh.co.uk/masterclass.php

The Poetry Society, 22 Betterton Street, London WC2H 9BX; 020 7420 9880; www.poetrysoc.com

Skillset (Sector Skills Council for the Audio Visual Industries), Focus Point, 21 Caledonian Road, London N1 9GB; 020 7713 9800; www.skillset.org

The Writers' Guild of Great Britain, 15 Britannia Street, London WC1X 9JN; 020 7833 0777; www.writersguild.org.uk

# YOUTH WORK

## Personal adviser

Personal advisers are employed by local authorities in the Department for Children, Families and Young People, which in turn is part of social services. In some areas the service still uses the name 'Connexions', which was the former organisation that employed personal advisers.

The work of individual advisers will depend on their clients, and involve work with other agencies to broker access to specialist services. Most of an adviser's time will be spent in direct contact with young people, but some time will also be spent liaising with other organisations, working with parents and carers, and promoting links with the local community. There is also a certain amount of administrative work – producing accurate and up-to-date records to be shared with other professionals.

Personal advisers are based in a variety of settings, including schools, colleges, and youth and community centres. At times, advisers may be called out to deal with crises in young people's lives. Most jobs will involve evening and weekend work. Some local authorities will provide services during the evening and overnight, to respond to the needs of young people.

### Qualifications and Training

To become a fully qualified personal adviser it is necessary to hold a relevant qualification at S/NVQ level 4, or equivalent, although some personal advisers will be working towards this level during training en route to qualified status. In addition, all personal advisers will be required to attend either the Diploma for Connexions Personal Advisers or the Understanding Connexions training programme.

The minimum age for entry to training is normally 21 and a driving licence is usually required. All candidates undergo police checks, so anyone with a conviction for a crime against children is barred from this type of work.

## Personal Qualities and Skills

Advisers need strong communication and relationship-building skills to engage the trust and respect of young people. They need to be able to listen carefully and respond appropriately; a non-judgemental approach is essential. Personal advisers need to empathise with young people's concerns while maintaining professional and emotional detachment. A sense of humour, reliability, flexibility, good time management and team-working skills are also important.

## Salaries

Salaries vary between individual Connexions Partnerships. Trainees may start on £14,000 to £15,000; qualified staff with the Diploma for Personal Advisers between £19,000 and £21,000 (£23,000 to £25,500 in London).

# Youth and community worker

Youth work promotes young people's personal and social development, provides support to help them achieve and progress into independence, and enables young people to have a voice in their communities and in society. This is accomplished through work with individuals, with and in groups, and with communities. In many instances youth workers work in partnership with professionals from other sectors, such as schools and colleges, careers, health organisations, the police and social services.

Youth and community workers work in a range of settings, including youth clubs, schools, colleges, community centres, as personal advisers within the Connexions Service and other specialist agencies offering information, advice and counselling. Some workers also work in mobile centres and with young people on the streets and in cafés. There are currently around 3,000 full-time youth workers employed in England and a far larger number of part-time and volunteer youth workers. The introduction of the Connexions Service in England, which offers advice, information and guidance to young people aged 13–19, has led to substantial numbers of new posts for people with youth work skills.

In Scotland, youth and community work is combined with adult education under the generic term 'community education'.

## Qualifications and Training

For those seeking qualification as a full-time, nationally qualified youth worker, various routes, including full-time and part-time diploma and degree courses, postgraduate courses, and distance learning, exist. Detailed information on courses can be obtained from the National Youth Agency, directly or via its website. Details of training and employment in Scotland and Wales can be obtained from Communities Scotland and the Welsh Youth Agency, respectively.

NVQs in community work are available at levels 2/3 and 4. There is normally a minimum age requirement, ranging from 19 to 21 (18 for some degree courses), and applicants are usually expected to have substantial experience of work with young people or adults in community settings. This can be paid or unpaid. Mature entrants may be accepted without formal academic qualifications.

## Personal Qualities and Skills

An interest in and understanding of the issues that affect people's lives, plus patience, stamina and a sense of humour are all qualities demanded of youth and community workers. They must also be able to plan, record and evaluate their work.

## Salaries

Starting salaries are between £15,000 and £19,000, rising to £20,000 to £26,000 with experience. There is often part-time work available in this field.

National Youth Agency, Eastgate House, 19–23 Humberstone Road, Leicester LE5 3GJ; www.nya.org.uk

Welsh Youth Agency, Leslie Court, Lon-y-Lyn, Caerphilly CF83 1BQ; 029 2085 5700; www.wya.org.uk/english/home.asp

Communities Scotland, CeVe Unit, Thistle House, 91 Haymarket Terrace, Edinburgh EH12 5HE; 0131 313 0044; www.communitiesscotland.gov.uk

Youth Council for Northern Ireland, Forestview, Purdy's Lane, Belfast BT8 7AR; 028 9064 3882; www.ycni.org

info

## ZOOLOGY

## Zoo keeper

*see* Animals

## Zoologist

Zoologists work in either research or teaching. Zoologists study anatomy, physiology, classification, distribution, behaviour and environment of all kinds of animals, from insects to elephants. When working in zoos, they usually coordinate conservation breeding programmes, collection planning and general conservation strategies. A very small number find jobs in industry, mainly in pharmaceutical and animal foodstuff companies. Research zoologists will probably work in one of the many government-backed centres on a variety of projects, including animal behaviour, pest control and the population ecology of birds.

### Qualifications and Training

A degree in zoology, available at some universities, is needed for a career as a zoologist. Postgraduate training in specialisations such as entomology or nematology is also available.

### Personal Qualities and Skills

Zoologists should have a scientific mind and an interest in research. They should also have keen powers of observation and be patient and confident.

### Salaries

New graduates working as research or technical assistants earn around £19,000. Zoologists in research posts earn up to £28,000.

info

Zoological Society of London, Regent's Park, London NW1 4RY; www.zoo. cam.ac.uk/ioz

# Index

# Index of advertisers

With over 1,000 titles in printed and digital format, **Kogan Page** offers affordable, sound business advice

**www.koganpage.com**

You are reading one of the thousands of books published by **Kogan Page**. As Europe's leading independent business book publishers **Kogan Page** has always sought to provide up-to-the-minute books that offer practical guidance at affordable prices.

**KoganPage**